Athanasius
Kircher

Athanasius Kircher

The Last Man Who Knew Everything

edited by
Paula Findlen

ROUTLEDGE
NEW YORK AND LONDON

Published in 2004 by

Routledge
711 Third Avenue
New York, NY 10016
www.routledge-ny.com

Published in Great Britain by
Routledge
2 Park Square, Milton Park
Abingdon, Oxon OX14 4RN
www.routledge.co.uk

Routledge is an imprint of the Taylor & Francis Group.

Transferred to Digital Printing 2005

Library of Congress Cataloging-in-Publication Data

Athanasius Kircher : the last man who knew everything / Paula Findlen, editor.
       p. cm.
Includes bibliographical references and index.
    ISBN 0-415-94015-X (hb : alk. paper) — ISBN 0-415-94016-8 (pb : alk. paper)
    1. Kircher, Athanasius, 1602–1680. 2. Intellectuals—Germany—Biography. 3. Jesuits—
Germany—Biography. 4. Learning and scholarship—Europe—History—17th century.
5. Europe—Intellectual life—17th century. 6. Germany—Biography. I. Findlen, Paula.
    CT1098.K46A738 2004
001.2'092—dc22
                                                            2003022829

To Betty Jo Teeter Dobbs,
honorary Kircherian,
true Newtonian

Contents

Acknowledgments

When I first became interested in Athanasius Kircher in the mid-1980s, there were very few people, outside of the select members of the Internationalen Athanasius Kircher Forschungsgesellschaft (f. 1968) and the Australian scholar John Fletcher, who had ever heard of him. Among those who had, most probably feared for my sanity in choosing such an unpromising, perhaps even preposterous subject. I seem to recall being asked more than once, "So you want to write about that crazy polymath, that strange Jesuit—the man who got everything wrong?"

Fortunately, not everyone felt this way. My first thanks goes to Martha Baldwin, who spent an evening with me in Rome in 1987 discussing our mutual delight in Father Athanasius. John Heilbron, whose early interest in Jesuit natural philosophy filled Bancroft Library with many of Kircher's books, inadvertently contributed to the genesis of this project by making Berkeley a remarkable place to initiate this research. I have been fortunate to study at two different institutions that valued Kircher, since the University of Chicago—as Ingrid Rowland's recent catalogue, *The Ecstatic Journey*, makes apparent—also contains an excellent collection of Kircheriana that I used with great pleasure in 1985–86, prior to working with his manuscripts at the Gregorian University in Rome.

The current project is the direct result of a collaboration with Stanford University Libraries and a number of my colleagues and students here. I owe a special debt to Henry Lowood, John Mustain, Roberto Trujillo, Assunta Pisani, Michael Keller, and many others in Green Library, whose enthusiasm for acquiring Ella and Bernard Mazel's virtually complete collection of the works of Athanasius Kircher and his disciples led me to envision the workshop from which this volume originated. The result was a wonderful exhibit (beautifully designed by Becky Fischbach) that continues to exist on paper in the form of Daniel Stolzenberg's catalogue, *The Great Art of Knowing*. Stanford University Libraries, especially in the persons of Henry Lowood and Glen Worthey, also contributed material and technical support to the Athanasius Kircher Correspondence Project directed by Michael John Gorman and Nick Wilding, which came to Stanford in 2000–01 so that we might connect this digital manuscript archive (initially sponsored by the Istituto e Museo di Storia della Scienza in Florence, the Pontificia Università Gregoriana in Rome, and the Istituto Europeo Universitario in Fiesole) to our library holdings. The staff in Special Collections has humored my desire to page every last Kircher book in our collection while completing this volume—to all of them, many thanks.

The presence of Kircher materials at Stanford, however, was more of an effect than a cause of my revived interest in the subject. During the late 1990s, I began to get a growing number of inquiries from other scholars who told me that they, too, were interested in Kircher or, more generally, in the role of the Jesuits in early modern culture. It was quite clear that *something* was in the air—some occult force, as Kircher would have said, drawing the scholarly world back to him and his projects. Occasionally I would see Tony Grafton, and we would remind each other that we should try to get as many Kircherians together as we could. I spent four months at the Getty Center in Los Angeles in 1995, which enabled me to meet David Wilson—and perhaps equally important, allowed Barbara Stafford and me to acquire all of the remaining Kircher pins in the gift store of the Museum of Jurassic Technology. The following year, I moved to Stanford and discovered the pleasure of having a wonderful colleague in East Asian Languages and Literature, Haun Saussy, who shared my passion. Shortly thereafter, Umberto Eco put me in touch with Eugenio Lo Sardo as he was in the midst of completing his reconstruction of Kircher's museum for an exhibit at Palazzo Venezia in Rome in winter 2001. Eventually, just around the time when I was beginning to feel like I might have inadvertently been elected the temporary and quite unofficial president of a neo-Rosicrucian network whose password was "Kircher," I decided to make good on my promise. The result was a conference in April 2001.

This memorable event—complete with Kircher videos, Kircherian music, a reconstructed magnetic clock by Caroline Bougereau, and many other modern-day wonders—and the volume that resulted from it could not have happened without the generous support of the Dean of Humanities and Science, Dean of Research, Department of History, Program in the History and Philosophy of Science, and Science, Technology, and Society Program at Stanford University. I want especially to single out Rosemary Rogers and Margaret Harris, since both of them ensured that the conference, postdoctoral fellowship program funded by the Hite endowment, and related activities all went without a hitch.

Preparing a volume of this scope and complexity has required the assistance of a number of people. First and foremost, I would like to thank four doctoral students: Robert Scafe compiled the bibliography and performed many other tasks essential to the preparation of the final manuscript; Daniel Stolzenberg helped me to edit a number of the papers and generously shared his own considerable expertise and enthusiasm for Kircher with me; and Sebastian Barreveld has seen the final manuscript through copyediting and pageproofs. Derrick Allums became my collaborator in translating two essays from French. All of them have reminded me what wonderful and interesting graduate students come to Stanford, and what a pleasure it is to work with them. Bill Germano at Routledge Press has been a marvelous editor. His own passion for

Kircher led to our collaboration, and I have been very appreciative of his enthusiasm for this project. I also thank Gilad Foss, Danielle Savin, and Andrew Schwartz whose support of this project during production and copyediting was absolutely essential to its completion.

I also want to thank a number of key participants in the Stanford workshop whose contributions might otherwise not be evident: Caroline Bougereau, Jorge Cañizares-Esguerra, Brad Gregory, Vanessa Kam, Federico Luisetti, Peter Pannke, Assunta Pisani, Jessica Riskin, Pamela Smith, Mary Terrall, Anne-Charlotte Trepp, David Wilson, and Glen Worthey all contributed to a pleasurable weekend of kircherizing. Most recently, as an offering for Kircher's four hundredth birthday in May 2002, Lawrence Weschler and Tony Grafton provided several of us with an opportunity to revisit our papers at the New York Institute of the Humanities in order to answer that burning question: "Was Athanasius Kircher the coolest guy ever, or what?" Needless to say, it is no small irony that a Jesuit, whose name most people can't pronounce and whose books they mostly haven't read, has earned this kind of twenty-first century approval. Whether he will soon supplant Leonardo as a popular icon of the past remains to be seen and probably depends on whether we can reconstruct the mechanical singing chicken or the vomiting lobster and present them in a Kircherian cryptology that can only be read in one of his catoptric machines or seen through his magic lantern.

My heartfelt thanks goes to all of the contributors to this volume for sharing my delight in Athanasius Kircher and his world (with a special tribute to Stephen Jay Gould, who died as this volume was nearing completion—Steve brought his personal copy of the *Mundus subterraneus* to Stanford so that he could punctuate his comments about fossils by turning to just the right page). Kircher himself insisted that friendship was a kind of magnetism that bound the peoples of the world together through some sort of occult sympathy. I can only say that in my experience of the people interested in him today, he was absolutely right. Their generosity and learning, more than anything, has made this project possible and enjoyable. Their mania for Kircher has perhaps alarmed a number of unsuspecting listeners who are still wondering if the cat piano really existed, or in fact if Kircher really existed, but, then, that is all part of the story. It is up to the reader to decide if this is just another Rosicrucian hoax, or fragments of the record of a life that we can actually document.

I suppose it is not entirely inappropriate to thank Father Athanasius. What would he have made of all this attention surrounding the four hundredth anniversary of his birthday, as exhibits and events in his honor occurred in cities as far-flung as Palo Alto, Chicago, New York, Rome, Madrid, Wolfenbüttel, and of course, Fulda? Would he be pleased to have become a minor character in so many Umberto Eco novels, the inspiration for at least two experimental musical compositions, and now the subject of a permanent museum exhibit on Venice Boulevard in Culver City, California? I suspect he would have considered it nothing more than his due. About time, he might have said. Perhaps he had become just a little bit tired of taking a perpetual ecstatic voyage without any new admirers to gaze at his ascent through the cosmos.

September 2003, Rome

Introduction
The Last Man Who Knew Everything ... or Did He?
Athanasius Kircher, S.J. (1602–80) and His World*

PAULA FINDLEN

"Nothing is more divine than to know everything."
—Plato, as quoted by Kircher in the *Ars magna sciendi* (1669)

1. "Poor Old Father Kircher"

Around 1678, news of the imminent demise of one of the seventeenth century's most fascinating, daring, prolific, and frustrating intellects leaked out of the Roman College, the principal educational institution of the Society of Jesus. Antonio Baldigiani (1647–1711), one of the younger professors of mathematics, scribbled an urgent message in the margin of a letter to let friends in Florence know that the man they had read and ridiculed, revered and despised, was now a shadow of his former self:

> Poor old Father Kircher is sinking fast. He's been deaf for more than a year, and has lost his sight and most of his memory. He rarely leaves his room except to go to the pharmacy or to the porter's room. In short, we already consider him lost since he cannot survive many more years.[1]

The German Jesuit Athanasius Kircher did not die until 27 November 1680, at the ripe old age of seventy-eight or seventy-nine.[2] His body was buried in Il Gesù and his heart in the Marian shrine of Mentorella, south of Rome. Despite Baldigiani's mournful description of Kircher, reports of his demise were somewhat exaggerated. Kircher was still writing his own letters to correspondents as late as November 1678, when he apologized to one colleague for any sloppiness inadvertently caused by his "trembling hand."[3] A trickle of letters continued, though increasingly composed by assistants, until the winter of 1680 when deafness and senility brought this final chapter of an interesting life to a close.

Perhaps even more alarming to his younger contemporaries was the fact that Kircher continued to publish, in the twilight of his career as one of the greatest polymaths in an encyclopedic age. The accelerating output seemed to defy his diminished capacities: with the encouragement of his publisher

1

Joannes Jansson van Waesberghe (or Janssonius, as he was often called) in Amsterdam and the assistance of various associates, Kircher had become a bookmaking, knowledge-regurgitating machine. He was already the author of more than thirty books on virtually every imaginable aspect of ancient and modern knowledge. Each publication demonstrated his dizzying array of linguistic, paleographic, historical, and scientific skills, and each advertised his myriad inventions, possession of strange and exotic artifacts, and mysterious manuscripts. Every work reminded Kircher's readers of his intimate familiarity with popes, princes, clerics, and scholars throughout the world. But these considerable accomplishments were not enough. At the end of his life, Kircher was determined to do two things: make his peace with God, through repeated contemplation of Ignatius of Loyola's *Spiritual Exercises* and frequent pilgrimage to the Marian shrine he had restored in Mentorella; and complete his outstanding publications.[4]

Kircher and his publishers devised ever more ingenious ways to advertise the continued expansion of the Kircherian corpus. In 1676, the reviewer of *Arca Noë* (*Noah's Ark*) in the Roman *Giornale de' Letterati* commented with amazement: "This is the thirty-sixth printed volume emerging from the fertility of this mind, and he has seven others ready to see the light of day. He will notify scholars about them, as usual, at the end"[5] (Figure Intro.1). The *Arca Noë* (1675) was the last of Kircher's books to appear under his own name containing a list of his published and forthcoming works, a form of advertisement that he initiated in 1646. Of the seven promised books, only three appeared in print. We have no record of the lost *Ars analogica* (*Analogic Art*) and *Ars veterum Aegyptiorum hieroglyphica* (*Hieroglyphic Art of the Ancient Egyptians*), nor do we know the whereabouts of his *Iter Hetruscam* (*Etruscan Journey*), a controversial history of ancient and modern Etruria that had more than its share of problems with the Jesuit censors. Kircher's translation of the second book of the great medieval Islamic commentator Avicenna's *Canon of Medicine*, which he had been promising readers since 1646 and proudly advertised as being "translated from Hebrew and Arabic," also never appeared.

Readers of this list, and the final enumeration of Kircher's works published in Giorgio de Sepibus's *Romani Collegii Societatis Jesu Musaeum Celeberrimum* (*The Celebrated Museum of the Roman College of the Society of Jesus*) of 1678, were invited to enter a seemingly infinite theater of books, a veritable encyclopedia of the mind in which the question of when the next publication would appear constantly yielded new answers. Virtually every book was advertised as appearing in print at least several years before it was actually available for readers. In a characteristic act of self-promotion, Kircher announced the "imminent" publication of some books for over thirty years.[6] He and his publishers understood well the power of the desire for knowledge in an age of mechanical reproduction. Jansson advertised himself to Kircher's readers as the "Amsterdam bookseller and printer of Kircherian work" and encouraged readers to

Figure Intro.1. The Deluge, according to Athanasius Kircher's *Noah's Ark. Source:* Athanasius Kircher, *Arca Noë* (Amsterdam, 1675). Courtesy of Special Collections, Stanford University Libraries.

contact him to buy anything on the list of 1675. Responding to inquiries about books that were no longer available or had yet to be published, Jansson emended the list in 1678, placing a cross next to the titles of those books he could not provide. While this might initially strike us as an indication that the Kircherian corpus seemed to be on the verge of obsolescence, the final word on Kircher's publications in his museum catalogue was designed to leave readers with the image of an endless horizon of projects to be published. "Many others," Jansson or Sepibus wrote, "are preserved in his mind, which, if God gives them life, will see the light."[7]

Reading such lists is a poignant reminder of why Umberto Eco identified Athanasius Kircher in the introductory pages of *The Name of the Rose* as the possible source of quotations from Brother Adso of Melk's description of the medieval labyrinth of a library containing Aristotle's lost book on laughter. Kircher seemed to possess so many fragments of ancient wisdom that it was entirely plausible to imagine that he had once owned and partially transcribed every lost manuscript of any significance. His encyclopedias offered choice passages of forgotten texts to his readers in large folio volumes, dense with the fonts of many languages and laden with the promise of more knowledge yet to come. The fact that he was unable—or perhaps unwilling—to release all of his books and editions of the wisdom of the ages into print made him all the more interesting and enigmatic. Was Kircher the man who held the key to all the best secrets of knowledge? Or had he simply invented it all to meet the expectations of his readers?

In 1678, a characteristically heterogeneous array of Kircherian intellectual projects lay on the horizon. A second edition of Kircher's fascinating exploration of the physical forces organizing and transforming the natural world, the *Mundus subterraneus* (*Subterranean World*)—announced to readers as the third edition because Kircher, quite characteristically, seems to have counted the two volumes of 1664–65 as two separate editions—appeared that year. Giorgio de Sepibus, the curator of machines in the Roman College museum, filled with Kircher's possessions, experiments, and inventions, had finally published its long-awaited catalogue.[8] The following year, the gorgeously illustrated *Turris Babel* (*Tower of Babel*) attempted once and for all to explain how languages had multiplied and dispersed throughout the globe since the folly of Babel. It also offered a fascinating account of why the Tower could not reach the moon, since Kircher proved definitively for his readers that the weight and height of such an edifice would have decentered the earth—which of course had not happened. Simultaneously the *Tariffa Kircheriana* (*Kircherian Tables*) appeared, offering a detailed description of the miraculous Kircherian combinatorial art that would quickly allow all the princes and nobles of Europe— and presumably anyone else "occupied by more important business" who could read Latin—to master all of geometry and arithmetic. In fact, Kircher himself seems to have become exactly that sort of person by 1679—at least this was how his associates wished to describe him rather than acknowledging that he was no longer capable of completing his own books. Kircher consigned the final preparation of the *Tariffa* to Benedetto Benedetti, professor of mathematics at La Sapienza, who described how "new occupations of great moment" had obliged Kircher to offer him the privilege of becoming its editor.[9]

Quite appropriately, the ultimate word in Kircherian studies appeared the year of Kircher's death in the form of Johann Stephan Kestler's *Physiologia Kircheriana experimentalis* (*Experimental Kircherian Physiology*) of 1680. Kestler, who assisted Kircher in making his machines, "extracted from the vast works of the Most Reverend Father Athanasius Kircher" the fruits of his experimental labor, filling its pages with accounts of definitive tests and splendid machines that, according to Kircher and his disciples, helped philosophers discern the truths of science in their investigations of the natural world.[10] It was a fitting coda to a half-century's intellectual production. Finally someone—perhaps Kircher himself, since the project was completed in Rome in October 1675 though it lay unpublished for five years—had had the good sense to reduce Kircher's terrifying prolixity to the equivalent of a big, beautiful book of baroque Cliffs Notes. An anonymous contributor to the first volume of the *Philosophical Transactions* of the Royal Society acted on a similar impulse when he chose to translate a single experiment from Kircher's *Mundus subter-raneus* so that readers "who either have not the leisure to read Voluminous Authors, or are not readily skilled in that Learned Tongue wherein the said Book is written" might gain some appreciation for the content of this book and the widespread interest it aroused after its initial appearance in 1665.[11]

When Jorge Luis Borges fantasized about a scholar who devoted his erudition to summarizing and commenting on an imaginary five-hundred-page encyclopedia he had never written, Borges was thinking specifically of a project that contradicted the logic of Kircher's world.[12] Perhaps Borges had had occasion to read the Jesuit Caspar Knittel's *Via Regia ad omnes scientias et artes. Hoc est: Ars Universalis Scientiarum omnium Artiumque Arcana facilius penetrandi* (*Royal Road to All the Sciences and Arts. That Is, the Universal Art Easily Penetrating the Secrets of All the Sciences and Arts*) of 1682. This delightful tribute to Kircherian logic transformed his encyclopedias into a pocket edition that an ordinary seeker of knowledge should be able to afford and absorb. Epitomizing Kircher was no small task. We should celebrate this Prague professor for the diligence with which he presented his intellectual hero as a neoscholastic authority. For a brief moment, Kircher had become the new Aristotle who promised his disciples everything from greater eloquence and enhanced memory to a kind of physically induced omniscience that could only be retrieved by manipulating one of Kircher's famous "arks"—wooden combinatorial chests that contained numbers, words, music, in short, anything that might be automatically produced by a machine that combined things according to a predetermined logic that its inventor had programmed into the machine.[13] To my knowledge, Knittel's *Via Regia* was the last book that openly advocated Athanasius Kircher's approach to knowledge—a "Universal Lullian-Kircherian Art of Knowing and Examining"—as a *clavis universalis* that might unlock the mysteries of the universe. Just as Kestler had summed up his experimental method, Knittel sought to simplify Kircher's philosophy of knowledge as the final proof of its universality. We can only imagine how young students at the Carolinum, for whom this text was intended, responded to this innovative pedagogical program.

The Kircherian machine, a vast and lucrative publishing enterprise that existed between Kircher's quarters in Rome and the offices of his Amsterdam publisher Jansson, did not simply continue in the twilight of his career; if anything, it became even more efficient in the late 1670s in getting Kircher's ideas out to his public. It seemed as if every participant involved in the project—the author, the publisher, his disciples, and last but not least, the Society of Jesus—wanted to squeeze the maximum amount of words, ink, and profit out of this singular mind of the seventeenth century. In December 1674, Baldigiani marveled at the fact that "any strange thing that he writes would be published in Amsterdam." He confessed that he no longer discussed matters of science with Kircher "because I'm afraid of seeing myself published one day in one of his books as the author and witness of some gross error."[14] Kircher had become the *omnium gatherum* of the intellectual flotsam and jetsam of Rome. Other Jesuit professors, Baldigiani reported, had found themselves in the pages of such works as *Arca Noë*, agreeing with Kircher on matters they had never discussed in his presence. At the height of his career, Kircher created a kind of typographic labyrinth that temporarily trapped all the best minds of the mid–seventeenth century inside his books.

But Baldigiani need not have worried too much. Kircher's intellectual authority was decidedly on the wane in the late 1670s. As early as 1672, local Roman antiquaries declared Kircher's efforts to explain the history of ancient Lazio flawed beyond belief. Had Kircher even bothered to travel to Ostia to see its Roman ruins? Raffaele Fabretti, custodian of Christian relics and the ancient Roman catacombs, thought not. He wrote an entire treatise outlining the errors of Kircher's *Latium* (1671).[15] Such nagging concerns about the basis for Kircher's claims to expertise delayed the publication of his other great study of the history and monuments of the Italian peninsula, the *Iter Hetruscam*, for years, finally consigning it to the dustbin of manuscripts that were perpetually in production without ever being printed. If Kircher's knowledge of the ancient Latins was less than perfect, what could he possibly say about the Etruscans that would satisfy the new criteria of scientific antiquarianism that emerged in the late seventeenth century?

While younger Jesuits bristled at the suggestion that they shared his philosophical outlook, others philosophers came to the conclusion that Kircher's efforts at omniscience simply stirred the water in the pot without ever bringing it to a boil. In the final year of Kircher's life, a young Leibniz (1646–1716), who had written admiringly to the German Jesuit in 1670 after reading his work on China, reflected on the difference between his own youthful *Dissertatio de arte combinatoria* (*Dissertation on the Combinatorial Art*), which he had written in 1666, and Kircher's *Ars magna sciendi* (*Great Art of Knowing*) of 1669. Kircher, he concluded, "had not even dreamed of the true analysis of human thoughts any more than had the others who have tried to reform philosophy."[16] That same year, he published his first account of the calculus, one of his many demonstrations of what this new kind of analysis might yield. Leibniz would not visit Rome until 1689, almost a decade after Kircher's death. There he encountered Father Baldigiani, who was still trying to improve upon Kircher's account of how to make color penetrate marble.[17] By 1716, after decades of careful study of many of the ancient and modern languages and sciences that had interested Kircher, Leibniz left no doubt in his readers' minds that other dimensions of Kircher's work had also gone astray. After reading Kircher's many publications on Egyptian language and evaluating his translations of hieroglyphic wisdom inscribed on the obelisks strategically positioned in the main piazzas of Rome, Leibniz tersely remarked: "he understands nothing."[18]

Unfortunately for Kircher, this seemed to be the growing consensus by the second decade of the eighteenth century. In the 1670s, Roman scholars already joked about the pleasure of fabricating evidence, knowing that Kircher was "highly susceptible to suggestion."[19] Even loyal disciples like Knittel advertised his arithmetic mistakes when they redid his combinatorial tables.[20] Within a few decades, such comments became the basis for disparaging every aspect of his erudition. In 1715, a year before Leibniz dismissed Kircher's famous interpretive translations of the hieroglyphs, Johann Burkhard Mencke (1674–1732) immortalized the image of Kircher as the most foolish of polymaths in his *De charlataneria eruditorum* (*The Charlatanry of the Learned*) when he described three different pranks played on the German Jesuit. The first involved a purportedly Egyptian manuscript sent by one Andreas Müller to Kircher that he translated without recognizing it to be a forgery. The second involved the discovery of a figured stone on a construction site in Rome. Kircher was immediately called to the site to authenticate this "monument of antiquity" and offered "a beautiful interpretation of the circles, the crosses, and all the other meaningless signs." Finally, he received silk paper inscribed with Chinese-like characters. Unable to interpret it, he finally expressed his bewilderment as to its significance to the bearers of this gift. With great glee, they held it up to a mirror, and the following words appeared: *Noli vana sectari et tempus perdere nugis nihil proficientibus* ("Do not seek vain things, or waste time on unprofitable trifles").[21] Who was Kircher, then, at the dawn of the Enlightenment? He was a man unable to recognize truth from falsehood, a scholar with an imperfect grasp of the science of philology and linguistics, an archaeologist who did not know the difference between a Roman lamp and a Grecian urn, and an inventor of language who could not recognize the simplest cipher. Thrice fooled, in Mencke's parable of learned ignorance, Kircher could no longer convince others that he knew anything of worth. The great English historian Edward Gibbon was quite sure of it.[22]

Increasingly, Kircher's penchant for connecting every different kind of knowledge no longer resonated with an eighteenth-century audience. In a world of increasingly specialized and jealously guarded expertise, the lacunae in Kircher's scholarship seemed glaringly obvious. In 1760, for example, the abbé Jean-Jacques Barthelemy, Louis XV's Royal Keeper of the Medals, informed Parisian academicians that Kircher's interpretation of the famous Nile mosaic of Palestrina was just plain wrong. The Jesuit declared it a monument to the goddess Fortuna erected by the Roman dictator Sulla. Barthelemy tartly responded that this seemed odd since it struck him as an image of Egypt rather than a Roman allegory. How ironic, he reflected, that "the author of the *Oedipus Aegyptiacus*," the greatest and perhaps most demented encyclopedia ever written about ancient Egypt, could not recognize the object of his intellectual passion when he saw it.[23]

If this had been the actual Kircher, or perhaps we should say the totality of Kircher's contributions to various intellectual projects, then there would be little more to do than laugh with others across the centuries at this most deluded of polymaths. Mencke's devastatingly funny portrait of Kircher, and Leibniz's and Barthelemy's criticisms limit our vision only to what people saw *in retrospect*, and they do not do full justice even to that part of his place in the history of knowledge. It was not Kircher's ignorance but the complex and compelling nature of his intellectual convictions that led him down a particular path, which, it turns out, was not the road to modernity but a rather different project.

Discussing Kircher's astronomy, which took as its starting point the Tychonic system of the universe that had become the official Jesuit cosmology in Kircher's youth, the Dutch mathematician and inventor Christiaan Huygens remarked in 1698: "I have sometimes thought that one would have be able to expect better ideas from Kircher, if he had dared to state them freely. But since he didn't have this courage, I don't know why he didn't prefer to abstain entirely from this subject."[24] This mixed assessment of Kircher's failings in relation to his potential, however, masked the fact that Huygens's decision to write his own cosmic voyage emerged from his reading of the *Itinerarium exstaticum* (*Ecstatic Journey*) of 1656.[25] In other words, Kircher was a source of inspiration for a great deal of interesting work in the seventeenth and eighteenth centuries. Scholars read and responded to his encyclopedias because they represented an intriguing stage in the evolution of many different scholarly disciplines, often all in the same thick volume. The more scholars separated out diverse strands of knowledge, the more they resisted Kircher's worldview which was itself a dynamic entity that responded to the intellectual possibilities of mid-seventeenth century Europe. He belonged to an era that combined rather than divided, that took delight in finding unlikely connections in the service of a grand unified theory of absolutely everything.

The same year that Huygens reassessed Kircher's astronomy, a brief notice of yet another aspect of his science appeared in the 1698 *Philosophical Transactions*, in an account of acoustic experiments performed in Oxford that had been inspired by certain passages in the *Phonurgia nova* (*New Way of Making Sound*) of 1673. The article concluded that Kircher's arguments about sound moving more swiftly at its beginning than its end were correct.[26] There were many different accounts of Kircher in circulation, in part, because he offered such a wide range of subjects for people to contemplate, each in their own way on the cutting edge of new knowledge. He was a man who nimbly gathered data, absorbed new methodologies, and recognized what was interesting to know by the standards of his time. Kircher's strength lay in his ability to make the study of science, language, history, faith, and antiquity equally interesting to his readers. His weakness, of course, was the opposite side of this coin, since his talent lay in combining subjects rather than treating each as a specific field of knowledge whose skills demanded the patience and depth of expertise that he was often unwilling to acquire.

We can see these differences in contrasting accounts of Kircher in the early eighteenth century. The same year that Mencke published his satire of false erudition, the great New England scholar and preacher Cotton Mather (1663–1728) finished a manuscript entitled *The Christian Philosopher*. Printed in London in 1721 with the assistance of the Royal Society, of which he was a member, it repeatedly invoked Kircher as an authority to be juxtaposed with the likes of Robert Boyle, Robert Hooke, and Isaac Newton. "*Kircher* supposed the *Sun* to be a body of wondrous *Fire*, unequal in Surface, composed of Parts which are of a different Nature, some fluid, some solid: The Disque of it, a *Sea of Fire* wherein Waves of astonishing Flame have a perpetual Agitation." The Puritan divine was quick to add that both Hooke and Newton instead described it as "a solid and opake Body."[27] But Mather's gleeful description of the bubbling solar cauldron that Kircher conjured up in his astronomy suggests that while the sober words of his fellow members of the Royal Society won his mind, the poetic descriptions and vividly engraved images in a Jesuit encyclopedia captured his imagination (Figure Intro.2). Astronomy was not the only aspect of Kircher's work than interested Mather. He accepted Kircher's priority over another Fellow of the Royal Society, Samuel Moreland, in the invention of the speaking tube, and he repeated Kircher's description of the eruption of Mount Etna; Mather marveled at Kircher's account of stones that naturally imitated the form of a monk's garment, and took note of his description of fevers that caused worms to form spontaneously within the blood. Mather was equally fascinated by Kircher's account of the ability of music to move the soul. He also agreed with him that more research needed to be done on one of the many unanswered questions of natural history: did fish with lungs also have ears?[28]

This random assemblage of facts, culled from Kircher's books by the greatest scholar in early colonial New England, reminds us of the continuing appeal of Kircher's worldview well into the eighteenth century. His exuberant curiosity still spoke to readers in the decades after his death, and he was a priceless source of strange facts, interesting questions, and intriguing if at times unsatisfactory experiments. The early members of the Royal Society were all avid readers of Kircher's work.[29] Mather was considerably less disingenuous about his relationship to Kircher, who simply provided him with information, than his contemporary Leibniz, who neglected to tell his readers—perhaps because it was too obvious—that virtually every major scientific, linguistic, and historical project on which he embarked had been directly inspired by reading Kircher's works. To a lesser degree, the same might also be said of Newton, who never once cited Kircher, leading Voltaire to wonder whether Newton had plagiarized his account of the relationship between light and color from Kircher, as some had reported.[30] It turned out he had not. Instead it was

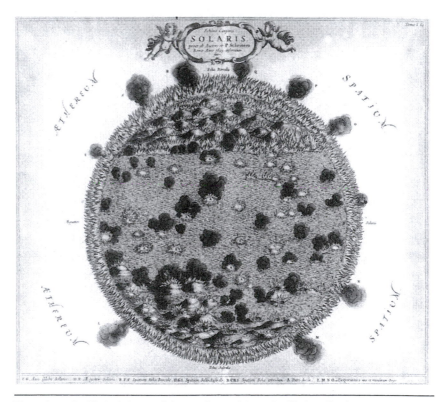

Figure Intro.2. Kircher's image of the sun. *Source:* Athanasius Kircher, *Mundus subterraneus* (Amsterdam, 1665). Courtesy of Special Collections, Stanford University Libraries.

Goethe at the end of the eighteenth century, in search of a science of optics to counter Newton's, who would rediscover Kircher. Nonetheless, a significant number of the most important attempts to create new sciences and reform knowledge in the second half of the seventeenth century emerged from an encounter with the ideas of this singular and beguiling figure.

2. A Clock and a Manuscript, or the Bearer of Secrets

If Athanasius Kircher was the most famous, or infamous, of scholars by the end of his life, he gave no explicit indication of this trajectory at its beginning. In the 1630s, as Kircher began to develop a European-wide reputation, the single most memorable fact about Kircher was that no one could spell his name correctly. Balthazard Kyrner, Baltazar Kilner, Kikser, Kircser, Father Anastasio[31]—the enigma of the German Jesuit who traveled south to escape the arrival of Protestants in his corner of the Holy Roman Empire seemed unusually difficult to resolve. Kircher's name, like the origins of his erudition, remained a puzzle even to those who opened their libraries to him, offered him their patronage, and assisted him in his quest to find a position worthy of his talents.

Kircher eventually achieved this goal when he was appointed professor of mathematics and oriental languages at the Roman College in 1633. He was subsequently relieved of his teaching duties in 1646 in order to devote all of his time to research, writing, and the entertainment of important visitors who came to Rome to see the famous Father Athanasius and his museum at the Roman College. Almost from the start, the scholarly community expressed their doubt about the nature of Kircher's erudition, while being tantalized by the promise of spectacular results. Kircher's success seems to have been due as much to his mastery of the art of intellectual dissimulation as it was also a product of his congenial personality, his good fortune with patrons and publishers, and his important position in the Society of Jesus. Put a different way, Kircher succeeded because seventeenth-century society wanted him to be successful. They had questions, and he provided answers. What more should they have wanted?

Born on 2 May 1602 in the small town of Geisa, the youngest of nine children in a pious and scholarly burgher family, Athanasius Kircher later described himself in his autobiography, published posthumously in 1684, as an accident-prone dullard. After his admission on 2 October 1618 to the Jesuit College at Paderborn, he was almost expelled from the Society of Jesus because of poor health when the college surgeon discovered open sores on his legs, the result of chilblains from a fall into an icy river. Though Kircher claimed to have studied Greek at the Jesuit college in Fulda as well as Hebrew under the tutelage of a rabbi—a sign that he was hardly witless—his initially quiet demeanor after his admission to the order made his earliest teachers despair of their new pupil. They soon discovered their mistake when, as Kircher immodestly recalled, he mastered the natural philosophy curriculum in less than two months, and successfully completed his novitiate in 1620.

As with many Germans of his generation, the brutal realities of the Thirty Years' War directly affected the course of Kircher's life. Perhaps this is one of the reasons that he remembered his youth as a serious of perilous encounters with the elements, disease, and war, in which divine intervention proved to be his salvation. Between 1622 and 1633, he led a peripatetic existence, studying and teaching at various colleges and trying to stay out of harm's way. A member of the Catholic minority in a part of the Holy Roman Empire that was largely Lutheran and Calvinist, Kircher was forced to flee to Cologne in January 1622 to avoid meeting an unpleasant fate at the hands of Protestant troops. One year later, having completed his philosophical studies, he found himself in Koblenz teaching Greek. In his spare time, he erected the first of several sundials that he made for various Jesuit colleges. At this point in his life, Kircher resolved to dedicate himself to two subjects: mathematics and languages.

By 1625, he returned to the town of Heiligenstadt, where his father had taught at the local seminary, and became an instructor in Hebrew, Syriac, and mathematics. When the archbishop of Mainz decided to visit, Kircher seized the opportunity to demonstrate a machine so fantastic that he was immediately accused of practicing black magic—but not by the archbishop, who invited him to Mainz for the next four years where Kircher installed another sundial while completing a four-year course in theology and initiating study of "Oriental languages."[32] Ordained in 1628, Kircher completed all but the final year of his tertiarship, the third stage of his probation as a Jesuit, in Speyer. At this moment, Kircher began to dream of two things that would preoccupy him for much of his life: the idea of becoming a missionary to the East and the possibility of deciphering the hieroglyphs. A chance encounter in the college library with a book on Egyptian hieroglyphics, probably Johann Georg Hörwart von Hohenburg's *Thesaurus hieroglyphica*, fueled the latter passion.[33]

Refused permission to go to the near East in 1628, Kircher spent the final year of his German interlude in Würzburg, where he was appointed professor of moral philosophy, mathematics, Hebrew, and Syriac at the Jesuit college in 1630. There he encountered his earliest disciple, Kaspar Schott (1608–66), who studied with Kircher and would later assist him in Rome, building machines, editing Kircher's works, and publicizing Kircher's boundless supply of inventions.[34] Kircher's preliminary studies of the "magnetic art" produced his first publication: a slim pamphlet entitled the *Ars magnesia* (*Magnetic Art*) in 1631. An earlier *Institutiones mathematicae* (*Institutions of Mathematics*), which Kircher wrote the previous year, remained unpublished because he left it behind when the Swedish army arrived in Würzburg in October 1631.[35]

In 1632, Kircher migrated to the Jesuit College in Avignon, never to return to the Holy Roman Empire. Appointed professor of mathematics and oriental languages, Kircher continued to pursue his twin passions as a scholar and a teacher. Having already developed a reputation as a builder of clocks and mathematical measuring devices for various German rulers and Jesuit colleges, he set to work building an elaborate sundial in the tower of the Jesuit College in Avignon that demonstrated his facility with using mirrors to direct the sun's rays across the wall to indicate not only the motions of the planets and the positions of the stars, but also the time differences throughout the world.[36] At the same time, he let local scholars know that he had two interesting artifacts in his possession: a sunflower clock and a mysterious manuscript by the Babylonian rabbi Barachias Nephi.[37]

Out of the ruins of Germany, two great secrets had been preserved for the Catholic world to decipher. The French scholarly community that Kircher encountered in 1632 found both of these items utterly fascinating. They watched him transform the college tower in Avignon into a mirror of the cosmos and marveled at his capacity for the most technical sciences and the most arcane languages—precisely the sort of knowledge greatly prized in the early seventeenth century. Kircher's reputation was made before anyone had authenticated either the clock or the manuscript. By the spring of 1632, the French lawyer, antiquarian, and savant Nicolas-Claude Fabri de Peiresc (1580–1637) in nearby Aix began to imagine that Kircher would help him unlock the mysteries of the Egyptian hieroglyphs.[38] At that point, Peiresc had not yet seen Kircher's mysterious manuscript, but desire only compounded his sense of optimism. Already in December 1632, scholars in Paris had heard of the German Jesuit who had copied an Arabic manuscript in the library of the elector of Mainz and promised that the knowledge it contained would enable him "to interpret all the inscriptions in Rome." By March 1633, Peiresc informed his younger associate, the philosopher Pierre Gassendi, that Kircher's manuscript, once properly transcribed and analyzed, would reveal "knowledge of things that have been unknown to Christianity for almost two thousand years."[39] A big claim indeed.

The initial image of Kircher, as a man in possession of fabulously important and difficult knowledge, received further confirmation as news of his sunflower clock traveled through the same correspondence networks. Kircher had already demonstrated his heliotropic plant, a nightshade whose seeds allegedly followed the motions of the sun when affixed to a cork bobbing in water, in Mainz; he now proceeded to demonstrate it in Avignon and Aix (Figure Intro.3). Peiresc described it admiringly as "a great miracle of nature," the best of the many "secrets of nature" that Kircher claimed to be able to explain. He begged Kircher for a copy of his recently published book on magnetism, plied him with his best Arabic dictionaries from his considerable library, and described Kircher's intellectual ambition as being "a little grander than the ordinary goals of his colleagues."[40] Kircher heightened the mystery of the sunflower clock by describing an encounter with an Arabic merchant in the port of Marseille who provided him with heliotropic seeds from an Eastern plant in exchange for a watch so small that it was contained within a ring.[41] Peiresc began to fantasize about bringing Kircher to Aix so that they might collaborate more easily. He was so taken with the German who possessed oriental wisdom that he encouraged the prior of the Jesuit College in Aix to discuss this possibility with the Jesuit General Muzio Vitelleschi in Rome.[42]

Yet even as Peiresc salivated at the prospect of working closely with this promising young scholar, he began to have doubts about the nature of Kircher's erudition. It took less than six months for the bloom to wear off the rose. Despite his best efforts to inspect Kircher's manuscript of the Barachias Nephi, Peiresc finally confessed to the antiquarian Claude Saumaise, he hadn't seen "even a copy of a single page" by November 1633. Kircher kept promising to improve his transcription, citing his "imperfect Egyptian" as a reason for the delay, but Peiresc began to wonder if there weren't other reasons. Two months earlier, he had caught multiple errors in Kircher's interpretation of the obelisk of Saint John Lateran in Rome.[43] And Kircher continued to dissimulate about the exact nature of the manuscript he possessed. Was Kircher really qualified to understand the relationship between Coptic and Arabic, let alone reconstruct the relationship

Figure Intro.3. The sunflower clock. *Source:* Athanasius Kircher, *Magnes, sive de arte magnetica,* 2nd ed. (Cologne, 1643). Courtesy of Special Collections, Stanford University Libraries.

between the ancient hieroglyphs and the modern languages of Egypt? Did he really own an interesting manuscript? Peiresc was no longer so sure.

Peiresc also began to express his reservations about the sunflower clock. Initially he believed it might offer the final proof of heliocentrism that Galileo's theory of the tides in his *Dialogue concerning the Two Chief World Systems* (1632) had failed to provide. This controversial book was in the hands of the Roman censors, and Galileo himself, much to Peiresc's dismay, was under interrogation by the Holy Office for the heresy of advocating Copernican astronomy. In Peiresc's correspondence with the Minim Marin Mersenne, one of the leading French natural philosophers of the time, we can observe the changing tone of his observations as his disillusionment with Kircher grew. Peiresc was a man who very much wanted to believe in Kircher's promise of linguistic and philosophical enlightenment; yet at the same time, he was a lawyer who demanded evidence as a precondition to belief.

In the spring and summer of 1633, all the important natural philosophers in France and the Netherlands discussed Kircher's sunflower clock. The trial of Galileo ended with his abjuration of Copernicanism on 22 June 1633, but discussion of Kircher's heliotrope continued. Mersenne was so intrigued by what he heard from Aix that he forwarded an account to Descartes. With characteristic caution, Descartes responded in July 1633 that if it were true, it was "most curious." But he added, "I still doubt the effect, though I nevertheless do not judge it to be at all impossible." Peiresc, on the other hand, living in closer proximity to Kircher, was not so kind. In October 1633, he told Mersenne that he had tried unsuccessfully to obtain a copy of the sunflower clock "by all means humanly possible" in order to test its properties. "I am of your opinion and don't believe in it any more than you do."[44] The clock, like the manuscript, seemed to be an object trapped inside a house of illusions. After Kircher's public demonstration of it in the Jesuit colleges of southern France, Peiresc concluded, quite rightfully, that it was no clock but a magnet.

After Peiresc's volte-face, we would expect him to have nothing to do with Kircher. In the summer of 1633, it seemed that Kircher's reputation had been ruined and the limits of his knowledge woefully exposed. Yet if this were the case, why do we find Father Athanasius departing for Rome in September of that year? Initially told to accept an assignment in Vienna (Kircher later boasted that he was to replace Johannes Kepler as the imperial mathematician), Kircher was preparing to return to the Holy Roman Empire. Peiresc, however, was determined to make use of Kircher to further one of his pet projects: the publication of Pietro della Valle's Coptic grammar and dictionary in Rome. He paved the way by using his contacts with General Vitelleschi to effect a transfer to Rome rather than Aix, and by writing one of the leading cultural figures in the Rome of Urban VIII, the antiquarian, naturalist, and collector Cassiano dal Pozzo (1588–1657), close confidant of Cardinal Francesco Barberini. In his letter of 10 September, Peiresc assured his Roman correspondent that Kircher's "most curious inventions and most unusual experiments" and the fruits of "his most exquisite mind" were worthy of papal patronage.[45] For the next two months while Kircher traveled south, uncertain of his final destination, Peiresc sent materials to dal Pozzo to assist in the continuation of Kircher's work on the Coptic grammar and dictionary, and to encourage the idea of investing in Kircher's linguistic skills. With great relief, he finally heard news of Kircher's arrival in Rome in mid-November 1633 and received confirmation of his appointment as professor of mathematics at the Roman College, where he succeeded Galileo's adversary, Christoph Scheiner, in this position.[46]

The idea that Peiresc considered Kircher useful in Rome is confirmed by the enormous amount of attention he lavished on Kircher's projects between 1633 and his own death in 1636. He endlessly pumped correspondents for news of Kircher's activities, offering advice regarding which projects Kircher should prioritize. He worried incessantly about the quality of Kircher's work. He used his Roman contacts to facilitate the Jesuit's access to the considerable manuscript holdings of the Vatican Library. For better and for worse, Kircher had become Peiresc's protégé, in part, because the French scholar was still hopeful about the editorial and philological aspects of the Jesuit's work, even as he questioned Kircher's interpretive abilities. When Peiresc heard that Cardinal Barberini had asked Kircher to interpret the Bembine Table, a prize antiquity engraved with mysterious characters that might aptly be described as the Renaissance Rosetta Stone, he began to wonder if the transcription of della Valle's Coptic manuscript, let alone that of the precious Barachias Nephi, would ever be completed (Figure Intro.4). "I did not expect that this good Father would get his hands on it so soon," wrote Peiresc in confidence. He worried that Kircher would misinterpret it, "having known his disposition during his year's sojourn in Avignon, where he allowed himself to be too easily diverted by the last thing that occupied him."[47] He also asked dal Pozzo to discourage Kircher from completing his latest publication on magnetism before finishing his editorial work on the two manuscripts.[48] In the next two years, to Peiresc's great embarrassment, Kircher began to unravel the secrets of some mysterious characters engraved on Mount Oreb in the Sinai. Peiresc considered it a modern forgery. He urged Kircher not to include this transcription in his *Prodromus Coptus sive Aegyptiacus (Coptic or Egyptian Forerunner)*.[49] As Kircher's prestige grew in Rome, everyone brought the learned Jesuit their best secrets. His stature grew by leaps and bounds as he attempted to answer virtually every pressing question of ancient faith. Kircher seemed increasingly autonomous from Peiresc's direction. Peiresc worried that his carefully laid plans to make the best knowledge of ancient Egypt available to a learned public had gone terribly astray. From Aix, he simply could not control Kircher's activities in Rome.

In the fall of 1636, shortly before Peiresc's death, Kircher's *Prodromus Coptus* finally appeared, published by the Congregation for the Propagation of the Faith in Rome. Praising his "erudition in secret exotic matters," the Jesuit censor Melchior Inchofer, who had played no small role in the condemnation of Galileo's *Dialogue*, judged it "a worthy beginning from which we may anticipate what will follow."[50] The *Prodromus Coptus* did not contain the Coptic dictionary, which eventually appeared in the *Lingua Aegyptiaca restituita (The Egyptian Language Restored)* of 1643. Instead it displayed many other choice examples of Kircher's linguistic virtuosity, including his account of a recently discovered Nestorian monument in China, brought to Europe's attention by Jesuit missionaries who first saw it in 1625, and his transcription of the Sinai inscription.[51] Antiquarians throughout Europe sharpened their quills to at-

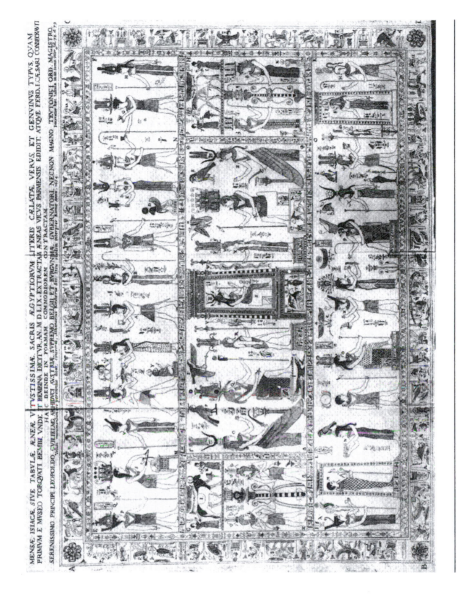

Figure Intro.4. The Bembine Table. *Source:* Athanasius Kircher, *Oedipus Aegyptiacus* (1652–55), vol. 3, p. 78. Courtesy of Bancroft Library, University of California, Berkeley.

tack all its errors. Peiresc cautioned them not to go too far. "Bad luck can be good in some things," he remarked proverbially.[52] Certainly Kircher did not dig deeply into the sources of his knowledge, nor did he take the time to establish sound proofs to shore up his conclusions. But, Peiresc reminded his colleagues, he was not a bad sort of Jesuit nor should he be entirely dismissed as a scholar. Early in the publication of the Coptic dictionary, he had declared that if Kircher could "break the ice and penetrate some tiny thing, perhaps with time one could overcome some other difficulties." For this reason, he warned his colleagues that "we should not caricature the Father in any way."[53] Kircher had opened the way for others to follow who could discreetly correct his errors without offending him or his patrons in Rome.[54] Besides, it was rumored in 1636 that Kircher was about to leave for the Levant at any moment. Good relations with Kircher and the Society of Jesus would ensure that European scholars had a steady supply of unknown manuscripts in foreign tongues for years to come.

Peiresc's attitude toward Kircher suggests a number of different things we might keep in mind. Quite evidently, he did not trust Kircher's antiquarian instincts any more than did the late-seventeenth- and eighteenth-century scholars who castigated Kircher, delighting in their discovery of his errors. Rather than perceiving Kircher to be an accomplished linguist and Egyptologist, as many others did throughout his career, Peiresc considered him to be a unique resource in facilitating the general project of recovering the past. Peiresc sagely observed that Kircher was the kind of scholar who "did violence to the authority of the ancients in establishing his conjectures."[55] But fundamentally he did not want to throw out the baby with the bathwater. Instead, he hoped that with his guidance, Kircher might become a unique conduit between the Roman world of antiquarianism, rich in manuscripts and artifacts with the promise of more to come through the Jesuit missionary networks, and the northern European world of scholarship that compensated for its relative paucity of original artifacts by establishing a more scientific foundation for the study of the distant past.

This view, however, was the perspective from Aix. What did people say in Rome? In November 1633, Kircher arrived in a city still recovering from the long shadow cast by the trial of Galileo.[56] He became the talk of the town. People came to the Roman College, the principal educational institution of the Society of Jesus, to converse with him and see his experiments. News of the wonders that Kircher brought to the papal city eventually found its way to Florence—or at least as far as Arcetri, where Galileo was under house arrest. In March 1634, two correspondents wrote to aging mathematician to tell him about what they had seen and heard about the young German. Both described in some detail Kircher's sunflower clock, which he displayed publicly in the crèche installed in Saint Peter's during Christmas 1637 as part of an exhibit of different clocks that told time all over the world.[57] As in the past, Kircher's inventions made him the object of considerable attention, inciting the curiosity of scholars in a new social and political environment. Peiresc and his friends did nothing to contradict this image, despite their skepticism about the clock.

In a classic misunderstanding of Kircher's origins, Raffaello Magiotti informed Galileo:

> Once again, there's a Jesuit in Rome who has spent a lot of time in the Orient. Besides knowing twelve languages and being a good geometer, etc., he has a lot of wonderful things with him, among them, a root that turns as the sun turns, and can serve as a most perfect clock.

Magiotti had seen a demonstration of the sunflower clock and heard that Kircher possessed copies of Arabic and Chaldean manuscripts, filled with "great secrets and histories." He also wrote of Kircher's promise to explain "everything contained in the obelisk of the Popolo." The "spectacle of so many novelties" made Kircher by far the most sought after scholar in Rome.[58] He was indeed a baroque magus bearing gifts from the East, a German newcomer in a city eager to embrace foreign scholars who helped promote the image of Rome as the capital of knowledge as well as of faith.[59]

Misperception is often as revealing as comprehension. If Kircher did not deliberately deceive his Roman audience, he in all likelihood chose not to disabuse them of the idea that he had actually been in the Orient. Perhaps the suggestive nature of this fantasy made it impossible for him to ever get there. If Kircher already seemed to have knowledge of the East, what would the Society of Jesus gain by actually sending him there? In 1637, after publishing his *Prodromus Coptus* with great fanfare, Kircher hoped that his bona fide credentials as a philologist and mathematician might finally win him passage to the Levant. Following a trip to Malta as the confessor of the recently converted Landgraf Friedrich of Hesse-Darmstadt, and in the midst of a brief assignment as professor of mathematics at the Jesuit College in Malta, he wrote a second letter requesting a mission to the Near East. General Vitelleschi quickly disabused Kircher of this idea, responding tersely in a letter of 7 January 1638 that he appreciated Kircher's "desire to go to the Orient," but the Society needed him at home. "Your Reverence must return to Rome."[60] There Kircher remained, save for his pilgrimages into the Roman countryside, for the remainder of his long and productive life. And it was in the papal city that he published the majority of his works on science and history, nature and culture, language and faith, inviting his readers to explore the connections among virtually every imaginable form of knowledge. But in the early years of his stay in Rome, Magiotti could report only one salient fact to Galileo: in more than three years, Kircher still had not given him a sample of the mysterious heliotropic root that he had discovered in the market of Marseille.[61]

3. The Making of a Baroque Polymath

Peiresc was absolutely right. Kircher had no desire to become simply an antiquarian. His vision of himself was as expansive as the city that became his

Figure Intro.5. The eruption of Mount Vesuvius in 1638. *Source:* Athanasius Kircher, *Mundus subterraneus*, 2nd ed. (Amsterdam, 1678). Courtesy of Special Collections, Stanford University Libraries.

home. Rome was a city of many sciences, a town filled with churches, palaces, monuments, and ruins, populated by artists, musicians, scholars, and theologians, all in service to some patron or another. Even if Kircher did not know he would secure a position in Rome, he soon became comfortable in this milieu. During his stay in Malta, Kircher made another instrument—the *Specula Melitensis* (*Maltese Observatory*)—and gave the Knights of Saint John instructions in how to use this miraculous mechanical microcosm that contained a planisphere, kept track of the Julian and Gregorian calendars, told universal time, charted horoscopes, and condensed all important medical, botanical, alchemical, Hermetic, and magical knowledge into a single cube known as the "cabalistic mirror."[62] He returned from his travels in southern Italy in 1638, having witnessed the eruptions of Mount Etna and Stromboli and climbed into the crater of Mount Vesuvius as it creaked and groaned under the strain of its geologic rhythms. Southern Italy was on fire, and Kircher was captivated by its spectacle of nature (Figure Intro.5). It took him over twenty-five years to write up the results of his investigations, beginning with his imaginative geological dialogue, the *Iter extaticum II qui & Mundi Prodromus dicitur (Second Ecstatic Journey)* of 1657, and culminating in his *Mundus subterraneus* of 1665.[63] But from that moment on, Kircher became convinced that understanding the natural world, in a broad sense, was as fundamental as deciphering the hieroglyphs. His work on magnetism continued to be a focal point of his investigations of nature, since Kircher saw the magnet as nature's hieroglyph—the key to understanding everything else.[64] Yet he also realized that there were many other puzzling natural phenomena that might yield information the magnet alone could not offer. Gradually his studies expanded to include virtually every crucial question of natural philosophy in the 1640s and 1650s.

At the end of the 1630s, mathematicians and natural philosophers throughout Europe knew several things about Kircher. They knew that he was somewhat ambivalent about the condemnation of Galileo and possibly open to discussions of heliocentrism. It was Peiresc who reported in September 1633 that Kircher did not consider the great Jesuit astronomer Christopher Clavius an anti-Copernican and maintained that younger Jesuit mathematicians such as Scheiner only adhered to Aristotle "out of necessity and obedience."[65] They heard that he was at work on an "invention for combinatorial composition," in other words, a music-making machine.[66] Finally, they considered him to be one of the leading advocates of the idea of universal magnetism, a notion that built upon the Neapolitan *magus* Giovan Battista della Porta's and the English physician William Gilbert's studies of the terrestrial magnet, and the German mathematician Johannes Kepler's concept that there was a central force, or *anima motrix*, organizing the motions of all planetary bodies.

Mersenne expressed some skepticism about the universality of Kircher's magnet and the novelty of his theories. He told a London correspondent in 1639 that "Antoine Kirker" and his Roman colleagues "claim that they will make us change our philosophy by speculating on the universal spirit that resides in this stone. Let's wait to see what it will be like in order to judge it." Mersenne provided observations for the table of magnetic declination published in the *Magnes, sive de arte magnetica (Magnet or the Magnetic Art)* of 1641, forwarding data from his English correspondents. Gassendi, Jesuit mathematicians and natural philosophers such as Christoph Scheiner and Niccolò Cabeo, and Jesuit missionaries in Goa, Macao, Canton, and the West Indies also contributed to Kircher's project.[67] The *Magnes* was the first work in which Kircher demonstrated his ability to create a global network of informants, using the combined resources of the Society of Jesus and the European-wide republic of letters to gather information. In this respect, Kircher earned the admiration of contemporaries who did not have access to his range of information. They eagerly read his book to see what he had done with their data.[68] They turned the pages in order to see what new instruments he had dreamt up in order to demonstrate the power of the magnet.

Galileo's disciple Evangelista Torricelli was the first to report the appearance of the long-awaited *Magnes*. From Rome in June 1641, he informed Galileo that the book was pleasing to behold, "enriched with a wealth of beautiful engravings." It contained many machines, described "with the most extravagant words." In Torricelli's opinion, it was a book full of excessive literary flourishes, abounding in epigrams, poems, and inscriptions "some in Arabic, some in Hebrew and other languages." Among its curiosities, however, he particularly admired Kircher's account of the music reputed to cure the tarantula's bite in Puglia. But ultimately he put the book down in utter frustration. "Enough: Signor Nardi, Maggiotti, and I laughed quite a bit." Such mixed reactions traveled north to Venice, where Fulgenzio Micanzio reported in December 1641 that he had heard that Kircher's *Magnes* was much like Scheiner's *Rosa Ursina*: once the straw was removed, no grain remained.[69] He had evidently been talking to readers such as Torricelli who did not appreciate the art of Kircher's science.

It took at least another year for northern European readers to complete their initial appraisal of Kircher's natural philosophy. The *Magnes* sold so well that a second edition appeared in 1643, and a third in 1654. In January 1643, Constantin Huygens finished reading a copy. He could not wait to tell Descartes what he thought. "You will find that it is not well-furnished but rather awful," he informed his friend. One week later, Descartes completed his own evaluation, famously declaring of Kircher: "The Jesuit has a lot of tricks; he is more charlatan than scholar."[70] He expressed enormous scorn for the sunflower clock, marveling at the idea that anyone should believe in a plant whose seeds had the power to do things in Arabia that they did not seem capable of doing in Aix, Avignon, or Rome.

Once again, Kircher seemed on the verge of losing all credibility. But perhaps there was more than a touch of jealousy in Descartes's comments? Kircher, after all, published his ideas on universal magnetism when the French philosopher was still in the midst of contemplating what to do with the different parts of his treatise, *The World*, which remained unpublished due to his fear of censorship after the condemnation of Galileo. The magnet, too, was extremely important to Descartes's philosophy that proclaimed all matter to be a product of extension and motion. Magnets helped to explain the forces organizing the movement of cosmic things through the microcosm of a terrestrial artifact. Newton also understood this when he initiated his youthful investigations into universal gravitation with a study of the magnet. In the fall of 1644, two English readers compared Descartes's account of the magnet in his *Principles of Philosophy* (1644) with the equivalent pages in Kircher's *Magnes*. "I think Kercher the Jesuit of the loadestone has prevented Des Cartes," concluded Charles Cavendish in a letter to John Pell, "for they differ little, as I remember."[71]

Had Kircher scooped Descartes? Surely not in any specific sense. Kircher's animistic philosophy and Cartesian mechanistic philosophy could not have been farther apart, which must have made it all the more annoying for the former to write extensively on an artifact of interest to the latter. But he had nonetheless declared the magnet to be "the key to all motion whatsoever."[72] Perhaps what annoyed Descartes in particular was the fact that Kircher celebrated the occult and divine qualities of the magnet with the resources of experimental philosophy at the very moment when the French philosopher wished to present the magnet as a great example of the physics (rather than metaphysics) of motion. In other words, Kircher had used the new physics of seventeenth-century science to arrive at the wrong result, and he inspired the entire scholarly community to contribute to the project. He had, once again, thrilled his readers by inviting them to contemplate a world of fantastic machines such as the "Universal Magnetic Horoscope" that efficiently if not entirely accurately told time in every major city where Jesuit missions flourished, setting the clock by noon in Rome (Figure Intro.6). Let us keep in mind that after his student years at the Jesuit college of La Flèche, Descartes had no particular love of the Jesuits.

Mersenne finally decided to resolve his own doubts about Kircher by going to Rome. He arrived in the papal city at the end of December 1644, bearing a copy of his *Harmonie universelle: Contenant la theorie et la pratique de la musique* (*Universal Harmony: Containing the Theory and Practice of Music*) of 1636. Kircher was then in the midst of finishing the first edition of his *Ars magna lucis et umbrae* (*Great Art of Light and Shadow*), his fascinating work on optics filled with spectacular demonstrations of the properties of light, published in 1646. It had just received approval of the Jesuit censors.[73] After several pleasurable days of philosophizing, in which the two fathers tested recent claims by Torricelli to produce a vacuum—which Kircher did not believe existed in nature—Mersenne loaned him the book. Kircher, then contemplating the idea of writing his own treatise on the science of music, "devoured my book on *Harmonie universelle* in four days ... ," Mersenne recalled. "He declared himself enraptured." Their mutual admiration grew, and Father Athanasius became expansive about his own plans for future publications. Kircher outlined the idea for his *Musurgia universalis* (*Universal Music-making*) of 1650, describing all the various combinatorial arts by which music might be produced artificially as well as naturally. He showed Mersenne "a lot of beautiful drawings" in his study and tantalized him with the "marvels" described in the forthcoming *Ars magna lucis et umbrae*.[74] Against his better instincts perhaps, Mersenne found himself captivated. In the heat of a discussion with Kircher, he wanted very much to believe in the Jesuit's peculiar form of wonder.[75]

Kircher's quarters at the Roman College were increasingly busy by 1644. One month before Mersenne's arrival, the English virtuoso John Evelyn

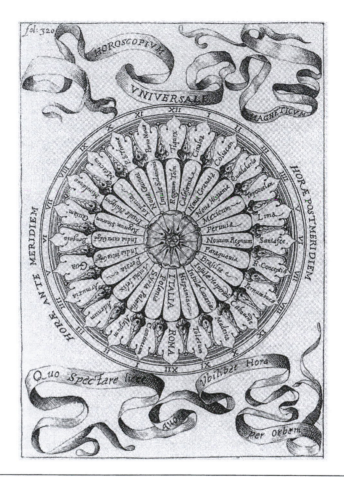

Figure Intro.6. Kircher's universal magnetic horoscope. *Source:* Athanasius Kircher, *Magnes, sive de arte magnetica* (Rome, 1641). Courtesy of Special Collections, Stanford University Libraries.

arrived in Rome to tour the city and see what Kircher was doing. Evelyn was well aware of the recent appearance of the *Lingua Aegyptiaca restituita*. He knew that Kircher was in the midst of completing his interpretation of the obelisk in front of Saint John Lateran for the new pope, Innocent X, since the two of them discussed this during the visit. Traces of Kircher's abundant scientific interests also lay scattered about his study. The variety of instruments and inventions that Evelyn described, in addition to hearing a lecture on parts of Euclid by Kircher, left an impression of an active and inventive mind at work: "with Dutch patience, he showed us his perpetual motions, catoptrics, magnetical experiments, models, and a thousand other crotchets and devices."[76] In Evelyn's and Mersenne's remarks, we can see the glimmerings of the kind of reputation that made Kircher a fixture on the seventeenth-century Grand Tour. He installed a speaking tube between his room and the gallery where he keep his inventions so that the custodian might call him when visitors appeared.[77] Presumably it worked the other way as well, so that visitors might occasionally hear the disembodied voice of Father Athanasius appear from nowhere like the Wizard of Oz.

It was around this time that Kircher, or perhaps his Roman publisher Ludovico Grignani, realized that it was good to advertise. The final pages of the *Ars magna lucis et umbrae* contained the first of Kircher's famous lists of publications. In addition to advertising seven books already in print, it drew readers' attention to eight other original works and eight translations yet to come. Among those "books ready to published if God grants me a long life" were the *Oedipus Aegyptiacus*, *Musurgia universalis*, *Mundus subterraneus* ("a vast and curious work," Kircher exclaimed), *Turris Babel*, an *Ars combinatoria* (surely the beginning of the *Ars magna sciendi*, since it promised a "new method for all sciences and arts" specifically addressed to "young men and the ignorant"), a *Magia mechanica* (eventually published by his disciple Schott under the title of *Technica curiosa*), and two works that seem forever lost to modern readers: the *Polypaedia Biblica*, which promised to extract the secrets of biblical knowledge, and *Concilium geographicum*, a reminder of Kircher's brief tenure as cartographer for the archbishop of Mainz.[78]

No wonder that Mersenne, Evelyn, and virtually every other visitor to Kircher's study were overwhelmed by the possibilities. But this was not all. To understand the breadth of Kircher's appeal at midcentury, we need to consider the rest of the list: a series of glorious translation projects that would have made Peiresc weep with joy while fearing for the quality of the results. Kircher promised translations of Syrian and Islamic manuscripts that would unlock the secrets of Eastern philosophy. He planned two additional translations of Arabic manuscripts—one a collection of geometric, optical, and astronomical fragments, the other an account of ancient Egyptian writing and law. In keeping with the finest scholarship of his day, Kircher also recognized the value of ancient polyglot manuscripts, promising his public a trilingual edition of Avicenna's *Canon of Medicine* in Arabic, Hebrew, and Latin; a Persian-Latin edition of Cato; and a manuscript containing "Arabic-Coptic-Latin Liturgies" that discussed the controversies between the Armenian and Latin churches.[79]

None of these translations ever appeared. But perhaps that was not the point of it all. In 1646, Kircher presented himself as a consummate encyclopedist whose knowledge of the arts and sciences rested on his ability to read virtually every ancient language of interest in Catholic Europe and whose reputation depended upon his access to rare and important manuscripts. He was a successful book-hunter in a city of ferocious bibliophiles. This was the message of his advertisement, and it was an image he had cultivated since the

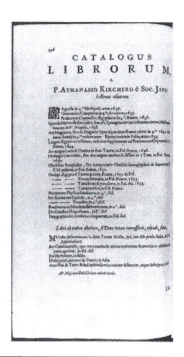

Figure Intro.7. "Catalogue of the Books by Father Athanasius Kircher." *Source:* Athanasius Kircher, *Mundus subterraneus* (Amsterdam, 1665). Courtesy of Special Collections, Stanford University Libraries.

1630s. Twenty years later, when Kircher revised his "Catalogue of Books by Father Athanasius Kircher" in 1665, he no longer felt the need to present himself as a translator of the ancients[80] (Figure Intro.7). The sources of his authority had not exactly changed, since he continued to be a man in possession of many secrets. But the location of this kind of knowledge no longer lay in arcane manuscripts alone. Rather it was increasingly found in the storehouse of knowledge— artifacts and inventions as well as books and manuscripts—that he displayed in the museum of the Roman College.[81] The increased propensity to view Kircher's books as a complete corpus only enhanced the sensation that Kircher was an authority beyond measure. In 1646, Kircher outlined a project to become a single-author *Encyclopaedia Britannica*. He largely made good on this promise. Like all good encyclopedias, his works bristled with inaccuracies and omissions. But they also allowed their readers to traverse the field of knowledge in its entirety, something that many other authors were unable—or unwilling—to do.[82]

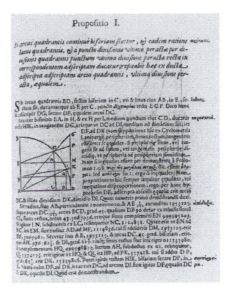

Figure Intro. 8. Squaring the circle, according to Kircher. *Source: Correspondence du Marin Mersenne Religieux Minime.* Ed. Mme Paul Tannery and Cornélis de Waard (Paris: Éditions du CNRS, 1965), vol. 9, p. 475.

After initiating readers into the mysteries of the magnet, Kircher could not resist solving another problem in the *Ars magna lucis et umbrae* that had puzzled mathematicians at least since the days of Pappus: he squared the circle borrowing a diagram from the medieval philosopher Ramon Llull. In the summer and fall of 1646, mathematicians throughout Europe laughed themselves silly over the result. Friends in Rome had warned Torricelli in advance that the results were risible. Kircher drew a line EF, bisecting radius AB at E, are BD at C. He concluded that the half-arc DC equaled tangent DF (Figure Intro.8). Logic dictated that this would be true for every half-arc, making a complete and perfect square. It was a beautiful visual proof since readers could literally, at least in their minds if not actually on paper, see the circle becoming a square.[83] The only problem was that it was an approximate rather than exact solution, ignoring the most basic tenets of mathematics since the Greeks. Kircher's ferociously precise and distinguished predecessor Clavius must have rolled over in his grave at the thought of a Jesuit mathematician at the Collegio Romano displaying such ignorance. News of Kircher's proof traveled from Rome to Florence to Paris. Torricelli sent the quadrature to Mersenne in July 1646. The response was a hearty bellow that echoed all the way across the Alps. "I wish I could hold back the force of my laughter when I think about the Kircherian squaring of the circle about which you wrote," Mersenne responded.[84] Torricelli found it so funny that he passed it on to the Jesuat mathematician Bonaventura Cavallieri for further amusement. Gassendi reportedly told his English friends, who admired the illustrations while skimming a copy in a Paris but concluded that such a book was not worth buying. Every mathematician in Europe, it seemed, turned to this particular page of the *Ars magna lucis et umbrae*.

One week after sharing a good laugh with Torricelli, Mersenne sat down to compose a letter to Kircher. He regretted that he still lacked his own copy of Kircher's "most beautiful book." They talked of recent astronomical discoveries and the things that the microscope might reveal. Finally Mersenne addressed Kircher's squaring of the circle. He reported what he had heard from Florence and Rome, concluding for the umpteenth time that such a solution was clearly false. While reserving judgment on how exactly Kircher had solved the problem in his book, Mersenne let his Jesuit correspondent know that such an approach to mathematics was deeply flawed, something he did not hesitate to publicize to colleagues in Paris and Aix in subsequent discussions. Perhaps Mersenne understood better than some other readers why Kircher had created such a flawed proof, which was, at its root, a kind of geometric hieroglyph, a symbolic conclusion to a centuries-old debate rather than a mathematical proof. Nonetheless he indicated his openness to other aspects of Kircher's work by concluding his letter with the following question: "And when can we hope for your music?"[85]

Other complaints about the first of Kircher's "Great Arts" emerged. The Minim Emanuel Maignan was deeply concerned about the potential overlap of his own work on catoptrics, the quintessential seventeenth-century science of mathematically rendered optical illusions, with sections of the *Ars magna lucis et umbrae*. Kircher later accused Maignan of plagiarizing his cylindrical mirror, to which Maignan responded defensively that two inventors might simultaneously arrive at the same conclusions. More critically, Constantijn Huygens observed that Kircher had completely misunderstood the art and science of the gnomon, the instrument used to cast the sun's shadow. Citing Plautus, he tartly observed of the Jesuits: "The greater the endeavor, the more often they produce worthless things." Huygens could not resist fantasizing about the idea of sending a strange tale about a prisoner in Antwerp who had the capacity to see through clothes for inclusion in Kircher's next edition. The joke—"There's one among you who has no shirt!"—was perhaps Huygens's way of reaffirming the adage that the emperor, or in this case a Jesuit, had no clothes. He told Mersenne that if Kircher included his anecdote in the next edition, it would truly be a "Great Art."[86]

Once again, we left with the paradox of Kircher's fame: throughout the 1640s, the republic of letters continuously found fault with Kircher's mathematics and natural philosophy and questioned his philology. At the same time, they asked for more. The year 1646 was by no means disastrous for Father Athanasius. He was relieved of any further obligation to teach. He attracted the attention of Pope Innocent X, who subsequently commissioned him to work with the sculptor Giovan Lorenzo Bernini in erecting one of the greatest monuments of baroque Rome, the Pamphili obelisk sitting atop Bernini's Fountain of the Four Rivers in Piazza Navona as of August 1649.[87] Interpreting the past was indeed a lucrative business in the papal city and so was the production of spectacle. We need to counterbalance criticism of Kircher with an assessment of his manifold success. While failing to convince individual readers of the merits of specific claims in his books, he intrigued all of them and persuaded other readers of the general soundness of his philosophical approach. Kircher did not intend his readers to linger very long on any singular insight that he had. Squaring the circle was a bust, but his approach to deciphering the hieroglyphs had triumphed at least in Rome and Vienna. He reminded his readers that the magnet was a crucial ingredient of experimental philosophy and intrigued them with his optical demonstrations. He and the team of engravers and printers who produced his books dazzled his audience, transforming ideas into images that even his critics were forced to admire. In the end, key aspects of Kircher's vision of knowledge succeeded, overcoming a sort of perpetual skepticism about the merits of his scholarship.

There was a reason Maignan worried that the *Ars magna lucis et umbrae* might eclipse his own work. Filled with beautiful engravings of Kircher's optical games—perspective glasses, magic lanterns, distorting mirrors that transformed blobs of paint into elegant portraits of princes and prelates—it was a startling and seductive book that invited its readers to participate in the game of knowledge, which was an art more than a science. The *Musurgia universalis* would do this equally effectively, when it brought forth page after page of fantastic music-making machines (Figure Intro.9). It appeared in the Jubilee Year of 1650, when the entire world flocked to Rome to celebrate a triumphal moment in the history of the Catholic Church. Kircher was at the center of it all. His *Obeliscus Pamphilius* (*Pamphilian Obelisk*) dazzled its readers with his ingenious reconstruction of the hieroglyphic inscriptions on the side of the obelisk that had been hidden to his view as it lay on the ground. This important new monument in the Eternal City confirmed his pronouncements about the importance of Egyptian wisdom to Catholicism. His books were in the hands of missionaries, scholars, and princes. He had worked with Matteo Marione to redesign the hydraulic organ of the Quirinale.[88] He was one of the most visited and celebrated men in the city. Even the Medici paid him a visit when the learned Leopoldo, brother of the Grand Duke and patron of the Galileian Accademia del Cimento, came to town for the Jubilee.[89]

The only thing lacking was an appropriate space in which to stage Kircher's apotheosis. This materialized in the form of a museum. In 1651, the Roman patrician Alfonso Donnino, secretary to the *Popolo Romano*, donated his collection to the Roman College. Donnino's bequest obligated the Society of Jesus to create a public museum that would be worthy of its donor and that would

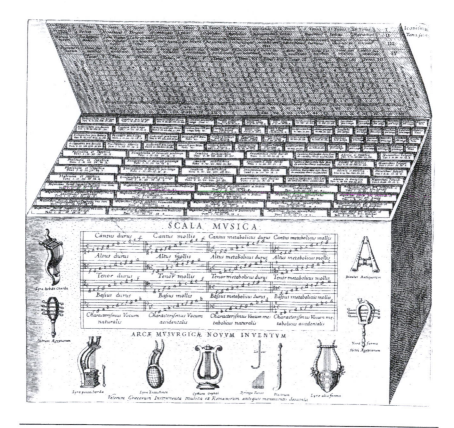

Figure Intro.9. Kircher's music-making "ark." *Source:* Athanasius Kircher, *Musurgia universalis* (Rome, 1650). Courtesy of Special Collections, Stanford University Libraries.

display his collection, composed predominantly of antiquities and paintings, in an appropriate fashion.[90] The Jesuits welcomed the opportunity to house a museum in their premier college. Inhabiting a city filled with cardinals' collections and aristocratic galleries, they understood the appeal of making the Collegio Romano into one of the leading museums of Rome. They appointed Kircher its first curator.

Kircher now had the forum that he had sought and a more public space to fill with his discoveries and inventions, which had previously been housed in his private quarters and a small gallery. In many respects he was the heir to a collection of instruments and papers inaugurated by distinguished predecessors in the chair in mathematics such as Clavius.[91] In characteristic fashion, Kircher enhanced this image by combining the traditional material culture of a mathematician with the possession of other kinds of artifacts that advertised the global reach of the Society of Jesus and informed his particular brand of encyclopedism. Surrounded by antiquities, curiosities, and inventions, he seemed like an oracle of knowledge, a kind of baroque Leonardo who had decided to write forward rather than backward—and publish it all.

Visitors came in increasing numbers to see Kircher in the midst of the Society of Jesus's collection. He was perceived as a famous collector and author, a man who not only wrote about the most interesting ideas in his books but who also possessed the most interesting things in his museum. One visitor described Kircher's endless penchant for demonstrating the mysterious powers of the magnet in the gallery and predicted that he "would frighten cardinals with the ghosts" of the magic lantern.[92] Kircher was so confident of the attractions of the collection that he helped to create over the next few decades that in 1671 he declared: "No foreign visitor who has not seen the Roman College museum can claim that he has truly been in Rome."[93] Whether he created knowledge was a subject that the scholarly community continued to debate, but no one denied his ability to produce spectacle.

4. Oedipal Adventures and Ecstatic Voyages

The year that the Roman College museum opened its doors to the public, Kircher was preparing the first volume of his massive *Oedipus Aegyptiacus*, one of the most eagerly anticipated books of the mid–seventeenth century.[94] In the summer of 1651, a young Anne Conway asked her father-in-law Lord Conway about "new books" that discussed the relationship between Christianity and philosophy. She received the following recommendation by September: "there is great hope we may be the wiser for it this yeare by the help of Kircherus."[95] Unfortunately, Conway never recorded her opinion of the book, if she ever had the chance to read it. Leopoldo de' Medici was not so taciturn. Upon receiving the third volume in June 1655, he wrote that the delays in publication had only increased "the desire with which the universe of virtuosi have waited to acquire the Egyptian Oedipus."[96]

Kircher's *Oedipus Aegyptiacus*, printed in four parts between 1652 and 1654 and finally made available to readers with its publication as an entire volume in 1655, represented the culmination of his research on Egypt[97] (Figure Intro.10). Dedicated to a multiplicity of patrons and overflowing with poems and epigrams by scholars who celebrated Kircher's virtuosity in enough languages to make one think that the entire world knew him, it was a book so complex in its production that it required special fonts to print the sections in many of the Eastern languages. Weighing in at a modest two thousand pages and underwritten by multiple patrons, including the Holy Roman emperor Ferdinand I, who contributed two-thousand *scudi* to the cost of its production, the *Oedipus* was Kircher's broadest and boldest statement about the meaning of Egypt in the mid–seventeenth century.[98] Having edited and translated key Coptic manuscripts in the first decade of his residence in Rome, and subsequently having explained his principles of translation in his *Obeliscus Pamphilius*, Kircher

Figure Intro.10. Kircher's image of himself as Roman Oedipus. *Source:* Athanasius Kircher, *Oedipus Aegyptiacus* (Rome, 1652–55), vol. 1. Courtesy of Special Collections, Stanford University Libraries.

now sought to bring together all the different strands of his reading, observing, and translating to create a complete portrait of the legacy of Egypt for his own times.

Kircher's Egypt was a veritable hieroglyph of the world, an ancient civilization of knowledge that contained true wisdom, *prisca sapientia*, even as it succumbed to the temptations of idolatry. It was the beginning of the forked path of truth and error, containing both the most sublime secrets that God had left humankind and evidence of the deep roots of human folly and arrogance in the face of the divine. Most importantly, however, the *Oedipus* provided a historical point of departure for understanding the history of civilizations and faiths. Jewish Kabbalah, Persian magic, Islamic alchemy, Chaldean astrology, Zoroastrian mysteries, and many other ancient sciences all crowded the pages of this dense encyclopedia. But antiquity was not Kircher's only point of reference, nor did he confine his remarks to the territory of ancient Egypt. The *Oedipus* traced the fate of hieroglyphic wisdom in virtually every known society. In an age in which reports of Aztecs temples, Mayan calendars, Brazilian cannibals, Chinese mandarins, and Japanese Buddhists inspired European curiosity about other cultures, Kircher helped his readers to see the commonalities within the overwhelming diversity of languages, faiths, and cultures. He underscored the universality of Christianity, not only by upholding the argument—already discredited by Isaac Casaubon at the beginning of the century—that the Hermetic Corpus anticipated the truths of Christianity, but by finding analogous evidence of Christianity in far-flung parts of the world.[99]

Egypt spawned a thousand idolatries, but it was also the home of the Trinity. The history of knowledge, in short, was a meditation on everything that was possible, everything that had once been known but was now virtually unknowable. Discerning readers found Kircher's account of Egypt filled with praise of civilizations he should have abhorred as an ordained Catholic priest. The Jesuit censors did their best to tone down Kircher's enthusiastic descriptions of magical, kabbalistic, and religious practices that were not properly Catholic and chastised him repeatedly for not taking a sufficiently critical view of his pagan sources.[100] But they never entirely succeeded in convincing Kircher's readers that he really meant to condemn the pagan mysteries that he deciphered. In book 3 of the *Oedipus*, for example, Kircher explicated in great detail the message of the mysterious Bembine Table, which he took to be a cosmological affirmation of Isis as the universal goddess of wisdom.[101] This bronze tablet, now acknowledged as a Renaissance forgery, was precisely the artifact Peiresc had told him *not* to explain.

Kircher subsequently published two more books contributing to his study of Egyptian artifacts in Europe: the *Ad Alexandrum Obelisci Aegyptiaci interpretatio hieroglyphica* (*Hieroglyphic Interpretation of the Egyptian Obelisk for Alexander VII*), of 1666, which described and interpreted the obelisk erected atop Bernini's elephant in front of Santa Maria sopra Minerva for Alexander VII in June 1667; and the *Sphinx mystagoga* (*Mystagogical Sphinx*) of 1676, which interpreted two mummies transported from Memphis to France by a collector. These later works provided further opportunities for him to reaffirm his skill at decoding the hieroglyphs, demonstrating his skills at the kind of symbolic analysis that was increasingly challenged by other scholars.[102] Despite Peiresc's warning about the limits of Kircher's philology, a succession of popes and scholars placed their confidence in his ability to unlock the mysteries of Egypt. Kircher was so pleased with his success in 1655 that he had the Dutch engraver Cornelis Bloemart create a printed portrait he could circulate to admiring patrons and disciples.[103]

Kircher's disciple Schott later reported that his master was so exhausted from the Herculean effort of completing the *Oedipus Aegyptiacus* while also working on the still unpublished *Mundus subterraneus* that he fell into a deep sleep that produced his *Itinerarium exstaticum (Ecstatic Journey)* of 1656.[104] Whether probing the heavens was a natural antidote to the rigors of symbolic interpretation, it seems in retrospect to have been part of the frenzy of activity that possessed Kircher in his fifties. By this time, he had begun to attract a series of capable assistants to aid him in the task of producing knowledge and populating the Roman College museum with new machines. Schott, for example, seems to have been specifically invited to Rome in the summer of 1652 to improve the quality of Kircher's publications after he caught several errors—and a potentially embarrassing bit of plagiarism—in some of Kircher's early publications.[105] As Schott left for a position at the Jesuit college in Würzburg in 1655, the duration of his stay in Rome coincided exactly with the period in which the *Oedipus*, *Itinerarium*, and *Mundus* were all in various stages of completion and a third edition of the *Magnes* was in preparation. Someone in Rome was worried that Kircher's reach in this crucial moment might exceed his grasp. Ultimately Schott devoted the remainder of his career to editing and defending Kircher's works.

The fall of 1655 was one of the busiest and most crucial moments in Kircher's life. His *Oedipus* was finally published, and the manuscript of his *Itinerarium exstaticum* was in the hands of the Jesuit censors. While some censors expressed serious doubts about the orthodoxy of Kircher's astronomical reverie, his "remarkable dream" nonetheless appeared in print despite murmuring that he had not sufficiently condemned heliocentrism and propagated a cosmology that was "dangerous to faith."[106] The fact that the *Itinerarium* was dedicated to the most famous convert to Catholicism, Queen Christina of Sweden, who had recently abdicated her throne and was en route to Rome, was not unimportant. Christina became Kircher's Isis in the Egyptian pageantry of baroque Rome. She entered the city with great fanfare in December 1655. Kircher had been preparing for her arrival since October, creating new machines with the help of Schott, completing the dedication to his book, and finding appropriate gifts to offer a queen during her visit to his museum on 31 January 1656. Quite appropriately, Kircher offered Christina an Arabic manuscript and a commemorative obelisk celebrating her visit in thirty-three languages.[107] More than twenty years after his arrival in Rome, Kircher was still the bearer of mysterious manuscripts, but he had also become their official translator.[108]

By the end of the year, Kircher found himself in a plague-infested city, scrutinizing the causes of pestilence beneath the microscope and considering how understanding contagion might further his comprehension of the natural world.[109] Briefly a plague expert, Kircher nonetheless did not aspire to becoming a medical researcher. As the 1650s drew to a close, he immersed himself in a world of natural and experimental curiosities. He allowed his recently departed colleague Schott to publicize the machines they had made together. From Würzburg, Schott embarked on an ambitious program to advertise the machines of the Roman College—and more generally, the instruments of the Society of Jesus—and the experiments performed with them.[110] By this point in time, Kircher had begun to routinely delegate the construction and description of his fabled machines to younger Jesuits.

In the throes of completing the long-awaited *Mundus subterraneus*, Kircher continued to find new forms of diversion for his capacious intellect. He began to research the history, nature, and antiquities of the Roman countryside—a project that would eventually culminate in his *Latium* (1671). During an expedition from Tivoli in 1661, he discovered the ruins of a mountaintop church containing a wooden Marian shrine, located on the very spot where Saint Eustace had been converted to Christianity by a vision of Christ in a stag's antlers. Kircher ultimately restored the shrine of Mentorella and made it into a place of pilgrimage, receiving visitors there every Michaelmas (29 September).[111] Perhaps this spiritual projection of restoration offered Kircher not only a respite from his busy routine at the Roman College, where growing numbers of visitors appeared expecting to meet with Father Athanasius and see a few of his famous demonstrations, but also some consolation, as a few of his publication projects floundered.

In the spring and fall of 1660, Kircher sent three works to the Jesuit censors: the *Ars magna sciendi* (*Great Art of Knowing*), *Iter Hetruscum* (*Etruscan Journey*), and *Diatribe de prodigiosis crucibus* (*Investigation of Prodigious Crosses*). The final work, a short treatise on crosses that had appeared naturally from the volcanic ash showering Naples after the eruption of Vesuvius, appeared quickly in 1661. But the other two publications languished due to the critical reports he received from his fellow Jesuits.[112] The problem in both instances was quality. In an age in which dozens of philosophers, among them Bacon and Descartes, had put forth bold new methodologies for attaining knowledge, Kircher's "great art" seems to have only inspired a reader such as Knittel. An anonymous English reviewer shared this view when he wrote in 1669 that Kircher "pretends by a new and Universal Method ... to enable men to discourse and dispute, innumerable ways, of every thing proposed, and to acquire a summary and general knowledge of all things." He concluded tartly: "Of what Use this Doctrine may be for the attainment of knowledge with more ease or advantage, the sagacious Reader may Judge."[113] Similarly, the idea of a German who had barely seen Tuscany writing the definitive work on its history and nature outraged some of the Tuscan Jesuits, who found the work riddled with errors. Increasingly Kircher was told by the learned members of his order that they, like many of his readers, expected better—rather than faster—results from one of the great minds of the century. They allowed the *Diatribe* to be published, but nonetheless let Kircher know that they did not think much of it.

Despite these publishing problems, in 1661 Kircher was one of the most sought after authors in Europe. Printers fought over the right to publish him. The winner in this contest was Jansson of Amsterdam, who received the exclusive rights to publish Kircher's work in the Holy Roman Empire, England, and the Low Countries in the winter of that year, in return for paying Kircher the princely sum of 2,200 *scudi*.[114] Encyclopedism was indeed a lucrative business—a further reminder that Kircher was giving his public exactly what they wanted, even if the Jesuits themselves harbored some doubts. Beginning with the *Mundus subterraneaus* in 1665, virtually all of Kircher's subsequent works were published in Amsterdam. Jansson ensured a wider distribution of his books in Protestant Europe, improved the quality of the illustrations, and facilitated the translation of two of Kircher's most popular works—the *Mundus* and *China monumentis illustrata* (*China Illustrated through Its Monuments*) of 1667—into Dutch and, in the latter case, French.[115] Jansson's broad distribution network made it possible for members of the Royal Society to find copies of Kircher's encyclopedias in London by the mid-1660s. Samuel Pepys and Henry Oldenburg bought new copies in the bookstalls of London, while the Royal Society curator of experiments, Robert Hooke, contented himself with either buying used editions of Kircher at half-price or purchasing loose copies, which he had his niece Grace bind in their rooms at Gresham College.[116] It is no wonder that Kircher thanked Jansson personally, of all his publishers, when he sat down to write his autobiography.[117] Starting in the 1660s, he became an author created by Rome, funded by Vienna, and produced in Amsterdam.[118]

Although Kircher was unable to publish his *Ars magna sciendi* until 1669, he found an immediate and enthusiastic audience for a related work, the *Polygraphia nova et universalis* (*New and Universal Polygraphy*) of 1663. Copies were distributed widely among European rulers in order to persuade them that Kircher had solved the ultimate diplomatic problem of the post-Westphalian age: how to communicate with one's neighbors without becoming a polyglot. Solving the problem of Babel was both a spiritual and political endeavor. Language could be placed in a box—yet another Kircherian ark whose levers, when properly manipulated, could translate phrases from one language to another or, better yet, create a simple cipher, a baroque Esperanto for all important conversations. Kircher invited his readers to practice mechanical translation with phrases designed to encourage them to have the kinds of conversations he thought really mattered, as exhibited in the following phrase: "Know that I am very ill content with you because you woulde not sende me your booke."[119] For more delicate communication about secrets of state, Kircher offered a solution to the problem of an insecure courier service in the form of a combinatorial form of secret writing (*steganographia*) designed to keep messages hidden from all but the intended recipient. Several disciples were so enthralled by Kircher's steganography that they wrote to him in code.[120]

With the appearance of Kircher's *Mundus* in 1665, natural philosophers throughout Europe once again had an opportunity to examine the quality of his evidence and conclusions. Writing to Benedict de Spinoza that year, Henry Oldenburg suggested that it was the former that made the book worth reading:

> I have turned over part of Kircher's *Subterranean World*, and all his arguments and theories are no credit to his wit, yet the observations and experiments there presented to us speak well for the author's diligence and for his wish to stand high in the opinion of philosophers.

One month later, Oldenburg expressed a far more critical view to Robert Boyle. After attempting to replicate some of Kircher's experimental conclusions, he reported that the "very first Experiment singled out by us out of Kircher" had failed, "and yt 'tis likely the next will doe so too." Perhaps Oldenburg recalled the sharp pronouncement of Christopher Wren, who considered Kircher and Schott experimental "jugglers" who were not serious about knowledge.[121] The Jesuits felt otherwise, but it was perhaps an indication of the Royal Society's anxiety that their own experiments not be taken lightly that they sought to distance themselves quite sharply from Kircher's methodology.

The *Mundus subterraneus* was a work designed to rival the *Oedipus* in its claims for universal erudition. It unlocked nature's hieroglyph by explaining the system of the earth that produced a wide variety of compelling natural phenomena, from erupting volcanoes to the most puzzling fossils. It attacked traditional alchemy while offering up a newly pious version of the transmutation of substance. Most importantly, it described nature in the broadest geographic sense, building on the kind of data that had made the *Magnes* an equally impressive example of Jesuit empiricism at work. Kircher thanked the Society of Jesus for allowing him to write a truly global natural history by encouraging its missionaries to send him a steady stream of reports and artifacts.[122] The *Mundus* was not a work written to meet the Royal Society's criteria of an experimental report of natural phenomena. Kircher's experiments were like his machines: demonstrations of principles that he already knew and wished to reveal to his audience. But it was a rich source of information for many seventeenth-century readers who, like Cotton Mather, used its illustrations to imagine the geocosm and mined its data in support of their own research.

During the 1660s, Kircher reached the apex of his career. A visible and controversial figure in the Society of Jesus, he enjoyed the patronage of popes and emperors and a continuous correspondence with scholars and missionaries throughout the world. While he had been celebrated as a specifically Roman phenomenon in the 1650s, in the next decade he became a truly global author, an expert on Asia as well as Egypt with disciples throughout the world.[123] Kircher single-handedly was able to muster more information and produce more books than the entire membership of the early Royal Society, or really any learned academy of this period. Understanding the value of these new scientific institutions, Kircher attempted to correspond with them, offering the resources of his religious order in return for access to their information and possibly honorary membership.[124] The Royal Society's fear of papists led them to refuse any formal correspondence with the Jesuits, though they published a great deal of Jesuit material in the *Philosophical Transactions*. And as we know, they read Kircher, whose ecstatic authorship exhibited precisely the sort of unbridled enthusiasm, demonstrable religious conviction, and subjectivity of knowledge that the new philosophy in theory if not always in practice sought to suppress.

5. Father Athanasius Kircher's Dream

It was around this time that Father Athanasius told his disciple Schott about a strange dream he had had, which Schott published in 1667 as "The Dream of Father Athanasius Kircher." Deathly ill, to the point that even his physicians despaired of his recovery, Kircher asked if he might self-medicate. He received permission to enter the Roman College pharmacy, where he took a soporific potion of his own devising that induced "a deep and most delightful dream that lasted the entire night." What did a sick, sweaty, half-delirious Kircher fantasize about at the end of the 1660s? Schott, of course, was happy to supply the answer: "He dreamed that he had been elected Supreme Pontiff." Kircher's dream was a fantasy of a society in his own image, a universal celebration of knowledge and faith in the heart of the Eternal City. Princely embassies traveled to Rome to congratulate him, and all the peoples of the world rejoiced. Many nations and peoples erected churches and Jesuit colleges in Rome and "many other things for the propagation of the Catholic faith."[125] When Kircher awoke, he was entirely cured, much to the amazement of his physician.

Dreaming of becoming pope was not exactly a subject designed to induce a peaceful, thaumaturgic slumber for a priest whose life hung in the balance. But Kircher was no ordinary man. He did, in his own way, aspire to rule the globe; after all his years in Rome, advising popes and cardinals about obelisks and secrets, he had more than his share of ideas about the nature of good spiritual leadership. Having lived to an age when cardinals typically became eligible for the papal tiara, Kircher's fantasy in his sixties serves to remind us that his ambitions transcended his specific intellectual interests. He had a vision of how knowledge might transform the world.

At the heart of Kircher's quest for omniscience lay a strong conviction that the world would be a better place if knowledge perpetuated the true faith. Unable to become a missionary, he celebrated apostolic endeavors in virtually every publication. He strove to unlock the mysteries of the past in the belief that they might help his own world to understand why Christianity was no longer united. Kircher's Catholicism was quite heartfelt, and his belief in the possibility of miracles was sincere. Let us pause for a moment to imagine Kircher's papacy. What would it have been like? A pansophic utopia perhaps, in which perfectly polyglot citizens trained in the Jesuit colleges explored the possibilities of knowledge through a series of machines. A world in which every piazza had an obelisk and every library contained Kircher's books. Most importantly, a world that was no longer divided by faith but united through it. This was a dream of many theologians and philosophers of the early modern period, and it was an idea that died slowly and reluctantly. Perhaps the last image of Kircher's papacy—the holy reign of Oedipus or perhaps Eustachius I—should be an image of Kircher in his tiara and papal robes, opening a copy of the *Polypaedia Biblica* that he promised his readers in 1646 but was unable to complete, speaking of God to all the nations of the world in all the tongues unleashed by Babel.

Sometimes dreams are better than realities. In the 1670s, Kircher found himself increasingly under attack. He had made so many pronouncements on such a variety of subjects that readers began to respond. Skeptical Protestants denied the Jesuit discovery of a Sino-Syrian monument in China in 1625, leading Kircher in his *China momentis illustrata* to attempt to prove the existence of an artifact he had never seen. Salomon de Blauenstein insisted that Kircher's attack on alchemy in the *Mundus* was a vicious piece of propaganda against Paracelsian doctrines.[126] After reading the *China illustrata*, the Tuscan naturalist Francesco Redi felt compelled to publish a letter to Kircher explaining the deficiencies of his claims for the miraculous curative qualities of the snakestone, a missionary artifact that allegedly sucked poison from a wound by sticking to the surface of the skin and sympathetically extracting venom. Kircher responded by having his disciple Gioseffo Petrucci publish the *Prodromo apologetico alli studi Chircheriani* (*Apologetic Forerunner to Kircherian Studies*) of 1677[127] (Figure Intro.11). Attacking the "envious and strident ignorance of his unjust accusers," Petrucci painted a portrait of Kircher as he wanted to be remembered: a judicious experimenter who carefully weighed all the evidence before coming to any conclusions. Emphasizing Kircher's skepticism about natural phenomena, Petrucci countered the image of his master as a gullible consumer of tall tales about strange things by presenting him as the logical heir of Galileo. Citing Kircher's unparalleled knowledge of non-European nature, he quoted Augustine as a cautionary tale for disbelieving readers: "Some credible things are false, just as some incredible things are true."[128] Petrucci invited readers to examine Kircher's own words in order to see the distortion that occurred in the characterization of his master in the words of critics. He promised to remove anything from his *Prodromo apologetico* that readers found to be false.

Three years later, when Johann Kestler published his *Physiologia Kircheriana experimentalis*, the apologies for Kircher's erudition seemed only to multiply. Noting that ordinary readers had difficulty understanding the "divine

Figure Intro.11. Allegory of Kircher's omniscience at the end of his life. *Source:* Gioseffo Petrucci, *Prodromo apologetico alli studi Chircheriani* (Amsterdam, 1677). Courtesy of Special Collections, Stanford University Libraries.

genius" of Kircher, Kestler sought to clarify any inadvertent obscurities that had cropped up in previous publications. He defended Kircher against all critics who sought to tarnish his glory, enumerating the attacks on his master's most distinguished publications. Among them was the *Oedipus Aegyptiacus.* Some critics, Kestler wrote with amazement, believed that Kircher's explanation of the hieroglyphs was simply "a figment of his own mind."[129]

Kircher's dream of knowledge was indeed transitory. Had he not been so assiduous in leaving it behind in his many books, I might be accused of making him up.[130] Or quite possibly I have simply borrowed him from the pages of modern fiction, examining the philosophical novels of the twentieth century—Borges, Calvino, and Eco in particular—to enrich the past with the fantasies of the present. "I'm not a bibliophile," declares one conspirator in Umberto Eco's *Foucault's Pendulum*, "but this was just something I had to have. It's the *Mundus subterraneus* of Athanasius Kircher, first edition, 1665."[131] Possessing Kircher has indeed become a modern bibliophile's fantasy, and he is as enigmatic, polymorphous, and seductive as the hieroglyphs he tried to interpret.

The last few years have seen an enormous resurgence of interest in Father Athanasius.[132] His machines are being replicated, his museum has been reconstructed, and scholarly interest in his work is at an all-time high.[133] This volume is the product of a new reassessment of Kircher that is now under way, as he ceases to be, in the words of a group who named their awards in cinematography after him, "an incredibly obscure historical figure" and is well on his way to becoming one of the important subjects through which we can understand the complexity of his world.[134] In his own time, Kircher was a barometer of virtually every intellectual transformation of the seventeenth century. He translated, collected, invented, experimented, and published. He shamelessly self-promoted, earning periodic warnings from his Jesuit superiors that he was violating one of the key principles of his faith—humility—in being so openly proud of his intellect. Very little of interest escaped Kircher's attention. As a result, he provides us with a fundamental perspective on what knowledge was in his time, how it could be known, and how it should be communicated.

It can rightly be said of Kircher that he was much more than the sum of his parts, and far more interesting because of it. "Thus, entirely unexpected, Father Kircher is here again," wrote Goethe at the dawn of the nineteenth century.[135] Kircher continues to surprise us throughout the centuries with the things he knew as much as with the things he obviously did not know. His intellectual creativity and fierce devotion to his life's work deserve our respect and perhaps even our admiration. His sense of the world, as it was at the height of the seventeenth century—an age of global missions and empires with sharp political, religious, and geographic divisions muted by acts of diplomacy, an age of empiricism put to the test by competing methodologies of knowledge, and an era in which a profusion of operas, concerts, and plays, of baroque churches and dramatically rendered piazzas, transformed theatricality from a philosophical ideal into a multidimensional sensory experience—was uncanny. To understand only Kircher's failures is to miss his successes. To study Kircher only as a singular personality or to consider a single work by him without understanding its relationship to the whole is to remove him, quite artificially, from the world that brought him into existence. By examining Kircher's activities in full, we can begin to see his version of the seventeenth century in clearer perspective: a global republic of letters enamored with a new vision of the past and the promise of a new science, a society shaped by the Jesuits and their missions, and a world that transformed Rome into one of the great capital cities of all time.[136]

Athanasius Kircher was neither the first nor the last man who claimed to know everything.[137] Every generation has its Kircher. But it is not always clear who such people are or what role they fulfill in contemporary society. To claim that we have lost this idea is to misunderstand the dream of omniscience and its persistence in a modern guise. Of course it is hard to imagine omniscience gaining the sort of institutional validation and widespread approbation that Kircher enjoyed in his lifetime. Studying Kircher allows us to examine the practical and political as well as the philosophical and spiritual dimensions of such a project. It pushes us to the brink of an abyss and fills our heads—at least temporarily—with some modicum of the wisdom that Kircher tried to convey in his books and exhibits. It reminds us that authors who become machines eventually break down, just as Kircher's own inventions did at the Roman College when he was no longer there to tend them.

Of course it is tempting to conclude by noting that Kircher is a reminder of why Descartes chose to forget everything he knew in order to understand something. If Kircher could not read many of the ancient texts that were his most precious sources, so we, too, cannot really read Kircher. But Kircher and his publishers understood that there were many different possible ways of absorbing the message of his books. We can *look* at them, as a young Otto Bettman did, growing up in the midst of his father's collection of Kircher's works in a town in Weimar Germany not far from Kircher's birthplace. Bettman, who fled Nazi Germany for the United States in 1935 with two trunks full of images, among them some of Kircher's famous engravings, would later say that looking at Kircher's images inspired his early interest in collecting prints and photos—the nascence of the Bettmann Archive, one of the greatest visual repositories of the twentieth century.[138]

Kircher has played a significant role in spurring the imagination, both in his own lifetime and ever since. In the middle of the nineteenth century, Edgar Allen Poe wrote a short piece entitled "A Descent into the Maelström," which was inspired by his reading of a passage in the *Mundus*. While he found Kircher's views "idle," he nonetheless confessed that when he saw the swirling vortex off the coast of Norway known as the maelstrom, Kircher's explanation "was the one to which, as I gazed, my imagination most readily assented."[139] By the late twentieth century, Kircher came to embody a kind of quirky modernity for a novelist such as Italo Calvino, who fantasized about a man reconstructing Kircher's captoptric theater of the *Ars magna lucis et umbrae* in his home in order to conceal himself—and ultimately being unable to discern his reality amidst the profusion of simulacra.[140] And there is surely much more to say about Umberto Eco's recurrent use of the ghost of Kircher in his novels. Think of Father Caspar Wanderdrossel in *Island of the Day Before*, a demented, polyglottish polymath who transformed a ship going nowhere into a floating cabinet of curiosities.

The essays that follow chart some of the possible directions for studying Kircher and his world. I have chosen not to summarize the essays in this introduction but rather to introduce Kircher himself by examining how his reputation developed and changed across a century. Studying Kircher is a collective project. Even a volume such as this one cannot do justice to the many important and interesting subjects that an examination of Kircher raises. This project is at once biographic and episodic, and it is the product of a collective conversation of a group of scholars who have all taken an interest in Father Athanasius for distinctly different reasons. It seeks to recover Kircher the man and the intellect, but also Kircher's society in the broadest possible sense—his sources of inspiration and information, his friendships, and those whom he inspired to kircherize. *Kircherizing* probably should become a word of ordinary usage in the twenty-first century, just as *kircherian* was in his own lifetime. It describes a way of thinking and being that competed with all the other epistemologies in play in the seventeenth century: Aristotelian, Platonic, Hermetic, Lullian, Baconian, Galilean, Cartesian, Newtonian, and so forth. This, after all, was the empire of knowledge of which Father Athanasius dreamed. During his imaginary papacy, the entire world conversed peacefully and harmoniously because they kircherized.

Notes

Thanks to Michael John Gorman, Anthony Grafton, Tamara Griggs, Antonella Romano, Ingrid Rowland, and Daniel Stolzenberg for suggestions and additional bibliography.

1. Biblioteca Medicea Laurenziana (hereafter **Laur.**), Florence, *Redi*. 219, fol. 204r (Father Antonio Baldigiani to Francesco Redi, Rome, n.d.). Baldigiani was professor of mathematics at the Collegio Romano until 1707.
2. There is some debate as to whether Kircher was born on 2 May 1602, as his autobiography records (Kircher 1684b, p. 1), or born in 1601. By contrast, in November 1678 he described himself as seventy-seven in a letter to Hieronymus Langenmantel. Langenmantel 1684, p. 85. The British Library possesses a rare copy of his *Vita admodum Reverendi P. Athanasii Kircheri, Societ[atis] Jesu* (shelfmark 701.b.55).
3. Kircher's final days are well summarized in Reilly 1974, pp. 179–182. The quote is from Langenmantel 1684, p. 86. See Noel Malcolm's essay for further discussion of Kircher's place in the republic of letters.
4. The story of Kircher's special relationship to the sanctuary in Mentorella is recounted in Cascioli 1915–16.
5. *Giornale de' Letterati* VII (Rome, 1676), in Gardair 1984, p. 272n28.
6. Compare the list in Kircher 1646, n.p. (can be paginated as p. 936: "Ad Lectorem") with Kircher 1665c, vol. 1, p. 346, Kircher 1675, n.p. ("Elenchus librorum a P. Athanasio Kirchero è Societate Jesu, editorum"), and Sepibus 1678, pp. 61–66.
7. Sepibus 1678, p. 64. Kircher's publication history is recounted more fully in Fletcher 1968 and Hein 1993.
8. Kircher 1678; Sepibus 1678. For more on the museum, see Findlen 1994, 1995, 2001a, and 2001b.
9. Kircher 1679a and 1679b (quotes from sig. A4r, sig. A7v). It is much more likely that Kircher's infirmities were the real reason he turned it over to Benedetti. On this work, see Corradino 1996.
10. Kestler 1680 (quote is from title page).
11. Anon., "An Experiment of a way of preparing a Liquor . . . ," *Philosophical Transactions of the Royal Society of London* 1 (1665–66): 125.
12. See Jorge Luis Borges's foreword to *The Garden of Forking Paths* (1941) in Borges 1998, p. 67.

13. Knittel 1682, esp. p. 60.
14. Laur., *Redi* 219, fol. 141r (Baldigiani to Francesco Redi, Rome, 16 December 1674). The subsequent discussion of *Arca Noë* appears in Laur., *Redi* 219, fol. 179r (n.d.). For a discussion of Kircher's publishing, see Fletcher 1968; Nummedal and Findlen 2000.
15. Fabretti 1741, vol. 3; cf. Kircher 1671b. See Griggs 2000 and 2002.
16. Gottfried Wilhelm Leibniz, *On Universal Synthesis and Analysis, or the Art of Discovery and Judgment* (ca. 1679), in Leibniz 1969, p. 230. See his correspondence with Kircher in Friedlander 1937.
17. Robinet 1988, p. 90.
18. Leibniz, *Discourse on the Natural Theology of the Chinese* (1716), in Leibniz 1994, p. 134.
19. Laur., *Redi* 219, fol. 141r (Baldigiani to Francesco Redi, Rome, 16 December 1674).
20. Knittel 1682, pp. 18–19. See his "Tabula Combinatoria aut potius Permutatoria" between these two pages, in which Knittel noted four errors of calculation in Kircher's table that had inspired his own. He kindly attributed the mistakes to the printers ("sine dubio vitio Typothetae"). Knittel was very much like Schott in being supportive of Kircher's project while attempting to correct and improve upon it in order to uphold his master's reputation.
21. Mencke 1937, pp. 85–86.
22. Grafton 1997b, pp. 182–189.
23. Griggs 2000, esp. p. 45.
24. Huygens, *Cosmotheoros* (1698), in Huygens 1888–, vol. 21, pp. 770–771. Readers may recall that the Danish astronomer Tycho Brahe constructed a geoheliocentric cosmos that combined the structure of Ptolemaic astronomy with new data from post–Copernican astronomy, creating a cosmos with two centers—the earth and the sun—around which different planets orbited.
25. For further discussion of this work, see Camenietzki 1995a and the contributions of Carlos Ziller Camenietzki and Ingrid Rowland to this volume.
26. Mr. Walker, "Some Experiments and Observations concerning Sounds," *Philosophical Transactions of the Royal Society of London* 20 (1698): 436.
27. Mather 1994, p. 35.
28. Ibid., pp. 106–107, 124–125, 169, 186, 265–266, 268. This kind of question suggests that Mather read Kircher as the culmination of a long tradition of encyclopedias discussing wonders, prodigies, and *problemata*; see Daston and Park 1998.
29. Reilly 1958.
30. Findlen 2000.
31. These misspellings reflect the variety of ways in which scholars in France and Italy wrote his name in the mid-1630s. Balthazar Kitzner was a philosophy professor at Würzburg, further compounding the confusion about which German scholar had emigrated to Avignon and subsequently Rome.
32. The majority of information in this section is from Kircher 1684b (quote p. 35). See Fletcher 1970, pp. 53–54; Hankins and Silverman 1995, p. 14, for his sundials.
33. Marrone 2002, p. 39.
34. Gorman and Wilding 2000 offer a complete bibliography of Schott's works.
35. John Fletcher, "Kircher and Astronomy: A Postscript," in Casciato et al. 1986, p. 130. The original manuscript of Kircher's *Institutiones mathematicae* is housed in the Badische Landesbibliothek, Karlsruhe, Cod. St. Blasien 67. Kircher's magnetic theories have been well studied in Baldwin 1987.
36. Kircher 1635.
37. On the former, see Hankins and Silverman 1995, pp. 14–36; on the latter, see Peter Miller's chapter in this volume.
38. See Aufrère 1990 and Miller 2000 for more on Peiresc's world; and Fletcher 1972 on Kircher's relations with his French correspondents.
39. Peiresc 1992, p. 38n35 (Peiresc to Samuel Petit, 14 December 1632); Peiresc 1888–94, vol. 4, p. 295 (Peiresc to Pierre Gassendi, 2 March 1633).
40. Peiresc 1888–94, vol. 2, p. 528 (Peiresc to Monsieur Du Puy, 21 May 1633) and p. 534 (idem, 30 May 1633); see Hankins and Silverman 1995 for a fuller discussion. On the importance of secrets in early modern science, see Eamon 1995.
41. Kircher 1641, p. 737.
42. On the episode in Marseille, see Kircher 1641, p. 737. For attempts to bring Kircher to Aix, see Romano 1997, p. 13; Romano 1999, pp. 387–388; and her epilogue to this volume.

43. Peiresc 1992, pp. il-l and 37–38 (Peiresc to Claude Saumaise, 14 November 1633). In fact, Kircher had shown Peiresc exactly one page on 3 September but nothing more, as Peter Miller and Daniel Stolzenberg have discussed in their more extensive study of this episode.

44. Mersenne 1932–88, vol. 3, p. 459 (Descartes to Mersenne, 22 July 1633) and p. 504 (Peiresc to Mersenne, 13 October 1633). See also Hankins and Silverman 1995, p. 16.

45. Gassendi 1992, p. 218; Peiresc 1989, p. 112 (Peiresc to Cassiano dal Pozzo, 10 September 1633). On Cassiano dal Pozzo, see especially Freedberg 2002.

46. The broader institutional culture of Jesuit science is well discussed in Baldini 1992 and 2000; Feldhay 1987, 1995, and 1999; Harris 1989 and 1996; Romano 1999; and Feingold 2002. The best starting point for understanding the Society of Jesus in general is O'Malley 1993; and Giard 1995.

47. Peiresc 1992, p. 63 (Peiresc to Saumaise, 4 April 1634).

48. Peiresc 1989, p. 140 (Peiresc to dal Pozzo, 29 June 1634). In this, he succeeded, since Kircher's *Magnes, sive de arte magnetica* did not appear until 1641.

49. Peiresc 1983, p. 91 (Peiresc to Gabriel Naudé, 5 June 1636). On the culture of forgery, see Grafton 1990.

50. Kircher 1636, sig. ++2v. I have used the translation in Rowland 2000, p. 88.

51. See Cipriani 1995; and Marrone 2002, pp. 40–45.

52. Peiresc 1992, p. 330 (Pieresc to Saumaise, 29 November 1636). This letter also discussed the rumor of Kircher's mission to the Levant (p. 331).

53. Peiresc 1989, p. 134 (Peiresc to dal Pozzo, 4 May 1634).

54. Peiresc 1888–98, vol. 5, p. 458 (Peiresc to Lucas Holstenius, 2 October 1636).

55. Peiresc 1989, p. 161 (Peiresc to dal Pozzo, 29 December 1634).

56. Redondi 1985; Biagioli 1993.

57. Galilei 1968, vol. 16, p. 64 (Giovanni Giacomo Bouchard to Galileo, 18 March 1634); vol. 17, p. 50 (Raffaello Magiotti, 21 March 1637).

58. Ibid., vol. 16, p. 65 (Bouchard to Galileo 18 March 1634). The Roman context of Kircher's work is discussed in Eugenio Lo Sardo's and Antonella Romano's contributions to this volume.

59. On Roman science in this period, see Romano 2002 and the special issue of *Roma moderna e contemporanea* 7 (1999): 347–598 edited by Antonella Romano on "Roma e la scienza (secoli XVI–XX)."

60. Archivio della Pontificia Università Gregoriana, Rome (hereafter **APUG**), *Kircher*, MS. 561, fol. 18r.

61. Galilei 1968, vol. 17, p. 18 (Magiotti to Galileo, 16 May 1637).

62. Kircher 1638. This work is more easily accessible in Schott 1664, pp. 427–477. It is tempting to think of this instrument as an ingenious combination of a Rubik's cube and a kind of late Renaissance PalmPilot, since it provided its users with absolutely every piece of crucial information they needed in the form of a physical puzzle that worked when each of the five cubes below the pyramid were manipulated. Kircher claimed that it had 125 different uses.

63. These projects have been studied in Findlen 1994; Nummedal 2001; Okrusch and Kelber 2002; and in Stephen Jay Gould's contribution to this volume. The publication date of the *Mundus* has typically been reported as 1664, but closer examination reveals that it did not appear until 1665.

64. Baldwin 1987 and 2001a.

65. Peiresc 1888–98, vol. 4, p. 354 (Peiresc to Gassendi, 6 September 1633). The original phrase is *par force et par obediance*. It was Scheiner who informed Kircher of the outcome of the trial; Mersenne 1932–88, vol. 3, p. 452 (Scheiner to Kircher, 16 July 1633). See Camenietzki 1995a and Ingrid Rowland's contribution to this volume for further discussion of the unorthodox aspects of Kircher's cosmology.

66. Mersenne 1932–88, vol. 6, p. 30 (Giovan Battista Doni to Mersenne, 27 February 1636).

67. Kircher 1641, pp. 115, 439–441, 444, 453–455, 457, 469, 481–483. Mersenne 1932–88, vol. 9, pp. 31–38 (Mersenne to Kircher, 20 January 1640), and p. 107 (Mersenne to Theódore Haack, 12 February 1640). Michael John Gorman's contribution to this volume discusses the nature of Kircher's information network in greater detail.

68. See John Pell's assessment of how Kircher used data he and Mersenne provided in Mersenne 1932–88, vol. 11, p. 244 (Pell to ?, 17/27 August 1642).

69. Galilei 1968, vol. 18, p. 332 (Torricelli to Galileo, 1 June 1641) and p. 372 (Micanzio to Galileo, 14 December 1641).

70. Mersenne 1932–88, vol. 12, p. 10 (Huygens to Descartes, 7 January 1643) and p. 29 (Descartes to Huygens, 14 January 1643). The second letter is translated in full in Hankins and Silverman 1995, p. 19 (my own translation modifies this slightly).

71. Ibid., vol. 13, p. 228 (Cavendish to Pell, September/early October 1644).

72. Kircher 1643b, in Scharlau 1969, p. 6.

73. See Baldini 1985 for the general system of censorship; Harald Siebert's essay in this volume discusses Kircher's relationship to the system of Jesuit censorship, as does Stolzenberg 2004.

74. Merseene 1932–88, vol. 13, p. 320 (Mersenne to Boulliaud, 16 January 1645).

75. The definitive study of this larger subject is Daston and Park 1998.

76. Evelyn 1955, vol. 1, pp. 105–106, 124.

77. Kircher 1673, p. 112. For more on Kircher's famous speaking devices, see Reilly 1974, p. 141; and Godwin 1979, pp. 70–71.

78. Kircher 1646, p. 936 (unpaginated but after p. 935). For Kircher's work as a cartographer, see Kircher 1684b, p. 34.

79. This final manuscript was, in all likelihood, Kircher 1653.

80. Kircher 1665c, p. 346.

81. Findlen 1994, 1995, and 2001a; Lo Sardo 2000.

82. On early modern encyclopedism, see Blair 1997; Vasoli 1978; and Luisetti 2001.

83. Kircher 1646, pp. 316–324. To understand the problem with Kircher's proof, make a circle with a two-inch radius. DC equals $1/2\ \pi$ (1.5708) while DF is 1.525. The smaller circle, the smaller the difference between DC and DF, making Kircher's proof a plausible approximation. The fact that the diagram was not to scale may have made the proof even funnier for some readers.

84. Mersenne 1932–88, vol. 14, pp. 366–367 (Torricelli to Mersenne, 7 July 1646); Galluzzi and Torrini 1975, vol. 1, p. 326 (Mersenne to Torricelli, 15 September 1646); see also pp. 272–273, 305–307, 314, 561 for other information in this paragraph. For an appreciative assessment of the treatise as a whole, see Corradino 1993.

85. Mersenne, 1932–88, vol. 14, p. 472 (Mersenne to Kircher, 22 September 1646). This negative response did not discourage Kircher from publishing other mathematical works; see Kircher 1665a and 1679b; and Schott 1660 and 1668.

86. Ibid., p. 636 (Huygens to Mersenne, 26 November 1646). On Maignan, see pp. 55–56, 420–421.

87. Kircher 1650b; Iverson 1968, pp. 86–88; Cipriani 1993.

88. Latanza 1995. Like Kircher's earlier building of sundials, this episode serves as a reminder that he was quite adept with machines.

89. Goldberg 1988, p. 19.

90. Archivum Romanum Societatis Iesu (hereafter **ARSI**, *Fondo Gesuitico* 1069/5, cassetto III, n. 1. *Atto originale antico di consegna al N[ost]ro Museo della Galleria di Alfonso Donnino* (1651). See Casciato et al. 1986; Lugli 1986; Findlen 1994, 1995, 2000, and 2001a; and Lo Sardo 2001.

91. Gorman 1999.

92. Huygens 1888–, vol. 3, p. 48 (Father Guisony to Christiaan Huygens, 25 March 1660).

93. APUG, *Kircher*, MS. 560 (VI), fol. 111 (Rome, 23 October 1671), in Rivosecchi 1982, p. 141; see also MS. 559 (V), fol. 140 (Rome, 17 October 1670).

94. Pastine 1978. This work is now being carefully studied in Daniel Stolzenberg's forthcoming dissertation; see Stolzenberg 2003, 2004, and forthcoming.

95. Nicholson 1992, pp. 31, 34.

96. Galluzzi and Torrini 1975, vol. 2, p. 229 (12 June 1655).

97. Daniel Stolzenberg's forthcoming dissertation, "Egyptian Oedipus: Antiquarianism, Oriental Studies, and Occult Philosophy in the Work of Athanasius Kircher" (Ph.D. diss., Stanford University, 2003) offers the richest account of this fundamental aspect of Kircher's work. As with a number of Kircher's works, there is some dabate about the dates of publication of the *Oedipus*. While the volumes were printed between 1652 and 1654, none were released until 1655, hence latter date on the colophon of volume three. Thanks to Daniel Stolzenberg and John Mustain for consulting with me or how to do the dating of these complicated texts.

98. Kircher 1684a, p. 61.

99. The classic study of Hermetic thought in the Renaissance remains Yates 1964.

100. See Stolzenberg 2004 and Harald Siebert's essay in this volume for a further exploration of Jesuit censorship of the *Oedipus*. Daniel Stolzenberg's and Anthony Grafton's essays in this volume explore aspects of the *Oedipus* in greater detail.

101. Kircher 1652–55, vol. 3, pp. 80–160. Readers may wish to contrast his interpretation with the earlier ones offered by antiquarians such as Lorenzo Pignoria and Herwart von Hohenburg.

102. Despite his early insight into the relationship between Coptic and the language of the ancient Egyptians, Kircher never thought that hieroglyphs might be phonetic rather than symbolic. He was too much an heir of a Neoplatonic vision of Egypt first articulated in the late fifteenth century. See David 1965; Iverson 1993; and Stolzenberg 2003.

103. Angela Mayer-Deutsch's essay in this volume discusses the images of Kircher during and after his lifetime.

104. Kircher 1660, p. 3. This text is discussed in greater detail in Ingrid Rowland's and Carlos Ziller Camenietzki's contributions to this volume.

105. APUG, *Kircher*, MS. 61, fol. 280r (Palermo, 10 June 1652). See Gorman and Wilding 2000, pp. 256–257. The information in this section relies on their book in general. The only other serious study of Schott to date is Hellyer 1996.

106. Biblioteca Nazionale Vittorio Emanuele, Rome, *Fondo Gesuitico* 1331, fasc. 15, fol. 223r (*Mira Kircheri in suo Itinerario Exstatico Audacia, Presumptio, ac Temeritas*). See Camenietzki 1995a, p. 30; Hellyer 1996, pp. 333–335; and Rowland 2000, p. 100.

107. See Findlen 2001a for a more detailed account of this visit and Åkerman 1991 on Christina of Sweden in general.

108. Kircher would continue to bestow rare manuscripts upon important patrons into the 1660s, for example, his gift of a tenth-century Syriac version of the Gospels to Duke August of Braunschweig-Lüneberg, duke of Wolfenbüttel, in March 1666. See Kuntz 1987.

109. Kircher 1658. This period of Kircher's life is discussed in greater detail in Martha Baldwin's contribution to this volume. On Kircher's microscopy, see Torrey 1938; Belloni 1985; Wilson 1995; esp. pp. 155–158; and Strasser 1996.

110. Schott 1657, 1657–59, 1660, and 1664.

111. See Kircher 1665b and 1671b; and Kircher 1684b, pp. 63–64, 70, 76–77; also Cascioli 1915–16.

112. See Harald Siebert's essay in this volume. The *Ars magna sciendi* did not appear for nine years (Kircher 1669), and the *Iter Hetruscum* never appeared.

113. *Philosophical Transactions* 4 (1669): 1093.

114. Fletcher 1988b, p. 9. This arrangement allowed Kircher to maintain his relations with Roman printers, who continued to publish his works in the early 1660s and would publish his *Tariffa Kircheriana* (1679) at the end of his life.

115. Jansson translated the *China monumentis illustrata* into Dutch (1668) and French (1670), and the second (1678) edition of the *Mundus* into Dutch in 1682. A partial translation also appeared in English in Nieuhof 1673.

116. Godwin 1979, p. 67; Rostenberg 1989, pp. 53, 72, 117. The English reception of Kircher's work is discussed in Noel Malcolm's contribution to this volume.

117. Kircher 1684b, p. 62. Thirty-six printers in Italy, the Holy Roman Empire, France, and the Netherlands published Kircher's books. See Hein 1993 for a more detailed discussion of the publication history.

118. Readers should not forget how central Hapsburg patronage was to Kircher's career; see Evans 1979.

119. Kircher 1663, pp. 142–144. Kircher's approach to language is discussed in Eco 1995; Wilding 2001a; and the contributions of Haun Saussy and Nick Wilding to this volume.

120. Ceñal 1953.

121. Oldenburg 1966, vol. 2, p. 567 (London, 12 October 1665) and, p. 615 (London, 21 November 1665); Shapin and Schaffer 1985, p. 31.

122. Kircher 1665c, vol. 1, sig. ***r. Stephen Jay Gould's contribution to this volume offers a fresh view of Kircher's account of fossils.

123. The essays by Carlos Ziller Camenietzki, Michelle Molina, and Florence Hsia as well as my other article in this volume discuss the image of Kircher as a global author.

124. Findlen 2002, p. 267. See Reilly 1958 on the role of Jesuit information in the Royal Society; and Harris 1996, 1998, and 1999 for a discussion of Jesuit information networks.

125. Schott 1667, pp. 455–456. I thank Michael John Gorman for bringing it to my attention. See Gorman and Wilding 2001, p. 232.

126. Grafton 1997b, pp. 150–154; Blauenstein 1667.
127. The snakestone debate is reconstructed in Baldwin 1995; and Nocenti 2002.
128. Petrucci 1677, p. 184. This text explicitly invokes Galileo's *The Assayer* as its model in establishing a scientific methodology and epistemology.
129. Kestler 1680, sig. *4r. Like Petrucci's defense, Kestler's compilation was in all likelihood written in collaboration with Kircher.
130. A number of visitors to David Wilson's exhibit on Kircher at the Museum of Jurassic Technology in Culver City, California, seem quite sure that *he* has indeed made Kircher up. Anton Haakman was also accused of making him up after completing a documentary on the Athanasius Kircher Society; see Haakman 1995, p. 144.
131. Eco 1989, p. 441.
132. The most recent works are Rowland 2000; Lo Sardo 1999 and 2001; Stolzenberg 2001; Marrone 2002; Athanasius Kircher 2001; Beinlich et al. 2002; Magie des Wissens 2003. Readers should compare them with earlier studies of Kircher such as Scharlau 1969; Reilly 1974; Pastine 1978; Evans 1979; Godwin 1979; City of Rastatt 1981; Rivosecchi 1982; Casciato et al. 1986; Gómez de Liaño 1986; Baldwin 1987; Fletcher 1988a; Merrill 1989; Leinkauf 1993; Hein 1993; and Findlen 1994. The article literature on Kircher is cited throughout the essays in this volume.
133. No modern Kircher fan should miss David Wilson's efforts to reconstruct some of Kircher's machines in the Museum of Jurassic Technology, a place that has the feel of the magic lantern whose invention is often wrongfully attributed to Kircher. Stanford University Library also owns a magnetic clock created by Caroline Bougereau with the assistance of Michael John Gorman. Examples and copies of the original machines exist in a number of European museums, such as the Museum for the History of Science in Florence and the Herzog Anton Ulrich-Museum, Braunschweig.
134. See the Web site (www.soisawthismovie.com) for a description of "The Athanasius Awards for Excellence in Achievement in Motion Pictures."
135. Goethe, "Theory of Colors" in Haakman 1995, p. 18.
136. Antonella Romano's epilogue treats these issues in greater detail.
137. I hope readers are aware that this is hardly the only book with this title, a sign that we continue to be intrigued by men who knew "everything."
138. One of the reasons the Bettmann Archive became well-known is because CBS asked him to select an image to illustrate radio. He used Kircher's famous image of a speaking tube to create an award-winning advertisement. See Otto Bettmann, *Bettmann the Picture Man* (Gainesville: University Press of Florida, 1992), pp. 8–9; and *New York Times* (4 May 1998), p. A17. Thanks to Ella Mazel, the original creator of the Athanasius Kircher collection in Special Collections at Stanford University Libraries, for bringing this story to my attention.
139. Poe 1978, vol. 2, p. 583. This essay originally appeared in 1841.
140. The novel in question is *If on a Winter's Night a Traveller*.

The Art of Being Kircher

1

Kircher's Rome

EUGENIO LO SARDO

The Town

Look at a map of the period. Look down on Rome—the southernmost point of Europe—torn to shreds by wars, attacked to the south by malaria, surrounded by a bitter sea full of strife and dread, infested by pirates. Ninety thousand people were separated only by the Adriatic, the Apennines, and a hundred galleys—which Venice kept always ready for war—from the ruinous regions of the infidel and from the even more hated Orthodox Christians, "foremost enemies of the Holy See." To the north its spiritual hegemony was threatened by the vacillations of the French and the sledgehammer blows of the kings and princes of the Reformation. The small Italian states—Tuscany, Savoy, Parma, Modena, and the republic of La Serenissima—were rent with internal conflict, as were Poland, Austria, and Spain. Still, these powers acted as dikes to protect the Catholic Church from the Protestant world, which was itself showing signs of division. Gustavus Adolphus himself, the king of Sweden, was on the point of converting at the time of Urban VIII.

Further south lay only Naples and Palermo. But the south was an outpost for Spain, a faithful ally and an invader at one and the same time, prepared in its pride to flaunt before the pope the power of its armies and fleets to force the spiritual leader to serve the designs of the Christian king. The sea, which lay at the gates of the city, at Ostia, was utterly perilous. It took very little to fall into the hands of the pirates. The green flags adorned with silver crescents infiltrated far into the deepest inlets of the Tyrrhenian Sea. With swift incursions they sacked and plundered, putting shipping and the supply of grain and provisions at serious risk. The battle of Lepanto had halted the fleets that had terrorized the West under Barbarossa and Dragut, but this had not been enough to put a stop to the constant drain from piracy, even if the balance of the exchanges between the two sides was perhaps shifting in favor of Christianity.[1]

This was the town in which Kircher arrived. He had himself tasted the surprises that the sea held in store, especially on the busiest routes of the upper and middle Mediterranean, and he had even explored the front line of Christianity, the wedge dividing East and West: Sicily and Malta. The invincible fortress of the Knights remained the most faithful ally of the Holy See. It was a thorn in the side of the great Ottoman hound, a gathering point for the armed fleets of the Genoese, the papacy, and the Order of Saint Stephen, which year after year intercepted the cargoes of merchandise going from Egypt to Costantinople in the straits between Cyprus and Rhodes.

This difficult situation, very present to the mind of a seventeenth-century man, began to have its ill effects only in the second half of the century. In Kircher's time Rome seemed at the height of its splendor. "I felt that I was appearing publicly in the theater of the world," wrote Galileo, referring to the Eternal City in the foreword to the *Dialogue concerning the Two Chief World Systems* (1632). This was the stage on which to "show the foreign nations that as much is known on this subject in Italy and especially in Rome as transalpine wisdom could possibly have imagined."[2] Thirty years later Kircher used the same words when he stated that "my Gallery or Museum is visited by all the nations of the world and a prince cannot become better known in this theater of the world than have his likeness here."[3]

Three Popes

When Kircher arrived, Rome dominated the artistic and intellectual world of Europe. All came to the Eternal City for inspiration—not, as they do now, to view the ruins of antiquity.

The French painter Nicolas Poussin—friend of the Roman antiquarian and naturalist Cassiano dal Pozzo, who was putting together his "paper museum" (*museo cartaceo*) in via dei Chiavari—studied perspective there and took the first steps of his successful career. He was one among many in that flowering of illustrious names such as Bernini, Borromini, and Pietro da Cortona who animated the artistic life of the city. But this fascinating and dazzling splendor concealed a precarious economic foundation, one that sustained the city and the papacy only with enormous effort.[4]

It was a splendid setting for the Barberini family, one dimmed only by the compromise with the Spanish party over the Galileo affair in 1633. The French scholar Nicolas-Claude Fabri de Peiresc had recommended Kircher to Francesco Barberini, the cardinal *nipote* and, since 1628, secretary of state. Francesco was an enlightened prince, a graduate of the University of Pisa *in utroque iure*. Lucas Holstein was the family librarian, and the prince had his own scientific cabinet, of which a description still exists in the Montepellier library. "Life is but a dream" (*La vita es sueño*), wrote Calderon de la Barca the same year that Kircher landed in the pope's capital. Rome thrived on wonders, the wonders of architecture and art. Its power was a spiritual one in the literal sense of the word: it had no armies, no rich trade fairs, no ports, no gold mines in Peru.

In a few decades, Sixtus V's city plan was profoundly transformed. The list of the buildings and artistic works completed at that time is astonishing: the colonnade of Saint Peter's, the ponte Sant'Angelo, the Chiesa Nuova, the Oratorio dei

Filippini, the Tempio della Pace, Palazzo Barberini, and Piazza Navona, Sant'Ivo, and the University to cite only a few of the architectural marvels of seventeenth-century Rome. Rudolf Wittkower aptly summarizes this extraordinary effort by noting that: "The anti-aesthetic approach to art of the period of the militant Counter-Reformation was now replaced by an aesthetic appreciation of artistic quality." The Jesuits too went through a deep metamorphosis: "mundane interests in wealth, luxury, and political intrigue [. . .] replaced the original zealous and austere spirit of the Order."[5]

Kircher found himself perfectly at home in this world. The Barberini appointed him to head a commission for the interpretation of the hieroglyphs, and he became professor at the Collegio Romano. He thanked the family by dedicating the *Coptic or Egyptian Forerunner* (*Prodromus Coptus sive Aegyptiacus*) (1636) to Francesco Barberini. Urban VIII's death, however, brought a dramatic change in the papal court. The hopes of the "new philosophers" for a humanist and scientific renewal of the Italian cultural life, already quenched by Galileo's trial, ended abruptly. When free living had already gone too far, Virgilio Malvezzi wrote to Evangelista Torricelli, it was time to rein in free speech.[6] The Spaniards imposed a Pamphili pope, Innocent X, and the French party in Rome was in dire straits. Antonio Barberini had to escape to France, and as soon as possible, the other members of the family followed him. A deep crisis divided the people. That "imperfect neutrality" among the Christian powers, lead by Urban VIII, was broken, and the property of his heirs was impounded. Olympia Pamphili—the "nobildonna" who refused to pay for the coffin of her brother-in-law, the pope—dominated the life of the capital and emptied the coffers of the papacy. Rome was also declining on the European political scene. In 1648, the papal envoy, Fabio Chigi, was not invited to sign the Treaty of Westphalia, which ended the Thirty Years' War. It was the first time in Europe that peace was made without papal intercession.

Kircher, as usual, swam with the current. He was under the protection of the Habsburgs and worked for the Pamphili family for the midcentury Jubilee. With the end of the Pamphili era, the wind shifted again. Chigi, a Senese humanist descendant of the magnificent banker and patron of Raphael, Agostino Chigi, ascended the throne under the name of Alexander VII. The new pope, a man of refined aesthetic taste, was personally linked with the German polymath. They met for the first time in Malta in 1637. Soon after Kircher left, Fabio wrote to him a letter full of kindness and consideration.[7] The pope was only three years older than the Jesuit. He was a skilled diplomat, having spent twelve years in Germany, an able politician, and a member of the republic of letters. Alexander was the founder of the new library at the University of Rome, designed by Borromini, which in his honor is still called the Biblioteca Alessandrina. Many common interests linked them, principal among them being the passion for the Egyptian mysteries and the Hermetic tradition.[8] Kircher would remember his friend and protector all his life, dedicating to him two books and a wooden obelisk, on which he called Alexander a master of ancient wisdom, an oracle of culture, and a reborn Osiris. A similar dedication on the same obelisk was offered to Christina of Sweden, who had been greeted by Alexander with great pomp on her arrival in Rome. The former queen of the northern country was "sanctified" as Isis reborn. The gods of Egypt were back on the Tiber shores.

Kircher's Square Mile

In the middle of the seventeenth century, Piazza Navona became the center of Rome, and the centerpiece of that square was the Fountain of the Four Rivers that Bernini completed, with the intellectual assistance of Kircher, in 1651. A good fountain, Bernini supposedly said according to his first biographer, should always have a true or metaphorical meaning.[9] Certainly, everything in this splendid masterpiece suggests the idea of the spiritual primacy of the pope, a supremacy both historical and actual. The fountain was intended to be the theatrical set to be seen by thousands of pilgrims during the great Jubilee of 1650. The obelisk, symbol of the sun, with the Pamphili dove on the top, is set on a base of rocks (the Church) and caves (the instincts, or Sin) from which the four most important rivers of the world spring (Figure 1.1). It is an idea often illustrated in Kircher's books. As in many symbolic systems with multiple meanings,[10] reading Bernini's work is a question of interpretation. The fountain can be read as an image of the Earthly Paradise—the origin of the four rivers—but also as an image of the faith's diffusion to the four continents (Australia was not yet discovered). According to Kircher, everything, even the mathematical proportion of the pyramid, had to be carefully interpreted.

The Nile's head remains half veiled (although Pedro Pais had discovered the river's source in 1618) to emphasize the mystery of the Egyptians' ancient wisdom. The Rio de la Plata is represented as a bearded man with a circlet on his thigh, enlightened by apostolic revelation, with a dragon-like armadillo, the Guaranì "tatù,"[11] lying at its feet. The Danube is old, like Europe. The Ganges River statue stands with a rudder in its hand. In between the Nile and the Ganges, a palm tree, a symbol of the Phoenix, is bent by the wind. There is a kaleidoscopic plurality of symbols and of links among them, but it is easy to decipher the central meaning of the whole: the spiritual supremacy of the pope. Thus a political program was transformed into a beautiful masterpiece.[12]

Not far from the Piazza Navona the church of the University of Rome, Sant'Ivo alla Sapienza, Borromini's masterpiece, introduces different meanings within a dominant idea: the limitations of mankind. "Sapientia edificavit sibi domum" wrote Borromini on the manuscript plan of the church.[13] Three hundred years later, Vincenzo Vespignani added on the high altar: *initium sapientiae, timor Domini*—"the fear of the Lord is the beginning of

Figure 1.1. Gian Lorenzo Bernini's Fountain of the Four Rivers in Piazza Navona. Credit: the author.

knowledge,"[14] where the Lord is not only the Father figure but infinite wisdom. Human beings always strive to reach new limits, and when they achieve those, they look for other challenges. As in the Fountain of the Four Rivers in Piazza Navona, in Sant'Ivo we can find a palimpsest of meanings, many of them related to Kircher's studies and iconography. Though there is no evidence of direct links between the "Gothic" architect and the German scholar, the two had a great deal in common. Both worked in Rome under Francesco Barberini's patronage, both enjoyed Innocent X's consideration, and both were very religious men—the first being a "cavaliere dell'ordine di Cristo," the second a Jesuit.

The church, finished in 1660, displays the arms of the Barberini and Pamphili families and, inside and outside the dome, Chigi's mountains and stars (Figure 1.2). The floor, an octagon with a cross at its center and black and white alternate tiles, looks like an oriental "mandala," with energy springing from the center toward the periphery and from the periphery to center again, in a tidal hypnotic motion. The flames on the lantern, according to several scholars, represent the Holy Spirit and the bond established between God and mankind. Human pride is thus punished by God but redeemed by the pentecostal miracle.[15] Just like Kircher's *Tower of Babel* (*Turris Babel*) (1679), the dome looks like a zigurat and the spiral "tiburio" another tower of Babel. The

Figure 1.2. The church of Sant'Ivo in Rome. Credit: the author.

themes of Kircher's work, in other words, found their expression in the religious architecture of the city.

Following the road from Piazza Navona to the Collegio Romano, another two hundred meters further on, we leave behind the Pantheon—the living demonstration of the superiority of the ancients—and arrive in the Piazza della Minerva. In this square of the Dominican Order, the Jesuits' most aggressive enemies, Bernini, with Kircher's aid, designed a little elephant carrying an obelisk and presenting his rear end to the Inquisition Tribunal[16] (Figure 1.3). At the base of the statue the inscription reads: "Alexander VII erected this obelisk once dedicated to the Egyptians' Pallas [Isis], to the divine wisdom, and to the deipara mother."

An International Network

The Collegio Romano, standing on the ruins of the temple of Isis in Campo Marzio,[17] faces on its southern side the Dominicans' compound and library. In the school's courtyard the fornices of the arches are walled up, but the windows of Kircher's gallery are still visible. The museum was founded in 1651, following a donation to the Order by Alfonso Donnini, the secretary of the Roman Senate. Thanks to Kircher's genius, his collection, now blended with the Jesuits', soon became the most famous in Rome and one of the best in Europe.

Figure 1.3. The obelisk in front of Santa Maria sopra Minerva. *Source:* Courtesy of Special Collections, Stanford University Library.

Every museum reflects the impure colors of the world. Kircher's reflected the colors of Rome; to understand it and the cultural life of the pope's capital, it is necessary to broaden one's horizons. Rome, as we have seen, was an international town surrounded by enemies. It had to find a way around these obstacles in order to increase its spiritual influence, just as in Columbus's day it was necessary to look for the East by going West or to turn around the African coast to reach India. The Jesuits were well suited to this task, for they were the most powerful missionary organization in the field. The followers of Loyola were spread over a great part of the known world, including all the countries subject to the Spanish and Portuguese monarchies, the imperial domains, China, India, Poland, and Russia (for some years). They strove to recapture England, and they struggled with all their might to retake ground from the Protestants. They even had a mission in the territory of the Grand Seigneur, the sultan at Costantinople. Kircher, as one of the most prestigious Jesuit intellectuals for over forty years, was a point of reference for generations of these missionaries. The effort to expand Rome's global influence is thus an essential background for understanding his work.

The state of the faith was constantly being monitored. Reports from the furthest corners of the earth arrived at the Roman Curia, where strategies were devised and human resources apportioned. The power of the Jesuits—who were in a position to weave schemes of international espionage using missionaries in China, Russia, and France—was a matter of concern to the popes themselves. The Propaganda Fide followed them with a watchful and critical eye. In 1676, Odoardo Cybo, secretary to the Congregation, drew up a lengthy report on the state of Christianity whose account of the history of the last century frequently dwelt on the operations of the Company of Jesus. "In the time of Innocent X," reads the manuscript, the Catholic religion "made great progress in Germany, Africa, and East India." In Europe it had had the unexpected success of converting the queen of Sweden, who could not, however, "move those heretics by her example to embrace the Catholic faith, even though she made the holy and glorious gesture of giving up such a great kingdom for the sake of religion." In Germany the Hanseatic cities remained the stronghold of the "most depraved heretics." There were struggles everywhere on the continent of Europe to suppress heterodoxy and to conquer new territory. Asia, "for the most part in the hands of the infidel," was not overlooked. The few Christians who lived there were "replete with the errors of Arius, Nestorius, Dioscurus, Eutychius, and other heretics and schismatics, all in league with their patriarchs in disobedience to the head of the universal church," even though the Holy See was working zealously for the conversion of these peoples. Still, they had scant success, "either because the Turks, who rule there, will not permit anyone to change religions unless they accept Mohammedism, or because the patriarchs and the metropolitans keep this hatred for the church of Rome alive out of ignorance and avarice."[18] It was best to trust divine providence.

In this detailed picture of the global ambitions of Catholicism, Japan occupied a preeminent position. Francisco Xavier, made a saint in 1622, had taken the Christian message to Japan and had made great progress in a very short time, "particularly in the city of Nagasaki." Leaving the rich lands of the East, where the legend of Marco Polo was still current, Cybo's report came then to Ethiopia, a vast country inhabited by Christians (Copts), who spoke many different tongues but had a common written language. Their king was known in the vernacular as Prester John, and their spiritual guide was the Patriarch of Alexandria. The Jesuits had gotten that far, and they claimed to have found the sources of the Nile. Many other kingdoms and countries were analyzed by the secretary of Propaganda Fide, always with some disdain for the work of the Jesuits, who often came into conflict with the secular priests because "by their custom" they wanted to "be alone."[19]

Odoardo Cybo's analysis was not lacking in insight, but he did not pay enough attention to the reasons for the decline of the Catholic countries of the

Mediterranean. The economic and moral crisis was a signal to the whole world that was under Rome's spiritual leadership. Italy became progressively more reclusive. News increasingly filtered by ecclesiastical intermediaries arrived distorted and watered down. The great maritime powers to the north were winning the economic battle, and the response was to take even more provincial and defensive positions. In ecclesiastical circles there was always the fear that things might get out of hand, and it was felt necessary to keep the peninsula under tight control. Florence, the official residence of the English ambassador, was placed under special surveillance. Many heretics were there, as in nearby Siena. Moreover, foreigners and Protestants abounded in Rome itself, not only passing through but settling down there for months or years at a time. Here they "threw themselves into vice," preparing malicious satires directed against the Roman court and even, "to great outrage," eating meat on Fridays. The Protestant preachers found plenty of food at Rome for their pestilential sermons, which kept people in their heresy. "Merchants, clerks, pimps, and other wretches, . . . taught them about evil," while "in the house of opera girls and disreputable women," they learned wickedness with people of higher rank. Yet not everything that came from outside was harmful. The great influx of foreigners made the Holy City famous, and it was observed that those who had spent time in Rome refrained from persecuting Catholics.

Port cities like Leghorn were another source of infection, and these posed a constant threat to the well-being of the faith. There was more freedom of conscience there, there were foreign residents of every religion, and banned books circulated. This made the arrival of peoples from different parts of Europe a constant threat to orthodoxy, even while Romans welcomed them in the hope that they would understand the heart of Catholicism better. Travelers were questioned minutely at the gates of Rome in a search for suspicious books. To be found with a copy of Boccaccio could expose one to grave risks, as would possession of the writings of those learned Germans who, according to the censors, laid out heretical doctrines with the pretended purpose of refuting them.[20]

Until the middle of the century, the decline and the crisis were not perceived. The better minds were sharpening their weapons to acquire souls, spices, and gold, and the most effective weapons, those in which the Eternal City was most proficient, were those of propaganda. If one does not grasp the global dimension of Catholicism and of Rome, one also will not understand the meaning of the many works of Athanasius Kircher, of his use of images, or of his very sophisticated pedagogical and apologetic apparatus. In 1667, Kircher dedicated his *China Illustrated* (*China monumentis . . . illustrata*) (1667), a book that was widely read and reprinted many times, to Emperor Leopold I, the most munificent of patrons. Beginning with the frontispiece, the book was a clever piece of propaganda for the missionary work of the Company of Jesus. The image portrays Matteo Ricci and Adam Schall holding open a map of China, and from the clouds Saint Ignatius and Saint Francisco

Xavier praying for divine assistance for the work of their brethren. The book was a great success. It offered a myriad of firsthand geographic information on many little-known countries, on recent journeys of exploration, and on the customs, religions, and flora and fauna of those countries. The entire work was furnished with splendid illustrations and was written in a flowing style combining just the right amounts of learned citation and Kircherian whimsy.

New countries had been explored and mapped by the missionaries following the policy of inculturation dictated by Saint Francis Xavier. "Inculturation" meant understanding the languages and customs of people in order to preach the Gospel. This was the peculiar Jesuit practice that resulted in a public condemnation by Innocent X of the so-called "Chinese rites."[21] The theological debate notwithstanding, the policy of inculturation produced a fruitful harvest of knowledge, including dictionaries, grammar books, maps, and geographic reports. Kircher was at the center of this world, and if the Company needed to struggle to maintain its position in the competition with other religious orders and with the Propaganda Fide, the museum was certainly an effective tool. There the Jesuits emerged as tireless and attentive travelers and observers.

The Museum

Under Kircher's stewardship, the museum of the Collegio Romano became a sort of philosophical gymnasium, an exercise space for the mind[22] (Figure 1.4). Following Ignatius's views, he quickly grasped the power of classical scholarship and of images. Heir to the great metaphysical systems of antiquity, and their careful interpreter, the German Jesuit used his weapons with consummate skill. For him, symbols and religion were the same thing: the most neutral image had a hidden meaning, both for the unlearned and for those initiated into the sacred mysteries. Like nature itself, as Eugenio Garin has written in reference to the works of the fifteenth-century humanist Marsilio Ficino, symbols concealed "a soul, a meaning." To stop at the surface, not to get down "to the deepest spiritual meaning," is therefore tantamount to a pernicious error. "To understand the significance" it is necessary "to seek the source," and this source "is the light and the wisdom of God." Every one of Kircher's images is infused with this message. They reveal the religious and devotional context from which they sprang, the spirit that led to the building of grandiose churches dedicated to the greater glory of God and his servants, and that inspired the heroism of people who, convinced that they were carrying out a mission of salvation and regeneration, abandoned everything to carry the message of Christ to the corners of the earth. To get to the root of things means to immerse oneself in a timeless reality, "living in eternity, beyond any discussion, any conviction."[23]

Kircher's museum helps us understand the human and religious reality of baroque Rome, with its passion for Hermetic wisdom, obelisks, and antiquities. In three years of research for the Rome exhibition re-creating his mu-

Figure 1.4. Athanasius Kircher greeting visitors in the center of the Roman College museum. *Source:* Giorgio de Sepibus, *Romani Collegii Societatis Iesu Musaeum Celeberrimum* (Amsterdam, 1678).

seum, we did not find a single representation of the crucifix (any more than there was in Scipione's Galleria Borghese). In place of representations of Christ on the cross, the museum was filled with machines, wooden obelisks, infant skeletons, animals, Roman burial vases and heads, mosaics, coins, and so forth. Kircher himself was on display, and with him the Eternal City. Italo Calvino aptly captured this projection of one man's ego in a passage inspired by Kircher: "It is my image that I want to multiply [in a mirror], but not out of narcissism or megalomania . . . on the contrary, I want to conceal, in the midst of so many illusory ghosts of myself, the true me makes them move . . . I am a man with many enemies, whom I must constantly elude."[24]

Notes

1. Lo Sardo 1999.
2. Galilei 1975, p. 8.
3. Findlen 1995, p. 641.
4. Stumpo 1985.
5. Wittkower 1958, p. 90.
6. Redondi 1983, p. 369.
7. Archivio della Pontificia Università Gregoriana, Rome (hereafter **APUG**), Chigi to Kircher on 13 March 1638.
8. See letter in APUG Chigi to Kircher, "eruditissime vir," 19 June 1639.
9. Baldinucci 1682, p. 84.
10. See Dante, *Convivio*, 1, 4.
11. Baldinucci 1682, p. 103. A stuffed armadillo was on display in Kircher's museum.
12. Cipriani 1993, passim; Rivosecchi 1982, passim.
13. AS Roma, Università, vol. 198.
14. Proverbs 7.
15. Portoghesi 1992, p. 212.
16. A sufficient reason to hold Kircher and Bernini in high esteem! The elephant is akin to the one in *Hipnerotomachia Poliphili*.
17. Mazza 2001.
18. Cibo, O. *Rapporto sullo stato della fede cattolica*. Archivio di Stato di Roma, Biblioteca, MS 466.
19. Ibid.
20. This suspicion had fallen on Abbot Tritemius, for example.
21. The condemnation of these policies, whereby the Chinese Christians were allowed to follow their traditions on occasions such as marriages and funerals, was subsequently modified by Alexander VII.
22. Sepibus 1678.
23. Garin 1973, p. 110.
24. Calvino, Italo, 1981. "If on a Winter's Night a Traveller." trans. Wiliam Weaver. San Diego: Harcourt Brace. pp. 162–3.

2

Reverie in Time of Plague

Athanasius Kircher and the Plague Epidemic of 1656

MARTHA BALDWIN

While Athanasius Kircher was enormously productive throughout his long life, the years of 1655–57 caused him particular consternation and disruption. At this juncture in time, Kircher faced considerable challenges—and it was not at all clear that he would be able to extricate himself with any sort of grace from his numerous problems. Obstacles seemed to arise at every turn—his patronage ties that he had so carefully cultivated over many years were disintegrating before his eyes; his research agenda had gone awry, and he was quite conscious of having promised more scholarly work than he was in a position to deliver; his right to publish his abstruse works was now being viewed with suspicion within his very own Society of Jesus; his loyal friend and disciple, Kaspar Schott, was sent away from Rome to return to the German provinces. And when plague broke out in Rome in the spring of 1656 and lingered well into 1657, Kircher was deeply moved by the prospect of his own mortality, by the destruction of life around him, and by the possibility of far greater casualties. How did Kircher weather such a stormy period in his life? And what do his actions in these years tell us about strategies he developed to handle crises in his future? I would argue that scrutiny of this troubled phase of Kircher's life gives the historian a particular insight into both the personality and the coping mechanisms of this elusive figure.

Patronage Problems

With the final illness and subsequent death of Pope Innocent X in January 1655, Kircher was aware he had lost a patron. While he might have been joyful at the election of Fabio Chigi as the new pope, Kircher was much too savvy an operator to assume that the new pope, whom he had fortuitously met almost two decades earlier in Malta, would take keen interest in his work as a natural philosopher. Indeed, it had been papal and patronly interest that so far had in large part directed Kircher's early research agenda toward Egyptian matters. In 1655, as Innocent X lay dying, Kircher must have been both profoundly pleased and deeply relieved to see the final volume of his *Egyptian Oedipus* appear in print. The multiple typefaces and lavish illustrations of the volumes had been painfully costly, and Kircher had relied upon the substantial financial subsidies of his patrons for the publication costs.

Kircher's foresight, if not clairvoyance, in protecting himself in the event of the death of his patrons can be seen in the strategy of his letters of dedication in the *Egyptian Oedipus*. When the first volume was published in 1652, Kircher had dedicated the entire volume to the Hapsburg emperor Ferdinand III, his faithful patron. But as the later volumes were issued, Kircher must have considered having a multivolume work dedicated exclusively to one patron, albeit a generous one, a waste of important opportunities to forge further patronage relationships. Hence he struck upon the strategy of dedicating individual chapters or long sections to a new group of individuals, all the while maintaining the facade that Ferdinand was his chief sponsor. By the time the final volume saw the light of day in 1655, Kircher was dedicating particular sections to various princes, dukes, archbishops, scholars, and diplomats. Hoping, although ultimately unsuccessfully, to sponge up some of the largesse of the Medici in Florence, he dedicated one short chapter to Leopoldo de'Medici. Moreover, the final and crowning chapter—on the theology or theosophy of the ancient Egyptians—Kircher dedicated to the Italian "Fabio Chisio," then identified only as the bishop of Imola and as a pious cardinal. While Kircher praised Pope Innocent X's recognition of Fabio Chigi's skills as a papal bureaucrat, Kircher noted that he himself valued other virtues of the bishop—namely his humanity, his piety, the sweetness of his morals, his modesty in living, and his freedom from all taint of ambition.[1] Assuredly, Kircher did not take this last-named quality at face value, since Kircher allowed fate—or divine will—a large role in explaining the vagaries of human history.

Undoubtedly, Kircher had sniffed the failing health of Innocent X, whose final illness had been slow and whose death on January 7, 1655, had come as no surprise. With a keen nose for papal favors, Kircher had no doubt been aware in 1652 that Innocent was rewarding Chigi with the bishopric of Imola and with a cardinal's hat a bit later. Kircher may also have learned about, as had others in papal circles, the debts and numerous disgraces of Pamphili's cardinal nephew. But did Kircher know that Chigi would be named the next pope? Assuredly, Kircher could not have known this when he penned the dedicatory epistle to the final chapter of his massive *Egyptian Oedipus*. Moreover, the parties who would elect the new pope were split into numerous factions—French, Spanish, old defenders of the Barberini interests, and newer defenders of the Pamphili family.[2] Such machinations baffled even those far closer to the Curia than Kircher. Moreover, Chigi would not be elected until April, some five months after the death of Innocent. Thus, Kircher appears simply to have hedged his bets, assessed his chances, and astutely sized up what little he had to lose (and how much he might gain) by dedicating a chapter of his book to a contender for the next papacy.

While Kircher's move in 1655 might strike us as brilliant, his moves in 1656 do not seem so fortuitous. When the first part of his *Ecstatic Journey* appeared in 1656, Kircher did not dedicate the book to the new pope. Never one to put all his eggs in one basket, Kircher boldly pursued new avenues of patronage. Hence he chose to dedicate the provocative little volume to neither popes nor Teutonic princes, his faithful and reliable sources of patronage. Instead, he dedicated the book to the newest and most dazzling figure on the patronage scene at Rome, Queen Christina of Sweden.[3] Kircher would be neither the first nor the last to be deceived in his expectations of Christina's generosity and well-filled purse. Indeed, the pope himself had once harbored hopes that the new convert to Catholicism would offer considerable financial resources to various causes of the papacy. In fact, the Venetian ambassador claimed the pope had wasted unconscionable amounts of money on receiving Christina in style.[4]

Following the lead of the papacy, the rector and provincial of the Jesuits at Rome Jesus clamored for recognition from Christina, who honored the Collegio Romano with two lengthy visits in January of 1656.[5] Kircher made special efforts to show her his museum and some of his experimental apparatus and boasted of this in his later works.[6] But Kircher, too, soon found his hopes of finding patronage from the Swedish queen gone up in smoke.

As Kircher was beginning to reckon with the consequences of the death of Innocent X and coming to terms with his need to curry the favor of Alexander VII, he was struck one year later with the news of the death, in April 1657, of his most reliable and most generous patron, Ferdinand III, the Holy Roman emperor. The death of Ferdinand III was certainly a blow to Kircher, and he had no reason to count on the favors of Ferdinand's son, Leopold, who was known for neither his father's piety nor his concern for the arts. But despite his anxiety, Kircher recognized that it would have been foolish not to at least attempt to ingratiate himself with Leopold. Thus Kircher decided to dedicate his next book, the *Second Heavenly Journey or Subterranean Forerunner,* to the young king of Hungary and Bohemia in the hopes of continuing in the good graces of the house of Hapsburg.[7]

In summary, as the summer of 1657 drew to a close, it was not at all clear to Kircher where to turn for new patrons. The working relationships and steady stream of favors he had come to count on from Innocent X and Ferdinand III had evaporated. Their successors, and more importantly the purses of their successors, remained unknown. But rather than succumb to the vagaries of misfortune, Kircher proved himself plucky in the face of adversity, willing to grovel at the feet of new patrons, persistent in ferreting out such patrons, and tenacious in cementing old alliances. While whimsy would never be the trademark of his patronage style, he would prove himself remarkably resilient—and successful—in his quest for new patrons.

Kircher's Research: An Agenda Gone Amuck

In addition to facing problems related to patronage in 1655–57, at the very same time Kircher confronted the painful reality that his research agenda had run seriously amuck. In 1655, Kircher had boldly moved away from the Egyptian subjects of his early research and had tackled the more controversial subjects of astronomy and cosmology. But his 1656 publication on his new interest in the heavens, the *Ecstatic Journey*, had brought with it unanticipated animosity from within the Society of Jesus.[8] Such a reaction may well have surprised Kircher, as he had taken several precautions against having his work viewed as too sympathetic to the heretical Copernican cosmos. He had gone out of his way to make his work appear hypothetical or fictional, rather than factual or observational. The very title of the work, "ecstatic heavenly journey," emphasized the trance- and dreamlike nature of the whole treatise. Moreover, in the text Kircher had included several overt affirmations of his theological orthodoxy and had claimed himself a believer in the Tychonian compromise system. However, despite these protestations of the author, the anonymous Jesuit censors were not ones to have the wool drawn over their eyes. Although they allowed Kircher's book to be printed in Rome, Kircher must have been severely chastened by the experience. He may have grasped fully for the first time just how close he had come to the fire when it came to matters of Jesuit censorship. His ecstatic dream about heavenly matters had turned hellish.

What was Kircher's strategy in dealing with the disapproval of his conservative Jesuit censors at Rome? If Kircher had been humbled, he was certainly not bowed by his experience. He was not about to make his own writings palatable to conservative Aristotelians. Instead, he proved himself a wily negotiator of trouble. While he did nothing overtly to disturb further the conservative Jesuit theologians at Rome, he did not roll over in defeat. Letting the matter rest for a while, Kircher had his student and disciple Kaspar Schott bring out a second edition of the work in 1660, and this time he saw to it that a German, not a Roman, publishing house printed the work. Never fainthearted, Kircher even went to the extreme of having Schott publish and respond point by point to the ridiculously conservative criticisms of his Roman censors. Schott was not the first to attempt to make the upholders of orthodoxy look like men unwilling to accept the modern evidence of the telescope, and he hammered away at Kircher's censors with the tenacity and conviction of Galileo's defenders decades earlier. Since Kircher was in Rome and Schott in Germany at the time of the appearance of the second edition, the whole affair was made to appear as if Kircher had played no part in the matter. But clearly Schott had undertaken the second edition with the full approval and connivance of his master.[9] More importantly, the strategy of avoiding printing presses in Rome, a policy clearly elaborated in the wake of the 1656 publication, would soon be put into play for the remainder of Kircher's life. When it came to handling subterranean fire, Kircher would not be burnt twice.

In addition to encountering unexpected hostility to his cosmological ideas, Kircher realized in 1656 that his planned schedule of publication was seriously delayed. Since the publication of the stunning and massive *Egyptian Oedipus*,

Kircher had announced his intention to publish another massive work, the *Subterranean World*. He had even accepted money from Ferdinand III as an advance for his efforts on the new blockbuster. To Kircher's dismay, the work was turning out to be far more exhaustive than he had anticipated, and the collection of information, both from published texts and from correspondence networks, was taking the author far more time than anticipated. In 1656, Kircher probably did not realize that the publication of the *Subterranean World* would take another decade, but he clearly grasped that it was years away from its once targeted date. With death of Ferdinand III in 1657, Kircher was further worried that his work, conceived and well under way, would not come to fruition without the further subsidies of his now dead Maecenas. Kircher was on the horns of dilemma: should he abandon the project, given that its size and contents were getting out of control, or should he continue to work on it, trusting blindly that finances would take care of themselves in due course? While what happened ultimately may seem clear to us centuries later, I would argue that the outcome was not at all obvious to the anxious Kircher in 1656. Stung by his tardiness in fulfilling his promised publication, yet proud of his ability to plumb the depths of any subject to its very bottom, Kircher agonized over how to proceed.

His decision, made in early 1657, was to affirm publicly his intentions to proceed on the work and to advertise its future production by giving his patrons and readers a taste of what would follow. I am reminded here of the similarity of Kircher's strategy to our modern bookseller's tactic of publishing one chapter of a book on the Internet in the hopes that the reader, once enticed by a snippet, will purchase the whole book. Thus, in November 1657 there appeared Kircher's *Iter ecstaticum ii*, or a second ecstatic journey. He designed this both as a continuation of his celestial ecstatic journey and as an apology for his failure to complete his promised magnum opus on schedule. This book has almost entirely escaped the notice of historians, and it is frequently bound with either his treatise on plague or his work on cosmology. Although its contents have been superseded by the *Subterranean World*, which appeared almost a decade later, scrutiny of the "prodromus," as Kircher himself called the 1657 production, sheds significant light on how Kircher handled his crises of 1656–57. Kircher chose to dedicate his "Subterranean Forerunner" to the Hapsburg prince, Leopold Ignatius, whom he addressed as the "worthy son of a worthy father."[10] In choosing Leopold, Kircher showed himself a shrewd analyst of Hapsburg politics: Leopold would be crowned Holy Roman emperor in the next year. However, the son had inherited neither his father's munificence nor his father's interest in Kircherian projects. Like the effort to extend himself to Queen Christina of Sweden, this would prove to be a patronage attempt not as amply rewarded as he might have hoped.

In his letter to the reader of the "Subterranean Forerunner," Kircher laid bare his rationale for writing up and publishing his yet unfinished work. Since so many men of great name had long urged the work upon him and since he had so long promised the work, he argued, the learned world merited the shorter version so that they could be assured that his promises were not idle. Such a protestation protected Kircher from being perceived as a laggard and turned him into a stalwart scholar who was interrupting his own research agenda for the sake of a community of learned men panting to have news of his brilliant researches and experiments. Kircher next laid bare a laundry list of his reasons for having delayed the production of his magnum opus: the project required "innumerable" and time-consuming experiments; an exhaustive study of the writings of ancient and modern geographers; and an extensive network of correspondence to gather reports of mountains, rivers, lakes, and volcanoes. Furthermore, an outbreak of plague at Rome had considerably derailed his production; the tragic death of Ferdinand III had cost him much emotional anguish; and the lack of necessary subsidies was also retarding the completion of the project. In short, Kircher lamented, he truly felt as "astonished and shocked as if stung by an unlucky and sinister throw of dice."[11] Bad luck had dogged the faithful author; he had been forced to put aside the project until he could be more optimistic about the fate of his next colossal work.

Did Kircher's decision to publish the "Subterranean Forerunner" meet its stated goal of allaying the demands of the great men who awaited his work so anxiously? There is absolutely no evidence that Kircher's readership was dissatisfied with the slow speed of his scholarly output. Rather than take his protestations at face value, the historian would do well to see this book as Kircher's ploy to troll for patrons. The bait he chose to use would be tales of an underwater boat journey to caves filled with dazzling phosphorescent fish. Not shy of tantalizing his reader with lurid stories, Kircher had his submarine enter into the gaping jaws of a whale so huge that Cosmiel, the angelic narrator, would point out the lungs, stomach, and intestines. Kircher realized shrewdly that such theatricality woos audiences. After admonishing his readers about the expense, both in time and money, of gleaning titillating reports from places as exotic as the Amazon River basin, Kircher left his readers of this short book with a clear implicit message: anyone wishing to hasten the production of the magnum opus, please send money at once to Rome.

Schott's Abrupt and Unanticipated Departure

The death of Innocent X in January 1655 was not the year's only disturbing event for Kircher. Equally upsetting may well have been the removal of his devoted friend and dedicated assistant, Kaspar Schott. While reassignment of personnel at the whim of the Jesuit superiors was standard operating procedure for members of the Society, Schott's abrupt notice to depart the Collegio Romano must have caused Kircher particular regret. The two men were bound together by shared intellectual interests, by their German childhood, and by their chafing at conservatives within their own Society. Schott and Kircher had crossed paths briefly in their earliest years at Würzburg, where they had been new members of the Society of Jesus. When the Jesuits at Würzburg had been forced to disperse by the approach of the hostile armies of Gustavus Adolphus in 1631, the two had become separated for decades. After their separate hasty and desperate flights from their homeland, Kircher surfaced at Avignon and then was in Rome by 1633; Schott first turned up at the Jesuit college at Tournai (Belgium) and then spent nearly two decades teaching at various Jesuit colleges in Sicily. In contact with Kircher by letter from Sicily, Schott was able to convince Kircher that he could be a helpful editor of his mathematical works. By August of 1652, Schott had received a summons to the Collegio Romano to work as Kircher's assistant. That Kircher could have arranged for Schott's being called from the hinterlands of Palermo to the headquarters at Rome suggests Kircher's rising influence within the Society. Moreover, Schott appears to have early on won the respect of Kircher by pointing out several mistakes in Kircher's mathematical texts. The relationship between Kircher and Schott during their three-year collaboration at the Collegio Romano deserves further study, but it was to end swiftly, much to the disappointment of each man, in 1655. Just as Innocent X had died and while his succession remained uncertain, the Jesuit General Goswin Nickel directed Schott to return to the German province of Franconia, where he was assigned to teach mathematics first in Mainz and later in Würzburg. Schott stayed in Würzburg, to his regret, until his death in 1666.[12]

Schott's abrupt departure from Rome struck Kircher at a particularly inopportune moment. The advice and encouragement of Schott must have been particularly valuable as Kircher faced the exceptional scrutiny and opprobrium of the Jesuit censors of his *Ecstatic Journey*. While we need not take every word about their relationship at face value, Kircher would always speak glowingly of Schott's assiduous scholarship and his personal dedication to his mentor. For example, when Schott published his enormous *Cursus mathematicus* in 1661, Kircher wrote the prefatory letter to the reader and drove home the point that "tyrones mathematicos" (mathematical beginners) were lucky to have the more difficult parts of mathematics explained to them by such a talented master.[13] To have had his disciple whisked away to the German hinterlands, even the familiar ones of his childhood, must have been bitter medicine indeed.

Plague in Rome and Its Consequences for Kircher

The arrival of plague in Rome in the spring of 1656 came as no great surprise to the learned community of physicians and papal administrators at Rome. Ecclesiastical and sanitary officials were studiously following reports of the outbreak of a quite virulent epidemic at Naples. The papal appointee, Hieronomo Gastaldi, carefully reviewed reports of plague cases in the towns between Naples and Rome as the epidemic traveled northward to the Papal States. By the time the first cases were reported in Rome, the papal sanitary bureau had been fully organized and given broad emergency powers to administer the city in the best interests of its citizens. All but eight of the city's gates were shut to traffic for the duration of the epidemic; those remaining open were under strict surveillance. The sanitary board had set up *lazzaretti* (pesthouses) for the afflicted and houses of quarantine (*case contumaciali*) for suspected carriers; physicians, surgeons, and phlebotomists were strictly prohibited from leaving the city; burials and disinfection of houses were strictly regulated.[14]

By the time the plague disappeared in mid-1657, Romans would consider themselves lucky to have endured such a mild epidemic. In 1656, however, no citizen was assuming the epidemic would not be a harsh one. Kircher appears to have been profoundly moved by the death at Rome consequent to the plague epidemic and more particularly by the prospect of his own death. Though he publicly lamented the interruptions to his research, Kircher did not spend his time idly. Instead he used the epidemic to his best advantage.

Although Kircher never acknowledged openly how the plague benefited him personally, we can see in retrospect that he had chosen to play his cards well in this crisis. Undoubtedly, the plague epidemic served to distract attention from the important charges of heresy surrounding Kircher's 1656 publication of his work on cosmology. Distraction, as all politicians know, can work wonders and make seemingly intractable problems disappear overnight. By the time the plague had vanished in 1657, there was no talk of further investigation of Kircher's alarmingly unorthodox cosmological ideas. And his rapid production of two less threatening works, namely the "Subterranean Forerunner" and his treatise on plague, further helped to hide the troubling issue of his unorthodox cosmology so patently expressed in his work eight months earlier.[15]

Moreover, the plague epidemic presented Kircher an opportunity to cement his allegiance with the new pope and to cast off his guilt and anxiety over the difficulties in proceeding with the *Subterranean World*. How could he be faulted for turning his mind from speculation about the underground architecture of the earth to the more practical and dire matter of a plague epidemic in his very city, his beloved Rome? Furthermore, Kircher shrewdly recognized that a treatise about the plague would offer him an opportunity to praise the sagacity of the new pope in safeguarding the Holy City. Thus, when the rapidly conceived and hastily executed *Examination of Plague* was ready for publication in early 1658, it came as no surprise that Kircher had dedicated it to the new pope. Much to his delight, Kircher found his efforts to enlist Alexander VII as his patron did not go unnoticed. By the time the plague was lifting, Alexander had sent Kircher an Egyptian scarab decorated with hieroglyphs to translate.[16] At the very end of the plague treatise, Kircher constructed a chronological table of plague epidemics occurring throughout the world. Here he claimed that although the Neapolitans had been struck *ad ultimum exitium*, the Romans had suffered far less. Not one to miss an opportunity for an ingratiating remark, he surmised that the plague struck Rome "more softly as if it were honoring the sanctity and piety of the Pontiff."[17]

Kircher's decision to write and publish a treatise on plague had not been part of his long-range research agenda. Rather, like the later appearance of mysterious crosses in the linen of Neapolitans shortly after an eruption of Vesuvius in 1661, Kircher's decision to write this book was formulated in direct response to a single, if disturbing, event. I do not want to suggest that Kircher's interest in plague was purely Machiavellian. Medical matters and pharmaceutical issues were beginning to intrigue him more and more in the later decades of his life, and the plague epidemic allowed him to consider medical matters more forthrightly. Kircher had broached medical topics in his early work on magnetism, wherein he claimed that the actions of antidotes inside the diseased human body were analogous to magnetic actions.[18] Similarly in his *Egyptian Oedipus*, Kircher had reviewed the sophisticated medical practices of the ancient Egyptians.[19] But later in his life, Kircher would become increasingly intrigued with medical alchemy and with chemically prepared pharmaceuticals. His *Subterranean World* would include lengthy sections concerning medical alchemy on the elaborate sympathies and correspondences among astral bodies, specific plants, and the organs of the human body. As he was granted increasing prestige and power within the Society, he could boast of having at his fingertips a well-equipped chemical laboratory where he patiently tested and experimented with chemically prepared medicines.[20] By the last decade of his life, Kircher would engage in a highly visible debate with one of the greatest physicians of Tuscany, Francesco Redi, over the efficacy of one particularly fashionable medicament, the snakestone, which reputedly originated in the heads of cobra snakes of India.[21]

But Kircher's later sustained and deep interest in medical matters should not be taken for granted when we examine his tribulations of 1656. Indeed Kircher had reasons to be hesitant about claiming to write as a medical authority. Most importantly, the Society of Jesus since its inception had agreed not to meddle in the medical profession, and the Jesuit hierarchy had faithfully adhered to this professional proscription, which had been duly recorded in the Constitutions. Kircher may have had hints that the hierarchy might condone certain interests in medical matters, as the preparation of chests of medicines to be sent out with Jesuit overseas missionaries was becoming well known.[22] But given the Jesuit censors' reception of his astronomical dream, he had good reason to worry.

Hence Kircher was clearly on the defensive when it came to writing about medical matters and candidly acknowledged in the opening pages of his treatise that he was not a "medicus." Such a sensitivity of Kircher to transgressing professional boundaries is particularly striking, for Kircher clearly had a sense of himself as *not* beholden to traditional boundaries of knowledge. He had not felt any need to apologize for his lack of expertise in any of his earlier works— be they Egyptian, musical, magnetic, optic, or linguistic. But in 1657, bristling at the recent reprimands from his astronomical censors, Kircher felt compelled to assert his medical credentials in his treatise on plague. Hence the opening pages of his plague treatise contain letters of approval and endorsement from three Roman physicians who were willing to vouch for Kircher's ability to speak authoritatively about medical matters. The reader finds letters from one Ioannes Benedictus Sinibaldus, professor of practical medicine in the Roman Athenaeum; from Paulus Zacchias, "medicus Romanus;" and from Hieronymus Bardi, identified by Kircher as an iatrochemist practicing in Rome. Sinibaldus remains an elusive figure to historians, but Kircher identified him as a conservative Hippocratic physician. Careful to ingratiate himself with Sinibaldi, in the text of the book Kircher carefully included the physician's preferred remedy (applications of hot cloths drenched in wine and sulfur to make the plague victim sweat), although he himself gave them only tepid endorsement.[23] Paolo Zacchias's interest in medicine, like Kircher's, was more learned than practical. He was writing a treatise on medical jurisprudence, which was published posthumously in 1661 and which would go through numerous editions in the eighteenth century. Girolamo Bardi had published a popular treatise on medicine in the Bible and enjoyed a reputation as a learned physician in Rome. Kircher proudly identified him as physician to the pope.[24] Thus, by soliciting prefatory letters from the three men, Kircher made sure they all loaned their medical authority to vouchsafe the contents of his volume on plague.

Kircher also assured his readers that he had conferred with the keepers of the infirmary at the Collegio Romano, but since there is no evidence that plague struck men living within the college, we cannot assume that Kircher had much contact, if any, with the sick. Similarly, he claimed that he had had long discussions with James Alban Gibbes, an English expatriate and physician living in Rome, but we have no evidence that Gibbes treated plague victims.[25] While flaunting his friendships with such physicians might have suggested to his readers that Kircher moved easily in medical circles, it is plain he preferred bookish theorists to skilled practitioners.

Kircher had also covered himself on the question of permissions to publish. The book contained a letter signed by the Society's general, Goswin Nickel, who declared that since the work had been approved by certain excellent doctors of medicine, he gave it his permission as well.[26] It is also clear from reading both the *Second Ecstatic Journey* and his treatise on plague that this was the period when Kircher was becoming steeped in alchemical literature, a subject of paramount importance to the shaping of his medical theories. Solitude, even enforced solitude, had yielded substantial rewards in extensive time for reading. Thus, Kircher would write that he had studied plague in order to find relief from the horrid silence of the city, the enforced closing of the Collegio Romano, and the disruption of his ordinary scholarly projects.[27]

What were the issues concerning the plague that intrigued Kircher? Kircher was no physician, and not the least interested in treating the sick or alleviating their pain and suffering. Kircher's treatise reveals instead a man consumed by the theoretical and intellectual issues lurking behind the medical disaster. Of all the burning issues, Kircher most wanted to know: What caused plague? How was it contagious? What stars, if any, were responsible for plague? Could the medical profession offer effective therapeutics for the afflicted or effective prophylactics for the exposed? Could plague be spread intentionally by evil persons? Could plague be contracted from the power of the imagination? What could a common man do to preserve his health in time of plague?

As he attempted to answer these questions in his treatise, Kircher made a clearly crafted endorsement of a materialistic and atomistic conception of disease. Drawing on Stoic philosophy, medieval matter theory, and Helmontian medical ideas, Kircher unfolded his philosophy of *panspermia*. While Kircher had mentioned such "universal seeds" or agents of fertility in his earlier works, he here envisaged invisible but material seeds that penetrated the fine openings of the skin and spread plague throughout the human body. He would later elaborate his notions of how poisonous substances act in the human body in the *Subterranean World*, but he had clearly grasped the essence of his theory in the plague epidemic. More importantly, it was the epidemic that made him realize how important his microscopic observations would be to his natural philosophy. Kircher had been performing observations with his microscope for at least a decade before the plague, and he had illustrated simple microscopes in his *Great Art of Light and Shadow* of 1646. But it was in his treatise on plague that Kircher first set forth a detailed description of his microscopic observations. He did so in order to promote his theory of spontaneous generation, a crucial component of his explanation of the origin of plague from the rotting cadavers of animals, insects, and humans. This, too, would be a matter he would return to often in his later works.

The theoretical thrust of Kircher's treatise on plague can disguise his quite jaundiced view of medical practice in general. Kircher evinced little faith in the medical profession. He stated plainly (and correctly) that no available medical treatment was effective against plague. "Since no thereapeutic treatment works, the best effort man can make is for prophylactics," he lamented.[28] While he held a deep conviction that there existed no poison in the natural world that did not have a natural antidote, Kircher conceded that the appropriate antidote for plague was not yet known to man. Only slightly more optimistic about preventive measures, Kircher reviewed the extant medical practices and protested that many were ineffective, and more were outright dangerous. After surveying common practices of wearing chemically prepared amulets, drawing blood, consuming syrups composed of powdered viper dust, and purifying the air by burning fragrant woods, Kircher advised his reader that flight from the city was the only reliable remedy. And should flight be impossible, as it surely was in the 1656 emergency, cleanliness and amulets of dead toads were about all to be trusted.

Surviving Difficulties, Sustaining Friendships

Given the quite pessimistic note of his treatise on plague, what can be said about Kircher's more personal response to the plague? Had Kircher felt threatened by the plague, or did he proceed with his altered publication program with his head down, heedless to the personal dangers the epidemic might hold for him? I would argue that Kircher was profoundly fearful at the time of the epidemic. His autobiography recounts his numerous narrow escapes from death by disease and accident, including a miraculous cure from gangrene as a youth.[29] At the end of his life, his escape from plague may have seemed foreordained, but there is little reason to maintain that he believed this at the time. When he wrote at the very time of the plague outbreak, Kircher stated that fear greatly elevated one's chances of succumbing to plague. Moreover, he noted that literary men were especially afflicted. In a particularly self-revealing statement he acknowledged that "literary men are most disturbed of all when the first news of an outbreak arrives; they are especially agitated with melancholic perturbation; they always have the image of death in front of them; and thus it happens that the chamber of their blood and spirits goes rigid."[30]

How had Kircher survived this bleak period in his life? Confined to the Roman College, shut off from his correspondence networks, fearful about contracting a deadly pestilence, and brooding about his own literary output, Kircher did not wallow in despondency. Instead he used this time of enforced isolation to forge strategies for both his publications and his patronage that would serve him well for the next decade of his life. The bitterly felt departure of Schott did not prohibit a successful scholarly partnership and flourishing friendship. Soon after his arrival in Germany, Schott would take up his pen to defend charges laid against Kircher's *Ecstatic Journey*. In fact, Schott appears to have been successful in drumming up sympathy for Kircher and for his unorthodox work among members of the Society of Jesus. Thus, when Schott's 1660 edition of his master's work appeared, newly entitled *Iter exstaticum coeleste*, or the *Celestial Ecstatic Journey*, Schott published not only his own defense, but that of another German Jesuit, Melchior Cornaeus, whom Kircher appears never to have known personally. Cornaeus's defense of Kircher must have been especially welcome, since he taught scholastic and polemical theology, not natural philosophy, at Mainz and Würzburg and hence represented the same faculties as assuredly did his anonymous critics.[31] In his later years, Kircher would employ yet again the strategy that had served him so well with the *Ecstatic Journey*, namely having other sympathizers take up his defense and keeping his hands unsullied in the fray. Thus, when Kircher became embroiled in a particularly vitriolic argument over spontaneous generation with Francesco Redi, Kircher let his disciple at the Roman College, Giuseffo Petrucci, take up his cause and appeared to remain unruffled by the passionate issue.[32] Similarly, Petrucci's publication bears the stamp of Kircher's behind-the-scenes approval and enthusiasm.[33]

In addition to trumpeting Kircher's genius throughout Jesuit houses in Germany, Schott also supported, and may well have advised, Kircher in his decisions about publication strategies. Schott's hasty departure from Rome at the behest of his Jesuit superiors had not left him time to oversee the publication of his own early work on mechanics and hydraulics, his *Mechanica-Hydraulico Pneumatica*. Despite having received permission to print the book in Rome from Goswin Nickel on the eve of his departure (the imprimatur is dated 23 January 1655), Schott chose not to leave his manuscript in Kircher's or his printer's hands at Rome. Instead, he carried it with him to Germany, where he was forced to let it languish for a full year until he successfully submitted it to the Jesuit authorities in the Province of the Upper Rhine.[34] By the time the book finally saw the light of day in May of 1657, Schott had discovered that the internal Jesuit censors in Germany were far more receptive than those in Rome to works openly enthusiastic about natural magic and anti-Aristotelian teachings regarding the vacuum. Moreover, Schott's decision to print this small book, rather than his own magnum opus, his *Magia universalis naturae et artis*, may well have been made in collaboration with Kircher, who was simultaneously devising a similar strategy about his *Subterranean World*. Indeed, Schott's apology for delaying his production of what would become a behemoth, prolix four-volume work echoes Kircher's lamentations in his short version of the *Subterranean World*—the work would be enormous, requiring great labor and zeal, and finishing it would not be possible without some relief from burdensome teaching duties.[35]

Whatever may be said of Kircher's friendship with Schott, it was clear to each man that this was not a friendship between equals. Schott always considered Kircher his intellectual superior and paid deference to his master throughout his life. Schott's own accomplishments in the field of physics were not insignificant (indeed, Schott grasped long before Kircher the importance of Boyle's and von Guericke's experiments with the vacuum pump), but it was not lost on Schott that Kircher lived in Rome and had access to books and princes that a humble teacher in a gymnasium in Franconia could never dream of.

Moreover, Kircher may well have leaned heavily upon Schott's example in forging his own determination to plow on with his massive undertaking of the *Subterranean World*. Schott, after all, beat his master to the punch in producing poundage per annum. He churned out his *Magia universalis* in a dazzling two-year's time. By the time volume 3 appeared in 1658, Kircher may well have been painfully aware of being outstripped by his underling. Despite Schott's kind words to his master, Kircher refused to allow his former assistant to dedicate the volume to him and insisted on his choosing another

Maecenas. Perhaps aware of Kircher's embarrassment, Schott dedicated the volume instead to Mary, Mother of God, "my guardian angel," in the hopes of pleasing the implacable master.[36] That Kircher would ultimately catch up and surpass the output of his distanced student had much to do with his outliving Schott by more than a decade. (Schott had died in 1666; Kircher would not die until 1680.) Rivalry, albeit friendly fraternal or paternal rivalry, has stimulated more than one man to publish.

Although Schott and Kircher each suffered their own difficulties as scholars, I want to ask how Kircher endured his *annus horribilis*. Inspired no doubt by Schott's example and encouraged by his friendship and protection, Kircher did not allow his quite significant troubles to overwhelm him. In time he would publish all his books outside of Rome, most of them with the Protestant Dutch printing house of Janssonius. Kircher would emerge from his year of troubles with new energy for his *Subterranean World*, new interests in alchemy and medicine, and new confidence in his patronage relationships. While much of Kircher's survival seems the result of his willful and courageous resilience, we should not lose sight of the fact that the arrival and departure of the plague were none of his doing. Yet Kircher cagily used the events to his best advantage, namely to allow his serious troubles with the Jesuit censors to dissipate in the heat of the crisis. Hindsight might blind us to the considerable challenges to his physical survival and to his prodigious scholarly productivity, which we are now inclined to see as inevitable. But despite the gloss he might later put on his tribulations, we might well ask whether his dreams during this year were more likely ecstatic reveries or nightmares.

Notes

1. Kircher 1652–55, vol. 3, dedicatory letter to book 11.
2. Alexander VII had become bishop and cardinal in 1652 and was rewarded for twelve years able diplomatic service in Germany in his deft handling of the Jansenist controversy. On papal politics during Alexander VII's tenure, see M. Rosa, "Alessandro VII," in *Dizionario Biografico degli Italiani* 3:205–215.
3. Kircher 1656, letter of dedication. For a further elaboration of Kircher's patronage strategies, see Baldwin 2002.
4. Corraro 1664. Corraro enumerated Alexander VII's expenditures on urban renewal and on the Vatican Portico, but he roundly condemned money wasted on the pope's reception of the queen of Sweden. He noted, "it cannot be denied, that such great Spirits do extremely thirst after Glory and Renown" (p. 8).
5. For a description of Christina's visit to the Collegio Romano and the elaborate festivities performed for her, see Villoslada 1954, pp. 276–277; Findlen 1995, pp. 633–636, and 2001a, pp. 39–48; Gorman 1999, pp. 170–189; Åkerman 1991.
6. Kircher mentioned Christina's visit in his *Mundus subterraneus*. For a discussion of the alchemical apparatus in his laboratory, see Baldwin 1993, pp. 41–64.
7. Kircher 1657, letter of dedication.
8. A fine analysis of the content of Kircher's *Iter exstaticum coeleste* and a review of the controversies it stirred within the Society of Jesus is found in Camenietzki 1995a. See essays by Daniel Stolzenberg and Harald Siebert in this volume. The article contains a detailed review of the objections of the anonymous Jesuit censors.
9. Ibid., pp. 23–27. Camenietzki gives a full analysis of the audacity of Schott and Kircher in circumventing the normal censorship channels of the Jesuits. One censor accused Kircher of "audacia, presumptio, ac temeritas" (p. 28).

10. Kircher 1657, letter of dedication.

11. Ibid., p. 8. "Sed sinistioris aleae iactu veluti attonitum stupefactumque aliquantisper."

12. On Schott's career as a mathematician in Germany, see Hellyer 1998 and 1996.

13. Schott 1661. The letter by Kircher extolling the wisdom of Schott accompanied the recommendations of other learned men, including Balthasar Conrad, another Jesuit professor of mathematics, and Adam Kochansky, a Polish Jesuit and colleague of Schott's at the Jesuit college in Würzburg.

14. Girolamo Gastaldi (1616–85), a papal bureaucrat, was appointed by the newly elected Alexander VII to be in charge of Rome during the time of the plague. Gastaldi wrote up his experiences as the supervisor of public health in a lengthy tome entitled *Tractatus de avertenda et profliganda peste politico-legalis*. Gastaldi's efforts were later rewarded. He would be named archbishop of Benevento, cleric of the Camera, and commissary general and general treasurer of the papal army. He was named cardinal in 1673 by Clement X. See N. Marsili, "Girolamo Gastaldi," in *Dizionario Biografico degli Italiani* 52: 532–533.

15. For the problems Kircher faced with respect to Jesuit censors, see the essay by Harald Siebert in this volume.

16. For Kircher's relations with Alexander VII, see Bartola 1989.

17. Kircher 1659. The unpaginated chronology of plagues appears at the very end of this edition, and is missing in the Roman edition six months earlier. The German edition has a preface by Christian Lange, professor of medicine at Leipzig.

18. Kircher 1654, pp. 542–545. See also Baldwin 2001b.

19. Kircher 1652–55, vol. 2, pp. 388–433.

20. Kircher 1665, vol. 2, pp. 404–408, 279–280. See also Baldwin 1993, pp. 46–54.

21. Baldwin 1995.

22. See Harris 1996, pp. 311–315, and Harris 1989.

23. Kircher 1658, p. 214.

24. Paolo Zacchia (1584–1659) wrote *Quaestiones medico-legales opus* (Avignon, 1660); Girolamo Bardi (1604–167) entered the Society of Jesus in 1619, but had left because of his ill health in 1625. Among his publications are *Medicus politico catholicus* (Genoa, 1644) and *Theatrum naturae iatrochimicae rationalis* (Rome, 1653).

25. Kircher 1658, preface. Gibbes had contributed a laudatory poem in English for the publication of Kircher's *Egyptian Oedipus* (vol. 2, preface).

26. Ibid., preface. These letters are not paginated.

27. Ibid., letter to reader.

28. Ibid., p. 165.

29. Kircher 1684b.

30. Ibid, p. 132.

31. On Schott's defense of Kircher and his cosmological treatise of 1656, see Hellyer 1996, pp. 333–335; and Camenietzki 1995a.

32. Petrucci 1677. On Kircher's relations with Redi, see Baldwin 1995, pp. 394–418.

33. On Petrucci's uncritical defense of his master, see his *Prodromo* (1677), especially his letter of dedication and pp. 6, 11, 24, 26.

34. See the imprimaturs, "Monitum ad lectorem" and "Occasio Operis," in Schott 1657. Schott includes von Guericke's experiments on pp. 441–488 and dedicates this part of the book to Kircher. He writes, "You are an ocean, an immense ocean on account of your fine and inexhaustible erudition. I was first your student (*discipulus*) in our Würzburg university, then your associate (*socius*) in literary matters at Rome" (p. 441).

35. Ibid., p. 2. "Quoniam vero Opus, ut dixi, vastum erit, multiq laboris ac studii, nec nisi subsisivis horis, quas ordinaris occupationibus subtrahere licebit, perficiendum." Schott may well have been angling for a release from teaching duties such as that granted Kircher with his status as scriptor. Schott's output of publications is absolutely staggering—he produced eleven titles between 1658 and his death in 1666.

36. See Schott's letter to Kircher of 10 October 1658 published at the head of Schott 1657–59, vol. 3. Schott wrote of Kircher, "Whatever I know, I know through you. You have conferred upon me innumerable favors over the course of many years. . . . Your innumerable and almost daily letters to me make manifest your good will upon me."

3

Kircher and His Critics

Censorial Practice and Pragmatic Disregard in the Society of Jesus*

HARALD SIEBERT

The extent of Kircher's literary production is one of the most amazing facets of this outstanding Jesuit in his time. In the fifty years of his writing career, he wrote nearly thirty books (counting only first editions). Including subsequent reissues and reprints, there are, altogether, about forty-five printed works that appeared in his lifetime, not to mention translations into several languages and posthumous editions.[1] Only two of these books had been published before Kircher arrived in Rome. Appointed as professor of mathematics at the Collegio Romano, his real mission in coming to Rome was to write a book on Egypt.[2] The *Coptic Forerunner* (*Prodromus Coptus*), his first publication, appeared in Rome in 1636; his last, the *Tower of Babel* (*Turris Babel*), in 1679. While he lectured for only four academic years,[3] his main activity until his death was writing, as well as building the collection of the world's most famous museum and maintaining a worldwide network of correspondents on all scientific matters. The support he had from his Order in producing this stupendous number of books was a freedom to write, yet not to write whatever he pleased. Every single Jesuit written work had to pass through internal censorship before being reexamined by the Holy Office and finally printed.[4]

In 1550, Ignatius Loyola, the founder of the Jesuit Order, had already proclaimed that all members should think and speak as one. Censorship had been instituted in order to ascertain the Society's doctrinal unity in publications as well as in oral communications by censoring books and opinions.[5] The frame of Jesuit doctrine was set by following Saint Thomas Aquinas in theology and Aristotle in philosophy. Neither yielded a well-defined set of convictions that produced unanimity. Moreover, in the Renaissance, Aristotle was given many voices by the proliferation of a number of commentaries offering different interpretations. At the beginning of the seventeenth century, Aristotle was rejected in favor of new scientific thinking as well as adapted and further transformed. Thus the idea of a uniform Jesuit philosophy in teaching and writing posed certain difficulties. These tensions led to a reorganization of the mechanisms of censorship, beginning in the 1580s, and also produced new attempts to define legitimate and illegimate philosophies in relation to Jesuit orthodoxy, culminating in lists of prohibited propositions that appeared in their final form in the *Ordinatio pro studiis superioribus* in 1651.[6]

At the time Kircher arrived in Rome, the system of Jesuit censorship was well established. In 1597, the order's General Claudio Aquaviva had founded the College of Revisors (*Collegium Revisorum*) that consisted of five members called Revisors General (*Revisores Generales*) representing the five assistancies of the Society of Jesus: Italy, Spain, Germany, France, and Portugal.[7] The College of Revisors had its seat at the Collegio Romano and began its work in 1601. The first rules governing censorship were codified in the same year.[8] These rules represent the first draft of what later became the Rules for Revisors (*Regulae Revisorum*) issued at the eighth Congregation (1645–46) and reaffirmed at the tenth Congregation in 1652.[9] Besides practical aspects these rules prescribed what Revisors should observe when examining books, and they detailed what is expected of Jesuit publications, and what is not to be tolerated.[10]

The Revisors General held no other office and only examined books they received from the General of the Order. They acted in an advisory capacity to the General, who was free to follow his own judgment. Besides approving or censoring publication, they could enjoin the author to make changes and to emend or delete passages. According to the Rules, the Revisors were supposed to work in secret and exercise discretion. They sent their judgment of each work in a letter to the General, who could then choose to pass on a copy to the author. Books with sufficiently theological content were examined by at least three Revisors. Writings without theological import merited examination by at least two Revisors.[11] Usually, one Revisor played a key role in writing the letter that would be sent to the General of the Order. Censorship in Jesuit Provinces worked similarly. For practical reasons provincial censorship became more and more independent from Rome, even though the foundation of the College of Revisors in Rome was meant to centralize Jesuit censorship by also verifying provincial judgments. In the Provinces, censors gave their judgment to the Provincial, who decided at his discretion what to do. Instead of the *imprimatur*, Provincials gave the *facultas* as license for printing.[12] In addition to the formal system of censorship, there were other Jesuits consulted as specialists. Since these "censors extraordinary" played a particularly important role in examining books of natural philosophy, language, and history, they examined Kircher's writings more often than did the Revisors General.[13]

This essay uses the censorship reports on Kircher's works to shed light on the interaction between the author and his censors. Jesuit censorship allows us to see how the Society of Jesus viewed Kircher's intellectual production and to what degree they allowed him the latitude to work freely. The censorship reports tell a story of Kircher, his books, and his censors, from which we will consider only a few episodes. First, however, a deeper understanding of our sources is needed. To facilitate and shorten the following description of documents, a list of all censorship reports is included in the appendix.[14]

Six of the thirty codices of censorship documents kept in the Roman Archive of the Society of Jesus discuss Kircher's books. Since the extant documentation of Jesuit censorship is far from being complete, there were more of them.[15] Even for books for which we have reports, the documentation is not always complete. Altogether, forty-eight letters have survived (including three copies, one addendum, and one letter written in defense of a given approval[16]). These censorial letters cover almost thirty years of Kircher's literary production beginning with censorship reports on his *Coptic Forerunner* and ending with those on his *Subterranean World* (*Mundus subterraneus*) (1665). The seemingly high number of extant letters (for only seventeen books of Kircher) is due to censoring practice. Depending on the matter treated in the book, the censors wrote individual letters rather than simply appointing one person to reflect the group's opinion. Thus, for some of Kircher's books there are letters from different censors that are not always in agreement. Furthermore, censors evaluated books consisting of several volumes tome by tome. Hence, censorship could reflect either an individual or a group opinion. Despite losses, the extant censorship reports cover the period in which Kircher acquired his stupendous reputation for omniscience.

1. Censoring Kircher

The censorship reports on Kircher's books varied widely in information, as we would expect in light of the fact that the results did not produce a uniform judgment. The censors neither agreed on what they thought of Kircher's work in general nor had the same response to each individual book in their reports to the General. We can roughly classify the reports into five different categories that allow us to understand better the interaction between Kircher and his censors. All but one (the defense letter of Le Roy) of the forty-eight documents can be described within the following categories:

1. *Simple approval:* Nine of Kircher's books received thirteen letters of simple approval. The censors judged that these works could be published because they neither offended the Christian faith nor infringed upon Jesuit doctrine.[17]

2. *Approval with comment:* The censors approved six of Kircher's books in ten reports with additional commentary. Many such reports comment positively on Kircher's achievements and his advancement of various sciences, highlighting the book's utility for students as well as for the republic of letters.[18]

3. *Conditional approval:* Twelve letters offer conditional approval for eight of Kircher's books. The censors approved publication only if certain passages were emended or deleted. They refer to those passages by quoting or summarizing Kircher. Such letters identify general or recurrent errors while also providing page numbers for specific points to be canceled or corrected. Because of laconic censors, missing page

numbers, and the missing manuscripts, not every censored passage can be identified in the printed version of the book.

4. *Disapproval:* The censors recommended to the General that he not permit the publication of four of Kircher's books.

5. *Confirmation:* In four letters concerning four of Kircher's works, the censors verify that he has revised the text according to the terms of a conditional approval. Subsequently the General gave his *imprimatur*. Although every book that Kircher published that received conditional approval probably went through this process, only four extant letters of this type survive.

All of these documents give us further chronological information about Kircher's publishing. In them, we can see such details as when he began or actually finished a work, and how long publication was delayed. Excluding letters of simple approval and confirmation, more than the half of all extant documents yield further information how Kircher's fellow Jesuits received his books, ideas, and personality. Yet surprisingly, only slightly more than a third of the documents (17/45), whose text comprises thirty-six of the sixty-six total pages that have survived, demonstrate the censors' strong intervention, by having passages modified or canceled, or the whole book suppressed. Thus, influencing publications in a concrete manner seems to be only a minor part of the censors' activity, though it did indeed affect eleven of the seventeen books by Kircher whose examination we can document.

Given the extent of interventions, we can presume that the practice of censorship had consequences for Kircher's literary work. However, only half of the censors' comments concerned themselves with issues of content. Interestingly, the other half dealt with the formal or literary qualities of his works. The censors frequently critiqued Kircher's style, focusing on such issues as language, exposition, attribution of sources, and missing translations. Above all and almost always, they faulted him for bragging.[19] In other words, thinking about the constructive aspects of censorship, Kircher's fellow Jesuits did the work of editors. Only the other half of their intervention was concerned with content censoring. Thus here the *filtro censorio* was equally applied to maintaining uniformity of doctrine and quality of publication.[20] The quality of Kircher's work reflected on the entire Society of Jesus.

How significant was the censorship of Kircher's work? In other words, how much was Kircher actually hindered in writing and publishing what he wanted? Let us return to the four letters of disapproval. For example, in 1657 the *Scrutinium pestis*, Kircher's treatise on the bubonic plague, was not approved because medicine had been excluded from Jesuit teaching since the founding of the Order.[21] The censors considered Kircher not competent to treat medical matters because he had no medical education. They did allow him to publish the parts regarding physics by suggesting that he insert them in some of his other publications (for example, his *Second Ecstatic Journey*, examined by them on the same day). Permission to publish the *Scrutinium pestis* as a whole (*prout iacet*), however, was denied by the censors François Duneau and François Le Roy.[22] In a separate paragraph at the end of the letter, the third censor, Celidonio Arbizio, suggested that theologians should not censor medical writings. While reaffirming that the book should not be published, Arbizio added: "Unless they were examined and approved by some eminent physician."[23] Contrary to his fellow censors, Arbizio gave the book a second chance if it was sent to experts. Obviously the General agreed with this viewpoint. After being reexamined by several physicians, the book was published in 1658.[24]

At the same time, the Revisors were examining another writing of Kircher. We have three censorship reports on the *Second Ecstatic Journey* (*Iter exstaticum secundum*), the continuation of Kircher's ecstatic exploration into the terrestrial cosmos. These letters suggest an uncertainty about what to do with this book, since they include a letter of conditional approval, followed by a confirmation, but also a letter of disapproval. Just three days after he had put his signature to the conditional approval, Duneau wrote to the General Goswin Nickel[25] in order to convince him not to permit the printing of the *Second Ecstatic Journey*. He justified his seemingly contradictory viewpoint by referring to the fifth rule for Revisors General. This rule insisted that all censors affix their signature to the majority opinion, while also allowing any censor who disagreed to explain his reasons to the General separately.[26] Duneau explains in his separate letter to the General that he disagreed with his fellow censors, Le Roy and Arbizio, as he had previously disagreed with them in the censorship of the *Ecstatic Journey* (*Itinerarium exstaticum*), for reasons of prudence. He reminded the General vividly of what a scandal the publication of the latter provoked.[27] The similarities between the *Ecstatic Journey* and the *Second Ecstatic Journey* formed the basis of Duneau's argument against publication. In addition, he alleged further reasons for his disapproval, partially repeating what Kircher had already been criticized for and asked to change in the previous letter of conditional approval: its haste and childishness, Kircher's boastfulness and disobedience, his incorrect explanation of the motions of the sea, and various philosophical statements contradicting Aristotle's authoritative view of the natural world. Duneau's intervention, however, failed in achieving its goal: the *Second Ecstatic Journey* was published. Nevertheless, his letter seems to have had some effect on the General. As we can see from the imprimatur of the published *Second Ecstatic Journey*, it was not the General Nickel who permitted printing, but quite unusually the Roman Provincial that gave the *facultas* (see the appendix). Perhaps Nickel felt a certain caution in becoming directly implicated, should this new imaginary voyage provoke another scandal. Yet he was not sufficiently worried to prevent Kircher from publishing it.

The 1660 censorship of Kircher's *Great Art of Knowing* (*Ars magna sciendi*)—a single report signed by the whole college of Revisors General—

presents us with a different kind of problem.[28] The five censors, among them Duneau and Le Roy, were very disapproving of the book. They did not censor Kircher for illicit theories, nor for having maintained forbidden propositions or having contradicted Jesuit teaching. Quality was the sole criterion. They thought it was a poor book and took only one page to make this clear. The censors blamed Kircher for promising much more than he produced. Primarily, they did not see that his "art" would yield anything, and they certainly did not see it living up to Kircher's proposal that his new method would become everyman's means for acquiring knowledge. Instead they noted that his combinatorial method could be understood only by learned men, and not even particularly well by them (Duneau and Le Roy were doctors of theology). Those who had yet to learn this art would be completely confused and overwhelmed by the redundancy of rules, examples, and terms, many of them ill-defined. The censors also noted that Kircher's explanations were often contradictory and imprecise. The words he used did not have any common meaning. In his demonstrations he mostly begged the question (*petit principium*) instead of proving his propositions. In short, the censors made clear that the *Great Art of Knowing* was in no way useful or instructive; they also accused it of deceiving the reader. The censors concluded that since it did not meet the requirements for Jesuit publications, neither the Society's nor the author's reputation would benefit from its printing.[29]

The same year, Kircher got still another disapproval for a book that is lost today. Despite its title, the *Etruscan Journey* (*Iter Hetruscum*) did not recount Kircher's fantastic adventures from yet another ecstatic trip to the ends of the earth or throughout the cosmos. The journey instead was a more prosaic tour of the region of ancient Etruria, presenting a historical account and a description of its present state. In contrast to the previous "journeys," the *Etruscan Journey* was obviously not a narration of a fictitious voyage. However, if we believe the censorship report, it was fantastic in its own way. Being a work of profane literature, it was examined by two censors extraordinary. They gave their judgment independently; one sent a letter of simple approval, while the other, Domenico Ottolini (Ottolinus), wrote the longest censorship report we have on a single work by Kircher. He delivered his judgment in form of a letter with an addendum. He disapproved of the *Etruscan Journey* for three reasons, each substantiated by numerous examples taken from the book.[30] Born in Lucca, Ottolini knew at least one of the towns Kircher described very well. He judged the book primarily in response to Kircher's account of Lucca. In this section alone, Ottolini found so many errors concerning history, geography, institutions, and buildings that they became a three-page addendum to the general letter of censorship. Here Ottolini concluded that what he personally knew for a long time about Lucca is almost all wrong or invented (*commentita*) in Kircher's book. Anyone knowing Lucca, even just a little bit, would recognize that Kircher's descriptions of the town and its buildings were false. Even those who knew nothing of Lucca would see for themselves that his descriptions were riddled with errors.[31] Given the large number of blatant mistakes and inventions, Ottolini suggested that Kircher's account of Etruria might also be incorrect in regard to other towns and places.[32]

Ottolini attributed the factual errors of the *Etruscan Journey* to a lack of diligence that he observed in Kircher's book in general: contradictions, incoherence, and improbabilities. In addition, Ottolini reproached him for not being up-to-date in his reading on ancient Etruria.[33] Ottolini anticipated a serious consequence of the deficient quality of Kircher's work, if it were published. The shortcomings in his account of several important towns, but also villages and castles, were bound to offend their citizens as well as their political leaders. Since being accurate as well as well-read in the appropriate literature were two of the requirements for Jesuit publications in the Rules for Revisors, showing that Kircher conspicuously failed to meet these expectations would probably have sufficed to suppress the book, as we have already seen in the case of his *Great Art of Knowing*.[34] With his third reason, however, Ottolini singled out an aspect explicitly not tolerated by the Rules, namely, that Jesuit publications give offense to nations, provinces, or persons.[35] Since he presented this as a consequence of Kircher's lack of diligence in researching his subject, the whole book appeared to be offensive. It did not meet Jesuit standards of publication, and its public appearance would be harmful to the Society.[36] Ottolini's arguments were convincing. The *Etruscan Journey* never appeared.

The censors' disapproval of the *Second Ecstatic Journey* and the *Scrutinium pestis* was without consequences, except for a delay in publication. Duneau's objections could not prevent the publication of the *Second Ecstatic Journey*. In the case of the *Great Art of Knowing*, the results were more serious. Although Kircher finally published the summa of his combinatorial studies in 1669, we do not know how much of the book's content changed because of the censors' report nine years earlier. For the same reason, we cannot know if the censors' severity in 1660 was justified. Since the text had not been approved, a second examination of the *Great Art of Knowing* was necessary. To get his book approved, Kircher ostensibly had to make substantial changes to the primary version. We have no documents from a second examination of the *Great Art of Knowing*, which must have taken place between 1663 (date of the latest letter preserved) and 1665 (*imprimatur* of the published book; see the appendix). Lacking these documents, we can only surmise that the disapproval of the *Great Art of Knowing* had consequences for its content and that the final version differs from what Kircher had intended to publish earlier. This is even more probable when we see what happened with the *Etruscan Journey*. For this work, we have evidence that Kircher worked on some revisions, even though the book never appeared.

Perhaps Kircher had received a copy of Ottolini's addendum. He certainly knew that his mistaken account of Lucca was a reason for disapproval. In order to correct his text on this point, he began a correspondence with a scholar in Lucca, Giovan Battista Orsucci (1632–86), who sent him an account of the

Republic of Lucca.[37] Having himself received several letters from Kircher, Orsucci had probably given him additional information in letters that are now lost. By May 1666, Kircher may already have received all the necessary information from Orsucci he needed for emending his passages on Lucca, since in his following letter he reports on the results of a second examination of his *Etruscan Journey*.[38] Strangely enough, a month before, Kircher had written that he would have already sent his book to his publishing house in Amsterdam if there had not been a war. These plans suggest that Kircher was confident enough that the book would be approved this time. In 1665, he had already advertised this book at the end of his *Subterranean World*. Despite being advertised again in 1667 (this time in Kircher's *China monumentis illustrata*), under its full title and as ready for print, the book had not even got past the censor the following year.

In December 1668, Kircher explained to Orsucci that the censors had not yet approved the work solely because it might give grounds for some nearby rulers to take offense, although concerning Lucca, he was quick to add, there was nothing that could offend anyone.[39] Either Kircher had misinterpreted the reasons for the first disapproval or he knew only about the content of the addendum, where he was blamed for shortcomings solely in his account of Lucca.[40] Whatever he might have revised in his text in the meantime, the offensive character as interpreted by Ottolini remained. The flaws in the censors' eyes finally turned out to be fatal for Kircher's *Etruscan Journey*. In his last extant letter to Orsucci, on 17 February 1669, Kircher confessed that he had given up hope that the book would see the light of day, if the General did not pass it to some other censors.[41] It is unlikely, therefore, that Kircher continued his efforts at revision and resubmission. For this publication he may have transformed his *Etruscan Journey* into a *Tuscan Atlas* (*Atlas Thuscus*) that above all should have been a rich source of maps and illustrations.[42] In the end, the book on Etruria never appeared, though Kircher's publisher was still advertising the *Etruscan Journey* in 1678.[43] This time Kircher had capitulated to censorship, but this time only. His other books were all published. Moreover, he had already found his own way to cope with censorship.

2. Disregarding the Censors

How did Kircher respond to his censors? When writing to the General on 4 May 1657, Duneau stated several arguments against the *Second Ecstatic Journey*. In his final point, he reemphasized what he had already stated in the beginning: "The two other Revisors approved the book only on the condition that a large part should be deleted and another part emended."[44] Stressing the extent of changes that the censors required reinforced Duneau's personal opinion that the General should suppress the whole book or have it reexamined by other censors. To make this appear even more advisable in Kircher's case, Duneau added: "especially, as we know from experience, that in his books hitherto printed the author has not emended all that I wanted to be corrected."[45] The final argument is the strongest Duneau put forward, since all examinations and all corrections were in vain if books were printed without being revised according to censorship. Alleging that Kircher disregarded censorship was a serious accusation. Since Duneau had become Revisor General only four years earlier, having examined two of Kircher's printed books, this statement seems a bit problematic. By 1657, Kircher had published eleven books in twenty-three years of living in Rome. Thus Duneau's own experience of Kircher's publication history was rather limited and did not justify the general terms in which he made his accusation, presenting Kircher's disregard as a known fact (*experientia constat*) that was evident in his books printed up to that point (*hactenus impressis*).

It is possible, however, that Duneau based his accusation on the experience of Kircher that the College of Revisors had hitherto. Did its members know that Kircher did not correct his books before printing, as enjoined by the censors? Duneau's statement is ambiguous. Further support is needed for his allegation, since his motives were clear: he wrote to the General in order to convince him not to allow the publication of the *Second Ecstatic Journey*. The stronger his denouncement of Kircher, the riskier it was for the General to support publication and the more likely that Kircher would have his book suppressed as a penalty for former as well as current transgressions. Remember that it was not the General Nickel but the Roman Provincial who gave the facultas for the publication of the *Second Ecstatic Journey*. For this reason Duneau's letter may have had some effect, though no major consequences: the *Second Ecstatic Journey* was published, Kircher's next book came out the following year, and there do not seem to have been any disciplinary measures taken against Kircher.

However, Duneau was not the first person to suggest that Kircher disregarded the censors. Five years earlier, in 1652, in the report on the first tome of the *Egyptian Oedipus* (*Oedipus Aegyptiacus*), Nicolaus Wysing, one of the five Revisors General and probably the chairman[46] for this censorship, made a separate statement at the end of the letter:

> I fear that the work done by the Fathers Revisors censoring this book will not be of much use: Recently yet in that *Synopsis* he has complied with the censure of the same fathers only as far as and how he himself wanted to. Further in person he told me once that he had noticeably augmented his book *Obeliscus Pamphilius* after it had been examined by the censors; and so I hear that he has also boasted somewhere that because of his experience in these things he can safely make use of this practice. Finally I have seen too that in a work to be printed (i.e., at the time of printing), Father Athanasius has once changed things at least regarding the order in such a way that it could not easily be detected if he has observed or ignored the censure. As it seems to me that this may extremely prejudice our censorship, I have considered that it should be made known to the providence of His Father.[47]

Thus Wysing, too, denounced Kircher to the General for disregarding and eluding censorship. Furthermore, he gave explicit details of Kircher's tactics. Changing and adding anything after the censors had examined the book was explicitly forbidden and punishable according to the Rules for Revisors General.[48] Much more serious,

Wysing impugned Kircher's intent because he felt that Kircher had rearranged his text during publication in order to make the censored passages irretrievable. He had not made all the corrections imposed on him by the censors as condition for publication, and instead he rearranged the order of passages in the book in order to conceal his noncompliance. More strongly, Wysing accused Kircher of integrating whole new parts into his *Pamphilian Obelisk* (*Obeliscus Pamphilius*) while it was in press. Publishing a book that partly had been neither examined nor approved, he plainly had circumvented the Jesuit system of censorship.

Certainly any Jesuit author who so blatantly disregarded the system should have been subjected to some punitive measures. But why would Kircher himself have reported his illicit practice to Wysing? He probably did not know Wysing was one of the censors of the *Pamphilian Obelisk*, but he would have known that he was a General Revisor (Wysing had been called to the Collegio Romano to accept this position). Did Kircher openly dare to defy a censor in person? If he did not know that Wysing was a Revisor General when he allegedly made these remarks, he was nevertheless defying the system of censorship—for neither the first nor the last time—and boasting loudly enough about it to be heard by a Revisor General. Here we see the bragging Kircher, as he is characterized in so many censorship reports, who felt that his rights as an author superseded the wishes of the censor.

In his accusation, Wysing mentioned by title two books in which he had witnessed Kircher's disregard. For Kircher's *Pamphilian Obelisk* he had written a letter of conditional approval two years before. His claims that Kircher integrated a whole new part into the book going to print are hard to verify. The manuscript no longer exists, but there are two censorship reports on the *Pamphilian Obelisk*. Comparing them with the printed work does not make clear if Wysing's accusation is grounded. The *Synopsis* he cited as a *recent* case of Kircher's disregard can only be the *Idea oedipi Aegyptiaci* that Wysing examined just two months before his denunciation. This *Idea of the Egyptian Oedipus* is a work that is unknown to us. However, it must have been published, or at least Wysing claimed to have seen it in print. Otherwise Wysing's statement would not make sense. A "Synopsis" is also mentioned in another censorship report on the *Egyptian Oedipus*.[49] It appears to have been an overview of the *Egyptian Oedipus*.

Fifteen years earlier, an "Idea or Outline of the Egyptian Oedipus" had appeared in Kircher's *Coptic Forerunner*.[50] Similarly, several parts of the *Egyptian Oedipus* also contained overviews, each called "*Synopsis*," placed at the beginning of different sections. These synopses are not simply condensed tables of contents, which appeared at the end of each tome, nor did they follow strictly the order of the text or the expressions and headings as used in the text. The synopses were in some way independent from the printed book; they may have been written before the *Egyptian Oedipus* had its definitive form. Perhaps the overviews of all tomes had been printed together under the title *Idea of the Egyptian Oedipus*—a title under which Kircher had previously outlined his work in a similar form. The unknown *Idea of the Egyptian Oedipus* is probably a collection of these synopses published later within the *Egyptian Oedipus*. Confronting the synopses of the *Egyptian Oedipus* with the censorship report on the *Idea of the Egyptian Oedipus* further supports this idea.[51]

Why would Kircher have printed an overview before publishing the book itself? He could have made use of this printed survey for promoting his book and winning further patronage. The printing of the *Egyptian Oedipus* was a lengthy and very costly affair. Perhaps the printed outline made the project more attractive to patrons. However, we have no evidence of this reason for publishing the *Idea*. Moreover, the *Idea* remained unknown to outside readers. An internal reason for printing the book's overview in advance is more likely. The censorship report tells us that the censors were considering whether the first part of the second tome of the *Egyptian Oedipus* could be printed, "in order to preserve the whole work's distribution as certified by the already printed Synopsis."[52] Thus the printed survey served as a guideline for examining subsequent parts of the book. Having approved the outline of the work, the censors could hardly cancel or completely disapprove of entire sections. Restraining censors from substantial interventions in judging, the printed synopsis functioned as a guarantee for the whole project. Subsequent censoring would be limited to less relevant issues than the work's form, intention, and argument. Kircher's long-planned *Egyptian Oedipus* would safely appear as long as he followed the structure and content of the printed synopsis. This may have been the sole reason for printing beforehand the synopses of all parts of the work under the title *Idea of the Egyptian Oedipus*.

Confronting the censorship report on the *Idea of the Egyptian Oedipus* with the later published synopses, we can see how Kircher disregarded his censors. The letter of conditional approval singled out four passages to be emended, quoting the text of the manuscript and prescribing clearly how to revise it in order to present the outlined work in a more modest way.[53] Where Kircher had written that his first Syntagma would reveal the Nile's origin, up to now "unknown" (*incognitam*), the censors wanted him to write "not so exactly perceived" (*non ita exacte perspectam*). Instead of promising in his fourth Class many things so far "by nobody known" (*a nemine intellecta*), following the censors he should have promised only things "not so easily known" (*non ita facile intellecta*). Kircher saved as much as possible from his more appealing wording in the printed version of the synopses. He had simply added in both cases "perhaps" (*forsan*). In the latter he replaced "by nobody known" with "not by anyone known." In the third passage, forced by the censors to emend the "unheard-of" (*inaudita*) theory by adding just "perhaps" (*fortassis*), Kircher now disdained to make further use of this modifier. In the printed version, his theory instead becomes one "given by nobody as I know" (*a nemine, quod sciam, tradita*). Thus Kircher here again refused to revise his text as prescribed, sticking to his superlative diction.[54] What appears to be not much more than a play of words was in the end still a censure. To disregard these injunctions was to disregard the system of censorship. Since nothing substantial was at stake here, Kircher's form of disregard may indeed have been a provocation. Perhaps Wysing took this seriously because he had chaired the committee. When he accused Kircher of having complied with the censure "only as far as and how he himself wanted to," Wysing indicated his own intransigent attitude as a censor who had not received the respect he felt he deserved.

As far as we know, there were no consequences for Kircher's misbehavior. Perhaps the circumstances may account for this. Wysing accused Kircher in a letter he wrote to Alexander Gottifredi just ten days after the latter had been elected General.[55] He was trying to impress the Society's new leader with his account of Kircher's lack of discipline. Perhaps he hoped that the new General would not notice what we can now see clearly: the several instances reported by Wysing were actually all related to only two of Kircher's books (see the appendix). When Wysing denounced Kircher in 1652 for having rearranged the order of a book in press, he might have meant the *Pamphilian Obelisk*, if it was really based on his own experience as a censor (*expertus quoque sum*). In this instance, he was right to question Kircher's sincerity in making changes, since comparing the printed work with Wysing's letter of conditional approval yields at least one clear case of disregard. Wysing asked him to indicate that what he quoted from Konstantinos Psellos was an error in faith. Kircher, however, chose not to add this comment to his Greek and Latin quotations.[56]

Six weeks after Wysing denounced Kircher's lack of discipline, General Alexander Gottifredi died. Before his death, he received the letter of confirmation and signed the *imprimatur* for the first tome of the *Egyptian Oedipus*.[57] Thus the censorship for this tome was finished, and Gottifredi's successor, General Goswin Nickel, received the censorial letters for the following parts of Kircher's *Egyptian Oedipus*. It was Nickel, however, who had received the censorship report on the *Idea of the Egyptian Oedipus*, as he had been Vicar General of the order, so he surely knew something of these controversies. As it turns out, however, Gottifredi's sudden death as well as Wysing's departure from Rome in the same year ensured that there were no consequences.

Perhaps it was Kircher's experience in eluding censorship that led him to boast of this fact. On 9 February 1652, the members of the College of Revisors had signed the letter of confirmation for the first tome of the *Egyptian Oedipus*. Given his intransigence in regard to Kircher's synopsis, Wysing would hardly have been willing to compromise about the content of another work censored under his leadership. It is unlikely that he would have given his signature to the letter of confirmation if he had realized that Kircher, again, had disobeyed his orders. Once again, this letter was sent to Gottifredi in Wysing's hand. The censors confirmed that the first tome had been corrected according to their instructions.[58] However, comparing the printed tome with the censorship report reveals that Kircher, once again, had not made all the changes. Either the manuscript the censors saw to verify Kircher's corrections was not the same one that went to press, or they did not do their work diligently enough. Or perhaps not all of the censors were as intransigent as Wysing, who in accordance with rule 5 for Revisors had to follow the majority in signing the letter of confirmation, even if he did not agree with it personally. Wysing's participation seems to warrant the conclusion that the censors did their work diligently. But perhaps this is one of Kircher's examples of how he used "his experience in these things" to elude the censors, possibly by changing his text for its examination and thereafter revising it further to his satisfaction once he had the censors' approval.

The first volume of the *Egyptian Oedipus* appeared when Wysing was about to leave Rome in late 1652, or had already departed. Under close examination, Kircher had a lot to do to satisfy his critics. The censors had pointed out nine general features and fourteen passages in detail that they wanted him to emend. They criticized Kircher no less than ten times for exaggerating in describing himself and praising his work. What he might have lost in self-description by revising these self-laudatory passages, he probably regained largely by taking up the censors' suggestion to shorten his preface ("Prooemium") and to begin his book by writing something about his project in general.[59] This foregoing description as proposed by the censors became Kircher's "Propylaeum agonisticum," which he placed at the beginning of tome 1 before the preface.[60] He also profited from censorship by learning that the Rhone does not traverse Lake Zurich, which, as the censors remarked, everyone knows "who has once taken a glance at a map."[61] Changing his Lake Zurich to Lake Geneva, Kircher get rid of a passage that was a bit embarrassing for someone who even on the same page pretends to explain the origin of European rivers by a theory of subterranean reservoirs that would be fully demonstrated only in his *Subterranean World*.[62] Since this work was published thirteen years later, the censors could not understand how the Swiss Alps should be the origin of so many rivers arising far away from Switzerland. Hence they wanted Kircher to correct what obviously must be false.[63] Here, however, Kircher did not follow them, since it was thus his theory and further an occasion to draw attention to another forthcoming work that was widely advertised and anticipated.

Making use of censorship seems not to have changed anything in Kircher's attitude to the censors. Kircher continued to show a certain contempt for his censors beyond 1652, demonstrating his disrespect most clearly in a letter that he sent in response to a censure, probably in 1654. That spring Kircher received a copy of the report on the third tome of his *Egyptian Oedipus*.[64] The censors had approved printing only on condition that several changes be made. In general the practice of sending copies of the judgment (without the signature of the censors) allowed censors and authors to communicate with each other, to the extent that the author had the opportunity to reply to his censors. When authors seized this opportunity, they usually did so by composing lengthy letters of defense in order to justify their writing and to salvage as much as they could. Sometimes this gave rise to an exchange of several letters between the author and his censors.[65] Kircher did not take this approach, however. He did not even consider it worth his time to find a clean sheet of paper on which to write his response to his critics. Instead he made his comments right on the copy of the censors' judgment, simply annotating in between the lines the several points of the censure (see appendix). This nonchalance might even suggest that his annotations were made for personal use only. But the fact that Kircher sent it back to the censors in this form manifests his irreverence for their authority. The copy annotated in his hand and filed together with the original judgment is preserved in the archive of the *Curia generalis*. Where he agreed with the censors, he seems to have made a few minor changes. Where he disagreed, the offending passages remained and were printed.

3. The Holes in the System

In 1657, Duneau referred to Kircher's indiscipline as to a known fact (*experientia constat*)—a fact that we now know was already apparent to Wysing in 1652. Duneau arrived in Rome the same year that Wysing departed for Germany. They did not necessarily meet. Wysing was replaced by Le Roy. Duneau was called as Revisor for the French assistancy, replacing Honoré Nicquet (Honoratius Nicquetus, 1585–1667), and took up his job only in 1653.[66] Although Wysing did not want his fellows to know of his denunciation,[67] they certainly knew about Kircher's illicit practices, from Wysing himself, from their greater experience, and also perhaps from hearsay. Thus Kircher's indiscipline was somehow a known fact at least among the Revisors during the five years between the two accusations.

While the censors knew what Kircher was likely to do to books in press, they did not seem to have any way to prevent his transgressions. Kircher continued to neglect following the censors' recommendations, or at least followed them only as far as he chose. Further comparison between the censorship reports and the printed works shows not only that Kircher neglected to make all the changes in the first tome of the *Egyptian Oedipus*, but also that he ignored the censors' advice about what to do with the second tòme, before Wysing departed, as well as with his *Ecstatic Journey*, which was examined by Duneau. How did he get away with it? We have no information about any disciplinary measures taken against him. Obviously there were none. He continued to publish books. The four parts of the *Egyptian Oedipus* appeared between 1652 and 1655.[68] From 1656 to 1658, he brought out a book a year, and in between he published the third edition of his *Magnet* (*Magnes*) (1654).

Recall that Kircher did not even emend everything in the *Second Ecstatic Journey*. Duneau had warned in his letter that Kircher would not follow the censors' advice. Here, at least, the General may have reacted to some degree by not giving the *imprimatur*. We can interpret this as a form of criticism he adopted toward a book likely to provoke a scandal similar to the one occasioned by the *Ecstatic Journey*. The Revisors verified the manuscript of the *Second Ecstatic Journey* and signed a letter of confirmation.[69] For the printed version, however, Kircher had not reduced the three dialogues to two, nor did he remove the figure of Hydriel, the watery spirit who appeared in the first dialogue as the mouthpiece for

Kircher's geology. His disobedience could be read merely from the title of his published book. Duneau had denounced Kircher to the General precisely for not having made all the changes in his printed works, and this was true even in the critical case of the *Second Ecstatic Journey*.

But we should hardly be surprised by this. Perhaps what is surprising is that Wysing and Duneau both expected Kircher to fully obey the injunctions. It seems to have been the case that not all censors were as intransigent as these two, perhaps reflecting disagreements within the Society of Jesus regarding what counted as orthodoxy. The experience they had as Revisors denouncing Kircher was roughly comparable. Wysing had been in his fourth year and Duneau in his fifth at the time they made their accusations. Both had censored two of Kircher's printed works. Their experience was equal and equally less than that of their fellows. Both being of sanguine character,[70] they were zealous enough to verify also the printed versions. Since changing the corrected text while the work was in press was forbidden by the Rules for Revisors, they were certainly not the only ones to have thought that this stage mattered in controlling the appearance of books in print. But they were the only censors who decided to take Kircher's disregard of the system seriously enough to denounce him to the General.

How seriously did Jesuit authors take the censors' injunctions in general? We might interpret Kircher's pragmatic disregard as a certain degree of tacit freedom that the system granted. Kircher felt free to ignore his censors, but he did not ignore censorship totally. He did not print anything without approval, nor did he publish anything that was explicitly forbidden. Yet how can we reconcile his definition of obedience with the rule about not changing the text after it had been examined and corrected?

> If further it happens after the correction that the author without the superiors' knowledge adds or changes anything that is of any moment, the superiors would consider punishing him severely according to the gravity of the offense.[71]

This last passage of rule 15 for the Revisors attached conditions to the punishment as well as to the changes for them to be illicit. Only modifications "of any moment" mattered. Superiors punished these changes according to the gravity of the offense. In other words, an insignificant modification could be made even after the manuscript had been corrected. The definition of a modification "of any moment" was open to interpretation. This gave Jesuit authors *room to maneuver*.[72]

If, as his books went to press, Kircher only made modifications that he himself considered insignificant, he could do so with an easy conscience. If there were Revisors who would verify the printing and did not agree with him on this point, then they passed on their dilemma to the judgment of their superiors. Punishment was at their discretion. Thus, should they agree with Kircher on the insignificance of his modifications, there was no offense and hence no punishment. Yet Kircher would still have had problems integrating a whole new part into a book that had already been corrected, as Wysing had reported regarding the *Pamphilian Obelisk*. Even this, however, would have been legally possible. The rule refers only to those changes and additions that the author makes without his superiors' knowledge (*insciis Superioribus*). If Kircher had informed them, the integration of a new part would obviously not have been illicit. In the end, Kircher depended on his superiors to do what he did safely. In the last instance, he relied on his good relations with the General.

Reminding ourselves that any decision within the Society of Jesus depended quite a lot on the General may seem rather obvious. Certainly the General was not only free to follow the censors, but also to alter the conditions they had imposed for printing.[73] However, he would do this at his own risk and could get into conflict with his Revisors if they felt strongly about a particular book.[74] Nevertheless, the General could and did decide which corrections Jesuit authors had to make, which in some instances entailed relieving them from some or even all of the censors' injunctions. Such a practice was, in essence, a second judgment. No other document exists, beyond the printed book itself manifesting the disregard of the censors' injunctions, that verifies to what extent discrepencies between the General and the Revisors played a role in giving Kircher the freedom to disobey the latter. The letters of confirmation regarding Kircher's books make it clear that he was not always exempted from following the rules of the system, even if he did not make all the changes requested. Since the censors confirmed that the manuscript had been corrected, Kircher could not have been entirely freed from injunctions by the General. This brings us back again to the last passage of rule 15 above. According to this passage, Kircher needed superiors to count on in case the Revisors decided to check the printed work. For this kind of support, perhaps not even the General was always needed. The Roman Provincial and the rector of the Collegio Romano, for example, were of higher rank than the Revisors within the Society of Jesus. They fit the definition of superiors, as mentioned in the rule.[75]

Careful reading of the decisive passage of rule 15 shows that there was a hole in the system of censorship—a hole, however, that was open only to those who were in good standing within the Order and who had good relations with their superiors. Kircher occupied exactly this sort of position with the Society. We do not know with certainty if Kircher knew the rules or knew them well enough to have construed these possibilities in coping with censorship. But he was the most prolific Jesuit author of the mid–seventeenth century, so who but Kircher would know how to work the system? If Wysing's report was correct, he at least considered his pragmatic disregard sufficiently orthodox to be willing to mention it directly to a Revisor General. Obviously he was right to say that "because of his experience in these things he can safely make use of this practice."[76]

After the *Second Ecstatic Journey*, the next book examined by the Revisors was the severely disapproved *Great Art of Knowing* in 1660. We know that they dealt with it harshly, even though it eventually was published. This, however, is the last report signed by Revisors General regarding Kircher's books. Thereafter, the extant letters are all written by censors extraordinary—specialists in each of Kircher's individual subjects rather than permanent members of the College of Revisors with long experience reading Kircher. In the same year, Kircher had his *Ecstatic Journey* reissued by his friend Kaspar Schott and under his friend's name in Würzburg. After 1665, Kircher published nearly all his books in Amsterdam. They appeared with a Roman *imprimatur,* but regarding their censors we have no documents. We can only suggest how Kircher's relation to censorship may have developed further.

After the disapproval of the *Great Art of Knowing* in 1660, Kircher's writings were exclusively given to censors extraordinary (see the appendix). The subject matter treated in these writings only partly accounts for this practice. A book on miracles such as Kircher's *Investigation of Prodigious Crosses* (*Diatribe de prodigiosis crucibus*) could have just as well been examined by the Revisors General. Since the latter examined the *Second Ecstatic Journey,* it is rather surprising that not even one of the numerous censorship reports on Kircher's *Subterranean World* was written by a Revisor General.

Jesuits acting as censors extraordinary for Kircher had a different attitude toward censorship than the official position of the Revisors General. Censors extraordinary did not simply approve whatever Kircher wrote. In these final years, he received two conditional approvals and one disapproval for which we have documents. In general, however, the censors extraordinary seem to have been less conservative than the Revisors General.[77] For example, they noted Kircher's incongruities with Aristotle but did not make him revise the text.[78] Some of Kircher's censors extraordinary seemed to plainly contradict the system they supposedly upheld. The team of censors extraordinary that examined Kircher's *Investigation of Prodigious Crosses* took almost a whole page to list arguments against its publication. But they did not force Kircher to wait for their approval: "if the author, however, decides by himself to publish it right now, we indicate some things to be emended before."[79] Publication, it seems, was now at the author's discretion. One censor extraordinary, Philippus Rochaeus,[80] literally collaborated with Kircher in the final stages of preparing the *Subterranean World* for publication. He approved it after going over errors "which the author, partly in my presence, corrected very promptly and with religious modesty, and partly promised that he would correct completely."[81]

The Rules for Revisors forbade this kind of trust and collusion, yet Rochaeus did not hesitate to mention it openly in his censorial letter to the Vicar General Gian Paolo Oliva.[82] Oliva seems to have been satisfied, since Rochaeus wrote two reports on the second tome of the *Subterranean World* the following year. Censoring Kircher had become an act of collaboration with the Society's famous author. The system continued to offer some modest supervision, but it also ensured that his books would appear.

Giving books only to censors extraordinary might have been a way to avoid further conflicts between the Revisors, Kircher, and also perhaps the General himself. Kircher's critics, Le Roy and Duneau, remained Revisors General as long as Kircher published books. Certainly both were familiar with Kircher's disregard of censorship, and both had judged Kircher's *Great Art of Knowing* severely in 1660. The disapproval of this book may have precipitated a crisis in Kircher's relation with the College of Revisors General as well as brought about the turning point in the Society's censorship of his works. Thereafter, he somehow opted out of the system by directing his book manuscripts to the censors extraordinary. Since it was always the General who decided who should examine Kircher's books, Oliva played no small role in this affair. In the end, respecting the College of Revisors General and its rules turned out to be less important for the Society of Jesus than the glory that Kircher's publications could win for their Order.

Notes

*   I thank NaFöG Berlin and the DAAD for my research stay in Rome, Justin Erik Halldór Smith for proofreading my essay, and Paula Findlen for helping to edit the English and for her suggestions concerning the conclusion of this essay. I thank Daniel Stolzenberg for sharing with me his transcripts of the censorship documents for Kircher's *Oedipus Aegyptiacus* and *Obeliscus Pamphilius*. He discusses these in "Utility, Edification, and Superstition: Jesuit Censorship and Athanasius Kircher's Oedipus Aegyptiacus" in *The Jesuits II: Cultures, Sciences, and the Arts, 1540–1773*, ed. John O'Malley, Steven Harris, T. Frank Kennedy, and Gauvin Bailey (Toronto: University of Toronto Press, forthcoming). Stolzenberg will also publish the transcripts of the judgments in a separate article. I also thank Michael J. Gorman and Nick Wilding for their Athanasius Kircher Correspondence Project.

1.   The actual number of his published books still varies in different accounts: Sommervogel 1890, vol. 4, col. 1046–1077; Casciato et al. 1986; Lo Sardo 2001, pp. 25–28.
2.   Kircher 1652–55, vol. 1, fol. 43r–v, for the Egyptian project that brought him to Rome.
3.   Villoslada 1954, pp. 335, 325.
4.   On Jesuit censorship, see Lamalle 1981; Baldini 1985; 1984b; 1984a; 1992, pp. 75–119; Hellyer 1996; Gorman 1996; 1998, pp. 156–158; and Romano 1999, pp. 23–25, 511–516, Romano, 2000, 241–60. This internal censorship, however, did not prevent Jesuit books from appearing on the Index of Prohibited Books; Reichmann 1914, p. 154. On the Holy Office and Robert Bellarmine as a censored censor, see Godman 2000; regarding Kircher and censorship, see Camenietzki 1995a; 1995b, pp. 173–183; Siebert, 2002; censorship reports on Kircher are noted in Baldini 1985, pp. 44–50; 1992, pp. 91–94, 110–113. Hein 1993, pp. 305–311.
5.   *Monumenta Ignatiana* 1934–38, vol. 2, p. 356; Baldini 1992, pp. 78–79. On the origin of a *Censura opinionum* besides the *Censura librorum*, see Baldini 1992, pp. 83–84.
6.   The text of the *Ordinatio* can be found in Pachtler 1887–94, vol. 3, pp. 77–97; and Archivum Romanum Societatis Iesu (hereafter **ARSI**), FG 657, fols. 641–667. On its role in censorship, see Baldini 1992, pp. 82–83, 107n24; Hellyer 1996, pp. 325–335. On Jesuit doctrine, Mancia 1992.
7.   Baldini 1992, pp. 84–87. Names of Revisors and periods of office are listed in Rome, Biblioteca Nazionale Centrale Vittorio Emanuele (hereafter **BNVE**), FG 1666. The members are not necessarily of the nationality they represent in the College of Revisors, and in some years not all assistancies had a Revisor. Claudio Aquaviva, General 1585–1615: see Sommervogel 1890, vol. 1, col. 480–491; vol. 8, col. 1669–1670.
8.   See ARSI Instit. 46, fols. 61r–v, and Rom. 2, fols. 58r–v. Baldini 1992, pp. 85, 108n36.
9.   A second draft of these first rules written after 1616 can be found in ARSI, Instit. 117, II, fols. 587r–588r. A copy of the 1645–46 text is in BNVE, FG 1387, n. 22. Baldini 1992, 109n42, 43. For the version of tenth Congregation, see *Institutum* 1892–93, vol. 3, pp. 65–68, and the modification in rule 15 in *Institutum* 1892–93, vol. 2, pp. 374–375.
10.   *Institutum* 1892–93, vol. 3, pp. 66–67, no. 6 references the *Ratio Studiorum* (1599) in relationship to censorship practice. See Lukács, *Monumenta Paedagogica*, 1965–92, vol. 5: 380 (5, 6), 383 (1, 2, 6, 8, 10, 11), 386 (2–5), 395 (2, 3). For decretum 55 of the fifth Congregation (1593/94): *Institutum* 1892–93, vol. 2, pp. 272–274 (now "decretum 41").

11. Rules for Revisors no. 2: *Institutum* 1892–93, vol. 3, p. 65; for the rules of 1601, paragraph 1: Baldini 1992, p. 85.
12. On provincial censorship, see Hellyer 1996; and Heigel 1881.
13. There are nineteen reports from Revisors General and twenty-nine from censors extraordinary. Kircher himself had been counselor censor; for his intrigue regarding Giambattista Riccioli see Gorman 1998, pp. 139–144. Censures written by Kircher are preserved in Archivio della Pontificia Università Gregoriana, Rome (hereafter **APUG**) 558, fols. 80r–81v; APUG 561, fols. 103r–v, 101r–v; APUG 563, fols. 102r–v.
14. The reports are listed in chronological order. The names of Revisors General are printed in capitals. The names are in the Latin or vernacular form used by the censor. The censorship reports on Kircher are: ARSI FG 656, fols. 194r–196v; FG 661, fols. 29r–34v; FG 663, fols. 133r–135v, 306r–v, 312r–327v, 327ªr–v; FG 667, fols. 609r–613v, 615r–619v; FG 668, fols. 389r–401v; FG 675, fols. 247r–248v.
15. There are no reports for works after 1665, and the report on the *Lingua Aegyptiaca restituta* (Rome, 1643) is missing. If the "Thesaurus linguae Coptae" (ARSI FG 667, fol. 619r) really is the Coptic lexicon published in *Lingua Aegyptiaca* (despite the early date of the censure), then according to the Rules for Revisors, there must have been at least a second censorship report according to the Rules for Revisors that discussed its other aspects. *The Report of Specula melitensis* (Naples, 1638) is not missing; it was certainly examined and approved, as Kircher was not yet back in Rome. The second editions of *Magnes* (Cologne, 1643) and *Scrutinium pestis* (Leipzig, 1659) were not examined; they were printed with the Roman *imprimatur* of the first edition, and *Magnes* additionally with a *facultas* for the printer (signed on 13 March 1643 by Gosvinus Nickel, Provincial of Lower Rhine).
16. In this letter (ARSI FG 675, fol. 247r–248r), Franciscus Le Roy refutes six forbidden propositions that an anonymous critic had deduced from Kircher's *Itinerarium exstaticum* (*Ecstatic Journey*). This letter had been used by Kaspar Schott for writing his *apologeticon* of Kircher in the second edition of the book under the title *Iter extaticum coeleste*, 1660, pp. 485–509 (here pp. 491–509). See Camenietzki 1995a; and 1995b, pp. 173–183. Siebert, 2002.
17. Here the censors refer to standard negative definitions given in the Rules for Revisors, specifying what books must not contain (*Institutum* 1892–93, vol. 3, pp. 66–67, rules 6, 7). Simple approval can be short—a simple statement without justification approving publication: ARSI FG 663, fols. 324r, 327ªr.
18. Such comments typically suggested that a work more than satisfied the criteria for publication and were at the censors' discretion to offer (*Institutum* 1892–93, vol. 3, p. 67, rule 8). In these cases, censors seemed to promote publication. Kircher got only two approvals with comment from a Revisor General (ARSI FG 667, fol. 616r).
19. Eleven of sixteen censures blamed Kircher for bragging. Modesty had to be observed by Jesuits, e.g., *Institutum* 1892–93, vol. 3, pp. 13–14, 67 (rule 8).
20. For these two kinds of censorship, Hellyer 1996, p. 325; Baldini 1984b, p. 573; 1984a, p. 17.
21. On the Jesuits and medicine, see *Monumenta Ignatiana*, 1934–38, vol. 2, pp. 470, 471.
22. ARSI FG 661, fol. 31r (censorship report on *Scrutinium pestis*). F. Duneau (Franciscus Dunellus, 1599–1684), Revisor General for the French assistancy 1653–83; Sommervogel 1890, vol. 3, col. 279–280, vol. 9, col. 265–266, vol. 11, col. 1685; Delattre 1949–57, vol. 1, 443–445; Rivière 1910. F. Le Roy (1592–1679), Revisor General for the German assistancy 1653–77; Sommervogel 1890, vol. 7, 255–256; Delattre 1949–57, vol. 2, pp. 258, 1188, 1283.
23. ARSI FG 661, fol. 31r. C. Arbizio (Celidonius Arbicio) was the Revisor General for the Spanish assistancy, 1651–57.
24. Three *testimonia* from Roman doctors in *Scrutinium pestis*, 1658, fols. 7r–8r; those from Hieronymus Bardi (9 June 1657) and Paulus Zacchias (s.d.) are in APUG 558, fol. 159r and APUG 564, fol. 130r.
25. Goswinus Nickel (1584–1664), General from 1652 to 1664; Sommervogel 1890, vol. 5, col. 1706–1707; Crombach 1932–35.
26. *Institutum* 1892–93, vol. 3, p. 68, rule 5.
27. Camenietzki 1995a, pp. 26–27. Siebert, 2002. In 1646, Duneau himself provoked a scandal, while rector of the college of Auxerre, publicly insulting the Sorbonne, the Jansenists, and local notables present during one of his sermons. For more on this scandal, see Rivière 1910.
28. ARSI 663, fol. 135r.
29. See Rule for Revisors no. 8; the Society's reputation is to be protected by all writings (rule 6): *Institutum*, 1892–93, vol. 3, p. 67.

30. The letter is in ARSI FG 663, fols. 314r–315v; the addendum referred to in the letter as "folium distinctum" is in ARSI FG 663, fols. 317r–318r (copy in ARSI 663, fols. 312r–313r). The letter of simple approval is in ARSI FG 663, fol. 316r. On Ottolini (Dominicus Ottolinus, 1623–94), Sommervogel 1890, vol. 6, col. 8–9.

31. ARSI FG 663, fol. 314r.

32. ARSI FG 663, fol. 314r, and especially ARSI FG 663, fol. 318r.

33. ARSI FG 663, fol. 314v. Kircher's *Latium* (1671) had been criticized for the same reason by the Italian archaeologist Raffaele Fabretti (1618–1700). Fabretti's corrections are dated 3 April 1672, published in Saggi 1735–41, vol. 3, pp. 221–236. See Silvia Bruni 2001, pp. 335–342.

34. Surpassing mediocrity was another requirement for the quality of Jesuit publications (*Institutum*, 1892–93, vol. 3, p. 67, rule 8). It is a vague formula that Ottolini seeks to substantiate by listing factual errors and deficient diligence on Kircher's part, while claiming that his work did not rise to the level of mediocrity: ARSI FG 663, fols. 314r, 315v. This formula, introduced by General Muzio Vitelleschi in 1616, was open to interpretation and gave rise to a controversy between Sforza Pallavicino and his censors: Costantini 1969, pp. 104–107; Baldini 1992, p. 89.

35. *Institutum* 1892–93, vol. 3, pp. 67–68, rule 7.4 and in general, rules 6, 15. See also Hellyer 1996, pp. 324–325n20.

36. ARSI FG 663, fol. 315v.

37. This account is preserved in APUG 559, fols. 24r–26v, with a letter from Orsucci dated 10 June 1663 (APUG 559, fols. 23r–v). Kircher's letters to Orsucci are in the Archivio di Stato, Lucca (hereafter **ASLu**). See Laurina Busti in Lo Sardo 2001, pp. 350–351. She mentions also a *relazione* and two copies of it, sent to Kircher in 1663, that might be the same account as preserved in APUG 559, fols. 24r–26v.

38. Kircher's letter of 14 May 1666 in ASLu., G.B. Orsucci, n. 47, let. n. 164, c. 417. See Kircher's letter "dopo poco più di un mese" in ASLu., G.B. Orsucci, n. 47, let. 169, c. 432 (Busti in Lo Sardo 2001, p. 350). Duke August of Braunschweig-Wolfenbüttel also expected an imminent publication, as discussed in a late letter to Kircher in June 1666: APUG 555, fols. 81r–v.

39. Kircher, 15 December 1668, in ASLu, G.B. Orsucci, n. 47, let. 269, c. 683 (Busti in Lo Sardo 2001, p. 350).

40. Yet Kircher received an account of another ancient Etrurian town, Orvieto, from Vincenzo Durante in 1661 (APUG 564, fols. 128r–129v), a subject on which he was criticized only in the letter of disapproval and not in the addendum.

41. ASLu, G.B. Orsucci, n. 47, let. 280, c. 742. We wonder why Kircher claimed that his *Iter Hetruscum* had already been approved "after a severe and long censorship" in a letter to Leopoldo de' Medici on 16 April 1661; see Mirto 1989, pp. 140–141. I thank Michael John Gorman for having brought this correspondence to my attention.

42. Mirto 1989, pp. 132–134. Langenmantel 1684, p. 75. Kircher never refers to his later attempt to publish a book on Etruria as the *Iter Hestrucum* in his letters to Florence (Mirto 1989, pp. 149–150, 159–162) or to Augsburg (Langenmantel 1684, pp. 64–68, 70–77, 78–83: calling it an *Atlas Thuscus*).

43. See Sepibus 1678, pp. 61–66, esp. 64. According to Sommervogel 1890, vol. 4, col. 1073, the manuscript was sent to Jansen in June 1678. He still planned to publish the book in 1688; Mirto 1989, p. 134.

44. ARSI *FG* 661, fol. 30v.

45. ARSI *FG* 661, fol. 30v, 34r (the letter is separated by interposed folios).

46. The whole letter (ARSI FG 668, fols. 398r–399r) is written in Wysing's hand. He may have also presided over the censorship of the first part of the second tome of *Oedipus Aegyptiacus* before leaving for Germany in 1652 (ARSI Rom. 81 Cat.brev. 1650–1656: already absent *sub finem anni* 1652). He became rector of the college in Dillingen and Altötting, and he died in Munich in 1672. Born in Lucerne in 1601 and called to the College of Revisors General in 1649 (BNVE FG 1666), he spent a short period in an office often held for a lifetime. Sommervogel 1890, vol. 8, col. 1309–1311, gives 1647–52 for Wysing's stay in Rome.

47. ARSI FG 668, fol. 399r: This separate paragraph signed by Wysing on 1 February 1652. The letter (ARSI FG 668, fols. 398r–399r) is signed by all Revisors General of 1652 except for Arbizio.

48. Rule 15 (last sentence): *Institutum* 1892–93, vol. 3, p. 68.

49. ARSI *FG* 668, fols. 391r–392v, esp. 391r : "impressa iam Synopsi."

50. Kircher 1636, pp. 333–338.

51. Synopses in *Oedipus Aegyptiacus*, vol. I: fol. 2v; II.1: fol. 1v; II.2: fol. 1v. The censorship report on the *Idea oedipi Aegyptiaci* (ARSI FG 668, fol. 389r) is in Wysing's hand and covers half a letter page. The three tomes mentioned in the report are those of the *Oedipus Aegyp-*

tiacus and not tomes comprised by the *Idea* itself (Kircher's books of several tomes are all examined separately tome by tome; see the appendix). Four passages are censored; three can be identified in the *Oedipus Aegyptiacus* (the fourth is related to the third tome, where there is no Synopsis in the printed book).

52. ARSI 668, fol. 391r: "ad salvandam totius operis distributionem, impressa iam Synopsi consignatam."
53. ARSI FG 668, fol. 389r.
54. Kircher 1652–55, vol. I: fol. 2v; II.1: fol. 1v.
55. Alexander Gottifredi (1595–1652) was elected General on 21 January 1652, and he died on 12 March 1652. Since he had been Secretary of the Society under Muzio Vitelleschi (General, 1615–45), Gottifredi was certainly not unfamiliar with questions of censorship. On Gottifredi, see Sommervogel 1890, vol. 3, col. 1623–1624.
56. ARSI FG 668, fol. 390r; Kircher 1650a, p. 270. The passage in question was "not only the souls were produced from seed, but also all higher orders of being have their origin from it."
57. The original imprimatur signed by Gottifredi (12 February 1652) is kept in APUG 561, fol. 12r. See note 68.
58. ARSI FG 668, fol. 397r: "correctionem Tomi primi [. . .] factam esse ad mentem Patrum Revisorum, in data super eo censura expressam."
59. ARSI FG 668, fol. 398v.
60. Kircher 1652–55, vol. 1, fols. 36r–45v (no page numbers).
61. ARSI FG 668, fol. 398v.
62. Kircher 1652–55, vol. 1, pp. 55–56.
63. ARSI FG 668, fol. 398v.
64. The copy with Kircher's annotations is in ARSI FG 668, fols. 401r–v, and the original report addressed to the General Nickel is in ARSI FG 668, fols. 400r–v. Kircher also received a copy (APUG 561, fols. 91r–v) of the report on *Oedipus Aegyptiacus*, t. II.2 (ARSI FG 668, fols. 396r–v).
65. Baldini 1992, p. 86.
66. BNVE FG 1666.
67. ARSI FG 668, fol. 399r.
68. The actual year of printing is given by the colophon at the end of each tome of *Oedipus Aegyptiacus*. It is missing in tome I and varies for tomes II.1, II.2 (each giving 1654 instead of 1653 on the title) as well as for tome III (giving 1655 instead of 1654). The *imprimatur* of tome III in 1655 was given for all three tomes. The *imprimaturs* for the single tomes preserved in APUG are not printed (APUG 561, fols. 12r, 13r, 14r); they reflect the respective dates of the printing licenses that appear on the titles of the tomes.
69. ARSI FG 663, fol. 134r. There were only three Revisors in 1657.
70. Thus they are described in the order's second catalogue; Wysing: ARSI Rom 59 Cat.trien. 1649–1651, fol. 280v, no. 61; Duneau: ARSI Rom 60 Cat.trien. 1655–1658, fol. 61v, no. 29.
71. *Institutum* 1892–93, vol. 3, p. 68.
72. Hellyer 1996, p. 320.
73. *Institutum* 1892–93, vol. 3, p. 68, rule 15 (second half), indicates such a practice in regard to the Provincial who should send his Revisors' censures to the General and wait until the General decides what actually had to be emended.
74. BNVE FG 1387, no. 23, fols. 381r–382r (written between 1644 and 1646) mentions a conflict between the General and his Revisors in regard to maintaining uniformity of doctrine in publications.
75. BNVE FG 1666; Baldini 1992, p. 86.
76. Kircher, quoted according to Wysing's separate statement: ARSI FG 668, fol. 399r.
77. Revisors General were mostly conservative: Baldini 1992, p. 82.
78. ARSI FG 663, fol. 327r: censorship report on *Mundus subterraneus*, t. II.
79. ARSI FG 663, fol. 306r: "Si tamen haec statim edere apud se statuerit, [. . .]."
80. Philippus Rochaeus is not in Sommervogel or Polgár.
81. ARSI FG 663, fol. 319r.
82. Gian Paolo Oliva (1600–1681), General 1664–81. He was elected Vicar General on 7 June 1661 in order to assist the desperately ill Goswin Nickel. This include acts of censorship. See ARSI FG 663, fol. 321r (Oliva signing *imprimaturs* for Kircher's books) and the appendix. On Oliva, see Sommervogel 1890, vol. 5, col. 1884–1892; vol. 9, p. 729; Suppl.; col. 615–616; and Polgár 1980–90, vol. 3.2, p. 604.

Book censored	Censorship report Date and place of censorship		ARSI
Prodromus Coptus	1635-Apr-12	Colleg. Rom.	FG 656 196r
	1635-Apr-22	Colleg. Rom.	FG 656 194r
	1635-Apr-23	Domus professa	FG 656 195r
Thesaurus Coptae linguae	1636-Feb-06	Romae	FG 667 619r
Magnes	1639-Nov-28	Colleg. Rom.	FG 667 609r
	1639-Nov-28	Colleg. Rom.	FG 667 610r
Ars magna lucis	1644-Dec-17	Romae	FG 667 611r
	1644-Dec-17	Colleg. Rom.	FG 667 612r
	1644-Dec-28	Domus professa	FG 667 613r
Musurgia universalis, t. II	1648-Jun-06	Colleg. Rom.	FG 667 616r
Musurgia universalis	1648-Jun-08	Romae	FG 667 618r
	1648-Jun-09	Colleg. Angl.	FG 667 615r
Musurgia universalis, t. I	1648-Jun-14	Colleg. Rom.	FG 667 617r
Obeliscus Pamphilius	1649-Nov-02	no place	FG 668 394r–v
	1649-Nov-11	no place	FG 668 395r
	1649-Nov-17	Colleg. Rom.	FG 668 390r–v
Idea oedipi Aegyptiaci	1651-Dec-02	no place	FG 668 389r
Oedipus Aegyptiacus, t. I	1652-Jan-31	Colleg. Rom.	FG 668 398r–399r
	1652-Feb-09	Colleg. Rom.	FG 668 397r
Oedipus Aegyptiacus, t. II.1	1652-May-05	Colleg. Rom.	FG 668 391r–392v
Magnes (third edition)	1652-Aug-14	Colleg. Paenit.	FG 668 393r
Oedipus Aegyptiacus, t. II.2	1653-Jul-20	Colleg. Rom.	FG 668 396r–v
Oedipus Aegyptiacus, t. III	1654-Apr-25	Colleg. Rom.	FG 668 400r–v
			FG 668 401r–v
Itinerarium exstaticum	1655-Nov-07	Colleg. Rom.	FG 661 29 r–v
	1655-Nov-13	Colleg. Rom.	FG 661 33r
Iter exstaticum II	1657-May-04	Colleg. Rom.	FG 661 32r
Scrutinium pestis	1657-May-04	Colleg. Rom.	FG 661 31r
Iter exstaticum II	1657-May-07	Colleg. Rom.	FG 661 30r–v, 34r
	1657-Jul-23	Colleg. Rom.	FG 663 134r
Scrutinium pestis	1657-Oct-23	Colleg. Rom.	FG 663 133r
Ars magna sciendi	1660-May-15	Colleg. Rom.	FG 663 135r
Iter Hetruscum	1660-Sep-04	Domus professa	FG 663 316r
Diatribe	1660-Oct-07	Romae	FG 663 306r–v
Iter Hetruscum	1660-Nov-12	Romae	FG 663 314r–315v
			FG 663 317r–318r
			FG 663 312r–313r
Mundus subterraneus, t. I	1662-Mar-25	Colleg. Hibern.	FG 663 319r
	1662-Apr-16	Romae	FG 663 320r
Mundus subterraneus	no date	no place	FG 663 321r
			FG 663 322r
Polygraphia nova	1662-Nov	no place	FG 663 323r–v
	1662-Nov-24	no place	FG 663 324r
Mundus subterraneus, t. II	1663-Jun-25	Colleg. Hibern.	FG 663 326r
	1663-Jun-27	Romae	FG 663 325r
	1663-Jul-03	Romae	FG 663 327r
	1663-Jul-25	no place	FG 663 327a r
Itinerarium exstaticum	no date		FG 675 247r–248r

Document type	Censors	Imprimatur Date
approval with comment	JORDINUS Antonius	1635-Apr-23
approval	BIDERMANNUS Jacobus	
approval	Käpfel Guilielmus	
approval	Lommelinus Ignatius	
approval	Rethi Jo. Baptista	1639-Nov-30
approval with comment	Giattinus Jo. Baptista	
approval	Cripsius Joannes	1644-Dec-18
approval	Rethi Jo. Baptista	
approval with comment	Inchofer Melchior	
approval with comment	NICQUETUS Honoratus	1648-Jun-16
approval with comment	Fabri Honoratus	1648-Jun-16
approval	Cripsius Joannes	
approval with comment	Perez Antonius	1648-Jun-16
approval on condition	Fabri Honoratus	no date
approval with comment	Santius Leo	
approval on condition	WYSING Nicolaus	
approval on condition	ARBICIO Celidonius, D'ABREU Sebastianus, NICQUETUS Honoratu, ROSSI Joan. Bap., WYSING Nicolaus,	
approval on condition	D'ABREU Sebastianus, NICQUETUS Honoratus, ROSSI Jo. Baptista, WYSING Nicolaus	1655-Jan-12
confirmation	D'ABREU Sebastianus, NICQUETUS Honoratus, ROSSI Jo. Baptista, WYSING Nicolaus	
approval on condition	ARBICIO Celidonius, D'ABREU Sebastianus, ROSSI Jo. Baptista, WYSING Nicolaus	in tome I
approval on condition	Fabri Honoratus	1653-Oct-29
approval on condition	ARBICIO Celidonius, LE ROY Franciscus, ROSSI Jo. Baptista	in tome I
approval on condition	ARBICIO Celidonius, DUNELLUS Franciscus, LE ROY Franciscus, ROSSI Jo Baptista	in tome I
copy of FG 668 400r–v		
approval on condition	ARBICIO Celidonius, DUNELLUS Franciscus, LE ROY Franciscus, ROSSI Joan. Bap.	1655-Nov-15
confirmation	ARBICIO Celidonius	
approval on condition	ARBICIO Celidonius, DUNELLUS Franciscus, LE ROY Franciscus,	1657-Aug-02
disapproval	ARBICIO Celidonius, DUNELLUS Franciscus, LE ROY Franciscus	1657-Nov-01
disapproval	DUNELLUS Franciscus	1657-Aug-02
confirmation	ARBICIO Celidonius, DUNELLUS Franciscus, LE ROY Franciscus	
confirmation	DUNELLUS Franciscus, LE ROY Franciscus	1657-Nov-01
disapproval	BASSANUS Michael, DUNELLUS Franciscus, LE ROY Franciscus, LEYTANUS Martinus, SOTELO Franciscus de	1665-Sep-01 1666-Jul-19
approval	Casilius Ant.	
approval on condition	Estmor Michael, Fabri Honoratus, Richeomus Antonius	1661-Jan-21
disapproval	Ottolinus Dominicus	
add. FG 663 314r–315v		
copy FG 663 317r–318r		
approval	Rochaeus Philippus	1662-Apr-19
approval with comment	Maurus Sylvester	
approval with comment	Leone Franciscus Maria	1662-Apr-19
copy of FG 663 321r		
approval on condition	Esparza Martini	1662-Dec-02
approval	Barrolus Daniel	
approval	Rochaeus Philippus	1662-Apr-19
approval	Maurus Sylvester	
approval with comment	Talbot Gilbertus	
approval	Rochaeus Philippus	
defense letter	LE ROY Franciscus	

(continued)

Book censored	Signed by		Date	Book published Place
Prodromus Coptus	Vitellescus Mutius	Praepositus Generalis	1636	Rome
Thesaurus Coptae linguae Magnes	Vitellescus Mutius	Praepositus Generalis	1641	Rome
Ars magna lucis	Sangrius Carolus	Vicarius Generalis	1646	Rome
Musurgia universalis, t. II	Carrafa Vincentius	Praepositus Generalis	1650	Rome
Musurgia universalis	Carrafa Vincentius	Praepositus Generalis	1650	Rome
Musurgia universalis, t. I	Carrafa Vincentius	Praepositus Generalis	1650	Rome
Obeliscus Pamphilius	Montmorency Florence de	Vicarius Generalis	1650	Rome
Idea oedipi Aegyptiaci	Nickel Goswinus	Praepositus Generalis	1652	Rome
Oedipus Aegyptiacus, t. I				
Oedipus Aegyptiacus, t. II.1			1653 (1654)	Rome
Magnes (third edition)	Nickel Goswinus	Praepositus Generalis	1654	Rome
Oedipus Aegyptiacus, t. II.2			1653 (1654)	Rome
Oedipus Aegyptiacus, t. III			1654 (1655)	Rome
Itinerarium exstaticum	Nickel Goswinus	Praepositus Generalis	1656	Rome
Iter exstaticum II	Rho Joannes	Praepositus Provincialis Provinciae Romanae	1657	Rome
Scrutinium pestis	Nickel Goswinus	Praepositus Generalis	1658	Rome
Iter exstaticum II	Rho Joannes	Praepositus Provincialis Provinciae Romanae	1657	Rome
Scrutinium pestis	Nickel Goswinus	Praepositus Generalis	1658	Rome
Ars magna sciendi	Oliva Joannes Paulus	Praepositus Generalis	1669	Amsterdam
Iter Hetruscum Diatribe	Nickel Goswinus	Praepositus Generalis	1661	Rome
Iter Hetruscum				
Mundus subterraneus, t. I	Oliva Joannes Paulus	Vicarius Generalis	1665	Amsterdam
Mundus subterraneus	Oliva Joannes Paulus	Vicarius Generalis	1665	Amsterdam
Polygraphia nova	Oliva Ioannes Paulus	Vicarius Generalis	1663	Rome
Mundus subterraneus, t. II	Oliva Joannes Paulus	Vicarius Generalis	1665	Amsterdam
Itinerarium exstaticum				

"The Censors' Report with Kircher's Comments"
source: ARSI, FG668, f.401rv

Admodum Rev[erende] P[ate]r N[oste]r G[e]n[era]lis
Legimus tom. 3. Oedipi Aegiptiacia P. Athanasij Chircher, et illum iudicamu
luce dingum; censemus tamen debere in aliquibus perfici, et corrigi.

1. Continere videtur in stilo notabilem inaequalitatem iam enim eligan-
    ter, iam nimis humiliter loqitur. [Kircher: *Quantum decursu operis
    fieri poterit, praestabimus desideratam emendationem*].
2. Authoritates Grecorum interdum solum latine refert, ut pag. 268 Pla-
    tonis verba. et pag. 345. verba Dionisij Areopagitae; interdum solum
    graece illas refert; melius se geret author, si eas, et graece et latine
    simul reponat. [Kircher: *factum est quod praeceperant Censores*]
3. Citationes et remissiones ad obeliscum Pamphilium, et repetitiones
    ex ipso sunt pene innumerae in hoc tomo; posset in his adhiberi
    aliquis modus; ne tedium pareret lectoribus. [Kircher: *Alius modus
    non est **nisi** ut citentur loca obelisci Pamphilij; si ita visum fuerit cen-
    soribus quibus tamen in praecedentibus censuris non placuit tantarum
    ex obelisco Pamphilio authoritatum repetitio.*]
4. In titulo et praefatione ad Imperatorem, et in operis decursu, aliqua in-
    serit author in sui commendationem, quae videntur redolere iactan-
    tiam; in quibus innuit se supra reliquos omnes mortales in hac rerum
    notitia excellere. [Kircher: *omissa sunt quae iactantiam redolent.*]
5. titulus est longior et intricatior quam par sit. [Kircher: *emendabitur*]
6. fol. 4. Hierogliphicum definit sacrae rei simbolum saxis [Kircher:
    sacris AEgyptiorum monumentis] insculptum, non apparet cur hi-
    erogliphica ad saxa restringi debeant in definitione. [Kircher: *dico me
    definisse hoc loco hieroglyphicum pro communi sensu philologorum,
    neque eorum definitio logica est [/] emendavimus tamen ubi apparet.*]
    fol. 6. [*sic*] Trismegistum ait fuisse regem maximum Aegipti, et tamen
    subiungit floruisse tempore Abrahe Primo Faraone rerum in Aegipto
    potiente. [Kircher: *haec vera sunt uti fuse in Obelisco Pamphilio
    docuimus fol. 35 & 97 alibique simul*]
8. fol. 2. dicit nullam esse gentem tam barbaram, quae non utatur carac-
    teribus. Contrarium liquet ex Canadensibus, et alijs. [Kircher: *moder-
    abitur assertio; hisce praepositio; Vix ulla natio.*]
9. fol. 8. ubi de filijs Noe et de Cam loquitur, sensus est obscurior, nec
    satis videtur coherens. [Kircher: *locus totus FG 668 401 rv Oed.aeg. III
    [locus totus emendatus est*]

X. fol. 20. Magna videtur polliceri de Bracmanum Caracteribus, cum postea,
quae de illis scribit non respondeant praemissis. [Kircher: *emendatus est locus*]

Xi fol. 159. ex mente Aegiptiorum dicit Crucem ansatam esse potissimum contra adversas potestates noctu dominantes amuletum, idque alias repetit. digna est haec eruditio, ut alicuius scriptoris authoritate roboretur. [Kircher: *vide Obelisc. Pamphil. lib. 4. hierogrammatistas 20, ubi ex Mars [ilio], Ficino alijsque assertam eruditionem confirmamus.*]

Xii. Dum agit de Caracteribus Sinicis, dicit se, illa quae tradit accepisse a P[at]re Michaele Boim legato misso ad summum Pontificem ab Imperatore, et duabus Reginis Christianis, et ab Imperatore Sinarum Catechumeno; remittimus iudicio Paternitatis V[est]rae, an expediat ista scribi ab authore ? Romae 25. Aprilis 1654.; [Kircher: *omnia omissa sunt, earum legationum P. Boym*]

"Quasi-Optical Palingenesis"

The Circulation of Portraits and the Image of Kircher*

ANGELA MAYER-DEUTSCH

Indeed, statues and images, since they are long-lasting, seem by direct inspection not only to refresh the memory about absent persons, but also to represent a certain optical palingenesis of those deceased.

—Theobald Müller, 1577[1]

And if the expense were not so great, I would make the whole German Nation into a name: but I must cut my coat according to my cloth.
    —Kircher to Johann Georg Anckel, librarian and adviser of Duke August of
        Brunswick-Lüneburg, 16 July 1659[2]

In this essay, I explore some ways in which images, texts, and names may be combined in order to produce a certain form of presence of absent individuals, which is suggested by the term *effigies*. The ancient use of the term implies the plastic, three-dimensional representation of the body in Roman, medieval, and early modern funeral rituals. *Effigies* is the most frequently used term for a portrait in postmedieval Latin, and quite often it still bears the meaning of forming a physical image to produce a memorial presence of the deceased. The complex memorial function of portraits—similar to the function of naming the dead in liturgy—as well as the self-promotional function of circulating portraits, forms the basis for my investigation of the role of portraits in the museum and life of Athanasius Kircher.

Paolo Giovio (1483–1552), whose collection is the subject of the above quotation from Theobald Müller, was a physician, courtier, bishop, and above all, the historian and custodian of the most admired portrait gallery of the sixteenth century. He was patronized by the Farnese and Medici families, and visited by princes, artists, collectors, and scholars. That Giovio understood the history of the world as a history of outstanding personalities is evident from his numerous publications and from the *Museo Giovio*, the collection of portraits displayed from 1537 on in his villa near Como. His lifelong publication project, the *Elogia* or *Brief Lives of Illustrious Men*, provided a literary image of historic personalities. The first part, devoted to writers, was published in 1546;

the second, on military men, appeared in 1551. Corresponding portraits hung in Giovio's gallery, but the published works did not include their reproductions, although Giovio had written to Daniele Barbaro of Venice in a letter of 1544 that "without the [accompanying] image the panels would seem completely mute and without spirit (*genio*)."[3] The fact that the texts were published without images to give them life, probably due to technical and above all financial problems, must thus have been a great disappointment for Giovio. Only after his death was a selection of the images published (the 1575 *Elogia* and the *Vitae* of 1576–78). Nevertheless, these works need to be considered as texts with illustrating portraits—*Bildnisvitenbücher* was the German term— not as "portrait-books," whose focus is the image. Only the *Pictures of the Musaeum Iovianum Made by Artful Hand from Life* (1577), in which the epigraph appeared, could be called a genuine portrait-book.

The portraits in the *Museo Giovio* were meant to be "painted biographies," and their value lay in their communication of the character, physiognomy, and "likeness" of the subject, rather than in their aesthetic quality or the reputation of their author.[4] Giovio wanted "true" portraits derived from supposedly "authentic" pictures of the subject, and not merely from literary, perhaps imaginary descriptions. Most of his works were thus copied from objects: medals, coins, drawings, woodcuts, paintings (miniatures, frescoes, and paintings on canvas or panel), and sculptures.

The declared aim of the museum was the *optical palingenesis*[5] of the dead, meaning their optical rebirth or reproduction. What, then, did Giovio intend to achieve with his museum? He sought to create a metaphorical reincarnation of people who, having lived at different times, would not otherwise be able to inhabit the same time and space, nor communicate with one another. Painted "ad vivum," in the sense of a substitute for the absent person, and depicted with the greatest possible physiognomic resemblance, this rebirth promised to create a deeper impression than that formed by images in the unassisted memory, in literary recollections, or in the auditory impressions used by preachers. Following Alberti's popular statement that pictures impress the soul, viewers of the painting were to be affectively moved, first and foremost, and only secondarily taught.

Also at stake was the old *paragone* between word and image and the discussion of the reliability of the senses, in which it was claimed that appealing to the eye impresses more deeply than appealing to the ear. Since Giovio (or his editor) used the word "optical" instead of "visual," the idea of projection might also have been at work. This idea culminates almost a century later—it seems to me—in Kircher's projections of pictures of the Resurrection on the walls of his museum, with the help of the *magic lantern*.[6] In his letter to Anckel, the adviser of the German duke August of Brunswick-Lüneburg, Kircher writes that "if the expense were not so great," he would hang portraits of all Germans in his gallery and thereby "make the whole German nation a name." His addressee, August, was a duke of minor importance, for whom the placement of his likeness in the gallery would have had much greater meaning than for more powerful rulers, as Paula Findlen has observed.[7] In this case the picture—in its arrangement on the wall—makes the name and not the other way round; this stands in marked contrast to the world of Giovio, where (despite the general shift toward the image) the name still comes first. Occasionally, sixteenth-century portrait-books included names without a corresponding image—the print simply shows an empty frame—but never images without a corresponding name. This shift becomes evident in a wider sense in the emblematic world of Kircher: in the *Musaeum Kircherianum*, in addition to the portraits, optical renderings of phrases or emblems, and architectural images were occasionally projected on the walls. A famous (though in reality rather unspectacular) "experiment" demonstrated by Kircher was the so-called palingenetic experiment, or vegetable Phoenix, whose product, a small "plant" formed in vitriol, was shown in the museum until cold weather caused it to break. The "plant" supposedly grew out of its own ashes without sunlight and resembled the legendary Phoenix rising from its ashes.[8] Kircher saw in this an analogical demonstration of the biblical account of the Resurrection. Perceiving the inherent emblematic qualities of this demonstration, Kircher employed it to commemorate Queen Christina of Sweden's celebrated conversion to Catholicism. Kircher showed the queen the demonstration twice during her two visits to his museum.

The theme of regeneration and rebirth (*palingenesis*) was therefore treated differently in the museums of Giovio and Kircher. But there were parallels: the term *optical*, already used by Giovio with reference to a sixteenth-century portrait gallery, nicely links the experience of the portrait gallery to the experience of the optical demonstrations that took place a hundred years later in the *Musaeum Kircherianum*.

"Scholarly" Portraiture

In the fifteenth and sixteenth centuries, portraits were mainly realized in the media of fresco, oil painting, the bust, and the tombstone. A major transformation in the fabrication and distribution of portraits came with the introduction of portrait medals and portrait miniatures, the printing of one-page portraits, as woodcuts or engravings, and later on, portrait-books.[9] The common feature of these forms of portraiture is the potential to circulate multiple copies.

Medals, with the help of emblems, promoted the status of their inventor and fostered patronage relationships.[10] Scholars distributed them as personal gifts, as did princes and noblemen. In 1519, the Flemish artist Quentin Metsys designed a medal of a scholar, Erasmus of Rotterdam, of which various examples circulated in lead and bronze.[11]

Portrait miniatures became an esteemed form of art and memento from around 1530 until the nineteenth century. Hans Holbein was one of the early leading practitioners of the genre. Miniatures could be kept in one's pocket or in little drawers, might be set into jewelry or snuffboxes, and were used "to humanize relations among people [. . .], to be bestowed by the subject upon respected colleagues."[12] It is this "humanizing" or familiarizing aspect of miniatures, medals, and portraits in circulation that provided their value in patronage relations, as will be shown later.[13]

The tradition of painted, drawn, or etched individual portraits of scholars began with Hans Burgkmair's etching of Conrad Celtis, the so-called *Sterbebild* of 1508. This image, conceived by Celtis himself while still alive and composed in the manner of a Roman tombstone monument, clearly anticipated the scholar's eventual memorialization after death. As discussed below, this theme received its most extensive treatment in the portrait galleries. Cranach's etchings of Luther (c. 1525), Durer's portraits of Philipp Melanchthon and Erasmus of Rotterdam (1526), and Holbein's various portraits of Erasmus dating from the 1520s and 1530s followed the *Sterbebild*. These representations of scholars in their studies were based on the much older tradition of images of authors and of dedication images in illuminations. Representations of Saint Jerome, the writing saint, in his study provided the iconographic basis for almost all subsequent scholarly portraiture from the thirteenth century on. In the fifteenth and sixteenth centuries, ordering portraits became quite fashionable and their execution was highly valued. The fact that Durer was so highly compensated for his portraits prompted Lorenz Beheim, canon of Bamberg, to say in 1517: "Tanti est contrafacere."[14]

Some scholars and artists, Erasmus and Durer among them, pointed to the general problem that the portrait of a scholar suggested expressing the ancient commonplace that a scholar's character would be better expressed through his writings than his portrait. This topos had a very long tradition in the aforementioned *paragone* of the *artes* (visual arts versus poetry), which drew upon discussions concerning the reliability of the senses (the eyes versus the ears). Durer's famous portrait of Erasmus (1526) refers to this skeptical commonplace by integrating a Greek inscription (which translates into English as "the bigger, better, more important will be shown by the writings") in his engraving. He found it on the reverse of Quentin Metsys's medal of Erasmus (1519), which Durer himself possessed.[15] The tradition of the representation of a special group of scholars, namely mathematicians and astronomers,[16] began with Hans Holbein's portrait of the mathematician and astronomer Nicolaus Kratzer in 1528. Printing permitted this tradition to develop and establish itself quickly.[17] Two principal features characterized its iconography: the representation of the person at half-length in a physical space, and the activity of the hands at a worktable with instruments of measurement and writing. These images appear to serve a kind of collective commemorative function.

The Image of Kircher as an Engraved *Effigies*

The various etchings, lithographs, and drawings of Athanasius Kircher from the seventeenth to the nineteenth centuries depict him at half-length, only once set in a physical space occupied with objects and furniture. The (mainly posthumous) paintings show him at half- or full-length, sitting in a room at a table with books, papers, and instruments close at hand. These surviving portraits depict him as a scholar—specifically a mathematician—and in one case as a scholar and collector.

There is an apparent tension between the Jesuit Order's crucial emphasis on poverty, humility, and modesty and the existence and circulation of the *effigies* (portraits) of distinguished Jesuits. As Michael John Gorman has emphasized, the theological mistrust of portraiture among Jesuits can be traced to the Society's founder, Ignatius of Loyola: "In so far as Ignatius's life story, in particular his spiritual disciplining after his injury at the battle of Pamplona, came to serve as a model for those entering the order, it is worth mentioning in the context of self-effacement that Ignatius never allowed his portrait to be painted while General of the Society—future portraits had to rely heavily on sketches made at his deathbed and several death masks."[18] Theological mistrust, the fear of honoring the images themselves rather than their prototype, was reinforced by the aforementioned topos concerning the inadequacy of the visual representations of scholars. Consequently, no portraits exist for many Jesuit scholars, including Christoph Grienberger and Kaspar Schott. This attitude appears to be reflected in the fact that almost all the known portraits of Kircher derive from a single image, an etching that reached its most refined state in 1664, quite late in the scholar's life (see Figure 4.1).

The earliest known portrait of Kircher was made for his fifty-third birthday, 2 May 1655, the first year of Alexander VII's papacy.[19] It was never included in any of his publications. The half-length portrait is not fully worked out, but remains a preliminary sketch. It presents the middle-aged Kircher against a dark, roughly hatched, neutral background. His bearded but juvenile face with a slight smile looks attentively at the viewer. Kircher's clothes are similar to those worn by Christoph Clavius (one of Kircher's predecessors as professor of mathematics at the Roman College) in an engraving by Francesco Villamena from 1606: simple underclothes, *mantello*, and *berretta*.[20] The portrait was made by the Dutch engraver Cornelis Bloemaert II (1603–92),[21] son of the painter Abraham Bloemaert.

A disciple of his father, as well as Gerard van Honthorst and Chrispijn van de Passe the Elder, Bloemaert was called first to Paris and then in 1633 to Rome. In Rome, Joachim von Sandrart worked with him, as did Theodor Mattham and other known engravers of the famous *Giustinian Gallery* (1635–37), the (unfinished) catalogue of the Marchese Giustiniani's collection of antiquities and paintings. Bloemaert remained in Rome until his death in 1692, working in collaboration with some of the most famous artists of the Roman High Baroque. Ironically in the context of this essay, the biography by his contemporary Filippo Baldinucci describes the elderly, modest artist as so far removed "from any desire for worldly applause that, although it was sought with much insistence and almost forced upon him, he never consented a portrait to be made of his person."[22] He was known for his engravings of genre and religious paintings by Baburen, Honthorst, Rubens, Blanchard, and Poussin. His work was highly valued by his contemporaries, mainly for his ability to convey painterly values, chiaroscuro above all, through the engravings. Bloemaert portrayed several princes and clergymen including Emperors Ferdinand III (for Kircher's *Egyptian Oedipus*, vol. 1) and Ferdinand IV; Antonio, Francesco, and Taddeo Barberini; and the two Dutch prelates Adriaen van Oorschot and Merten Conincx.[23] He also made the frontispieces of Kircher's *Pamphilian Obelisk* (1650) and *Egyptian Oedipus* (1652–55).

In 1655, both Kircher and Bloemaert were nearing the peak of their careers. Kircher recently had been made custodian of the officially founded museum of the Roman College, and he had published thirteen books with the help of his imperial and papal patrons; he had been relieved from his teaching duties to devote himself completely to his studies and expensive publications and to the construction of elaborate machines, partly on view in the museum. Bloemaert owned a house on the Via Capo le Case in Rome and had twelve Dutch assistants working for him.[24] The length of his biographies, as prepared by Sandrart and Baldinucci, bespeaks his high position in the Eternal City. He worked for various patrons and made "exquisite prints which he produced without interruption in almost infinite number."[25] It is quite probable that Kircher himself or his Jesuit superiors at the Roman College commissioned the portrait. Since Bloemaert had already made the frontispieces for two of Kircher's works and portrayed important people from Kircher's circle of patrons and clients, it would have been only natural to ask him to execute the portrait. Perhaps it was intended to be incorporated in the publication of the descriptions of machines in Kircher's museum. The print's unfinished state might then be linked to significant delays in the preparation of this publication, which was originally planned in expectation of the spectacular visit of the so-called Phoenix, the newly converted Queen Christina of Sweden. In October 1655, Kircher asked Lucas Holstenius, Vatican librarian, to provide financial support for this project. The grant was not given, a special publication on the museum appeared only in 1678, and Queen Christina instead received other emblematic presents at the conclusion of her visits to the museum in January 1656. Kircher's disciple Kaspar Schott worked on the planned publication while staying with Kircher in Rome from 1652 to 1655. Schott's *Hydraulic-Pneumatic Mechanics* (1657) consists of an exhaustive description of the hydraulic and pneumatic machines found in Kircher's museum. In the preface to this work, he announces the imminent publication of the museum's catalogue.[26]

The 1664 elaboration of Kircher's portrait[27] adds a subtitle to the picture, which has been given an oval format (Figure 4.1). The keyhole perspective into

Figure 4.1. Cornelis Bloemaert II, *Portrait of Athanasius Kircher*, 1664/1678. *Source:* Giorgio de Sepibus, *Romani Collegii Musaeum Celeberrimum*, p. 1. Courtesy of Stanford University Libraries, Stanford.

the fictive space vaguely recalls a Roman tombstone monument with the figure in an alcove.[28] Underneath the oval is a pedestal to which is attached a piece of paper bearing an inscription. It reads: "Be it painter or poet, both will say in vain: it is he. The world of the antipodes knows his *face* as well as his *name*. James Alban Gibbes, Professor of Rhetoric in Rome" (my emphasis). This inscription refers to the well-known *paragone* between the painter and the poet, crucial for early modern art theory. It may also suggest a wide distribution of this etching (from one antipode of the world to the other) and perhaps refers to the magnetic poles of the antipodes, and thereby to the central role of magnetism in Kircher's natural philosophy. Kircher regarded magnetic attraction and repulsion as the *lingua franca* of all creation. But above all the inscription explicitly links the two issues with which I am concerned in this essay: portrait (face) and name. The 1664 engraving contains other novel elaborations. A shelf with books is pictured to Kircher's left, and an artfully gathered curtain appears in the back of the room, seen to his right and above his head, which lends the subject a certain dignity (as in the painting at Ingolstadt, discussed later on). These additions provide the viewer with the calm and sober scholarly context of the bedroom (*cubiculum*) as the room for study, as well as with the spectacular, courtly context of theater and representation linked to Kircher's museum. This etching later served as the model for many painted, drawn, or engraved portraits of Kircher, found today in various libraries, museum archives, and private collections.[29]

"I Have Kissed It Two and Three Times"

The humanistic tradition of scholars and poets sending epitaphs to friends developed in Germany at the beginning of the sixteenth century with Hans Burgkmair's aforementioned etching of Conrad Celtis, the so-called Sterbebild (1508), whose iconography was still very close to the Roman tombstone portrait. This tradition transformed into the habit among scholars of sending and exchanging not only epitaphs but also printed portraits. During the sixteenth century, woodcuts and engravings of famous scholars like Erasmus or Melanchthon increasingly became part of the stock-in-trade of print sellers, joining the more traditional images of miracles and saints, and leaflets describing monstrous births.

In 1611, Johann Reinhard Ziegler, publisher of Chistoph Clavius's complete works, wrote to one of Clavius's assitants in Rome to discuss the publication of the first volume: "To honor Father Clavius, he [the bishop of Bamberg] is taking care to ornament the front of the work with an engraved title page at his expense. He even wishes for the likeness of Father Clavius that has been circulating in Germany to be reprinted. If it is not a good representation, be patient, as the book itself will certainly express the mind."[30] The letter suggests that the portrait circulated in Germany, possibly in exchange for other portraits. The last sentence might express not only doubt about the aesthetic quality of the image, but also the aforementioned ancient skeptical commonplace concerning portraits of scholars in general.

Few sources discuss the reasons for requesting an engraved portrait or portrait medal.[31] Perhaps the reasons were felt to be self-evident. But the reasons for sending them were quite explicit, as we will see. Kircher gave the unpublished and unfinished portrait of 1655 to his publisher Joannes Jansson van Waesberghe, who had a new engraving prepared from it,[32] first published in 1665. In 1661, Jansson secured exclusive publishing rights to Kircher's works in the Holy Roman Empire, England, and the Low Countries. The 1664 engraving was printed in publications such as Subterranean World (1665),[33] China Illustrated (1667), and Museum of the Roman College (1678):[34] Kircher's "face and name" stood for Rome, caput mundi, and the museum; they functioned as a mirror of the outside world that was to be distributed not only far away (China) but also deep into the (subterranean) world. The portrait was eventually printed on fly sheets (loose or bound into printed works) listing Kircher's available publications. As such, the 1664 print would have served an important role in Jansson's efforts to turn his author into a marketable commodity.[35]

Only ten weeks after Kircher's birthday in 1655, the portrait was received at Mainz by Schott, who answered: "I have kissed it two and three times, but even more I would have wished to do with Your Reverence that which Cardinal Brancacci and Monsignor Beutinger have done." Unfortunately, we can only speculate what activity that was. Schott hoped that Kircher would send more copies of his portrait "because a lot of people want to have it, and I would like to give it to several Signori and Princes."[36] Schott may have used it as a present, together with presentation copies of his and Kircher's books. He tried to promote Kircher's affairs as well as his own, especially with the elector archbishop of Mainz and bishop of Würzburg, Johann Philipp von Schönborn (who had called Schott to Würzburg).[37] The engraving served to initiate discussions among important people regarding Kircher and his books.[38] It was also part of an intricate system of exchange: Four years later, in March 1659, Schott wrote from Würzburg to Rome, describing the return of a promised *effigies*.[39] He had wanted to give it to the prince-abbot of Fulda, Joachim of Gravenegg, together with some books by Kircher, who had written to Gravenegg the previous month,[40] hoping for financial support of his expensive *Egyptian Oedipus* (1652–55)—Syntagma VIII in the third volume was dedicated to Gravenegg. Shortly before Schott received Kircher's portrait intended for the prince-abbot, Gravenegg answered Kircher's letter from February, sending no money but only an engraving of his likeness.[41] In the summer of 1659, Schott finally gained an audience with Gravenegg: he reported that the prince-abbot was now interested in Kircher's works and posed many questions.[42] Schott in turn dedicated his edition of Kircher's *Ecstatic Journey* (1660) to the prince-abbot.

The portrait accompanied not only books but also other gifts, such as natural objects, medicaments, delicacies, and manuscripts. In March 1666, for example, Kircher sent the 1655 engraving with his manuscript of the Gospels written in Syriac in 945—"which is more dear and precious to me than any other thing"— to Duke August the Younger of Brunswick-Lüneburg (1579–1666), "as an ornament of his most famous library."[43] In July 1666, three coins, specimens of a new minting from the ducal mines, arrived in Rome, accompanied by August's portrait, the second one sent to Kircher. As John Fletcher writes: "Fa. G. P. Oliva [current General of the Society of Jesus], overwhelmed by August's exemplary likeness, has taken one of the coins away to show to his frequent visitors. The cardinal-landgrave Friedrich of Hesse-Darmstadt, in whose conversion (1637) Kircher claimed to have been instrumental, had similarly carried off the portrait of August, boasting of the German blood he shared with the duke."[44] As part of an earlier strategy to gain the duke's patronage, in 1656, Kircher had already asked for a likeness of the duke to hang in his portrait gallery.[45] It seems that Kircher perceived the value that hanging the portrait in his gallery would have in the eyes of the duke, and the logical *contrassegno* after its late arrival in 1659 was a letter describing the framing of the engraving in gold and its good placement among all the illustrious princes and popes.

Visitors of Kircher and the museum, on the other hand, often received asbestos stones or Kircher's portrait as a gift.[46] The identification of Kircher with his museum, called the *Musaeum Kircherianum* in contemporary correspondences and travel accounts, made such a gift a logical consequence.

Although the sources found so far are relatively few, I suggest that the circulation of portraits played an important role in the competition for patronage. Kircher sent his portrait to people abroad and gave it to his visitors in Rome. His "currency of fame" (*Scher*) worked on two levels: the circulation of words (books and letters) and of images (illustrations, emblems, and portraits). The circulation of the latter placed Kircher's image "out there" in the world, just as the images of people from "out there" in the world hung in Kircher's gallery.

The Image of Kircher: Painted Portraits

Most of the printed, painted, or drawn portraits of Kircher after the engraving of 1664 refer in one way or another to this original image as their principal source. This claim is substantiated by two of the three known paintings of Father Kircher made in 17th and 18th centuries. Today these are found in the storerooms of the Galleria Nazionale di Arte Antica in Rome, in the priests' seminary at Fulda, and in the Stadtmuseum of Ingolstadt (the only one currently on view).

The oil painting on panel from the Galleria Nazionale di Arte Antica in Rome, on view recently in the Roman exhibition "Il Museo del Mondo," is the only portrait of Kircher that decidedly differs from Bloemaert's etching[47] (Figure 4.2). It was previously shown in the 1930 exhibition "Roma Secentesca," whose catalogue still gave "Museo Kircheriano" as the provenance of this work,[48] supporting the hypothesis that it was commissioned by Kircher's superiors or himself. Sabina Carbonara judges the anonymous work to be Flemish on account of its strong realism.[49] Allowing for the fact that the current state of the panel is not very good, and that the original colors might have been more vivid, I would nonetheless judge the brownish colors to be discreet and modest in comparison with the two other paintings. Apart from the scarves (on the head, beneath the *berretta*) hanging down on either side of the face, the clothes are the same as in the engravings. Like the others, it is a half-length portrait. In this version, however, his face is beardless, and the bulbous nose and the asymmetry of the eyes—its "strong realism" (Carbonara)—cause the painting to appear much more intimate and personal, less official, than the two other paintings. Perhaps this reflects the post-Tridentine expectation, formulated most extensively by Gabriele Paleotti, that portraits—all too often narcissistic exercises in unchristian self-aggrandizement—should depict the sitter with a radical realism.[50] In contrast, art critics

Figure 4.2. Anonymous, *Portrait of Athanasius Kircher*, second half of seventeenth century. *Source:* Courtesy of Galleria Nazionale di Arte Antica, Rome.

writing from the academic perspective that was predominant up to the end of the seventeenth century judged the realistic portrait to be much inferior to the idealized portrait.[51] Despite its intimate character, or maybe precisely because of its representation of the individual "character" that was so prized in most portrait galleries, I would not exclude the possibility that this portrait hung in the portrait gallery of the museum. The spirituality that this kind of memorial portrait was supposed to convey, due to its realism, gives me further reason to think it may have hung in the gallery.[52] It is not mentioned in the 1678 catalogue, but Kircher rarely missed an opportunity for self-promotion, making it quite likely that some such portrait was included in his gallery. Again, the provenance in the 1930 catalogue suggests this possibility. "Father Athanasius Kircher has augmented"[53] reads the interesting and somewhat strange inscription at the bottom of the painting. Does this refer simply to the size of the painting (65 × 50 cm), or to Kircher as an "augmented person" in the sense of a person that became quite famous, with reference also to the other illustrious portraits in the gallery?

A large, intensely colored eighteenth-century painting of Kircher is now in the Hrabanus Maurus Hall of the priests' seminary at Fulda[54] (Figure 4.3). Kircher had attended the Jesuit school at Fulda from 1612 to 1618. The commemorative painting was made before 1756 as part of a series of twenty-four portraits ordered by the Jesuits, most of them executed by Johann Andreas

Figure 4.3. Emanuel Wohlhaubter, *Portrait of Athanasius Kircher*, before 1773. *Source:* Courtesy of Erich Gutberlet, Großenlüder.

Herrlein (1723–96), court painter at Fulda, or by his workshop. Popes, students of some importance for the college and the papal seminary, as well as saints and scholars of the Jesuit Order were portrayed.[55] Most of these paintings come from the Jesuit college and the papal seminary (today, the Vonderau Museum), but the provenance of the Kircher portrait is not certain. It was painted by Emanuel Wohlhaubter, Herrlein's predecessor as court painter.[56]

In the painting the Jesuit is shown almost at full-length, sitting on an armchair at a table, turning slightly to his right. The palette of colors includes very clear and intense greens (the back of chair, the tablecloth on the smaller table), blue and red (the *berretta*, the *mozzetta*,[57] the larger tablecloth, the vision of Christ), deep black (the *mantello*), and gold and silver tones, in contrast to the dark brown tones of the previously discussed painting.[58] A large sheet of paper with two drawings of an obelisk is lying on the table, probably a sketch for the large engraved folding tables included in the lavishly illustrated folio work the *Egyptian Oedipus*. In addition, we see, from back to front, an armillary sphere, an inkpot with a quill, a closed book, and two rulers. The last three objects are lying on the sheet, suggesting a working environment. In his left hand Kircher holds a slightly open compass. The right arm sits on the arm of the chair; his bearded face and eyes are turned toward the viewer. To his right is a small table with a dark green cloth, covered with five books. Of the three standing books, two spines are legible: the *Great Art of Light and Shadow* and the *Tower of*

Babel, books that relate to Kircher's profession as a mathematician.[59] The architectural background of the painting is not clear. On the left side we recognize either a visionary scene or a painting of that scene, probably intended to be a fresco because it is framed only at its bottom. Since the upper and right sections of the painting are cut off, we can see only the bottom-left part with gray clouds and sky, red and blue parts of a cloth around a person's legs, a hand with a yellow stick pointing (along an imaginary line) to the armillary sphere, Kircher, and the books on the small table to Kircher's right. According to Erwin Sturm the subject depicted is a vision of Christ.[60] On the left side we see the suggestion of a window with a gray windowsill, opening toward a square with an obelisk with a surrounding fence, rising steps, and the church of Saint Peter in the background. The Vatican obelisk was first encountered by young Kircher during his tertianship in Speyer in 1628, in Herwart von Hohenburg's work on hieroglyphics. It marked the beginning of Kircher's hieroglyphic studies, which culminated in the *Egyptian Oedipus* referred to by the drawings on the table.[61]

This painting, made almost a century after the scholar's death, is the only portrait representing Kircher as a mathematician. It features key topics of his studies, set in a space that commemorates his achievements: single items, such as the drawn and painted obelisks, the two identifiable books, and Saint Peter's function as a kind of optical mnemonic device to future students and visitors of the Jesuit college at Fulda.[62] The representation of the vision of Christ as the prime inspiration for each Jesuit seems crucial and is reaffirmed by the blue and red colors with which Christ, Kircher, and the cloth on the desk are depicted: Kircher's achievements (following a notion commonly applied to individual Jesuits as well as to the Society as a whole) were only possible with the help of Christ. Christ speaks through the works and resulting books of his obedient disciple, Kircher, whose autobiography is typically full of visions. This idea is familiar from the illustrations accompanying many Jesuit publications, in which divine hands work with depicted instruments, guide a princely hand with a scepter,[63] or simply symbolize divine inspiration, as is probably the case here.

The largest of the three paintings discussed here[64] belongs to the Ludwig Maximilian University Archive in Munich[65] and has been on view at the Stadtmuseum of Ingolstadt since 1992 (Figure 4.4). It is part of a series of four portraits of Jesuit astronomers made around 1730 by the Bavarian painter Christoph Thomas Scheffler (1699–1756). From 1719 to 1722, Scheffler worked as a journeyman for Cosmas Damian Asam. Afterward he joined the Society of Jesus and left again in 1725, which is likely the year in which the portraits were realized. The "double bass images" (framed in the form of a double bass) portrayed Kircher, Christoph Scheiner (1575–1650), Christoph Clavius (1537/38–1612), and Johann Baptist Cysat (1586–1657). Ingolstadt, as the domain of Scheiner and Cysat, and Rome, as the domain of Kircher and Clavius, faced

Figure 4.4. Christoph Thomas Scheffler, *Bassgeigenbilder*, 1725. Series of four portraits of Athanasius Kircher, Christoph Scheiner, Christoph Clavius, and Johann Baptist Cysat. *Source:* Stadtmuseum Ingolstadt. Courtesy of Ludwig Maximilian University Archive, Munich.

each other from the corners of the ceiling in the baroque Orban Hall of the Jesuit college.[66] This hall was erected around 1725 to house the large encyclopedic collection, focusing on instruments and paintings, gathered by Father Ferdinand Orban, S. J. (1655–1732).[67] Orban was professor of mathematics at Innsbruck and court preacher at various places, ultimately at Ingolstadt. Orban had repeated troubles with the Society due to disobedience and failure to observe his vow of poverty. Not only did his collection elicit criticism because "he showed it to noble women in his *cubiculum* for an hour or longer,"[68] but his very possession of the collection was deemed a violation of the vow of poverty: by an order of the General of 8 September 1708, the collection was declared the property of the college and no longer owned by Orban, who was demoted to the position of curator.

It is interesting to note the parallels to Kircher's museum: Orban's collection started as a mathematical museum[69] and received its objects mainly from Jesuit missionaries and noblemen. Its classificatory system was broadly modeled on the second catalogue of the *Musaeum Kircherianum*, published by Filippo Bonanni in 1709. Zacharias Conrad von Uffenbach's 1710 description of the collection states: "Indeed he is a regular Father Kircher, which [opinion] pleased him very much when I told it to him."[70]

The decorative program for the vault of the hall—consisting of stucco (in the form of a double bass and four-leaf clover), fresco, and oil paintings—was intended to integrate the collection within the unifying system of heaven and earth. Unfortunately, only the stucco and the four "double bass images" have survived. Placed above the astronomical sky with stucco reliefs of the sun, the moon, and the zodiac were once three large frescoes in the center (known to us only from preparatory sketches from around 1740), conceptualizing step-by-step the hierarchical worldview, made up of the four elements, the glorification of the arts and sciences, the allegory of theology, and the reigning wisdom of God (*Sapientia Dei*). Additionally, images of the four continents in the form of a four-leaf clover were also planned for placement around the central fresco of the allegories. They would have formed a parallel to the "double bass images."

In the painting of Kircher, the Jesuit is represented as a scholar in his stage-like study, distanced from the viewer through the device of a wooden pedestal, as in the other paintings from the series (Figure 4.5). All four paintings feature a low viewpoint, which would have looked quite natural when the paintings were *in situ*, but in their current setting, this effect causes the portraits to seem monumental and remote. The Jesuit is seated in the center of the painting, wearing (as in the other paintings of the series) the familiar outfit of the *mantello* and *berretta*, this time all black. His body inclines toward the viewer with arms extended. The chair is armless, adding to the immediacy of his presentation. To his left is a table with an inkpot and an open copy of his *Subterranean World* showing an image of Vesuvius ("Typus Montis Vesuvii" reads the text facing an image of lava streams) held and presented to the viewer by Kircher, while his other hand points with a quill to the same book opened on another page showing Mount Aetna erupting and the text "Typus Montis Aetna, ab authore observa(ti) A.o 1637" on the opposite page. A globe, a standard object in representations of the study, sits at the bottom of the painting in front of the table. To his right we see several large folios, placed on two levels. The one Kircher is pointing to, placed on the lower level, is propped open by another book and by the back of his chair. Some spines of other folios are legible: "Musurgia, Ars combinatoria, Musaeum, Ars Lucis et Umbrae, Mundus Subterraneus." On the wooden step of this stage, erected for Kircher and his books and objects, we further recognize single sheets featuring a combinatorial table

Figure 4.5. Christoph Thomas Scheffler, *Portrait of Athanasius Kircher*, 1725. *Source:* Stadtmuseum Ingolstadt. Courtesy of Ludwig Maximilian University Archive, Munich.

and, possibly, fossils, as well as a telescope in the background. The lower-right section of a landscape painting is recognizable on the wall in the background. Interspersed among the lower row of books, natural specimens are displayed, depicted in the manner of still lives: a tree of coral and grasslike plants, or perhaps the legs of birds. Above his head is a red gathered curtain, as in two other portraits from the series, emphasizing the scene's stagelike appearance. The colors are brown, beige, red, and black.

This painting employs the familiar iconographic devices of Saint Jerome in his study transferred here to a stage, which is not unusual in the iconography of this saint. As part of the decorative program for the vault of the museum (the Orban Hall)—a universal theater of the world reigned by the *Sapientia Dei*—the four portraits exemplify the astronomical endeavors of the Jesuits. Each of the four scholars is shown seated at a table in a baroque studio—with the emphasis on books (Kircher), instruments (Scheiner), the cross (Cysat), or specific commemorative objects (Clavius). This is the only known painting of Kircher as a scholar and—secondarily, since the objects are somewhat in the background—collector. We see Kircher in his "museum" in the contemporary meaning of the term, as defined for example in the standard compendium of museums, Caspar Neicklius's *Museographia* (1727): "a room for study containing books belonging to literature or erudition as well as various curious things."[71] The reference to the museum, made by the representation of natural specimens and the catalogue of the collection (*Musaeum*), functions as an exemplum of the museum of Father Orban, located in the hall underneath.

The paintings offer three distinct pictures of the Jesuit: one rather intimate and "realistic," one of the Jesuit mathematical practitioner, and one of the scholar and collector in his study, self-consciously presenting his written works. There were surely other painted portraits of Kircher, both contemporary[72] and posthumous, executed for portrait galleries in particular. Stanislaus Koprowski is known to have had a portrait of Kircher in Kraków; Ferenc Nadasdy had one painted and hung in one of his Hungarian castles.[73] Most of them are probably lost today.

Names and Faces on the Walls

The circulation and exchange of portraits, as well as their purposeful collection and presentation in a fixed place, gave rise to a widespread phenomenon in the sixteenth and seventeenth centuries: the portrait gallery. There were galleries of oil paintings or etchings, sometimes removed from portrait-books,[74] and galleries of mixed genre, such as was probably Kircher's. Standards of size, media, and aesthetic quality varied greatly. Such portraits almost always had dubious claims to authenticity, but despite the recurring refrain of "true likeness" associated with such galleries and with portrait-books, their ability to realize this goal varied greatly from case to case. Sources were not always specified and the opportunities for fraud were plentiful, as we see in the case of the London printer-publisher Peter Stent, who saw fit to use the copy of a Rembrandt etching of the artist's father as a portrait of Thomas More.[75]

The history of such galleries starts with Pliny the Elder and Vitruvius,[76] both of whom related the ancient habit of hanging portraits of relatives or famous personalities in libraries. The most famous examples in medieval and early modern times might be the row of busts in the Captioline Museum in Rome, the gallery of twenty-one busts of the Gonzaga family in the Palazzo Ducale of Sabbioneta near Mantua, and the Munich Antiquarium. Oil and fresco portraits were also realized in municipal halls, palaces, villas, castles, churches, and studies.[77] Federico da Montefeltro (1422–82), ruler of Urbino, displayed personally selected portraits of people worthy of emulation[78]— ranging from Moses to the contemporary Pope Sixtus IV—in his *studiolo* at the Urbino palace. His own portrait, of course, also appeared as a "true likeness." These portraits remained *in situ* until 1631, and all are extant today. They were painted in oil on panel and featured personalized Latin inscriptions at the bottom. Later on, woodblocks based on some of them circulated. To achieve these "true likenesses," Federico, much as Giovio would do some fifty years later, used models in fresco or oil, portrait medals, or manuscript miniatures. But by far the most famous collection, featuring around four hundred painted portraits, was that of Paolo Giovio, begun in 1521 and displayed from 1537 on in his villa near Como,[79] which was built expressly for that purpose.[80] Giovio engaged artists to make copies for his gallery, "truly taken" from the originals,[81] *in situ* or acquired from his powerful friends. The copies were to conform to a standard height of one and a half feet. Once the copies were realized to his specifications, the originals no longer interested him.[82] Biographical notes accompanied the paintings on the walls, affixed on pieces of paper beneath each painting, which were also published.[83] Giovio's museum spawned many others, stocked with copies of the copies.[84] Between 1578 and 1590, Archduke Ferdinand of Tyrol completed work on his painted portrait gallery at Ambras, a collection that only came to be exhibited after 1770.[85] The acquisition of these portraits was better organized and standardized than the process by which Giovio realized his collection. The archduke included a sample of the small, standardized size he had in mind for the images in his petitions to princes and in his instructions to his agents. After their arrival in Ambras, the oil-on-paper images were stretched on small wooden surfaces.

Such standardization was rather unusual at that time and depended of course on extensive financial resources. Kircher's gallery, by contrast, appears to have been a secondary effect of his solicitations for favor. The hanging of the portraits was probably done with minimal regard to size, media, artist, and aesthetic quality. The crown jewel of such galleries was that of Kircher's first patron and broker, the wealthy aristocrat, counselor of the Parliament of Aix, polyhistor, collector, and all-around *virtuoso* of the republic of letters, Nicolas-Claude Fabri de Peiresc (1580–1637).[86] "The collection," writes David Jaffé, "remains exceptional in not being another fashionable replica of the seminal 'famous men' portrait collection of the sixteenth-century historian, Paolo Giovio."[87] It was rather "an iconographical representation of a social reality: the nexus of patronage relations that governed French and European society."[88] He presented around eighty painted portraits, "old portraits" and "particular friends."[89] Among those portrayed in his study at Aix were Peiresc's teacher, the humanist Giovan Vincenzo Pinelli; the Dutch philosopher and polyhistor Hugo Grotius; the philologist Joseph Scaliger; the painter Pieter Paul Rubens; Cardinal Francesco Barberini, his secretary Cassiano dal Pozzo, as well as his librarian Lucas Holstenius; and Pope Urban VIII. Peiresc exchanged portraits with, among others, dal Pozzo and Pierre and Jacques Dupuy, royal librarians and custodians of the circle of correspondents known as the *Academia Puteana* in Paris. His list of portraits offered to the Dupuys in 1624 included names of the artists, indicating a rather unusual interest in artistic quality. This collection served as an exemplary model for Kircher's gallery of portraits. Likewise, Peiresc's gift of chests of books and manuscripts in the 1630s as well as "all his Egyptian Rarities" sent to Rome contributed materially to the basis of the vast encyclopedic collection that Kircher gathered over the following decades.[90]

Significantly, the first chapter of the very late catalogue of Kircher's museum—offering a description and summary of the museum's highlights—begins with the subject of portraits: the first chapter commences with a description of the entrance gate, decorated with bas-reliefs of Popes Alexander VII, Clement IX, and Clement X.[91] Later in this chapter, a very short passage describes some of the actual portraits, namely those of the house of Habsburg. If we can trust Sepibus's description, these were displayed throughout the *atrium*. The living representative of the Habsburgs, Leopold I, is described as present *in effigie* and therefore deeply inscribed in memory. It seems that the verbal presentation was more impressive than the portrait itself, an observation probably also true of the museum as a whole. As far as I know, there is no travel account that specifically discusses the gallery of portraits, which at that time was a standard part of any scholar's collection.[92]

Another passage (in chapter 4) begins with a general description of the situation of the gallery, stating that pictures and paintings (not only the portraits) covered almost every spot on the walls like a tapestry. The chapter separates the 123 various paintings or pictures (*variae picturae*) from the portraits (*effigies*), possibly suggesting a separate hanging of these two classes. The list of the people portrayed (more or less the only information provided) includes first the aforementioned popes (plus Urban VIII and Innocence X) and the Habsburg emperors (Ferdinand II and III, and Leopold I, as well as Archduke Leopold).[93] It continues with the "important" kings and princes (among them Phillip IV of Spain, Louis XIV, Queen "Christina Alexandra" of Sweden, Margherita of Austria, Grand Duke Ferdinando de Medici, Duke August of Brunswick-Lüneburg, and his son Albert) and individual scholars and missionaries (among them Christoph Clavius, "extraordinary mathematician", Adam Schall, and Giuseppe Ancieta). All portraits were sent as "a particular testimony of affection" for Kircher. For Kircher and Peiresc the panopticon mirrored first and foremost their nexus of patronage relations. The hanging probably varied with new papacies and possibly with future, new, or lost patrons. When, for example, John Bargrave (1610–80)—English virtuoso, canon of Canterbury, and traveler, whose collection is still kept in the Canterbury cathedral—visited the Medici gallery in Florence during his Grand Tour, he committed a faux pas, saying that the new picture of Cromwell, now "hung amongst the heroes," "spoyled all the rest." The reaction of the Grand Duke is related as follows: "At which he stopped, and did not know how to take it; but, at length, said he, 'On occasion it is as easily taken down as it was hanged up.'"[94]

The portraits were signs of honor not only for the museum and the Roman College but especially for Kircher himself: "I beg you to thank His Highness much for the portrait (*Abcontrafeyung*) by which you paid tribute to me, my museum, as well as my own person"[95] reads his response, after finally receiving the portrait of duke August of Brunswick-Lüneburg in 1659. His ambitions seem to have exceeded his financial means: "And if the expense were not so great, I would make the whole German Nation into a name: but I must cut my coat according to my cloth."[96] The importance of names with reference to images, made explicit in Gibbes's inscription for the 1664 engraved portrait of Kircher, seems to be confirmed by this formulation (to make somebody a name by hanging his portrait on the wall). Many of the optical experiments shown in the museum also employed names (of popes and emperors). The modern viewer does not expect the name of the sitter to form an essential part of the portrait. Thus one can say that for the modern viewer, the image comes before the name, which is of secondary importance. For medieval and for many early modern viewers, it was the other way round: the name (sometimes incorporated in the canvas itself) came before the image. It is no coincidence that the recitation of the name in liturgy, which forms the basis of remembrance, stands at the official beginning of the museum in 1651: the donor of one of the foundations of the collection, the Roman senator Alfonso Donnini, asked to be named in prayers for his salvation in the daily mass of the Jesuits.[97] Many of Kircher's correspondents were delighted to consider him the very embodiment of immortality, which derived to a great extent from his Christian name. Kircher was named for Saint Athanasius, the Greek Church Father, upon whose feast day he was born. Florid, more or less flattering epigrams, distichs, and puns exploited this play upon his name.[98]

According to his autobiography, published posthumously in 1684, Kircher had several visions during his life, signs from heaven revealing him to be a "chosen disciple" and often warnings of danger. The *Musaeum Kircherianum* was a place of learned conversation and illustrious spectacle intended to "convert" in the broadest sense of the term. The instruments used were optical, acoustic, and magnetic experiments that initially confused and amazed, and subsequently—in theory—"illuminated" and converted. The Jesuit Wilhelm of Gumpenberg explained the vision of Saint Eustachius in terms of image-wonder: it was the image of the cross with Christ, not the cross itself, that converted him.[99] It is perhaps no coincidence that Kircher chose the church of Saint Eustachius in Mentorella, near Guadagnolo, for reconstruction and retirement. Image and name are the basis of Jesuit spirituality. For Jesuits, it was the salvation of souls (with the help of images and names) that counted in the end, and not "the delight of the souls" mentioned so often with reference to the real—rather than the ideal—museum and its marvelous machines.

Notes

*   Thanks to Daniel Stolzenberg for his commentaries and careful editing of the English.
1.   Müller 1577, fol. 2r: "Statuae profectò & Imagines ob id ipsum, quòd diu durant, praesentique inspectione non memoriam tantùm absentium refricare, sed et palingenesian quondam opticam defunctorum repraesentare videntur."
2.   Herzog August Bibliothek (hereafter **HAB**) BA 376; printed in Burckhardt 1744–46, p. 148. Cited (with correction of the middle part: "wolt ich der gantzen Teutschen Nation einen Nahmen machen") in Fletcher 1986, p. 285.
3.   Cited in Clough 1993, p. 198, my translation.

4. This was a common feature of these galleries. The portrait was understood as an indicator of character, and it is interesting to see that della Porta used Giovio's book for his reflections on physiognomy. See Haskell 1993, chapter 2: "Portraits from the Past."

5. The word comes from the Greek παλινγενεσια; in pure Latin, *iterata generatio*. See Heinrich 1892, vol. 2, col. 1444. It later became synonymous with resurrection in the biblical sense, a use we will come across later with reference to Kircher's museum, in the form of the "palingenetic experiment" and experiments with the magic lantern.

6. See, for example, Sepibus 1678, p. 39.

7. "My Gallery or Museum is visited by all the nations of the world, and a prince cannot become better known 'in this theatre of the world' than to have his likeness here" (Kircher to Anckel, 7 March 1659, cited in Findlen 1994, pp. 386–387).

8. Scholars of the Royal Society were rather interested in the possibility of a plant growing without sunlight. Those who saw Kircher's experiment, or attempted to replicate it according to his instructions, remained unconvinced and deeply disappointed. See Gorman 1999.

9. In the second half of the sixteenth century, portrait-books of popes and emperors became a phenomenon in the main publishing centers of western Europe. Plates from these books were frequently removed for framing by those who could not afford a gallery of oil portraits. Such portrait-books exploited the relationship deemed by humanists to exist between personality and facial characteristics. Technical developments of printing in the sixteenth and seventeenth centuries permitted the mass production of detailed likenesses of individuals, whose quality often surpassed the crude woodcut portraits of the fifteenth century. See Clough 1993.

10. According to Stephen Scher, "it was a mark of great favor to be given one" and "above all, the medal is a very personal object [. . .]. It commemorates, memorializes, glorifies, criticizes, or even satirizes its subject." Scher 1994, pp. 15, 19.

11. See Treu 1959, pp. 26–28. The medal, in turn, inspired the composition of several engraved likenesses. Erasmus himself requested additional copies of the medal from time to time, which he sent to his numerous friends and patrons.

12. See The Cleveland Museum of Art 1951, p. 11.

13. Studies on the circulation of books are numerous. See, e.g., Chartier 1987; Johns 1998. In contrast, I do not know of any on the circulation and use of images, portraits in particular.

14. See Rupprich 1956, vol. 1, p. 259, no. 36.

15. In the second half of the sixteenth century, the problematic manifested itself even more sharply in the "*Bildnisvitenbücher*" of the Protestant humanist tradition. In 1575, Peter Perna of Lucca published Giovio's *Brief Lives* in the Protestant city of Basle, including etchings by Tobias Stimmer. Here, scholars are portrayed in text and image as an intellectual and religious elite. For some people, especially in the Catholic regions, this manner of aggrandizing individuals went too far. In Zurich, for example, the Council decided in 1586 to limit the sales of portraits of scholars "to the bare essentials" on the familiar grounds that the real portrait lay in the scholar's writings. See Staatsarchiv Zurich, B.V., 28, fol. 385v, cited in Mertens 1997, p. 246n80.

16. The types of the scholar and the mathematician are related and sometimes overlap in their iconography, as Petra Kathke (1997) has shown with an emphasis on sixteenth-century portraiture.

17. To name only a few examples: the etched portrait of the Löwener astronomer and mathematician Reinerus Frisius Gemma by Jan van Stalburch (1557); and an unknown mathematician by Martino Rota (see Kathke 1997, figs. 11 and 12) or the 1646 etching of J. F. Nicéron (1613–46) in which the mathematician is sitting at a table with instruments and perspective drawings, with the facade of a church in the background. See Mortzfeld 1986–, vol. 17, A 15032.

18. Gorman 1998, p. 73n8. See Lucas 1993, p. 63; and De Dalmases 1943–1965, vol. 3, pp. 240–241.

19. See Casciato et al. 1986, fig. 79, for the image belonging to the Smithsonian Institution Libraries, Special Collections. The plate measures 19 × 14.5 cm. The subtitle reads: "P. Athanasius Kircherus Fuldensis ê Societ: Iesu Anno Aetatis LIII. Honoris et observantiae ergò sculpsit et D.D.C. Bloemaert Romae 2 Maij 1655."

20. See Kühn-Hattenhauer 1979, p. 116. This portrait of Clavius—the last in a series of portraits of clergymen including Cesare Baronius and Roberto Bellarmine—is among the first to transfer the monumentality of the paintings of scholars or clergymen in interior

settings to prints. Kühn-Hattenhauer finds a close parallel in painted portraits of popes, for example, those by Titian. Although Jesuit clothing as such was highly unstable, the *mantello* and the *berretta* were quite usual for non-missionaries, scholars and students in particular.

21. Older secondary literature, such as Le Blanc 1854, p. 378, and Williamson 1964, p. 147, claims that the portrait was executed after the design of his father, Abraham Bloemaert (1564–1658), which Bloemaert specialist Marcel Roethlisberger denies. See Roethlisberger 1993, vol. 1, p. 518n49.

22. Cited in Roethlisberger 1993, vol. 1, p. 517.

23. See Wurzbach 1906, vol. 1, p. 112, and Roethlisberger 1993, vol. 1, p. 518n50.

24. As Sandrart describes it: "He remained in Rome, accumulated much cash . . ."; Sandrart 1675, p. 362.

25. See Baldinucci 1845–47, vol. 4, p. 600.

26. See Schott, 1657, p. 3. For a new edition of that work, see Gorman and Wilding 2000. I am grateful to Michael John Gorman for this information.

27. This etching was offered in 1958 by the German antiquarian Diepenbroick for 30.- DM, which seems to be an average price with respect to its neighbors in the catalogue. See Diepenbroick-Grüter 1954–63, vol. 7: "Big and decorative portraits," no. 742, p. 19. It is perhaps worth mentioning that Kircher did not figure under "beautiful, rare and interesting portraits," which might be an index of its ready availability in the 1950s.

28. See the aforementioned *Sterbebild* for Conrad Celtis (1508). The iconographic relation to these kinds of epitaphs seems to me more convincing than the relation to the flat, two-dimensional portraits of the miniatures.

29. Among the series of portraits in the Vonderau Museum at Fulda, there are several copies, which vary little from the 1664 print. Inv. no. II Ec 95/4 by Johann Friedrich Schmidt (1730–85) of Nuremberg (see also Österreichische Nationalbibliothek Vienna [hereafter **ÖNB**] Pg 174.096: I [2b]); no. Ec 97/4 is the wrong-way-round version by Andreas Frölich (second half of the seventeenth century); no. II Ec 98/4 is a nineteenth-century lithograph for the German translation of Kircher's autobiography by Seng (1901); and no. II Ec 139/4 is a pen lithograph by Charles Paul Landon (1760–1826; see also ÖNB Pg 174.096:I [2a]). Singer 1931, pp. 22–23, gives eight portraits of Kircher, adding two engravings (ÖNB Pg 174.096:I [1a and b]) and a woodcut to the list here. One of the eighteenth-century catalogues of the *Musaeum Kircherianum* (Contucci 1763–65) gives another, altered, and non-smiling version of Bloemaerts etching on the front of the first volume. See Stolzenberg 2001a, p. 25. In the collection of portraits of the Clendering Library, University of Kansas, there is a drawing in red chalk. See Clendering@kumc.edu/dc/pc/kircher02.jpg for the picture. I exclude here all portraits in the wider sense, published in the frontispieces of compendia by Kircher's disciples such as Kestler 1680 or Petrucci 1677.

30. Johann Reinhard Ziegler to Paul Guldin, Mainz, 14 May 1611, cited in Gorman and Wilding 2000, p. 41.

31. An earlier document on that issue is Willibald Pirckheimer's explanation for his request of an engraving of Durer, namely the (visual) presentation of an absent person and the imagined meeting with other (engraved) friends. See Mertens 1997, p. 244. This imagined meeting became real on the visual level in the institution of the portrait gallery.

32. See City of Rastatt 1981, p. 3.

33. The engraving sometimes seems to reinforce the pupils, as here, but it seems to me to be a variation in the printing quality rather than an elaboration.

34. The last one with a new date and age in the text around the oval.

35. See Fletcher 1988b, p. 8 ff. Unfortunately, I have thus far found almost no information on this issue.

36. Schott to Kircher, Mainz, 15 July 1655, Archivio della Pontificia Università Gregoriana, Rome (hereafter **APUG**) MS. 567, fols. 47r–v, cited (as well as the previous quotation) in Gorman and Wilding 2000, p. 17, my translation.

37. See Gorman and Wilding 2000.

38. See, for example, the description of Schott's first visit to Schönborn. The portrait is not mentioned, but he probably would have presented it to Schönborn had he already received it. See note 36. The visit to Schönborn occurred two days previously.

39. Schott to Kircher, Würzburg, 9 March 1659, APUG MS. 561, fol. 279.
40. Kircher to Gravenegg, 1 February 1659, published in Fletcher 1982, pp. 93–94.
41. Gravenegg to Kircher, 18 March 1659; the engraving is APUG MS 562, fol. 177.
42. Schott to Kircher, Würzburg, 20 July 1659, APUG MS. 561, fol. 288.
43. HAB, MS. 3.1.300. Aug.fol. Two documents, a dedication and an excerpt of a letter, precede the text of the Gospels. The dedication is placed above the bookplate, which contains the engraved likeness of Kircher. The quotes are from the letter and the dedication.
44. Fletcher 1986, pp. 292–293. It is not clear whether the coins also carried August's likeness.
45. See Findlen 1994, pp. 386–387.
46. See Findlen 1994, p. 225.
47. Galleria Nazionale di Arte Antica, inv. 5003. It measures 65 × 50 cm.
48. Galassi Paluzzi 1930, p. 17, no. 69.
49. For the hypothesis on the client, see also her short text in Lo Sardo 2001, p. 292.
50. See Paleotti 1961, pp. 117–509, especially pp. 332 ff.
51. See Kathke 1997, p. 14. That judgment, compounded by the facts that the artist was (and is) anonymous and that the aesthetic quality is deemed rather mediocre, as well as Kircher's diminishing fame, ultimately resulted in the painting's disappearance into the junk rooms and depositories of the Roman College and the Galleria Nazionale.
52. See Pommier 1998, p. 192.
53. P. "Atha.Kircher.adauxit," coming from *ad-augere, auxi, auctus* = to augment.
54. This is the former benedictine abbey at the cathedral of Fulda. It measures 132 × 110 cm. On the reverse of the canvas, the cropped, preexisting painting of a group of praying Franciscan monks is still visible.
55. See Sturm 1982, pp. 19–25; and 1984, p. 220.
56. It was included in the late baroque library furnishings of the college and as such, following the suppression of the college in 1773, entered the hall of the priests' seminary. Framed by a carved, ornamental frame, it was included as *Supraporta* on the south wall of the hall. Its croppings on the top and both sides are therefore either from that time or even earlier when it was included among the library furnishings of the Jesuit college. Originally the hall served as the winter choir, with windows giving on the high choir of the dome, through which ill monks could observe the mass. Later on, it was called Savigny Library, Athanasius Kircher Hall, and today Hrabanus Maurus Hall or the exegetic seminary.
57. It is the only portrait of Kircher with the *mozzetta* that I know, maybe because so many popes in *mozzettas* are portrayed around him.
58. I do not mean to suggest by this remark that it was based upon that model. The Roman painting was quite likely unknown to Wohlhaubter.
59. Though largely concerned with biblical history and linguistics, the *Turris Babel* also discusses the engineering aspects of the construction of the Tower of Babel, and on this account, the artist may have associated it with Kircher's identity as a mathematician.
60. We sometimes find such framed window-like vistas with scenes from the life of the portrayed subject. One example is the Netherlandish portrait of Petrus Canisius at his worktable (first half of the seventeenth century), showing Canisius's vision of his blessed parents in heaven. See Baumstark 1997, p. 521.
61. It might also be the obelisk in the center of Piazza della Minerva, transferred by the artist to Saint Peter's Square. Kircher's expertise was used in the process of translation, erection, and inscription of that obelisk, supported by Gian Lorenzo Bernini's elephant. This is an idea suggested by Eugenio Lo Sardo. The fact that the book depicted right next to the obelisk is *Ars magna lucis et umbrae*, largely devoted to sundials, might, as Michael John Gorman has remarked, refer to the projects of meridians that Kircher suggested to Pope Alexander VII in the 1660s.
62. Through these simple devices, both Kircher and his merits are quickly conveyed. This is not a picture of a real room but a memorial space for a former, superficially known pupil of the college.
63. To cite only two of many examples, there is the engraved frontispiece of Christoph Scheiner's *Pantograph* (1631), and Bloemaert's engraving of Ferdinand III in Kircher 1652–55, vol. 1.
64. It measures 183 × 183 cm.

65. Since 1784, when the university trustees of Munich ordered "the better paintings" of the Orban Hall transferred from the University of Ingolstadt to Munich. See Bayerisches Hauptstaatsarchiv München (hereafter **BHM**) GL 1489, no. 2.
66. The *Litterae annuae* of 1732 compares the museum at Ingolstadt with the one in Rome in an enthusiastic obituary on Orban. See BHM, Jesuiten 125 (1732), Ingolstadt, pp. 2–4.
67. See Hofmann 1994.
68. See Duhr 1928, p. 346, cited in Krempel 1968, p. 169.
69. Gonzales, General of the Order at that time, referred to it in its early stage of 1696 as an "apparatus of mathematics" (Duhr 1928, p. 346, cited in Hofmann 1994, p. 662).
70. Uffenbach 1754, p. 733, cited in Krempel 1968, p. 170.
71. See Neicklius 1727, p. 6.
72. Brian Merrill (1989, p. v) claims that Nicolas Poussin painted a portrait of Kircher, who taught him the rules of perspective. It is not mentioned in the literature on Poussin, and I suspect it does not exist.
73. Koprowski to Kircher, Krakòv, 1 March 1664, APUG MS. 563, fol. 288. On Nadasdy, see Rozsa 1973.
74. See Clough 1993, p. 186.
75. See Haskell 1993, pp. 52–53 (with picture).
76. Pliny, *Natural History*, book 35, 6 and 7, and Vitruvius, *De Architectura*, VI, chapters 3 and 6. See also Boehm 1985, pp. 76, 257.
77. Francesco Petrarch had devised a program of illustrious Romans for the hall of the Palazzo of Francesco "Il Vecchio da Carara" at Padua (1367–79). Giotto had painted two separate cycles of famous men in the Castel Nouvo of Naples and the Ducal castle of Milan.
78. Sometimes these examples substituted for the princely ancestors, as Sigmund Jacob Apin advises in his 1728 manual regarding collections of portraits for emperors without genealogical trees or for non-noble citizens.
79. See Pavoni 1985; and Klinger 1991.
80. He thought it was situated above the ancient ruins of the villa of Pliny the Younger.
81. "Ritratti veri e fidelmente ricavati dall'originale" (1549), cited in Pavoni 1985, p. 114.
82. See Pavoni 1985, p. 114.
83. See Clough 1993, p. 198 (with sources). The concept derived from the classical inscriptions on portrait busts, which gave brief biographical details.
84. Notably the one built in the Palazzo Vecchio of Florence (Sala della Guardaroba) in the mid–sixteenth century by Grand Duke Cosimo de' Medici and the one created shortly after 1551 at Guastalla by Ippolita Gonzaga. For the dissemination of these "Giovian" collections in Europe from 1552 on (the date when Cosimo I de' Medici let the portraits of the *Museo Giovio* be copied by an artist at Como), see Prinz 1979, pp. 603–664, including an iconographic catalogue from A–Z for Cosimo's collection, consisting of 488 portraits. In 1579, the Habsburg emperor Ferdinand of Tyrol, whose portrait was also featured in Giovio's collection, wrote to Giovio's heirs requesting permission to make copies for his gallery. His artist worked on this project for some two years.
85. Before 1770, the approximately one thousand little likenesses of 13.5 × 10.5 cm were stored in chests of the Kunstkammer. Today they are on permanent view in a separate section of the Viennese Kunsthistorisches Museum, together with the medals (!).
86. See Jaffé 1988 and 1994; Sarasohn 1993.
87. Jaffé 1988, p. 138.
88. Sarasohn 1993, p. 70.
89. These two classes were also differentiated by size: the old portraits were smaller than Peiresc's lifesize representations of his friends. See Jaffé 1988, p. 138.
90. See Kircher 1650b, sig. c1r, and his Vita, published by Langenmantel 1684, p. 43. See Wilding 1998.
91. Sepibus 1678, fol. 1.
92. See Schnapper 1988, pp. 123–133.
93. "All pictures sent by high magnificences and maecenas of the arts to the true author of the museum" (Sepibus 1678, fol. 6).
94. Cited in Bann 1994, pp. 11–12.
95. Cited in Burckhardt 1744–46, vol. 2, p. 148. My translation.
96. See note 1.

97. He further wanted to be buried in a tomb in the new church of Saint Ignazio (designed by Orazio Grassi), which flanked the college, with the epitaph "Alfonso Donnini, Tuscan citizen awaits here his resurrection of the flesh." See APUG vol. 35, VII, e, fol. 2r.
98. See, for example, Harsdörffer to Kircher, Nuremberg, 7 April 1656, APUG MS. 557, fol. 262; and Leibniz to Kircher, Mainz, 16 May 1670, APUG MS 559, fol. 166.
99. See his *Atlas Marianus*, no. 772, p. 819.

The Sciences of Erudition

5

Copts and Scholars

Athanasius Kircher in Peiresc's Republic of Letters

PETER N. MILLER

It is customary to date the beginning of Coptic studies in Europe to publication of Athansius Kircher's *Coptic or Egyptian Forerunner* (*Prodromus Coptus sive Aegyptiacus*) in 1636.[1] This is untrue in two ways. First, Kircher was preceded by Peiresc—indeed, he was set on to this subject by the Provençal antiquary—who began his inquiries in 1628. Second, as the title of his book indicates, he was never interested in Coptic for its own sake.[2] As famous as Kircher has become, and as forgotten as Peiresc, it bears remembering that at the time the relationship was reversed. Only in the decades after the latter's death in 1637 did the pupil's fame seem to burnish the teacher's.[3]

I. Provence

It was the Paris Polyglot Bible project that stimulated the serious study of the languages and history of the ancient and modern Near East that dominated the last decade of Peiresc's life.[4] News that Jean Morin planned to publish the Samaritan Pentateuch belonging to the Oratory in Paris, and that a Samaritan Targum was in the possession of Pietro della Valle, in Rome triggered a series of letters from Peiresc to his Roman friend, Girolamo Aleandro, in the summer and fall of 1628. But soon their correspondence, and also Peiresc's first letters to della Valle himself, turned from Samaritan to "Egyptian."[5] The survival of communities of Samaritan speakers encouraged him to believe that pockets of "Egyptian" might also be found in out-of-the-way places, just as vestiges of ancient European tongues survived in the Basque country, Brittany, and Wales.[6] Peiresc's longtime interest in late antique magical gems had acquainted him with "those Greek sounds mixed into that Egyptian language," and his hope was that della Valle's Egyptian texts would help unravel their meaning.[7] While their correspondence in 1629 and 1630 was dominated by discussion of how best to transport della Valle's Samaritan manuscript to Rome, Peiresc continued to ask for the Coptic material as well—indeed, it is in a letter of March 1630 that he first uses this word instead of "Egyptian"—but was told firmly that none would be forthcoming until the just-loaned Samaritana was returned.[8]

Peiresc's authority was moral and intellectual. But he was in Provence, della Valle, with the manuscripts, in Rome. Peiresc could not have been very surprised to learn, in March 1630, that della Valle had decided to charge the Franciscan Tommaso Obicini (di Novaria) with the task of preparing his Coptica for publication.[9]

Peiresc's real response to della Valle was to assemble his own team to study Coptic, beginning with Samuel Petit of Nîmes, and his own collection of Coptic materials.[10] An outbreak of plague and an urban revolt in Aix severely disrupted Peiresc's correspondence in 1630 and 1631. When Peiresc next wrote to della Valle, in May 1632, he was under the impression—falsely, as it turned out—that Obicini had died, reviving Peiresc's own ambitions. He informed della Valle that he had friends who had already made great progress on Coptic studies among whom was "a new person, most skilled in all the oriental languages, of the German nation, named Rev. Father Athanasius Kircser, Jesuit." He was possessed of "an ancient manuscript by a Babylonian rabbi, who wrote a treatise in Arabic on the rules and manner of reading the hieroglyphic characters on Egyptian obelisks. In which there is inserted some words in the ancient Egyptian language, for which he had found the interpretation of some, but not all, and which he could perhaps supply with the help of your Coptic vocabulary, which is more complete than ours and of any other author."[11] This is the first mention of Kircher in Peiresc's correspondence (that I have found), and also the first mention of that curious manuscript by the "Babylonian rabbi" Barachias Nephi.[12] More telling for what came later is that Peiresc seems less excited about the existence of a supposed key to hieroglyphics—what most thrilled Kircher, of course—than he was about the Coptic words that happened to be used in this document.

As he built his collection of Coptica—the letter to della Valle mentioned the recovery of a papyrus book covered in hieroglyphic characters—Peiresc reminded Petit of its resemblance to the strange inscriptions on gnostic gems.[13] In October 1632, Peiresc gathered his thoughts on Coptic in another letter to Petit, a copy of which he preserved in his dossier on oriental studies under the filing title "COAEGYPTII/ COPTITES."[14] Two weeks later, again to Petit, Peiresc announced the arrival in Avignon of the Jesuit refugee from Würzburg with his prized manuscript.[15]

It was in the same letter to Petit of February 1633, in which Peiresc noted that he had obtained for Petit the Coptic materials that François-Auguste de Thou had brought back from Egypt, that he heralded the impending visit of "this fine German Father, whom I have written to you about," with his ancient key to hieroglyphics.[16] A month later the visit was foretold for Easter.[17] Peiresc excitedly urged his friend and collaborator, Gassendi, to bestir himself from Digne to meet Kircher.[18] Easter came and went without Kircher, though he did send ahead some of his "protheories."[19] A month later Peiresc was still waiting.[20] Kircher finally arrived in mid-May 1633 and stayed for a few days.

Peiresc's report of the meeting to Cardinal Francesco Barberini pointedly emphasized that della Valle's Coptic lexicon remained useful.[21] In mid-June Peiresc learned that Kircher would bring the Barachias with him as soon as his schedule permitted—after the summer.[22]

The summer of 1633 was a busy one for Peiresc—and a tumultuous one. In July he hosted the rabbi of Carpentras for at least several weeks, established a long-lasting working relationship with two Capuchin monks just returned from Egypt, Gilles de Loches and Césaire de Roscoff, and held an audience with his agent in Cairo, Jean Magy. Notes on the meeting with the Capuchins were preserved by Peiresc in a memoir labeled "TURCS. ABYSSINS,"[23] and those on the visit with Magy under the title "*1631.1632 INCENDIE SOUBSTERRAIN EN ARABIE, et AETHIOPIE.*"[24] Peiresc's efforts to arrange a meeting between Kircher and these knowledgeable orientalists, however, came to nothing.[25]

In August, Peiresc received from Kircher the crushing news of Galileo's condemnation and abjuration. The same letter contained a vicious anti-Jewish attack on another of Peiresc's friends, Rabbi Salomon Azubi of Carpentras.[26] Peiresc defended both men, and the outburst seems not to have damaged Kircher in Peiresc's eyes. Despite a heat wave that had forced even Peiresc from his cabinet, Kircher let it be known that his work on the Barachias continued apace.[27]

Kircher finally showed up, with his precious Barachias, on 3 September 1633. Peiresc left several accounts of the meeting, the most detailed a memoir drawn up for his own records.[28] He seemed to have sensed a fraud right from the start. Was it because Kircher refused to let him copy out anything "but a page from the last part" of the book? or because it began exactly as he thought did the text of Horapollon? or because it included material Peiresc recognized from Herwarth von Hohenburg's *Thesaurus Hieroglyphicum*? or because Kircher failed to compare his results with the account in Ammianus Marcellenius, which Peiresc had once before brought to his attention? "I showed him this," Peiresc wrote, "and in the end made [it] clear, although with great pain." Kircher "did not concede until he saw himself caught out in the change of portraits, whereby he had omitted the most legitimate and accurate to follow that which was totally opposite and incompatible with the manner and antiquity that this image ought to evoke." Ever the philosopher, Peiresc described the episode as yet another lesson in human nature, "in which there was much to wonder at, how the human spirit is so easily surprised, and how imposture is sometimes so powerful—by which he was greatly ashamed at the end."[29] Peiresc's disappointment must have been tremendous.

Kircher's reaction to the meeting was even more dramatic: he fled Provence for Rome, not informing his patron and colleague until it was too late to stop him, and without collecting the letters of recommendation that would have honored Peiresc in soliciting his protection.[30] Peiresc ended up sending the letters separately, with some embarassment, to della Valle, to Cardinal Francesco

Barberini, and to his secretary, Cassiano dal Pozzo.[31] In these letters, Peiresc praised Kircher's erudition and even hailed his skills as an interpreter of ancient Egypt. After all that had transpired how—and why—could he do this?

A first answer was given by Peiresc scarcely a month later in a letter to the Dupuy brothers. He had just received some Arabic historical and astronomical texts from Egypt that, he thought, were "likely interspersed with Egyptian words and phrases, as was the Barachias of Father Athanasius, and which cannot be deciphered without the aid of the language of the Copts."[32] In other words, while Kircher was mistaken in proclaiming it a key to hieroglyphics, it did have some value as an aid for the decipherment of Coptic.

II. Rome

Kircher's departure for Rome was something of a defection, as if jumping from one research team to its rival. Just as della Valle's earlier decision to convey his Coptic manuscripts to Obicini had spurred Peiresc to build up his own collection and develop local resources for the study of Coptic, Kircher's flight led Peiresc to seek out native informants, to develop a much closer working relationship with French Capuchin orientalists either still in Egypt or recently returned home, and to upgrade his relations with other European scholars, most notably Claude Saumaise. In the end, the native angle failed to deliver any signal success.[33] The most learned of the Capuchins, Gilles de Loches, protested an ignorance of Coptic,[34] though not before eventually supplying Peiresc with a Coptic alphabet that has been described as "probably the first modern work on Coptic."[35]

The turn to Saumaise proved much more fruitful. In a letter written to Peiresc in July of 1633, and probably received just at the time of Kircher's visit, Saumaise announced that he had been devoting himself to Coptic for some time and "discovered there some beautiful secrets!" Like Peiresc, he came to this material from the study of magical gems.[36] A few months later, he explained that he had already "made a lexicon of some three or four hundred words" and also fabricated a rough-and-ready grammar. With more help he promised further successes in cracking the language of those inscriptions, with their mix of Greek, Coptic, "and sometimes even Syriac or Chaldaic words, as you have remarked so well."[37] Help was precisely what Peiresc would provide him.

In a letter to Saumaise of November 1633, Peiresc explained that in addition to his own experience with gnostic gems and news of della Valle's find, a third push to study Coptic was given him by "an Arabic manuscript by a Rabbi, Barrachias Nephi of Babylon, who put together a treatise on the hieroglyphic mysteries of the Egyptians, in which he interprets many figures, and gives diverse alphabets, that include some of these [Coptic] characters." But he could say little more than this because "I never could obtain the communication nor the copy of even one page, however often he [Kircher] testified to his good will."[38]

Information about Coptic materials in the libraries of Wadi Natrûn was relayed by Peiresc to his contacts in Egypt. In a memo to Jean-Baptiste Magy in

Marseille, the brother of Peiresc's chief agent in Cairo, Jean Magy, for whom it was probably intended, Peiresc gave instructions for the purchase of one such book.[39] In a separate annex destined for the eyes of Father Théophile Minuti only, then traveling on Peiresc's secret service in the Levant, he gave a particular command to seek out a volume of Arabic Church Councils said by de Loches to be at the monastery of Saint Macaire, for which he would pay up to thirty escus—the same amount he was prepared to spend on the original of the Ethiopic Book of Enoch, one of his most dearly sought after treasures.[40]

Despite these efforts Peiresc never gave up on Rome. He remained engaged with the key principals, della Valle and Kircher, and also with his most important Roman brokers, Cassiano dal Pozzo and Cardinal Francesco Barberini. In February 1634, for example, Peiresc turned back to della Valle, trying again to obtain his Coptic manuscripts even though the Parisians had still not returned his Samaritan Targum. Peiresc used both stick and carrot. He reminded della Valle that he "had since received and communicated up to five or six exemplars" of the Samaritan Pentateuch—as if della Valle's fame as the provider of a single Samaritan manuscript was a favor that could be rescinded if he now failed to share his Coptic ones—and that, in any event, the whole predicament with the Samaritan materials was the result of della Valle ignoring Peiresc's instructions about shipment. [41] But—now, the carrot—Peiresc also was willing to pledge as surety for the Coptic texts "my entire library and all the contents of my study, where is found some uncommon things" (*le obligo la mia bibliotheca intiera, et tutto lo studio mio, dove si trova qualche cosetta non commune*).[42] This was no small understatement, as Peiresc's collection was one of Europe's wonders.

We ought not to imagine that Peiresc was some unworldly monk who had to hold his nose all through this tortuous back-and-forth with della Valle. On the contrary, as a later letter to Saumaise makes clear, Peiresc, who after all as a humanist secretary at the court of Louis XIII had seen how politics worked up close, viewed negotiation as part of the hunt. "Since, being of the humor that I am, it seems that I find remedies easily enough in matters which seem very difficult, and entry into almost inaccessible places. If I happen to meet persons who wish to accommodate themselves to my sentiments, and who could secretly hold the addresses that I seek, having hardly encountered a greater obstacle than when one abandoned the chase," he would spare no effort.[43]

This time, however, Peiresc's efforts failed. He informed Petit at the end of March 1634 that della Valle had decided to consign the manuscript to Kircher.[44] But still he did not give up on Rome. Even as he pursued other possibilities, he kept writing to Cassiano dal Pozzo encouraging him to ask Cardinal Barberini not to burden Kircher with other projects, and to Kircher himself urging a similar self-control.[45] To better insulate Kircher against these demands, Peiresc even offered to assume the costs of publishing the Barachias to keep him free of any debt of obligation to Barberini.[46]

At the same time, Peiresc was not oblivious to Kircher's shortcomings as a scholar. As he shared with Saumaise in a letter of April 1634: "And not to hide anything from you, this sample led me to fear greatly that the work of the poor Barachias will be of little greater credibility than one had made us believe of it, and that these are but simple imagined conjectures of his time about the hieroglyphic figures that he sees, rather than a proper authentic tradition of the true manner of deciphering them."[47]

And yet, as if in the next breath, Peiresc offered another justification for continuing to work with Kircher rather than abandoning him to his Roman fantasies. "All the same," he continued, "since one must neglect nothing even though this author may not be able to give us a comprehensive knowledge of these mysteries, it would not be inconvenient if he had discovered to us some good thing, which he had almost done by conserving for us in writing some tradition of the idolatrous superstitions of these Indian or African peoples, who derive their origins from those of the Egyptians." The problem posed by the Barachias was the same as the much-mentioned gnostic gems: how to separate the practical magic from the historically valuable material—the ancient pagan beliefs—they also conserved.[48] A history of error—superstition, magic—could, therefore, still contain much information that was true. Kircher's Barachias might be flawed as a key to hieroglyphics and yet provide evidence about the place and time in which it was produced and, therefore, about Coptic.[49]

Indeed, even in July of 1634, Peiresc still considered Kircher as a member of his équipe. "There are today," he wrote to Gilles de Loches, "four or five very learned men amongst my friends who are working on this language of the Copts, and who have already made very excellent discoveries of its secrets and origins, principally of the primitive antiquity of Greek." Among them was "another of my friends, who is amongst the marvelously learned of this century, but who is not French, nor in the kingdom."[50]

Peiresc's handling of the Barachias manuscript illustrates his thoroughgoing historical approach—one that he shared with Saumaise but which was not shared with them by Kircher, whose real goal Peiresc justly characterized as "the sources of Egyptian philosophy" (le fonds de la philosophie Aegyptienne).[51] Their approach to Ethiopic diverged in the same way: Kircher joined several threads into a single sacred narrative, while Peiresc's questions teased them apart. For much of 1634 and 1635, Peiresc delved deeply into the relationship between Coptic and the languages of Upper Egypt and Ethiopia.[52] His explanatory model was drawn from what was known—or conjectured—about the relationship of European languages: confusions caused by "the migrations of peoples, the expulsion of the possessors of one land or town and its occupation by others; and then again sometimes the conquerors are content with domination and superiority rather than expulsion." All of these effects were most in evidence along frontiers, like that of France and Brittany, or France and Flanders, or Egypt and Ethiopia. As he explained to Saumaise, there were many modern parallels to the case of Coptic. "In our own times," he wrote, people seeking land had migrated to the back country of Provence from the Genoese Riviera, so that two languages were now conserved—the corrupted Genoese dialect, "which we call *figon*," and the "natural" vernacular, Provençal, with also some mixture between the two.[53] The very learned recipient of the letter found Peiresc's observations "extremely curious and very nice." [54]

Peiresc's comparative historical linguistics did have a theoretical backbone. After examining three Coptic Gospels that he had received from Egypt, he explained to Samuel Petit that he noticed something extraordinary in what amounted to the "preface" to Mark a statement that Saint Luke wrote his gospel in the city of Antioch in the twelfth year of the Emperor Claudius and the twentieth of the Ascension of Jesus Christ. "And this seems to me very much compatible," he concluded, "with true synchronism" (*compatible au vray synchronisme*).[55] Another letter, to the Capuchin Agathange de Vendôme in Egypt, mentioned the prefaces to his Coptic gospel "in which I find many good things to note for the true synchronism, and to conciliate the diverse opinions of the Fathers on this matter."[56] Comparative chronology à la Scaliger probably accounts for the term's origin; Peiresc, like his friend and collaborator John Selden, developed it into a term of art for antiquaries.[57]

III. *Prodromus*

A letter from Kircher written on 8 February 1635 mentioned to Peiresc the existence of a "Prodromus Coptus-Aegyptiacus." This manuscript, preserved in Peiresc's papers, constitutes the nucleus of what later became the *Prodromus Coptus*.[58] After so many discussions, one would have thought that its arrival would have been a cause for celebration, or at least comment. But Peiresc's long reply of 30 March, despite being very much concerned with Coptic matters, focuses on the old familiar theme: Kircher's work habits. Nor does the presentation copy bear the mark of intensive handling. Failure to debate the *Prodromus* is a fundamental feature of Peiresc's encounter with it, both before and after publication.

In his letter of 30 March, Peiresc began by cautioning Kircher that presenting theories as certainties would put his credibility at risk. That was why he insisted that any edition of a bilingual Coptic work, such as della Valle's manuscripts, include both the Coptic words and the Arabic translations. The reader, it is implied, should not have to take one scholar's word on faith.[59] As for the Barachias manuscript, he always believed what Kircher only now had come to see. "For your Barachias I was always a little dubious, which you never dared admit to me as you have done now." Peiresc offered his own art of extracting the diamond from its rough setting—elsewhere, he described this as enjoying the rose amidst the thorns—as a model for how Kircher should handle the Barachias manuscript.[60]

Peiresc returned again to the question of how to make use of a text more or less shot through with barbarism, superstition, or plain falsification. This ability to isolate out the meaningful from the dross was especially necessary with magical texts. The "weak spirits" (*esprits faibles*) sought supernatural prophylaxis. *Esprits forts*, perhaps by definition, and certainly by contrast, learned to read them against the grain. They were more concerned with the quest for meaning: the "formulae, uses and routines of the ancient religion of the pagans which very often reveal, albeit at a great distance, the mysteries that the priests of the idols affect in order to render them more venerable. And this," Peiresc concluded, "is what could best serve the design of your *Oedipus*, and to decode not only your Egyptian hieroglyphs, but an infinity of other mysteries, and the most abstract, of the pagan theology." [61] Any pretended magical potency reflected more what was already in the eye of the beholder than "any secret supernatural virtue."[62]

For these reasons, Peiresc advised Kircher not to discard the parts of the Barachias manuscript that he thought useless, but to recognize that they might be of interest to other people, in other places, at other times.[63] To help Kircher do this, Peiresc offered to serve as his editor, going over the text for worthy bits that might have been discarded—though Peiresc warned that he had no taste for magical and occult forces. "In advance I declare myself very unsophisticated in these matters and that I believe not only that this is all deceptive boasting (*forfanteries abusives*), but that they have no more force and virtue than those who are persuaded of it."[64]

Even though Peiresc's own interest in Coptic had been piqued by studying magical gems, magic as such held no claim over him. Those who believed in it, like those who consulted auguries or read their future in games of chance, were of a different temperament. Peiresc quickly added, however, "that this is said between us, not intending at all to dislodge you from your sentiments, to which I will always be prepared to defer, if after you have heard me out, you persist in your opinion."[65] Nevertheless, Peiresc could not keep his skepticism to himself. As if tweaking Kircher, Peiresc told him about the enchanted sword of Gustavus Adolphus, which hung in the cabinet of one of his Aixois friends, and whose blade was engraved with "the symbols or characters of your Barachias, if my memory doesn't mislead me"—in short, with hieroglyphics. Of course, Peiresc observed dryly, whatever magic they possessed did not help the late king of Sweden. This type of interpretation would never hold up, Peiresc speculated, "if we were better informed of the intention of the author." On this small battlefield the historian again confronted the mystagogue.[66]

Only after saying all this does Peiresc come around to acknowledging receipt of "the preface to your *Prodromus*." Rather than commenting on its contents, Peiresc reproved Kircher for using ignorant secretaries whose faulty transcription of oriental languages had exasperated him. Having tried and struggled to get the characters right in his own copy, "I lost patience with it"—

and this from one whose patience was a watchword wherever *bonae literae* were honored. Peiresc's final word is a comment on the whole: "It is better to go a little more slowly and acquit oneself better."[67]

The eventual appearance of the *Prodromus*, surely the signal event of 1636 for any European orientalist, did not elicit from Peiresc any sense of satisfaction at a project brought to a successful completion. In part this reflects Peiresc's view of Kircher, one confirmed again in the spring of 1636 by a short essay Kircher sent him on an inscription found at Mount Sinai.[68] Peiresc's assessment of the essay is severe. He complained to the Dupuy brothers that Kircher had "imagined to himself" the whole interpretation, as if it had "come to him through the spirit." [69] He asked the Dupuy brothers to check with François-Auguste de Thou, who had visited the site in 1629 and could provide visual testimony (*tesmoing occulaire*), "because I greatly wonder if this is true, or supposed, totally made up and forged at pleasure. . . . Nevertheless," Peiresc concluded, "I hardly have the courage to send you his interpretation which seems to me scarcely supported, nor scarcely like nor appropriate to the place where it is." When Peiresc decided in the end to send it, he enjoined them not to circulate the essay "so as not to detract too much from the reputation that this good man had acquired, which has certainly rendered him a a little too credulous in matters that are of very difficult explanation. And I truly fear that what he will undertake with hieroglyphic characters will be the same."[70] To Naudé, Peiresc wrote that he found the proofs unbelievable. "I will urge him not to put it in his *Prodromus* so as not to run the risk of doing harm to the rest."[71]

Nor did Kircher's publication have much of an effect on Peiresc's research agenda. The summer of 1636 saw him pursuing his quest for Coptic materials in the libraries of Cairo and Lower Egypt as if nothing had changed.[72] The arrival of the *Prodromus* was registered, quietly, in a letter to de Loches in September 1636, and solely in terms of its pre-publication history, not its contents.[73] To Lucas Holstenius, in the Barberini household, Peiresc had a hard time disguising his feelings.[74] To Kircher himself, Peiresc offered congratulation but also admonition. "Judging from the work you are doing now," he wrote, "you can improve a lot." He added: "You understand well what I am telling you."[75] In a later letter he insisted again on the usefulness of a less dogmatic approach. At such a great distance from the past, many ordinary things could appear as mysteries and mistakenly shape the interpretation of the past. "It is for this reason that you will find it very well not only to guarantee nothing, but to fix nothing, and to leave to everyone the full liberty of judging all this material, whether in general or in particular."[76]

By the end of 1636, comments about Kircher and Coptic become very sparse.[77] Peiresc spoke most openly in his letters to Saumaise. By the end of November, both men had finished reading the book, and neither much liked it. In his long letter of the 29th, Peiresc tried to make the best case for being nice to Kircher, but he did not hide his true feelings. He described the *Prodromus* as "this poor book" whose reading must have provided Saumaise with some "exercise and escape from a few hours' boredom." He was sorry that he was unable to furnish "a pasture more worthy of your rare spirit." Here Peiresc's humanity took over. He insisted to Saumaise that his work

> will certainly be well received by everyone and be even more praiseworthy and glorious if you spare that poor man, as you promised me and which I accept with all my heart and take as a particular favor. Not that this poor man did not merit being rapped on the knuckles, since he has dispensed so many things that were not permissible to him, and presumed for himself more than he was owed. But if you will pardon him, you will not fail to make a meritorious work, since it is not from malice that he failed but rather from the habit of letting himself be persuaded by all things at the slightest appearance without knowing to deepen them and excavate the unknown truth.

Kircher was a decent man (*fort bontif*) who judged everyone by his own standards and consequently was surprised when proof was actually demanded. In Provence, for example, he advocated, "innocently, among his friends, all sorts of things however incompatible with the spirit of the Company with which he was engaged, such as concerning the movement of the earth according to the suppositions of Copernicus, with the infinity of consequences that follow, as well as concerning other maxims right conforming to those of the liberties of the Gallican Church. [All] which merits respecting and caring for him, totally differently from what one would have done otherwise."[78]

This is extraordinary stuff. We can now add a third reason for Peiresc's continued support for Kircher even after he suspected fraud. He explained to the Dupuy brothers in October 1633 that the Barachias manuscript was worth pursuing because it contained words that might be Coptic and so could contribute to its decipherment. To Saumaise in April 1634, he stressed the value of the manuscript as a guide to the beliefs of the world in which it was composed—even if this was not, in fact, the age of hieroglyphics. Now, Peiresc emphasized something very different: his sense that on the grand political issues of the day, freedom of thought and civil sovereignty—*which transcended philology*—he and Saumaise and Kircher were really on the same side. This is what merited special consideration.

There was also a fourth, eminently practical, reason for indulging Kircher. Peiresc observed that Kircher was "almost at the point of going off to the Levant, where he could make great discoveries of books and aid not only the public in general, but you and me and other particular persons," all of which he might be less inclined to do if Saumaise savaged a book that came to him from Peiresc. "Refutations not always being so necessary," Peiresc commented, "and if you were to judge that there were any that were inevitable, I pray you modify them and conceive them in terms as sweet as he could believe." Peiresc wanted to make sure that any criticisms Saumaise offered would not look like an expression of ill will against either Kircher or his Company but rather "like when a brother talks to a brother or a son to his father."[79]

By 15 December 1636, Peiresc had received Saumaise's list of corrections to the *Prodromus* (probably sent with his letter of 18 November, to which Peiresc's was a reply). He lauded Saumaise's intellectual method, reading passages "each in its own place, according to the true sense of the author and the appropriateness of the language"—almost the opposite of Kircher.[80] But he also praised Saumaise's moderate tone. "This spirit of peace and charity," he concluded, "could not be more recommended to my taste."[81] In concluding, Peiresc reminded Saumaise to "spare all that could concern the honor of that poor man who is transported and persuaded by things so poorly founded and so flimsily conceived and put in writing." But Peiresc wasn't finished. Whenever Saumaise came across something, "whether Arabic or Coptic or whatever, where he could merit your approval, you would give me a good amount of pleasure, and more, to use the occasion to praise it with some small paean to his good will or whatever other thing you could do for the love of me." Saumaise, too, would benefit from this charity, as he would be praised by all the men of letters "who will see and will easily recognize the charity that you will have used in sparing him, when he had merited repoach for his easy credulity and mistakes." [82] After all, Kircher was only human. "For to praise only those impeccable gentlemen, I don't know if there will ever be found any who might be so exempt from all sorts of human failings."[83]

What is left unsaid is as important as what is said: these letters contain no discussion of the book's content. And yet the *Prodromus* is a deeply Pereskian book—several of its parts actually came to Peiresc in manuscript form prior to publication.[84] Its dedication to Cardinal Francesco Barberini as chief promoter of oriental studies, and its attempt to put Coptic in context, to understand language both as a product of history and as evidence for historical argument, were loosely consistent with Peiresc's own approach. And Peiresc was himself given pride of place, ahead even of della Valle, as one who by "armed appeal forced [him] to undertake the work."[85] But there were also differences—and these turn this story of what did not happen into evidence for the state of antiquarian oriental studies in the first half of the seventeenth century.

First and foremost, the *Prodromus* is one of the last great intellectual achievements of the Counter-Reformation papacy. Beginning with Gregory XIII, Rome looked confidently to Eastern Christianity, and to the intellectual riches of the East more generally, for proof of its universal sway. These Roman resources are rehearsed in the book's first few pages. After the various permissions—from the General of the Jesuit Order, and the master of the Sacred Palace—came a series of panegyrical poems in Hebrew, Arabic, Samaritan, Armenian, Ethiopic, and Syriac (in various scripts), all contributed by Easterners resident in Rome. Their authority in oriental matters was deployed to lend credibility to Kircher's argument.[86] But their presence also demonstrated that this was not to be read as the work of one man only; the *Prodromus* stood for the work of a whole cadre of scholars. However impressive Peiresc's international network, it was defined as much by the absence of this institutional structure. He lacked precisely the resources that Kircher could, and did, so gaudily deploy. (One wonders how carefully they read Kircher's work before they signed on; perhaps they didn't think anybody else would either.) Indeed, much of Peiresc's effort with Francesco Barberini was to insert himself *into* this network and try to harness its power for his own purposes. But his peripheral status was an inescapable reality.

Second, in the dedication to Cardinal Barberini, Kircher described the work as an introduction (literally, "prodromus") to his major treatment of Egypt, the *Oedipus Aegyptiacus* (1652–55).[87] In this mammoth work, the flights of fancy that Peiresc lamented, and which in his own lifetime he strove to rein in, were fully indulged. Amidst them, however, there is also the kind of late humanist scholarship that was so common among Peiresc's friends. Kircher's attempt in the *Prodromus* to explain the similarities between Coptic and Ethiopic through a history of the Church in northeast Africa is conducted through the use of sources. The analysis of the discovery of the famous "Nestorian Stone" in western China in 1625 is done by publishing the accounts of the Jesuit missionaries who discovered it and by representing the stone itself, reprinting its text, and supplying it with a translation. Even the sober-minded Laudian orientalist Bishop Brian Walton took seriously some of Kircher's linguistic history.[88]

And yet, as Peiresc so often lamented, this approach was applied with too much haste and too little self-criticism. The explanation of the spread of Christianity to East Asia, in which discussion of the Nestorian Stone played a major role, looked historical because proof-texts were always adduced. But upon closer inspection, the evidence melted into assertion and hypothesis.[89] Kircher's discussion of the relationship between Coptic and hieroglyphics, the real reason for the book's existence, and presented at length in the book's concluding chapter, was equally tendentious.

A third feature of the work had less to do with Kircher than with Kircher's residence in Rome. If he had remained in Avignon, or even if he had been relocated to Vienna, as was initially planned, it is less likely he would have emphasized quite so much the role of the early Church as an agent in the history of the Near East. Nor could one imagine Peiresc, friend and admirer of the Protestants Joseph Scaliger, Samuel Petit, Hugo Grotius, Giulio Pace, and Claude Saumaise, recruiting the study of Coptic for the war against the Reformed Church (even if Peiresc did always call it "la religion pretendu reformée").[90] Or of his being interested in Ethiopia solely for its value in explaining the Christian penetration of Asia.[91] Further evidence of Kircher's different citizenship in the republic of letters is his reliance on Baronius as an authority. The scholarship of this hero of Counter-Reformation controversialism had been ridiculed by northern European scholarship by the time Kircher took up his pen. Yet in the book that Kircher wrote, like those composed by Baronius himself half a century earlier, ecclesiastical history explains everything and drives all doubts before it.

Because Kircher treated hieroglyphics as a symbolic language, he never considered it necessary to root its study in that of other languages, whereas for Peiresc the history of languages was the great key to the history of civilization. Moreover, Peiresc pursued this inquiry through what we would call field-work—sending investigators to find out what was spoken where and when, and to retrieve as much evidence as possible. Kircher's focus on religion also limited the evidence that he considered; his discussion of Ethiopia, for in-stance, relied solely on liturgical materials.[92] The complexity of Peiresc's his-tory of language, with its interest in the gradations between Coptic and Ethiopic, is reduced in the *Prodromus* to a simple equation between the history of language and the history of the Church. Travelers' accounts and the evi-dence of manuscripts is exchanged for a reliance on liturgy—the bulk of the argument in chapters 2 and 3 ("The practices of the Copts" and "The Coptic-Ethiopic Church translated to other parts of the world") is carried through printing of prayers in these languages, their transliteration, translation, and commentary. Peiresc's flights of comparative history led to a more compli-cated view of the past, while Kircher's strove for the ultimate simplicity: unity.

Kircher would not do Peiresc's bidding, would not be his kind of scholar. For that we may be thankful: he has made it possible for posterity to accompany him through the European marvelous and off into outer space. But we ought also to be a little sad: for an intelligence too hungry for the celebrity of instant fame to commit to that intergenerational project of the advancement of learn-ing that often leaves its initiators wreathed not in laurels but obscurity.[93]

Notes

1. See D. Allen 1960, 1970; David 1965; Pastine 1978; Rivosecchi 1982; Strasser 1988a; and Cipriani 1993, chapter 2.
2. See Gravit 1938; and Bresson 1988.
3. Kircher's praise is published in Kircher 1643a and 1650b and cited in Gassendi 1657, pp. 283–286. Kircher published panegyrical poems in Aramaic, Samaritan, Georgian, and Coptic in the "Panglossia" (Bouchard 1638), pp. 88, 90, 93, 96. On this, see Chaine 1933.
4. See Miller 1997a, 2001c.
5. Peiresc to della Valle, 25 September 1628, Vatican, Archivio Segreto Vaticana (hereafter **ASV**), Arch. Della Valle-Del Bufalo 52, fol. [1]. Peiresc to Aleandro, 27 November 1628, Vat-ican, Biblioteca Apostolica Vaticana (hereafter **BAV**), MS. Barberini-Latina 6504, fols. 226r–v. See Miller 1997b, 2001a.
6. Peiresc to Aleandro, 27 July 1628, BAV, MS. Barb.-Lat 6504, fols. 216r–v; 25 September 1628, BAV MS. Barb.-Lat 6504, fols. 219r–v; 26 October 1628, fol. 224v.
7. Peiresc to Aleandro, 25 September 1628, MS. Barb.-Lat 6504, fol. 219v; 26 October 1628, fol. 224r; 27 November 1628, MS. Barb.-Lat 6504, fols. 226r–v. Peiresc to della Valle, 26 No-vember 1628, Aix, Bibl. Méjanes MS. 213 (1031), p. 65. See Miller 2001a.
8. Peiresc to della Valle, 7 June 1629, Aix, Bibl. Méjanes MS. 213 (1031), p. 75. Della Valle to Peiresc, 27 July 1629, Paris Bibliothèque Nationale, Paris (hereafter **B.N.**). MS. Dupuy 705, fol. 189. Peiresc to della Valle, 4 March 1630, Aix, Bibl. Méjanes MS. 213 (1031), p. 77.

9. Della Valle to Morin, (21 March) 1630, Morin 1682, p. 167. Lantschoot 1948, p. ix; Peiresc to della Valle, 9 October 1630, Aix, Bibl. Méjanes MS. 213 (1031), p. 84.
10. Peiresc to Petit, 5 October 1630, Carpentras, Bibliothèque Inguimbertine (hereafter **Carp., Bib. Inguimb.**), MS. 1875, fol. 244v.
11. Peiresc to della Valle, 19 May 1632, Vatican, ASV Arch. Della Valle-Del Bufalo 52, fol. [4v].
12. See discussion Stolzenberg 2003, ch. 1, sec. 5.
13. Peiresc to Petit, 14 July 1632, Carp., Bib. Inguimb, MS. 1875, fol. 250. This letter was accompanied by the loan of three Coptic manuscripts (B.N., Nouvelles acquisitions françaises [hereafter **N.a.f.**], 5169, fol. 49r, for 18 July). By the next month, Peiresc was preparing to send Petit his three Coptic manuscripts. Peiresc to Petit, 14 August 1632, Carp. MS. 1875, fol. 249v.
14. Peiresc to Petit, 1 October 1632, MS. Lat. 9340, fol. 273; MS. Carp. 1875, fol. 251.
15. Peiresc to Petit, 14 October 1632, Carp. MS. 1875, fol. 251v.
16. Peiresc to Petit, 18 February 1633, Carp. MS. 1875, fol. 252v; Peiresc to Petit, 18 February 1633, MS. Carp. 1875, fol. 252v.
17. Peiresc to Petit, 8 March 1633, Carp. MS 1875, fol. 253v. At the same time that he was urging Petit on, Peiresc still hoped for success on the Roman tack. Peiresc to Petit, 19 March 1633, Carp. MS. 1875 fol. 258.
18. Peiresc to Gassendi, 2 March 1633, Peiresc 1888–98, vol. 4, pp. 295–296. Gassendi 1657, year 1633, p. 85.
19. Peiresc to Dupuy, 4 April 1633, Peiresc 1888–98, vol. 2, pp. 488–489; Peiresc to Gassendi, 5 April 1633, Peiresc 1888–98, vol. 4, pp. 300–301.
20. Peiresc to Dupuy, 16 May 1633, Peiresc 1888–98, vol. 2, p. 521.
21. Peiresc to Barberini, 19 May 1633, Vatican, BAV, Barb.-Lat 6503, fol. 50r; see also Peiresc to Dupuy, 21 May 1633, Peiresc 1888–98, vol. 2, pp. 528–529.
22. Kircher to Jean Ferrand, S. J., 4 June 1633, Carp., Bibl. Inguimb. MS. 1831, fol. 131.
23. Carp., Bib. Inguimb., MS. 1864, fol. 259. The text is printed in Aufrère 1990, p. 115.
24. Carp., Bib. Inguimb. MS. 1864, fol. 263, and B.N. MS. Fonds français (hereafter **F.fr.**) 9532, fol. 42, both indicate that Magy was in Aix on 29 July 1633.
25. Peiresc to Kircher, 3 August 1633, Rome, Archivio della Pontificia Università Gregoriana, Rome (hereafter **APUG**) 568, fols. 370r–371v. I cite the letters of Peiresc to Kircher from the transcription made by Nick Wilding in Appendix 2 of his dissertation (Wilding 2000) and thank him for making these available to me. I have checked them against the originals on-line at "The Correspondence of Athanasius Kircher: The World of a Seventeenth-Century Jesuit," http://kircher.stanford.edu.
26. I discuss this episode more fully in Miller 2004.
27. Peiresc to Kircher, 17 August 1633, Aix, APUG 568, fols. 198r–v.
28. Carp., Bibl. Inguimb. MS. 1864 fols. 228–229; printed in Bresson 1992, pp. 380–382. See also Peiresc to Gassendi, 14 September 1633, Peiresc 1888–98, vol. 4, p. 361. Compare this latter with Gassendi's formal, public account of Kircher's visit (1657, year 1636, p. 85).
29. Bresson 1992, p. 381.
30. He left Aix and was in Marseille on the 6th, whence he sent Peiresc a hurried farewell letter. Kircher to Peiresc, 6 September 1633, B.N. F.fr., 9538, fols. 228bis r–v.
31. Peiresc to della Valle, 7 September 1633, Vatican, ASV Arch. Della Valle–Del Bufalo 52, fol. [6]ʳ; Peiresc to della Valle, 10 September 1633, Aix, Bibl. Méjanes MS. 213 (1031), p. 97; Peiresc to Barberini, 10 September 1633, BAV Barb.-Lat 6503, fol. 60. Peiresc to Cassiano, 10 September 1633, Peiresc 1992, pp. 111–112.
32. Peiresc to Dupuy, 24 October 1633, Peiresc 1888–98, vol. 2, p. 631.
33. Peiresc to Agathange de Vendôme, 17 May 1635, Valence 1891, p. 135; Cassien de Nantes to Peiresc, 27 July 1635, Valence 1891, p. 158.
34. Gilles de Loches to Peiresc, 6 May 1634, quoted in Omont 1892, pp. 491–492. Copies of the letter are found in Paris, B.N. MS. Varia Coptica 150; MS. Latin. 9340. Indeed, we know that a list of his oriental manuscripts that was drawn up upon his return, probably for Peiresc's benefit, contained not a single Coptic book (B.N. MS. Latin 9340, fol. 304).
35. Gravit 1938, p. 15. The text survives in B.N. MS. Latin 9340, fols. 238–254.
36. Saumaise to Peiresc, 20 July 1633, Tamizey de Larroque 1972, vol. 1, pp. 229–230.
37. Saumaise to Peiresc, undated, Carp., Bib. Inguimb. MS. 1810, fol. 161.
38. Peiresc to Saumaise, 14 November 1633, Bresson 1992, p. 38
39. B.N. MS. Latin 9340 fols. 112r–v.

40. "Record du Sr. de Peiresc au Sr. Jean Ba. Magy de Marseille avec priere de ne le communiquer à personne, qu'au R.P. Théophile Minuti tout seul . . . S'il y à moyen de faire le voyage de St. Macaire, qui n'est que de trois journées, il faudra tascher de recouvrer au moins une coppie bien correctement transcripte du libvre qui est en la bibliothecque du Monastere des Cophtes, contenant quatre Conciles Arabiques, Et s'il y avoit moyen d'obtenir le volume original, je n'y plaindrois pas une trentaine d'escus." B.N. MS. Latin 9340, fols. 112v–113r.

41. Peiresc to Della Valle, 9 February 1634, Vatican, ASV Arch. Della Valle-Del Bufalo 52, fol. [8]v.

42. Ibid., fol. [9]r.

43. Peiresc to Saumaise, 4 April 1634, Bresson 1992, p. 62.

44. Peiresc to Petit, 21 March 1634, Carp. MS. 1875, fol. 268v.

45. Peiresc to Saumaise, 4 April 1634, Bresson 1992, p. 55; Peiresc to Della Valle, 6 April 1634, Vatican, ASV Arch. Della Valle-Del Bufalo 52, fol. [10]r; Peiresc to Cassiano dal Pozzo, 6 June 1634, Peiresc 1992, p. 139; 29 June 1634, p. 140; 7 September 1634, pp. 146–147; Peiresc to Cassiano, 3 November 1634, p. 157; 29 December 1634, p. 161; Peiresc to Kircher, 3 June 1634, Rome, APUG 568, fols. 372r–v.

46. Peiresc to Kircher, 6 September 1634, Rome, APUG 586, fols. 374r–v.

47. Peiresc to Saumaise, 10 April 1634, Bresson 1992, p. 81. Saumaise agreed. Saumaise to Peiresc, 10 June 1634, Bresson 1992, pp. 382–383.

48. Peiresc to Saumaise, 10 April 1634, Bresson 1992, p. 81.

49. In a dejected letter at year's end to to Cassiano dal Pozzo, Peiresc could still observe, "Et sempre si scopriranno du buonissime cose nelle sue fattiche." Peiresc to Cassiano, 29 December 1634, Peiresc 1992, p. 161.

50. Peiresc to de Loches, 3 July 1634, Valence 1891, p. 59.

51. Peiresc to Kircher, 3 June 1634, APUG 568, fol. 372r.

52. Saumaise to Peiresc, 1 June 1635, Tamizey de Larroque 1972, vol. 1, pp. 266–267. Peiresc to Cassien de Nantes, 29 September 1635, Valence 1891, p. 190. I hope to discuss Peiresc's Ethiopic studies elsewhere.

53. See Peiresc to Saumaise, 22 May 1634, Bresson 1992, pp. 91–93.

54. Saumaise to Peiresc, 2 September 1634, Bresson 1992, p. 386.

55. Peiresc to Petit, 23 August 1635, MS. Carp. 1875, fol. 276.

56. Peiresc to Agathange de Vendôme, 10 August 1635, Valence 1891, p. 162.

57. See Woolf 1990, p. 219.

58. Kircher to Peiresc, 8 February 1635, B.N. M.S. N.a.f. 5173, fols. 25–27; *Prodromus Copto-Aegyptiacus*, B.N. MS. Latin 9340, fols. 258–272; also MS. Dupuy 663, fols. 95–106.

59. Peiresc to Kircher, 30 March 1635, Rome, APUG 568, fol. 364r.

60. Ibid., fol. 364v.

61. Ibid., fols. 364r–v.

62. Ibid., fols. 364v–365r.

63. Ibid., fol. 364r.

64. Ibid.

65. Ibid.

66. Ibid., fols. 364r–v. For the sword, see Secret 1977.

67. Ibid., fol. 364v.

68. The manuscript is MS. Dupuy 488 fols. 161–163, which is copied with Kircher's letter of 1 April 1636.

69. Peiresc to Dupuy, 22 April 1636, Peiresc 1888–98, vol. 3, p. 474.

70. Peiresc to Dupuy, 13 May 1636, Peiresc 1888–98, vol. 3, p. 484.

71. Peiresc to Naudé, 5 June 1636, Peiresc 1983, p. 91.

72. Peiresc to Agathange de Vendome, 22 July 1636, Valence 1891, pp. 245–246.

73. Peiresc to de Loches, 23 September 1636, Valence 1891, p. 269.

74. Peiresc to Holstenius, 2 July 1636, Peiresc 1888–98, vol. 4, p. 441.

75. Peiresc to Kircher, 30 October 1636, Rome, APUG 568, fol. 216r.

76. Ibid., fol. 218r.

77. Typical is the passing reference in Peiresc to Cassiano, 31 October 1636, Peiresc, 1992, p. 254.

78. Peiresc to Saumaise, 29 November 1636, Bresson 1992, pp. 319–321.

79. Ibid., p. 331.

80. Peiresc to Saumaise, 15 December 1636, Bresson 1992, p. 352.

81. Ibid.

82. Ibid., p. 353.

83. Ibid.
84. For example, the letter of Father Emmanuel Diaz describing the Nestorian Stone, which is labeled by Peiresc "*1625/* SINARUM/ Inscriptio Christiana" (Carp., Bib. Inguimb. MS. 1831, fol. 147), the interpretation of the inscription at Mount Sinai, sent in a presentation copy to Peiresc as "Scripturae mirabilis et toto oriente celebratissimae in monte Sinai rupi cuidam incisae" and dedicated to Francesco Barberini (B.N., MS. Dupuy 488, fols. 161–162), and the précis of the work as a whole, *Prodromus Copto-Aegyptiacus*, (B.N., MS. Latin 9340, fols. 258–272; also MS. Dupuy 663, fols. 95–106).
85. "inter principem sane non immerito locum obtinet Amplissimus Dominus Nicolalus Fabricius de Pereisc Christianissimo Regi a secretis concilijs armata deprecatione extortum aggrederer, idque ab alijs derelictum, ad incudem revocarem." Kircher 1636, pp. 4–5.
86. Even those Peiresc had found risible, like his interpretation of the strange inscription at the foot of Mount Sinai.
87. Kircher 1636, [††2]v.
88. Walton 1657, XV.6–8, p. 100; Wilding 2000.
89. He posits the existence of "lingua Syra Ecclesiae Copto-Aethiopicae," and then, on the basis of the Nestorian Stone, he assumes that it was from Ethiopia that the East was made Christian. Kircher 1636, pp. 49–50.
90. Kircher 1636, pp. 44–45.
91. Pastine 1978, p. 186.
92. Pastine 1978, pp. 85, 119.
93. The author wishes to thank Anthony Grafton and Alastair Hamilton for their comments on earlier versions of this paper.

6

Four Trees, Some Amulets, and the Seventy-two Names of God

Kircher Reveals the Kabbalah

DANIEL STOLZENBERG

Although it is the work of a Kabbalist precisely to read one thing but understand it in a different way, nevertheless he will keep to the inviolable rule that good must be understood as good and bad as bad, lest he apply black to white or day to night.
—Johannes Reuchlin, *On the Art of Kabbalah*[1]

The Kabbalah occupied a privileged position in the reconstruction of ancient wisdom underlying Athanasius Kircher's interpretation of the "hieroglyphic doctrine." Although his syncretic method tended to equate the traditions of all cultures, he believed in an especially close relationship between Egyptian and Hebrew wisdom. "The Hebrews have such an affinity to the rites, sacrifices, ceremonies and sacred disciplines of the Egyptians," he wrote, "that I am fully persuaded that either the Egyptians were Hebraicizing or the Hebrews were Egypticizing."[2] According to Kircher, the true Kabbalah preserved the same Adamic wisdom that Hermes Trismegistus encoded in the hieroglyphs, while the "Rabbinic superstitions" found in many kabbalistic treatises were closely related to Egyptian idolatry. On this ground he believed that he could use the Kabbalah to interpret hieroglyphic inscriptions, and his works frequently drew on kabbalistic sources. The second volume of his magnum opus, *Egyptian Oedipus* (*Oedipus Aegyptiacus*) (1652–55), contains a 150-page treatise on the *Kabbalah of the Hebrews*, a systematic treatment of the Kabbalah that deals in turn with the mystical nature of the Hebrew alphabet and various hermeneutic methods based on its manipulation; the kabbalistic names of God and their use in mystical prayer; the doctrine of the ten sefirot or divine numerations; and what Kircher calls the "natural Kabbalah," which, as with the other divisions, contains both a true doctrine and a false one, the latter corresponding to what Kircher calls kabbalistic magic and kabbalistic astrology.

This essay looks at Kircher's treatment of the Kabbalah through the investigation of a single diagram (Figure 6.1). The plate in question, labeled the "Mirror of the Mystical Kabbalah," is placed at the conclusion of Kircher's

Figure 6.1. *The Mirror of the Mystical Kabbala. Source:* Kircher 1652–55, vol. 2, part 1, p. 287. By permission of Stanford University Libraries.

lengthy treatment of the divine names, of which it is a kind of visual summation or distillation, although parts of it also relate to his later discussions of kabbalistic astrology and magic. In analyzing this image, I aim to bring out in an encapsulated form several themes relevant not only to Kircher's study of the Kabbalah but also to his studies of esoteric traditions more generally. Kircher's representation of the seventy-two names of God provides an outstanding example of the congruence of Kircher's studies of non-Christian wisdom (despite their frequent heterodoxy) with the universalist ideology of the early modern Catholic Church. The emphasis on amulets, evident in the diagram and throughout the treatise, is indicative of the idiosyncratic marriage of early modern antiquarianism and occult traditions that shaped Kircher's hieroglyphic studies. Finally, the analysis of Kircher'sources—visual as well as textual—shows how he crafted his work from a pastiche of borrowed materials and nonetheless made an original intepretation.

Kircher's monumental interpretation of the Egyptian hieroglyphs appeared in a series of volumes published in Rome in the first half of the 1650s, though he had begun the project almost twenty years earlier. First off the press was the *Pamphilian Obelisk* (*Obeliscus Pamphilius*), a preliminary study published in the Jubilee Year 1650 to celebrate Pope Innocent X's reerection of an ancient obelisk with hieroglyphic inscriptions in the Piazza Navona. This was followed by the three volumes (the second bound in two parts) of the *Egyptian Oedipus*, funded by Emperor Ferdinand III, which presented Kircher's full treatment of the "hieroglyphic doctrine." The final volume contained translations of most of the known hierolgyphic inscriptions in Rome—where many obelisks and other Egyptian artifacts had been imported in the days of the Roman Empire—as well as examples communicated to Kircher from other parts of Europe and the world.

Kircher believed that the hieroglyphs had been invented after the Flood by the Egyptian sage Hermes Trismegistus to encode the pure wisdom he had revived from the antediluvian patriarchs. But later generations of Egyptian priests corrupted Trismegistus's teaching, mixing it with superstitious magic, and thereby created an ambiguous hieroglyphic legacy that was passed on to other civilizations, where it was preserved in scattered texts. Thus Kircher's interpretation of the hieroglyphs involved lengthy expositions of various non-Egyptian traditions supposed to contain elements of the pure Hermetic wisdom, as well as the corrupt Egyptian superstitions, including the Chaldean Oracles, Pythagorean verses, Orphic hymns, Arabic magic, and the Hebrew Kabbalah. According to Kircher, the purest core of the Kabbalah was unlike the other strands of the "ancient theology" (*prisca theologia*) in that it did not depend on Egyptian wisdom but rather constituted an independent tributary of the same antediluvian tradition. As for the superstitions found in both traditions, the vectors of influence were bidirectional, leading Kircher to declare that the beliefs of the Egyptians and the Hebrews are so similar that "whoever borrowed from whom, they can scarcely be told apart."[3] In "The Mirror of the Mystical Kabbalah," Kircher dramatically depicts both the pious and superstitious dimensions of the Kabbalah as they pertain to the doctrine of the names of God.

Kircher based his diagram on an earlier work by the French Jewish convert turned Christian Kabbalist, Philippe d'Aquin, called the *Interpretation of the Tree*

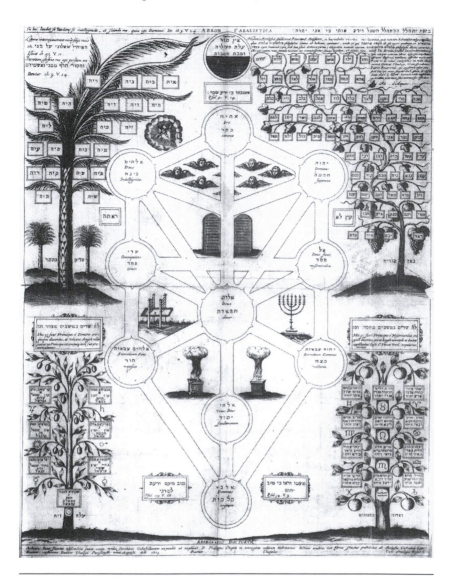

Figure 6.2. Philippe d' Aquin's *Tree of the Kabbalah. Source:* D'Aquin 1625. Bibliothèque Nationale, Paris. Cliché Bibliothèque Nationale de France.

of Kabbalah[4] (Figure 6.2). But Kircher has taken great liberties, using the original diagram as a template in which to insert his own rather different kabbalistic interests. D'Aquin's figure is dominated by a diagram of the ten sefirot—the kabbalistic tree *par excellence*—surrounded in the corners by four trees symbolizing various kabbalistic doctrines. Kircher's diagram removes the sefirotic tree, which he treats separately in a later section of the treatise, and replaces it with a man-

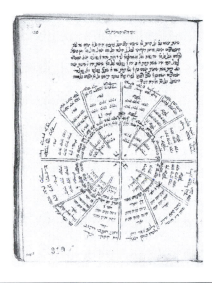

Figure 6.3. Kabbalistic diagram of the Hebrew names of God, from the manuscript of Moses Cordovero's *Pardes rimmonim* used by Kircher. *Source:* Biblioteca Apostolica Vaticana (BAV) Neofiti 28, fol. 319r. © Biblioteca Apostolica Vaticana (Vatican).

dala-like sunflower bearing the names of God. (The central part of Kircher's diagram was probably inspired instead by a diagram in Moses Cordovero's *Pardes rimmonim* [Garden of pomegranates], which, although much simpler, likewise shows the different divine names radiating in a circular pattern from the Tetragrammaton in the center and culminating in the seventy-two names of God arrayed along the circumference[5] (Figure 6.3). The central image also suggests the influence of James Bonaventure Hepburn's *Virga Aurea*. This broadside, printed in Rome in 1616, contains an engraving of the Virgin Mary inside a stylized, radiating sun, beneath which are displayed seventy-two alphabets, many of a fantastic or magical nature.[6]) He also does away with d'Aquin's palm tree, for which he has no need. But Kircher's use of a vine to hold the seventy-two divine names, an olive tree associated with the seven planets, and a fruit tree[7] with the signs of the zodiac—all are dependent on d'Aquin. Kircher does not, however, follow d'Aquin's discussion of the symbolic significance of the different species of trees, which consequently come to seem arbitrary. It is characteristic of Kircher's citation techniques that he never mentions d'Aquin.[8]

The central, sunflower-shaped part of the diagram illustrates key parts of Kircher's exposition of what he considers the good, pious part of the Kabbalah of divine names, which is expounded in chapters 4 to 7 of *Kabbalah of the Hebrews*. The first five rings represent what was by Kircher's day a standard Christian interpretation of the Kabbalah, which purported to discover confirmations of the Trinity and the divinity of Jesus Christ in Jewish kabbalistic doctrines about the names of God.[9] Emphasis on the four-, twelve-, forty-two-, and seventy-two-letter names of God was a common feature of Christian treatments of the Kabbalah, already found in influential early works by authors such as Pietro Galatino and Johannes Reuchlin.[10]

The centermost circle contains the Tetragrammaton, the most sacred and ineffable four-letter name of God, understood in the Kabbalah as the origin of all other divine names, which are depicted in the diagram as radiating outward from the Tetragrammaton (Figure 6.4). The attentive viewer will note, however, that the Hebrew name of God in the middle of the diagram contains five, not four, letters. In the Christian Kabbalah the Tetragrammaton, (YHVH), was equated with the so-called Pentagrammaton,   (YHSUH), a variant of the name of Jesus formed by inserting the Hebrew letter *shin* (printed in the diagram in openface) in the center of the Tetragrammaton. According to this Christianized interpretation of the Kabbalah, the name of Christ, the true Messiah, made the ineffable name of God pronounceable. "Jesus Christ," Kircher writes,

> the center of all nature, in whose name all the other divine names are concentrated, God and man, has shown the four-letter name, which was formerly secret and concealed but is now revealed and explained by the Teacher himself, to the future world. Here the figure shows the diffusion of the divine name יהשוה whose figure (*typus*) was formerly the four-letter name יהוה. Just as the Sun illuminates, makes fruitful, and animates all things by diffusing its rays through all the world, so the power and efficacy of the name JESUS, who is the Sun of justice, vivifies and preserves all things by diffusing itself through all things.

Just as the word took on flesh though the incarnation, the letter *shin* in the middle of the Tetragrammaton "connects the divine and the human on equal terms."[11] The ineffable Tetragrammaton is associated with the Old Dispensation and is described as the *typus* of the five-letter name, which represents the universal New Dispensation. Kircher here is closely following a line of interpretation originally put forward a century and a half earlier by Johannes Reuchlin, one of the first Christian students of the Kabbalah, and subsequently widely diffused.[12]

Since the Messiah, Jesus Christ, is synonymous with the Tetragrammaton, their representations are interchangeable, and the circle devoted to the Tetragrammaton contains, in addition to the Hebrew Pentagrammaton יהשוה, the monogram of Jesus IHS in Latin characters, and three *yods* written above the Hebrew vowel *qamats*, which Kircher explains as a form of the Tetragrammaton symbolizing the Trinity.[13] Written inside the openface letters of the IHS are four Hebrew phrases taken from the Bible, which are taken to refer to the Tetragrammaton.[14] The equation of Christ with the Tetragrammaton is reinforced by the image of Jesus placed among the divine names.

Figure 6.4. The four-, twelve-, and forty-two-letter names of God. *Source:* Kircher 1652–55, p. 287, vol. 1, detail. By permission of Stanford University Libraries.

The first name to radiate from the Tetragrammaton is the twelve-letter name of God, which Kircher gives as   : the Father, the Son, and the Holy Spirit (Figure 6.4).[15] Between these twelve letters are interspersed the names of twelve divine attributes. From the twelve-letter name emanates the forty-two-letter name, which Kircher gives in two versions, the first of which is very similar in meaning to the twelve-letter name. In English it reads: "God the Father, God the Son, God the Holy Spirit, Three in One, One in Three." In his exposition of the twelve- and forty-two-letter names, Kircher attributes these Trinitarian interpretations—which he prefers to those based on the superstitious letter combinations of more recent rabbis— to a certain "Rabbenu Hakadosch."

Unlike Reuchlin's doctrine about the name of the Messiah, which is based on the application of genuine kabbalistic techniques to Christian apologetic ends, these interpretations of the twelve- and forty-two-letter names of God are based on forgeries. The Trinitarian teachings of Rabbi Haccados first appeared in a small book published in Rome in 1487 by a Spanish Jewish convert named Paulus de Heredia. The *Letter of Secrets* supposedly contained Latin translations of letters exchanged by Rabbi Nehuniah ben Hakanah (a great rabbinic sage of the first century A.D. and, according to medieval legend, a master of the Kabbalah) and his son. The texts are filled with bogus quotations from Jewish sages and authoritative texts like the Zohar, which are made to expound the Kabbalah's supposed Christological and Trinitarian core. Among the forgeries within the forgery are numerous passages from a nonexistent treatise called *Galerazaya* or *Secretorum revelator* (Revealer of secrets) attributed to Rabbi Haccados, editor of the Mishnah, which set forth the Trinitarian interpretations of the names of God. These doctrines became widely diffused through quotation in later works, in particular Agostino Giustiniani's 1516 polyglot psalter and the works of Pietro Galatino.[16]

The second forty-two-letter name displayed in Kircher's diagram, is authentically Jewish-kabbalistic, being derived from the first two verses of Genesis according to a method of letter substitution, and is devoid of Trinitarian or Christological significance (Figure 6.4). It is surprising that Kircher includes this name in this part of the diagram, which otherwise appears to be meant as a representation of good, non-superstitious Kabbalah, because in chapter 4 of *Kabbalah of the Hebrews* he derides and condemns the method by which it is derived, calling it "the lowest of the combinatory arts."[17] A third ring contains forty-two "grades of being" (*gradus entium*), corresponding to the letters of the forty-two-letter names.

Up to this point, Kircher's representation of the names of God has been entirely conventional and derivative. From the forty-two-letter name, however, emerges the seventy-two-letter name of God—or more properly, the seventy-two names of God—and here things become more interesting. In place of the traditional seventy-two 3-letter Hebrew names of God that one would expect to find in this place, Kircher gives seventy-two 4-letter names of God associated with seventy-two nations that make up humanity (Figure 6.1). As one would expect from Kircher, the roster is truly global, including New World inhabitants such as the Mexicans, Filipinos, Canadians, and Californians, as well as the Japanese, Chinese, Ethiopians, and so forth. Philology—as so often—falls victim to Kircher's greater purpose. The English, for instance, worship "Good," not God; the Italians *Idio*, not *Iddio*. This part of the diagram illustrates an argument set forth in chapter 7 of *Kabbalah of the Hebrews*, which contains the treatise's most concentrated exposition of the Christian Kabbalah. Here Kircher places the claim that all the nations of the world possess a divinely-inspired four-letter name of God on par with the classic argument about the wonder-working, five-letter name of Christ and its identity with the Tetragrammaton. "Since the world was created for man," Kircher explains,

> and all mankind is divided into seventy-two families, as attested by holy scripture, hence arose the name of seventy-two letters, or the seventy-two names, in which the whole order of nature is aptly expressed together with the seventy-two names of the Angels presiding over all nature.[18]

A label identifies the tree in Kircher's diagram as "The Mystical Tree Planted in the Middle of Paradise for the Salvation of the 72 Nations, whose fruit are the 72 Names of God."

Traditionally, the seventy-two names of God refer to a series of three-letter Hebrew names that are generated from three verses of Exodus 14, which each, mysteriously, contain exactly seventy-two letters. When the three verses are written in three rows, seventy-two 3-letter names can be read in the vertical columns. (The resulting names appear in the leaves of the vine at the top of Figure 6.1.) Kircher discusses the mystery of these names in chapter 6 of *Kabbalah of the Hebrews*, mostly following Moses Cordovero's exposition in *Pardes rimmonim*.[19] He explains that these seventy-two divine names of God, and the equal number of angel names produced by adding the suffixes *-iel* or *-iah*, represent different divine virtues or attributes—the multifarious effects in the created world of the one, undivided God represented by the Tetragrammaton. These seventy-two powers or intelligences correspond to an equal number of classes of created things and preside over the seventy-two families that make up humanity. Thus, in Kircher's words, they aptly express the whole order of nature. According to Kircher, there is no danger in these names, inasmuch as they accurately describe the attributes of God; it is only their abuse in the practice of superstitious amulets that must be shunned and condemned. Nevertheless, when it comes time to present the seventy-two names in the central diagram, Kircher replaces the classic Hebrew names derived from Exodus 14 with the polyglot seventy-two 4-letter names supposedly revealed to all mankind.

A Hebrew passage quoted by Kircher from the *Pardes rimmonim* (but ultimately dependent on the *Sefer bahir* [Book of illumination]) describes the seventy-two 3-letter names as branches of "a great tree in the middle of paradise," which draw their power and sustenance from the three verses of Exodus. Kircher calls this "the tree planted in the middle of paradise for the salvation of the seventy-two peoples and nations of the world," thus identifying it with the tree bearing the seventy-two 4-letter names that appears in the diagram in the following chapter.[20] In the Jewish sources, the seventy-two names of the angels that preside over the same number of families composing humanity have a theurgical and magical significance: the angel names are supposed to possess the power to influence corresponding supernal forces.[21] For Kircher, who rejects these magical practices, the significance of the divine names lies instead in their representation of the totality of humanity. By replacing the esoteric Hebrew names with names for God in seventy-two languages representing all mankind, he has turned the Kabbalah of divine names into a universal revelation and a promise of salvation to all peoples.

A first step toward such a universalizing interpretation of the Kabbalah of divine names had been made a century earlier in a work published by the Franciscan kabbalist Arcangelo da Borgonovo. In an interpretation of one of Pico's kabbalistic conclusions, Borgonovo describes how the Israelite priest of the Old Testament was commanded to carry a golden plate inscribed with the Tetragrammaton, in order that the sacred rites would be performed in the name of God, the source of "every influence and favor." Furthermore, Borgonovo explains,

> he used to carry a mantle with seventy-two pomegranates because, being the only legal, true, and legitimate priest among all the priests of the world, he alone could beseech [God] not only on behalf of the Israelites, but on behalf of all the peoples of the world, of which there are seventy-two. He also used to carry seventy-two bells, in alternation with the pomegranates, with which he would call forth the seventy-two princes who preside over the seventy-two languages.[22]

Kircher—whose familiarity with this passage is revealed in a section of the *Oedipus* manuscript that was removed from the printed work—leaps from Borgonovo's description of the Israelite priest calling on the power of the divine name on behalf of all the world to the claim that all the nations of the world have known the name of God.[23] It is to be noted, Kircher asserts, that the name of God among all nations typically has four letters, the result not of human decision but of "a certain divine instigation." Kircher took this notion from Marsilio Facino, who observes in his commentary on Plato's *Philebus* that "everyone calls God by four letters," and gives several examplease of God's four-letter name in different languages that are also found in Kircher's diagram.[24] These names emanate from the Tetragrammaton in the same way as the twelve- and forty-two-letter names Kircher explains:

> So by this it seems to be indicated that everything in the world receives sustenance by the power and efficacy of this name; and thus all the peoples and nations of the world are bound to respond to so many gifts of divine goodness under the true cult of one religion diffused through the world.[25]

Along similar lines, Kircher argues that the Hebrew Tetragrammaton itself was known to ancient pagan wise men. The Egyptians received the doctrine of the Tetragrammaton directly from the Hebrew patriarchs and encoded it in a hieroglyph (Figure 6.5). Likewise, Pythagoras expressed the doctrine of the

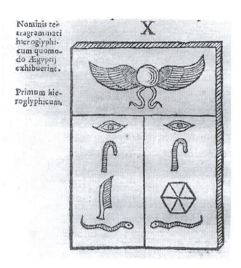

Figure 6.5. The Tetragrammaton encoded in an Egyptian hieroglyph. *Source:* Kircher, 1652–55, vol. 2, part 1, p. 282. By permission of Stanford University Libraries.

Tetragrammaton in the tetractys, or mystical set of four (here Kircher again follows an argument first made by Reuchlin[26]), and Orpheus did so allegorically through the figures of Muse, Dionysus, Apollo, and Venus. In its totality, Kircher's tree of divine names depicts the dissemination to the entire world of the names of God emanating from the primordial Tetragrammaton, which itself encodes the doctrines of the Trinity and the divinity of Christ.

The central figure of Kircher's diagram is thus a symbol of the universality of Christian truth. As such, it can be advantageously compared to another tree-shaped diagram, the image of the "universal horoscope of the Society of Jesus" in Kircher's *Great Art of Light and Shadow* (*Ars magna lucis et umbrae*) (1646), which graphically depicts the global reach of the seventeenth-century Church, and the Jesuit Order in particular, by simultaneously displaying the time of day in every Jesuit outpost around the world[27] (Figure 6.6). Kircher's kabbalistic tree is a kind of Jesuit emblem—note again the oversized Jesuit monogram, IHS, which Kircher has placed at the center with the other names of Christ. It can be read as a map of the original, universal distribution of truth to humanity, which served as the preface and ideological basis for the early modern missionary campaign depicted in the "map" of the tree of the universal horoscope. Though this ancient heritage of truth and piety was obscured and corrupted over time, vestiges of it remain amid the idolatry and superstition of heathen peoples. This claim is one of the central arguments of the *Egyptian Oedipus*. The notion of such a common religious past suggested the existence of a relatively receptive groundwork on which Christian teachings

Figure 6.6. *The Universal Horoscope of the Society of Jesus. Source:* Kircher 1646, p. 553. By permission of Stanford University Libraries.

could be cultivated among distant races of infidels. It thus offered a justification for the proselytizing missions of the Jesuits, whose "accomodationist" missionary strategy allowed a considerable degree of syncretism in interpreting native traditions and adapting them to Catholicism.[28]

It is worth pointing out that in this interpretation, the historical uniqueness of the ancient Jews is greatly diminished if not obliterated. The teachings of the Kabbalah and the possession of a four-letter name of God belong to all humanity. This is just one example of Kircher's tendency to undercut Jewish historical uniqueness—the unintended and heterodox consequence of his emphasis on the common origins of human cultures. Furthermore, it is noteworthy that Moses and the revelation at Sinai are almost entirely absent from Kircher's histories. Most Christian interpretations of the Kabbalah described Moses as the source of the Kabbalah, just as most versions of the *prisca theologia* derived pagan wisdom from Moses and the Pentateuch.[29] Kircher, however, preferred to trace both to Adam and located the dispersion of the primeval wisdom to the gentiles in a pre-Mosaic biblical past. This interpretation undercuts the significance of the Old Dispensation to the Jews by robbing them of their unique role as guardians of pre-Christian truth. In addition, Kircher's implicit depiction of a universal Old Dispensation takes away from the significance of the New Dispensation, whose universality no longer appears novel. The claim that a continuous tradition of true wisdom and religion begins with Adam, the common father of mankind, may support a Catholic universalist vision, but it could suggest a disturbing question: What more had God to teach mankind by the revelation of the Law or the incarnation of Christ?[30]

Kircher's diagram is completed by three additional trees. Here, in the margins, we enter the territory of *nugae Rabbinorum*, "Rabbinic rubbish." In the left-hand corner is an olive tree, identified as "The Mystical Tree Containing the 7 Planets, the Members of the Body and the Presiding Angels." The right-hand corner depicts "The Pomegranate Tree Containing the 12 Signs of the Zodiac, the 12 Tribes of Israel, and 12 Revolutions of the Name of God" (Figure 6.7). Kircher reveals the meaning of both trees in his discussion of "Kabbalistic Astrology," in which he explains that they represent kabbalistic amulets meant to attract the beneficent influences of the heavenly bodies and their presiding angels. The olive tree depicts seven planetary seals, each composed from one of the seven 6-letter names that make up the forty-two-letter name of God (the second of the two versions discussed above), together with a corresponding part of the human body and the corresponding planetary angel. Thus the seal of Saturn contains the first part of the forty-two-letter name of God,   , the right eye, and the name of the angel Raphael who rules over them.[31] This seal is supposed to ensure long life, while others ensure peace, wisdom, grace and beauty, wealth, and so forth. The pomegranate tree represents similar

Figure 6.7. Trees representing kabbalistic amulets. *Source:* Kircher 1652–55, vol. 2, part 1, p. 287, details. By permission of Stanford University Libraries.

seals, which, Kircher explains, are based on the signs of the zodiac matched with the twelve permutations of the letters of the Tetragrammaton. He attacks these practices as superstitious and warns the Christian reader to avoid them.

Kircher's third tree (in truth, a vine) at the top of the image depicts the seventy-two 3-letter names of God derived from Exodus 14 (Figure 6.1, top). As we have seen, Kircher's attitude toward these names is ambivalent. As representations of divine attributes they present no danger, and he refers to the seventy-two angels presiding over all nature in his description of the part of the diagram that is meant to represent the pious doctrine of the divine names. But, according to Kircher, superstitious rabbis also use these names to construct impious amulets. In a way, the diagram of the vine is doing double duty, representing both pious and impious doctrines of the names derived from Exodus 14. The caption beneath the vine is keyed to two pages: one corresponds to Kircher's approving discussion of the divine names that emerge from the Tetragrammaton/Pentagrammaton; the other corresponds to his disapproving discussion of their abuse in amulets meant to appease guardian angels.[32] "Let the reader know," Kircher writes before explaining, in detail, how the amulets are constructed, "that sometimes under a shining Angel a black tail is found, when there is nothing so holy that the enemy of the human race will not use it under the pretext of divine worship in order to destroy souls."[33]

All three of the outerlying trees thus represent bad Jewish magical practices involving amulets. Strictly speaking, such practices are not part of the Kabbalah proper. Rather, they belong to an independent tradition of Jewish popular magic based on the power of divine and angelic names, though, as we have seen, they absorbed kabbalistic elements.[34] Kircher identifies his source for these practices as a Hebrew book entitled *Shimmush Tehillim* or the *Use of the Psalms*, which is not a kabbalistic treatise but a popular manual for performing this kind of Jewish magic. When the Vatican Library (which possesses several manuscripts of *Shimmush Tehillim*) catalogued Hebrew manuscripts in the 1660s, such treatises were listed separately from other kabbalistic treatises under the rubric of "Practical or Magical Kabbalah," revealing an awareness of the difference between such practices and the speculative and mystical traditions, even if Jewish popular magic was associated with the term "Kabbalah" in a broad sense.[35]

Thus it is worth asking why such magical practices involving amulets, which were relatively marginal to the Kabbalah, receive so much attention from Kircher, more attention than either his Jewish or Christian sources would warrant. An important part of the answer lies in Kircher's fascination with amulets and talismans in and of themselves, a fascination indicative of the motivating role that ancient and exotic objects played in his study of esoteric traditions. The primary purpose of these objects in Kircher's work was not to provide evidence of kabbalistic theories, much less to show how to put such theories into practice. Rather, it was the theories that were brought into discussion in order to explain the objects, whose illumination was the primary task. The objects came first, the theoretical framework followed.

This puts Kircher's studies in a markedly different context from that of Renaissance Neoplatonism and Hermetism—though Kircher is usually viewed simply as an untimely continuation of those traditions. It is not that Kircher was uninterested in the possibility of finding profound truths in these traditions, but this was not his chief motivation for studying them. His study of the hieroglyphs and esoteric traditions is best understood in the context of the passion for studying inscriptions, artifacts, and old and exotic manuscripts that was shared by many contemporaneous scholars—that is to say, antiquarianism.[36] Kircher had staked out a reputation as an interpreter of exotic objects, and his perceived expertise in esoteric traditions constituted part of his credentials to be such an interpreter.[37] That is to say, he studied these traditions in large measure because they offered a framework for interpreting objects and thereby illuminating distant cultures—a goal that had antiquarian value independent of any profound wisdom they may or may not contain. Thus, for Kircher, esoteric traditions were tools of antiquarianism, even if the results were different from what we normally associate with that term. In this light, the side of Kircher's studies that reached its apex in the *Egyptian Oedipus* may be seen as the offspring of an encounter between early modern antiquarianism and Renaissance occult philosophy.

To a large extent, the *Egyptian Oedipus* represents Kircher's peculiar implementation of a research program he adopted under the influence of the aristocratic antiquarian and patron of learning Nicolas-Claude Fabri de Peiresc during their association in the 1630s. Its peculiarity does not lie in its focus on esoteric subject matter per se, for other antiquarians of the time, including Peiresc, who strike us as more sober-minded than Kircher, were also interested in the study of hieroglyphs, esoteric oriental texts, and artifacts associated with magic. Peiresc, for example, had a large collection of "gnostic" amulets, whose investigation he promoted, and even Kircher's notion of using the Kabbalah to translate hieroglyphs was foreshadowed in a letter by Peiresc.[38] Having mastered Roman and Greek antiquity in the course of the sixteenth century, by the seventeenth many antiquarians and philologists increasingly turned their attention to the wonders of the East. Kircher's peculiarity with respect to more sober antiquarians rather lies in his relative lack of critical acumen and scholarly rigor in the implementation of a shared research program. If antiquarianism is usually associated with a skeptical attitude, fastidious attention to detail, and a preference for accumulating factual information rather than advancing speculative hypotheses, Kircher's work may well seem to represent its antithesis. (Indeed, his success among those receptive to his methods may be attributed in part to his ability to offer a kind of comprehensive finished product that more rigorous scholars, because of their rigor, could not.) However, the point is not the degree to which Kircher fell short of the scholarly model represented by antiquarianism, but that this was his model. The two-thousand-page *Egyptian Oedipus*, with all its recycling of Late Antique and Renaissance Neoplatonist and magical traditions, may read like a "Summa Magiae" or a "phenomenology of the occult,"[39] but formally the work was an interpretation of some (especially perplexing) ancient inscriptions, the most antiquarian of genres.

The Kabbalah, then, provided the theoretical context in which Kircher considered Jewish magical artifacts and practices, such as amulets, which consequently took on a disproportionate role in his exposition. This kind of "esoteric antiquarianism," practiced with different degrees of scholarly rigor by different practitioners, should be recognized as a factor in the continued interest in the esoteric lore associated with Renaissance magic and Neoplatonism during the seventeenth century.

But it was not only scholars and collectors who were interested in these matters. Amulets were not only, or even primarily, objects from the past to be displayed in the antiquarium; they were also widely in use in popular magical practices. In the section of the *Oedipus* devoted to "Hieroglyphic Magic," Kircher describes two "kabbalistic amulets," which he claims he was approached to explain not only by curious acquaintances but also by the Holy Office of the Inquisition, which obviously had a practical interest in the matter. As he often does in such matters, Kircher presents his discussion as a public service to the Christian reader: since it can be difficult in some of these cases to discern the false from the true, he will explain things so that should the reader come across such an amulet, he may recognize its impious nature and avoid jeopardizing his soul.[40]

Describing one of these amulets, a certain "magical coin," Kircher explains that if one considers its surface, all seems sacred and divine, but beneath the surface lurks a black scorpion's tail ready to sting overly credulous souls.[41] It is in fact a superstitious Jewish amulet, and Kircher uses his knowledge of the Kabbalah to explain its inscriptions. The nature of the coin is somewhat ambiguous; although it is written in Hebrew, the front is composed of various names of Jesus, and there is even a picture of the Christian savior in its center (Figure 6.8). Kircher, who is convinced of the Jewish provenance of the amulet, interprets the presence of Christ's image and names as a nefarious attempt to lure Christians into superstition as well as an example of the Jewish penchant for blaspheming Christ.[42] It is more likely, however, that this amulet was produced by Jewish converts to Christianity who continued to practice Jewish magic within the framework of their new religion by calling on the power of the name of Jesus along with Jewish names of God and the angels.[43]

Whatever its provenance, this amulet has particular relevance to this discussion because of its striking resemblance to another image: Kircher's diagram of the kabbalistic tree of divine names. Both figures have a face of Jesus Christ at their center, surrounded by various divine names laid out in concentric rings. Indeed, some of their inscriptions are identical: like the diagram, the amulet bears the five-letter name of Christ in the center of its front side, and its back side features (in addition to the twelve permutations of the letters of the Tetragrammaton and the names of the angels Uriel, Gabriel, Michael, and Raphael) the same four Hebrew phrases inscribed by Kircher in the openface letters of the monogram IHS.

Kircher's diagram, besides being a Jesuit emblem of Catholic universalism, can also be read as a pious Christian-kabbalistic amulet—an apotropaic talisman to ward off superstition through the power of the name of Christ. At the center are several forms of the "wonder-working" divine name of Jesus, as well as a portrait of the Savior. Christ's force radiates outward through derivative forms of the divine names, reaching all humanity, and ultimately repels the superstitious magical Kabbalah of the rabbis, which is forced to take refuge in the

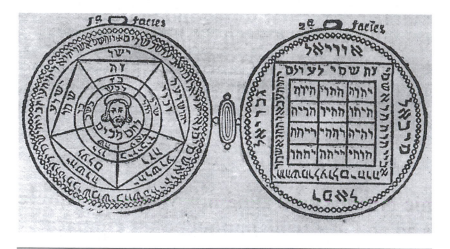

Figure 6.8. A kabbalistic amulet. *Source:* Kircher, 1652–55, vol. 2, part 2, p. 475. By permission of Stanford University Libraries.

corners—not unlike the heroic Society of Jesus, fighting heresy and superstition and spreading truth in the four corners of the globe.

Notes

1. Reuchlin 1993, p. 311.
2. Kircher 1652–55, vol. 1 fol. b1v.
3. Kircher 1652–55, vol. 2, part 1, p. 359.
4. Aquin 1625. The original work is very rare, and the plate even more so, as it is lacking in many copies. I have consulted a photograph of a loose print of the diagram that belonged to Nicolas-Claude Fabri de Peiresc, which is now deposited with Peiresc's manuscripts at the Bibliothèque Nationale in Paris; Bibliothèque Nationale, Paris MS. Latin 9340, fol. 7. I thank Peter Miller for bringing this to my attention. Secret 1985, Pl. 15, reproduces a 1735 reprint of the diagram, which is quite faithful to the original. The frontispiece to the modern Italian translation (Aquin 1993), however, bears little resemblance to the original. For d'Aquin's explanation of his diagram, I have to rely on the Italian translation.
5. Cordovero's *Pardes rimmonim* was a major source of Kircher's treatise, although Kircher did not know the author's name and referred to the work simply as "Pardes." Kircher consulted a manuscript of the work at the College of Neophytes, now Biblioteca Apostolica Vaticana (hereafter BAV) MS. Neofiti 28. The diagram is found at fol. 319r. The immediately preceding pages of the manuscript bear marginalia by Kircher.
6. See Mély, 1922, which reproduces the entire broadside. Hepburn was a Scottish Franciscan and curated Oriental manuscripts at the Vatican Library.
7. D'Aquin has an apple tree, while Kircher has a pomegranate—though in Latin a pomegranate is a "Punic apple," *malum punicum*. Kircher does not explicitly identify the lower-left tree as an olive but it resembles one, and that is how the corresponding tree is identified by d'Aquin.
8. The treatise on the Kabbalah, like the rest of the *Oedipus Aegyptiacus*, is heavily annotated with citations to sources. The citations, however, are not reliable as an indication of Kircher's actual encounter with the sources—indeed, they are often positively misleading. Many of Kircher's quotations from and references to Hebrew and Aramaic primary sources are taken secondhand (often along with ready-made Latin translations) from unacknowl-

edged Latin authors. At the same time he omits any reference to many of the secondary sources on which his work is dependent.

9. On the Christian Kabbalah, see Secret 1985, 1992; Scholem 1997; Dan 1997; Faivre and Tristan 1979; and Blau 1944.

10. Galatino 1518, bk. 2; Reuchlin 1993, bk. 3.

11. Kircher 1652–55, vol. 2, part 1, p. 287. Also see pp. 232–238 for his discussion of the mystical Trinitarian significance of the Tetragrammaton.

12. Reuchlin 1494. See Zika 1976. In addition to Reuchlin's *De Verbo Mirificio*, Kircher cites Arcangelo da Borgonovo 1557. (Here as elsewhere Kircher mistakenly gives that author's name as "Novoburgensis.")

13. Kircher 1652–55, vol. 2, part 1, p. 235.

14. In Kircher's translations these are: "hoc nomen meum in aeternum" (this is my name for eternity); "Domine, nomen tuum in aeternum Deus"(Lord, your name for eternity is God); "Deus virtutum hoc nomen meum" (God of powers this is my name); and "Ego Deus, hoc nomen meum" (I am God, this is my name). Ibid., p. 287.

15. The Hebrew text in the diagram is frequently corrupt, due to the artist confounding similarly shaped letters such as *kaf* and *bet* and transposing letters. Here as elsewhere I have corrected the obvious mistakes and followed the more reliable Hebrew names given in the body of Kircher's text.

16. On Heredia and the *Epistola secretorum*, see Scholem 1997. Forgeries by Jewish converts—primarily Heredia's *Epistola secretorum* and the interpolations in the otherwise reliable translations of kabbalistic texts prepared by Flavius Mithridates for Givoanni Pico della Mirandola—played a decisive role in the genesis of the Christian Kabbalah. On Flavius's translations and their influence, see Wirszubski 1989.

17. Kircher, 1652–55, vol. 2, part 1, p. 251. Kircher's inclusion of this divine name in the table may indicate that he did not consider it so superstitious as he felt compelled to state. In his explanation of the diagram (which occurs in a later section of the treatise than his initial negative description), he describes the second forty-two-letter name neutrally, giving no explanation of its significance or method of composition: "And these are the two divine names of forty-two letters; the first disclosed (*explicatum*) [i.e., the Trinitarian name attributed to Haccados], the second secret (*arcanum*) [i.e., the name derived from letter combinations] . . ." Ibid., p. 287.

18. Ibid., p. 288.

19. Ibid., pp. 267 ff.

20. Ibid., p. 273.

21. The theurgical significance involves the use of the angel names in mystical prayer, described by Kircher; ibid., p. 274. The less religiously magical significance of the names is only implicit in the kabbalistic sources, but becomes explicit in Jewish magical practices based on the construction of amulets with the seventy-two angel names, as discussed below.

22. Arcangelo da Borgonovo 1569, p. 1. Borgonovo's discussion of Christ as the Tree of Life may also have inspired parts of Kircher's intepretation; ibid., pp. 21–28.

23. The relevant passage of Borgonovo appears, uncited, in the original manuscript of *Oedipus Aegyptiacus*, Biblioteca Nazionale Centrale Vittorio Emanuele, Rome (BNVE) MS. Ges. 1235, fols. 125r–v. Kircher removed this section after the Jesuit Revisors, who reviewed the text prior to publication, called attention to the fact that he had plagiarized from Borgonovo; see Archivum Romanum Societatis Iesu (hereafter ARSI) FG 668, fol. 392. See Stolzenberg 2004 and Stolzenberg forthcoming. It is now known that Borgonovo had himself plagiarized much of his text from the work of his deceased teacher, Francesco Giorgi; see Wirszubski 1974; Secret 1974. Hepburn's *Virga aurea* (see above) was likely another link in the chain of association that led Kircher to this vision of the name of God in seventy-two languages.

24. Allen, 2000 pp. 142–5

25. Kircher, 1652–55, vol. 2, part 1, p. 287.

26. See Zika 1976, p. 128.

27. On this diagram considered as a Jesuit emblem, see Michael John Gorman, "The Angel and the Compass: Athanasius Kircher's Geographical Project," in this volume.

28. See Mungello 1985. On the congruence of Kircher's studies of the hieroglyphs and other occult traditions with the ideology of the post-Tridentine Church, see Cipriani 1993; and Pastine 1978.

29. On the *prisca theologia*, see Walker 1972, esp. pp. 1–2. Beginnning with Pico, most Christian interpreters of the Kabbalah traced that tradition to Moses, but Jewish views were less uniform; Altmann 1987, p. 7.

30. By these comments, I do not mean to attribute to Kircher an explicit and deliberate anti-Christian argument, but only to point out certain implications that may be easily derived from his line of argument. The fact that ancient Jews and pagans knew Christian mysteries does not, of course, contradict the most important rationale for Christ's incarnation, the redemption of the original sin. It is notable, however, that the original sin is all but absent from Kircher's account of the transmission of Adamic wisdom to postlapsarian posterity.

31. In fact, in his explanation of the amulet (Kircher 1652–55, vol. 2, part 1, p. 352), Kircher gives the six-letter name as   . But this appears to be an error, as it is inconsistent with the forty-two-letter name (as given in Kircher 1652–55, vol. 2, part 1, p. 258) of which it is supposed to be the beginning. The text given in the diagram is even more corrupt.

32. Each of these amulets is composed of one of the seventy-two angel names written with a corresponding verse from the psalms. Kircher, 1652–55, vol. 2, part 1, pp. 274–281. Kircher also discusses the amulets based on the seventy-two names, along with the amulets represented by the olive and pomegranate trees, in the chapter on kabbalistic astrology. Ibid., pp. 352–353.

33. Ibid., p. 271.

34. By this I mean that these popular practices involved neither the type of theurgic activity directed toward affecting the realm of the sefirot nor the ecstatic practices meant to induce divine union, which constitute the practical dimensions of the two main divisions of the Kabbalah. (See Idel 1988.) Rather, practices such as the use of amulets described in the *Shimmush Tehillim*, although they sometimes employed elements derived from the Kabbalah—such as the names of God constructed by kabbalistic hermeneutic techniques—were popular practices used to attract good fortune and repel bad in the mundane realm of daily life. On "practical Kabbalah," see Scholem 1978, pp. 182–189, who observes: "Historically speaking, a large part of the contents of practical Kabbalah considerably predate those of speculative Kabbalah and are not dependent on them. In effect, what came to be considered practical Kabbalah constituted an agglomeration of all the magical practices that developed in Judaism from the talmudic period down through the Middle Ages."

35. Giulio Bartolocci, "Morè Makòm. Index Materiarum Authorum & titulorum librorum M.S. Ebraicorum Bibliothecae Vaticane, Palatinae, & Urbinatis" (1661): BAV Vat. Lat. 13197–13199. "Cabala Practica, Magica, etc." in vol. 3, fols. 239–246. The distinction between these works and those defined simply as "Cabalistae" is explained at vol. 1, fols. 137–138: "Until now we have listed kabbalistic books which are called Work of Creation and Work of the Chariot (*Maassè Bereschith, et Maassè Marchevà*); which deal with the external works of God (*de operibus dei ad extra*), the divine attributes, and the rewards and punishments owed to men according to their works. Now are noted Kabbalistic codices which are called operatory, for the very reason that they [the authors] boast that they can produce many marvels and supernatural effects by the invocation of certain good names or evil spirits."

36. The classic descriptions of early modern antiquarianism are Momigliano 1966, 1990.

37. Kircher's professional identity as an interpreter of mysterious objects and inscriptions can be seen especially clearly in Kaspar Schott's portrait of Kircher in his preface to the first volume of the *Oedipus*: "Benevoli Lectori," Kircher 1652–55, vol. 1, fols. c2r–d1v. It is true that the amulets represented by the trees in the diagram are not physical specimens but texts meant to be written on paper or parchment—they are practices more than objects. Nonetheless, inasmuch as his interest in amulets in general was fueled by antiquarian interest in physical specimens, the point holds. Furthermore, Kircher's discussion of the written amulets is based, as he stresses, on information culled from unpublished Hebrew manuscripts, making their exposition a kind of antiquarian endeavor. The other kabbalistic amulets described by Kircher (discussed below) were specific specimens, described by Kircher as "coins" (*nummi*), the archetypical object of antiquarian study.

38. This dimension of Peiresc's antiquarianism emerges clearly in Agnès Bresson's edition of his correspondence with Saumaise and others: Peiresc 1992. Peiresc refers (with some skepticism) to the efforts of a M. St.-Clerc to interpret a hieroglyphic inscription "by the Kabbalah" in a 1632 letter to d'Aubery; Peiresc 1888–98, vol. 7, 221. An example of Peiresc's promotion of the study of "gnostic" amulets from his collection is treated in Barb 1953.

Peiresc also sent Kircher an Arabic magical seal from his collection, which he interpreted in Kircher 1652–55, vol. 2, part 1, p. 392. None of this is to deny that Peiresc's interest in such matters was much, much more circumspect than Kircher's, and there is no doubt that he would have been greatly dismayed by the *Oedipus Aegyptiacus*, despite its frequent homages to him, had he lived to see its publication. On Peiresc's antiquarianism more generally, see Miller 2000.

39. Evans 1979, pp. 440–441.

40. Kircher 1652–55, vol. 2, part 2, p. 474. Kircher's reference to the Inquisition's desire for him to publish this material is clearly intended to deflect criticism that his detailed descriptions of illicit magical practices were too dangerous to be published. Precisely this complaint was made regarding Kircher's descriptions of magical seals by the Jesuit censors charged with reviewing the *Oedipus* manuscript, apparently to no avail: "Thus it does not seem permissible for the author to lay out how each superstitious seal may be composed and arranged in practice for superstition and magic. Nor does the author do enough when he reproves the aforesaid seals as superstitious and to be shunned, since some curious and insufficiently God-fearing individuals might esteem them and put them to use." ARSI FG 668, fol. 396r.

41. Kircher 1652–55, vol. 2, part 2, pp. 474–475.

42. Ibid., pp. 476–477. Also see pp. 477–478 on Jewish blaspheming against Christ.

43. A version of this same amulet, as well as other similar kabbalistic amulets in use among Jewish converts at the end of the seventeenth century, is described by Bartolocci 1675–93, vol. 4, pp. 158–165, 233–235. The seal in question is depicted at p. 162.

7

Kircher's Chronology*

ANTHONY GRAFTON

It is tempting to think that Gershom Scholem might have read the work of Athanasius Kircher. For a powerful elective affinity links the two men. Like Scholem in the years around 1920, so Kircher in the years after 1620 found himself committed, to his own surprise, to a scholarly work of redemption. He would spend his life collecting and repairing the broken fragments of a lost tradition. Scholem dedicated himself to the Kabbalah at a time when kabbalists rejected history and talmudists scorned mysticism. Kircher made himself the master of Egyptian studies after decades in which Counter-Reforming popes and Calvinist professors had competed to exorcise Egypt and its hieroglyphs from the Western tradition. Like Scholem, Kircher succeeded marvelously at his task. In his later years in Rome, he became the acknowledged expert on Egyptian hieroglyphs and other ancient scripts and languages, the creator of a renowned research center and collection, the author of a series of weighty and respected, if unsalable, books, and the scholarly adviser on dizzyingly theatrical urban projects dominated by obelisks.[1]

Like Scholem, Kircher had to confront and deal with the scholarly work of an erudite sect, specialists in criticism whose method gleamed with the frightening destructive power of a brand-new power saw. Scholem wrestled with the votaries of the *Wissenschaft des Judentums*: nineteenth-century scholars like Leopold Zunz and Heinrich Graetz and their twentieth-century disciples. These men applied the analytical and philological methods of German philology to Jewish sources. By doing so, Scholem argued in a famous lecture, they had made it possible to rethink the Jewish past, but they had purchased their triumphs at a terrifyingly high price. They threatened to relegate vital parts of Jewish tradition to the dustbin of history.[2] Kircher, for his part, struggled with the work of experts on technical chronology: sixteenth- and seventeenth-century scholars like Joseph Scaliger and Kircher's Jesuit confrère Denis Petau. These men linked philology with astronomy and compared the Bible with secular histories like that of Herodotus. By doing so, they rewrote ancient history, replacing its traditional, vague foundation dates with precise, exotic new ones like that of the accession of Nabonassar to the throne of Babylon on 26 February 747 B.C. At the same time, however, they threatened to gut history of its providential order, and even to reduce it to chaos. The templates that had traditionally revealed the purpose and order of the chaos of regnal years and battles, invasions, and inventions that filled the columns of traditional world chronicles—for example, the scheme of the Four Monarchies, derived from the prophetic vision of Daniel—disintegrated under scholarly scrutiny. As early as 1566, Jean Bodin noted that Daniel's scheme lacked room for the largest monarchies of his day, the Spanish and the Turkish, as well as great ancient ones like those of the Chaldeans and the Parthians. The neatly ordered, teleological world history purveyed by textbooks, dramatized by millenarian sermons, and dazzlingly illuminated by Albrecht Altdorfer's *Battle of Alexander* collapsed into a disorderly heap of empires without end.[3]

Worse still, the neatly defined, relatively short time line of the Bible began to fray. Aztec and Chinese chronologies, which scholars avidly collected and discussed, stretched back, apparently, as far as ten or twenty thousand years before the birth of the Messiah. So, according to no less an authority than Plato, did Egyptian history. By the end of the sixteenth century, chronologically informed heretics asserted—among many other worrying propositions— that the world was far older than the biblical account stated. Giordano Bruno made clear, in one of Zeus's speeches in The Expulsion of the Triumphant Beast, that only "certi magri glosatori" tried to reduce the six thousand years that stretched alarmingly, according to good ancient authority, between Zoroaster and Plato to harmless lunar months. He died on the Campo de' Fiori for this chronological heresy, among many others.[4] Across the confessional divide and at the other end of Bruno's Europe, Christopher Marlowe asserted, in the hearing of an informer, "That the Indians and many authours of antiquity have assuredly written of above sixteen thousand years whereas Adam is proved to have lived within six thousand years."[5] In the 1650s, Isaac la Peyrère published the first extensive effort to prove a similar thesis from the Bible and from pagan historians. His short Latin book provoked multiple refutations even though it omitted most of the most telling technical evidence then known against the biblical chronology.[6] Spinoza's *Tractatus*, though chiefly concerned with different issues, also helped to inspire radical rethinking of the status of the Old Testament.

No wonder, then, that seventeenth-century Catholic thinkers who took an interest in chronology often viewed the field with anxiety or melancholy. Chronology threatened orthodoxy—indeed, it threatened certainty. The Cistercian abbot Paul Pezron, writing in 1687, insisted that chronologers who followed the shorter chronology of the Hebrew Bible—as most experts had—could not accommodate the history of Egypt and China within the short period, less than 2,500 years, which it allowed between the Flood and the birth of Jesus. Only by accepting the longer chronology of the Septuagint, the ancient Greek translation of the Old Testament, could Catholics hope to defend the Bible against the Jews, pagans, and *esprits forts* who sought to deny its authority.[7] This position provoked a vigorous refutation from the Benedictine Jean Martianay, who redoubtably defended the Hebrew text. A similar controversy between Georg Horn and Isaac Vossius shook the Protestant world at the same time.[8] The ancient records seemed at once scanty and contradictory, and the notorious problems they raised were mind-bendingly complex. Chronology's stakes became frighteningly high: as Pezron put it, "time, which consumes all things and seems to want to relegate everything to eternal oblivion, has virtually deprived the human race of knowledge of its extent and antiquity."[9]

Kircher—as Thomas Leinkauf has shown in his wonderful study of the Jesuit's philosophy—firmly believed in continuity, in the order of being as in the order of history.[10] But historical continuity required a continuous chronology, as Kircher implicitly acknowledged when he equipped his works with long tables of the names of rulers and their dates, and as he explicitly asserted more than once. These features of Kircher's work have attracted far less attention from modern scholars than his magnificent illustrations of Babylonian and Egyptian monuments. Their neglect is understandable enough. The discipline of chronology itself fell into oblivion as long ago as the eighteenth century—at least in up-to-date circles. Even moderns who respected erudition— like Edward Gibbon—found chronology slightly absurd. As a precocious teenager, to be sure, Gibbon exhausted himself trying to weigh the chronological systems of Scaliger, Petau, and others: "the Dynasties of Assyria and Egypt," he recalled, "were my top and cricket-ball: and my sleep has been disturbed by the difficulty of reconciling the Septuagint with the Hebrew computation." But the historian's erudite songs of innocence eventually turned into cautious songs of experience: "at a riper age I no longer presume to connect the Greek, the Jewish and the Egyptian antiquities which are lost in a distant cloud: nor is this the only instance in which the belief and knowledge of the child are superseded by the more rational ignorance of the man."[11] Chronology, in other words—especially the sort that most interested Kircher—became a synonym in the age of reason for mindless pedantry and foolish efforts to solve insoluble problems. The very name of the discipline seemed, and seems, to demand the adjective "mere."

In the sixteenth and seventeenth centuries, however, chronology occupied a prominent place in scholars' mental topographies of the world of learning. In recent decades, few have had the desire—fewer still the patience—to find their way through the numerical and linguistic brambles that sprout on the thousands of folio pages that Joseph Scaliger dedicated to chronology—not to mention the sources that he drew on and the even more voluminous reactions that he provoked. Yet Scaliger's two massive books, the *De emendatione temporum* of 1583 and the *Thesaurus temporum* of 1606, won him every distinction that scholarship could bring a Calvinist in the years around 1600. His rewards ranged from efforts at plagiarism and sharp critiques by Jesuits—a point to which I will return—to a chair at the most innovative university in Europe, that at Leiden, and not just an ordinary professorship at that, but a full-time research post that made him the envy of his successors, who had to teach as well as to compile massive folios. In Kircher's time, in other words, chronology mattered; it even seemed exciting.

When Kircher set out to do chronology, moreover, he entered intellectual territory into which others had already cut roads, and in which certain areas had long been settled. Failure to recognize this fact has often led modern scholars astray. Consider one small example. In the *Tower of Babel* (*Turris Babel*) (1679) and elsewhere, Kircher raised the question of how the human race could possibly have increased so rapidly in a mere 275 years after the Flood as to enable Nimrod to rear his tower. A demographic thought experiment assured him that no problem existed. If each of the sons of Noah had a son and a daughter each year, and all of them lived and began to procreate when they reached thirty, the rules of the combinatory art showed that the population of the earth could have become as large as 23,328,000,000 by the time of the Tower of Babel.[12] Kircher offered this argument as his own, and it looks characteristically quaint. In fact, however, it was only a new version of what had become almost a tradition by his time. Abraham Bucholzer and others had already carried out similar computations. Walter Raleigh used them to show that Egypt and other lands had already been inhabited before the Flood: "in the infancy of the first age, when the bodies of men were most perfect, even within 130 years (the same, if not a greater) number might be increased; and so within 70 years later (that is, by such time as the world had stood 200 years) as well Assyria, Syria, and Egypt, might be possess'd before the flood, as they were within the same time after it."[13] Kircher's efforts at historical demography, like Raleigh's, represented a highly traditional effort to apply the tools of logic—and mathematics—to the austere family dramas of the Old Testament.

To enter Kircher's chronological universe is anything but simple, however—even for one who knows the literature of the field. Like many contemporary scholars, he liberally cited the earlier polymaths on whose works he drew. On inspection, however, Kircher's lists of secondary sources show surprising omissions. By the seventeenth century, every serious student of chronology, Catholic, Lutheran, or Calvinist, agreed on the identity of those who had made it a rigorous discipline. Pezron, for example, held that the greatest authorities had led their followers down a series of wrong paths, since they insisted on following the shorter Hebrew chronology. Yet even he wrote with special respect of Joseph Scaliger, "one of the great men of our time, and especially expert in the study of time," and Denis Petau, "who absolutely commands this field of study," and who "never contradicted" Scaliger on the biblical text, "even though he never spares him where any other subject is concerned."[14] Gibbon, recalling his early obsession with the field, traced the development of its literature in the seventeenth century, naming a slew of names, almost all of them irredeemably obscure in his time (to say nothing of ours): "from Strauchius I imbibed the elements of Chronology: the tables of Helvicus and Anderson, the annals of Usher and Prideaux distinguished the connection of events. . . . In my childish balance I presumed to weigh the systems of Scaliger and Petavius, of Marsham and Newton."[15] The modern reader naturally expects the admirably well-informed Kircher to make similar references.

In fact, however, Kircher did not. Instead of citing Scaliger or Petau, he referred by preference to the annalistic chronologies and biblical commentaries of earlier Jesuits, Torniellus, Salianus, and Pereira, none of whom practiced chronology in its bravura high-tech form. At times, moreover, he almost went out of his way to cite old-fashioned texts and commentators. In the *Pamphili Obelisk* (*Obeliscus Pamphilius*) (1650), for example, Kircher set out to identify the first, Chaldean Zoroaster. He analyzed the name as a Chaldean compound meaning "forming idols of hidden fire." And he asserted: "that Zoroaster, that celebrated inventor of magic, was Ham, the son of Noah, and he received this name because of the marvels he worked with magical power."[16] A massive tower of evidence—not all of it obviously authoritative—supported this theory. Gregory of Tours, for example, described Ham, in his *History of the Franks*, as a magician and the inventor of idolatry, and explained that he was called Zoroaster when he passed over to the Persians. Other authors, primary and secondary, confirmed this view. One name in particular brings the reader up short: "Berosus," writes Kircher, "identifies this Zoroaster with Cham, whom he also calls Chameses, that is, shameless, the Saturn of the Egyptians."[17]

Every well-informed reader of ancient and modern chronology knew that two sets of texts by Berosus were in circulation. A Babylonian priest named Berossus recorded the traditions of his people for their Greek and Macedonian conquerors in the third century B.C. Fragments of his work, quoted variously by Pliny, Josephus, and a number of late Greek writers, had attracted the attention of Bodin and many other scholars before Scaliger collected them systematically. He published these texts, with an elaborate commentary, in 1598 in the second edition of his *De emendatione temporum*. The long appendix in which they appeared marked the first effort to produce something like the massive collections of fragments of the Greek historians assembled by philologists in the nineteenth and twentieth centuries.[18] But a history of ancient times in five books, extant only in Latin and also ascribed to Berosus the Chaldean priest, had reached an even wider public after its first appearance in 1498. This second Berosus usefully connected the Old Testament history of the Jews with the story of the other nations. He also deftly refuted the lies of pagans like Herodotus and Diodorus Siculus. His learned commentator, the papal theologian Giovanni Nanni, or Annius, of Viterbo, made these points even more clearly than Berosus did, in a commentary several times longer than the text. No wonder, then, that Kircher found his testimony helpful.[19]

Nanni, however, wrote not only the commentary on Berosus, but the text itself—as scholars had repeatedly pointed out. As Beatus Rhenanus put it, aptly quoting one of Erasmus's adages, "one of them milks the he-goat, and the other holds out the sieve."[20] Scaliger collected the genuine texts of Berossus in order to drive the false ones off the market. In quoting the Annian Berosus as a genuine ancient text, Kircher violated the normal rules of play for mid-seventeenth-century chronology.

The reference to an outdated and dubious source was not an isolated slip. In the *Turris Babel*, which appeared as late as 1679, Kircher repeated his identification of Zoroaster and revealed what was probably its original, intermediary source—even as he made clear that he recognized that the Latin Berosus was not the only one:

> The Annian Berosus [he writes] narrates that this Zoroaster was the same as Cham, the son of Noah, in book III of his *Antiquities*. Joannes Lucidus Samotheus writes this in Book II, chapter 5, and we follow him in the *Obeliscus Pamphilius*.[21]

Joannes Lucidus Samotheus was the pen name of an early-sixteenth-century chronologer, Giovanni Maria Tolosani, whose *Opusculum de emendationibus temporum* first appeared in 1537. This book is a primitive, annalistic history of the world, in which ample quotations from the Annian forgeries adorn an otherwise bare and unconvincing narrative. Lucidus did not always accept Berosus's testimony; he denied, for example, Berosus's claim that Noah had used astrology to predict the Flood, insisting that he had done so instead by divine revelation.[22] But he did quote Berosus's assertion that Cham, "who always studied magic and necromancy, obtained the name Zoroaster."[23] And he accepted, as Kircher would, that Ham bore the multiple names Chameses, Zoroaster, and Saturn, since this familiar euhemerist technique enabled him to fold Greek mythology into sacred history.

Zoroaster's date mattered to Kircher. Like Giordano Bruno, he knew that normally reliable ancient writers, starting with Xanthus of Lydia, had dated the Persian prophet to six thousand years before the time of Plato. Like Bruno, he also knew that the astronomer Eudoxus had tried to reduce Zoroaster's antiquity, probably at Plato's request, by interpreting the six thousand years as so many lunar months. And like Bruno, he found this effort to save the chronological phenomena unconvincing. By identifying Zoroaster with Ham, he could reveal the ancients' "error maximus" and defend the authority of the Scriptures. Instead of reducing the six thousand years to five hundred, he simply eliminated the whole account from history because it contradicted the Bible. It seems curious, to say the least, that Kircher relied for this central point neither on the numerous Jesuits who had devoted themselves to chronological and biblical studies, nor on the original text of the Annian Berosus, but on an early-sixteenth-century writer who showed no expertise in mathematics, astronomy, or philology.

Seen in the context of Jesuit scholarship, moreover, Kircher's tactics look even curioser. At the end of the sixteenth century, the Jesuit Antonio Possevino undertook the first of what became a series of full-scale attacks on Scaliger's chronology by members of the Society. In his massive effort to catalogue—and control—the intellectual resources available to Christian scholars, the *Bibliotheca selecta*, Possevino made clear that many scholars had gone wrong by trusting in the Annian forgeries. He then suggested that Scaliger himself—the very man who collected the original Greek fragments of Berossus and others—had made the same mistake.[24] This charge was a complete and no doubt deliberate falsification, which disgusted and enraged its victim.[25] But it appeared in an authoritative statement of Catholic cultural policy—one that, like the official censorship, set out to extirpate both theological and factual errors. When Kircher reposed faith in "the Annian Berosus," he seemed—to judge from Possevino—to join hands not only with a Catholic forger, but also with a contumacious heretic.

Kircher's approach to Egyptian chronology seems odder still. In the *Egyptian Oedipus* (*Oedipus Aegyptiacus*) (1652–55) he dedicated a whole section to the "physical-chronological question, whether Egypt was inhabited before the Flood, or not, and who its first kings were."[26] In this case too, everyone knew the basic problem. The chronicle of Eusebius, in the Latin recension of Saint Jerome, began with Abraham—and made him contemporary with the "sixteenth power of the Egyptians, which they call a dynasty."[27] This presumably meant that fifteen Egyptian dynasties must somehow have existed in the very short interval—some 350 years by the Hebrew computation—that separated Abraham's birth from the Flood (more precisely, they must have existed in the even shorter interval between Nimrod's kingdom, the first one, and Abraham).

Sixteenth-century chronologers struggled to assimilate this awkward information. What to do with information that seemed to threaten the chronological spine of sacred history? Reject it? Interpret it safely? Avoid controversy? Or search the apparently chaotic record for some hidden truth? Some scholars, such as Philip Melanchthon and Johannes Carion, adroitly suppressed evidence of conflict. They remarked only that the Kingdom of Egypt, though rich and powerful, had been secondary in age and prestige to Babylon—just as France, in modern times, was second in prestige to the Holy Roman Empire—and went on their way rejoicing.[28] Others wrestled with the apparent inconsistencies. Lucidus quoted Eusebius to the effect that the term *dynasty* must mean "a rule of some determined period"—but made no effort to explain why Eusebius's records did not begin with the first of them.[29] Still others strayed into more dangerous territory. The geographer Gerardus Mercator, for example, speculated that the Egyptian dynasties "must have been before the Flood." The question was clearly delicate—as is evident from the fact that Benito Pereira refuted Mercator at length, while even the bold Walter Raleigh, who went over the whole problem at length, took a *via media*. He criticized both Mercator, who had accepted the popular view that gave "too much credit to the Egyptian antiquities," and Pereira, who had dismissed them as "fables."[30]

Where others made dangerous suggestions, Scaliger put the chronological cat among the theological pigeons. In 1602, reading through the unpublished Byzantine world chronicle of George Syncellus, he discovered the list of Egyptian dynasties compiled by the priest Manetho of Sebennytus in the third century B.C. Manetho's lists made clear that the thirty-one Egyptian dynasties—including the first fifteen—were just that, long series of kings with distinct names. He duly provided these, along with their regnal years. The thirty-first dynasty ended, as Scaliger knew, in 329 B.C. with Alexander's conquest of Egypt. But the period from the first to the thirty-first dynasty covered, in Manetho, no fewer than 5,355 years. The first dynasty, accordingly, began not just before the Deluge, but before the Creation itself—and even before the beginning of Scaliger's Julian Period in 4713 B.C.[31]

Scaliger, as a pious Christian, complained of the "prodigious antiquity" of these dynasties. But he felt unable to reject them completely. So he postulated what he called a "period of proleptic time," time before Creation itself, in which he listed them. And he described what he had done, provocatively, as an example of the rhetorical figure of "oxymoron—the statement that something took place when time did not exist."[32] In 1606, when Scaliger's *Thesaurus temporum* appeared, his new evidence for Egyptian deep time set off explosive reactions in learned readers, most of whom were prepared in advance to see long chronologies as dangerous. Many experts firmly rejected both Manetho and Scaliger's dealings with the dynasty lists. "I don't see"—so Scaliger's close friend Isaac Casaubon wrote in his copy of Scaliger's book—"of what use these inventions of foolish peoples are for real history."[33] Jesuits, who had already identified Scaliger as a public enemy, sharpened their nibs. Petau, the Jesuits' designated technical chronologer, denounced Manetho's Egyptian dynasties as "forged and absurd" and lampooned Scaliger for being so foolish as to accept them.[34] Still others strove to insert the dynasties into Christian chronology, by treating them as simultaneous rather than successive or by using the longer chronology of the Septuagint, the Greek Old Testament, to accommodate them.

In the *Turris Babel*, which appeared in 1679, Kircher made plain that he followed Pereira, Torniellus, and Salianus—the conservative Jesuits who, like Petau, found proof in the Bible that "As there was no division of languages before the Flood, so there was also no division of nations. Hence there could not have been Egyptians before the Flood; far less could they have filled up some 15 dynasties that lasted 3317 years, and 74 more years of a sixteenth dynasty, as Scaliger and Africanus have it."[35] Kircher too declared, "on the basis of the irrefutable testimony of Sacred Scripture," that no individual kingdoms could have existed before the confusion of tongues at Babel. Once again he followed Lucidus, whom he quoted, in arguing that the first sixteen dynasties "must have been either fewer in number or very short." But he also made one curious concession: "When I mentioned the Egyptian dynasties at length in volume I of the *Oedipus Aegyptiacus*," he now wrote, "even before the Flood, that was not because I thought as much, but following the opinion of the Egyptians, the Arabs and Manetho."[36] Even though Kircher seemingly took back his original opinion, in other words, he referred readers to his older synthetic work on Egypt for a fuller account of his views.

More important, by the time Kircher wrote the *Turris Babel*, he evidently had come to regard his arguments in the *Oedipus* as somehow dangerous. And that is not surprising. By the 1670s, the works of La Peyrère, Spinoza, and others had made these questions increasingly controversial. A quarter of a century before, Kircher had treated Egyptian chronology in quite a different way. Even in the *Oedipus*, Kircher conceded that many regarded the dynasties as an invention. But he argued that men before the Flood had already known the art of politics as well as other arts and crafts. Kingdoms, in other words, had existed. Their inhabitants—who were giants, and long-lived—could have filled the world, as Noah's sons would, with a vast population (1,247,224,717,455, he estimated).[37] The sons of Noah, moreover, must have told their curious children about life before the Flood, and inscriptions on rocks and oral traditions would have preserved information about the antediluvian kingdoms. Plato, after all, had learned of the antediluvian wars of Atlantis.[38]

Even in this context, Kircher admitted that many found the Greek dynasties of Manetho and Scaliger manifestly absurd, and he never discussed Scaliger's analysis of the documents at length. Instead, he cited a later Leiden professor, Claude Saumaise, who mentioned that Chaldean and Egyptian astrologers had claimed they had carried on their art for tens of thousands of years—and cited a text that referred to thirty Egyptian dynasties. Kircher cited Saumaise, moreover, non-ironically. He carefully ignored Saumaise's characteristically biting remark, based on a passage in Pliny, that it was remarkable that the Chaldeans had observed the stars for so many thousand years without ever learning that the moon borrowed its light from the sun.[39] But Saumaise provided no more conclusive arguments or evidence about Egyptian antiquity than Scaliger did. Kircher found his chief support for arguing that the Egyptian kingdom predated the Flood in a very different quarter of the republic of letters. As he himself put it: "I know that many will dismiss dynasties like these as pure inventions, and rubbish. In fact, I recall that I too shared this opinion, until, once I had gained more solid knowledge of "Eastern traditions and sources," I finally found that they are not so spurious as many might think."[40] The identity of these "Eastern traditions and sources," and the circumstances in which Kircher obtained and used them, reveal much about the privileged intellectual position he occupied in Rome, at the center of an intellectual whirlpool where all new philological and historical results eventually washed up—and about the central role of chronology in wide-ranging local and international discussions.

Kircher relied chiefly on two informants, one of whom had been dead for about a century and a half. The prolific Arabic writer Jalāl al-dīn al-Suyūtī (1455–1505), a proud native of Cairo, wrote among a vast number of other works a history of Egypt.[41] This—like a number of earlier local histories in Arabic—emphasized the achievements of the Egyptians in Pharaonic and Hellenistic times.[42] Al-Suyūtī and other writers, some of whom he cited, stated clearly that a whole series of Egyptian kings had ruled before the Flood. Kircher quoted these statements at length, in Arabic and in accurate Latin translations. They enabled him to narrate many curious details about the magical achievements of a number of individual Egyptian rulers—like the skilled magician Mesram, who used his art "to carry out great things, and it is said that he tamed a lion and rode it, and it is said that while that king rode, demons carried him, sitting on a throne, until he reached the middle of the Ocean, and he established there a bright citadel, and in it he put an idol of the sun, and he carved his name in it."[43] Kircher admitted that "the philologists of our day" would see these strange texts, with their tales of wise kings and powerful talismans, as mere "apocrypha." But he insisted that he could not have omitted them, "both because these histories are unknown to the Latins, and because I have found some tiny spark of the truth hidden even under the ashes of these barbarous accounts."[44]

Kircher drew a pregnant, intellectually generous moral from this discovery: "I think that not everything that stinks of myths and inventions should immediately be rejected. The Arabs have many things, unknown to the Greeks and the Latins, which, I might hope, if the learned should apply their skills to publishing them, would bring great profit to the Republic of Letters, with regard to many matters that have long been the objects of debate."[45] Far from setting out his new material with the reserve that Scaliger and Saumaise had shown, in other words, Kircher resonantly announced its importance. His commentary made clear that wise scholars would emulate his example and be willing to find the tiny fragments of historical tradition that a shattered tradition might conceal. Few scholars of the time responded so openly to such challenging material.

Kircher did not turn up the new evidence on his own, nor was he the first to see its bearing on traditional Christian chronology. His second, living informant was his friend, the Maronite scholar Abraham Ecchellensis, who served as the king of France's Arabic translator, taught Arabic in Rome, and catalogued the Vatican's oriental manuscripts; Echellensis turned up al-Suyūtī's work among a batch of Arabic manuscripts he obtained in Pisa and gave to Cardinal Francesco Barberini. He quoted the text himself while preparing his own translation of a much less challenging text—the thirteenth-century Arabic chronicle of the Christian Copt Ibn ar-Rahib, which he brought out in 1651.[46] Ibn ar-Rahib's chronology fit comfortably within the biblical framework. But Ecchellensis pointed out, in his commentary on the text, that al-Suyūtī had recorded Egyptian claims to a history that stretched back for tens of thousands of years.[47] Kircher began studying al-Suyūtī's work as early as 1636. Lucas Holstenius, the learned bibliophile who served as librarian first for the Barberini and then for the Vatican, wrote to Peiresc in that year that "the most remarkable [of the books obtained by Ecchellensis] is an Egyptian chronicle that runs from the Creation down to St. Louis's expedition. Kircher, who has received this manuscript and describes it as genuinely remarkable, will write a detailed account of it for you."[48] Kircher's conversations with Ecchellensis may well have turned on the two men's similar approach to source criticism. In the preface to his own work, which appeared just before the *Oedipus*, Ecchellensis argued fiercely that "since we do not understand the languages" that the Egyptians and Chaldeans had used, and their histories were not accessible, one must draw on Arabic historians for detailed information about them.[49] From the tall pages of minutely detailed works of baroque scholarship rises the low, unexpected hum of lively, forgotten conversations about the nature of biblical time and the value of new historical sources.

The language both men used shows how boldly Kircher speculated as he tried to reconstruct ancient chronology. He felt able to defy the fellow Jesuits on whom he normally relied, and whom he always cited—so long as he did not have to rely on Scaliger's Greek sources when doing so. It seems likely that Abraham—a feisty soul who spent much of his time from 1645 to 1653 in Paris, where the limits of permissible discussion on sacred history were wider than in Rome—had a substantial impact on him. And it seems certain that Kircher himself, from the 1630s to the 1650s, attacked these matters with a boldness that startled and even frightened his older, more discreet self, as the openness of the midcentury made way for the era of the Rites Controversy.

Kircher conceded the difficulties involved in establishing a solid Egyptian chronology. But he eloquently evoked the "propensity, basic to my nature, to work out things of this sort," which had led him—in a characteristically heroic metaphor—"to break through this isthmus as well." Chronology, Kircher insisted, played an essential role in his larger enterprise of restoration. And the "traditions and monuments of the Orientals" proved that the Egyptian dynasties somehow belonged to the field. Like Scaliger, in other words, Kircher accepted the historicity of Manetho's dynasties, at least to some limited extent. He thus made his own the thesis that antediluvian history was far richer, and could be reconstructed more completely, than normal exegetes of the Old Testament believed.

Kircher saw Hermes Trismegistus, after all, as the restorer of primeval doctrines as well as the creator of hieroglyphs. It made perfect sense to have him reconstruct—among other lost arts—those of a lost Egyptian kingdom. And two other sets of arguments that Kircher developed also reveal his belief that he could retrace the history of antediluvian culture. In the *Arca Noë* he drew from Josephus the tale of the two columns set up by Seth, one of stone and one of brick, with the secrets of nature inscribed on them. These showed that the peoples before the Flood had had "all the arts necessary to human life," and even "commerce, without which human society could hardly be preserved" (one hears the Jesuit's voice especially clearly here). Commerce, of course, could not exist without writing—which the antediluvian giants had also used to record their deeds, traditions, and sciences for posterity.[50] In citing and interpreting this material as he did, Kircher came strikingly close to the *esprits forts*. Gulielmus Sossus, for example, made a character in his dialogues *De numine historiae* assert that the historian Nicholas of Damascus could have used Seth's columns to learn "deep historical secrets" not attested in the Bible. Josephus in turn could have learned from Nicholas, as well as from Moses: "Josephus owed much of his enlightenment to gentiles. For in his day, almost all the knowledge of the antediluvians survived on public monuments."[51]

In another case Kircher came even closer to Scaliger than he had when he extended Egyptian history, though again he never said as much. Scaliger followed tradition in one respect at least in the *Thesaurus temporum*, his second great book on chronology. He folded the history of languages into the larger history of nations, tracing the development of ancient alphabets from that of the Samaritans to what he saw as the late, square-character Hebrew script still in use in his own time and, as he brilliantly conjectured, to Greek as well.[52] Kircher rejected Scaliger's particular scheme and offered his own, much more capacious history of human and angelic alphabets in its place. Unlike Scaliger, moreover, he firmly insisted that the Hebrew of the Old Testament was the oldest language. But he also told Ferdinand III, who asked him to work out a sort of genealogy of all the languages in existence, that the task was impossible. When a printer dropped a form of type, Kircher pointed out, the characters that had once been organized in words scattered into random, meaningless groups on the floor. The same thing had happened to human languages in history. The infinite vicissitudes of human affairs and the numberless minglings of peoples had made it impossible to disentangle their stories.[53] Here Kircher—as he no doubt knew—came very close to Scaliger, who used the words for God in the various European languages of his own day to assemble them in groups—but refused to push back behind what he called the ten or eleven "linguae matrices," a term that recurs in Kircher, to a Hebrew (or any other) original.[54] Close study of time did not reveal the comforting presence of orderly change—though it did enable both Kircher and Scaliger to make fun of their predecessor in these fields, Goropius Becanus, who had argued at length that the patriarchs spoke something like Dutch in the Garden of Eden.

Kircher's convergences with Scaliger are suggestive. For Scaliger, as he sailed the stormy philological seas of Manetho's Egyptian dynasty lists for the first time, found himself embarked on a voyage from which there was no turning back. Evidence he could not reject showed him a history measured not in the Bible's shallow time, but in a new and scary deep time. As he told the students who lodged with him, "I am doing the history of 8,000 years, according to the pagans"—8,000 years, not the 5,600 allowed by the Hebrew Bible or even the 6,800 allowed by the Septuagint.[55]

Kircher, presumably, found himself making the same discovery in the 1640s and 1650s. While he contemplated the history of the world and its nations, their beginnings receded vertiginously even as he read the sources—rather as the limits of space receded while he observed and computed the movements of the stars. Even in the more cautious 1670s, he still strewed his new works with clues to the location and import of his older discoveries.

Did Kircher consistently see time as deep and history as without a clear beginning? Certainly not—or as certainly as we can say anything, given the deliberate ambiguity and complex wit of Kircher's language, which makes all attempts at interpretation tentative.[56] After all, Kircher never explained why he found Arabic accounts of Egyptian pre-history—which contained plenty of manifestly implausible statements, by normal standards—more credible than Manetho's dynasty lists, which previous Jesuits had rejected as absurd. F. Scott Fitzgerald remarked long ago that the test of a first-rate mind is its ability to entertain contradictory ideas and still function. Fitzgerald would have found much to admire in Kircher. At times—as in his spectacularly detailed chapters on the cities of Nimrod and Semiramis in the *Turris Babel*—Kircher wrote as if he could think himself back into the past. A magnificently hyperbolic application of that primeval Jesuit discipline, composition of place, enabled him to rebuild the Tower of Babel and the Hanging Gardens, stone by stone and arch by arch, from the tiny references to them in his sources. The antiquary could raise not just individuals, but cities, from the dead. In these moods, Kircher probably thought—as many other Catholics did—that the longer chronology of the Septuagint could accommodate most of the new history he had discovered.

In other moods, however, Kircher could deny that it was possible to restore the identity of much more recent monuments. "Here at Rome," he wrote in one magnificent rant, "we see every day the insanely massive structures that the ancients built. If you seek them, you can't find them. If you do find them, all you see are half-buried corpses. They believed that they were rearing structures that would last forever. But now, though scarcely sixteen hundred years have passed, only their vestiges survive. . . . This is how the unfair lot of mortals makes the wheel of vicissitude turn, so that nothing is stable, firm and solid. How many great palaces, gardens equipped with every form of delight, do we see, whose authors we do not know? And as things pass from the possession of one to those of many others, so little by little they fall into complete oblivion. Not a hundred years pass before villas and palaces, coming into the possession of other families, lose all memory of whose they were at first."[57]

This splendid tirade—one directed as much against Kircher's Rome, the city of palaces, as against Nimrod's Babylon—shows the extent of the Jesuit's ability to entertain ideas about the past that were in sharp tension with one another—a skill to conjure with in the seventeenth-century heyday of the paradox. Kircher, who confidently called whole ancient cities back to life, could also feel and express the antiquary's characteristic nostalgia for an irrecoverable past. The master of historical time could evoke time's destructive tooth as eloquently as any epigrapher or numismatist.[58] In these moods, Kircher—like Scaliger—may well have contemplated the mysteries and terrors of deep time.

For all his doubts, Kircher did not hesitate to teach his brightest pupils about his discoveries. And at least one of them, the brilliant Sinologist Martino Martini, applied his teacher's methods to even more radical effect.[59] When Martini reached China in the 1640s, he found that the Chinese—like the Egyptians—preserved a solid annalistic tradition—one that set their first seven kings solidly into the period before the supposedly universal Flood. Like a good Jesuit, Martini made fun of these boastful pagans who extended their history too far: "And clearly, the Chinese annals contain many absurdities, so far as both the ages of men and the regnal years of kings are concerned. Should we trust these writers, historical time would have to be extended far backwards, thousands of years before the flood."[60] Jesuits had realized well before Martini arrived that Chinese historical traditions seemingly reached back to great antiquity, and their efficient communications network rapidly brought the news to Europe. By 1636, the ex-Jesuit Agostino Mascardi argued in his elaborate treatise on the art of history that Chinese historians had preceded Moses. He supported this thesis by quoting a letter from the Milanese Jesuit Celso Confaloniere to Cardinal Federigo Borromeo. Confaloniere had described a Chinese account of the earliest kings as "the oldest book that they have, and according to their histories it was written in the time of the Patriarch Abraham. In my opinion it is the oldest text in the world, because it was written more than five hundred years before Moses wrote."[61] For the most part, Martini followed Jesuit precedent in arguing that the plausible segments of early Chinese history could be accommodated within the more generous biblical chronology of the Septuagint, and he read his Chinese historical sources through a normal Christian lens.[62]

At the same time, however, like his ambivalent teacher, Martini admitted that the Chinese had been skilled astronomers and record keepers, whose works seemed to deserve a measure of credibility. They seemed, indeed, to have made the first astronomical observation ever recorded—an achievement that made it absurd for Europeans, "whose name did not yet exist," to call them barbarians. Martini denied that he "wished to claim so much authority for them as to make us alter our shorter chronology of the Flood."[63] Nonetheless, he narrated Chinese history, so far as he could, following the Chinese time line, which began 784 years before Noah's Flood. Still hesitant when he summed up, he admitted that Chinese traditions about events before the Flood might be inventions. But at the same time, he went so far as to suggest that these accounts might also have been preserved within the Ark—just as "learned men hold that many other things, which are relevant also to our religion, were saved from oblivion there"—a clear reference to what Kircher taught him, very likely on his return to Rome in 1654, about the way that Egyptian historical traditions survived the Flood.[64] Martini's less contentious efforts to identify the early Chinese kings with the Hebrew patriarchs also closely resembled Kircher's way of folding pagan and sacred histories together. Evidently then, Kircher did more than devise a new and radical chronology of Egypt. He encouraged learned friends who knew even more languages than he did to push such arguments even farther—as Martini did, so successfully that his Chinese chronology would help to shake the faith of generations of *philosophes*.[65]

Historians have often noted that the discovery of China radically challenged traditional ways of writing world history.[66] Certainly, the irreducible new facts about China, some of them directly imported as material objects and others vividly described in Jesuit annual letters and histories, helped to destroy old chronologies and cartographies. But Martini did more than any other single writer on China to attack the certainties of chronologers, forcing even pious historians to extend history beyond the period allowed by the Hebrew text of the Old Testament. And Kircher prepared him to do so. The discovery of ancient Egypt, the result of an expedition carried out in libraries rather than trading ports, opened the teacher's eyes and helped him hone his pupil's intellectual tools to the sharpness needed to cut through traditional schemas.

Chronology, as Kircher practiced it, became as theatrical as architecture and as ecstatic as a subterranean or celestial journey. It offered him a superb stage, one on which he repeatedly demonstrated his ability to dance across tightropes from which almost anyone else would have fallen. Yet chronology was more than theater: it was also endless, pointed disputation. As a chronologer, Kircher dwelled both in the familiar shallow time of Annius of Viterbo and the dangerous deep time of Joseph Scaliger; he listened to the dangerous siren songs of Abraham Ecchellensis and sang seductively himself to Martino Martini. When he drew up long, dry tables of Pharaonic names and long, citation-stuffed passages on the dates of useless men, he reported on the results of conversations that ranged across a dozen delicate subjects, from the credibility of historical sources to the nature of historical time. No wonder, then, that Kircher—and so many of his contemporaries—found the subject anything but dry or pedantic. Chronology offered them a privileged glance at mysteries—the forgotten origins of the Egyptian and Chaldean traditions that played so prominent a role in the public spaces of Kircher's Rome.

Notes

* Warm thanks to Paula Findlen, Michael Head, Peter Miller, Ingrid Rowland, and Daniel Stolzenberg for comments on and criticism of the arguments advanced here, to Nicholas Standaert for his counsel on the history of Sinology and for discussion of many other subjects, to Michael Cook for generous help with matters Islamic, and to Nancy Khalek, who with great generosity, enthusiasm, and erudition identified and translated Kircher's Arabic quotations.

1. For recent excellent surveys of Kircher's interest in Egypt, see Rowland 2000, pp. 15–19, 87–95; and Stolzenberg 2001c, pp. 115–125; 2001b, pp. 127–139.
2. See, e.g., Biale 1979; Dan 1987; and Schäfer and Smith 1995.
3. Bodin 1579, I, pp. 298–304; Brown 1939, pp. 70–75.
4. See Grafton 1995, pp. 15–31.
5. Strathman 1951, p. 201.
6. Grafton 1991, pp. 204–213.
7. Pezron 1687.
8. Allen 1949; Klempt 1960; Raskolnikoff 1992, pp. 163–220; Grell 1995, vol. 2, pp. 791–881, 1200–1204.
9. Pezron 1687, p. 1.
10. Leinkauf 1993.
11. Gibbon 1966, p. 43.
12. Kircher 1679a, p. 9.
13. Raleigh 1736, vol. 1, p. 90. See in general Allen 1949.
14. Pezron 1687, pp. 8–9.
15. Gibbon 1966, p. 43.
16. Kircher 1650b, pp. 12–13.
17. Ibid., p. 14.
18. Grafton 1997a, pp. 124–143.
19. See most recently Rowland 1998.
20. Rhenanus 1551, p. 39. Warm thanks to K. J. Weintraub for pointing out the Erasmian source of the expression.
21. Kircher 1679a, p. 44.
22. Samotheus 1545–46, fol. 16r.
23. Ibid., fols. 20v–21r.
24. Possevino 1593, vol. 1, p. 92.
25. Scaliger 1629, p. xlviii.
26. Kircher 1652–55, vol. 1, pp. 65–68.
27. Eusebius 1923, p. 17.
28. Carion 1557, pp. 33–34.
29. Samotheus 1545–46, fols. 20r–v.
30. Raleigh 1736, vol. 1, pp. 89–92. Raleigh's resolution of the problem rather resembles Kircher's, though it rests on different evidence.
31. Grafton 1983–93, vol. 2, pt. Iv.
32. Scaliger 1606, p. 309.
33. Casaubon, MS. note in his copy of the *Thesaurus temporum*, ibid.: Cambridge University Library Adv.a.3.4.
34. Petau 1757, vol. 2, p. 19.
35. Salianus 1641, vol. 1, pp. 198–199.
36. Kircher 1679a, p. 112.
37. Kircher 1652–55, vol. 1, pp. 69–70.
38. Ibid., pp. 70–71.
39. Ibid., p. 72, apparently citing Saumaise 1648, praefatio ad lectorem, fols. [c8r]–d r.
40. Kircher 1652–55, vol. 1, p. 71.
41. On al-Suyūtī see in general, Sartain 1975; *The New Encyclopedia of Islam*, s.v. al-Suyūtī, by E. Geoffroy; and Salem 2001. Kircher also quotes, in this context as elsewhere, an author he here calls Abenephius, whose work I have not been able to identify. But almost all of his detailed information comes from al-Suyūtī.
42. Rosenthal 1968, pp. 154–156; Cook 1983, pp. 67–103. Suyūtī seems to draw on the strand of historical thought that Cook calls "Hermetic," of which he writes: "The material is in general somewhat heterogeneous in character, but the dominant note is one which a European audience can readily associate with the *Magic Flute*" (71).
43. Kircher 1652–55, vol. 1, p. 73, quoting al-Suyūtī 1903, vol. 1, pp. 14–15. Most of the passages Kircher quotes in his discussion of antediluvian Egypt come from this section of Suyūtī's work, vol. 1, pp. 13–15.
44. Kircher 1652–55, vol. 1, p. 74.
45. Ibid.

46. On Abraham Ecchellensis, see della Vida 1939, esp. p. 6n 3; Fück 1944, pp. 159–160; and Rietbergen 1989, pp. 13–41. A fascinating contemporary portrait appears in a letter from Lucas Holstenius to Giovanni Battista Doni, 4 December 1644, in Mirto 1999, pp. 135–137.
47. Ecchellensis 1651, pp. 181–182.
48. Holstenius 1817, p. 275.
49. Ecchellensis 1651, pp. 144–147.
50. Kircher 1675, pp. 205, 208.
51. Sossus 1632, p. 196.
52. Thomas Basson, 1606, Scaliger, *Animadversiones*, p. 103.
53. Kircher 1679a, pp. 218–219.
54. See Scaliger 1610, pp. 119–122; and Droixhe 1978, pp. 60–63.
55. Lefebvre 1669, vol. 2, p. 216. Cf. Grafton 1983–93, vol. 2.
56. Note that Kircher, who cited the forged Berosus of Annius of Viterbo as an authority, also referred to him as "Berosus Apocryphus" (Kircher 1675, p. 208). Such paradoxes are common in his work.
57. Kircher 1679a, p. 22.
58. On antiquarianism and nostalgia in this period, see Miller 2000; and Stolzenberg 2001b.
59. On Martini's work on Chinese chronology and history, see in general Pinot 1932, pp. 200–202; Van Kley 1971; and Witek 1983, pp. 223–252. On the larger context, Walter Demel offers rich information in Demel 1986. Martini's relations with Kircher are documented in their correspondence, in Martini 1998. On the larger intellectual history of the Jesuits' Chinese enterprise, see, e.g., the contrasting accounts of Spence 1984; Mungello 1985; and Jensen 1997. For an interesting look at current research, see Smith 2002, pp. 7–12.
60. Martini 1658, pp. 9–10.
61. Mascardi 1859, p. 21.
62. See Collani 1998, and Collani 2000, pp. 147–183, summarized as Collani 1996. Nicolas Standaert, to whom I am greatly indebted, informs me that Martini may have drawn information from Sima Qian's *Shiji* (ca. 145–90 B.C.), but that his main sources were the *Zizhi tongjian (gangmu) qianbian (Prologue to [The String and Mesh of] the Comprehensive Mirror for the Aid of Government)* by Jin Lixiang (1232–1303) and the *Zizhi tongjian gangmu (The String and Mesh of the Comprehensive Mirror for the Aid of Government)* by Zhu Xi (1130–1300), as well, perhaps, as shorter chronological lists.
63. Martini 1658, pp. 20–21.
64. Ibid., p. 27.
65. On the impact of Chinese chronology on European discussion, in addition to Pinot and Van Kley, see Klempt 1960; Rossi 1984; and Ramsay 2001.
66. See, e.g., Van Kley 1971.

The Mysteries of Man and the Cosmos

8

Athanasius Kircher, Giordano Bruno, and the *Panspermia* of the Infinite Universe

INGRID D. ROWLAND

Quapropter dum tutus iter sic carpo, beata
Conditione satis studio sublimis avito
Reddor Dux, Lex, Lux, Vates, Pater, Author, Iterque:
Adque alios mundo ex isto dum adsurgo nitentes,
Aethereum campumque ex omni parte pererro,
Attonitis mirum et distans post terga relinquo.
　　　　　　—Giordano Bruno, "De Immenso et Innumerabilibus," I.i.19–24

Athanasius Kircher was first summoned to Rome from France in 1634, to take up a chair in mathematics at the Jesuits' Roman College in the immediate wake of Galileo Galilei's trial and condemnation for heresy. The holder of this chair in mathematics also taught astronomy, and hence Kircher inherited the position, the study, and the astronomical instruments of his predecessors—most notably the great Christoph Clavius, creator of the Gregorian calendar and the first person to invite Galileo to lecture in Rome, but also Galileo's more recent adversaries: Orazio Grassi, Christoph Grienberger, and Christoph Scheiner, this last personage a particularly bitter rival of the sharp-tongued Tuscan scientist.[1] In 1633, Kircher had admitted to friends in Avignon that several of the most prominent Jesuit astronomers, including Clavius and Scheiner, actually believed in a Sun-centered, Copernican universe; the tone of Kircher's remark suggests that he must have shared these Copernican convictions as well. Whatever these men's private beliefs may have been, a conservative Jesuit curriculum, adopted in 1599, compelled them to teach an Earth-centered cosmology, as Kircher explained:

> The good father Athanasius . . . could not restrain himself from telling us, in the presence of Father Ferrand, that Father Malaperti and Father Clavius themselves in no way disapproved the opinion of Copernicus—indeed they would have espoused it openly had they not been pressed and obliged to write according to the premises of Aristotle—and that Father Scheiner himself did not comply except under compulsion and by obedience.[2]

It was one matter to discuss cosmology in Avignon, and quite another to do so in the heart of Rome, and at first Kircher gave no indication in his writings, published or unpublished, that his own ideas might depart from the orthodox Catholic universe, whose Earth stood motionless at its center, orbited by the Sun, the planets, and the sphere of fixed stars. Old blind Galileo, under permanent house arrest in his house outside Florence, stood as too vivid a reminder of how perilous the conflict between good science and good faith could become. For his first twenty years in Rome, Kircher refused adamantly to write specifically on the subject of cosmology, although he wrote copiously about nearly every other subject under the Sun, including mirrors, clock-making, the ancient Egyptians, magnetism, optics, and acoustics. Indeed, one of Kircher's more ambitious early studies, *Magnes, sive de art magnetica* (*The Lodestone or the Magnetic Art*) (1641), his large book on magnetism, energetically denounced both Copernicus and Kepler—although he also managed to make it clear that he did so, like Clavius, Grienberger, and Scheiner before him, "under compulsion and by obedience":

> The truth is that anyone who examines these matters a bit more thoughtfully will clearly see that the motion of the longitude of the Planets can be adjusted much more easily, quickly, and truly to the hypothesis of a fixed earth than a mobile one; just as the Ptolemaic and Tychonian hypotheses are to be preferred by many parasangs over this Copernican one, and perhaps I would be able to demonstrate this at greater length here if I did not fear overstepping the limits of my Establishment.[3]

> About our Kepler, Imperial Mathematician, it is fair to say that whereas no Mathematician is better and more subtle than he, yet no one is worse as a Physicist; hence I vehemently lament that the divine teachings of such a great man should be so shamefully besmirched by his Physical blatherings, as he shows all too well in this present Copernico-Pythagorean contrivance.[4]

In 1656, however, Athanasius Kircher changed his mind about writing his own treatise on cosmology. The stimuli for this change may have been several, but the most insistent of them must have been the presence at the Collegio Romano itself of his onetime student and close collaborator, Father Kaspar Schott. A first-rate experimentalist with reserves of energy that seem nearly to have matched Kircher's own, Schott also seems to have spoken his mind far more forthrightly than his diffident, elusive mentor. And one of the subjects on which the younger man seems to have expressed himself with great insistence was Kircher's obligation to write a book on astronomy.

Kircher had another literary stimulus as well, in the person of the recently elected pope, Alexander VII (reigned 1655–67), a former Sienese prelate named Fabio Chigi who had first met Kircher in 1637 and remained a friend ever after. As cardinal and the Vatican's secretary of state, Chigi had already helped to sponsor publication of one of Kircher's most ambitious works, the huge four-volume *Oedipus Aegyptiacus* (*Egyptian Oedipus*) (1652–55); as pope he continued to press his learned friend for scholarly contributions that ranged from brief book reviews to manuscript pamphlets to printed books of every size, shape, and length. A man of exacting personal integrity and deep religion, Chigi had become an intellectual figure of international prominence during his career as papal nuncio to Germany in the 1640s, a diplomat whose ties, like Kircher's, extended from freethinking Protestants to conservative Catholics. Progressively deteriorating health and the declining political position of the Papal States would quickly take their toll of Chigi's papacy, but the mood at his election in 1655, both in Rome and abroad, was unusually optimistic, and this is the atmosphere in which Athanasius Kircher finally committed this thoughts on cosmology to writing, and then to print.

Still hoping, surely, to avoid controversy as much as possible, Kircher published his work on cosmology as fiction, as the revelations of a dream that he called an "ecstatic heavenly journey," *Itinerarium exstaticum coeleste (Ecstatic Celestial Journey)*. To set the scene, he told what seemed to be an autobiographical story (its basic truth would later be confirmed by Kaspar Schott). After an evening concert at the Collegio Romano had ended with a long discussion between Kircher and the musicians, who began to retune their instruments (two viols and a theorbo) to the microintervals of various ancient musical scales, a rapturous Kircher (named Theodidactus, "taught by God," for the purposes of the dialogue) lay down to an unusually sound sleep. He dreamt that he found himself lying in a verdant meadow, where he was suddenly roused by an angel with shimmering wings and eyes like burning coals. This personage, who went by the appropriately celestial name of Cosmiel, offered to escort Theodidactus through the secret recesses of Heaven and Earth, an offer Theodidactus eagerly accepted.

Although Kircher's readers should have been prepared by this setting to read a Christian version of Cicero's *Somnium Scipionis*, a dream-essay whose cosmic travels provided a tour through the range of ancient Roman virtue and its heavenly rewards, in fact the *Itinerarium exstaticum* brought them something quite different: it quickly turned into a lover's pilgrimage in the spirit of Dante's *Divine Comedy*; Theodidactus occasionally addressed Cosmiel, who served as his Beatrice, in the smitten tones of the bride in the *Song of Songs*. Cosmiel, however, was no genteel Beatrice by nature; despite his seraphic politeness, the angel was given to speaking his mind—and bluntly at that. Athanasius Kircher's exuberant sense of humor never lurked too far beneath the erudite surface of his many books, but in the *Itinerarium exstaticum* it came to the fore with particular emphasis, especially in the repartee between Theodidactus and his sharp-witted angelic escort. Nor did the extraordinary vividness of Kircher's imagination lie far beneath the book's surface. From the dreamy meadow where man met angel to the outer reaches of the firmament, Kircher-Theodidactus described his physical surroundings with all the imaginative precision of a longtime practitioner of Ignatius Loyola's *Spiritual Exercises*, which accustomed every Jesuit to placing himself through acts of imagination in Heaven, in Hell, at the foot of the Cross. Few Jesuit fathers, however, would have dared to describe the cosmos in which the *Itinerarium extaticum coeleste* would soon place Theodidactus and Athanasius Kircher.

The universe through which Cosmiel guided his charge that ecstatic evening dispelled nearly every tenet of the Aristotelian cosmology that Kircher was bound by the Jesuit curriculum to teach as accepted fact. Gone were Aristotle's crystalline spheres made of a celestial fifth element or quintessence, as Theodidactus, the dream-Kircher, discovered when Cosmiel propelled him smoothly through the Earth's atmosphere and into outer space—space, the angel revealed, was a yielding fluid rather than a brittle solid. In midflight, man and angel turned back to admire a vision of the distant Earth that only the astronauts of the twentieth century would eventually observe with their own eyes. Safely arrived on the Moon and protected by Cosmiel's vial of celestial droplets from expiring in the rarefied lunar atmosphere, Theodidactus inquired about the dark areas his telescope had revealed on the Moon's surface. The angel answered by dropping him abruptly onto a roiling lunar sea to show him that the dark areas were oceans as watery as Earth's own. (As Kircher was a notorious prankster himself, it may not be surprising that Cosmiel shared his idea of a joke.) As Theodidactus, buffeted by lunar whitecaps, exclaimed at the real Moon's discrepancy from Aristotle's account of it, Cosmiel scoffed that Aristotle was wrong about a great many things.

> You are mistaken, and greatly so, if you persuade yourself that Aristotle has entirely told the truth about the nature of the supreme bodies. It is impossible that the philosophers, who insist upon their ideas alone and repudiate experiments, can conclude anything about the natural constitution of the solid world, for we [angels] observe that human thoughts, unless they are based on experiments, often wander as far from the truth as the earth is distant from the moon.[5]

Together man and angel noted that if the Moon and all the other heavenly bodies were made of the four standard elements rather than a celestial quintessence, there was this advantage to the situation: it was possible to be baptized everywhere in the universe.

From the Moon, angel and Jesuit proceeded on to the sphere of Mercury, then on to Venus, and then to the Sun. Here, for the first time, they encountered a remarkable force called *panspermia rerum*, the universal seminal power of things.

Panspermia rerum had made its first appearance in Kircher's writings in 1641, in *Magnes*, his large book on magnetism, where he declared that "it must be known that the earth, as the common mother and womb of all things, also contains the seeds of all things in herself."[6] Later in the same work he specified that Earth was "pregnant with a certain panspermia or universally generative mix of seeds,"[7] and he explained that "individual Plants are made from a certain one and the same panspermia in the earth according to the condition and quality of the soil in which they are planted."[8] Here *panspermia* denoted the power of fertility through which the Earth produced the observable variety of plants and, by extension, animals. (It derived, as shall be seen below, from one interpretation of Aristotle's theory of *entelecheia*, the idea that things contained the potential for their final development just as seeds contained, in potential, the form of the plant, animal, or person they were designed to become.) In another passage of *Magnes*, Kircher also attributed the figments of imagination to *semina*, seeds, animated by formative power (*vis plastica*).[9]

In the *Itinerarium exstaticum*, however, *panspermia rerum* had developed, like the rest of Kircher's cosmology, into something quite different from the teachings of Aristotle. Cosmiel now described *panspermia* not as a passive quality of the womblike Earth, but as an active quality carried on the liquid fire by which the Sun's rays penetrated liquid space to reach the Earth's surface:

> The whole mass of this solar globe is imbued, not with one single property, but rather with a certain universal seminal power (*panspermatica quadam virtute*), by means of which, as the nature of the various parts of the sun, in various ways, hides its riches within the hidden bowels of the Solar World, a fiery liquid, blended in various ways, touches things below by radiant diffusion . . . and produces various effects. [10]

Fertility, in other words, was projected like light and heat on the rays of the Sun. In the long treatise *Ars magna lucis et umbrae* (*The Great Art of Light and Shadow*) (1646), Kircher had noted that not only light and heat, but also smells, fertility, and figments of the imagination could be projected by a process he called "ray-throwing," *actinobolismus*, an idea that initially defied the grasp of Theodidactus when Cosmiel presented it: "But, O my Cosmiel, I do not understand how that multiple panspermatic power can exist in the Sun's globe." Cosmiel, ever eager to inculcate the importance of scientific experimentation while aiming a blow at Aristotle, replied:

> I do not want to you take *panspermia* in the sense in which the seeds of earthly things really contain [them] in actuality [this was Kircher's version of Aristotle's entelecheia and the version of *panspermia* he had described in his earlier *Magnes*]; but rather in a virtual sense of emanation. I'll make you understand the whole thing by means of a familiar experiment. If you liquefy various kinds of different metals with different qualities in the same crucible, it is certain that all these species of metals will liquefy into a single liquid . . . and yet its vapor will diffuse the various qualities of the different metals individually, both healthful and noxious. You should imagine that by analogy the same thing happens in the solar globe in the same manner. The parts of the solar globe are not all homogeneous and of the same nature and quality, as the Aristotelians believe, but are endowed with various properties as the divine wisdom has designed Nature according to its art.[11]

This solar *panspermia*, in other words, was quite a different quality from what we might describe as the embryonic potential in earthly phenomena that

Kircher had described as *panspermia* in *Magnes* some fifteen years before. Furthermore, Cosmiel's presentation of the Sun as a body subjected to constant disturbance parted ways definitively with the Aristotelian Sun's changeless perfection. But the dialogue's most radical cosmological ideas were still to come: they emerged when the *Itinerarium exstaticum* pushed beyond Saturn into what Theodidactus anticipated would be the realm of the fixed stars. Bracing himself for impact with the heavenly crystal, the cringing father instead ran into Cosmiel's scathing wit:

> My Theodidactus, now I truly see that you are excessively simple of mind, and more gullible than average when it comes to believing anyone else's opinion. The crystalline sphere you are looking for cannot be found in nature, and there is no basis for the idea that the stars are fixed on such a sphere. Look around, examine everything around you, wander the whole Universe, and you will find nothing but the clear, light, subtle breeze of the great ethereal Ocean, enclosed by no boundaries, that you perceive all around us.[12]

Theodidactus soon learned that the fixed stars only looked fixed because he and all other earthly creatures observed them from such incalculably great distances. In fact, Cosmiel showed that each individual star in the firmament behaved exactly like the Sun, shedding heat and light, and was surrounded by planets of its own. Many of these stars, moreover, were far larger than the Sun itself, and at least as charged as the Sun with that novel quality called *panspermia rerum*. As Cosmiel explained:

> Because the supreme Archetypal mind is so full of ideas for possible things, he wanted to establish this universe, to the extent that the capacity of its passive potential permits, with a numberless variety of spheres, differing in all their powers, properties, brightness, shape, color, light, heat, influences, and content of latent seminal principles according to the ineffable plan of the archetype.[13]

With this description of a universe consisting of a "numberless variety of spheres," the *Itinerarium exstaticum* courted real trouble. Cosmiel described a cosmos that existed on a scale so immense that Johannes Kepler had actively shrunk back from it (in a letter to Galileo of 1610); Galileo himself had only dared allude to the possibility in oblique language.[14] In Kircher's day, indeed, there were only two modern accounts of a universe so immense and so limitless: the fifteenth-century German cardinal Nicholas of Cusa had arrived at an infinite universe in the second book of his treatise *On Learned Ignorance*, arguing that the motions of Earth, stars, and planets were all relative to one another in a cosmos without center and without circumference. A century later, Cusanus's universe had been developed in far greater detail by the sixteenth-century Italian philosopher Giordano Bruno, but Bruno, for his pains, had been burned at the stake in Rome in 1600 as an "obstinate and pertinacious" heretic and his writings consigned shortly thereafter to the *Index of Prohibited Books*.[15] Although Cosmiel and Theodidactus mentioned Cusanus explicity in their discussions, the details of their cosmos, and Kircher's, could only have derived from reading Giordano Bruno.

Influenced by the theories of his fellow southern Italian Antonio Telesio, Bruno had divided the infinite cosmos into two types of heavenly bodies: hot stars, or "suns," orbited by colder planets. Bruno called these cold planets "earths" in his 1591 poem "De Immenso et Innumerabilibus":

> Sun and Earth are the primal animals, first among species
> Of things, and from the primal elements they have
> been fashioned,
> They in themselves contain the archetype of every compound,
> Whence all the dry parts conjoin with all the parts that
> are humid,
> And in amid them thereafter when air has been interjected
> Then they create great caverns, of ever burgeoning vastness.
> Thus what lies latent in small scale can be observed
> when it's larger
> What may be hidden in parts, may be revealed in its wholeness.[16]

With his usual candor, Cosmiel had evidently described the same kind of universe, composed of hot stars and cold planets, both kinds of heavenly bodies shot through with a continually changing mix of elements and subject to unending turbulence.

Bruno also claimed that the infinite universe carried the seeds of its own propagation everywhere. His cellmates in inquisitorial prison in Venice reported: "He said that God needed the world as much as the world needed God, and that God would be nothing without the world, and for this reason God did nothing but create new worlds."[17] Cosmiel's description of God is remarkably similar: "the supreme Archetypal mind . . . so full of ideas for possible things, [that] he wanted to establish this universe, to the extent that the capacity of its passive potential permits, with a numberless variety of spheres."

The fertility of Bruno's universe derived from a single, all-pervasive world soul that mixed with the four chemical elements to create and then to dissolve living compounds. In Bruno's view, the elements themselves broke down on the smallest scale to atoms, and he chose, like the Roman philosopher-poet Lucretius, to express his atomic theory in the difficult medium of Latin hexameter verse.

Kircher's Cosmiel, on the other hand, denounced atomism with some energy; still, his account of God as an all-pervasive force in the universe paralleled Bruno's world-soul in nearly every respect, and *panspermia rerum* exhibited most of the qualities exhibited by Bruno's atoms, those minimal units of nature to which the heretic philosopher sometimes applied the Lucretian term *semina rerum*, "the seeds of things." Indeed, as Kircher well knew,

Greek *sperma* and Latin *semen*, which both meant "seed," were perfectly synonymous—not only as words, but as ideas.

Athanasius Kircher certainly read Giordano Bruno; he would say so openly on page 4 of a late work, the *Ars magna sciendi* (*Great Art of Knowing*) of 1669, there referring to a posthumously published set of Bruno's commentaries on the mnemonic art of the thirteenth-century Catalan mystic Ramon Llull.[18] Cosmiel's description of the universe shows that Kircher had obviously read Bruno's cosmological works as well. Yet if the Jesuit censors who lodged a complaint against the *Itinerarium exstaticum* in 1656 detected traces of Giordano Bruno's thought in Kircher's writing, they did not say so; instead, they took the author to task for having postulated an infinite universe, pinning the ultimate blame on Copernicus:

> To be sure, Kircher on occasion reproves the condemned opinion of Copernicus about the motion of the earth, lest (he says on p. 28) he be seen to assert anything contrary to the decrees and institutions of the Holy Roman Church: nonetheless, throughout his entire book he carefully constructs all the evidence that Copernicus first brought in to establish and defend the motion of the earth, and he weakens all the arguments by which that error is usually refuted under a great weight of reasoning. From whom, if not from Copernicus and his followers, did Kircher accept that immensity of the firmament that he inculcates ad nauseam, and that error about the distance of the fixed stars from the earth?[19]

This censure apparently went no further than the Jesuit superiors in Rome (who preserved it in their records and authorized at least one manuscript copy now in Naples); unlike Bruno and Galileo, Kircher could count on the continued favor of the pope, his old friend Alexander VII. Furthermore, unlike Giordano Bruno, Cosmiel, echoing Cusanus, contended that the immense universe surrounding himself and Theodidactus only appeared to be boundless—it was perfectly finite in the eyes of God. By emphasizing this last detail, Kircher was able to drive a fine but crucial distinction between Bruno's heresies and his own orthodoxy, however unorthodox it may have been. As Cosmiel told Theodidactus, quoting the Psalmist: "Only God, the Creator of all things, counts [the] multitude [of the stars] and calls them by name."

By 1659, Kircher's onetime student and close collaborator, Kaspar Schott (who was perhaps the real-life model for the angel Cosmiel), proposed publishing a revised edition of the *Itinerarium* in Germany. In the course of this revision, Schott, a formidable scholar in his own right, supplied his mentor's book with a slightly revised title, *Iter extaticum* (*Ecstatic Journey*), and a copious body of annotations, some his own, some the work of Kircher himself. This new version of the dialogue was printed in Würzburg in 1660. Schott used it to launch an implicit challenge to Kircher's Roman censors, citing Giordano Bruno among other indexed authors in support of his own cosmological contentions (some of which differed with Kircher as well). Schott's revised *Iter extaticum* also included a direct reply to Kircher's Roman censors, on which the two of them collaborated. Whether because it was published in Germany, beyond the reach of the Roman Holy Office, or because of the pope's protection, or both, the *Iter extaticum* would be spared by the censors and ultimately reprinted in 1671.

In 1665, Athanasius Kircher published one of the great books of his career, *Mundus subterraneus (Subterranean World)*, a huge, expensive folio tome packed with big, costly illustrations and do-it-yourself volvelles. *Mundus subterraneus* was also a truly international publishing venture, produced simultaneously in Catholic Rome and Protestant Amsterdam, where it represented the first fruit of what would become a long-term, lucrative collaboration between Kircher and the Dutch firm of Jansson and Weyerstraet. Kircher dedicated *Mundus subterraneus* to Pope Alexander VII, his patron and longtime friend. In its pages he would develop the idea of *panspermia rerum* to its fullest extent, presenting it as the property that had enabled God to transform primordial chaos into every sort of matter in the universe:

> It can be established from the Sacred Book of Genesis, that GOD GREATEST AND BEST created nothing immediately, whether plant, animal, or any other thing of mixed species, but rather than these were drawn forth from nothingness through the Chaotic Mass (for which God simultaneously created *panspermia* and the universal seed of Nature) so that as if from a preexisting entity He produced all things: the heavens, the stars, minerals, plants, and animals. [20]

Kircher now specified the chemical composition of this *panspermia rerum* as a "pregnant mixture" of salt, sulfur, and mercury, which, when combined with vapor and heat, produced life itself:

> It may properly be asked in this context what this *panspermia* and seminal power that produced all things was. I say that it was once a material spirit made up either of a more subtle heavenly breeze or a portion of elements, and that it was once a spirituous Sulphurous-saline-mercurial vapor, the universal seed of things, created by GOD together with the elements, the origin of all the extant bodies that have been created in the world.[21]

If Kircher's early *Magnes* had restricted this *panspermia* to Earth alone (which he understood both as one of the four elements and as a physical entity), *Mundus subterraneus* fearlessly claimed that the universal seed existed in every part of the universe, cleverly exploiting the ambiguity of the word *mundus*, which could refer either to the Earth in isolation, or to the whole cosmos:

> Divine Providence designed the Earth or Geocosmos in such an order and location that it would serve as a base and final end or all created nature, in which as if in the lap and passive principles of all nature all the other bodies of the World would be sown, and spread their seeds and the energy of their power . . . hence [Nature] is impregnated by the power of the circling stars and mixtures of seminal principles.[22]

Typically, Kircher bolstered his contentions by tracing them back to ancient wisdom. *Mundus subterraneus* dutifully cites the Bible and the Church Fathers as primary sources:

> Holy Genesis teaches openly that the seeds of things (*semina rerum*) were created together with the Earth: "And God said: Let the earth bring forth green plants and make seed and fruit-bearing trees bearing fruit according to their kins, and let their seed be upon the Earth. And it was so." Thus *panspermia*, or the spermatic mixture of all things, was created at the same time as the Earth.

> And thus from the holy Oracles of Moses, which we should rightly put parasangs ahead of all other certainties of human knowledge, it can be established that in the beginning GOD the creator of all things created the Matter that we call Chaotic out of nothingness; for glorious GOD created all things at once, including something in the nature of compounds and material substances that would be produced subsequently, but lay as it were hidden under a certain *panspermia*. . . . He did not eliminate chaotic matter straightaway, for he wanted it to last until the consummation of the world, first in the beginnings of things, then up to the present day carried in the *panspermia* of all things . . . which opinion almost all the monuments of the Holy Church Fathers harbor, and especially the *Hexameron* of Saint Basil.[23]

In a short manuscript treatise written during the reign of Pope Alexander VII, and therefore at approximately the same time as the last drafts of *Mundus subterraneus*, Kircher observes that awareness of *panspermia* first developed in ancient Egypt, and it was symbolized by that ubiquitous Egyptian image of the scarab beetle rolling his ball of dung:

> The figure of a scarab with spread wings is taken from the primeval school of Egyptian mystagogues, which they called the sun-god . . . because of the similarity and analogy between the work of this beetle and the work of the sun. . . . For just as the scarab gives life and fertility to his ball while rolling it from East to West by infusing it with seed, so the sun-god, by orbiting the globe, gives it life and fertility by the means of the same *panspermia rerum*, and fills it with every kind of thing.[24]

The scarab and his ball of dung thus provided a vivid demonstration of Kircher's conviction that putrefaction bred life, by spontaneous generation as well as sexual reproduction; his own fertile imagination thereby matched that of those ancient Egyptians who had originally turned a ball of dung into a symbol of the Sun.

Panspermia in *Mundus subterraneus* borrowed its specific outlines from Paracelsus, who had first proposed that salt, mercury, and sulfur were the primal compounds of the physical world. Kircher, like most of his contemporaries, denounced the great alchemist vocally while helping himself liberally to his best ideas.[25] *Panspermia* also constituted the chemical version of another Paracelsan triad: fire, water, and air, the three elements occurring on Earth that were not Earth themselves. Kircher, characteristically, referred the chemical triad of salt, sulfur, and mercury to the Holy Trinity:

So that a single thing would be seen as established with triple power, in which glorious GOD impressed the sign of his ineffable and adorable Trinity on his primordial creation as a future principle for all things; hence, not without merit, we observe that this Saline-sulpurous-mercurial spirit, like the universal seed of Nature, can be called one substance distinguished in three powers, the proximate cause of all things.[26]

But the cosmic sperm of *panspermia rerum* also exploited a verbal distinction with a subtlety that might only be called Jesuitical. Kircher employed a Greco-Roman compound phrase, *panspermia rerum*, to describe the universal seeds of things, but he also used the phrase *semina rerum*, and this was one of the terms by which the Epicurean poet-philosopher Lucretius had referred to atoms, a usage subsequently adopted by Giordano Bruno.

In a sense, the stretch in Athanasius Kircher's cosmos from *semina rerum* to *panspermia rerum* was no more than a stretch from the Latin term for seed, *semen*, to the Greek *sperma*. It was simply a dangerous stretch, one that Kircher explicitly denied in *Mundus subterraneus* along with denials of many other doctrines to which he actually subscribed. But like atoms, *panspermia rerum* allowed Kircher to postulate a universe that was consistent throughout its infinite extent. However vocally he might decry atomism, the seeds at the heart of *panspermia* acted just like Bruno's atoms in binding that infinite universe together, and endowing it with the ubiquitous fertility that atoms and the world-soul provided for Giordano Bruno. In the early years of the twentieth century, the great Swedish chemist Svante Arrhenius (who won the Nobel Prize in Chemistry in 1903) would propose that the universe, now securely accepted as infinite and composed of atoms, carried spores of life throughout its infinite reaches, some of which had landed on the earth to create life there; Arrhenius called this phenomenon *panspermia*.[27]

Despite its potential perils, Kircher's presentation of *panspermia rerum* reveals why the clever father survived for an entire natural life span to practice his dangerous art. He continually quoted the Bible in support of his contentions, no matter how radical, and unlike Galileo, who as a layman was discouraged from speculating on theology and exegesis of the Bible, Kircher was a Jesuit priest, entitled to expound on theology and the Bible to his heart's content. But Kircher also brought in Talmud, scarabs, obelisks, and experimental evidence, and he cowed his opponents with Babel towers of fact, working the subtleties of argument with the deftness that has been proverbially associated with his Order. Kircher's cosmology and its attendant concept of a universal *panspermia* also show that however dramatically the eight-year trial and gruesome public execution of Giordano Bruno had been designed to prove that the heretic philosopher was a lone and terrible fanatic, the performance failed. Bruno's books had been read by Kepler, Galileo, and Athanasius Kircher, and they were enough to change the course of natural philosophy. For both Bruno and Kircher argued with passionate eloquence that nothing but an infinite universe did justice to an omnipotent God, and once the idea of that vastness immeasurable had been conceived, it really did burst the crystalline spheres of Aristotelian physics. What Giordano Bruno said of himself in *De Immenso* might as well have been said of Theodidactus when he first climbed onto the wings of Cosmiel for their *iter exstaticum coeleste*:

> Hence as I make my journey, secure and sufficiently happy
> Suddenly I am raised aloft by primordial passion;
> I become Leader, Law, Light, Prophet, Father, Author,
> and Journey.
> Rising above this world to the others that shine in their splendor
> I wander through every part of that ethereal country
> Then, far away, as they gape at the marvel, I leave them
> behind me.[28]

Notes

1. See Kircher 1641, pp. 431–433.
2. Kircher's statement is found in a letter from the French scholar Claude-Nicolas Fabri de Peiresc to the French royal astronomer, Pierre Gassendi, 27 August 1633: "27 Aoust * 1633. Et toutefoys le bon P Athanase que nous avons veu passer icy bien à la haste, ne se peult tenir de nous advoüer, en presence du P Ferrand, que le P Malapertius [Charles Malapert, French Jesuit who worked in Poland and Douai] et le P Clavius mesmes n'improuvoient nullement l'advis de Copernicus, ains ne s'en esloignoient guieres, encores qu'on les eusse pressez et obligez d'escrire pour les communes suppositions d'Aristote, que le P Scheiner mesmes ne suyvoit que par force et par obediance aussy bien que luy qui ne faict pas de difficulté d'admettre au corps de la lune, non seulement des montaignes, des vallées et des mers ou estans, mais des arbres et des plantes, et mesmes des animaulx, pourveu qu'on en veuille excepter et exclure les plus parfects et d'admettre aussy que la terre face une reverberation sur le globe de la lune, de la lumiere du soleil, qui responde à celle que faict la lune sur la nostre." Peiresc 1893, vol. 4.
3. Kircher 1641b, p. 572: "verum qui haec paulo pensiculatius scrutatus fuerit, manifesto videbit, longitudinis Planetarum motus, multo facilius, expeditus, et verius iuxta terrae fixae hypothesin, quam motae, erui posse; ut vel ex hoc ipso Copernicanae hypothesi, Ptolomaica, et Tychoniana hypothesis multis parasangis praeferri merito debeat; quae fusius forsan hoc loco demonstrare possem, nisi limites instituti meae transire vererer."
4. Ibid., p. 551: "Keplerus noster, Mathematicus Caesareus, de quo id dici merito potest, ubi Mathematicus eo nemo melior et subtilior, nemo peior, uti Physicus est, ut vehementer doleam tam eximium virum divina illa μαθήματα, Physicis suis nugamentis tam turpiter commaculasse, quod cum in aliis, ut in hoc praesenti Copernico-Pythagoraeo machinamento satis ostendit."
5. Kircher 1660, pp. 97–98: "Erras tu summopere, si Aristotelem de iis rebus, quae ad supernorum corporum natura pertinent, omnia vera locutum esse tibi persuadeas . . . fieri enim non potest, ut Philosophi, solis suis cogitatis insistentes, repudiatisque experientiis, quidpiam solidi circa naturalem Mundi constitutionem concludere possint; conceptus enim hominum, nisi experimentis fulciantur, tanto saepe numero a vero aberrant longius, quanto hunc globum Lunarem a terreno longius distare videmus."
6. Kircher 1641b, p. 717: "sciendum est, terram, uti communis rerum mater est et matrix, ita rerum omnium quoque semina in se continere."
7. Ibid., p. 718: "terram . . . panspermia quadam sive omnigena seminum mistura foetam."
8. Ibid., p. 722: "ergo singulae Plantae ex una et eadem panspermia quadam facta[e] tellure pro conditione et qualitate terreni, cui inseruntur."
9. Ibid., p. 836.
10. Kircher 1660, p. 201: "Hoc tibi certo persuasum habeas, totam hanc solaris globi molem, non una tantum facultate, sed panspermatica quadam virtute imbutam esse, qua quidem

pro diversa diversarum partium solarium natura, intra abdita Solaris Mundi viscera divitias suas abscondente, humor igneus diversimode tinctus, per radiosam virtute varia et multiplici imbutam diffusionem inferiora attingit, et pro subiecti cuiusvis natura diversos effectus producit."

11. Ibid., p. 202: "Sed o mi Cosmiel, illud non capio, quomodo multiplex illa panspermatica facultas in Solis globo inexistere possit. Cosmiel. Panspermiam non eo sensu accipias velim, quod terrenarum rerum semina in se contineat actu et realiter; sed virtute quadam eminentiali. Faciam tamen, ut totum capias per familiare tibi experimentum. Si in crucibulo quodam varias metallorum virtute discrepantium species liquefeceris, certum est, metallicas species liquefactas unum numero liquorem exhibere, [203] tametsi omnibus metallorum confusis facultatibus plurimum discrepet, ut ex diversis colorum generibus liquido patet; cuius quidem vapor pro diversa natura metallorum, nunc salutiferas, nunc noxias qualitates diffundit. Pari modo et analogia in solari globo fiere existimare debes. Sunt in solari globo non omnes partes, uti Peripatetici existimant, eiusdem facultatis seu naturae homogeneae, sed variis virtutibus, prout divina sapientia per artem suam Naturam in suos eas fines disposuit, dotatae."

12. Ibid., p. 341: "Mi Theodidacte, iam vere video, te nimis simplicis ingenii esse, et ad quorumvis sententias amplexandas plus aequo creduli. Sphaera illa crystallina, quam quaeris, in rerum natura non reperitur; stellas autem huiusmodi sphaerae infixas esse, nullo prorsus fundamento nititur. Gyra oculos, lustra omnia in circuitu, perambula singula, totum Universum peragra, neque aliam tamen, praeter hanc, quam sentis, limipidissimam aetherei Oceani nullis finibus conclusi, volubilem, subtilissimamque auram reperies."

13. Ibid., p. 361: "Et quoniam supremus ille Archetypus intellectus infinitis omnium possibilium rerum ideis foetus est, ita mundum hunc, quantum passivae eius potentiae capacitas permisit, innumera globorum, qui omnes viribus, proprietatibus, claritate, figura, colore, luce, calore, influentiis, latentibusque seminalium rationum foeturis different, varietate iuxta inexplicabilem archetypi rationem constitutum voluit."

14. Kepler 1610, fol. 10r.

15. See, most recently, Gatti 2000.

16. Bruno 1884, V.ix:

Sol vero et Tellus sunt prima animantia, primae
Sunt rerum species, primis conflata elementis,
In seque archetypum cunctorum compositorum
Comprendunt, coeunt ubi sic humentia siccis
Partibus, inque suis interiecto aere primas
Concipiunt magnas, quo sunt mage vasta, cavernas.
Quod latet in parvo, licet in magno ergo videre,
In totoque patet quod pars occultat ubique . . .

17. Firpo 1993, p. 268: "disse che Dio havea tanto bisogno del mondo quanto il mondo di Dio, e che Dio non sarebbe niente se non vi fosse il mondo, e che per questo Dio non faceva altro che crear mondi nuovi."

18. Llull 1617.

19. Biblioteca Nazionale Centrale, Rome, Fondo Gesuitico 1331, fasc. 15, fol. c209r: "Tertio licet aliquoties ille [sc. Kircherus] damnatam Copernici de telluris motu sententiam reprobat, ne quid (inquit pag. 28) sacrae Romanae Ecclesiae decretis et Institutis contrarium asserere videatur: passim tamen toto suo libro, et penitus adstruit omnia, quae ad statuendum, propugnandumque telluris motum primus invexit Copernicus; argumentaque enervat omnia, quibus error illi magno rationum pondere solet refelli. A quo enim, nisi à Copernico, eiusque sectariis illam Kircherus [208r] ipse accepit, quam ad nauseam inculcat firmamenti immensitatem, et enormem stellarum fixarum à terra remotionem?"

20. Kircher 1665c, vol. 2, p. 350: "Constat ex sacro Genesis volumine, DEUM OPT. MAX. nil immediate, sive plantam, sive animalem, aut aliud quodcunque mixtum spectes, creasse, sed mediante Chaotica massa ex nihilo educta (cui panspermiam et universale Naturae semen concreaverat) veluti ex praesupposito subjecto cuncta, coelos, sidera, mineralia, plantas, animalia produxisse."

21. Ibid., p. 327: "merito hoc loco quaeri potest, quaenam fuerit illa panspermia et vis seminalis rerum omnium productrix. Dico fuisse, spiritum quondam materialem seu ex subtiliori caelestis aurae sive ex elementorum portione compositum, fuisseque vaporem

quondam spirituosam [Sulphureo]-salino-mercurialem, semen universale rerum, Elementis a DEO concreatum originem omnium eorum, quae in Mundo condita sunt entium corporeum."

22.   Ibid., vol. 1, p. 103: "Tellurem itaque sive Geocosmum divina providentia eo ordine et situ disposuit, ut cum veluti basis et ultimus finis totius naturae conditae futurus esset, in quem veluti in totius naturae gremium principiumque passivum, omni reliqua Mundi sperni corpora, sua spermata et virum energias diffunderent; Certe id ex se et sua natura quietem postulare videbatur, animi locomotiva facultate destitutam; hoc enim pacto aptius ambientum astrorum viribus, seminaliumque rationum miscellis impraegnata subdebatur."

23.   Ibid., p. 109: "Accedit, quo universa Telluris moles iam ante, pro necessitate uniuscuiusque climatis, semina unicuique rei propria sibi concreata habebat, quae caloris obstetricantis virtute foecundata, animataque in innumerabilium rerum sobolem emerserunt. Telluri vero semina rerum concreata, aperte sacra Genesis docet [1:110] Et ait: *Germinet Terra herbam virentem et facientem semen et ligum pomiferum faciens fructum iuxta genus suum, cuius semen in semetipsis sit supra Terram; Et factum est ita.* Terrae itaque panspermia seu omnium rerum spermatica commistio concreata fuit. Quoniam vero haec panspermia nec dum ex potentia in actum educebatur ante aquarum separationem, Aridaeque detectionem, sed virtute indigebat ex alto, cuius influxibus conservata, semina rerum in germina, folia, flores, fructus educeret: hinc statim subnexuit Genesis, Solis, Lunae, stellarumque productionem, iuxta quarum influxus luminosoque actinobolismos ita Terram disposuit, ut inde pro certa temporum climatumque consitutione infallibilis vegetabilium effectus consqueretur: atque adeo principium activum passivo, paranympho Deo, conjunctum, tum primum totius vegetabilis naturae propagationem continuavit."

        Ibid., vol. 2, p. 327: "Ex sacris itaque Mosaicis Oraculis, quae merito omni humanae cognitionis certitudini multis parasangis anteferre debemus, constat, conditorem omnium DEVM in principio rerum Materiam quondam, quam nos non incongrue Chaoticam appellamus, ex nihilo creasse; gloriosus enim DEVS creavit omnia simul; intra quam quicquid in natura rerum mixtarum substantiarumque materialium postea producendum erat, veluti sub πανδπΣρμια quadam confusum latebat: Divinus enim Architectus, praeter hanc materiam, et animam humanam, nil de novo creasse, ex ipso Sacrae Paginae textu patet; eo quod ex hac unica materia chaotica, veluti ex subjacente materia et Spiritus divini incubitu iam foecundata, postea omnia, et coelos et elementa, atque ex his compositis tam vegetabilium quam animalium species (excepta anima rationali) solo omnipotentis vocis imperio eduxerit . . . quaeque postea per seminalem virtutem iis concessam sese perenni generatione propagare possent. Materiam vero Chaoticam non statim abolevit, sed usque ad Mundi consummationem durare voluti, ut in primordiis rerum, ita in hunc usque diem, panspermia rerum omnium refertam: perire voluerit, quam DEVS in principio ex nihilo produxit ex materia chaotica, quam sententiam plerorumque fere Sanctorum Patrum monumenta potissimum *Sancti Basilii* in *Hexamero* tuentur."

24.   Kircher, *Ad Illustrissimum et Reverendissimum Josephum Mariam Suaresium, Episcopum Dia* τριβιον *De Magico Gnosticorum Sigillo*; Biblioteca Apostolica Vaticana, MS. Vat. Lat 9064, fol. 84r: "In altera facie sigilli, scarabei figura expansis alis incisa videtur, ex prisca mystarum Aegyptiarum schola extracta; quam solare numen, quod Graeci ϛλιοκάνθαρον id est ob splendorem scarabeum solis dicebant, ob operum huius insecti ad operum solis similitudinem et analogiam, hoc pacto appellatum. Huiusmodi solare numen Gnostici in suis sigillis nullibi non obviis, veluti simia Aegyptiorum, nunc galli capite, galea clypeaque munitum, nec non serpentibus pedibus formidandum modo sub scarabei figura alata ceu mundi animam, uti in hoc cernitur, exprimebunt. Quemadmodum igitur Heliocantharus globulum suum ab Oriente in occidentem versatum infuso semine ad foecunditatem animat, it hoc solare numen orbem circumeundo e[a]ndem rerum πανδπΣρμία animat, foecundat, et omnigena rerum varietate replet."

25.   See Kircher 1665c, vol. 2, p. 258.

26.   Ibid., pp. 328–329: "ut una res triplici virtute constituta videatur, in qua gloriosus DEVS primordiali creaturae suae veluti rerum onmium futuro principio, Sacrosanctae ineffabilis et adorandae suae Triadis signaculum impressit: Unde non immerito hoc tanquam semen Naturae universale, Spiritum salino-sulphureo-mercurialem, unam substantiam triplici virtuti distinctum nuncupandum censuimus; proximum verum omnium principium, ele-

mentis quae huius vehiculum quoddam sunt, et materia remota, ab inito rerum inditum, et ad rerum omnium constitutionem, compositionemque a Deo Opt. Max. destinatum."

27. Arrhenius 1908.

28. Giordano Bruno, *De Immenso et Innumerabilibus* I.i. 19–24 in Francesco Fiorentino, ed. *Jordani Bruni Nolani Opera Latine con scripta*, vol. I, Naples: Domenico Morano, 1884, pp. 201–202.

9

Father Athanasius on the Isthmus of a Middle State

Understanding Kircher's Paleontology

STEPHEN JAY GOULD

Part I. Kircher Trapped at the Starting Gate of Mythical History

Charles Darwin, the most genial and generous of scientific revolutionaries, treated his creationist colleagues with equanimity rooted in confidence that his new world order would prevail both by utility and weight of evidence. Darwin's rare expressions of annoyance generally record his frustration at the emptiness of creationist arguments that seem to advance a particular case but actually explain nothing at all. For example, he demonstrates how evolution provides a simple and coordinated explanation for the various forms of striping found on the coats of all horse species—from the permanent and prominent coloration of zebras, to the occasional striping of aberrant horses, to the weak bands of color that often appear in hybrids between unstriped species, to the bands of color that sometimes form in juveniles but disappear in adult life—whereas creationist accounts, with their central premise of a separate creation for each species, offer nothing but empty verbiage about divine preferences for order or propensities to craft signals as aids for human understanding. Darwin compares this lingering mysticism in creationist arguments with a standard caricature supposedly by describing the foolish delusions of theologically tainted early paleontologists of Kircher's generation:

> To admit this [creationist] view is, as it seems to me, to reject a real for an unreal, or at least for an unknown, cause. . . . It makes the works of God a mere mockery and deception; I would almost as soon believe with the old and ignorant cosmogonists, that fossil shells had never lived, but had been created in stone so as to mock the shells now living on the sea-shore.[1]

Darwin's history of paleontology repeats a standard refrain of his day and (alas) our own—a conventional Whiggish account replete with heroes and villains, and constructed in three canonical stages of increasing light. In this account, each transition demolishes a previous bulwark of theological reaction as Western history unfolds in warfare between scientific enlightenment and religious impediment.[2] Butterfield may have coined "Whig history" to designate a progressivist view of political advance,[3] but scientists have always been the staunchest promoters of Whiggish narratives, as the ethos of the field virtually enjoins a linear concept of history as a pathway toward factual truth, the empiricist's analogue of superior morality or growing liberality as the *summum bonum* of an upward trajectory.

In the conventional tripartite account, paleontologists before the scientific revolution—described as "Aristotelian," "medieval," or "Renaissance" with decreasing degrees of disdain—could not even conceptualize fossils as organic remains, and they attributed these petrified likenesses of plants and animals to occult forces of the mineral kingdom, or to direct acts of divine showmanship or even humor. In Stage Two, gaining ground throughout the seventeenth century and taking hold in Newton's generation, the organic view finally prevailed as mechanism triumphed and mysticism receded. But theological constraints still demanded obeisance to the Mosaic chronology, and such restriction led to the minimally historical view that virtually all fossils (and the entire stratigraphic column) record the single paroxysm of Noah's flood. Finally, beginning with Buffon's mid–eighteenth-century presentation, and prevailing in the British school from Hutton to Lyell, "deep time" triumphed and the fossil record became the archive of an immensely long history of organic change (although not yet explained in evolutionary terms—a fourth great step that would not be taken until 1859).

Consider, for example, a standard account of the history of paleontology in these three stages, as presented in 1909 by the leading French paleontologist, Charles Depéret:

> The Middle Ages retained the ideas of Aristotle, and almost unanimously adopted the theories of the spontaneous generation of fossils or petrifactions under varying formulas, such as plastic force, petrifying force, action of the stars, freaks of nature, mineral concretions, carved stones, seminal vapors, and many other analogous theories. These ideas continued to reign almost without opposition till the end of the sixteenth century. . . .
>
> The seventeenth century saw little by little the antiquated theories of plastic force and of carved stones disappear, and the animal or vegetable origin of fossil remains was definitely established. Unfortunately the progress of paleontology was to be retarded for a long space of time by the rise and success of the diluvian theories, which attributed the dispersion of fossils to the universal deluge, and endeavored to adapt all these facts to the Mosaic records. . . .
>
> Yet there were, among these partisans of the Flood, a few men of worth, whose principal merit, outside their too frequent extra-scientific speculations, was that they deeply studied fossils and spread the better knowledge of them by exact representations. This task of the description and illustration of fossil animals was especially the work of the scholars of the eighteenth century which was

the age of systematic zoology. From all quarters they set themselves to gather and collect fossils, to study and describe them.[4]

This tripartite and triumphalist history misstates the generalities of paleontological learning badly enough to arouse the ire of any scholar; but if one wished to specify a person or event maximally misserved by this resilient falsity, the Jesuit polymath Athanasius Kircher (1602–80) has certainly received the shortest end or the worst shake (choose your favorite metaphor for unfairness)—however understandable, if lamentable, the reasons. Triumphalist tales need villains in several categories, with direct political persecutors ranking foremost (Urban VIII in the standard version of Galileo's ordeal), and a particular caricature of an intellectual stick-in-the-mud standing just behind—the role traditionally assigned to Kircher in the tripartite account.

In the standard Anglophonic (and Protestant) version, Kircher could hardly avoid his miscasting in such a role by later historians.[5] As a powerful Jesuit, and at least "semiofficial" scholar and natural historian in the Papal See, and as a contemporary, if aging, counterpart to Newton, Boyle, Halley, and Hooke, Kircher became (and has remained ever since) the foil of modernism, the optimally available synecdoche for all the lingering scholasticism and theological constraint that modern science had to overcome. Thus, the "sound bite" on Kircher's paleontology places him as the last significant rearguard inhabitant of Stage One, the last "medievalist" who denied the organic nature of fossils and attributed their origin to occult (or divine) forces acting in the mineral kingdom—in other words, as the last important obstacle to paleontology's victorious entry into the second stage, where a mechanical worldview and a rejection of final causation would potentiate the advance of this discipline into its next phase of basic understanding: the key recognition of fossils as remains of ancient organisms.

Three developing and interrelated arguments summarize the aim and organization of this essay: (1) debunking (in Part II) the tripartite and triumphalist account of paleontology in general; (2) demonstrating, in particular, that no Stage One of inorganic darkness ever existed (also in Part II); and (3) finally, and in greater particular, documenting (in Part III) that Kircher never advocated an inorganic origin for most fossils (and showing, moreover, that the primary questions Kircher asked of the fossil record, and his basic classification and conceptualization of the mineral kingdom, precluded such categories in any case).

Therefore, as a prelude to making this general argument sensible, perhaps even interesting (at least as an exercise in basic fairness both to a fascinating individual and to the intellectual strengths and subtleties of his maligned age), I must first document the establishment and longevity of the Kircherian legend. This parody of heroic history depicts Kircher as a Jesuitical dark knight who tried to serve his church and Moses's literal chronology by describing a pristine earth, imbued with symbols of unchanging order, as expressed in the similar appearance (and medically useful power) of rocks that look like organisms, and the living creatures that occupy similar positions in the other kingdoms of nature's overarching and harmonious unity.

Kircher's contemporaries, as we shall see, generally reported his views with fair accuracy (although often with some confusion, as Kircher himself honestly discussed his own doubts and puzzlements on key issues). A glance at the most influential accounts of the history of paleontology written during the eighteenth and nineteenth centuries reveals that the myth of Kircher's anachronistic residence in Stage One had already congealed, as his name became associated with a lingering belief in the inorganic nature of most fossils. The great four-volume compendium of Knorr and Walch,[6] filled with the most beautiful plates ever printed and endowed with the most obsessively thorough review of printed literature ever attempted, states in the historical introduction to Part 2:

> Most naturalists of this century held the exclusive opinion that these bodies of the mineral kingdom, which looked so much like shells, had no relation with actual shells in the sea, but were formed instead by a secret and special power (*virtu*) of the mineral world. The partisans of this opinion differed among themselves about the best manner for expressing this conviction. . . . Several of them named this power *vis plastica;* others a *mineralis formativa;* others as a joke of nature, while still others attributed these objects to a universal spirit, an Archeus—a petrifying, or architectural, or form-giving spirit. Others gave the name of *aura seminalis* to this power, as they tried to seek the cause for the formation of petrified shells in a vegetative principle inherent in the mineral kingdom. . . . All these absurdities flow from Aristotle's principle of spontaneous generation, and the *vis plastica* of Avicenna and Albert the Great. The latter scholar transmitted the idea to the Scholastics. Nevertheless, the views of this [seventeenth] century would have been more reasonable if the great authority of Kircher and Gassendi had not so strongly supported this error [of spontaneous generation]. Kircher, in particular, was not ashamed to designate Avicenna's *vis plastica* (for he had carefully studied this Arab philosopher) as a *spiritus lapidificus, architectonicus* or *plasticus.*[7]

At the close of the nineteenth century, the great German paleontologist and compendiast K. A. von Zittel published an astonishingly detailed listing of almost any paleontological claim ever advanced, or any study ever undertaken. Zittel wrote, in the conventional misunderstanding and dismissal of Kircher as a reactionary wed to theological doctrine as the source of an ahistorical perspective defining Stage One:

> The origin of solid rocks was ascribed to a power within the earth, called the *vis lapidifica*, which bound the elements together, strengthened them, and then gave them different forms through a *spiritus architectonicus* or *plasticus.* . . . As examples of "figured stones" [a common name for fossils in Kircher's time], a large

number of drawings were presented, which either depicted the figments of an overheated fantasy, or must have been drawn as outright falsifications. For Kircher, most figured stones, even bones and teeth, were manufactured by a *vis lapidifica* and *spiritus plasticus*. However, he did grant an organic basis to lithified fishes, fossil wood, leaf impressions, lignite, and also certain molluscan shells. Nonetheless, these remains clearly had no historical meaning for Kircher. The biblical creation story satisfied him completely.[8]

If we turn to the two most important Anglophone works written in the twentieth century on the history of paleontology, F. D. Adams in *The Birth and Development of the Geological Sciences* at least grants Kircher's belief in the organic nature of *some* fossils, but otherwise he repeats the conventional view of Kircher as a reactionary advocate of occult forces in the mineral realm:

> Athansius Kircher, a member of the Jesuit Order and a prolific writer, gives an extended account with many illustrations, of wonderful markings and forms which are found in rocks. Among them are the letters of the Greek and Latin alphabets, various geometrical figures, representations of the heavenly bodies, of trees, castles, animals of different kinds, the human form, as well as certain strange outlines which, as he presents them, seem to carry a suggestion of supernatural meanings. These latter, like those given by other writers in this period, represent the products of a glowing and highly imaginative fancy, inspired, in some cases at least, by an earnest desire to read into these obscure figures a deep religious significance, as the direct revelations of the Creator of the world. Kircher held that most of these had been brought into being through the action of a *Spiritus Architectonicus* or *Spiritus Plasticus*, but thought the forms of leaves, mussels, fish and bones were the remains of living things.[9]

In the most incisive and distinguished book ever written on the history of paleontology (by a superb paleontologist who then enjoyed a second career as an equally eminent historian of science), M. J. S. Rudwick confines his commentary to the mythology of Kircher's residence in inorganic Stage One:

> The explanation that Hooke opposed was, in his own words, the view that fossils owed "their formation and figuration" to some "kind of *Plastick virtue* inherent in the earth". The continuing popularity of this view, stemming as we have seen from the Neoplatonism of the previous century, owed much to the work of one of the most prolific and versatile scholars of the age, the German Jesuit Athanasius Kircher (1602–1680). Kircher's highly popular encyclopedia on *The Subterranean World* . . . described the "geocosm" of a static Earth in terms of an extended organismic analogy with the microcosm. The stony matter of "fossil objects" was attributed to a "lapidifying virtue diffused through the whole body of the geocosm," and their form to a "*spiritus plasticus*" analogous to that which controlled the development of an organism. . . . No stony resemblance or likeness was too implausible for Kircher to believe, and he decorated his work with a fantastic collection of supposed natural "images."[10]

And so the legend persists, with Kircher depicted as the last "pre-modernist" holdout against the consequences (for the earth's age, and for historicity in general) of an organic origin for petrified remains in the geological record.[11] Finally, being far from sinless on this matter, I must at least cast a stone my way and cite my own previous obtuseness and willingness to accept the traditional view rather than to read Kircher's own words, since I previously described Kircher in similar terms.[12]

Part II. Against Tripartite Triumphalism: No Consensus Ever Existed for Interpreting Fossils as Inorganic Sports of Nature

If Stage One of the tripartite Whiggish tale—the supposed "pre-modern" consensus that described fossils as inorganic sports of nature—never existed at all, then Athanasius Kircher, obviously, could not have played his assigned role as an anachronistic, finger-in-dike, theologically benighted anti-empiricist who tried, from his antique conceptual prison in literal sight of the papal throne, to stem the modernist tide by defeating its novel weapons of Cartesian mechanism and Baconian inductivism. Several books could (and should) be written to debunk this persistent myth of paleontology's erroneous foundation, but I will only outline the general argument here, as the case seems so overwhelming in its barest bones, and as Kircher's fascinating and truly different paleontology presupposes the undoing of this inorganic legend as a first step toward proper comprehension. The outline of this Part II proceeds as three major contentions, linked in logical order, with each expressed in a series of subarguments:

A. The supposed temporal sequence of three stages in the interpretation of fossils—from belief in inorganic origins, to acceptance of organic origin with deposition restricted to the singular event of Noah's flood, to recognition of organic origins with changing form and composition through substantial time—never characterized the history of paleontological understanding.

1. These three positions cannot designate a progressive advance of scientific understanding through time because all three arguments were simultaneously and prominently "in play," starting with the first printed paleontological texts. In fact, the two earliest accounts from the opening decades of the sixteenth century, written by the two greatest thinkers of the time, present the same scheme in designating *all three positions* as the full range of major alternatives. Moreover, both men also concur in defending the third, and supposedly "last," stage as their favored opinion.

In his Leicester Codex, written during the first decade of the sixteenth century, Leonardo da Vinci discussed three major theories for interpreting marine fossils on mountaintops: the inorganic theory (which he ridiculed unmercifully); the Noachian attribution (which he rejected with a set of brilliant arguments, both observational and quasi-experimental—calculating, for example, how far a cockle shell could travel during a forty-day storm from its original oceanic residence to a burial site now far inland, and judging the distance too great for granting any credibility to this explanation); and the hypothesis of the supposed third stage, not nearly ready to make an entry according to the Whiggish account, that land and sea had frequently changed positions during the earth's lengthy history, with current mountains occupying the sites of former seas (the opinion that Leonardo supported, and that he recognized as the standard argument of classical scholars from Hippocrates to Strabo).

One might claim (as indeed I once did,[13] and quite erroneously) that Leonardo's parsing, which had no influence upon later history because his notebooks remained unpublished and unknown to scholars for several centuries, only records his personal and superior insight, and not the standard view of the time—so that the tripartite model might still hold, with Leonardo's personal status as far "ahead of the curve" deemed admirable but entirely invisible. However, even this nuanced version of conventional history, potentially validating the traditional assessment of Kircher as a reactionary mired in Stage One, cannot be sustained, because another great Italian intellectual of the early sixteenth century, Girolamo Fracastoro of Verona, presented exactly the same classification of three competing interpretations, and he also voiced his support for the "modernist" third view—but quite publicly in a statement prominently reported in nearly every seventeenth century work of note in paleontology and general natural history.

In this account, Torello Sarayna, a noted lawyer and antiquary (who published his description of Fracastoro's response in 1530), became puzzled by the plethora of marine fossils found while quarrying local stone to rebuild the fortifications of Verona. Recalling that such classical scholars as Theophrastus and Pliny had written of petrifaction, Sarayna asked his friend and learned natural historian about the nature of fossils. Fracastoro, the greatest scholar and physician of his time, now best remembered for describing and naming syphilis in a long and elegant Latin elegy entitled *Syphilus sive morbus Gallicus*, responded with the same threefold set of possibilities that Leonardo had privately penned into his Leicester Codex—thus indicating that this taxonomy of potential solutions for a recognized problem had already become conventional 150 years before Kircher's *Mundus subterraneus*.

The standard scientific account of Fracastoro's judgment first appeared in the 1622 catalogue of Francesco Calzolari famous museum in Fracastoro's natal town of Verona, where a full section of text bears the prominent title *Magni Fracastorii sententia de proposita questione*. In this text, Sarayna reports Fracastoro's rejection of the inorganic and Noachian hypotheses, and his firm support for the third view: "Thus did he [Fracastoro] conclude that these [fossils] were once real animals, and that they had been cast up there [upon the mountains] by the sea, and initially born in the sea. . . . This then was the teaching of our most illustrious antiquary Fracastoro."[14]

Interestingly, the first modern printed defense of this third position (in an explicit section devoted to the argument, not just as a passing comment)—that fossils are petrified remains of organisms, thus suggesting an ancient earth with frequent changes in positions of land and sea—probably occurs in one of the most famous humanistic treatises of the time, the *Genialium dierum* (*Book of Pleasant Days*) published in 1532 by the Neopolitan legal scholar Alexandro ab Alexandri (1461–1523), who wrote: "I remember seeing hard stone in the mountains of Calabria, a great distance from the sea, in which a large number of marine shells are amassed and congealed together with the marble into a single body."[15] As a Renaissance humanist who revered the writings of ancient Greece and Rome as the apogee of attainable wisdom, Alexandri writes to affirm an old consensus, now expressed in a work of modern humanism, and not to expound anything controversial from a realm he would have recognized as a novel enterprise called "science."

2. Contrary to the claim of Darwin's opening quotation, and to the standard dismissal of the inorganic alternative as an explicitly anti-intellectual rearguard tactic of dogmatic theologians, I have never read a defense of inorganic origin framed as God's test of our faith, or as a divine joke or mere sport, or (more seriously and conspiratorially) as the work of demons out to undermine the Lord's work. Yes, defenders of the inorganic argument did often refer to fossils as *lusus naturae*—literally, "sports of nature." But this phrase implied no trickery of direct divine emplacement, and it only invited scholars to consider mechanisms and forces active in the mineral kingdom whereby forms resembling plants and animals might be generated within rocks.

3. Very few scholars who wrote on paleontological matters ever believed that *all* fossils should be attributed to inorganic causes of the mineral realm. At most, and for good reasons explored below, some particularly difficult objects of no obvious relationship to organisms received such an interpretation. I do not deny that a few early scientists did espouse a general inorganic view.[16] But I suspect that the common impression of a truly potent and pervasive inorganic theory, as so often portrayed by Anglophone historians and scientists, arises from the peculiarity that in the late seventeenth century, but only there and then with such force and influence, a fully inorganic conception was developed and strongly defended by a group of prominent English scholars and scientists—Martin Lister, Edward Lhwyd, and Robert Plot, in particular. Nonetheless, and even then, the more prominent group of Robert Hooke, John Woodward, and John Ray explicitly countered with persuasive arguments for organic origin. Still, this late-seventeenth-century English episode does represent the only high-water mark for a genuine, if short-lived, "school" of prominent inorganicists among participants in debates about the meaning and nature of fossils—so Anglophone scholars may be excused for falsely extrapolating a parochialism to a generality.

B. No good or compelling general reason ever existed to inspire or encourage a belief in the inorganic nature of all (or even most) fossils.

1. Of the two potential rationales for pervasive inorganicism—that theology (or general *Weltanschauung*) compelled, or that limitations of empirical knowledge impelled—the first claim of comfortable fit with a larger worldview cannot be sustained. Nothing in sixteenth- or seventeenth-century Christian theology, either Catholic or Protestant, commanded (or even implied) an inorganic view of fossils as more consonant either with basic belief or with understandings of the earth's age and history. In particular, an organic interpretation of fossils did not threaten traditional views of a young earth, created just a few thousand years ago, essentially in its present constitution, and with all living forms fashioned directly by God in six days of twenty-four hours—if only because fossils, viewed as remains of organisms, could comfortably be ascribed to consequences of Noah's flood. (No seventeenth-century scholar had yet recognized the potentially threatening pattern of a set of anatomical changes, expressed through vertical sequences of strata, with successively lower—now recognized as older—layers containing an ever higher percentage of extinct forms looking less and less like modern organisms.)

2. The second potential reason—that honorable misunderstandings about the empirical nature of fossils implied an inorganic interpretation—can also cite no supporting rationale. In particular, proponents of an inorganic Stage One have frequently claimed that the well-known phenomenon of petrifaction—the composition of many fossils as rocky material known only from the mineral kingdom and not as organic matter (even as hard biological "stuff" of shell or bone)—forced pre-modern naturalists to regard fossils as inorganic even though the objects bore such an uncanny resemblance to organisms. But petrifaction (the active transformation of organic matter to mineral substances) had been recognized, accepted, and extensively discussed by scholars for centuries. Avicenna wrote at length about the stony nature of many organic remains. Most influentially, Albertus Magnus devoted substantial sections of his treatise *De mineralibus*—the "standard" pre-Renaissance volume on the general subject—to discussions of petrifaction, including his documentation of petrifying springs and ponds, recognized throughout Europe, where people could place such objects as crowns, shoes, or bird nests, and retrieve them later, converted to stone.[17]

C. In Kircher's time, scholars could cite entirely reasonable arguments—both theoretical and empirical—for claiming that some fossils had formed entirely in the mineral kingdom, and not as remains of organisms.

More subtly, the principal taxonomies for fossils, as suggested by general worldviews of Kircher's time, did not even conceptualize the problem in terms of a fundamental dichotomy between organic and inorganic modes of origin. Thus, the basic framing of paleontology's subject matter did not suggest, at least for Kircher and most of his contemporaries, a primary intellectual task of dividing a general category of "things in rocks that look like organisms" into two basic piles labeled "remains of genuine organisms" and "products of the mineral kingdom that happen, for whatever set of complex reasons, to resemble organisms."

1. Various scholars, with Cardano in the mid–sixteenth century as perhaps the most famous exponent (particularly in the chapter on stones in his *De subtilitate* of 1550), did not sharply distinguish an inorganic mineral kingdom from the organic world of vegetable and animate nature. Rather, they viewed all matter as imbued with the spark of life but in varying degrees, forging a rising chain of being, with mineral objects less endowed and animals most strongly pervaded by this universal force. Under such a worldview, the weaker "life force" of the mineral kingdom might generate objects looking like their more vital counterparts in botanical and zoological realms. But such fossils would not be conceived as inorganic "mimics" or symbolic analogues of plants and animals. Indeed, a primary distinction of organic from inorganic makes little sense at all under such a continuationist conception of natural reality.

2. In another view held by some sixteenth- and seventeenth-century natural philosophers, but often mistakenly portrayed as the canonical or nearly universal belief for validating the supposed Stage One of general consensus about the inorganic nature of fossils, pervasive correspondences supposedly linked the three realms of matter (animal, vegetable, and mineral). Such a system illustrated God's sensible and harmonious creation of a static and deeply meaningful world order, and it also guaranteed that each distinctive object in any kingdom shared a common form with designated counterparts in each of the other two kingdoms. However, the composition and mode of origin for each of the three objects might differ profoundly, for the overarching correspondence recorded an ideal unification, not a likeness of material construction. Thus, an inorganic rock in the mineral kingdom might look just like a fish, and the similarity might record deeply meaningful unification in God's design for a sensible cosmos. But the fossil itself would remain inorganic in origin and structure.

I do not deny that Neoplatonic arguments of this form enjoyed substantial support and respect. But few naturalists ever invoked such a conception of nature to defend an inorganic origin for all, or even most, fossils. And although Kircher himself did advance such theories of correspondence, especially for identifying the medical potential of certain plants by their similarity in appearance to afflicted human organs and parts, he never used these Neoplatonic ideas to justify an inorganic origin for most petrified fossils that looked like plants and animals.

Incidentally, an exaggerated account of influence for this "correspondence theory" has generated the most common canard about a mythical Stage One of general belief in the inorganic nature of fossils. In decrying the inorganic view as benighted mysticism and theological apologetics, critics usually suppose (as Darwin did in my opening quotation) that inorganicists attributed the genesis of fossil "mimics" for plants and animals to the mysterious action of something called a *vis plastica* (plastic virtue), or some other Latinate mumbo jumbo recalling Molière's famous mock on pre-modern medicine: the foolish physician's empty claim that opium puts a person to sleep because the drug contains a "soporific virtue."

Because the meaning of various claims regarding forces called *vis, spiritus, virtus,* or *succus* does become important in understanding the views of Kircher and earlier scholars, two preliminary comments about this general terminology should help clarify the actual intentions behind such invocations:

(i) No tendency can be more misleading in historical analysis than our temptation to backread modern sensibilities into interpretations of older usages—as detractors of Kircher have so consistently done in branding all talk about *vis* and *spiritus* as theological impediment and mysticism seen through modern secular glasses and the false model of warfare between science and religion. So I do not want to err in the other direction by trying to assimilate these terms to an admittedly imperfect understanding of questions posed in a manner that modern empiricists would regard as reasonably congenial with the aims of science as now understood.

Nonetheless, and after grappling for many years with the usage of such terms by sixteenth- and seventeenth-century scholars, I have developed the strong impression that most invocations of *vis, spiritus, virtus,* or *succus*—when designated as a source for the origin of fossil forms—advance no claim for an intrinsically intractable operation that can only be viewed with wonder or attributed to ineffable divine power beyond human understanding. Kircher and other scholars invoked these terms to describe sources, forces, and causes that they did not understand, but that they regarded as potentially knowable—a scholarly enterprise that might be aided by giving a name, albeit little more than a vague label, and if only to focus attention toward possibly fruitful paths of inquiry. After all, if crystals form in a regular and repeated pattern, some kind of force must ordain the geometry. A name like *spiritus architectonicus* (a term actually used by some naturalists) may not push understanding much beyond the Molièreian void, but at least the label identifies a problem for exploration. I have developed a strong sense, in reading these texts, that Kircher and colleagues did not commit the error of thinking that they had identified a solution by creating such names within a classification of potential modes for nature's action.

(ii) We must recognize the Aristotelian background and context of this discourse. In using such labels, Kircher clearly wished to honor and separate the key Aristotelian categories of form and matter. Some of the hypothetical causes labeled as *vis* or *virtus* did refer, rather vaguely to be sure, to the "mysterious" (but only in the sense of presently unknown, rather than formally and permanently intractable) bases for the genesis, within rocks, of shapes with detailed resemblances to plants and animals—in other words, to the form-giving properties of the Aristotelian distinction. But other relevant forces, also labeled as *vis* or *spiritus*—for example, the *spiritus lapidificus* invoked by many naturalists of the time—designated the "matter-making" rather than "form-giving" aspect of the Aristotelian dichotomy. In other words, a *spiritus* for matter did not designate the source of a fossil's form or shape, but rather the substance of its composition. In particular, the *spiritus lapidificus* established a name for whatever process caused the petrifaction of organic matter into mineral substance—the well-known (if poorly understood) process of material transformation so essential to the comprehension of fossils as *organic* remains!

3. If the first two reasons—a model of rising degrees of vitality through all kingdoms of nature rather than a sharp distinction of inorganic minerals from living vegetables and animals, and a theory of symbolic correspondence for common forms fashioned by different processes in all three kingdoms—establish theoretical bases for regarding at least some fossils as inorganic in origin, then a third set of rational justifications for the same conclusions should be designated as empirical. Most common fossils look so much like organisms still inhabiting the earth that an organic explanation could hardly be doubted, at least by scholars of Kircher's experience and intellectual acumen. But a few fossils—particularly the highly regular, apparently crystalline parts of extinct organisms with no close modern relatives—remained supremely puzzling well past Kircher's generation, and these could easily suggest a conclusion of inorganic origin. Most notably, the common belemnites—regular, crystalline, cigar-shaped internal shells of an extinct group of cephalopods broadly related to modern squid—puzzled scholars well into the eighteenth century, when specimens with surrounding soft parts were finally discovered. In a notable debate of the late 1720s, for example, the British organicist John Woodward (who strongly upheld the organic nature of fossils as relics of Noah's flood) advanced an inorganic interpretation for belemnites,[18] while his Swiss colleague Louis Bourguet supported an organic origin for belemnites, but incorrectly identified them as teeth of fossil fishes or marine reptiles.[19]

Part III. Kircher's Complex and Rationalist Taxonomy for the Genesis of Fossils, with Most Categories Identified as Remains of Organisms or Results of Their Activities

If the primary thinker of a representative time has been systematically misread—not only in a general way, but in a manner precisely opposite to his actual intent—then our comprehension of this period and subject stands in serious disarray, and in need of radical reformulation. We face such a situation for Kircher's paleontological views. Kircher ranks not only as the leading scholar of his generation, but also as an exemplar of something far more important—that is, as the last great advocate for a pre-modern view of the natural world, a subtle and fascinating mode of thinking that Newton's generation would soon render obsolete and, therefore, hard to recover or comprehend for people trained to think so differently about the origins and causes of material objects.

In particular, so long as we continue to parrot the conventional claim that Kircher supported an inorganic origin in the mineral kingdom for most fossils that look like the remains of plants and animals, we cannot accurately depict the central features of his natural philosophy. I therefore devote this article's final major section to a reanalysis of Kircher's paleontological views. I will focus my general argument upon two propositions, each primarily explicated by Kircher in his most famous and extensive text about the earth, the *Mundus subterraneus* (1665); but each defended as well by a "smoking gun" of explicit commentary in two earlier works, the *Itinerarium exstaticum* (part two) (1657) for the first proposition, and the *Diatribe de prodigiosis crucibus* (1661) for the second claim.

For my *first proposition*, I will demonstrate that *Kircher regarded most fossils as remains of organisms*, that he never upheld the inorganicist interpretation conventionally attributed to him, and that he understood petrifaction as a key argument for the organic genesis of stony fossils. In the *second proposition*, I will then show that *Kircher's limited categories for inorganic origin of some fossils lie embedded within a broader taxonomy that does not utilize organic versus inorganic as a basic, or even an important, criterion for a* fundamentum divisionis; and that, even here, Kircher established at least two subcategories of this taxonomy for organic remains (or products of the activities of organisms). (Modern paleontologists would designate the objects of these two subcategories as genuine fossils by the standard definition—that is, as evidence for ancient organisms, broadly construed as body parts, impressions of body parts, or records of the behaviors of organisms.)

Thus, of Kircher's two major categories, the first includes the petrified three-dimensional remains of ancient organisms, whereas the second embraces all other forms found in the mineral kingdom that look like organisms and other objects of human concern. Because the majority of examples in this second category also record the substances and activities of ancient organisms, Kircher obviously advocated an organic origin for most mineralogical objects (all items in his category one, plus most items in his category two) that strongly resemble plants and animals in their general form and detailed organization.

This analysis of Kircher's actual views on fossils must begin with a reminder that in his day, and extending through the eighteenth century, the term *fossil* (from the past participle of *fodere*, "to dig") referred to any object found in (and extracted from) the mineral realm. Thus, in Kircher's usage, fossils include both objects resembling plants and animals, and anything else of a mineralogical nature that might attract our attention as a discretely definable form or substance. In fact, the decision to forge a primary distinction between objects that look like plants and animals because they originated as organisms (the restricted sense of *fossil* used today), and items of inorganic genesis that happen, for whatever reason, to resemble forms of human interest, identifies a primary episode of intellectual change in the history of scientific ideas. Interestingly, this important change began with a decision to distinguish the remains of ancient plants and animals as "extraneous fossils" (or some similar adjectival restriction) because they had entered the mineralogical realm from one of nature's other two kingdoms, and to call the remaining objects of truly mineralogical origin "intrinsic" or "native" fossils, as products of the mineral kingdom *ab initio*. For reasons that no one has properly traced, the term *fossil* survived only as a description for the extraneous category, and it fell from use for intrinsic objects of mineralogical origin.

A. The First Issue of the Nature of Three-Dimensional Petrifactions

Kircher presented his major statement about the operation and physical character of the earth in a massive and lavishly illustrated two-volume folio work, published in 1665 as *Mundus subterraneus*. Kircher follows a venerable tradition in regarding our planet as an active system, treated as a macrocosm with parts fully corresponding (and maintaining cycles of self-sustaining activity) to the microcosm of the human body—hence Kircher's famous plates of volcanoes and internal magma chambers as the earth's cycling heat (matching the bodily warmth that sustains human activity), and interior lakes and streams as the earth's water (of the four Greek elements), matching the suffusion of the human body with blood.

Nonetheless—and this Kircherian conviction becomes crucial in understanding his views about fossils—Kircher drew a sharp distinction, based on the Aristotelian properties of life as a rising series toward a human pinnacle (vegetative, sensitive, and rational), between the two living kingdoms imbued with these powers and the third, mineralogical, kingdom that featured properties of growth, cycling, movement, and sustainability but did not manifest the spark of true life. Kircher writes in the introduction to volume 2, book 8, on the composition of the mineral kingdom:

> Two kinds of seminarium must be considered here, the first for inanimate bodies, including all those formed in the womb of the earth, and comprising the genera and species of minerals, rocks and metals; the other, or spermatic force, is vegetative or sensitive [i.e., animate], without which nothing at this [higher] scale of Nature can be achieved.

Because he believed that the mineralogical world did not manifest powers of true life, Kircher had to find other explanations (than direct production by life forces in the mineralogical kingdom) for the abundance of forms in rocks (a large proportion of "fossils," by the broad definition then in use) that strongly resemble either plants or animals, or products of human art (including apparent pictures of buildings and cities in marble, or putative representations of such complex religious scenes as Mary holding the infant Jesus or Christ dying on the cross, as exposed on natural surfaces of banded agates). How can we understand the genesis of these apparent products of life within a kingdom not imbued with actual powers of life? This key question motivates the two sections that might be called "paleontological" by modern definitions in book 8 of *Mundus subterraneus.*

Kircher begins by drawing a primary taxonomic division between two kinds of apparently "organic" images within rocks—three-dimensional petrifactions, and "pictures" of organisms, or scenes of human artifacts, on the surfaces of rocks and gems: "Figures in rocks may be considered in two different modes, either as found on smooth surfaces of flat rocks, or as made of the solid rock itself, transformed in various ways."[20] At this stage of the argument, we encounter the first factor that has led to such entrenched misunderstanding of Kircher's paleontological views. Kircher wrote two discrete sections on paleontological fossils in *Mundus subterraneus,* one for each of the two categories mentioned just above (two-dimensional pictures on surfaces of rocks and three-dimensional petrifactions). But his first paleontological text in *Mundus* treats the two-dimensional pictures (and other miscellaneous forms) in chapters 8 and 9 of section 1 ("De lapidibus in communi") of book 8. Book 8 covers everything lifelike found underground, including rocks that only mimic living forms, but also treating animals, men, and even demons that dwell beneath the earth's surface—"On the stony substances of the earth; on bones and horns and fossils, and also on subterranean animals, men and demons."

In this first paleontological discussion of chapters 8 and 9 in section 1, "About remarkable natural pictures of works, forms, figures and images, which are drawn on rocks and gems; and about their origins and causes," Kircher includes memorable illustrations to accompany his text, and these have often been reproduced in subsequent scientific and historical publications. Kircher's figures include letters of the alphabet, turrets of castles, John the Baptist in his camel hair coat, and Mary holding the infant Jesus. Obviously, Kircher did not interpret these figures as remains of organisms (or fossils in the modern sense)—so later commentators have assumed that Kircher must have regarded most fossils as inorganic in origin if he discussed fossils of this sort first.

But two fairly evident observations directly contradict the inference that because some of these initial, and admittedly striking, pictures show objects of inorganic origin, Kircher must therefore have ascribed all, or at least most, fossils to inorganic causes. First, this initial discussion also includes pictures of ordinary organic fossils, especially two full-page images of fish skeletons.[21] Second, and more crucially, Kircher may have placed this discussion of two-dimensional "pictures" first, but he clearly regarded his second category of three-dimensional petrifactions as far more common in nature, even if less puzzling in origin or striking in appearance. However, and unfortunately in retrospect, he treated this other category of petrified organic remains in the *subsequent* section 2 of book 8, entitled "On the transformation into rock of liquids, salts, herbs, plants, trees, animals and men, or on the petrifying force."

How could Kircher have expressed himself more clearly—even stating his conclusion in the title of the section itself—in asserting the organic origin of petrified three-dimensional fossils, the more common category for objects in rocks that look like plants and animals? In fact, Kircher begins his discussion of this category by stating that the indubitably organic origin of such forms need hardly be stated at all—and then appending a clear picture [Fig. 9.1] of a mass of fossil shells evidently so formed. Kircher writes: "I will not speak here of the innumerable oysters, clams, snails, fungi, algae and other denizens of the sea that have been converted to stone, because these are obviously found everywhere in such a state, and hardly merit any mention."[22]

Why, then, has the myth of Kircher's firm or exclusive allegiance to inorganicism taken such hold? I would suggest two reasons as primary sources for this pervasive error. First, the myth suits our Whiggish desires for linear progress in science, and for bad guys at the beginning of modernity—especially (under the model of warfare between science and religion) for a powerful Jesuit, and semi-official papal scientist, as chief villain. Second, Kircher did grant first place, at least in order of composition, to his smaller category of two-dimensional forms and other miscellaneous items, and to the even smaller subcategories for "pictures" with inorganic origins in this general group. He also, as stated above, included some memorable illustrations of these inorganic pictures. Thus, both from laziness and by inclination, we tend to stop reading when we encounter our expectations right at the outset—and we never realize that most of the subsequent text treats the vast majority of fossils with evident organic origins. I suspect that Kircher presented the inorganic pictures first because he found them most interesting and puzzling, and he saved the obviously organic majority for later documentation of uncontroversial matters. How could he have anticipated that later commentators would so confuse his highlighting of rare puzzles with a supposed underlying of canonical causation?

We need little beyond this bare internal evidence to prove that Kircher regarded his second category of organic petrifactions as the source of most fossils. But two additional points seal the case and emphasize the fallacy of the conventional claims that a scholar of Kircher's caliber upheld an inorganic orthodoxy for the origin of fossils as a dying gasp of theologically indoctrinated pre-modern natural history.

1. Lest one think that Kircher's relegation of petrifaction to second place in *Mundus subterraneus* denotes a permanently subsidiary ranking for this organic category in Kircher's thoughts, a "smoking gun" from an earlier work targets an opposite viewpoint. In 1656 and 1657, Kircher published the two parts of his *Itinerarium exstaticum*, his contribution to the interesting genre (dating at least to Cicero's *Somnium Scipionis*) of imaginary journeys as devices to discuss the philosophy or speculative science of distant times and places. In part 1, Kircher (as a character named Theodidactus) travels throughout the heavens, and in part 2 (published in 1657) to the underwater

Figure 9.1. Kircher's illustration of a mass of petrified shells. From *Mundus subterraneus*. Author's personal copy.

and underground realms of earth. Part 2 ends with an explicit "Prodromus" (so called) for his forthcoming *Mundus subterraneus.*

Interestingly, book 5 of this prodromus, entitled *Metalloscopus,*[23] presents a putative order of chapters for what would become the geological book 8 of *Mundus subterraneus.* But instead of listing the two-dimensional pictorial fossils and other forms of problematic origin in first place (the eventual sequence in *Mundus*), Kircher here follows an order of relative importance, rather than personal puzzlement, and lists the organic categories first, followed by the confusing two-dimensional pictures in distinctly subsidiary place. In the outline for book 5 of his 1657 prodromus, chapter 1 will treat metals, and chapter 2 earths. Chapter 3 will then discuss *organic* remains in their putatively original state, not yet even petrified: "On bones found in the earth, unicorns, tongue stones [sharks' teeth, as Kircher knew], supposed bones of giants, fossil wood, coal, and the causes thereof."

Chapter 4 then moves on to organic material that has become petrified, but whose kingdom of origin can scarcely be doubted. Note Kircher's stress on the variety and ubiquity of such organic remains: "On various and innumerable things converted into rocky substance; for example, animals, fossils, humans, quadrupeds. . . ." Fifthly, and only in last place, Kircher finally proposes to treat the two-dimensional puzzles that eventually came first in *Mundus subterraneus:* "On diverse stones and marbles striped with pictures; and on the causes thereof." I believe that this original ordering records Kircher's unchanging assessment of the relative ranking in abundance among mineralogical objects that strongly resemble organisms or human products—and that forms with organic origin clearly and always dominate.

2. We should also consider the length and care that Kircher lavished upon his treatment of petrifactions in *Mundus subterraneus.* This chapter may have followed a discussion of more puzzling two-dimensional forms, but Kircher's dense and incisive arguments, especially his efforts to provide criteria for distinguishing true petrifactions from false claims, prove the importance he granted to the subject of fossils with organic origins. He begins with a chapter on the history of scholarly recognition (*Variae rerum in lapides conversarum observationes*), focusing on Albertus Magnus, but going back to Theophrastus and Avicenna, and even to the original example of organic material converted to mineral matter: *de statua uxoris Lot* (on the statue of Lot's wife)!

A second chapter then treats stones that grow within the bodies of living organisms, from kidney stones in humans to bezoars in goats, for if rocks can form within living creatures, why can't entire organisms turn to rock after their death? In the third chapter, my favorite, Kircher then brilliantly dissects the history of claims for petrified bones of giant humans.

Kircher presents a series of functional and mechanical arguments against the stability of such large creatures. If, for example, gigantic statues of humans collapse under their own weight without massive supporting struts, why should an actual person be viable at such dimensions? In my personally favorite argument, he doubts that creatures this big could be fed: "What food would be sufficient for such gluttony? Surely an entire herd of sheep or goats would be required for minimal sustenance every day."[24]

In a more forensic mode, Kircher even suggests why we may have been fooled into accepting some large objects as bones of human giants. First, some specimens may be actual bones, but of elephants rather than humans. Second, certain naturally formed and rounded vacuities in mountains, if filled by clays that then harden into rocks, might well be mistaken for giant skulls of humans. Kircher finally concludes in no uncertain terms: "An accounting of these stories of giants therefore shows then to be empty and ridiculous."[25]

The concluding chapters of this disquisition on petrifaction, covering claims for unicorns, other kinds of horns, fossil woods, and coals, also shows Kircher's powers of reasoning at their best. He dismisses most historical arguments for the mythical unicorn, but correctly notes (including an illustration as well) that the straight tooth of the narwhal (a creature related to whales and found in Scandinavian waters) resembles the supposed form sufficiently well to serve as a natural source for the ancient legend.

B. The Second Issue of "Pictures" in Rocks and Other Curious Forms

All fully consistent and truly useful taxonomies embody theories about the objects under classification. The preliminary expression of a guiding theory usually resides in the taxonomist's choice of a *fundamentum divisionis*, or primary criterion invoked to establish the basic categories for a chosen system of order. When paleontology became codified, by the late eighteenth century, as the study of life's long history of temporal changes as recorded in organic remains deposited within the earth's strata, the distinction of these organic remains (now exclusively granted the name *fossil*) from other rocky configurations that might be mistaken for organisms or human artifacts became the primary task of the new science. In this context, the obvious *fundamentum divisionis* for "complex forms in rocks that look like organisms or signs of their activities" became the representation of something "truly organic" and therefore a genuine fossil *versus* something inorganic in origin and therefore not a fossil.

This distinction became so overridingly important, and so blessedly obvious, that scientists and historians then tended to backread this *fundamentum* into the taxonomies used by earlier students of the mineral kingdom, and to judge this older work by the anachronistic criterion of success in separating organic remains (true fossils) from misleading "mimics" of organisms (such as dendrites, the uncannily leaflike structures formed inorganically by precipitation of manganese sulfate on rock surfaces). But many of these earlier scholars, including Kircher, did not conceive the separation of organic remains from other complex forms found in rocks as their primary goal—although they certainly understood this problem and did not disregard its salience or theoretical importance.

Kircher recognized a large, and clearly majoritarian, category of fossils (in his broad definition of the term) as former organisms, or parts of organisms, later transformed in material composition by petrifaction. But because he did not utilize a *fundamentum divisionis* of organic *versus* inorganic, his specification of a clearly organic first category does not imply that his second major category, to be discussed in this final section, must have been established exclusively to house inorganic forms that looked like organisms or human artifacts—although most previous commentators have made and used this assumption (especially since Kircher began his paleontological chapters by describing this second major category) to label Kircher as a partisan of the inorganic theory for the nature and origin of fossils.

But for Kircher this second category, although established as a counterpart to his first category of three-dimensional petrifactions, was not conceived as a repository for inorganic forms that might be confused with organic petrifactions. Rather, Kircher established this second category to express and address a different problem better tuned to his own concerns (and not anachronistically responsive to the issue that would become paramount once science discovered the age of the earth and its history of organic change through time).

I have struggled, trying many approaches and formulations, to gain sympathetic entry into Kircher's subtle and unfamiliar intellectual realm. But I now suspect that Kircher's own conceptualization of the central problem about fossils may best be stated in the following way: rocky things can obviously look like organisms if they once were organisms and their original form has been preserved by petrifaction (the first category). But what set of forces and causes can make stony substances look like organisms or the products of human activity if, in fact, these particular stones never were organisms?

Kircher united the set of reasons for this puzzling second situation ("organic" forms in the mineral kingdom that never were organisms) into a quadripartite taxonomy defining his second category. We shall see that some of these reasons require the presence or activities of organisms (thus making the resulting objects fossils by modern definitions), whereas other reasons invoke no organic precursors or causes at all. But Kircher's second category does not become incoherent or senseless simply because, by modern standards, some objects within his scheme derive from organisms whereas others do not—for all objects included within this second category share Kircher's own defining property for residence therein: they look like organisms but are not the transformed substances of actual organisms.

I stated previously that this second category united forms found on surfaces of rocks (as opposed to the three-dimensional organic petrifactions included in the first category). Indeed, the great majority of objects in this second category do share this property of actual (or effective) two-dimensionality, but the more accurate and theoretically cogent definition for residence in this second category should be stated more broadly (and defined more "negatively" with respect to objects in the first category)—for this second category includes *all* mineralogical objects that look like organisms or human artifacts but are *not* derived from actual organisms later petrified to mineral composition. In other words, Kircher could explain more readily (since petrifaction had long been understood) how things that once were organisms could still look like organisms when transformed to mineral matter (remember, as well, Kircher's allegiance to the Aristotelian distinction of form and matter, and his consequent understanding of petrifaction as a process that changes matter but not form). But he faced deeper problems with things that looked like organisms but *never were actual organisms*—and he established his second category to address this problem by uniting these puzzling forms under a single rubric. (The great majority of such puzzles did address effectively two-dimensional forms, so he used this rough-and-ready descriptive criterion to admit most items into this second category, even though he defined the category itself in broader causal terms.)

In his major discussion of this second category (chapters 8 and 9 of section 1 of book 8 in *Mundus subterraneus*), Kircher presents a fourfold classification of subcategories to parse the full domain.[26] This quadripartite system became quite well known to Kircher's contemporaries and to paleontologists of the next generation or two—as cited, for example, in Scheuchzer's *Herbarium diluvianum* (as he tries to ascribe fossil plants to Noah's flood, but recognizes that dendrites, inorganic precipitates that look uncannily like leaves and stems, may not be true plant fossils); in Beringer's infamous *Lithographiae Wirceburgensis* (1726), as he argues that his carved and fake fossils cannot be phony because their solidity places them outside the inorganic subcategories of Kircher's second category; and in Knorr and Walch.[27]

1. *The first subcategory as clearly defined and inorganic.* For his first subcategory of mineralogical objects that look like organisms but cannot be petrified bodies of once-living creatures, Kircher cites a reason, obvious in retrospect (and probably uncontroversial in his own time as well), but expressing nonetheless a keen grasp of foibles in human perception and psychology. Kircher simply reminds us that resemblances between rocks and organisms may be entirely fortuitous and accidental—the products, in other words, of our vigorous imaginations, just as we see pictures in clouds and the forms of old men, recumbent gods, or threatening animals in the craggy peaks of mountains. Kircher writes:

> Consider how the human imagination leads us to see such a variety of things in heavenly clouds—now flying dragons; then ships, mountains, cities and castles; then crosses, human figures, and similar fantasies composed of clouds and represented in our imaginations. . . . Indeed there is nothing, actually produced by

nature without such intentions, that will not be seen by our imagination as similar to something of human concern.[28]

Kircher ends this section with an interesting discussion on the porous nature of rocky substrates, the tendency of liquefied salts and other mineral substances to flow into these channels and vacuities, and the later hardening of these infillings by the *vis lapidifica*, or solidifying forces active throughout the planet and responsible for giving form to flowing substances, including the initial coagulation of earth from the primal chaos of Genesis 1. Inevitably, some of these hardened infillings will look like organisms or artifacts of human culture—thus explaining, for example, the frequent discovery of letters or simple geometric figures expressed as veins of quartz or calcite. (Many later sources have assumed that Kircher meant to depict some direct miraculous power of God imposed upon rocks.[29] But Kircher presented this figure merely to illustrate his first mode of accidental but entirely natural production of rocky "pictures" with salience for human concerns.)

2. *The second subcategory as inorganic in material composition, but including fossils (recording the accurate forms of organisms) by modern definitions.* I believe this second subcategory, more than any other, proves my central contention that Kircher's general category for "things in rocks that look like organisms but are not petrified remains of organisms" does not indicate his allegiance to a general theory of fossils as inorganic in origin. For the objects of this second subcategory are remains of organisms (and therefore fossils by modern paleontological usage), although formed of inorganic matter that *did not replace* an originally organic substance by petrifaction.

I had long been puzzled, before reading Kircher's text with care, at the figures of genuine fossil fishes presented by Kircher among his motley collection of two-dimensional forms of evidently inorganic origin (the towers and turrets of Florentine marble on page 30, or the famous letters and geometric figures of page 23)[30] (Figure 9.2). But a proper understanding of the actual *fundamentum divisionis* for Kircher's second category dissolves the apparent paradox (for Kircher's *fundamentum*, as previously discussed, does not contrast organic with inorganic, but rather distinguishes organic origin followed by later mineralogical replacement *versus* "organic" appearance not arising from initial composition as organic matter).

As any modern paleontologist would immediately recognize, Kircher is groping, in this second subcategory, toward a definition and understanding of what we now call *casts* and *molds*—that is, either impressions made by organisms upon soft materials that later become lithified (to form a mold that accurately preserves the form of the organism as the impression left upon the sediments), or replicas of organisms made when soft materials (usually clays or sands) fill up the vacant spaces left by these impressions and later harden into rocky materials themselves (thus forming what paleontologists call a cast

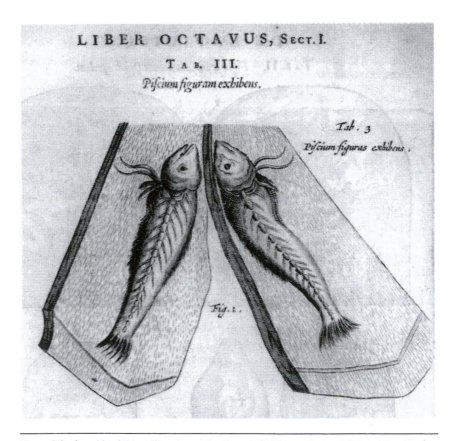

Figure 9.2. One side of this split rock contains the petrified bones of a fossil fish, but the other side preserves only an impression of the fish, not any actual petrified remains. From *Mundus subterraneus.*

of an organism—and corresponding, in this case, to our ordinary vernacular understanding of the process of casting as well).

The point may seem obvious in our current understanding of fossils. For a modern paleontologist, an object is a fossil of an organism whether it originates as a direct petrifaction of the original organic material itself (the shell of a mollusk later turned to stone, for example), or whether it preserves the form of the original organism as a cast of secondary material that filled up an accurate impression made by the shell upon surrounding sediments. Of course, we distinguish the petrifaction from the cast because we recognize the different modes of production, one more direct than the other. But both are fossils in our terminology and conceptualization, because both accurately record the form of the ancient organism, albeit secondarily for the cast and directly for the petrifaction. After all, if we possessed only the cast of Michelangelo's *David* (now standing exposed to the weather in the loggia of Florence) and had lost the original (now protected in the Accademia Museum), we would still know the basic form, size, and design of Michelangelo's conception.

So we now designate both the petrified original and the mold or cast as a fossil. But consider the question from the standpoint of Kircher's own and rather different *fundamentum divisionis*, however strange or unfamiliar to us today— mineral objects that look like organisms because they *are* petrified organisms *versus* mineral objects that look like organisms but never were actual organisms. Molds and casts fall into Kircher's second category, even though we now unite them with petrifactions in our present taxonomies. Once we penetrate Kircher's mental categories, his odd placement of excellent molds and casts (presenting highly accurate representations of organic forms, as in the casts of fossil fishes in Figure 9.2) into a larger category populated mostly by inorganic objects begins to make sense within Kircher's own system of questions.

In any case, the molds and casts of Kircher's second subcategory include a large subset of objects that all modern paleontologists regard as fossils and use as important and reliable evidence for the forms and activities of ancient organisms. (Incidentally, anyone who doubts Kircher's keen understanding of the highly accurate preservation of organic forms as molds and casts under this second subcategory should read his discussion on the impressing of fish bodies into clays, the subsequent decay of the fish itself, the preservation of an impression in the lithified clay, and the resulting "inorganic" representation of a truly organic form with its final conclusion that such objects must be interpreted "not as bones, but as a true and genuine picture of the animal, impressed in this manner into the rock."[31])

3. *The third category as a problem for Kircher, but as the best illustration of his honorable struggle to understand the puzzling phenomenon of objects made by (or referable to) organisms that are, nonetheless, not vestiges or transformations of the organisms themselves.* By studying Kircher's third and fourth subcategories, we can best appreciate his struggles to resolve modes of generation that he does not adequately understood, but that he clearly wishes to bring under the rubric of rational explanation rather than miraculous production. Kircher had succeeded with his first two subcategories—for the first included pure accidents that required no additional rationale for their formal similarity to organisms, whereas the second elucidated a clearly verifiable mode for rendering true shapes of organisms without ever incorporating or transmuting the actual substances of the organisms themselves. However, with his third subcategory, Kircher now has to face the prospect of explaining mineral forms that look like organisms, and seem to require some input from organisms (for the resemblances cannot be dismissed as accidents of our vivid imagination), but where the source of organic influence has not been identified in any satisfactory way. The casts and molds of the second subcategory required only that organisms impress their shapes into soft clays that later hardened into rocks. But the forms of this third subcategory seemed to imply the diffusion or oozing of some actual organic substance (but not the entire organisms itself) into a rock—and Kircher had no good explanation for how such a feat might by accomplished.

Kircher described this third category in a confusing statement as "from some kind of singular occurrence leading to the squeezing out of some kind of figure in some way."[32] Kircher's own colleagues noted the ambiguity and lack of clarity, and they often became confused themselves. For example, Scheuchzer, in the 1723 edition of his *Herbarium diluvianum*, tried to grasp the meaning of Kircher's third subcategory, but then mixed up Kircher's invocation of "accidente" (referring in this case, I think, only to accident in the sense of unusual occurrence) with the citation of accident in the sense of fortuitous resemblance, used by Kircher in his first subcategory. Scheuchzer therefore quoted Kircher's definition and then expressed his puzzlement by appending the following sentence: "But I would like to know how such an accident differs from the case of something called fortuitous. Do these accidents refer to truly singular happenings or to some general kind of occurrence?"[33]

I find Kircher's text fascinating in its floundering, with so little clarity or success, after something quite specific—a way of emplacing some organic influence into a rock, in order to engender at least the partial form of an organism, when the organic influence cannot be ascribed to the easier and well-understood process of petrifaction for a discrete organism. Kircher struggles with various suggestions of limited plausibility: True plant seeds cannot grow to mineralized plants within rocks, but could fragments or even pulverized dust of plants get into rocks and somehow mobilize the *vis lapidifica* of the mineral kingdom to generate at least a partially plantlike configuration?[34] Could the cadaver of an animal fall upon a rock, and mineral salts then carry some aspect of the organic form, if not deeply into the rock, at least onto its surface in some permanently engrafted form?[35]

I offer no defense for the cogency of Kircher's suggestions, but I would contend that his struggles illustrate two important points directly contradicting our usual deprecations of his explanatory style. First, we must at least acknowledge that Kircher is struggling to devise some testable natural explanation, rather than relying upon an appeal to mysticism or miracle beyond the ken of rationality. Second, we must note how the speculative character, even the far-fetched nature, of Kircher's propositions display his eagerness to embrace organic influences upon the genesis of fossils that look like plants and animals, thus further refuting the conventional view of Kircher as the last inorganicist holdout against modernity in the explanation of fossils.

4. *The fourth subcategory as a fascinating key to Kircher's commitment to natural causation (when at all possible), even for depictions of specifically religious scenes in natural objects; or why (even in inappropriately anachronistic terms) we may regard Kircher's general approach as scientific in our modern sense of this term.* With this fourth and final subcategory (although Kircher adds a fifth and sixth on pages 43–44, as slight variants upon the same general theme), Kircher faces yet a different, and in many respects more difficult, problem from those suggested by other two-dimensional forms. How can he explain truly complex pictures found in rocks, often of religious scenes, and often including several figures in proper theological orientation along with appropriate letters of text (INRI on crosses, or the name of Jesus written under his image, for example)? Clearly, such mineralogical versions of human artifacts cannot be organic fossils in the usual sense, but how could any ordinary and natural force of the mineral kingdom generate such complexly meaningful forms either? Indeed, the problem raised by this last subcategory seems to transcend any previous concerns about organic or inorganic origin, or about Kircher's own *fundamentum* of organic appearance due to genesis by transforming of actual organisms *versus* organic appearance for other reasons. Instead, the key question has now switched to an arguably more general and more important inquiry about whether such complex forms can be explained naturally *at all*, or whether they require suspension of natural laws and direct production by divine fiat.

The basic observation that Kircher directs his entire effort, throughout all his discussions of fossils, toward elucidating and defending potentially natural modes of causation, and toward rejecting any direct appeal to supernatural production, provides our best insight into his strong preferences for rational or experimental resolution. (Obviously, as a seventeenth-century Jesuit scientist and devout Catholic, Kircher accepted the theoretical legitimacy of God's supernatural intervention as a potential explanation for any profound curiosity seemingly outside the aegis of nature's ways. But in putting his preferences for naturalistic explanation so evidently before his readers, and in defending this scholarly modus in the very realm of large, old, and mysterious underground phenomena that might be regarded as an optimal locus for supernatural action, Kircher shows his primary dedication to what we would, even now, regard as "scientific" styles of explanation above all.)

Some of these mineralogical "pictures" seem so complex, and so unlikely to arise without some entity's conscious intent, either human or divine, that Kircher first wonders whether an actual human painting placed between two flat pieces of marble, with the entire "sandwich" then tightly bound and buried for some time, might lead to the seepage of colors from the painting into the rock, with sufficient preservation of the form of the image as well. So Kircher tries some experiments along these lines and reports success:

> Thus, in order to submit this question to some experiments, I painted various little images, which I placed between two plates of marble and left covered and undisturbed for several months. I then opened up the tables after this passage of time; and, behold, and marvelous to say, I found several figures, including the sacred name of Jesus among them, not only impressed upon the surface of the stone, but also penetrating right to the base.[36]

This explanation of human production, Kircher then admits, may work for mineralogical pictures found on rocks at the earth's surface, but how shall similar pictures found in rocks buried deeply underground be explained? Perhaps, Kircher suggests, people used to hide such objects in caves or deep within the earth, either because they once lived in such places or because they buried the items to escape religious persecution.

But Kircher must still address the more general and troubling issue of whether naturalistic explanations of this (admittedly far-fetched) type will always suffice, or whether appeals to supernatural origin must now finally be faced and admitted. After all, Kircher affirms, many of these pictures do portray scenes that God and his angels might well desire to place on display for humans, either as portents or as signs of divine instructions or displeasures. At this point, Kircher invokes, as devout scientists have frequently done both in his time and before and ever since, the Aristotelian analysis of causality to preserve the possibility of affirming both natural production and purposeful divine intention at the same time.

After all, to say that God directly desired and ordained the mineralogical production of such pictures does not force one to the conclusion that God used supernatural means to carve images directly. To invoke Aristotle's terms, the final cause (or purpose) of the picture may well reside in God's intended design as a portent or signal, but God may still superintend the actual production of the object by efficient causes (mechanical modes of production, following the exclusive and restricted meaning of the term *cause* in modern science) governed by ordinary operations of natural law. In asserting this argument to save natural causality while acknowledging God's direct interest in making these particular objects, Kircher presents the following title (as a marginal label) for the final subsection of his discussion: "How God, with the cooperation of Nature, produces such prodigious images." Kircher then writes in the accompanying text: "I say that the administration of divine providence is accomplished through the mediation of many secondary causes."[37]

To generalize this important theme in his short discussion within *Mundus subterraneus*, Kircher refers his readers to an earlier work of 1661, "our work on prodigious crosses observed on linen clothing of people in Naples," where he laid out a full taxonomy of possible causes and then opted, as here in his explanation of mineralogical pictures, for execution of these divine desires entirely by the action of ordinary natural laws: "for instance, by using natural executors for divine providence, that is, by the combination of natural causes."[38]

Kircher's *Diatribe de prodigiosis crucibus* presents his most compact and fully developed argument for preferring rational explanations, scientifically ascertainable as proceeding by the ordinary action of nature's laws, over appeals to miraculous agency that can only be admired but not causally comprehended in any useful way to guide our future discoveries and actions. Kircher wrote this book to ascertain the probable cause of crosses that began to appear on clothing and other objects in Naples, right after the eruption of Mount Vesuvius in 1660.

Kircher presents a taxonomy of three alternatives for explaining prodigious phenomena from a special time and place: First, God may simply have ordained these occurrences miraculously and outside the ordinary course of nature.[39] Second, angels or demons may have constructed these prodigies by using natural means and forces, but in combinations and intensities so far beyond the powers of human duplication or understanding that we would still not be able to comprehend the reasons and origins. Third, the ordinary laws of nature may have sufficed to produce these items when and where God desired their appearance. In this third case, human investigation and intellect will be able, at least in principle, to understand the causes and origin of these prodigies.

After much analysis and incisive observation based on distinctions and separations—that, for example, the crosses appeared on clothing made of linen but not of wool; and that crosses only formed under certain conditions of temperature and moisture—Kircher strongly advocated the third alternative of natural causation, with its happy consequence of maximal accessibility to human understanding. The crosses formed as lines made of fine dust emitted by the volcano and coagulating into streaks that often took the form of crosses when concentrated into folds and creases on certain kinds of cloth under definite climatic conditions.

I close with two figures from my personal copy of Kircher's *Diatribe*, for these unique illustrations so clearly point to the practical utility of naturalistic explanations, whereas appeal to miraculous agency can only inspire awe, but not rational understanding (Figures 9.3 and 9.4). My copy found its way to Mexico, and to a convent school for girls, where at least two students read the work diligently. My title page (Figure 9.3) contains the naively moving inscription of a young female student: *Ego Maria Petronilla Enriquez de Suzman hunc librum legi a prima usq[ue] ad ultimam paginam.* ("I, Maria Petronilla Enriquez de Suzman, read this book from the first to last page.") Second, and more importantly for the interests of science—and I rest my case for admiring Kircher as a rationalist and exponent of empirical investigation on this humble illustration of genuine utility—one of the readers drew a sketch on the book's final blank page. Here (Figure 9.4) this reader used Kircher's experimental approach, and his arguments about how the dust emitted from Vesuvius might gather upon surfaces in the form of crosses, to show how certain foldings might provide substrates for the shapes that Kircher had described and advocated. And by such humble and fruitful activity, so strongly abetted, if not directly inspired, by the power of Kircher's writings upon empirical methods and preferences, human curiosity prevails, and knowledge advances.

Figure 9.3. The title page of my copy of Kircher's 1661 *Diatribe*, with a charming testimony of thorough study written by a convent schoolgirl in Mexico.

Part IV. Coda

I wish to add a final word of admiration for Kircher by suggesting one more correction, and proposing one more amendment to thwart the harmful mythology that has depicted this great Jesuit scholar as a reactionary theological dogmatist, actively retarding or even subverting the progress of science: in spending so much time reading the *Mundus subterraneus* and other works by Kircher, I have developed enormous respect, not so much for the power of his insights and assertions, but for the *quality of his doubts*, and for his willingness to grope and struggle with material that he understood only poorly by his own admission.

In a famous essay, T. S. Eliot remarked of Alfred, Lord Tennyson's longest and most celebrated poem, *In Memoriam*, that the Victorians had revered the work for the supposed power of its religious convictions, but that he, quite to the contrary, had discovered the poem's greatness in the character and quality

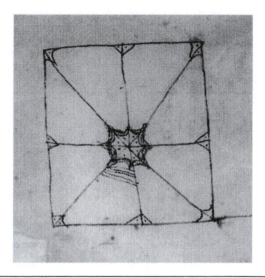

Figure 9.4. A drawing made by an early reader of my copy of Kircher's 1661 *Diatribe*, showing how the reader tries to understand and illustrate Kircher's theory about the natural formulation of images of crosses on folded clothing.

of Tennyson's profound doubt and non-resolution. I therefore, in agreement with Eliot but transferring my application to Father Athanasius, give the last line to Kircher himself by citing the literal last words (effectively never read, one may be quite sure) of the *Mundus subterraneus*—the footnote in small type on the very last page, inserted right after the end of the index. Kircher apologizes for any remaining typographical errors in the text, explaining that he had been absent from Rome during the time of publication and had not been able to read the proofs carefully. He thus ended by begging his readers' indulgence for his human failings, and by reminding everyone of a wise old saying about generosity: *Sic quandoque bonus dormitat Homerus*—And thus, sometimes, even good Homer nods.

Notes

1. Darwin 1859, p. 167.
2. An influential model, fallacious and harmful in equal doses, and largely codified in two of the great publishing successes of the later nineteenth century—Draper 1874; and White 1896.
3. Butterfield 1931.
4. Depéret 1909.
5. However unpleasant the reminder, British and American scholars should not underestimate the role of Catholic stereotyping, however generally "polite" and non-virulent these days (as opposed to former potencies well-known in English history, but perhaps less acknowledged in their American versions as the "Know-Nothing" and other anti-Catholic movements of our past). Let the sinless cast the first stone, but I do not see how anyone could defend an argument that among the Abrahamic religions, Roman Catholicism has in general been less friendly or more oppositional to science than any other. Unfortunately, however, Draper's (1874) initial formulation of the "warfare model" between science and

religion stated the highly prejudicial views of a committed anti-Catholic who felt that Protestantism could make a fruitful peace with science, whereas Roman Catholicism must be suppressed for modern thought to prevail.

6. Knorr and Walch 1768–77. I quote from my French edition.
7. Ibid. 1768, pp. 24–25. I am responsible for all translations.
8. Zittel 1899, pp. 31–32.
9. F. Adams 1954, p. 255.
10. Rudwick 1972, p. 56.
11. The most recent treatment of Kircher's geological work also emphasizes these aspects of his natural philosophy. Nummedal 2001, p. 41.
12. Purcell and Gould 1992, p. 81.
13. Gould 1998.
14. Ceruto and Chiocco 1622, pp. 407–410.
15. Alexandri 1532.
16. Encelius in *De re metallica* of 1557, for example. See Gould 2002a and 2002b.
17. In retrospect, many cited examples of petrifaction did not represent active replacement of organic by mineral matter (as in petrified wood), but rather a simple encrustation of objects by mineral substances precipitated from surrounding waters. But Albert and his colleagues did not distinguish true petrifaction from encrustation. In any case, they knew that organic material could turn to stone, and that the mineralogical composition of many fossils therefore did not argue against an originally organic nature.
18. Woodward 1728.
19. Bourguet 1729.
20. Kircher 1665c, vol. 2, p. 37.
21. Ibid., pp. 34–35.
22. Ibid., p. 48.
23. Kircher 1657, pp. 233–234.
24. Kircher 1665c, vol. 2, p. xx.
25. Ibid., p. xx.
26. Ibid., pp. 22–45.
27. Scheuchzer in my French edition of 1723, p. 28; Beringer 1963, pp. 72–75; Knorr and Walch 1768–77.
28. Kircher 1665c, vol. 2, p. 37.
29. Adams 1954.
30. Kircher 1665c, vol. 2, pp. 34–35.
31. Ibid., p. 38.
32. Ibid., p. xxx.
33. Scheuchzer 1723, p. 28.
34. Kircher 1665c, p. 40.
35. Ibid., p. 41.
36. Ibid., p. 42.
37. Ibid., p. 43.
38. Ibid., p. 44.
39. Kircher 1661, p. 25

10
The Angel and the Compass
Athanasius Kircher's Magnetic Geography

MICHAEL JOHN GORMAN*

In October 1639, the Jesuit missionary Martino Martini found himself adrift in the Atlantic. On route to Goa, the Portuguese vessel that contained nine Jesuits destined eventually for the Chinese mission had met with catastrophic conditions. The boat, along with its companion vessel, was forced to make an unplanned forty-six-day stop on the Guinean coast that drained its supplies, infected its passengers with horrific maladies, and forced a return to Lisbon. "To tell the truth to Your Reverence," Martini wrote to his erstwhile mathematical mentor at the Collegio Romano, Athanasius Kircher, "the land and sea along that coast generally called Guinea appear to have been damned from all eternity, such are the heat, the rain, the pestilence, things that you would never believe."

Dejected at their aborted mission, the Jesuits and their companions turned back toward Portugal, passing close to the Azores, where Martini noticed the abundant Sargasso grass floating in the water. In addition to indicating to the mariners their position with respect to the islands, Martini noted, the round berries of the flaxlike sea grass were reputed to be an indispensable remedy for gallstones.

On 1 October, the vessel was hit by a violent storm. "The water was higher than mountains." With all sails taken down except for one the size of a sheet, the boat was driven along by the wind for almost seventy leagues. After the winds had finally subsided, the nobles and sailors on board entertained themselves by making bets as to their distance from the Portuguese coast.

Martini, armed only with a chart on which he had been tracking every step of the ship's voyage, and a compass specially adapted to allow him to calculate the declination of the magnetic needle from true North, defeated both noblemen and mariners in his calculations. "I said that we were to the East of the island of Terceira and only one hundred leagues from the mainland." In exact accordance with Martini's predictions, the ship arrived in Portugal early in the morning of 14 October.

How did a Jesuit priest with almost no seafaring experience defeat the estimates of seasoned navigators with expert knowledge of sea currents, winds, and marine phenomena? Martini's reasoning went thus: "if we had been to the West of the Azores, the magnet should have declined to the West, but as it declined to the East, we could not have been to the West. Some said that we were in the midst of the Islands, but I demonstrated that this could not be true, as, even though we were at their latitude we did not see them, and that was impossible." Skeptics challenged Martini, wondering why, given that the islands extended for 120 leagues from east to west, they had never been seen during the course of the storm. "Precisely because even before the storm we were to their East," rebutted Martini, supporting his claim with a detailed mathematical analysis of the ship's meandering route. "I write this," Martini flattered Kircher, "not so as to praise myself, but so that Your Reverence may see all that I have learned from you, especially in the field of magnetic declination."[1]

Martini had spent a mere two months as Athanasius Kircher's "private disciple in mathematics" in the Collegio Romano, but this brief apprenticeship, occurring shortly after Kircher had taken up the post of mathematics professor, apparently had a transformative effect on him. At the end of the sixteenth century, Christoph Clavius had created a private mathematical academy in the Collegio Romano, with the express goal of providing advanced training to those destined to teach mathematics in Jesuit colleges in the different provinces, and to those destined for the Chinese mission, for which mathematical skills were regarded as particularly relevant. Matteo Ricci, the most famous representative of the first generation of Jesuit missionaries to China, was himself an alumnus of Clavius's original academy. The academy really consisted in informal advanced training that took place in the bedroom of the senior mathematician of the college, also known as the "mathematical museum" (*musaeum mathematicum*), where valuable instruments and mathematical manuscripts were kept under lock and key. After the death of Clavius's successor, Christoph Grienberger, control of the mathematical museum and the serious task of training senior mathematicians in advanced trigonometry, astronomy, and hydraulics passed to the more playful hands of Athanasius Kircher, who rapidly transformed the sober mathematicians' bedroom into a dazzling showcase of speaking tubes, perpetual motion machines, sunflower clocks, optical tricks, and hydraulic devices, only later to be transferred into the more commodious halls of the *Musaeum Kircherianum*.[2]

Martini's floating microcosm—his cabin aboard ship, filled with charts, astrolabes, quadrants, compasses, and the astronomical works of Clavius, Peter Apian, and Tycho Brahe—is a fascinating mirror of Kircher's *cubiculum* in the Collegio Romano. While Kircher would draw heavily on Martini's reports in compiling *The Magnet, or on the Magnetic Art* (1641), Martini used the mathematical techniques he had learned from Kircher during his two-month apprenticeship in Rome to demonstrate his navigational superiority over the ship's pilots. Pitting his own book knowledge, charts, and instrumental abilities acquired from Kircher against the accumulated experience, dead reckoning, and reliance on natural signs of the Portuguese mariners, Martini claimed multiple victories. On his subsequent voyage to Goa, his judicious use of the magnetic needle saved his ship, carrying the viceroy of the Indies, from certain destruction on a shoal of treacherously sharp rocks.[3]

In his aspirations to universal knowledge, Athanasius Kircher relied crucially on Martini and his ilk, Jesuit missionaries inflamed by their Ignatian training to endure every sacrifice to advance the glorious achievements of their Order. Conversely, the mathematical skills of Jesuit missionaries, in addition to their willingness to nurse the sick, hear confessions, and even parade as flagellants during Easter week, helped ensure them a welcome place aboard the heavily charged Portuguese ships destined for the Indies.[4]

Kircher's audacious attempt in the late 1630s and early 1640s to carry out a great "Geographical Plan" (*Consilium Geographicum*), aimed at harnessing the global network of Jesuit missionaries in order to reform geographic knowledge and to resolve the problem of calculating longitude at sea, constitutes a vivid demonstration of the nature of the organic connections between Kircher's Roman cell, on the one hand, and the missionary spaces inhabited by Jesuits like Martini, on the other. The global distribution of Jesuit missionaries was absolutely essential to Kircher's attempt to reshape terrestrial geography—by fixing the longitudes and latitudes of Jesuit missions and colleges—and to reform navigation—by devising a foolproof method for calculating longitude at sea.

The primary "enabling technology" for Kircher's project was correspondence—frequent epistolary contact with mathematically trained Jesuits. In his essay in this volume, Noel Malcolm argues convincingly that Kircher's "oracular" correspondence was atypical of the fluid, multidirectional model of correspondence endorsed by the seventeenth-century Republic of Letters. Kircher's Geographic Plan constitutes a particularly striking example of his conception of the role of the centralized accumulation of correspondence in the reform of natural knowledge, and it makes explicit the monarchical power structure that characterized his epistolary community. The ultimate failure of his geographic project, which quite literally vanished, as we will see, and his dispute with Jesuit astronomer Giambattista Riccioli over the relative merits of global correspondence and exquisite local instrumentation, illustrate a clash between two contrary social models for the prosecution of research in astronomy and geography.

In his *The Magnet, or on the Magnetic Art*[5] Kircher outlined his proposal for a *Magnetic Geography* that would be magnetic in two respects—both in seeking magnetic solutions to geographic and navigational problems and in drawing the observations performed by mathematicians, navigators, and missionaries throughout the world together in Rome, as if by some occult force of attraction.[6] Kircher likened his project to the reform of the calendar reform carried out under Pope Gregory XIII in 1582, suggesting that just as the convergence of the authorities of pope, princes, and universities had reformed the temporal order governing religious and civil affairs, so might a similar initiative allow geographic knowledge, clearly in disarray, to be reformed.

Like the Gregorian reform of the calendar, Kircher argued, geographic reform could not be carried out by a single individual. Instead, it was seen to require a "unanimous conspiracy of mathematicians." The religious orders were particularly suited to such a task, but most appropriate of all was the Society of Jesus, "distributed throughout the whole globe, provided with men skilled in mathematics and, above all, enjoying a unanimous harmony of minds."

Kircher was urged to embark upon the reform of geographic knowledge through the use of Jesuit informants by a number of sources, especially the General Muzio Vitelleschi, who ordered him to compose a "Geographical Plan" (*Consilium Geographicum*), "a treatise in which I would display the methods and procedures for restoring Geography, and would explain by what means, with which instruments, and in which place, state and time observations might be carried out fruitfully. I would try to show briefly and clearly that this business would not be difficult work for the religious orders." Kircher's plan for a Jesuit-led global observational imperative would go far beyond mere cartography: "I would also provide instructions for what they should observe about the flux and reflux of the tides, the constitution of lands and promontories, the natures and properties of winds, bodies of water, rivers, animals, plants and minerals, and, finally, about the customs, laws, languages and religious rites of men."[7]

Although Jesuit missionaries, from Matteo Ricci to José de Acosta, had been enormously active in accumulating observations of just this kind in the first century of the Society's existence,[8] at the beginning of the second century Kircher wished to discipline and coordinate such reports. By doing so, he would avail of the mobility, mathematical expertise, and self-effacing obedience of his Jesuit colleagues. Inscribed into Kircher's larger geographic project was an attempt to resolve the recalcitrant navigational problem of calculating longitude at sea, a problem of the utmost importance for navigation in the seventeenth century. Latitude calculation was simple (given clear skies)—measure the angular elevation of the pole star at night, and you had your latitude. Longitude calculation, without a mechanical clock that could remain reliable during a sea voyage, was a very different matter.[9]

A huge number of solutions to the longitude problem were proposed after Philip III offered a perpetual pension of six thousand ducats to anyone who could find a workable method of maritime longitude determination in 1598. Galileo had proposed using the eclipses of the newly discovered satellites of Jupiter as a

Figure 10.1. Jan van der Straet (Stradanus), *The longitudes of the globe discovered by the declination of the magnet from the pole, Source:* From the series *Nova Reperta*, circa 1600. Courtesy of Stanford University Libraries.

"celestial clock" that sailors might consult to determine their position, a project frustrated by the difficulty of making accurate telescopic observations of the Jovian moons aboard a moving ship.[10] Oronce Finé, followed by Jean-Baptiste Morin, proposed an immensely complicated method involving the movement of the moon against the background of the fixed stars, of which Kircher later complained that its use required the mathematical ability of a Euclid or a Ptolemy.[11] Michael Florent van Langren attempted to use the motion of the terminator shadow across the lunar disk as a painfully slow celestial sundial.[12]

Kircher approached the problem in a different way, through magnetic variation—the deviation of a compass needle from North as determined by the pole star—a technique previously suggested by Giambattista della Porta in the late sixteenth century and by mathematicians and navigators in England.[13] The famous series of engravings of *New Discoveries* carried out in the late sixteenth century by the Flemish artist Jan van der Straet, or Stradanus, and printed by Jean Galle included, along with such celebrated inventions as gunpowder, eyeglasses, and the printing press, an illustration of "the longitudes of the globe discovered by the declination of the magnet from the pole" (Figure 10.1). In the illustration, a sailor aboard a ship in stormy seas calculates the position of the meridian by observing the position of the sun, and he compares it with the direction of the magnetic needle to calculate the declination.

Despite the unbridled optimism of Jan van der Straet, however, it was by no means obvious to most navigators in the early seventeenth century just *how* the measurement of magnetic declination could allow longitude to be calculated at sea. The Jesuit missionary Cristoforo Borri, who traveled to Macao and Indochina between 1615 and 1622, was reputed to have discovered a method. Kircher clearly knew about Borri's efforts, and endeavored to use Martini to discover further details of his method. The technique, at least according to Martini, seems to have involved the construction of a chart mapping points of equal magnetic declination, an azimuthal compass (i.e., a magnetic compass equipped with a sighting device or shadow-casting device to allow the astronomical meridian to be determined), and a technique for measuring the declination at any time of day.[14]

In 1639, Marin Mersenne wrote to Gabriel Naudé in Rome in 1639 to suggest that Kircher should "order some Reverend of the Society in each college, by whatever means possible, to note the variation of the magnet and the height of the pole star accurately. Let him order that one or another lunar eclipse be observed in these same houses and colleges." "If this task were completed," Mersenne continued, "and if the authority of the supreme pontiff would lend itself to this task, the result would be that some time under the happy auspices of Urban VIII we would know the magnetic variation of the whole world, the altitudes of the pole star, and the longitudes so long sought after."[15] Mersenne's suggestion was similar in tone to one made some years before by Pierre Gassendi, who proposed to Kircher's patron Nicholas-Claude Fabri de Peiresc that either Urban VIII or his nephew Cardinal Francesco Barberini should incite missionaries to make accurate eclipse observations to reform the geographic art.[16] Interestingly, Gassendi did not restrict his suggestion to the Jesuits, having made previous use of the observational powers and mathematical expertise of other peripatetic Counter-Reformation orders such as the Capuchins and the discalced Carmelites in collecting reports of eclipses.[17]

While Peiresc and Gassendi could use Capuchins and discalced Carmelites to transfigure the Mediterranean, however, the Atlantic space remained far less accessible to their network of informants. Additionally, while eclipse observations might allow longitude to be established at a terrestrial location, they were of little use to a lost ship's captain unless his predicament happened to coincide with a lunar eclipse.[18]

Kircher responded swiftly to Mersenne to inform him that he had already embarked on just such a project.[19] Having performed numerous observations of the magnetic declination during his own peregrinations through Europe, and armed with the observations collected by his predecessors in the Collegio Romano, he wrote to distinguished mathematicians throughout Europe to solicit their measurements of the magnetic variation of their place of residence. He hoped that in this way they "would all be inspired to perform careful observations to determine this variation and other matters with which our Geographical Plan is concerned." The outcome of this first attempt was disappointing. Kircher had "almost no news at all from the more famous mathematicians."[20] This required a change of plan. Taking advantage of a meeting of the Procurators (responsible for the financial affairs of each Province of the Jesuit Order) in Rome in November 1639, Kircher asked each Procurator to solicit observations of local magnetic declination from the Jesuit mathematician resident in the different cities of his Province.[21] In addition to sending observations, each mathematician was to explain in detail exactly what precautions had been taken and what type of equipment had been used. Unlike the more famous mathematicians, a great number of their Jesuit contemporaries responded immediately.[22]

Kircher published their observations along with those made by others in his *Magnes*. In recognition of the labors of his Jesuit helpers, performing observations of the magnetic variation in places as far apart as Goa, Paris, Macao, Alexandria, Constantinople, and Vilnius, Kircher published their names in a large table reporting the magnetic declination and the latitude of the place at which the observation was made (Figure 10.2). Behind this table lies an enormous amount of labor, in the performance of observations in different urban centers, their transmission to Kircher, and their tabulation.

Politically, it has often been observed that the Jesuit Order has a monarchical organizational structure, with great emphasis on obedience to commands issued to the periphery from the Roman center.[23] Such a structure, to be contrasted with the capitular structure of the older monastic and mendicant orders, clearly lends itself extremely well to projects like the measurement of global magnetic variation. [24] One of Kircher's more expert correspondents on magnetic matters, the French Jesuit Jacques Grandamy, made the congruence of absolute power and global observation very explicit when he suggested in a book published four years after Kircher's *Magnet* that kings and princes should order their subjects to measure magnetic variation diligently in the cities under their rule, and that the General of the Society of Jesus should order his subordinates—Jesuit priests and lay brothers in different parts of the world—to do the same.[25] Although Kircher makes frequent reference to a "Republic of Letters" in his works, both he and Grandamy are clearly conscious that in the world in which they live, the command of an absolute authority, whether secular or clerical, was the most effective way of galvanizing observers into action.

The letters sent to Kircher by his Jesuit informants reveal the difficulties of constructing a collective experimental enterprise. Joannes Ciermans, writing to Kircher from Louvain, writes in highly charged language:

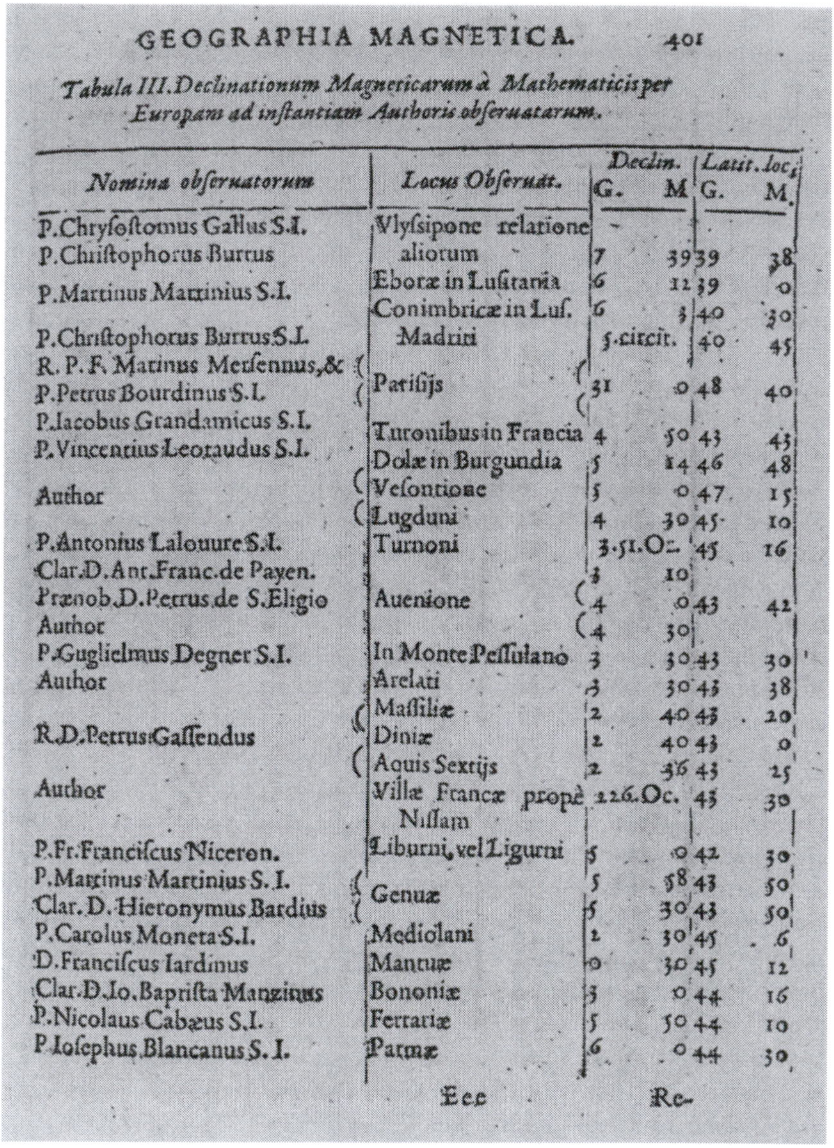

GEOGRAPHIA MAGNETICA. 401

Tabula III. Declinationum Magneticarum à Mathematicis per Europam ad inſtantiam Authoris obſeruatarum.

Nomina obſeruatorum	*Locus Obſeruat.*	Declin. G.	Declin. M	Latit. loci G.	Latit. loci M.
P.Chryſoſtomus Gallus S.I.	Vlyſsipone relatione				
P.Chriſtophorus Burrus	aliorum	7	39	39	38
P.Martinus Martinius S.I.	Eboræ in Luſitania	6	12	39	0
	Conimbricæ in Luſ.	6	3	40	30
P.Chriſtophorus Burrus S.I.	Madriti	5.circit.		40	45
R.P.F. Marinus Merſennus,&					
P.Petrus Bourdinus S.I.	Pariſijs	31	0	48	40
P.Iacobus Grandamicus S.I.	Turonibus in Francia	4	50	43	43
P.Vincentius Leotaudus S.I.	Dolæ in Burgundia	5	14	46	48
Author	Veſontione	5	0	47	15
	Lugduni	4	30	45	10
P.Antonius Lalouure S.I.	Turnoni	3.51.Oc.		45	16
Clar.D.Ant.Franc.de Payen.		3	10		
Prænob.D.Petrus de S.Eligio	Auenione	4	0	43	42
Author		4	30		
P.Guglielmus Degner S.I.	In Monte Peſſulano	3	30	43	30
Author	Arelati	3	30	43	38
	Maſſiliæ	2	40	43	20
R.D.Petrus Gaſſendus	Diniæ	2	40	43	0
	Aquis Sextijs	2	36	43	25
Author	Villæ Francæ propè Niſſam	2.26.Oc.		43	30
P.Fr.Franciſcus Niceron.	Liburni, vel Ligurni	5	0	42	30
P.Martinus Martinius S.I.	Genuæ	5	58	43	50
Clar.D.Hieronymus Bardius		5	30	43	50
P.Carolus Moneta S.I.	Mediolani	2	30	45	6
D.Franciſcus Iardinus	Mantuæ	0	30	45	12
Clar.D.Io.Baptiſta Manzinus	Bononiæ	3	0	44	16
P.Nicolaus Cabæus S.I.	Ferrariæ	5	50	44	10
P.Ioſephus Blancanus S.I.	Parmæ	6	0	44	30

Eee Re-

Figure 10.2. Table of magnetic declinations. Note the predominance of Jesuit (S.I.) observations. The two columns on the right-hand side show the magnetic declination and the latitude, respectively. *Source: Kircher,* Magnes, sive de arte magnetica *(*The Magnet, or The Magnetic Art*), 1643, p. 401. Courtesy of Stanford University Libraries.*

Although the sky here is cold and cloudy, this is not true of my breast, under which something is warm and lives in ready obedience to Your Reverence. To accumulate together in the Father that which you estimate to bring splendor to his name and to that of our Mother, the Society, you will have a strong helper in me if you wish. For we know that it is not for one man to repair (*instaurare*) astronomy and geography, but requires the works of many mathematicians to be gathered together in one.[26]

In Lithuania, on the request of the Provincial, Oswald Krüger took time away from his cooking duties to observe the magnetic declination of Vilnius and two neighboring towns and wrote to the Polish Provincial to encourage Jesuit mathematicians in the Polish province to do likewise.[27]

A correspondent in Mainz, a city where Kircher had previously taught for several years, though keen to send Kircher his measurements, was unable to be of any use because the marauding Swedish armies had taken every mathematical instrument in the Jesuit college, down to the last pair of compasses.[28] At the other end of the scale, Jacques Grandamy boasted of a new instrument he had designed to measure both magnetic declination and inclination, or dip, with the utmost accuracy.[29] Others clearly did not understand what they were supposed to do, and asked Kircher for clarification, meanwhile sending observations of questionable meaning. Along with the numerical measurements, Kircher's obedient observers often sent diagrams and other information to make their observational practices as transparent as possible to the "mathematical prince of our Society" in Rome.[30]

Occasionally the task of observation was delegated by Kircher's correspondents to their subordinates: "The declination of the magnet from the Meridian, required by Your Reverence, has been investigated by Master Gaspar Schiess, the private mathematical disciple of Fr. Cysat," Jacobus Imhofer wrote to Kircher from Innsbruck on 15 January 1640. "He has used various needles, all of which disagree with each other, some indicating 4, some 6 and some 10 degrees [of declination]. He says that he is waiting for the arrival of Fr. Cysat, who has the best magnets locked-up, and that he will then make observations most diligently and send them to Your Reverence."[31] Jesuits worldwide begged Kircher to turn them into more efficient measurers. "If Your Reverence has some information about this practice," wrote Jacques Durand, "I would be most grateful if you could send it to me."[32] Some sent reflections of a philosophical nature, querying the source of terrestrial magnetism and Gilbert's suggestion that the earth was a large magnet. Others reported on magnetic magic, particularly Francis Line's magnetic clock composed of globe suspended in water that rotated to indicate the hours of day and night, reputedly driven by a cosmic force emanating from the sun.[33]

Martino Martini himself provided Kircher with a vast number of measurements made during his voyages, from Portugal to Cape Verde and the Azores, from Goa to Macao. Martini was also perhaps most optimistic among Kircher's correspondents about the possibility of solving the famous problem of longitude. A letter he wrote to Kircher from Goa, later published proudly in the *Magnet*, claimed that "the discovery of longitudes by the magnet is no longer held by me to be impossible, indeed, I believe it has already been discovered." Martini's extravagant claim was followed by a description of a technique for using a chart marked with magnetic meridians to calculate longitude.[34]

However, a number of correspondents wrote independently to advise Kircher of some anomalous observations recently performed in England. The measurements of magnetic declination performed in Limehouse by William Borough, Edmund Gunter, and Henry Gellibrand appeared to show a decrease in magnetic declination between 1580 and 1634.[35] Mersenne, Gassendi, Pierre Bourdin, and Jacques Grandamy all reported the same phenomenon to Kircher in their letters and speculated on its possible causes.[36] Similar changes had been observed by Jesuit mathematicians in Rome and Bologna. Although Kircher recognized the difficulty that such observations posed to his project of using charts marked with lines of equal declination to calculate longitude—if magnetic declination in a single locale was unstable, the value of such charts would be at best temporary—he was hesitant to pronounce on the cause of this phenomenon, and effaced many of the cosmological speculations of his informants from the published work.

There is a fine balance, in this episode, between acknowledging the fallibility of the single observer or instrument and emphasizing the immense power of a Jesuit experimental collectivity. Kircher's reaction to the observations of the English mathematicians, which were eventually to quash hopes for a geomagnetic solution to the problem of longitude, is indicative of this tension. Every observer was born with original sin in Kircher's world. "A perfect observation, free of all error and falsehood could only be carried out by an angel," he claims in *Magnes*, so mere mortals must acknowledge their fallibility before jumping to conclusions of the nature of terrestrial magnetism or other questions of cosmological import. "While I assert this," Kircher continues, "nobody should think that I wish to detract from the most useful and absolutely necessary study of observations. I only wish to show how much caution, circumspection, industry and indefatigable labor is required in making observations, for them to be reliable."[37]

Kircher's *Great Art of Light and Shadow* (*Ars magna lucis et umbrae*) (1646) renewed Kircher's promise to publish his *Consilium Geographicum* for the collective restoration of all terrestrial knowledge. In the meantime, he provides his readers with a *Horoscopium Catholicum*—a composite sundial in the form of an olive tree representing the different provinces of the Jesuit Order that Kircher displayed to visitors to his museum in the Collegio Romano[38] (Figure 10.3). When a stylus was placed in each Province, and the device positioned

Figure 10.3. *The Catholic Horoscope. Source:* Kircher, *Ars magna lucis et umbrae* (*The Great Art of Light and Shadow*). Courtesy of Stanford University Libraries.

vertically so that the Roman time was given correctly, the clock allowed the time in all the different Jesuit provinces to be read. In this way, the viewer could perceive that the Society of Jesus was performing its religious duties—masses, confessions, sermons, and catechesis—throughout the world, day and night, with no interruption and in all known languages.[39]

Following emblematic themes developed in the *Image of the First Century of the Society of Jesus* (*Imago primi saeculi Societatis Iesu*) (1640) celebrating the first centenary of the Jesuit order, Kircher's universal horoscope is the apotheosis of Jesuit globalism and pious synchronicity. Initially a cruciform version of the paper instrument was displayed, and dedicated to the new General Vincenzo Carafa on the day of his election.[40] Surmounted by a Habsburg eagle, carrying an Austrian (*Austri-acus*) compass needle, a feature removed from the Amsterdam edition of the *Ars magna* for the peace of mind of a Protestant readership, the olive-tree sundial was designed so that the shadows of the small gnomons, when aligned, spell the abbreviated name of Jesus, IHS, which appears to "walk over the world" with the passing of time, like the synchronized, uniformly trained members of the Jesuit order who used the abbreviation as their symbol. Kircher's idealized Jesuit geography, placed on display to visitors in the Roman center, situated the prime meridian emphatically in Rome.

But what of the great Geographical Plan? Giambattista Riccioli wrote to Kircher in 1642 to ask when the *Consilium Geographicum* might at last appear in print. Riccioli had collected a vast number of observations himself, and conducted a lengthy series of experiments on precision time measurements using pendulums that he applied to making eclipse observations. In some ways providing a competing model to Kircher's distributed information community, Riccioli surrounded himself with local disciples willing to observe pendulum oscillations for consecutive periods of up to twenty-four hours at a time, and with extremely precise observational instruments.[41]

Riccioli's impatience to see Kircher's *Consilium Geographicum* in print was in vain. In the 1654 edition of the *Magnes*, edited and amplified by Kircher's disciple Kaspar Schott, it became clear that the great Geographical Plan would never be revealed. "When I was keeping the work, composed with no small effort, amongst other things, in my Museum, and waiting for the right moment to publish it for the good of the Republic of Letters," Kircher wrote, "it was secretly removed by one of those people who come to me almost every day from all over the world to see my Museum."[42] Kircher's project for a universal reform of terrestrial knowledge through the concerted agency of the Jesuit Order was stolen!

The mysterious theft of the *Consilium* from Kircher's museum conveniently relieved him from the need to produce a method for determining longitude by magnetic declination, an obligation that had become increasingly complicated by further observations of the temporal instability of declination, despite the optimism of Kircher's Jesuit disciples for the magnetic reform of geography and hydrography. Even before the disappearance of the *Consilium*, Kircher's longitudinal concerns had swung decisively landward. He wrote to Gassendi in 1642 to say that Cardinal Francesco Barberini was urging him to coordinate eclipse observations, in the same way that he had coordinated measurements of magnetic declination two years previously.[43] As with the declination observations, Kircher demanded that his informants on eclipses provide him with all of the details of the circumstances under which the observations were carried out, and with the names of those who were present as "indicators (*indices*) and witnesses of the said eclipses."[44]

Giambattista Riccioli probably received a similar request at this time. In any case, he wrote to Kircher shortly afterward to say:

> I have exquisite instruments (*organa*) in which, for reasons explained in an astronomical work that I have in my hands, I place my trust more than in those of Tycho himself, even though that great man got very close to the truth. I also have four of ours [i.e., Jesuits] who are extremely well trained and are both my witnesses and my assistants in conducting observations.[45]

In the end, it was Riccioli, not Kircher, who published a *Reformed Geography*, incorporating many of the observations previously published by Kircher into his tables and adding observations performed by himself and supported by the financial resources of the extremely wealthy Grimaldi family of silk merchants.[46] Well before he did so, however, he was subjected to a process of censorship that reveals something of the tension between local and non-local modes of natural investigation in the Jesuit Order.

On 24 November 1646, Riccioli was forwarded a copy of an anonymous censure from Rome. The letter requested him to "send to Rome that part of his work which is entitled 'On my own Discoveries,' so that it can be known what he will put forward that is new with respect to the most excellent artificers Tycho, Kepler and Lansberg whose expenses in this matter of such great importance were supported for all their lives by Emperors and Kings." The anonymous censor also asked, "What methods and instruments were used to observe the motions of the stars," and insisted that Riccioli "should also send that part of the work which he calls Instrumental Geography, so that it can be known from this what method he will use in emending and assigning the true longitudes of regions. For this is a task not for a single man, but such as deserves *the unanimous collaboration of all the mathematicians of the Society.*"[47]

The tone of the censure clearly recalls Kircher's geographic project, and indeed the handwriting of the anonymous text is a convincing match with

Kircher's letters from the period, providing further confirmation of his authorship.[48] Riccioli sent a chastened official response to the Roman censor, but Kircher sent a further, private letter to him at this time that included a number of more damning criticisms voiced by other people both inside and outside the Jesuit Order.[49] To this second letter, Riccioli responded at some length.[50]

Dismissing as absurd the criticism that he, a theologian, should not engage in mathematics because it was "unbecoming for a single person to profess two different faculties," Riccioli invoked a number of illustrious polymaths, ranging from Thales to Tycho Brahe and Kircher himself. "To speak freely to you," he continued to Kircher, "it was worthwhile procuring a vacation from theology, and refusing the administrative offices that I was offered more than once, acquiring from whatever source the money necessary for the construction of instruments and observational glasses, and wearing away my health by so many long night vigils, that all of whatever mind I had, nay, not mind, but back and upper-arms, has been expended as if from rolling a great weight ahead of me."[51] Riccioli also defended himself strenuously against the accusation that he relied solely "on the judgments of [his] pupils," inverting the traditional Jesuit hierarchy of authority.[52]

The following objection, however, was that Riccioli was a "private man"— "that is, as I interpret it, that I do not supply the expenses necessary for this business, but that they are supplied by my disciples from most noble families, Fr. Alfonsus Gianoti rector of this College, Marquis Cornelius Malvasia and, in the first place, by the Grimaldi, a most opulent family of this city."[53] Riccioli did not deny the charge—"Certainly our metal instruments are present in the college, and I did not create them out of nothing."[54] However, the expenses incurred in instrument building were justified by their capacity to enhance the reputation of the Society for mathematics and to bring direct returns:

> To inspect and to be witnesses on one occasion or another, were not only ours [i.e., Jesuits], but also other men of this city, and they were astonished by the agreement of the different instruments, directed toward the same star, to the minutes. And, among others the same Rocca [i.e., Giannantonio Rocca] remarked that he would trust (hold back your envy of the word) my observations no less than those of Tycho himself. Dr. Antonio Roffini was so captivated by [the instruments], that although he was previously hostile to ours [i.e., the Jesuits], he will bequeath his library, most richly provided with mathematical books, to our College.[55]

Perhaps most revealingly, Riccioli politely refused Kircher's request that he should move to Rome:

I say sincerely that there are reasons why I cannot do so without great damage to my work. Where you are, I cannot hope for the instruments and the books that, in addition to the library I already mentioned, I am given freely by the Marquis Malvasia, P. Cavalieri, P. Ricci, Dr. Manzini and others who are extremely well provided with them, far less the enormous gnomon that I use in the church of S. Petronius. Two Coriolians, engravers of figures in wood that are so fine that they seem to be in copper, and who are now obliged to me, as is the caster of new print-characters; the said D. Cornelius Malvasia Vexillifero, now a Senator, who encourages me and helps to cover my expenses together with the Most Eminent Cardinal [Girolamo Grimaldi], who also expects the book to be dedicated to him—all of these, I say, I cannot hope to find elsewhere.[56]

Where Athanasius Kircher saw the acquisition of natural knowledge as operating through a centralized global epistolary network of Jesuits, Riccioli's project was irretrievably local. Apart from his own body, he could not even send the parts of his book that Kircher requested from Bologna to Rome because "the affectations of my health and my stomach pains" rendered copying out the different parts of the book an impossibly arduous task.[57]

Local patronage, books, instruments, artisans, and Ignazio Danti's utterly immobile meridian line in S. Petronio—a fitting foil, perhaps, to Kircher's universal Jesuit horoscope—conspired to prevent Riccioli's removal to Rome.[58] Where Kircher concentrated his energies on marshaling a distant community of observers, Riccioli cultivated close local friends and disciples. Too close, occasionally—his celebrated relationship with Francesco Maria Grimaldi extended to allowing the latter to shave him and cut his hair, and the tendency for the older Jesuit to entertain his younger disciple in his bedroom late at night, after the other members of the community had gone to bed, led to rumors reaching the ears of the General, who obliged Riccioli, against his protestations of health problems, to move from Parma to Bologna,[59] where Grimaldi would eventually join him.

When Riccioli published his extremely influential *New Almagest* (*Almagestum Novum*), stripped of the part containing the descriptions and illustrations of his expensive instruments that had so worried the Roman censors, he acknowledged his human fallibility in the frontispiece, by giving angelic wings to the figure of the goddess Astrea, in explicit acknowledgment of the truth of Kircher's claim that perfect observations were only possible for an angel[60] (Figure 10.4).

Kircher's ideal observer was not an angelic individual, however, but a distributed collectivity of disciplined Jesuits, equipped with mathematical skills, azimuth compasses, and an efficient postal system. Kircher's geographic project was rooted in a particularly vivid vision of the role of his Order in the reform of natural knowledge, a vision of synchrony, uniform training, and the centralized accumulation and publication of missionary reports.

Figure 10.4. Frontispiece showing Astrea, goddess of justice, as a winged angel. *Source:* Giambattista Riccioli, *Almagestum Novum* (*New Almagest*), 1651. Courtesy of Stanford University Libraries.

Kircher's Epistemology

He is likewise one of the most naked and good men that I have seen, and is very easy to communicate whatever he knows, doing it, as it were, by a maxim he has. On the other side he is reported very credulous, apt to put in print any strange, if plausible story that is brought unto him. He has often made me smile.
—Robert Southwell, letter to Robert Boyle, 30 March 1661[61]

The question of Kircher's "working epistemology" is rarely addressed seriously. Rather than considering Kircher as possessing a particular conception of the correct path to knowledge, he is frequently subjected to alien epistemological standards based on the rejection of precisely the kinds of knowledge he strove to accumulate. Unsurprisingly, when these standards are applied, with their emphasis on certain and demonstrable knowledge, Kircher fails to make the grade and his more exotic claims are heaped with ridicule.

What, however, if Kircher never had any intention of creating certain and demonstrable knowledge? What if his more humble goal was to accumulate and disseminate a body of probable knowledge that would, in time, be rejected or more strongly accepted as more facts came to light? More specifically, what if his ultimate concern was to create a social structure that would be optimally suited to the accumulation of probable, *not* certain, knowledge? Kircher's approach to natural philosophy would then be very similar to the probabilistic stance of Jesuit theologians with regard to moral philosophy criticized so scathingly in Pascal's *Provincial Letters*.[62]

While we await a wholesale reevaluation of Kircher's philosophy of knowledge, the history of the conception and execution of Kircher's Geographical Plan offers us a small but revealing window on Kircher's working conception of the relationship between natural knowledge and the senses. In seventeenth-century Jesuit culture, certainties and experiential knowledge belonged to entirely different categories, and ultimately emanated from different sources.[63] This position was expressed emblematically in the frontispieces to numerous Jesuit works on optics, perhaps most eloquently in Kircher's own *Great Art of Light and Shadow*, which depicts the sources of knowledge in descending order of clarity: sacred authority, reason, sense (aided by instruments), and profane authority (Figure 10.5). Making instrumentally produced knowledge more than probable was simply nonsensical from this point of view, one somewhat resonant with that of one of Kircher's most avid readers, Robert Boyle. Like Boyle, Kircher endeavored to craft a practical, social solution to the problem of knowledge, but the solution he settled upon—a centralized correspondence network of obedient Jesuit missionaries—was rather different from Boyle's meticulously detailed experimental histories.[64]

Kircher's presentation of himself as a mediator of the opinions and observations of others rather than a forger of new dogmas and certainties was, more-

Figure 10.5. Frontispiece Athanasius Kircher, *Ars magna lucis et umbrae* (*The Great Art of Light and Shadow*), 1646. *Source:* Courtesy of Stanford University Libraries.

over, a position that was well adapted to the intellectual climate in Rome during Muzio Vitelleschi's thirty-year reign as General of the Jesuit Order, a period characterized by increasingly fervent persecution of Jesuits who deviated from Aristotelian orthodoxy in matters of natural philosophy.[65] Kircher's angelic observer, azimuth compass in hand, embodies a powerful epistemological stance, at the center of which lies individual sensory weakness and fallibility.

Notes

*   I am very grateful to Noel Malcolm, Simon Schaffer, Moti Feingold, Paula Findlen, and Nick Wilding for comments, criticisms, and stimulating arguments relating to previous versions of this paper.

1.   Martino Martini to Kircher, Evora, 6 February 1639, Archivio della Pontificia Università Gregoriana, Rome (hereafter, **APUG**) 567, fols. 74r–75v, published in Martini 1998, vol. 1, pp. 61–69. On Martini, see also Demarchi and Scartezzini 1996. All documents cited from the Kircher papers in APUG may be consulted online via the Athanasius Kircher Correspondence Project, http://kircher.stanford.edu.

2.   On Clavius's mathematical academy, see Clavius 1992, I.1, pp. 59–89, and Gorman 2002. On Kircher's museum, see especially Findlen 1995. On the mechanical devices in the museum, see Gorman 2001.

3.   Martino Martini to Muzio Vitelleschi, Goa, 8 November 1640, Archivum Romanum Societatis Iesu (hereafter **ARSI**), Goa 34 1, fols. 81r–86v, in Martini 1998, vol. 1, pp. 97–140.

4.   On Jesuit involvement in Portuguese trade networks, see the important study by Alden 1996.

5.   Kircher 1641b. Interestingly, Stanford University's copy of the first edition of *The Magnet* [shelfmark QC751 .K58 1641] belonged to the important baroque architect and mathematician Guarino Guarini (1624–83). On Kircher's *Magnes*, and his magnetic philosophy in general, the most comprehensive study remains Baldwin 1987. See also Hine 1988. For an interpretation of Kircher's collection of data on magnetic declination different from that offered here, see Baldwin 2001a, p. 33.

6.   Kircher 1641b, Lib. 2, Pars Quinta. *Geographia Magnetica*.

7.   Kircher 1654, p. 293. The first reference to Kircher's Geographical Plan that I have been able to find is in a letter from Martino Martini to Kircher, sent from Évora in Portugal on 6 February 1639. In this letter, Martini writes: "I am awaiting the *Magnetic Philosophy* [i.e., the *Magnes*] and the *Mathematical Plan (Concilium Mathematicum)*" (Martini 1998, vol. 1, pp. 57–70). The "mathematical plan" to which Martini alludes is almost certainly Kircher's Geographical Plan, suggesting that Kircher may have conceived it as early as 1637, when Martini was studying magnetic declination with him in Rome.

8.   For an analysis of the relationship between travel and data gathering in Jesuit culture, see Harris 1996 and 1999; and Hsia 1999a.

9.   There is an enormous literature on the longitude problem, but see especially Andrewes 1996; and Bedini 1991.

10. Van Helden 1996.

11. Kircher 1646, p. 552.

12. See Van de Vyver 1977.

13. See Bennett 1987, pp. 53–55.

14. Martini to Kircher, Lisbon, 16 March 1640, in Martini 1998, vol. 1, pp. 87–92. On Borri, see Petech 1971; and Mercati 1951.

15. Marin Mersenne, [Treatise on the magnet, 1639?], BL Add. MS. 4279, fols. 145r–146v, in Mersenne 1932–88, vol. 8, pp. 754–762, on p. 761.

16. Gassendi to Peiresc, n.d., n.p., published in Gassendi 1658, t. VI, p. 90.

17. See Gassendi to Diodati, Aix, 23 April 1636, in Gassendi 1658, t. VI, pp. 85–90, on p. 88. On Peiresc and Gassendi's attempts to coordinate eclipse observations made by missionaries, see especially Wilding 2000, pp. 132–139.

18. Before changing to magnetic variation, Kircher also attempted to use Jesuit missionaries to gather measurements of lunar eclipses with the help of a paper *Rota Geographica* that he distributed to correspondents. See Kircher, letter to an unidentified Jesuit, Rome, 14 October 1636, APUG 561, fols. 83r–84v.

19. Kircher to Mersenne, Rome, 23 December 1639, Houghton Library, Harvard University, Fms. Lat. 306. 1 (3) [a copy, apparently in the hand of Gabriel Naudé]. This letter is not published in the Mersenne correspondence (Mersenne 1932–88).
20. Kircher 1641b, p. 430
21. ARSI Congr. 7, fols. 46r–48v: *Acta Congregationis Procuratorum anni 1639*. Two of the Procurators present at this congregation, P. Pierre Cazré and P. Nithard Biber, subsequently corresponded with Kircher directly. See APUG 567, fol. 192r (Cazré) and APUG 567, fols. 128r, 172r (Biber).
22. Kircher 1641b, p. 430.
23. Démoustier 1995.
24. On this point, see O'Malley 1993, p. 354, and the revealing comments made by Jeronimo Nadal in his Dialogus II (1562–65), in Nadal 1962, pp. 601–774, on pp. 764–770 (*De ratione gubernationis*), especially p. 767.
25. Grandamy 1645, p. 83.
26. Ciermans to Kircher, Lovanij 7. Martij 1640, APUG 567, fol. 90r.
27. Oswald Krüger to Kircher, Vilnius, 21 July 1639, APUG 567, fol. 53r.
28. Henricus Marcellus to Kircher, Mainz, 1 May 1640, APUG 567, fol. 213r.
29. Grandamy to Kircher, Touron, 9 May 1640, 557, fols. 400r–401v, on fol. 400r.
30. Henricus Marcellus to Kircher, Mainz, 1 May 1640, APUG 567, fol. 213r.
31. Jacobus Imhofer to Kircher, Innsbruck, 15 January 1640, APUG 567, fol. 177r.
32. Jacques Honoré Durand to Kircher, 12 March 1640, APUG 567 fol. 202r.
33. Lorenz Mattenkloth to Kircher, 8 March 1640, APUG 567, fol. 159r; P. Grégoire a St. Vincent to Kircher, 8 March 1640, APUG 567, fol. 24r–v. On Line's magnetic clock, see Hankins and Silverman 1995, pp. 14–36.
34. Martino Martini to Kircher, Goa, 8 November 1640, in Martini 1998, vol. 1, pp. 71–86.
35. Gellibrand 1635. On this episode, see Pumfrey 1989.
36. See APUG 557, fols. 41r–56v, and Kircher 1654, Lib. II. Pars V, Caput VI, p. 340.
37. Kircher 1641b, p. 483.
38. See Kircher 1646, p. 553.
39. Ibid.
40. Kircher 1646, facing p. 554.
41. On Riccioli's time measurements, see Koyré 1953; and Galluzzi 1977. On Riccioli's early training, see Baldini 1996. On Riccioli's cosmology, see Dinis 1989, which includes an extremely useful intellectual biography (chapter 1).
42. Kircher 1654 p. 294. For the true anguish of Kircher's predicament, it is hard to do justice to the original Latin: "Dissimulare hic non possum animi mei iustum dolorem, quem ex iactua praefati consilii Geographici precepi: cum enim opus non sine vigilijs elaboratum, inter alia in Musaeo meo conservarem, tempusque opportunum in lucem publicam litterariae Reipublicae bono emittendi praestolarer; ab uno illorum, qui quotidie paene Musaei inspiciendi causa ad me undique confluebant, clam subductum est."
43. Kircher to Gassendi, Rome, 13 February 1642, published in Gassendi 1658, vol. VI, p. 446.
44. Ibid.
45. Riccioli to Kircher, Bologna, 5 July 1642, APUG 561, fols. 177r–178v, published in Gambaro 1989, pp. 44–52, on p. 44. For an excellent analysis of astronomical culture in Bologna during Riccioli's time, see Heilbron 1999.
46. Riccioli 1661. For Riccioli's consideration of the longitude problem and magnetic declination, see Lib. VIII, *Geomecographus*, Cap. 12–16.
47. ARSI FG 662, fol. 477 r, published in Gambaro 1989, p. 40, and retranscribed (with amendments) in Baldini 1996, p. 176n55, emphasis added.
48. Gambaro (1989) adduces no hypothesis concerning the authorship of the *censura*, whereas Baldini (1996) explicitly dismisses the possibility of Kircher's authorship on the basis of a later letter from Riccioli to Kircher. However, the letter in question, discussed below, refers not directly to the anonymous *censura*, but to a letter, now lost, from Kircher to Riccioli reiterating some of the points in the original censure and adding a number of other points of contention concerning Riccioli's way of life. It is from these *other* points (particularly the inability of a single person to be proficient in two different faculties simultaneously) that Riccioli dissociates Kircher. Taken in its entirety, the existing evidence is entirely compatible with Kircher's authorship of the original anonymous *censura* of ARSI FG 662, fol. 477 r.

49. Riccioli to the Roman censor, n.p., n.d. [Bologna, between 24 November and 22 December 1646?], published in Gambaro 1989, pp. 70–76.
50. Riccioli to Kircher, Bologna, 22 December 1646, published in Gambaro 1989, pp. 77–81.
51. Ibid.
52. Ibid., on p. 78.
53. Ibid.
54. Ibid.
55. Ibid.
56. Ibid., p. 81. See Riccioli 1651, sig. *Ar–A2r, letter of dedication to Prince Cardinal Girolamo Grimaldi. For the involvement of Francesco Maria Grimaldi in the work, see sig. A2r.
57. Ibid. Riccioli's decline in bodily powers during the period prior to the publication of the *Almagestum Novum* is corroborated by the *Catalogi Triennales* for the period: on 15 May 1645 his "*vires*" are reported to be "*mediocres*," by 15 September 1649 they have become "*imbiscelles*," and by 1 October 1651 they are reduced to "*debiles*." See ARSI Ven. 40, fols. 18v, 48v: #11 (for 1645); ibid., fols. 94v, 125v: #16 (for 1649); ibid., fols. 178r, 204r: #14 (for 1651).
58. On the use of meridian lines in churches, including S. Petronio, to perform astronomical observations see Heilbron 1989 and, especially, 1999, pp. 82–119.
59. See Muzio Vitelleschi to the Provincial for the Veneto, 13 September 1636, ARSI Ven. 1, fol. 318v, cited in Baldini 1996, p. 174n40.
60. Riccioli 1651, Pars Prior, XVII.
61. Boyle 1772, vol. 6, pp. 297–300.
62. On Jesuit probabilism, see especially Kantola 1994.
63. Ashworth 1989. For an important discussion of sources of knowledge in seventeenth-century natural philosophy, see Dear 1995. On the epistemological underpinnings of "preternatural philosophy" in the early modern period, see Daston 2000, especially pp. 27–29.
64. On Boyle's experimental histories, see Shapin and Schaffer 1985; and Shapin 1994.
65. On Vitelleschi's measures to curb Jesuit *libertas philosophandi*, see Gorman 1996 and 2002; and Costantini 1969. For Kircher's own difficulties with the censors, see Camenietzki 1995a.

Communicating Knowledge

11

Magnetic Language
Athanasius Kircher and Communication

HAUN SAUSSY

Languages are not the product of a reason that is present to itself.
—Turgot, *Remarques critiques*

Every machine is a reasoning machine, in so much as there are certain relations between its parts, which relations involve other relations that were not expressly intended.
—Peirce, "Logical Machines"

1.

The *Polygraphia nova et universalis* (*New and Universal polygraphy*) of Athanasius Kircher offers little that was new in the world of cryptography or language theory in 1663. What retains the attention is rather the packaging, the ways in which several kinds of concern are brought together and made to mirror one another around a central axis that would be the nature of language. The work's table of contents promises the following:

Section I.
The Reduction of All Languages to One.

Section II.
The Extension of One Language to All.

Section III.
A Techno-logia; or, a universal Steganographic Secret operating by combinations of things; whereby, through a technique impenetrable to the human mind, one may transmit one's secrets to another in nearly a thousand ways.[1]

Each of these inventions had been prefigured or described in detail by others, including some of Kircher's correspondents and eventual recipients of presentation copies of the work. Section I, the Reduction, offers an international code in which words will be represented by a two-part symbol—one part referring to the meaning of the word (as recorded in a table of vocabulary items), one part indicating its grammatical function (as represented by the morphology of the Latin language). The ancient precursor of this nomenclator is the "Tironian notes," a hieroglyphic shorthand reputedly invented by Cicero's secretary. Gustavus Selenus had proposed making these "notae" the basis of an international written language, in a book published in 1624 and sent to Kircher in 1664, after the publication of *Polygraphia nova*.[2] Kircher's immediate model is a code composed by a mute Spanish Jesuit in the 1650s, elaborated on by Kircher in a manuscript circulated in 1660, and concurrently published in another version with a special ideographic script by Johann Joachim Becher in 1661.[3] Kircher rounds out these inventions with a polyglot dictionary. Section II, the Extension, is another kind of dictionary of equivalences, only the use of this dictionary is to supply a word as the substitute for a letter: what the user copies down is a message in flowing Latin prose, which the reader decodes by checking each word against the columns of a special table and recovering the letter that the word replaces. This artifice is drawn, with acknowledgment, from the work of Johannes Trithemius, whose *Polygraphia* had been cleared of the accusation of sorcery by Selenus's 1624 publication. Section III consists of substitution ciphers and letter keys, a set of cryptographic techniques put into circulation nearly a hundred years earlier by Vigenère.[4] What is particularly Kircherian, however, is the way in which these devices are drawn together into a single project and made to reflect other themes of his lifelong investigations.

2.

The reader of Athanasius Kircher's writings on language is always cheated, sometimes amused. Kircher promises us great things—the Reduction of all Languages to One, or the Extension of One Language to All, for example: practical communicative solutions based on the resolution of age-old linguistic problems. What he delivers, however, is something rather less imposing. The two great discoveries announced in the chapter titles of *Polygraphia nova* turn out to be mere typographic artifices. The Reduction is a numbered vocabulary list, by the aid of which one could conceivably, at most, hold an awkward conversation with a person possessing a similarly numbered list in another language. The Extension is a slightly more complicated code, in which whole words of Latin (or any other language, should anyone produce translated editions of Kircher's work) are used to indicate single letters.[5] The message conveyed by these single letters can, it is true, be couched in any alphabetic language, but there is not a very deep relation between the poles of the "extension" Kircher so grandiloquently promised.

To look at the chapter titles, the "axis" common to sections I and II would seem to be the relation between *all languages* and *one language* (the universal receiver-language, the language into which all languages would be translatable). Acts of communication between the poles of "all" and "one" would be rendered possible, one might think, by something like the essence of language:

that which remains identical to itself despite every possible variation. But when we inspect the content of the chapters, this promise turns out to be empty. The "oneness" that makes possible the "reduction" in section I is a declared semantic identity among synonyms (an identity always debatable in every particular), but the "oneness" on which hinges the "extension" in section II is a matter of equivalences arbitrarily established between words and individual letters, it being assumed that these letters are generally adoptable for noting any language. It is as if section I defined the essence of language as meaning, but section II defined that essence as form (as units of script). But no further or deeper essence of language comes to bridge form and meaning; or perhaps it is of the essence of Kircher's baroque linguistics to put a blank, a missed connection, in the place of that essence. As if to confirm that the victory is with non-semantic form, section III conveys exclusively permutations of letters, any letter being an adequate replacement for any other letter, given a rule that accounts for the substitution. Whether reduction or extension, Kircher's solution to the ancient problem of Babel sidesteps language in all its complexity, substituting for the variety of languages and the composite character of any particular language a roughly symmetrical pair of parlor games.

This deception or disappointment—the magic trick that never quite comes off, at least for readers of our day and age—is an essential accompaniment to the reading of Kircher. At certain points we find him acknowledging it himself, as his grand visions and equally grand commissions bump up against the limitations of his means. As if in a dialectic of the imaginary and the feasible, the architecture of *Polygraphia nova* has parallels throughout Kircher's writings.

Language for Kircher partakes of two domains: a sympathetic network linking the particles of the cosmos together, and a technology of language based on the shuffling of letters. At rare moments it appears that it might be possible for the two domains to coincide. At least, that is Kircher's desire, that is what he often promises us as a horizon of research; but what is most apparent to our eyes is always the yawning gulf between. In studies of Kircher, the division between his aims and his results often appears in the form of the Janus motif: Kircher, the man with one foot in Renaissance mystagogy and the other in seventeenth-century science, or the simultaneous inhabitant of the universes of Descartes and Hermes Trismegistus.[6] To divide a man up in this way is, it seems to me, not quite to take him seriously; it amounts to saying he was such a patchwork that he couldn't know his own mind. Was Kircher aware of his doubleness, and if so, how did he address it? What does communication mean for Kircher, that it should take such varied forms in his oeuvre?

Whatever particular domain of nature or art Kircher focuses his attention on, it sooner or later provides an occasion for applying knowledge to problems of communication. In *Magnet, sive de arte magnetica* (*Magnet, or the Magnetic Art*) (1643), the fascinating because unexplained play of forces between magnetized objects even when held at a distance from one another suggests the

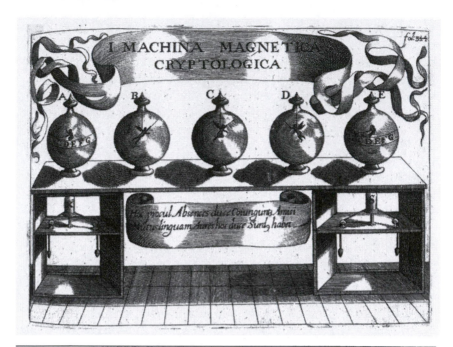

Figure 11.1. *I. Machina Cryptologica. Source:* Athanasius Kircher, *Magnes* (Cologne, 1643). Courtesy of Department of Special Collections, Stanford University Libraries.

fabrication of a "Machina Cryptologica," a sort of magnetic telegraph (Figure 11.1). The "machine" consists of a series of bottles, each stoppered by a well-lubricated magnet, the magnets all strong enough and near enough to attract or repel one another. When the stopper on the far left of the series is twisted, causing an attached pointer to indicate a letter of the alphabet, the remaining magnets one by one spin in "sympathy," so that the last of the series, also fitted with an alphabetic label and pointer, will give a readout corresponding to the first (Figure 11.1). Less a cryptographic device than a semaphoric one, the "machine" is fully plugged into the energetic circuits of Kircher's universe.[7] The attraction and repulsion of magnets is only the plainest evidence for the same forces that account for the surprising cures achieved by application of snakestone or the playing of tarantella music; the arrangement of the planets and the sun around the earth; and the lives and loves of plants, animals, and men. A chapter title in *Magnes* gives the category label for these startling phenomena: we live in a "Mundus magneticus, sive catena magnetica" (a magnetic world, or a magnetic chain). The sole key to nature, says Kircher, is the unity among dispersed things, the "rerum omnium naturalium Magneticus in hoc Universo nexus" (the magnetic tie among all the natural things in this universe).[8] There is distance—always; but there are forces that overcome distance,

Figure 11.2. *II. Machina Cryptologica. Source:* Athanasius Kircher, *Magnes* (Cologne, 1643). Courtesy of Department of Special Collections, Stanford University Libraries.

and we can harness these forces to serve the primary human need to send messages. Perhaps the need to send messages is simply another form of those forces. (In this spirit, Kircher presents himself to a potential patron as "drawn by some unknown strength or power, some sort of magnetism" to open a correspondence with him.[9]) Thus the possibility of communication across spaces of separation is a natural potential that the clever scientist (or natural magician) puts to work.[10]

A magnetic universe is essentially communicative or representative, as is symptomatized by Kircher's difficulty in making a secret communication device that is not also a broadcasting station (Figure 11.2). Representation, in turn, works as do the numerological puzzles and magic squares Kircher borrows from Cornelius Agrippa of Nettesheim, who had ascribed them to the Egyptians:

> The Egyptians believed that by using these very numbers, they could bind to their service the spirits of this world. . . . This much at least is certain, that beneath all this there lies something analogous to the highest orders of ideas, which, were anyone able to extract it from the confused mixture (*miscella*) of worldly objects by using some artifice akin to this one, I am sure that nothing in the investigation of natural things would be closed to him.[11]

The structure of knowledge is hardly different from that of communication: identification of a "sameness" or "unity" hiding in the mingled disorder of things as they appear to us, and prodigious travel through nature along the epistemological shortcuts thus revealed.

At times, nature showed an indulgent face to Kircher's "magnetic" and "sympathetic" explanatory framework:

> I have seen a complete crucifix in an agate-stone. . . . In bits of tufa rock, I have seen a whole alphabet whose letters were formed of variously shaped veins in the stone. . . . At the same time, I caught a butterfly in the garden of our residence, on whose wings nature had accurately imprinted the face of our Savior.[12]

These signs and images are simply concretizations of the "concatenated influence" (*concatenato influxu*) that holds the world together and binds it to its divine source.[13] A powerful, revelatory language like that of the ancient Egyptians reveals the connection, the nexus, among things; weaker languages merely partake of the "miscella."

3.

It was doubtless because of Kircher's gift for expressing the symbolic web of the universe that he received one of his most difficult royal commissions. As Kircher puts it at the beginning of his *Polygraphia nova*:

> Once while the most wise Emperor Ferdinand III was engaged in one of those familiar discussions of literary matters to which he resorted in order to be released from the world's weight pressing on his shoulders, the question came to him: whether there might exist a universal language by means of which someone might correspond with all the peoples of the world; and as there was no one capable of providing a sure ground for such a language, it pleased his Holy Roman Majesty to commit to my feeble talents the solution of the problem proposed by him.[14]

A language permitting communication "with all the peoples of the world" would have been particularly handy for a seventeenth-century Hapsburg monarch whose domains covered several dozen distinct linguistic areas (including languages as far apart as Italian, Hungarian, Polish, German, and Croatian) and who had the Turks intermittently at his gates. What sort of idiom might Ferdinand III have had in mind when he issued his command, probably in the early 1650s?

The projects for universal languages that circulated in the first half of the seventeenth century promised, in general, to make language learning easy and universal (one would acquire, in a few hours' time, a single system of writing applicable to every language on earth) and, as a prelude to this universal writing, to draw all known languages back to their "original" or to their "primitive" form. The best-known version of a universal language project from this period is unfortunately unknown to us except through Descartes's response to it, written in a letter to Mersenne.[15] The project discussed by Descartes mingles purely technical considerations (simplification of grammar, the availability of a dictionary that could be translated into all existing languages) with historical ones (the proposition that by using the new language we might "explain the thoughts of the ancients through the words that they used, by taking each word as the true definition of the thing"): it would reunite what had been dispersed not only in space (French, Germans, English, Italians, and so forth) but in time (ancient Greeks, ancient Romans, contemporary French, Italians, and so forth).

Some aspects of the project discussed by Descartes recall Francis Bacon's praise of the Chinese writing system as a set of "Characters Real, which express neither letters nor words in gross, but Things or Notions; insomuch as countries and provinces, which understand not one another's language, can nevertheless read one another's writings."[16] And that is the only part of the project that Descartes found praiseworthy: "the whole utility I see resulting from this invention is its application to writing . . . with common characters for each primitive word, characters that would correspond to the sense, not the syllables."[17]

Insofar as they came equipped with a theory, the newly created languages that adopted the option of the "Characters Real" mostly held themselves apart from prior history, either presenting themselves as pure conveniences of communication or describing their new beginning as a chance to do away with the disputatious history of language and translation up to then. One of the rare exceptions is Pierre Besnier's 1674 announcement of a new universal language, *A Philosophical Essay for the Reunion of the Languages, or, the Art of Knowing All by the Mastery of One*. Besnier holds that: "First, there is a certain accord between the several languages, and that therefore they are attainable by comparison. . . . Secondly, that they are unquestionably founded upon reason."[18] Besnier's reason is etymology: in a series such as

cadere > caer > ker > cher > choir > déchoir

one can recognize the continuity between the different stages, though it is not easy to describe their motivation; both sound and meaning differ at every step, so that linguistic history is, for Besnier, an "alembic." "Reason" perhaps stands for the possibility of rationalizing the gap between any two adjacent transformations, not the series as a whole. To explain a language, says Besnier, you must have command of its whole history.[19] His is not (to say the least) a reductive epistemology.

Yet it must have been by beginning with something like the expectations that converge in Besnier—universality of application added to comprehensive historical elucidation—that Kircher's response to the emperor's commission eventually took its particular technical course. For as Kircher tells it, he began by seeking to reduce all existing languages to a set of common roots that would form the core vocabulary of the new language, but suddenly the same thing happened to me that might happen to a typesetter who has several pages of type laid out and ready for putting under the press: by some inexplicable chance the bonds dissolve and the letters rain down onto the floor, retaining no trace of their true former meaning and no longer capable of being brought back to their lost prototype. So it is with that near-infinite multitude and diversity of languages which, from the beginning of the world until now, has been exposed to so many changes of empire, so much mixing of diverse populations, and so many historical vicissitudes that I believe it most unlikely that a foundation common to all languages should be discovered.[20]

As a result of contemplating too closely the historical debris of language change, Kircher's mind, normally so attentive to the unifying sympathies and nexuses dispersed through the natural world, lost its power of connection ("dissolutis ligaminibus," as he puts it in his comparison). That is to say, the encounter with the irregular and capricious history of language causes the natural magician's explanatory framework to shatter. Language reduces Kircher to the condition bemoaned by a nameless professional code cracker of his time, who observed that

in dealing with ciphers, it is in the power of the most whimsical scribbler in the world to ordain the meanings of things as his own caprice determines. He can decide that today, 24 will stand for heaven and tomorrow it will stand for the earth. . . . [The decipherer] has no way of knowing if a certain cipher stands for A or B or C or some other letter of the alphabet, whether it is a syllable or a word or perhaps a null sign; he hesitates everywhere, doubts everything and can plant his mind on nothing that is solid. . . . It is easy to gain knowledge of an unknown through our previous knowledge; for that, all that is necessary is reasoning power and the syllogism does the rest; but to penetrate an unknown by means of another thing equally unknown is more than all philosophers of the world together can do.[21]

Rather than reply to the imperial command with an admission of failure, Kircher presented to the throne a "linguistic device" (*artificium linguarum*) bearing the proud titles of universal communication and penetration, but accomplishing those ends in oddly reduced fashion. Kircher's student Kaspar Schott describes the secrecy surrounding the first "publication" of what was later to be the *Polygraphia nova*:

Many years ago Kircher thought of a new device, which he called an *artifice of languages*; it enabled anyone to read and understand whatever unfamiliar language he wished, by making various arrangements of rods and combinations of the characters written on them. He demonstrated it once to the most august Kaiser Ferdinand III and to his brother, the most serene archduke Wilhelm Leopold, at that time governor of Belgium. Both of them were delighted with it, as this new and ingenious invention, worthy of great princes, deserved; and they decreed that it not be made public, but rather be reserved for their own use and that of their most august family. And it is for this reason that at no time, in the three years I spent offering my paltry scribal services to the Author of the device, was I able to obtain from Kircher that he show me, even as if through a crack, anything connected to it, except a great number of bare and uninscribed rods stored in a chest which was shaped like a pipe-organ.[22]

The chest's shape is the last relic of the language Kircher hoped to speak about language and nature. It echoes another expression of his view of the world as filled with divine forces, the analogy of the cosmos as an immense pipe organ in *Musurgia universalis* (*Universal Music-making*) (1650).[23] As Nick Wilding has observed, the closed system of circulation into which Kircher introduced his linguistic artifices (the very few patrons of high rank who received wooden chests with inscribed tallies, and the several dozen recipients of the *Polygraphia*'s first edition, every copy apparently destined to be presented with the author's compliments) is inseparable from the content of those artifices themselves. Composed in an atmosphere of secrecy, they are meant to facilitate communication not with the world in general, but only among other possessors of the gifts.

4.

Although the recipients of Kircher's "artifice" fall into two classes—the superior class, those who received wooden chests; and the second class, who received the printed book only—the book's content and illustrations are designed to supply a near equivalent to the experience of having and using a chest. At the conclusion of sections II and III comes a full-page illustration, with a poetic epigram to seal the importance and the symmetry of the artifices contained therein (Figure 11.3). The imagined wooden version of the "Extension" cipher is labeled:

> GLOTTOTACTIC ARK. . . . Good for writing letters throughout the whole world.[24]

The plate illustrating the box filled with slide-rule–like alphabetic permutations—a manual abbreviation of the work ordinary cryptographers would have performed on paper—says, in roughly parallel fashion:

> Steganographic
> Ark,
> containing a set of
> tablets.
> Through this Ark the combination of things is revealed
> to you.
> Whatever you wish to write, it returns to you in
> foreign tongues.[25]

Kircher is much taken with these "arks"—safeboxes as well as Noah's Arks, in the sense that much is enclosed in their small compass. His comment on the

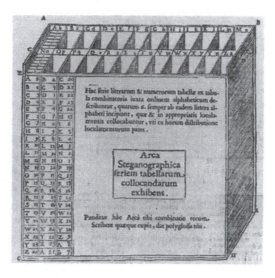

Figure 11.3. *Arca Steganographica. Source:* Athanasius Kircher, *Polygraphia nova* (Rome, 1663). Courtesy of Department of Special Collections, Stanford University Libraries.

second ark returns us to the perspective of a magnetic language that would reveal the unity of the world:

> By this means you may conceal numberless hidden meanings, either by veiling the key to your code under a single sentence or else by easily hiding a single secret under innumerable [word] meanings—sentences, observations, letters about any subject whatsoever, so that truly one may say that here "one is all, and all are one"; and the reason, briefly stated, is as follows. Since the tablets may be moved about as many times as there are combinations of the letters of the alphabet, it is clear, then, that there can be no end to this undertaking, as is demonstrated by the number 25852016738888497666640000 which represents the number of combinations of the 24 letters of the alphabet. . . . Surely there is no conceivable sentence occurring in any language which cannot be represented on the tablets; thus this narrow box and the letters enclosed therein surpass all the libraries of the whole world.[26]

Another attempt to formulate the essence of language, this time as permutation? But this apparently final and total dimension where "one is all, and all are one" leaves open many ambiguities in the application. No more than the first two trunks does the "steganographic ark" actually "return to you in foreign tongues" what you wish to write, it merely transposes your writing into new sequences of letters that look foreign in comparison with the first version. Only section I applied a method to linguistic content. The artifices of sections II and III gain their titles to a kind of universality by dislocating, in different ways, form and content: using a word to stand for a letter, in one case, and using a different letter to stand for each letter, in the other. The "reduction" and "extension" Kircher speaks of are not really continuous processes of growth or contraction, but processes of transposition and substitution that require new rules of reading, rules that the arks and the book *Polygraphia nova* itself contain. "Polygraphy" does not lead to a new understanding of language, not even to a new use of language, but only to new techniques for processing bits of language into different shapes.

And with this we are again before the unsatisfying division of Kircher into two epistemological personalities. An "enchanted" cosmos survives in Kircher's dreams of a more potent language, maintained by historical and literary allusion in perfect continuity with nature; but the execution of Kircherian "polygraphy" is disenchanted, flat, and profane, a mechanical substitution of letters for which a twenty-five-place number provides the chief poetic ornament.

5.

There would be much to say here about the first *Polygraphia*, that by Johannes Trithemius, who originated the word-for-a-letter device and some of the alphabet-substitution techniques refined by Vigenère. Here there is only room to draw a parallel with Kircher's two registers, as a matter of literary form. Trithemius had the poor judgment to write his treatise on codes and ciphers, *Steganographia* (*Disguised Writing*) (1608), in an allegorical form, instructing his reader to "summon spirits" who would "do your bidding" if called from this or that quarter of the compass by such sonorous invocations as this:

> The key and operation is under the principal spirit Pamersiel, anoyr madriel per ministerium ebru sothean abrulges itrasbiel. And nadres ormenu itules rublion hamorphiel. To these, submit your orders and exorcism.[27]

The book horrified a visitor to Trithemius's abbey, Charles de Bovelles, who denounced Trithemius for dabbling in magic.[28] Trithemius was never quite cleared of the charge, although he quickly wrote a new and less sinister book on cipher, *Polygraphia*, in which he protested his innocence and begged for the patronage of the emperor Maximilian.[29] *Steganographia* was not printed for another hundred years, and once published (by Protestants) was promptly put on the Index. More recently, Frances Yates still listed it as "a major Renaissance manual of conjuring."[30] And yet its invocations were decoded as long ago as 1624, when Gustavus Selenus picked out every other letter (more or less) of the nonsense words to make *anoyr madriel ebru sothean abrulges itrasbiel nadres ormenu itules rublion* into *nym die erste bugstabe de omni verbo* ("take the first letter of every word"), a recipe for decoding the next passage.[31] Trithemius's *Polygraphia* actually shows us the two halves of the Kircherian dilemma—"sympathetic magic" and "verbo-technology"—side by side. But the mystical and the pedestrian registers are here differently conjoined: rather than the grand perspectives of sympathetic semiology collapsing into the bathos of letter-juggling, in Trithemius the mystical or demonic register is merely an allegorical disguise for the flat, unextraordinary play of the letter, the Oulipian resources of combinatorics. The relation is not that between a promise and its (inadequate) realization, but between a deceptive coating and a humdrum core. With enchantment its delusive outside and mechanism its pragmatic content, Trithemius's *Polygraphy* reads like a critical inversion of the aims and claims of Kircher's. Except, of course, that Trithemius's artifice came first and Kircher's is expressly designated the *new* polygraphy.

6.

For Kircher, then, there is magnetic language and there is mechanical language. In the whole context of his work, the language machines of *Polygraphia nova* express the unbridged gap between perfect communication, that chain of magnetic forces, and profane communication, accomplished by copying letters one by one from inscribed sticks or dictionaries.[32] Machines, in Kircher as in many another baroque author, are signs, sensory appearances whose workings must be guessed at; and like the signs of language, they are easily misunderstood. The "theater of fine devices" exemplified by Kircher's museum stages a "baroque culture of special effects" that teaches moral lessons by tricking the spectator into awareness of her susceptibility to illusion.[33]

If the obsession with mechanical displays seems to relegate Kircher to a courtly or ecclesiastical corner of seventeenth-century culture, we have only to look at the notebooks of the young Descartes—dating from the months preceding his famous dream of philosophical revelation, and his first meditations on what would become the Cartesian method—to open up a larger perspective. Descartes's "Cogitationes privatae" (Private Thoughts) of 1619 includes several plans for mechanical devices that would startle the observer by their simulation of spontaneous, living action:

> Let us suppose a statue with iron in its head and feet, standing on a thin magnetized cable or iron rod. And let another rod or cable be set above its head, a bit higher, also magnetized but more heavily charged in some places than in others. And let the statue be holding in its hands a long staff like a tightrope walker's, hollowed out and connected to the spring that gives the automaton's principle of movement: at any light touch on the staff the whole statue will step forward every time it is touched and, each time it hits a more strongly charged part of the magnet, will jump spontaneously. At the same time instruments may be played.
>
> An Architean [i.e., mechanical] dove can be made with, between its wings, mills turning in the wind so that it will always pursue a straight course.[34]

The dove flies in a straight line as if pursuing an objective, the acrobat statue seems to respond to its environment and to dance in time to music: Descartes's youthful artifices counterfeit consciousness and intentionality, by giving the signs that permit us to recognize these properties in living beings, but of course their movements are determined by purely material causes.

For Descartes as for Kircher, the machine was an arena for eliciting fallacious guesses about causes, using hidden mechanisms (magnetic attraction, the self-adjusting rudder of a Dutch windmill) to simulate life. The machine must convince, and then fail to convince; the lesson it teaches lies in the difference between the way it appears from two perspectives (roughly, from the "front" and from the "back"). But simulacra are inherently ambiguous; they may be intended to make A counterfeit B, and succeed in making B counterfeit A. The observer's experience of a Cartesian machine would raise the question whether life—the thing simulated—was genuinely of a different order from its mechanical simulacrum. For animals and the human body, as far as Descartes's mature philosophy is concerned, the differences are only of degree: all are subject to physical laws, and a complete physical account of their behavior is doubtless possible. Language, for Descartes, is a different matter, since it consists trivially in physical articulation, chiefly in mental activity, and thought is not mechanically determined. The example of speaking automata occurs in *Discours de la méthode* (*Discourse on Method*) (1637), book 5:

> If any such machines bore a resemblance to our bodies and imitated our actions as closely as possible for all practical purposes, we should still have two very certain means of recognizing that they were not real men. The first is that they could never use words, or put together other signs, as we do in order to declare our thoughts to others. For we can certainly conceive of a machine so constructed that it utters words, and even utters words which correspond to bodily actions causing a change in its organs . . . but it is not conceivable that such a machine should produce different arrangements of words so as to give an appropriately meaningful answer to whatever is said in its presence, as the dullest of men can do.[35]

A language machine, then, is bound to fail. The mental is (by definition) not the mechanical. Syntax and contextual acuity, says Descartes, are not the sort of things that can be counterfeited by machines, as any human (even a dull-brained one will do) can demonstrate. Descartes's discussion leaves us (if we are convinced by it) with two widely separated objects: the faculty of language as exercised by humans, and the flat, inadequate attempts to mimic it with mechanical means. Inadequacy is, however, far from meaningless: Descartes is imagining baroque machines that, like Kircher's, defer, for the instant of amazement, their inevitable fall back into their true identity as defective imitations of God's handiwork.

Kircher's *Polygraphia nova* is an exhibition of language machines—a transposition onto the field of language of his speaking statues, dancing cherubs, and vomiting eagles. Its successive chapters seek to automate the operations of translation, coding, and even composition (though the fluent compositions generated by section II are without relation to the composer's intended meaning). The relation between input and output is, in every case, determinate, but the unprepared observer is supposed to be unable to recognize that.

The moment of the *Polygraphia* machine's greatest fecundity—that is, the point at which it most powerfully exceeds the observer's ability to second-guess it—is the declaration of its power to "surpass all the libraries of the world" and to express every possible sentence of every language. It attains the twenty-five-place number of its triumph through brute-force permutation, as the cryptographers would say, not by forming a hypothesis about the working of language. But this brutal, purely quantitative shuffling of signifiers suggests not a theory of language, but a verdict on it. Quirinus Kuhlmann's poem "Der Wechsel menschlicher Sachen" (The Mutability of Human Affairs) consists mostly of one-syllable nouns: except for the first and last words of each line, the remainder can be moved about freely with no noticeable change in meaning, giving, as the author proudly says, a total of 127×10^{64} possible combinations for the first four verses alone.[36] If the poet's aim is to impress on the reader the inconstancy of worldly things, his poem becomes an example of what it teaches; and if no particular word order seems preferable to any other, that too is a foretaste of wisdom. With an allusion to Kircher, Kuhlmann exclaims: "Consider the inner essence of wondrous permutation! Be assured that you will discover there the center of all languages (*das Centrum aller Sprachen*) and point out in play that which the world seeks in toil and fails, to its cost, to find."[37] Georg Philipp Harsdörffer's *Mathematical Recreations* (1651) includes a "Five-Layer Thought Ring of the German Language," an arrangement of concentric wheels inscribed with prefixes, vowels, consonants, and suffixes (choices that attest to a good sense of morphophonetic regularities in German) (Figure 11.4). Each position of the five wheels points to one of 97,209,600 possible German words, inevitably including "blind or meaningless" ones such as *fortgrorcht*.[38]

Neither Kuhlmann nor Hardörffer were concerned to lay bare the nature of language; rather, language was for them the material for an experiment as open-ended (and inconclusive) as the alchemical quest. An *art* (in the seventeenth-century sense, preceding the specialization of this term as something distinct from "science," "learning," and "industry") is a method for producing objects, and the art of which language machines are a part produces letter sequences, preferably in vast quantities and unrecognizable forms. "Any adequate masking of content is absent from the typical works of the baroque," Walter Benjamin observed. "The extent of the claims, even in the minor forms, is breathtaking. And they lack any feeling for the intimate, the mysterious. They attempt, extravagantly and vainly, to replace it with the enigmatic and the concealed."[39] This holds true even on the small field of the twenty-four letters.

The lesson of the machine is that no matter how marvelous, it is still not miraculous; no matter how many combinations a finite set of elements can produce, its number still falls infinitely short of infinity; and thus the tri-

Figure 11.4. *Fünffacher Denckring der Teutschen Sprache. Source:* Georg Philipp Harsdörffer, *Fortsetzung der mathematischen und philosophischen Erquickstunden* (Nuremberg, 1651). Courtesy of the Beinecke Rare Book Library, Yale University.

umphant display of large numbers stands for the exhaustion of language as much as for its fecundity. It is a melancholy Lullism. So Leibniz:

> Inasmuch as all human knowledge can be expressed by the letters of the alphabet, and as one can say that the person who has perfectly mastered the use of the alphabet, knows all there is to be known; it follows that one might calculate the number of truths of which human beings are capable, and thus determine the size of a work that would contain all possible human knowledge, in which there would be everything that could ever be known, written or invented—and even more, for it would contain not only the truths, but also all the false statements that can be uttered, and even expressions without any meaning. This investigation helps to show how small a thing man is in comparison to the infinite substance. . . . But supposing that we go ever forward . . . one day everything will be

exhausted . . . and it will necessarily one day have been literally true (*il faudrait toujours qu'il fût un jour vrai au pied de la lettre*) that nothing more can be said that has not already been said.[40]

7.

There are several ways of explaining Kircher's ideology of communication. Michel Foucault, in *Les Mots et les choses* (*The Order of Things*), characterized Vigenère, Duret, and (one would assume) Kircher as thinkers belonging to a pre-Cartesian "episteme" in which the doctrine of signatures, the conception of meaning as naturally inhering in the world and asking only to be discovered, was the chief avenue of understanding works of nature as well as of human invention.[41] But it is notoriously difficult to achieve harmony among the various voices presumed to represent a given episteme, even one so large as the Book of Nature. In Foucault's terms Kircher himself would have to be seen as internalizing the split between a doctrine of signatures and a mentality of two-dimensional classifications, a split that corresponds to the division between his Hermetic rhetoric, in which meaning is motivated by the constitution of the world, and his mathematical-cryptographic permutations, which could hardly succeed as cryptography unless they were to some strong degree undermotivated by meaning, intention, or natural constraints. The Foucault alternative leaves us with an incomplete Kircher, or with the traditionally Janus-faced Kircher.

Umberto Eco, in his *Search for the Perfect Language*, adopts the framework of contemporary semiotics to classify the language proposals among which Kircher's "Reduction" and "Extension" take their places: this is useful for drawing up a typology and tracing influences, but has the untoward effect of treating what seventeenth-century authors wrote as an anticipation (usually highly defective) of a science we now know in its maturity.[42]

I find it most useful to take Kircher as a fully competent player in a certain language game, and ask what that language game could have been. Historians who have worked toward reconstructing the social environment of seventeenth-century thinkers on language are of great help in this effort. Wilding's attention to the mode of circulation of Kircher's cryptographic texts, and Stillman's handling of the linguistic questions debated by the Royal Society, provide just the kind of information and analysis that have usually been missing from intellectual histories of the period.[43] To take the history of ideas as self-sufficient almost guarantees that half the story will escape us.

With such considerations in mind, we can pass beyond the observation that Kircher has failed to treat language consistently in his three sections, or to provide anything like a coherent theory about communication throughout his many writings. Yes, on the face of things Kircher's linguistic attitude is incoherent: at times Kircher imagines communication as an unimpeded flow of thought connecting entities already joined by a prior "sympathy," and at times he imagines it as a merely technical business of copying down letters and looking up entries in a dictionary. Language is a different object according to the different situations in which Kircher imagines and addresses it.

To reduce the problem to the dimensions of the *Polygraphia nova*, Kircher divides language into two and ascribes part of it to a universal register, primarily semantic, where the purpose of collocating dictionary entries is to make meanings and access to meanings problem-free. This is language in the register of the church: the "arithmetical nomenclator" was devised by a fellow cleric for use in a multinational, multilingual brotherhood implanted on five continents and monitored by a constant flow of documents in a standard language (Latin). The nomenclator simplifies and speeds up access to what the other person is trying to say (at least, that is what it does in principle, whatever the difficulties attached to its execution). A second register is reserved for different modes of communication: this is the register where the writer seeks to keep meaning private, to restrict access to a tiny number of qualified readers equipped with decoding devices. This is language as it is used in courts and diplomatic missions: the language of alphabetic substitutions, where what matters is not transmitting meanings in their immediacy but frustrating the unchosen reader, to the point of composing messages that deny they are private at all (the word-for-a-letter cipher). Competence in this second language is conferred by the bestowal of an artifact, the precious steganographic "ark." With its dictionaries and "arks," the Kircherian information workshop is divided between two languages, each passing for "language," and the difference between them is (roughly speaking) political. Instead of a linguistics or a theory of communication, we should see in Kircher's *Polygraphia nova* an essay in verbal technology, a set of methods for transmuting messages into new forms. But the reason for transforming a message into this or that form will depend on the purpose of communication. It is as if there were no category of language-as-such.

The moment, narrated by Kircher, where an attempt at making a universal linguistic science of some kind (whether this was to be a newfound code or a primordial idiom) fell apart and led to a mere linguistic technology is not irrelevant to the project of the *Polygraphia nova*. It leaves traces; these are to be seen particularly in the chapter titles, the introductory sections and closing paragraphs with their exuberant promises, and the cross-references to this work in other productions such as the *Ars magna sciendi* (*Great Art of Knowing*). The difference between the two registers is not just that between promise and delivery, it mirrors the two worlds among which Kircher—for all his oddities, an extremely sensitive and agile social actor—negotiated his career.

Kircher saw the communicative landscape as a hostile territory dotted with tiny pockets of qualified readers. The experience of the previous century, with its religious wars cutting kingdoms apart and separating areas of like belief and policy from each other, obviously weighed on his thinking, as it would have in the case of any traveler or letter writer in confessionally divided Europe. But across the hostile spaces or in the magnetic atmosphere above them, communication takes place, as for example between two pieces of mutually grafted skin, and Kircher supposes a system of forces or waves that the properly prepared observer will see at work everywhere. In other words, communication is sovereign, though perhaps not just now: for the time being, we talk to each other in the guarded codes of court and diplomacy. John Wilkins, veteran of one great religious war, saw what was at stake in the "Reduction of All Languages to One": the imposition of a single universal language, "repairing the curse of Babel," was unlikely "until some person attain the Universal Monarchy."[44] Kircher was, in his way, preparing the kingdom.

Notes

1. Kircher 1663, p. 2.
2. On Tironian notes, see Boge 1973; Trithemius 1518, book 6; and Arnold 1971, p. 59. On their potential as an interlinguistic communication device, see Selenus 1624, pp. 370, 394 (quoting Hugo 1617). On the correspondence between Selenus and Kircher, see Fletcher, 1986.
3. For descriptions of the Spaniard's and Becher's inventions, see Schott 1664, pp. 483–503; and Becher 1661. Kircher's "Novum inventum linguarum omnium," distributed in manuscript as of 1660, prefigures both *Polygraphia nova* and *Ars magna sciendi* (Kircher 1669). Two surviving manuscript copies of the "Novum inventum" are Biblioteca Apostolica Vaticana, MS. Chigiani I. vi. 225, and Herzog August Bibliothek, Cod. Guelf. 3.5. Aug. 4°. See Marrone 1986; Strasser 1979; and for Leibniz's dismissive comments, see Leibniz 1903, pp. 536–537.
4. Vigenère 1586.
5. For a description of these two artifices, see Wilding 2001a. For a contemporary critique of these devices as trivial mechanical substitutes for genuine speech, see Kuhlmann 1674. An artifice identical to the "Extension" had been published some years earlier in a popular edition, "for the recreation of honored ladies and growing youths," by Johann Just Winckelmann (see Weinsheun 1657). Winckelmann belonged to the circle of wits that gathered around Kircher's correspondent and occasional patron, Duke August of Braunschweig-Lüneburg.
6. Such assessments will be familiar to any reader of the scholarly record on Kircher: see, for example, Thorndike 1923–58, vol. 8, pp. 567–587; Godwin 1979, Rossi 1960, and Yates 1971. Marrone 1986, p. 85, speaks of "an apparent contradiction . . . an antinomy perfectly aligned with the polyhedric personality of Kircher."
7. Kircher 1643b, pp. 333–346. See also "Appendix Apologetica," Kircher 1663, p. 18. Kircher 1646, pp. 907–908, applies similar reasonings to telescopes and mirrors.
8. Kircher 1643b, pp. 463, 469. For scoffing at "old wives' tales" about flesh grafts and other cases of "like calling to like," see p. 334. But the credence accorded quite similar tales in book III of the same work leads one to suspect that the disprized stories had in common the fact that they were recounted by "plebei illi Philosophastri" (those lowborn pseudo-philosophers).
9. Kircher to Duke August the Younger, 18 January 1650. See Fletcher 1986, p. 284.
10. For an inventory of natural phenomena that can be used as communicative devices, see Kircher 1643b, pp. 334–335.
11. Kircher 1665a, pp. 144–145.
12. Kircher 1646, pp. 806–807.
13. Kircher 1676, p. 20.
14. Kircher 1663, p. 6. On this work and its history, see Wilding 2001a.
15. Descartes to Mersenne, 20 November 1629; Descartes 1969, vol. 1, pp. 76–82. As far as I can tell, Descartes is not mentioned once in Kircher's voluminous works.
16. Bacon, *Advancement of Learning* (1605), in Bacon 1968, vol. 3, pp. 399–400.
17. Descartes 1969, vol. 1, pp. 79–80.
18. Besnier 1675 (original edition Paris, 1674), p. 3. Besnier's essay is introduced here simply as an example of a type, not as the specific inspiration for Descartes or Kircher (that would be

impossible, given that Descartes's letter dates from 1629 and Kircher must have received his commission from Ferdinand III around 1655).

19. Besnier 1675, pp. 52, 62–63.
20. Kircher 1679a, p. 218.
21. Devos and Seligman 1967, pp. 1–3.
22. Schott 1664, pp. 479–480. On this restricted "publication" of wooden artifacts, see again Wilding 2001a.
23. See the illustration and description (chapter title: "In quo mundus organo comparatur") in Kircher 1650a, vol. 2, p. 366.
24. Kircher 1663, p. 85.
25. Ibid., p. 130.
26. Ibid., p. 141. For similar invocations of huge numbers drawn from combinations, see Harsdörffer 1651, p. 516; Alsted 1652, p. 14; Leibniz 1768, vol. 2, p. 375 (original publication 1665); Weinsheun 1692, p. 4.
27. Trithemius 1608, pp. 1–2. For evidence of Kircher's early interest in Trithemius, see Kircher 1643b, pp. 338–340, where the 1608 edition of *Steganographia* is dismissed as the unreliable concoction of "plebeian men." Arnold (1971, p. 188), continues to doubt the authenticity of the later books of *Steganographia*. Kircher and Schott both perform a great deal of recycling of Trithemius's various writings, not only the cryptographic texts but also his astrological history of humanity (Trithemius 1567). All three men were from the same region of southern Germany (Fulda–Würzburg). The Trithemius connection has most recently been explored by Eco 2001.
28. On this episode, see Schott 1665; Arnold 1971; and Victor 1978, pp. 33, 54–55.
29. Trithemius 1518.
30. Yates 1971, p. 208. Like Yates, other commentators take the last chapters of *Steganographia* as straightforward conjuring (for example, Eco 2001). But it is at least possible that a further sense hides beneath the necromantic rhetoric; the lesson of cryptography, as demonstrated by *Polygraphia*, is that the absence of a hidden meaning can never be proved, only supposed.
31. Selenus 1624, pp. 41–42.
32. "So it is that alphabetical script, as a combination of atoms of writing, is the farthest removed from the script of sacred complexes. These latter take the form of hieroglyphics" (Benjamin 1977, p. 175).
33. Alluding to Combe 1614. On Kircher's machines, their "special effects," and their educative functions, see Gorman 2001.
34. Descartes 1969, vol. 10, pp. 231–232. For an exact Kircherian parallel to the magnetic tightrope artist, see Gorman 2001, p. 68. The same notebook page contains Descartes's critique of the art of memory, as practiced by one Lambert Schenkel: Descartes maintains that memory is not a problem for the investigator who can hold the "chain of sciences" (*catena scientiarum*) in his head. Mnemonics is thus like a machine constructed in unconvincing imitation of knowledge (the chain): it substitutes adventitious links and detours for the rational chain itself. On this break with the traditional memory art, see Yates 1971, pp. 359–361.
35. Descartes 1985, vol. 1, pp. 140–141; original in Descartes 1969, vol. 6, p. 56.
36. Compare the poem as originally printed (reproduced in Maché and Meid 1980, pp. 268–269), and its ever-changing electronic implementation (Kuhlmann 1998). On Kuhlmann's theological ideas and correspondence with Kircher, see Gillespie 1978.
37. Kuhlmann 1960, p. 26.
38. Harsdörffer 1651, p. 517. *Fortgrorcht* was generated from the Beinecke Library's copy, on 10 November 1985.
39. Benjamin 1977, pp. 180–181.
40. Leibniz 1903, pp. 532–533.
41. Foucault 1966, pp. 3–35.
42. Eco 1995. Eco's remarks on *Polygraphia nova* in Lo Sardo 2001 resort to the now-traditional gesture of citing Borges's invented Chinese encyclopedia with its absurd categories (cf. Foucault 1966, p. 3).
43. Stillman 1995.
44. Wilkins 1668, p. 20.

12
Publishing the Polygraphy
Manuscript, Instrument, and Print in the Work of Athanasius Kircher

NICK WILDING

How did early modern intellectual and political elites view the nature and role of communication? What were the perceived deficiencies in systems of exchanging information, and what remedies were proposed? How were individual and group interests manifested in projects for the social reorganization of networks? This essay will approach these key issues to understanding the business of knowledge control in the early modern period by reconstructing the material circulation of letters, tracts, instruments, and printed books containing Athanasius Kircher's proposal for a new and universal language.

On 4 August 1663, Juan Caramuel Lobkowitz, one of the pillars of seventeenth-century Catholic erudition, wrote to his longtime correspondent, his "Mirror of Wisdom," Athanasius Kircher. The letter was remarkable, not so much for its content, but more for its choice of language: it is the only surviving example of a text written in Kircher's own invented universal language scheme.[1] Kircher had published, earlier the same year, a book called *The New and Universal Polygraphy* (1663),[2] which has long been recognized as an example of the early modern European obsession with constructing a single language to undo the curse of Babel, the confusing multiplicity of languages.[3] While the problem (as it was then conceived) of linguistic plurality occupied a wide variety of European intellectuals, from philosophers such as Descartes and Leibniz to religious and social reformers such as Campanella, Comenius and Hartlib, in the case of Athanasius Kircher we must look beyond some vague notion of a common "worldview" to explain why he wrote, circulated, rewrote and published his language scheme. This essay will attempt to take Caramuel's message out of the dusty *wunderkammer* of Renaissance intellectual curiosa, and explore its meanings by reconstructing the traces of power and writing it bore with it and which made it possible.

Our larger field of inquiry, which was also that of Kircher, is the relationship between the material culture of communication and what might be termed a grammatology (a study of the history and meaning of writing itself). Indeed, we find in Kircher's work a manipulation and transformation of terms such as "script," "language" and "writing" that provide us with the very opportunity of forging their history. Using a combination of new archival material and new approaches to that material, I hope to sketch out a moment in history where writing enters into a new contract with power. In the case of Kircher's universal language, indeed, the nature and practice of writing are reformulated in a spectacular attempt to rehardwire the centers and networks of desired political power—a new script for a new world order.

First, we should attempt to understand the workings of Kircher's invented language. The system worked by allowing a person using one language to write letters in a notation that a recipient could then retranslate into his own language. The universal language was made up of a series of thirty-two lists, numbered with Roman numerals and printed on separate pages, each containing a selection of thirty-two to forty phrases, names, places, dates, or numbers in five languages (Latin, Italian, French, Spanish and German). The total vocabulary of the language consisted of 1,048 terms. Each term, in all five languages, was given a value in the polygraphic code by its table number and position in that table. XVI.6 "meant" osculari, basciare, baiser, besar, Küssen, or translating all these terms into English, "to kiss." A basic Latinate grammar was provided by adding supplementary signs to the Roman and Arabic terms: N signifies nominative, and so forth. Words not included in the language's limited vocabulary were to be supplied in traditional script, and syntax was to be based on Latin word order.[4] Thus "XXVIII.10.XVI.23.Å Kircher" (the opening of Caramuel's letter) meant "Father Kircher, mirror of wisdom."

Two dictionaries, for encoding and decoding the language, were organized in a hybrid structure using both alphabetical and conceptual systems: the second dictionary, used for writing in the language, consisted of thirty-two tables. Tables 1–23 contained the alphabetically organized general vocabulary, while the remaining tables were organized under conceptual headings, in the following order: table 24 listed countries; 25, cities; 26, time; 27, proper names; 28, adverbs; 29, prepositions; 30, pronouns; 31, the main forms of the verb "to be"; and finally, 32, forms of "to have." The first dictionary, for reading a message into a vernacular, was similarly divided into two parts, with a general vocabulary, following Latin alphabetical order, and a second section, containing the other categories.

A few basic points need to be made about the form chosen for the "polygraphy." The system was a pasigraphy, or purely written language; no spoken form was ever deemed desirable. This may seem an inconsequential point, but in fact Kircher's prioritization of the written over the spoken is worth analyzing. The distinction may at first seem to be the classic philosophical debate between the conflicting claims of speaking and writing to represent truth. Certainly, this epistemological tension constantly resurfaces in early modern writings on writing. But perhaps Kircher's writing was something more specific than a pasigraphy: his concern, even in the printed text, was with producing less a language than a kind of universal cipher—a code open to all its recipients. This first, sociological fact goes hand in hand with two others: the second is generic or functional—the polygraphy was specifically designed to be good only for letter writing, not for the production of other texts—it consolidates epistolary bureaucracy; the third fact is technological—the character of the code was originally designed to be handwritten, not printed. This last fact may not be immediately obvious, as the polygraphy was, ultimately, printed. As we shall see later, a printable version of the vocabulary was a late development in its written form—all earlier versions contained drawn, iconic marks rather than Roman numerals. The polygraphy was thus designed for a particular type of information exchange—elites, in possession of its key, were meant to exchange handwritten letters (of a limited vocabulary) with other initiates. Far from being either universal, or a language, the polygraphy was, from the beginning, intentionally restricted, socially and philosophically.

How did this paradoxical creature, a book not meant to be published, a writing not meant to be printed, come into existence?

Kircher's own retrospective account of the genesis of his polygraphy, printed in the 1663 *Polygraphy*, is worth recounting. He explained that the suggestion for constructing a universal language came directly from Ferdinand III. Kircher remembers being

> at first distraught, then justly aware of my own stupidity, then terrified by the difficulty of the proposed subject, not being up to it, so I gave up any hope of undoing the knot. But with renewed spirit, driven on by the great agitation of my mind, I began to think over this invention, at least if I might be able to render it probable, even if not work it out in practice. Then, having examined the promises established by all the Combinatory Arts, and finding nothing to my taste in the reasons I had assembled, at last with the help of God the way occurred to me by which I hoped I could give the Emperor full satisfaction. The Emperor now being long-since dead, I showed this to Leopold I, son and successor of his glorious father, in a box divided into combinatory tables.[5]

The narrative seems simple: the emperor sets a puzzle, and Kircher solves it. But from Kircher's correspondence, it is possible to reconstruct the system of brokerage that allowed him to insert himself into this patronage system, and to understand why such a gift might have been of interest to the two emperors.

Kircher's *Polygraphy*, as he explicitly states, is a reworking of two texts by the German humanist scholar and abbot, Johann Trithemius: his own *Polygraphy* and a *Steganography*. Both works were widely read and discussed, generating a polemical charge of necromancy even during Trithemius' lifetime. The latter was a work on codes and ciphers that circulated throughout the second half of the sixteenth century in manuscript, was finally published in 1606 by Protestants, and immediately put on the Index.[6]

Kircher first entered this debate in 1640, in a private correspondence with the powerful Czech politician Bernhard Ignaz von Martinitz.[7] Up until 1640,

Kircher had published only on magnetism, sundials, mirrors and Coptic. It was this last subject that, for Martinitz, made Kircher a likely client for the courtly production of a Catholic steganography. He writes, in a section marked "N.B." by Kircher, that the *Introduction to Coptic, or Egyptian*[8] had shown him that Kircher was able to "penetrate the basis of the varieties of all languages."[9]

When Martinitz left for Vienna at the end of 1640, he made sure that Kircher had a secure channel to the emperor via his Jesuit confessor, Padre Johann Gans.[10] Court confessors played a crucial, if understudied, role in early modern political and intellectual life, not merely as powerful individuals, but as privileged nodes in the networks of religious organizations. Even though Kircher had previously served the emperor by inventing his "pantometer," a kind of mathematical Swiss-army knife, in 1631,[11] he used his confrere Gans to secure access to Ferdinand for his new projects. The next we hear of Kircher's steganographic work in the imperial court is through this contact, five years later, in 1645. Gans writes to say that he has received a "new steganography" for the emperor from Kircher.[12] The work is now lost, but it may well have been a standard Trithemian combinatory code.

With this paradoxical product, a copy of a code with no users, safely with the emperor, Kircher had to give his system value by constructing a network around it. He turned to the emperor's brother, Leopold Wilhelm, the governor of the Spanish Netherlands from 1646 to 1655, whom he had been courting in the late 1640s to accept the dedication of his *Universal Music-making* (1650),[13] via Leopold's Jesuit confessor, Johannes Schega in Brussels. Kircher's new patron expressed his desire to receive a new gift, which had apparently already been offered through Schega, of the "artifice of writing letters in any kind of language."[14] But the demands of polygraphy and steganography remained intertwined: a few months later, Schega, on behalf of the governor, asked Kircher to decipher a numerical code, as he was already considered to be a riddle-solving "Oedipus."[15] Again, the specter of Trithemius' codes entered the correspondence, with a request for Kircher to explain the more obscure passages.[16] Kircher seems to have responded, not with a discussion of the *Steganography*, but with his own cipher system, perhaps the same one he had presented to Ferdinand III six years previously.[17] This seems to be part of a renewed effort to establish an elite to use his code systems, because a few months later he wrote to Ferdinand, explicitly recalling his earlier work on Trithemius and displaying his new cryptographic discoveries in an accompanying tract.[18]

Organizing Knowledge

In the 1640s and 1650s, as we have seen, Kircher used two interrelated systems of steganographic communication: letters and tracts. In 1649, he had invented the first of his "Arcae" or "Cistae"—boxes containing a system of wooden slats with information on them, which could be manipulated to make calculations.[19] More a slide rule than a Pascalian computing device, they nevertheless made attractive presents to curious patrons. Cheap, portable, and full of promise, they were designed to reify any domain of knowledge. These organs, as they were also called, because they superficially resembled musical organs, formed a supplementary system of dissemination of polygraphic and steganographic systems. These economies of publication, epistolary, tractate, instrumental and printed, were not discrete and isolated, but always spilling into and running through each other.

Ferdinand III died in 1657, and was succeeded by his son, the seventeen-year-old Leopold I. Leopold's confessor was, yet again, a Jesuit, Philipp Müller. The early years of the new emperor's reign saw a concerted move by the Jesuits to reimpose a Counter-Reformation ethos on the empire through its leader.[20] This domestic consolidation also necessitated an attempt to create a new Catholic world order, and Kircher's exploitation of his preexisting patronage network to establish an international elite community for his universal language should be seen as part of this Jesuit policy. If the early steganographic works were created as a kind of courtly distillation of the exigencies of war, and the first polygraphic drafts as an idealized attempt to bring the postwar polyglot empire into harmony, the circulation of both steganographic and polygraphic manuscripts at the end of the decade may be seen as an attempt to extend this program into the field of international diplomacy.

Extending his role of virtual courtier beyond Habsburg circles, Kircher next attempted to bring the Medici rulers of Florence into his elite group, exploiting the relationship between Grand Duke Ferdinand II and Emperor Ferdinand III "by name, for genius in literature, and by family-ties."[21]

In November 1659, Kircher sent the first of his polygraphic organs to the Grand Duke. The existing letters between Rome and Florence show that the "promised artificial secret of languages, enclosed in a little box,"[22] was sent to the Medici court in an attempt to extend the domain of Kircher's imperial polygraphic patronage network. Kircher first mentions the "artifice of languages" to the Grand Duke on 8 November, claiming that it has already been "strongly desired for a long time by the Emperor and Archduke Leopold."[23] The gift of the "secret" gains its value by the restricted economy in which it has circulated, and its "novelty." In an undated letter, written shortly after this exchange, Kircher finally sent the organ.[24] The "secret" was shared only by Leopold I and Leopold Wilhelm, both described as "great patrons of my studies," a role obviously being offered to the Grand Duke too. To underline the secrecy of the supposedly universal language, Kircher also sent a steganographic manuscript.

This present of the "linguistic ark" and steganographic manuscript to the Grand Duke was coordinated with presentation copies of the "Artifice of a New Steganography" to Leopold I and Archduke Leopold Wilhelm[25] and the "Artifice of the Universal Language" to Bernhard Ignaz von Martinitz, Duke August of Brunswick-Lüneburg, Pope Alexander VII, and Leopold I.[26]

Kircher's letter of presentation to Leopold I explains that while the language is self-explanatory, the emperor's confessor Müller will be able to describe its workings in detail.[27] The language-gift functions at least three levels: one is practical and internal, in that it offers the "Supreme Transactor in human affairs" "advantages for the administration of Imperial matters"; at another level, the gift works as a kind of self-representation of Kircher's intellectual and spiritual unifying genius, which should be seen as a metonym for the entire Society of Jesus; it is also designed to consolidate the relationship between Müller and the emperor, in that it creates the professional role of Jesuit polygrapher to supplement the text, a role that may be replicated with every copy of the manuscript.

Leopold's response to the polygraphic manuscript was favorable: Martinitz wrote back to Kircher a couple of months later that "The Emperor wrote to me that he has received your new work titled The Reduction of All Languages to One, which he says he has sweated over and overcome with the Archduke, and that he wants me to deal with paying generously for the supply of the book."[28] This is the first mention of a shift from an economy of manuscript circulation to one of book publication.

The *Polygraphy* was eventually made up of three sections—the polygraphy, the steganographic letter, and a Trithemian combinatory code section, plus an apologetic appendix with separate pagination. These three parts had circulated in overlapping economies: the combinatory code may well have formed the lost steganographic treatises to Ferdinand III from the 1640s; the steganographic letter had been used to link Brussels, Vienna, and Florence; the polygraphy extended this network of alliances to Rome, Prague, and later, Wolfenbüttel.

The book publication of the three sets of manuscripts that had circulated in Kircher's restricted, but expanding, economy was to be dedicated to Leopold Wilhelm. He accepted his copy of the polygraphic manuscript in April 1660, in a letter that later became a posthumous letter of acceptance for all three systems.[29] The polygraphy, unlike the steganographic tracts, necessitated publication, for it to perform Kircher's task, in the archduke's words, of "rendering almost unilingual the people of the World's countries, who are mutually at odds with each other by such a variety of languages, bringing into harmony the dissonance of so many different and unknown voices by the most ingenious invention of signs common to all, and teach the natural stupidity of human tongues to correct itself with art and mute letters."

Educating the Prince

The momentum of the campaign was increasing, and an elite community of potential users was in place. For the polygraphy to gain real value, though, it had to be presented not just as a meta-language to an existing system, but as a formative instrument to be incorporated automatically into the next generation's statecraft. Kircher turned his attention towards the emperor's youngest brother, Karl Joseph. Via his Jesuit correspondents Johann Baptist van Hollant and Phillipp Müller, Kircher had indirect access to the prince. By 1660, Kircher had already sent the eleven-year-old prince a copy of the polygraphic manuscript, which van Hollant claimed he liked immensely.[30]

That the manuscript was actually read by its recipient, unlike so many other dedicatory tracts of the time, is shown by a comment forwarded by van Hollant from the young prince who was being subjected to Kircher's experimental pedagogics: in the published version of the polygraphic language, the manuscript's use of icons to organize the fifty-four tables of terms was replaced with thirty-two tables marked by Roman numerals. The manuscript version organizes its vocabulary conceptually: all the language's animals, as well as the terms "animal" and "quadruped," are found under the icon of a cow; instruments, from pens to ploughs, are designated by an icon of a compass, plus their corresponding number. For some of the more abstract terms, letters are used, which abbreviate the group's organizing principle; so "CB" (cibus) designates "food." The fifty-four categories derive from the Lullist Combinatory Art, the icons mainly from Kircher's interpretations of hieroglyphs. Kircher did not regard them as an arbitrary system, but as a way of gaining direct access to the universe as it really was. The icons were later to provide the conceptual vocabulary for *The Great Art of Knowing* (1669).[31]

In terms of the general development of artificial languages in the seventeenth century, the movement from a polygraphy based on an alphabetic word list to a conceptually based vocabulary has been seen as a critical paradigm shift. Kircher's production moves in the opposite direction, which has led some historians to regard it as the "wrong" direction.[32] Van Hollant's letter shows that far from withdrawing from an impending epistemological crisis, Kircher's transformation of his polygraphy from a conceptual to an alphabetic system was due to his patron's practical requirements. The supposedly fundamental paradigm shift was, in fact, all too easy to negotiate, and its explanation is rather banal: the eleven-year-old Karl Joseph found the little icons of angels, trees, and the like, too difficult to draw. Numerical codes were suggested as an easier option.[33] This point may seem insignificant, but it opens up two very different notions of early modern writing: Kircher used his icons because they were instrumental signs—leading, in themselves (and not via an arbitrary linguistic system), to enlightening meaning. Thus writing (or drawing) is seen as a means of access to a higher reality. For the prince, the graphic sign is above all a means of writing as a technology—its efficacy and ease is more important than the status of the symbol. The construction of philosophical symbolism comes into conflict with its writing, at the material level of sign production.

The campaign to educate the young prince into steganographic practices continued in 1661, when Kircher sent him another of his boxes of knowledge—this time a mathematical organ that contained thirty different disciplines, one of which was steganography.[34] The instrument required a user to explain and manipulate its workings, and Kircher proposed his friend the mathematician Godefrid Alois Kinner von Löwenthurm, the archduke's tutor, to act as an on-the-spot operator in Kircher's absence. Again, we see that Kircher's instruments are not just princely gifts, but ways of securing court functions for members of his network. The expertise required of such an instrument operator would later be published in book form by Schott,[35] but at this stage of Kircher's steganographic publication, the stress is laid on a different economy of knowledge, which is transferable only to specific sites and through chosen personnel.

Kinner accepted the role of instrument operator when the organ finally arrived in December 1661.[36] But the instrument was immediately found to contain many mistakes in its information, so Kinner also had to correct these embarrassing errors, in a letter accompanying Joseph Karl's thank-you note.[37] A few months later, Kinner received some additional explanations from Kircher, even though he had since discovered that the organ contained other problems, such as an inadequate section on fortification. One of the disciplines already covered by the pupil and his tutor was steganography, in which the young archduke excelled.[38] A year later, Kircher's organ market showed signs of expanding along the same lines as his steganographic manuscript network, as he sent a steganographic chest to his old cryptologist correspondent, Duke August of Brunswick-Lüneburg, as a present for his son Ferdinand Albrecht.[39]

The specificity of these organs, and the need for an operator well versed in their functions and a patron willing to be educated by a box, gave them a short practical shelf life. In 1664, Karl Joseph died, and the organ's status became problematic. Kinner inherited the organ, and he offered to publish an account of its workings with Schott.[40] But in 1666, before Schott had managed to publish the account of the organ, he, too, died. Kinner wrote again to Kircher, to inform him of the news, and ask if he knew what had become of the organ. He even suggests that it might have been buried with Schott, as though it had finally found its role as a postmortem prosthesis.[41] When the posthumous account, edited by Kinner, finally came out in 1668, the organ was still lost, and Kinner seemed to have given up hope of trying to find it.[42] Printing an account of an instrument did not only spread knowledge of the original, it could render the original redundant.

Into Print

With Karl Joseph's indirect demand for Kircher's "sacrifice" of his iconic system, the text for the book was now stabilized, and rather than sending a new round of manuscripts to incorporate the changes, Kircher moved toward a limited edition print run for the *Polygraphy*, which was kept out of the commercial market and only ever available as a gift from the author.[43]

The generally received view that early modern print guaranteed a standardization of scientific knowldge in its very repeatability has recently been challenged. Instead, it is argued, the practicalities of the printshop produced texts that were anything but uniform. Piracy undermined authorial control, and the supposed authority of print was constructed in long and difficult campaigns.[44] To this critique, one might add that a case such as Kircher's *Polygraphy* offers another corrective: the seventeenth-century printed book could also contain manuscript text, inserted in the process of both production and reception. Annotated copies transform the printed monologue into an active dialogue, and bear witness to a power relationship between author and 'reader' that modifies the notion of print as an end point in book production. At the same time, the author himself often modified his text, either at the level of correction or by inserting personalized frames into the book in the form of dedicatory notes or covering letters (which were often then pasted into the printed volume by the recipient). In the case of a limited edition gift publication, such as the *Polygraphy*, we see almost all copies of the text bearing some dedicatory note. Kircher's notes remove the book from the public market and reinsert it into the realms of epistolary networks and manuscript publications.

Kircher started sending out copies of his *Polygraphy* in June 1663.[45] The first examples seem, appropriately enough, to have been sent to the emperor, although Kircher's dedicatory letter no longer exists. Müller, the emperor's confessor, acknowledges receipt of two copies, sent 15 June.[46] Müller himself presented a copy to Leopold, while van Hollant presented the other copy to Karl Joseph. Indeed, this act of presentation may be seen as the central meaning of the book, for it seems unlikely that Leopold ever read his dedicated copy: the emperor was swamped with work for at least the next fortnight, and was still recovering from an illness. Karl Joseph, who would die the following year, was also in convalescence. In a letter sent a few days later, Kinner, whom Kircher had entrusted with the manipulation of his organ, made it clear that the Karl Joseph had still not had time to look at the book. Worse, he informed Kircher that his universal language had a precedent (of which Kircher seems unaware), in Johannes Becher's *Character*.[47] A month later, the potentially grave situation was looking much better: any notion of plagiarism had been reversed, and Karl Joseph, despite his illness, was taking a real interest in the polygraphic system, encoding and decoding letters. Kircher's dictionary was found to be too limited, "lacking even common words," so that a vernacular letter had to be rewritten several times before it could be put into the universal script. This made the writing of letters tedious. Far from being seen as a completed project, the printed *Polygraphy* was viewed by its first readers as just part of an ongoing process. In addition to offering critiques, Kinner already wrote that he hoped the next edition, from Kircher's Amsterdam publishers Jansson, would provide a fuller polyglot dictionary with a running numerical key.[48]

The next copies of the *Polygraphy* sent out by Kircher show the dissemination of prestige enveloping the book. On 20 June, copies were sent to Duke August of Brunswick-Lüneburg and his son Ferdinand Albrecht, who had previously received Kircher's steganographic manuscripts and organ. The work is described as being "destined for the recreation and use of Princes," and Kircher asks his recipients to forward other copies to Johann Friedrich of Lüneburg, in Hanover, and the electors of Saxony and Brandenburg.[49] These copies also are already inscribed with dedications. Kircher asks this favor of forwarding the books because of his "real poverty and want," but the system might also be viewed as creating a hierarchy of dissemination, with prestige filtered and added at each stage, in a way that would be lacking in a centralized network. These extra copies thus bear a double trace—the originary mark of production, from the book's posthumous dedicatee, Leopold Wilhelm (which is combined with the Imperial order to publish), and a secondary mark from Duke August. These copies, textually identical to those disseminated in Italy, for example, become almost another publication, as they gain the approval of the (Protestant) duke.[50] The book's content also necessitates this act of rendering visible the dynamics of its dissemination. To construct even a fiction of a potential community of polygraphic or steganographic writers, its members' identities must be signaled to each other.

The following day, 21 June, Kircher continued replicating the preestablished manuscript and instrument network in the dissemination of the printed text. Writing separately to Grand Duke Ferdinand II[51] and Leopoldo de' Medici,[52] Kircher again points out that the book is "fitting only for Princes." The *Polygraphy*'s imperial origin is stressed, but the book receives a rather different representation, as an experimental proof that resolved an apparently impossible paradox, for it to fit into the Medici's famous taste for experimentation and novelty. Kircher also represents himself as primarily a member of the Republic of Letters, rather than a Jesuit, to play the Medici courtier, and he even requests a contribution for his expanding museum from the Grand Duke. Again, the gift received only a formal acknowledgment that implied the book had not been opened. The Grand Duke said the book was judged to be "very useful, and really worthy of your famous and original intelligence."[53] Leopoldo's letter does not even mention the book's title, and it refers only to his pleasure in seeing pieces "so worthy of your virtuous tasks."[54] On the same day, Kircher sent a copy to Vincenzo Viviani, disciple and biographer of Galileo, and perhaps the most famous natural philosopher in the Medici court, but received no reply.[55]

In the following months, copies of the book were sent to a number of patrons, both potential and actual. Kircher, unfortunately, did not draw up a mailing list, but the responses preserved in his correspondence allow for at least a partial reconstruction of the network. Following the chronology of the responses, which may well offer only a refracted view of the order of mailing, we see that Italian and German princes were Kircher's ideal reader/users. From July to November, letters came from Castiglione, Naples, Turin, Heitersheim, Munich, Mantua and Prague.[56] Even before receiving the book, Heinrich Maximlian, elector of Cologne, wrote to thank the author for having given his agent in Rome a copy.[57]

These letters of reply, as one might expect, are formal and anodyne. Certain eulogistic adjectives recur: Kircher is curious, original, erudite and tireless. The volume is certainly appreciated as a gift—Ferdinando Giovanni di Gonzaga immediately says he will have the book bound, and send Kircher one of his medals (no doubt to be placed in Kircher's famous museum). But there is no talk of establishing a network of users for either the code or the polygraphy, no inquiries for the identities of the other recipients, no engagement with the contents of the book at all.

Almost the sole exception to this general observation is the response from Juan Caramuel Lobkowitz. He had been in correspondence with Kircher since 1644, on a variety of subjects: astronomy, music, mathematics, theology and philosophy. In the autumn of 1663, he was in the process of institutionalizing the Accademia degli Investigatori, a Baconian scientific research group linked to the Royal Society and the Accademia del Cimento. A Cistercian, Caramuel had received a Jesuit education at Madrid, and he became a staunch supporter of the Society.

As we have seen, the general initial response to the *Polygraphia* was of polite curiosity. For the work to have any intellectual impact, it needed some post-launch publicity, and Caramuel was the ideal figure to give his blessing to the scheme. His own works included treatments of steganography and universal grammar, his intellectual reputation, within orthodox Catholic circles, was unassailable, and he occupied a privileged position both internationally (with strong contacts in Rome, Vienna, and Madrid) and institutionally (both in the Vatican and Naples). His polyglot and polygraphic letter to Kircher of 4 August 1663, which opened this essay, combines these social and intellectual resources. It eulogizes the Emperor Leopold, Kircher's former patron, and Kircher himself. More importantly, it shows, both in its content and existence, that the language was not merely a curious idea, but could work practically. It was easy to learn, as is explicitly stated by the self-referential claim that the letter itself was written the same day Caramuel received the *Polygraphy*. And it gestured toward the construction of an initial community of language users, with its various translators offering multiple points of access to the "original" polygraphic letter via their translations into Italian, Spanish, French, German, and Czech.

The letter was copied, and the polygraphic version presented to Alexander VII. It seems that the letter was expressly written to be included in a second edition of the *Polygraphy*. In Caramuel's *Philosophical Critique* (1681), he claims that the book went through a second edition in Amsterdam in 1680, the year of Kircher's death, but this edition does not seem to exist.[58] In a letter to Leibniz, written in 1670, Kircher discusses the origin of the *Polygraphy* and claims that after the first edition in Rome in 1663, a second edition was published in Paris, and that a third edition is being prepared, with a ten-language dictionary, by Jansson.[59] Southwell's entry for Kircher in the *Library of Writers of the Society of Jesus* makes no mention of either the second or third edition.[60] In a letter dated 18 June 1664, Jansson and Weyerstraet say that they are waiting for the "Poligraphia" (it is not clear whether a new manuscript or a copy of the Rome edition is intended).[61] Two years later, they say, without explicitly mentioning the *Polygraphy*, that the Anglo-Dutch wars have held up all up printing work for the last two and a half years, blocking the supply of paper from France and making it "extraordinarily expensive."[62] In a rather nice historical irony, the book born out of wartime concern with the safe transmission of material messages had its own dissemination indefinitely deferred by another war.

Given this blockage of a direct line of reproduction and dissemination of the *Polygraphy*, its contents were filtered through the channels of Schott's publications. In 1664, his *Curious Technology* contained résumés of Becher's and Kircher's projects, repositioning them firmly within the tradition of hard technology that instrumentalization had made possible.[63] The year after, Schott produced an entire book devoted to steganographic and polygraphic systems. The *Steganographic School* positions Kircher's work within a long genealogy of steganographic and polygraphic projects, citing, in the introduction, Trithemius, Cardano, della Porta, Vignère, Puteanus, Hugo, Duke August, and Kircher. This marshaling of the history of writing was designed to provide a triumphal teleology, culminating in Kircher's work. But it also relativizes that position by offering alternative projects and a local explanation, in terms of patronage, which somehow undermines the proposed universality of the project. Kircher had attempted to avoid charges of parochialism by operating at the highest levels of patronage—the empire and the papacy—and then disseminating his project and authority in a trickle-down model. Already in Schott's publication, we see that the project has become just another "curiosity" for German princes (the *Steganographic School* is dedicated to the marquis of Baden and Hochbergen). The claims for universal authority from local sites of production could obviously be replicated in rival sites, and the period 1650 to 1670 witnessed a new multiplicity of universal languages, setting out to restore a unified, pre-Babel tongue.

In reconstructing the chronology of the production, dissemination, and consumption of the various stages and forms of the polygraphy, I hope to have shown that the relationship between a set of ideas and their material media is complex, self-modifying, and locally circumscribed. While the printed *Polygraphy*, for instance, uses a different graphic system from that of earlier manuscript versions, this has less to do with a deterministic link between the medium and the message, and more to do with the requirements of patrons and clients. That the very medium in which these requirements were brokered, the letter, becomes the object undergoing reformulation tells us that both these requirements and the letter were viewed as centrally important to the safe functioning of the court and the religious society. We might care to reevaluate Kircher's spectacular failure to unify the languages of the world in the light of his success in portraying the exchange of letters (the tool of the bureaucratizing state and the republic of letters) as a system, a system that could itself be circumscribed, manipulated, packaged and presented as a monopolistic gift. A gift that claimed for writing itself a new point of origin, that rendered writing the mark of the political fantasy of a universal, Catholic Empire.

Notes

1. Two copies, with slight variants, are at Apostolica Pontificia Università Gregoriana, Rome (hereafter **APUG**) 564, fols. 181r–184v, and APUG 563, fols. 187r–189v. A presentation copy for Pope Alexander VII, of the polygraphic version, is at Biblioteca Apostolica Vaticana (hereafter **BAV**), MSS. Chigiani, I. VI. 224, fol. 59v (reproduced in Marrone 1986). The Latin version of the letter is printed in Ceñal 1953, pp. 139–143.
2. Kircher 1663.
3. For general introductions to the field, see (in alphabetical order), Albani and Buonarroti 1994; Couturat and Leau 1903; Cram and Maat 1999; Eco 1995; Knowlson 1975; Rossi 2000; and Strasser 1988b.
4. For a detailed analysis of the language's structure, see McCracken 1948; and Eco 1995, pp. 196–200.
5. Kircher 1663, section 1; chapter 1.
6. On the fortuna of Trithemius, see Brann 1999.
7. On Martinitz, see Evans 1979, pp. 206–207. He was one of the recipients of Kircher's undated presentation manuscripts of the "Linguarum omnium nova arte ad unam Reductio," Österreichische Nationalbibliothek (hereafter **ÖNB**), MS. 9536, fols. 1r–24v (1659–60).
8. Kircher 1636.
9. APUG 556, fols. 314r–315v.
10. APUG 556, fols. 294r–295v. See also APUG 556, fols. 308r–309v, and APUG 556, fols. 289r–291v.
11. Schott 1660, introduction.
12. APUG 561, fols. 123r–v.
13. Kircher 1650a.
14. APUG 561, fols. 156r–v.
15. APUG 561, fols. 167r–v.
16. APUG 561, fols. 157r–v.
17. APUG 561, fols. 158r–v.
18. APUG 561, fols. 24r–v.
19. On these instruments, see Miniati 1989.
20. See Evans 1979, chapter 4.
21. Published in Mirto 1989, pp. 152–153. This article also transcribes the letters from Kircher in the Biblioteca Nazionale Centrale di Firenze to Ferdinando II, Cardinal Giovanni Carlo, Prince Leopoldo, and Antonio Magliabechi.
22. Mirto 2000, pp. 229–230. This letter is referred to in the postscript to APUG 556, fols. 63r–64v. See also APUG 556, fols. 63r–64v.
23. Mirto 2000, p. 229.
24. APUG 563, fols. 99r–v.
25. ÖNB, MS. 9545, fols. 1–40, and ÖNB MS. 11388.
26. This manuscript exists in three presentation copies: BAV, MSS. Chigiani, I., VI., 225, fols. 11r–37v; ÖNB, MS. 9536, fols. 1r–24v; and HAB Herzog August Bibliothek Wolfenbüttel MS. Cod. Guelf. 3.5. Aug. 4° fols. 1r–28v.
27. APUG 561, fols. 20r–v.
28. APUG 555, fols. 244r–245v.
29. Published in Kircher, 1663, p. 3; the original is at APUG 555, fols. 49r–v.
30. APUG 555, fols. 277r–v.
31. Kircher, 1669.

32. See Eco 1995, pp. 196–205. Eco regards Kircher's conceptually based system as "incongruous," adding, "It was perhaps the lack of internal coherency in this system of concepts that induced Kircher to abandon this line of research, and devote himself to the more modest and mechanical method used in the *Polygraphia*" (p. 205).

33. APUG 555, fols. 277r–v.

34. APUG 555, fols. 98r–v.

35. Schott 1668.

36. APUG 562, fols. 13r–v.

37. APUG 562, fols. 8r–v, and APUG 555, fols. 75r–76v.

38. APUG 562, fols. 128r–v.

39. APUG 555, fols. 282r–283v. The "cista" is conserved at the Herzog Anton Ulrich-Museum, Braunschweig, Kos 502. Reference from Strasser 1988b, p. 172.

40. APUG 562, fols. 3r–v.

41. APUG 562, fols. 151r–v.

42. APUG 564, fols. 1r–v.

43. Kircher 1679a, p. 219. Schott claimed that Ferdinand III and Leopold Wilhelm wanted to keep the language in the family: Schott 1664, pp. 479–480.

44. See Eisenstein 1979; and Johns 1998.

45. The book passed the Jesuit censors in November 1662 (reports by Martini Esparza and Daniello Bartoli are at Archivum Romanum Societatis Iesu, Rome, Fondo Gesuitico, 663, fols. 323r–v, 324r, "Censurae Librorum 1626–1663"). The General of the Society of Jesus, Oliva, gave permission to print the book on 2 December 1662. See also Schott 1664, p. 481.

46. APUG 562, fols. 74r–v.

47. APUG 562, fols. 129r–v, referring to Becher 1661.

48. APUG 562, fols. 11r–v. The edition never appeared.

49. HAB, BA N° 358, published digitally at http://www.hab.de/projekte/kircher/kircher.htm. August's dedicated copy of the *Polygraphy* is at HAB, 6. 1. Gram. 2°. Another letter of the same date, from Kircher to the duke's son, Ferdinand Albrecht, is conserved at HAB Fb 4° 52 (inside his copy of the *Polygraphy*). August's letter of acknowledgment is at APUG 555, fols. 21r–22v.

50. See APUG 555, fols. 116r–117v.

51. Mirto 2000, pp. 230–231.

52. Mirto 1989, pp. 142–143.

53. APUG 555, fols. 69r–70v.

54. APUG 555, fols. 55r–56v.

55. The copy, with Kircher's autograph dedication, is at the Biblioteca Nazionale Centrale di Firenze, Palat. 5–86, dated 21 June 1663.

56. APUG 555, at, respectively: fols. 55r–56v; 162r–v, 73r–74v, 57r–58v; 104r–105v; 59r–60v, 33r–34v.

57. APUG 555, fols. 71r–72v.

58. See Ceñal 1953, pp. 141–142.

59. Leibniz 1987, pp. 48–49. See also APUG 559, fols. 166r–v.

60. Ribadeneira et al. 1676, pp. 92–93.

61. APUG 562, fols. 167r–168v.

62. APUG 562, fols. 169r–170v.

63. Schott 1664, section 12, book 7, chapter 2, "A Universal Key to all the languages of the Whole World."

13

Private and Public Knowledge

Kircher, Esotericism, and the Republic of Letters

NOEL MALCOLM

The image of a "Republic of Letters" which we have today was fashioned in the late seventeenth and early eighteenth centuries. It is the image of an intellectual realm, open, collaborative, and above all universal in its scope and its aspirations. As Noël Bonaventure d'Argonne put it in 1700: "It extends throughout the world, and is composed of people of all nations. All languages, living and dead, are spoken there. Arts mingle there with letters, and the mechanical sciences also have their place in it."[1] The activities of this "republic" were conducted partly in print, and partly in conversation (in academies, salons, and coffeehouses); but perhaps its most characteristic medium was correspondence. Networks of correspondence, discussing points of scholarship, scientific research, and the latest publications, crisscrossed Europe and, in some cases, reached even further afield. This was a less public activity than communication in print, but it was seldom entirely private: letters could be shared, transcribed, and discussed with third parties. As Paul Dibon has put it: "It was a strict duty of each citizen of the Respublica literaria to *establish, maintain, and encourage communication*, primarily by personal correspondence or contact. . . . Every citizen was bound to widen the range of his correspondence and bring new citizens into the circle."[2]

If there is one person in the second half of the seventeenth century who appears to match all these requirements, it is Athanasius Kircher. His writings ranged through most arts and sciences; he seems to have known more languages, living and dead, than any other scholar of the age, writing in Latin, Italian, Spanish, German, Dutch, Greek, Hebrew, Armenian, Arabic, and Coptic, and reading in many more; and his correspondence did, to borrow d'Argonne's phrase, "extend throughout the world." Here, apparently, was not just an "archetype" of the Republic of Letters (as Dibon has described him) but a one-man walking compendium of it.[3]

Kircher's own descriptions of his research methods seem to harmonize quite closely with the Republic's ideals of collective intellectual endeavor. In the second preface to *Mundus subterraneus* (*Subterranean World*) (1665), he explained that he had sent letters of inquiry to "the most skilled men" in almost every European province of the Jesuit Order.[4] Introducing the *China illustrata* (*China Illustrated*) (1667) to the reader, he thanked his missionary colleagues Heinrich Roth and Johann Gruber for the information "they communicate unceasingly."[5] And in the general preface to the *Oedipus Aegyptiacus* (*The Egyptian Oedipus*) (1652–55), he wrote that in order to gather his materials "it was necessary to undertake a correspondence—at considerable expense—with the famous learned men, not only of Europe, but of Africa and Asia too, writing to each one in his own language."[6] His greatest debt, he announced there, was to Peiresc, "whose huge services to the Republic of Letters were so great, that they can never be obliterated by the forgetfulness of posterity."[7] References to the Republic of Letters were in fact very common in Kircher's prefatory statements about his own works. In the preface to the *Ars magna lucis et umbrae* (*The Great Art of Light and Shadow*) (1646), he said that having tested his work experimentally he now presented it "to the Republic of Letters"; that book, he coyly declared in the preface to his next publication, *Musurgia universalis* (*Universal Music-making*) (1650), "was, as I understood, not ill-received by the Republic of Letters"; apologizing for his slowness in publishing the *Oedipus aegyptiacus*, he noted that it had been "promised long ago to the Republic of Letters"; the same phrase was used for his *Mundus subterraneus*; and his *Arithmologia* (*The Science of Numbers*) (1665) would, he hoped, contribute "a not inconsiderable amount of enlightenment and profit to the Republic of Letters."[8]

Nevertheless, despite all these professions of allegiance to the Republic, and despite all his qualifications to stand as a model citizen of it, there are reasons for thinking that Kircher was not an 'archetype' of that Republic, nor even a representative of its mainstream. While the place he occupied in seventeenth-century intellectual life was certainly not an isolated one, it was not really central or typical. This is true not only of the contents of his theories (some of which will be discussed below), but also of his whole *modus operandi*. Consider, for example, the peculiar nature of his correspondence. Unlike other great managers of correspondence networks—Marin Mersenne, for instance—he was seldom engaged in multidirectional flows of information. In Mersenne's case, it is common to find that A writes to B, B discusses in return his own correspondence with C, A also writes to C commenting on B and asking C to pass on a letter to D, and so on. In Kircher's case, even sustained sequences of two-way correspondence are unusual. Instead, two unidirectional activities predominate: information gathering by Kircher for his own purposes, and the sending of queries to him by others. Of his 763 correspondents, 436 (57 percent) wrote to him only once.[9] Sometimes the queries related closely to his special expertise: for example, a Jesuit in Lyon sent him a drawing of an amulet with an unintelligible inscription, and received a long disquisition on the iconology of amulets in return.[10] But questions poured in on any and every topic: in a *cri de coeur* written to his friend Langenmantel in 1675, Kircher complained about the growing "multitude" of letters he received each week, full of "the most difficult questions about natural phenomena, and about other sciences."[11] His universal fame as an 'Oedipus', a riddle-solver, had established what John Fletcher has called "the common public view of Kircher as an accessible enquiry-office."[12] It is perhaps not surprising that, from all Kircher's own uses of the phrase "Republic of Letters," one gets no sense of a connection between the nature of such a republic and the nature of these letter-writing activities. Indeed, the sheer formulaic repetition of his references to it in his prefatory pages suggests that the term "Republic of Letters" functioned for him as little more than a token—a generalized way of gesturing toward his readership, and toward that intellectual common good to which any such publication was meant to contribute.

There was another problem. One of the key features of the Republic of Letters was its inter-confessional nature. Protestants and Catholics communicated more or less equally; theological topics were not altogether excluded from debate, but the participants tended to avoid the stamping grounds of controversial theology, discussing shared worries (such as Socinianism) and shared interests (such as new publications in biblical scholarship) instead. On these terms it was possible for a devout Minim friar (Mersenne) to correspond regularly and cordially with a professor of theology at the Calvinist stronghold of Leiden (André Rivet); indeed, one might say that the center of gravity of the entire Republic of Letters was its Franco-Dutch axis, connecting the vibrant intellectual life of Paris with that of the Dutch universities and printing houses. (Hence the importance, as intellectual intermediaries, of Huguenots in the Netherlands.) Kircher, on the other hand, was not only a Jesuit, but someone with a reputation as a proselytizer. The list of his correspondents is overwhelmingly Catholic—indeed, 238 of them (31 percent) were Jesuits—and despite his connection with an Amsterdam publisher, he never gained a personal entrée to the intellectual world that centred on the Dutch and northern German universities.[13] In the eyes of many northern Europeans (not only Protestants, but Gallicans too) there was something intellectually suspect about the Jesuits: they were thought to lack the proper spirit of criticism, using their skills and their learning to impress the public for ulterior purposes—whether proselytizing or maneuvring for social and political influence. Thus when Charles Patin described to a friend his recent visit to Rome in 1677, he observed somewhat sniffily that he had made no attempt to get to know Father Kircher: "although he also studies antiquity, he handles it in a rather suspect and Jesuitical way; I deal with it truly, sincerely and openly, as befits a historian."[14]

This "Jesuitical" charge could easily be combined with the more common accusation that much of Kircher's published work was not an original contribution to the world of learning, but an undiscriminating compilation of other writers' labors. As the Oxford mathematician Robert Payne put it in a letter to Gilbert Sheldon in 1650, having just read the *Ars magna lucis et umbrae*:

> The truth is, this Jesuit, as generally the most of his order, haue a great ambition to be thought the great learned men of ye world; & to that end write greate volumes, on all subjects, wth gay pictures & diagramms to sett them forth, for ostentation: & to fill vp those volumes they draw in all things, by head & shoulders; & these too for the most part, stolen from other authors. so that if that little, wch is their owne, were separated from what is borrowed from others, or impertinent to y^{eir} present argument, their swollen volumes would shrink vp to ye size of our Almanacks. But enough of those Mountebankes.[15]

Kircher was, then, not a fully integrated member of the European Republic of Letters: he was regarded by many as a somewhat dubious or marginal figure, and his own activities as a correspondent, though tireless and wide-ranging, did not really exemplify that complex circulation of knowledge that was the Republic's way of life. The differences, however, go deeper than that. For both the idea and the practice of the seventeenth-century Republic of Letters implied certain assumptions about the relationship between critical understanding and political life: a set of assumptions about knowledge and power that might be called the implicit ideology of the Republic. And while Kircher too had his own beliefs about the relationship between knowledge and power, the ideology they implied was fundamentally different.

A word of warning is needed here. Many of the modern studies of the Republic of Letters tend to read back into the seventeenth century those ideological descriptions of it that they find in the writings of the Republic's spokesmen in the early eighteenth. These are then combined with a curiously teleological version of Jürgen Habermas's argument about the emergence of a "public space," to create the impression that from an early stage the participants in the Republic were striving to establish a quasi-political entity, a public realm over and against the state.[16] The very use of the term "Republic," harped on by early-eighteenth-century publicists such as Jean Leclerc and Pierre Desmaizeaux, seems to encourage this: when Desmaizeaux calls the Republic of Letters "a state that extends throughout all states," it is easy to suppose that he is thinking of something that acts more or less politically, rivaling or even trumping the existing units of political power.[17] Some of the leading modern writers on the Republic of Letters have succumbed to the temptation to read back into the seventeenth century such quasi-political aspirations: thus Hans Bots, for example, emphasizes the desire of the learned world "to form its own state," and Françoise Waquet argues that the whole phenomenon of the Republic of Letters in the seventeenth century embodied a positive political program, consisting of ecumenism, irenicism, universalism, or even utopianism.[18]

In fact, as Waquet herself has demonstrated in some detail, the term "Republic of Letters" was used in many ways, most of which were devoid of political implications. Often the phrase was merely a synonym for *orbis literarius* (the literary world); frequently the term *respublica*, which we translate as "republic," was used in the more general sense of *res publica* (the common good), not implying, even analogically, any sort of statelike entity.[19] (*Res publica literaria* would thus mean the common good of literary people, not of the state as a whole.) Some of the classic texts that have been said to expound a theory of the literary "republic," from Decembrio in the fifteenth century to Saavedra Fajardo in the seventeenth, turn out on closer inspection to have no real connection with the concept of a republic at all.[20] It is true that some writers in the sixteenth and seventeenth centuries did make use of the political connotations of *respublica* in the phrase *respublica literaria*; but they usually did so ironically, often self-deprecatingly, to emphasize the *non*-political nature of the world of scholars, its detachment from the political—and confessional—world. As Anne Goldgar has written, summarizing her findings about the intellectual community of the late seventeenth century: "The 'public' my scholars cared about was each other. Their work was not primarily directed at public utility, their ideal society was not intended for general emulation, and the political aspect of their lives was to be divorced absolutely from their scholarship."[21]

If ideology is a system of justification for politics, then the ideology of the seventeenth-century Republic of Letters was a peculiarly negative one, an ideology of the non-political. As activists never tire of pointing out, any ideology of the non-political is still a political position, as it justifies, or at least inertially defends, the political status quo. Such an ideology is peculiarly well adapted for those who are not inclined to be ideologists; most members of the seventeenth-century Republic of Letters fell into that category, and their adherence to this ideology was simply implicit in their acceptance of the Republic's practices. They accepted that differences of political allegiance and religion could be set aside for their purposes; that some basic framework of state authority was required, to supply the conditions of security they needed for their work; that the rules of action that applied in the public, political world might have to differ from the ones they themselves adhered to in their personal and intellectual dealings with one another; and that some of the things set aside by them as "indifferent" (such as customary laws, religious practices, and social conventions) might be necessary components of authority and stability in the public realm. This ideology rests, therefore, on a distinction between the shared-private world of the scholars and the public world outside them. It draws on the neo-Stoicism of Lipsius; on the private/public dichotomy and the cultural relativism of Montaigne; and on the Machiavellian tradition, especially as developed by Cardano and Charron. Indeed, if this implicit ideology of the seventeenth-century Republic of Letters has any explicit exponents, they are Pierre Charron, Gabriel Naudé, and François de La Mothe le Vayer.[22]

Such an ideology is at least potentially radical in intellectual terms: within the Republic of Letters, critical thinking can dismantle all sorts of publicly accepted beliefs and superstitions. But it is thoroughly non-radical politically: it relies on, and defends, the powers that be. Generally, members of this Republic support the state; their natural political program is not ecumenist universalism, but a pragmatic Erastianism. Insofar as such a Republic of Letters has any political force or charge, it is directed not against the state but against the common people. The literati know that customs are absurd, that law is not grounded directly in nature, that religion functions as a political device; but they try to keep this knowledge to themselves. One could say, therefore, that the private/public distinction generates an esoteric/exoteric distinction too; but the esoteric in this case is not so much a body of positive truth or a doctrinal system as a type of critical analysis.

Not everyone, however, was a subscriber to this ideology. Exceptions included rationalists such as Hobbes, who believed that irrational superstitions among the general population would only become instruments of priestcraft, and that the rational principles on which the state was grounded could and should be taught to the common people.[23] Also set apart from this ideology were the evangelical universalists, such as Jan Amos Komenský (Comenius) and Samuel Hartlib, whose efforts were directed at universal reformation. Despite the obvious differences between Hobbesian rationalism and Comenian religious universalism, there were some formal resemblances between their positions: both were basically opposed to any theory of knowledge and power that hinged on an esoteric/exoteric distinction.

The case of Athanasius Kircher, on the other hand, is different yet again: he also stands apart from the ideology of the Republic of Letters, but he does have a theory in which the esoteric/exoteric distinction plays a significant part. Consider, for example, the use made of reports by travelers and missionaries about exotic foreign cultures. In the hands of a writer such as La Mothe le Vayer, such reports are used to demonstrate the variable, even absurd, nature of human custom and human beliefs: the message is anti-universalist, undermining faith in the *consensus gentium* (agreement of all peoples), and using ironic strategies to suggest that the practices of his own society may be intrinsically no more rational than those the missionaries describe. In Kircher's hands, however, just the opposite use is made of this material: he seeks out a common core, a common tradition or derivation that unites the foreign cultures and religious beliefs with his own.[24] His is a sort of crypto-universalism: it postulates a shared essence, but a hidden one.

That common core was the *prisca theologia* (ancient theology), the Hermetic wisdom, the body of esoteric knowledge associated with the ancient sage Hermes Trismegistus.[25] For Hermeticism played a central part in Kircher's philosophical system. Perhaps the strangest judgment ever passed on Kircher's work is that of Joscelyn Godwin, who notes, "Again and again in perusing Kircher's books I wonder . . . whether there is not a deliberate esoteric undercurrent at work," but concludes: "To attempt to connect him in any conscious way with the esoteric undercurrents of the seventeenth century would of course be totally implausible."[26] Kircher's relationship with the esoteric Hermeticist tradition was in fact strong, direct, and clearly stated in his work. It is true that he attacked alchemists, kabbalists, and astrologers (or, at least, bad astrologers—what he called "astrologasters").[27] It is also true that he sometimes explained apparent examples of "natural magic" in purely mechanical terms—such as the famous "speaking statue" of the Hermetic text *Asclepius*.[28] The Catholic Church's hostility to magic also placed real constraints on what he could write or say.[29] Yet even those constraints did not prevent him from publishing an entire treatise on natural magic—book 10 of his *Musurgia universalis*—in which he explained the principles of cosmic harmony from which the sympathetic correspondences of stones, plants, animals, and heavenly bodies were derived, noted that this was the secret wisdom of the ancient Egyptians (and of Orpheus, a "Magus Sapientissimus"), and set out a list of "The Practical Rules of Natural Magic," explaining how those correspondences could be "applied."[30]

Kircher presented the early history of this tradition of "secret wisdom" in the first volume of his *Oedipus Aegyptiacus*. The wisdom was imparted by God to Adam; through his descendants it was transmitted to Noah, and thus survived the Flood. Roughly three hundred years after the Flood, Noah and his sons and grandsons passed on this body of knowledge to a gifted Canaanite who was known as Idris to the Arabs, Thouth (i.e., Thoth) to the Egyptians, and Hermes Trismegistus to the Greeks. Hermes traveled widely through the ancient world before settling in Egypt as scribe and counselor to Misraim, the Egyptian king; there he helped to set up an ideal political order, based on the principles of harmony contained in the ancient wisdom. This was a monarchy in which the kings were advised (and their successors chosen) by wise philosophers and priests. Hermes knew that religion was essential for human society and government, and he set up an elaborate system of religious institutions, including colleges of priests, cantors, augurs, scribes, prophets, and "hierogrammatists." The task of the hierogrammatists was to inscribe the sacred doctrine on stone in symbolic hieroglyphs, the meaning of which was known only to initiates.[31] Unfortunately, however, these hieroglyphs were easily misunderstood by the common people. Before long, symbolic images (for example, the asp, lion, and dog, signifying royal virtues) were misread as pictures of gods or idols, and moral allegories (such as the stories of Horus, Typhon, Isis, and Osiris) were taken literally as narratives from a polytheist theology. This distorted version of the ancient wisdom, corrupted into polytheism and idolatry, then spread much further afield, undergoing further local modifications to give rise to all the heathen religions of the world.[32]

There is something deeply paradoxical about this whole account. According to Kircher, the cause of mankind's descent into error was "the levity and inconstancy of the human mind."[33] The uncontrolled activity of the common people, working on the mysterious images of the hieroglyphs, had quickly given rise to superstitious beliefs and idolatrous practices: this showed how essential priestly and political control must be to the maintenance of both political stability and theological purity. And yet the system of control devised by Hermes (and lauded by Kircher as the wisest system ever invented) included the use of priestly secrecy and the concealment of doctrine in mysterious hieroglyphs—which was precisely what had occasioned the growth of popular error. Readers might well be forgiven for thinking that the use of hieroglyphs was not Hermes's most brilliant achievement, but his most catastrophic mistake. And they might find support for that view in a passage elsewhere in Kircher's works, his invocation in the preface to his *Polygraphia nova et universalis* (*New and Universal Polygraphy*) (1663) of an Arabic proverb: "If you have a secret, either conceal it, or reveal it."[34] At first sight, this advice may seem superfluous: after all, what else can one do with a secret, except either keep it secret or reveal it? But that is not the point of the proverb. As Kircher explains, "conceal it" here means "conceal the fact that you possess a secret": the worst thing to do, therefore, is to let people know that you have a secret, but refuse to impart it to them. And yet that is exactly what was done by Hermes Trismegistus, the wisest of all the ancient sages.

Two simple questions thus arise. Why did Hermes not conceal even the fact that he possessed this secret knowledge? Alternatively, why did he not fully reveal its contents to the people? Kircher's answer to the first question is that religion is essential to human society: "without it, the union and agreement of human society cannot exist, and there can be no trust, no justice, no virtue."[35] (In thus appearing to justify religion on political-functionalist grounds, Kircher was an inheritor here of a Counter-Reformation adaptation of the Machiavellian tradition, in which it was claimed that true religion supplied an even more functionally efficient "reason of state" than any human wisdom.) The second question, however, presented—or should have presented—a more serious challenge to Kircher as a Christian theologian; if Jesus Christ had preached his Gospel openly to the common people, it was hard to understand the wisdom of Hermes' refusal to do so. Strangely, Kircher raised this vital question only once, when he asked, in his discussion of symbolism in volume 2 of the *Oedipus Aegyptiacus*, why the Egyptian priests had refused to reveal their entire doctrine to the people. "My answer," he declared, "is that they did this both to show due honor and reverence for sacred things, and to avoid the danger of errors."[36] He emphasized that the desire to honor sacred truths by protecting them from public view was natural and ancient, citing both the Pythagoreans and the Jewish kabbalists; he enlisted Christ himself in a tradition of at least partial concealment, noting that he taught a theology with three levels of meaning (natural, symbolic, and mystical); but above all, he stressed the need to prevent sacred wisdom from falling into the wrong hands.[37] This meant, in the first place, hiding it from the common people, who could not possibly understand it anyway. (Although he did not develop the point, this would supply a Kircherian answer to the criticism that Hermes' system of hieroglyphics actually promoted popular misunderstanding: the answer would be that the common people would always have misunderstood the esoteric doctrine, even if it had been spelled out to them.) And in the case of the secret doctrines of the Egyptians, "falling into the wrong hands" also had a more specific meaning: the Egyptian priests feared that if their doctrines and ceremonies were made fully public, neighboring states could make use of them, as the materials of operative natural magic, to send hostile demons to attack them.[38]

Fundamental to Kircher's argument here is a general assumption which might be called the basis of his political philosophy: the assumption that knowledge is power, and that the concealment or control of knowledge is therefore essential to the art of ruling. His only treatise on politics, *Principis christiani archetypon politicum* (*The Political Archetype of a Christian Prince*) (1672), gave special prominence to this theme: "there is no greater virtue in a wise prince," he declared, "than tenacity in keeping one's counsel secret."[39] The ancient image of Harpocrates, with his finger on his lip, was for Kircher a reminder of the need for silence and secrecy, both in religion and in government. Running through many of Kircher's works was a special interest in different types of "steganography," the art of secret communication—whether magnetic (in *Magnes* [*The Magnet*]), catoptric (in *Ars magna lucis et umbrae*), musical (in *Musurgia*), graphic (in *Polygraphia*), or numerical (in *Arithmologia*). Such arts would be of special use to political rulers; indeed, Kircher sometimes suggested that they belonged in the category of "arcana" to which only rulers should have full access. In a remarkable passage at the end of his *Ars magna sciendi* (*The Great Art of Knowing*) (1669), he listed various new arts that he was in the process of developing, beginning with his "steganographia universalis," and explained that Ferdinand III had urged him not to hasten their publication, for fear that "arcane matters of this sort, which are fit only for kings and princes—whether for their private mental recreation, or for serving the public good—might become objects of contempt if they were published and made known to all and sundry."[40] In a similar vein, Kaspar Schott's preface to the reader in the *Oedipus Aegyptiacus* began by noting that the Egyptian wisdom contained in Kircher's work was of a sort that was "fit to be communicated only to the priests and kings of the Egyptians, and to a few others who aspired to sacerdotal and regal dignity," and went on to say that Kircher received letters from princes all over the Christian world who "communicate secrets to him . . . and request from him the explanation of arcane matters."[41]

Kircher's political ideal was a union of wisdom and power: rule by a philosopher-king. He praised the Confucian polity of China in glowing terms: "the whole kingdom is administered by *literati* more or less in the manner of Plato's republic, so that Plato's wish seems to have been fulfilled in the Chinese monarchy—the wish he expressed when he said how happy that kingdom would be in which either the king philosophized, or the philosopher ruled."[42] In his prefaces and dedicatory epistles he lost no opportunity to conjure up the image of the royal philosopher, comparing Ferdinand III to Hermes, for example, or invoking the figure of Chosroes, the astronomer-king.[43] These were more than mere airy compliments to his dedicatees; they expressed one of his most central concerns. Indeed, the union of wisdom and power was central to his philosophy and his religion. The omnipotent God, who had ordered the universe, had made it possible for human beings to understand that order and, by understanding it, participate more fully in it; and the more fully they participated in it, the more they would be freed from their vices and filled instead with divine illumination, becoming increasingly deiform themselves.[44] The underlying model of religion here seems, despite all Kircher's no doubt sincere protestations of Catholic intent, to be more similar to Gnosticism than to orthodox Christianity.[45]

In his assumptions about knowledge and power, therefore, Kircher may have come close to the ideology of the Republic of Letters in some superficial ways, but in fact he differed from it profoundly. The surface similarities include a distrust or fear of the ignorant common people, and an acceptance of an element of "reason of state" (even, in *Principis christiani archetypon politicum*, an acceptance of the need for "dissimulation").[46] Both positions, as has been pointed out already, generate a kind of esoteric/exoteric distinction. But the underlying patterns of thought are quite different. In Kircher's case, the pattern is that of a spectrum or ascending scale of illumination, with the esoteric wisdom confined to those who are at the upper end of it; but it is in the end a single spectrum, an expression of that great scale of truth, being, and love round which the harmony of the universe is constructed. In the case of the Republic of Letters, the model is much more prosaic: just a shared-private space of critical discussion and communication, surrounded by a public realm. That public realm has a merely functional and instrumental value vis-à-vis the shared-private one; indeed, the public realm of the state can be justified in purely instrumental terms, which means that it can be founded simply on human convention. For Kircher, good government is the opposite of the merely conventional: the better it is, the more purely it embodies a cosmic principle of harmony and order.

Again, for the Republic of Letters it is just a contingent fact that a mass of common people exists outside the shared-private world of the Republic, not participating in its intellectual life and threatening it with their tendency to disorder. It is a fact, but need not be one. It might be possible to teach enlightened, critical thinking to the general populace; the borders of the Republic are both porous and expanding, particularly through the use of publications in the vernacular. For Kircher, on the other hand, it is not a contingent fact that a scale of being, or a scale of illumination, should exist: it is built into the nature of things. Individuals may move up that scale, but the higher wisdom will always be the preserve of those few who are at the higher end of it. The highest secrets of all will be reserved for princes and sages; other matters may be explained a little more generally; but even Kircher's one work of quasi-popular-ization, his *Itinerarium Exstaticum* (*The Ecstatic Journey*) (1656) is still in or-nate Latin, written at the request of an emperor and dedicated to a queen. The distinction between the esoteric and the exoteric arises necessarily from the difference between high and low in the nature of mankind; and that difference, according to Kircher, will always be there, because it reflects the harmony of the universe. As he put it in a chapter on "the symphonic nature of the political world" in his *Musurgia*: "The state could hardly survive, if all people in it were equal. . . . Divine providence so constituted men, that whilst one can reach the highest summit of wisdom, another is sunk in the abyss of ignorance, hardly differing from a beast."[47]

Notes

1. "Vigneul-Marville" (pseudonym of d'Argonne) 1699–1701, vol. 2, p. 60.
2. Dibon 1990, p. 159. Cf. also his essay "Communication épistolaire et mouvement des idées au XVIIᵉ siècle," reprinted in the same volume, pp. 171–190; Ultee 1987; and Waquet 1993.
3. Dibon 1990, pp. 177–178.
4. Kircher 1665c, vol. 1, sig. 3*1r.
5. Kircher 1667a, sig. 2*2r.
6. Kircher 1652–55, vol. 1, sig. b3r.
7. Ibid.
8. Kircher 1646, sig. 2†4r; Kircher 1650a, vol. 1, sig. 2†2r; Kircher 1652–55, vol. 1, sig. +4v; Kircher 1665c, vol. 1, sig. χ2v; Kircher 1665a, sig. 2+1r.
9. Fletcher 1988b, p. 139.
10. Matthieu Compain's letter to Kircher (30 September 1666) is Ponteficia Università Gregoriana, MS. 563, fols. 36–37. Kircher's reply (19 November 1666) is printed in Spon 1673, pp. 208–211. This letter by Kircher is omitted from John Fletcher's listing of the correspondence (Fletcher 1988c), and appears to have been entirely overlooked hitherto by Kircher scholarship.
11. Langenmantel 1684, pp. 56–58 (22 February 1675).
12. Fletcher 1988c, p. 139.
13. Fletcher 1988b, p. 5; Fletcher 1988c, pp. 140 (statistic), 145–146.
14. Cited in Waquet 1985, p. 136, n. 182 (20 December 1677).
15. British Library, London, MS. Lansdowne 841, fol. 33v (16 December 1650). Payne's notes on the *Ars magna lucis et umbrae* are in Chatsworth (Derbyshire, England), MS Hobbes C. i. 1. Cf. the dismissal of Kircher as a "Mountebank" by the distinguished Protestant scholar James Ussher in 1655: Evelyn 1955, vol. 3, p. 156.
16. See Habermas 1989. For an eloquent (but, I believe, mistaken) application of this to the seventeenth-century Republic of Letters, see Goodman 1994, pp. 12–23.
17. Desmaizeaux 1729, p. xxiv; cf. Leclerc 1701, p. 146, describing the Republic as "a country of reason and light, not of authority," and Henri Basnage de Beauval, cited in Broekmans et al. 1976, p. 113, calling it "a free country."
18. Bots 1977, p. 6; Waquet 1989b, esp. pp. 495–497.
19. Waquet 1989b, pp. 478–483.
20. Decembrio 1540 uses the phrase *politia literaria* (which would normally be translated "re-public of letters") in its title, but immediately explains (fol. 1r) that his word *politia* derives not from the Greek *polis* but from the Latin *polire*, meaning "to polish": the translation should therefore be "literary elegance," or perhaps "belles-lettres." Saavedra Fajardo's "re-public of letters" is a conceit far removed from any description of the practices of contem-porary literary life, a city populated by classical authors, with pens for cannons on its battlements, etc. (Saavedra Fajardo 1670). Fumaroli gives a misleading account of Decem-brio; he also misrepresents Samuel Sorbière, whose letter about the maxims of friendship (Sorbière 1660, pp. 401–407) he describes, quite unwarrantedly, as constructing a theory of the Republic of Letters out of the political doctrines of Hobbes: Fumaroli 1997, pp. 46, 56.
21. Goldgar 1995, p. 6.

22. The best accounts of this ideological tradition are Pintard 1943, pp. 539–564; Procacci 1965, pp. 77–106; Battista 1966; Keohane 1980, pp. 119–150; Castrucci 1981; Charles-Daubert 1985; and Taranto 1994, pp. 17–129. The version of Habermas's argument presented by Reinhart Koselleck is more convincing precisely because it is more attuned to this tradition: see Koselleck 1988, pp. 104–113.

23. I discuss this in "Hobbes and the European Republic of Letters," in Malcolm 2002, pp. 541–5.

24. On this major aspect of Kircher's work see Pastine 1978.

25. See the classic studies by Yates 1964 (pp. 1–189); and Walker 1972. A brief but valuable discussion of Kircher's adherence to this tradition is in Leinkauf 1993, pp. 246–254.

26. Godwin 1988, p. 32.

27. See, for example, Kircher 1646, p. 769 (attacking diabolic magic); Kircher 1652–55, vol. 2, part 1, p. 359 (attacking kabbalistic magic as a misuse of the kabbalah), and vol. 2, part 2, p. 140 (condemning astrology); Kircher 1669, p. 6 (criticizing astrologers and alchemists); Kircher 1672, p. 9 (denouncing astrologers, necromancers, magicians, and kabbalists). He did, however, defend the principle on which a true astrology could be based, arguing that God rules the corporeal world through "Intelligences," and that the system of correspondences on which the universe is organized includes division into nine celestial regions: Kircher 1656, pp. 362–363.

28. Kircher, 1650a, vol. 1, pp. 305–306. This line of argument was taken further by his follower Kaspar Schott, who did his best to remove from the term 'magic' any occult connotations: Schott 1657–59, vol. 1, esp. pp. 8–11.

29. See the summary of a second (undated) letter from Kircher to Compain (cf. above, note 10): "In another letter he apologized for not having given a detailed explanation of the lettering on the amulet, as he was forbidden to do so by the Holy Office, for fear that he might appear to be teaching magic" (Spon 1673, p. 212).

30. Kircher 1650a, book 10, esp. pp. 390–396. Frances Yates gives a somewhat misleading account of Kircher's remarks about magic, noting his denunciations of diabolic magic but giving, as the only example of his positive attitudes to magic, the merely mechanical "natural magic" of the *Ars magna lucis et umbrae*: Yates 1964, pp. 421–422.

31. Kircher 1652–55, vol. 1, pp. 113–116.

32. Ibid., vol. 1, pp. 144–159, 166–172, 241–245, 398–400.

33. Ibid., vol. 1, p. 241.

34. Kircher 1663, p. 5.

35. Kircher 1672, p. 7.

36. Kircher 1652–55, vol. 2, part 1, p. 127.

37. Ibid., vol. 2, part 1, pp. 27–28, 127–129. He returns to Christ's use of esotericism at the end of the work, quoting his admonition about pearls before swine: vol. 3, p. 579.

38. Ibid., vol. 1, p. 142.

39. Kircher 1672, p. 20.

40. Kircher 1669, p. 481 ("to all and sundry" here translates a contemptuous phrase taken from Horace, "lippis & tonsoribus," literally "to the blear-eyed and barbers").

41. Kircher 1652–55, vol. 1, sigs. c2r, d1v.

42. Kircher 1667a, p. 166.

43. Kircher 1652–55, vol. 1, sig. 2†1v; Kircher 1656, sig. +2v.

44. See, for example, the account of "purgation" and "illumination" at the end of Kircher 1652–55 (vol. 3, pp. 578–579).

45. The implicit unorthodoxy of Kircher's theology is a large subject, the exploration of which must lie beyond the bounds of this essay. It should be noted that there is extraordinarily little Christology in his theological writings; his frequent assertions of Trinitarianism, which might at first glance appear to express Christian orthodoxy of a non-Gnostic kind, are usually linked to triadic Neoplatonist metaphysics, and have almost no Christological content at all.

46. Kircher 1672, p. 22.

47. Kircher 1650a, vol. 2, p. 433.

The Global Shape of Knowledge

14

Baroque Science between the Old and the New World

Father Kircher and His Colleague
Valentin Stansel (1621–1705)

CARLOS ZILLER CAMENIETZKI*
TRANSLATED BY PAULA FINDLEN AND DERRICK ALLUMS

It is practically impossible for the contemporary historian interested in the affairs of modern science not to be slightly troubled when opening one of the large scientific folios of Father Kircher for the first time. The work is difficult to fit into the traditional academic schema and hard to understand. Traditionally historians have not seen Kircher's works as belonging to the domain of science, and a number of modern scholars have argued that the Jesuit "is not in the proper sense a scientist."[1] Nevertheless, we should recognize that in his own time many natural philosophers from all sides closely followed Father Kircher's publications and considered them serious works that allowed, or at least facilitated, knowledge of the world. Thus, a first question for the contemporary historian is presented: what was, or could be, "a scientist in the proper sense" in the seventeenth century?

My intention in this essay is not only to answer this question, but to keep in mind the fact that, as we have known for some time now, what was to become "science" in the following centuries was not yet defined. In fact, several different scientific projects competed for the attention of the learned in the mid–seventeenth century. Often the "scientist" of this period incorporated elements from various sources into his work, shaping his theses, propositions, and metaphysics from diverse ingredients. Today, we know all too well that the work of most of the men of science of this period was closer to a heterogeneous assemblage of research programs and methodological procedures than a coherent and unified march toward knowledge of the world. Kircher embodied this heterogeneity, perhaps better than any other natural philosopher of his time, because he choose to address such a wide range of subjects and read encyclopedically on each and every one.

To characterize some important elements of Kircher's scientific project, I have chosen to examine his intellectual relationship with a mathematician-missionary who was active in Portuguese America. This allows us to explore simultaneously the science that Kircher practiced and the diffusion of his ideas throughout the world.

1. Two Books, One Literature

In May 1685, the latest volume of the *Acta Eruditorum*, the Leipzig journal known throughout the Republic of Letters for its reviews of important books, announced the publication of Uranophilus Caelestis Peregrinus *The Heavenly Traveler Uranophilus* in Gand (Figure 14.1). The work was written in Salvador, Brazil, by Valentin Stansel, a Jesuit missionary. The advertisement described it in the following terms:

> Thirty years ago, on the model of voyages into ecstasy, Father Athanasius Kircher dealt with nature, virtues, qualities, composition, and structure of the fixed and moving stars. The author of *Uranophilus* has decided to write his book, either in imitation of Kircher or quite independently. In fact, it is not clear to us whether or not he was aware of his confrere's subject. In any case, it is not probable that Stansel was unaware of the book of such an important scholar of his own religious order. Furthermore, Kircher has read and cited works by him. It is hard to believe that he did not cite the *Iter*, if he had read it, given that the ideas of Kircher exposed in other works are defended and incorporated by this author.[2]

Father Stansel's text was a dialogue among three characters: Uranophilus (the author himself, literally lover of the skies), Urania (the muse of the sky), and Geonisbe (the muse of the earth). The work was organized around the various

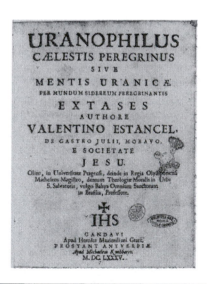

Figure 14.1. Frontispiece of Valentin Stansel, *The Heavenly Traveler Uranophilis. Source:* Valentin Stansel, *Uranophilus Caelestis Peregrinus* (Gand, 1685). Courtesy of the Biblioteca Nazionale Centrale Vittorio Emanuele II, Rome.

Figure 14.2. Urania and Geonisbe inspire Uranophilus's ecstatic journeys while he sleeps in a garden. *Source:* Valentin Stansel, *Uranophilus Caelestis Peregrinus* (Gand, 1685). Courtesy of the Biblioteca Nazionale Centrale Vittorio Emanuele II, Rome.

ecstasies during which Urania guided Uranophilus to a planet or some other specific part of the heavens. Between two consecutive ecstasies, they encounter Geonisbe and take advantage of the occasion to discuss what they had seen in the heavens and what had happened on earth during the absence of the two celestial characters (Figure 14.2). They use the occasion, of course, to talk about the town of Salvador and its environs. They discuss the specific geography of places, the current problems of the city, tropical nature and its woods, fruits, and flowers, surrounding dangers such as attacks by the Tapuias, and the passage of foreign scholars through the city. Quite remarkably, Stansel records the presence of monsters and sirens on the islands of the bay of Salvador. We will return to this subject later. Regarding natural philosophy, the themes discussed in the debates touch on the structure of the heavens, tropical nature, and still other propositions of scientists of the period.

The work of Kircher to which the author of the review refers is none other than the *Itinerarium Exstaticum* (*Ecstatic Journey*) published in Rome in 1656.[3] In that work, Father Athanasius described a voyage into ecstasy where the character Theodidactus—Kircher—enters into ecstasy and is taken up into the heavens by the angel Cosmiel. During the journey they discuss the structure and organization of the world as well as the principal astronomical theories of the period. Kircher's book enjoyed a remarkable fortune. At the same time, it also had difficulties being approved by the internal censors of the Society of Jesus, who found the content rather unorthodox in an age shaped by the condemnation of Galileo in 1633 for espousing Copernican-ism. This important fact might help explain the reasons for Stansel's apparent ignorance of Kircher's publication, which so resembled his own in many important respects.[4]

Both Stansel's *Uranophilus* and Kircher's *Itinerarium Exstaticum* belonged to a rather interesting seventeenth-century literary genre: imaginary voyages.[5] The development of philosophical thought between the sixteenth and seventeenth centuries, the maritime discoveries in an age of overseas exploration and conquest, the new theories of the heavens, and the appearance of the telescope and telescopic observations of celestial bodies considerably stimulated the minds of more than a few writers of this period. The idea of writing books that recounted voyages into the heavens and other planets became quite appealing. In place of the numerous commentaries on *The Dream of Scipio* of more ancient times, the seventeenth century witnessed the publication of celestial voyages based on the new astronomical knowledge produced since the diffusion of Copernicus's ideas. The German Lutheran astronomer Johannes Kepler's posthumous *Sommium* (1634), a moon voyage that he had worked on since his student days, set the tone for the discussion of the possibility of seeing the world from a different perspective.

Given the organization of Stansel's text, it was impossible not to notice that "the subject of this work is the same as that of the Ecstatic Voyage of Father Kircher," as the *Journal des Sçavants* pointed out in 1685.[6] Indeed, the similarities between Father Stansel's *Uranophilus* and the *Itinerarium Exstaticum* of his confrere Athanasius Kircher largely justified the suspicion of imitation. The two authors employed the same dialogue form, and both made their voyages ecstatic. Both writers used rather elaborate metaphors, hyperboles, analogies, and double entendres. The two books further resembled each other in their basic content and in the eclecticism of the theses they examined; both authors tried to discuss new scientific ideas without paying much attention to grand philosophical systems. They avoided presenting obvious facts or arguments in favor of a coherent and organized cosmology. Above all, they distanced themselves from the orthodox scholasticism and the tradition of Aristotelian commentary that were common in the schools at the time. It is obvious that Stansel's *Uranophilus* imitated the form of Kircher's *Itinerarium Exstaticum*. But beyond imitation, the commonality of their approach suggests a conceptual coherence to their intellectual ambitions. This makes the question of the author of the review in the *Acta* more interesting: did Stansel read the work of his fellow Jesuit?

In fact, the two Jesuits met each other in Rome in 1656, when Father Valentin was passing through on his way to Lisbon exactly at the time when Kircher's book was first being published. The Portuguese capital was the main port from which Catholic European vessels departed for the Indies. For several months, they worked together at the Collegio Romano. They maintained regular contact in the following years; Stansel entered into the network of Kircher's correspondents that he cultivated in every corner of the world where Jesuit missionaries and curious scholars could be found.[7] Beyond the usual information on the state of the Society of Jesus in Brazil, its tropical nature, and some astronomical observations he supplied to assist Kircher in providing Jesuit astronomy with the best-informed global network of observers that the world had ever seen, the missionary Stansel provided Father Athanasius with curious objects from Lisbon for the famous museum of the Collegio Romano.

Following his departure from Rome, Stansel worked in the colleges of Lisbon and Elvas, where he made observations of the sky and wrote some books.[8] On 19 April 1663, the missionary left for Brazil and remained there for the rest of his life. Father Valentin had already been a well-known astronomer and philosopher from the beginning of the 1650s before he left the University of Prague. He had written texts and participated in the academic culture of the city, defending, directing, and publishing theses. His activities were noticed by Bohemian scientists of his generation: Jacob Dobrzenski of Nigro Ponte, for example, made several references to him in his book *New and More Pleasing Philosophy on the Wonderful Spirit of Fountains* (*Nova et amenior de admirando fontium genio philosophia*) (1657).[9] This Prague physician tells us that the Stansel "museum," maintained at the university, was a place where experiments were performed and scientific instruments and machines were displayed in imitation of other, better-known collections in Europe, among which Kircher's museum at the Collegio Romano is perhaps one of the most important.[10]

A skilled mathematician, Stansel's astronomical writings were read and appreciated by a number of the best-known astronomers and natural philosophers at the end of the seventeenth century. In particular, the observations of the comet of 1668 he made in Brazil circulated in manuscript form and were even printed in a number of the most important European scientific periodicals.[11] It is certain that beyond the quality of his technical knowledge and the precision of his results, the place where he made his observations played an important role in the diffusion of his writings, in particular, of the book in question, *The Heavenly Traveler Uranophilus*.

2. The Order and Knowledge of the World

The cosmos in which *Uranophilus* strolls is not at all presented as something definitively organized. In Stansel's cosmos, we inhabit the antithesis of Bernard le Bovier de Fontenelle's *Conversations on the Plurality of Worlds* (*Conversations sur la pluralité des mondes*) (1686), which appeared around the same time.[12] In diametric opposition to what the Cartesian perpetual secretary of the Paris Academy of Sciences proposed—an ordered cosmos emanating directly from the acceptance of heliocentrism coupled with Descartes's idea of the vortex as the motive force in the cosmos—Stansel offered his readers a world governed by innumerable forces about which the natural philosopher, indeed science itself, had little to say. Stansel often reminded his readers that many things were "hidden from the human mind" (*recondita ab hominium mentibus*), before expounding his theories on the problems under examination. Even if he later advanced a plausible explanation of the facts, he always presented his theories as provisional, as though the world could be otherwise. The cosmos could be the way it was due to the action of celestial stimuli, or it could possibly be the result of the cosmic sympathies governing the relations between the microcosm and the macrocosm. The idea that the true "laws" of the world are hidden from men remained much stronger in the middle of the seventeenth century than one might believe at first glance.

To be sure, Stansel does not take questions about the general organization of the universe lightly. On the contrary, he vigorously defends, for example, the polycentrism of the world, which is more or less the geoheliocentric system of Tycho Brahe, a solution to the problem of incorporating the data of heliocentrism within a traditional Ptolemaic-Aristotelian universe that had been the official astronomy of the Society of Jesus for over a half-century.[13] But the most important questions for Stansel are not related to planetary movements, speed, the order of the planets, epicycles, and the like; these are only inventions for calculations. Through Urania's commentaries, Stansel informed his readers that he was concerned principally with the causes of these movements. In fact, during the second half of the seventeenth century, several solutions to this problem were presented. Stansel examines two of them: that of Kepler, who proposed the movement of the sun and magnetism as the driving force of the stars; and the more traditional solution of the force of divine intelligences in determining the motions of planetary bodies proposed by a number of theologians since antiquity. On this question, Stansel closely followed the opinions of his fellow Jesuit Kircher: he used arguments based on contemporary knowledge of magnetism to refute Kepler's theses, but accepted the idea of divine intelligences, which were readily assimilated into the current understanding of angelic forces, proposed in the arguments of classical theologians.[14]

Stansel's *Uranophilus* displays a world that is well-organized but not subjected in any way to a single, precise, and univocal logic, or if one prefers, a clear and distinct logic. Stansel seems to have abandoned the option of scientific coherence in the name of local and efficacious explanations of events. In one passage, after having adopted the solution of intelligent driving forces as a plausible explanation for heavenly movements, he examines the potential for atomistic theses to explain the same phenomena, and displays excitement at the possibilities opened up by Descartes's thought.[15] His particular manner of seeing the world effectively takes us back to the propositions of his illustrious correspondent in Rome, Father Kircher. As we have already remarked, the two made similar choices in the narrative form of their imaginary voyages. They also adopted explanations and evaluated theories in a similar fashion, discussing new philosophical ideas without calling into question a clearly established system of ideas.

Let me take the characteristic use of a genre of scientific experiment as an example of their approach. Kircher proposed "experiments by analogy" to explain the action of celestial bodies on the earth both in his works as a whole and in the *Itinerarium Exstaticum* in particular. This type of "experiment" was widely appreciated in the seventeenth century. In 1665, the astronomer António Pimenta, for example, acknowledged having taken an experiment capable of showing the formation of comet tails from the work of Niccolò Cabeo. Pimenta hung a glass ball filled with water in front of a candle and observed the formation of a cone of light on the other side of the ball. He maintains that this experiment would help astronomers and philosophers to understand the appearance of comets.[16]

To return to the activities of Father Athanasius, Kircher proposed an experiment capable of explaining the influences of Mars on the lives of men, when the characters of the *Itinerarium Exstaticum* are on this planet. He maintained that if one burned a sphere composed of bitumen, sulfur, and other substances in a closed room, then any man placed there would experience intense anger and worry, since the red planet governed these qualities.[17] Stansel cited this same experiment, proposing others for the effects of Saturn on the human mind, while always referring to the work of Kircher as the most authoritative source for this kind of experimentation. It is worth noting that the scientific missionary in Brazil assured his readers that he read all about these experiments in the *Great Art of Light and Shadow* (1646), not in the pages of the *Itinerarium Exstaticum*.[18] While the experiment is effectively described in the *Great Art of Light and Shadow*, the fact it also appears in a more recent publication that is far closer in form and style to the *Uranophilus* leads one to think that Stansel wanted to distance himself from the *Itinerarium Exstaticum* and was loathe to cite it.[19] In fact, the author of the review in the *Acta* was right to be suspicious of the feigned ignorance in the work of Father Valentin: it was impossible, really unthinkable, that he would not be familiar with the Kircherian dialogue. Kircher wrote this work at the height of his fame. It was widely diffused throughout Europe and every corner of the world where the Jesuits went. It is thus highly unlikely that a missionary-mathematician, who was in Rome in 1656 and in Lisbon the following years, would be unfamiliar with this volume.

But we can well understand the possible reason for Stansel's distancing himself from the work that he had seen published the year he passed through Rome and that belonged to the same genre as the one he was writing. The *Itinerarium Exstaticum* was subjected to internal censorship by the Society of Jesus, and it was the subject of rather lively discussions among Jesuit theologians who examined it at the College of Revisors (Collegium Revisorum).[20]

Father Valentin himself had already had problems with censorship when he attempted to publish "Vulcanus Mathematicus" *The Mathematical Vulcan Mathematicus*.[21] It is highly probable that he dissimulated the obvious connections between his *Uranophilus* and the *Ecstatic Volume* by pretending never to have read it. This remains a possible solution to the mystery of Stansel's apparent ignorance of Kircher's book. The affair also shows, however, that dissimulation was a part of the relations between Jesuit writers and the internal censors of the Society.[22]

Beyond what one might think about the relative independence and reluctant submission of scientific Jesuits to the disciplinary norms of the Order, Kircher's and Stansel's use of this "experiment by analogy" suggests that they shared other, more complex propositions. A somewhat less critical evaluation of the use of this "experience" might conclude that it served only to reinforce an idea in play at the time by means of an analogy of doubtful taste. However, Kircher appreciated the Neoplatonic philosophy of his time. He held dear the ideas of the fifteenth-century theologian cardinal and philosopher Nicholas of Cusa and the Hermetic theses that were passionately discussed during those years. One of the most important propositions to emerge from this philosophical ambiance is defended in the *Itinerarium Exstaticum* and elsewhere: that of the universal correspondence among created things. Father Athanasius followed in the cardinal's footsteps in these matters: the idea of creation *ex nihilo* implied that God made every worldly being from himself. Now, this is to say that the essence of each thing is none other than the essence of God. From this proposition, it is easy to conclude that *omnia in omnibus* (everything is in everything)—the cherished theme of Neoplatonism since the Renaissance.[23]

Kircher based his comprehension of the correspondence between things of the world on Cusa's ontology.[24] His explanation of the relations between the microcosm and the macrocosm, and the hidden virtues of plants, animals, and minerals, also fits nicely in this domain: the totality makes possible the connections between things. Thus, an experiment made in a room *could* reproduce the effects of the celestial influences on man; it sufficed to be thoroughly acquainted with the secrets of the connections between things. This reflection, however, leads to another conclusion: human realizations, too, are part of this chain of correspondences; that which is made by the human hand cannot escape the relations among things. Thus anchored in these ideas, Kircher built his research program: "we search for the connection of the whole Universe and also the connections among corporeal things by an original and new method."[25]

3. The Kircherian Scientific Program

In addition to sharing many specific things, both Stansel's *Uranophilus* and Kircher's *Itinerarium Exstaticum* offer us a good starting point for understanding Kircher's scientific project. While it is the proper role of a dialogue to investigate fundamental themes, to present what is essential and true about the state of knowledge, Kircher presented his particular way of conceiving the organization of the world in all of his voluminous scientific writings. Each work was conceived as a large encyclopedia in which knowledge was organized in an extensive way: in each book, Father Athanasius tried to expose the ensemble of known correspondences among all things. Thus, he explained tides when he wrote on magnetism; he exposed the principal astronomical theories when the subject was light; and so on. The fact that Kircher's theses confronted the most important questions science was posing at the time is an important reminder of why his scientific project endured so long. Thus, in the debates on magnetism, for example, and particularly in the controversy with the Tuscan physician and naturalist Francesco Redi, Father Athanasius made explicit certain elements of his thought that help us to understand better his basic notions. Martha Baldwin examined this debate several years ago, so I will not discuss it in further detail here.[26] Kircher and Redi disagreed in the 1660s about the virtues of the snakestone, a fantastic object from India that could be found in the head of a certain type of viper. It was said that the stone could heal people poisoned by the bites of other venomous beasts. It was enough to place the stone on the fresh bite: it would absorb the poison present in the victim's body. The poison left the stone when it was placed in a glass of milk or cold water. This marvelous object arrived in Europe toward the middle of the seventeenth century, via missionary networks, and its fabulous qualities were examined in several places on the Continent.

For the subject of this essay, we should concentrate on the epistemological questions that divide these two natural philosophers: Redi, the Florentine doctor, enlisted in the camp devoted to discrediting the "marvels of faraway lands" and knowledge founded on hearsay. Redi was a philosopher of the Galileian school active in Florence in the age of the Accademia del Cimento. For him, the regularity of nature's laws assured the natural order, and these laws acted on the entire earth. The singular virtues of special objects had no place in his world, nor could he easily accept the stone's effectiveness.

By contrast, relations of resemblance imposed by the nature of creation itself governed Kircher's world. The natural order was, in fact, nothing but the fabric of correspondences among things established by the act of creation. This same fabric assured the regularity of events. Kircher's notion of order permitted, among other things, the inclusion of singular virtues, marvelous things, and serpent stones. For Father Kircher, order lay in the harmony of the world and not at all in the laws of nature. The snakestone conformed perfectly to his idea of nature. The controversy between the two was therefore intense: Redi repeated experiments to prove his theses, while Kircher tried to explain the sympathies between the stone and the poison.

The matter was more important than it might seem. The novelties that the missionaries brought back bore witness to the success of the actions of European men of faith in the East. If they did not work as described, then a black stain would be thrown on the edifying reports of the missionaries. Father Kircher could not afford to miss an opportunity to put his scientific project at the service of such an important cause of the Society of Jesus, even though doing so meant risking his philosophical reputation.

Kircher's treatment of two other important questions, which have been thoroughly studied in the history of science and concern the mathematization of natural philosophy, can help clarify his way of conceiving the nature of human knowledge. In fact, the problem of falling bodies and the trajectory of projectiles attracted the attention of many scholars of the time, so Kircher could not remain silent on these matters. He agreed to debate this subject, but he always was careful not to participate too actively in these conversations. Moreover, the endurance of his project for knowledge, as attested by the confrontation between his ideas and those that have since enjoyed wider acceptance, remains an important way to evaluate their strength.

Father Athanasius analyzed the law of falling bodies and projectiles in two works: "Musurgia Universalis" *Universal Music-making* (1650) and the *Mundus Subterraneous Subterranean World* (1665). He explained Galileo's best-known conclusions without any difficulty. As he wrote, bodies fall according to square of time, which is to say that they fall at a distance proportionate to uneven numbers for each unit of time. Kircher's demonstrations are those of Tuscan philosopher and mathematician. Similarly, Kircher accepted Galileo's description of projectiles as well as his use of a parabola in his account. But it was how Kircher interpreted these results that differed so dramatically from the conclusions of Galileo. Kircher stripped them of their philosophical content; such results were mathematical constructions that did not belong to the realm of reality. Kircher did not believe that the "book of the world" was written in mathematical characters. For him, the falling of bodies according to the square of time remained a mathematician's artifice, a piece of *a posteriori* knowledge that was not connected to the natural world itself. Father Athanasius accepted Galileo's idea of falling bodies as either a description of appearances, a good technique for making knowable the approximate position of a falling body, or a useful instrument for the mechanical arts. But there was no question of taking a theorem, a mathematical construction, as an "intrinsic law" of the natural world.[27] The same can be said of planetary movements. According to Galileo, the mathematical world has no end, no Aristotelian final cause. Relations among events are determined in a univocal manner. There is no place in such a world for understanding cooperation between first and secondary causes, since the Galileian universe does not hide any secrets or messages to be decoded. Governed by Euclidean geometry, this world is determined and complete and thus shares no characteristics with the Kircherian world.

To the extent Kircher accepted that the relations among things could be described mathematically, it was because, for him, such a description could only

have local value—the shadow on the sundial and the movement of the sun—
or a practical utility, as in astrological prediction. Other rules, such as sympathy and influences, governed the fabric of correspondences among things, and
their logic could not be expressed by precise quantities. Furthermore, since
omnia in omnibus—all things are in all other things—and each specific thing
or event exists in relation to all others through a comprehension of the totality,
a mathematical treatment of these relations turns out to be unimaginable.

Kircher could not accept the idea that mathematics could be used to construct knowledge of the physical world, a description of appearances without
any possibility of generalization. Nonetheless we should recall that appearances
for him are not temporary manifestations of a fundamental essence about
which one cannot, or rather does not, want to say very much. Kircher makes
clear in his work in general, and in the *Itinerarium Exstaticum* in particular,
that things occur as the result of God's contraction, as he learned in his readings of the philosophy of Cardinal Nicholas of Cusa. According to Cusa, when
God wished to create the world, he had nothing other than himself to create
beings. Indeed, he derived all beings from himself by a process that he called
"contraction."[28] In effect, we are very far from debates about the treatment of
appearances, so dear to nominalism, that informed the question of alternative
world systems and their relationship to the physical reality of the universe since
the publication of Copernicus's *On the Revolutions of the Heavenly Orbs* in
1543. In any case, the Society of Jesus distanced itself from nominalism since
the founding of the Order. The decision to anchor their philosophical studies
in Thomist realism was made in the context of the scholastic discussions of the
second half of the sixteenth century. By Kircher's time, the debates revolved
around other questions, such as Neoplatonic and Stoic ideas.

The universe of Kircher, this organic world where all things relate to each
other, turned out to be open to innumerable possibilities that are unthinkable
in the fixed structure of the "laws of nature" of the Galilean world. Kircher's
universe could include serpent stones, sirens, giants, and dragons, for example.[29] Such things were possible even when they did not seem probable. For
Father Athanasius, to assert the "mathematical laws of nature" was tantamount to setting limits on the act of creation, which put the natural philosopher in the position of placing interdictions on the actions of God.

Given these philosophical presuppositions, Kircher's scientific project could
only follow the path of what he took to be the world of appearances: an enormous encyclopedia of the world with long descriptions incorporating analyses
of doubtful facts. This science could study any natural event or product of
man. There was no exemplary phenomenon that represented a synthesis of nature, as the law of falling bodies did for Galileo. There was no precise and
quantifiable universal law.

The work of the Kircherian natural philosopher was nothing more than the
identification of the place of each fact, examined in the ensemble of the world,

in the relations of sympathy that connected it to remote phenomena. But the idea according to which the universe was the *maximus contractus* also implied that each being appeared in all its integrity. Of course, if the relations among things are an expression of a sign left on a being created at the origin of the world, then appearance cannot be limited to something temporary, or opposed to essence as it was understood in sixteenth- and seventeenth-century philosophy. What we have here is a scientific program that studies appearances—a science of appearances. For Kircher, it must be recalled, the essence lay in the appearance. And the place of things in the totality of the universe could be grasped only by the study of appearances, thanks to this major fact of creation: *ex nihilo*. We are, in effect, far from the modern concept of "phenomenon"—a natural occurrence about which scientists can find some law of regularity, enumerating, quantifying, and understanding it in its connections with proximate causes. Kircher and his fellow Jesuits first asked the question regarding the place of appearance in the totality of creation.

Comprehending this aspect of Kircher's work helps one understand the enormous credulity that accompanied the studies of Kircher and other scholars who followed the same basic ideas: Stansel's belief in the real existence of mythological beings, such as dragons or the monster found on the coast of Portuguese America is a good example of this willingness to suspend disbelief.[30] There are no interdictions, no things that cannot exist. Since there are only appearances, it suffices that the appearance be real and that it have appeared to a reliable witness in order to enter it into the ranks of things that deserve to be studied.

Such a science could live easily with experimental demonstrations such as the experiment by analogy cited above. Appearance sufficed to reproduce the essential effects. Such a science could also absorb the most important results of the new science of Galileo or Descartes. We have already seen that Kircher and Stansel did so without much difficulty. It was enough to take the results of any new philosophy in a strictly local sense.

But it is clear that other important natural philosophers of the period could not easily accept the propositions of Father Athanasius. Beyond Redi's response, the Florentine scientific community at the end of Galileo's lifetime ridiculed the work of the Jesuit from his first publications. Evangelista Torricelli, for example, reported to Galileo, in the following terms, about the publication of Kircher's *Magnet, or the Magnetic Art* (1642):

> Two bits of news here: the death of Cardinal Pio, and the publication of Father Athanasius Kircher's book that has been greatly anticipated for many years. He is the Jesuit mathematician from Rome. The work is a rather thick volume on magnets: a volume rich with a great supply of beautiful engravings. You will find astrolabes, clocks, wind-meters, with a handful of most extravagant words. Among other things, there are a lot of small and larger decanters, epigrams, diptych, epitaphs, and inscriptions, partly in Latin, partly in Greek, partly in Arabic, partly in

Hebrew and other languages. Amongst the fine things is the score of that music that is said to be an antidote to the tarantula's venom. Enough said: Signor Nardi, Signor Maggiotti, and I laughed for quite a long time.[31]

Other important philosophers and mathematicians exchanged similarly unfavorable letters on the propositions and science of Kircher. Descartes called him a charlatan, and Constantijn Huygens did not see very much in his books.[32] In short, Kircher's project for the science of his time did not please some of the most active scientists of what is called the Scientific Revolution of the seventeenth century. But it must be recalled that what would eventually become "modern science" was still disputed and that the theories and dominant tendencies of this new science were not yet well defined. This explains the fact that the very honorable Robert Boyle of the Royal Society recommended that traveling naturalists verify the existence of the snake and the marvelous stone in the part of his scientific instructions concerning the Orient that did not appear in print until 1692.[33]

4. A Baroque Project for Science

Kircher's ideas were real solutions for knowledge offered in search of a new science. To not accept this aspect of his work is anachronistic. One cannot examine his basic propositions with the eventual shape of modern metaphysics in view, since it was just being born at this time. The refusal to take seriously Kircher's science risks restricting the study of the scientific life of this time to a group of well-organized and better-appreciated seventeenth-century natural philosophers. In the twenty-first century the battles of the Galileans or Cartesians have long been won; nothing justifies reviving the Redi-Athanasius debates. It is perhaps more satisfying to try to re-create the philosophical ambiance that sought the meaning of Kircher's propositions in his own time. Then we might be able to grasp important elements that contribute to our understanding of the complex relations between science and culture.[34] The examination of his thought and of the heterodoxy of its metaphysical foundations suggests rather important connections between scientific thought and manifestations of culture in the seventeenth century. This was, after all, the age of the baroque. It seems useful to inquire whether the project that Kircher shared with his colleagues can find its place within this broader cultural movement.

During the seventeenth century, the use of a scientific language full of imagery and rich with metaphors and allegories was common among a much broader set of scientific milieus than the rather restricted circle of "Kircherian scholars." One can find in the works of Redi, Galileo, and even Descartes interesting examples of the use of the resources of baroque literary style. They also used expressions that fit well with Kircher's project: "harmony of the world," "theater of the world," "proportions of nature," and still others. The point is not to identify typical expressions of baroque discourse in use by the natural philosophical community. Rather, it is a question of the meaning and role of concepts in a restless intellect that were translated into words and common expressions of the period. For Kircher and Stansel, these expressions are of fundamental significance. They translate an organic idea of the world, an idea of nature that equates it with a fabric of relations among things from which nothing can escape.

By contrast, if turns of phrases, figures, and expressions typical of baroque writing are effectively found in the scientific texts of the Galileian-Cartesian philosopher, they do not go beyond the limits of literary form or beyond an idea of harmony that is not at all Kircher's. Cartesians made use of these cultural resources, but the expression "harmony of the world" only had the function of embellishing their discourse and of suggesting precise numerical relationships between the things in the world. Kircherian and Cartesian philosophers meant two different things when they used this expression. The former group saw it as a specific way of conceiving the organization of the created world, while the latter group felt that "harmony" only recalled the beauty and perfection of the world.

Rather than reexamining Kircher's work from the point of view of his literary style, it seems more interesting to investigate the homology between the form of baroque writing and the presuppositions of Father Athanasius's ontology. This investigation produces rather interesting results, since Kircher's works found their most favorable reception, geographically and chronologically, precisely in those areas where baroque literature flourished in Europe and elsewhere, especially in the New World, where, for example, one finds Father Stansel, Sor Juana, and Don Carlos de Sigüenza y Góngora.[35]

The scholarship about baroque art and literature that has emerged since the early twentieth century suggests that the fascinating spell of appearances and of the instability of the world were important traces of the culture.[36] But, on the other hand, the problem of abusing allegory was also part of the arsenal of resources available to writers of the baroque period. Authors used allegories and metaphors in their works, but they themselves discussed the limits and conditions of allegorical discourse: Emmanuele Tesauro, Matteo Peregrini, and Baltasar Gracián are among those who examined this problem in the mid–seventeenth century. Yet still, if one takes into consideration the discussions of what was called *pensiero peregrino* (thought that travels), it will not be surprising to note that one of the strong cultural presuppositions in this period was the very idea that things and facts maintained reciprocal connections.[37]

Pensiero peregrino—traveling thought; *la pointe* sharpness or wit; *la agudeza*—witticism. These subtle metaphors made such concepts comprehensible by deciphering the established connections among ideas, sentiments, and events. A good example of wit in the literature of this time can be found in the works of the Jesuit Baltasar Gracián, one of the most accomplished writers of the Spanish Golden

Age. In the first words of his book *The Critic* (*El Criticón*), he writes the following phrase: "the island of Saint Helena (on the stairway from one world to another) served as the landing place of portable Europe, and a generous wind always blew, maintaining the Catholic fleets of the Orient in the middle of immense seas by divine clemency."[38] Portable Europe is the expression that serves him in order to describe the long voyages of the age of navigation and his work in distant lands. For the reader, it was a question of finding the place of an idea in a chain of correspondences in the world. Thus writing about a pilgrim or a path could easily lead to a reflection on the life of men in this world or on the paths to salvation, to cite only one of the best-known allegories of the baroque period.

It is surely profitable to view the things and events on which Kircher spent his intellectual energy as so many "witticisms": the snakestone, the crosses that appeared over Naples after the eruption of Vesuvius, fossils, experiments by analogy, and so many others. Using the baroque idea of witticism to try to explain the Jesuit's approach to the natural world effectively helps us understand the nature of his explanations. The experiment by analogy—whose importance is absolutely fundamental to understanding Kircher—should be interpreted as the reduction, at the level of the "laboratory," of baroque metaphor: the reproduction in a closed room of the influences of Mars on men, the enflamed ball that leads to the red planet. Kircher's understanding of facts or events was indeed comparable to the idea of baroque witticism. According to Kircher, the chain that connected one thing to another found its parallel in the chain that led readers from the metaphor to the idea hidden beneath it. This remains a rather promising hypothesis for approaching some understanding of the Jesuit's thought.

5. The Destiny of Outmoded Ideas

Following the precepts of Neoplatonic philosophy that were more common in the sixteenth and seventeenth centuries, Father Kircher organized his thought around his conception of totality. He was always interested in building a discourse that examined the whole. His studies were never limited to a single event taken in isolation. Above all, his goal was always to ask questions in relation to that totality, to explore the principal relations among things, and to the place of each of them in the ensemble of the universe. This put him in diametric opposition to the most important transformations of the thought of his period, or more precisely, to those transformations that have been *recognized* as the most visible signs of scientific modernity. A significant part of modern scientific discourse developed precisely in opposition to the notion of the sympathies and correspondences and influences among things. Thus, it is not surprising to see all of Kircher's work forgotten for the past three hundred years. This essay, which describes the main features of Kircher's thought, helps us understand the difficulty in accepting his oeuvre as a kind of *scientific* work. The paths that science eventually chose did not accept Father Athanasius's basic propositions. Moreover, Kircher was Jesuit. For a long time, this single fact served to reinforce the idea that his propositions could have no relation to scientific thought. It is enough to recall Jules Michelet's protests against "the men in black" to realize the problem.[39]

This problem was still more profound in regard to the work of Father Valentin. We should consider the fact that he worked in Salvador, capital of the Portuguese colony in the New World. This played an important role in his situation, given the fact that the principal philosophical and scientific debates of the seventeenth century did not pass directly through Portugal, as they had two hundred years earlier. Indeed, the work of Stansel was thrown into oblivion due to the aforementioned evolution of scientific ideas, the disappearance of his intellectual network, and his situation as a colonial scholar. In Portuguese America his history was no different. There—where he had earned a certain prestige among his fellow Jesuits and in the broader colonial culture, in particular due to his controversy with Father Antônio Vieira—twenty years after his death almost no one concerned themselves with his writings.

The natural philosophers in Kircher's entourage, including Father Valentin Stansel, were victims of the same neglect. Disciples such as Kaspar Schott, Giuseffo Petrucci, and so many others also fell into oblivion. Only in the past century have the ideas of these natural philosophers again emerged as worthy of study, as we have reevaluated baroque culture and reorganized the history of science. Finally, the conceptual effort to put together again two domains of culture that were for the longest time apparently so far removed suggests a promising approach to pursuing this subject further. But we are still very far from solving the complex problems that follow from the proposal to examine scientific thought under the instruments of literary criticism.

Notes

*   The author thanks the CNPq for having made the research for this essay possible.
1.   Corradino 1990, p. 24.
2.   *Acta Eruditorum* 1685, p. 235.
3.   The work was published two more times in Würzburg in 1660 and 1671, augmented with short explanatory texts by Kaspar Schott and other documents. These editions were published under the title *Iter Exstaticum*. I have used the last edition.
4.   Cf. Camenietzki 1995a.
5.   Many authors have examined this genre. See the bibliography of Schatzberg et al. 1987, but especially Nicolson 1948.
6.   *Journal des Sçavants* 15, 1685, p. 309.
7.   The archive of the Pontificia Università Gregoriana contains several letters sent by Stansel to Kircher. They have been available now for several years electronically through a digital archive at the Istituto e Museo di Storia della Scienza in Florence and at Stanford University, thanks to the efforts of Michael Gorman and Nick Wilding. The URL of the Stanford site is http://kircher.stanford.edu.
8.   See the bibliography at the end of the volume.
9.   Dobrzenski 1657, p. 113, and others.
10.   Lo Sardo 2001; and Findlen 1995.
11.   Isaac Newton, for example, cited Stansel's work in his *Principia Mathematica*. Newton 1687, p. 507–508; *Le Giornale dei Letterati* 9 (September 31, 1673) also cites it on pages 134–136; the *Philosophical Transactions* cite the same observations in vol. 9, 1674, pp.

91–93. Ten years ago Stansel's observations of the comets were studied in Casanovas and Keenan 1993.

12. Fontenelle 1686.

13. Lattis 1994.

14. Stansel supports this idea through the mouth of Urania: "Planetas, caeteraque tam errantia quam inerrantia astra, ab intelligentiis sive angelis circumago." Stansel 1685a, p. 69.

15. He cites Descartes on many occasions and critiques his heliocentrism. Cf. Stansel 1685a, p. 104.

16. Pimenta 1665, p. 34.

17. Kircher 1671a, p. 252.

18. Stansel 1685a, pp. 134–135.

19. Kircher 1646, p. 544.

20. In fact, though the Collegium Revisorum censured it, the book was nevertheless published. This provoked an internal discussion in the Society. Camenietzki 1995a.

21. The document of censorship of this work is still at the Archivium Romanum Societatis Iesu, *Fondo Gesuitico* 672, fol. 35. The book was censured, among other reasons, for the Cartesian theses it presented and defended.

22. Dissimulation has been strongly associated with the Jesuits for a long time. Since the appearance of the work of Rosario Villari, scholars have also seen it as an important resource for understanding baroque culture. See Villari 1987; and the recent volume of the journal *Sigila* (2001) devoted to this subject.

23. "Ita Universum per natura in omnibus omnia est, & ita omnia quoque in mundo, tametsi nobis occulta, & humano ingenio incomprehensa proportione connectic, ut tamen perfecte conspirent: & quamvis innumeri in mundo globi incomprehensa proportione connectit, ut tamen perfecte conspirent; & quamvis innumeri in mundo globi sint nobis incogniti, & extra omnen sensuum comprehensionem longe remotissimi; ita tamen per naturam, quae est ars Dei, & spiritus universorum, seu anima mundi, apte connectuntur, & per motum in tantam harmoniam concinnantur, ut unum sine altero, sine totius dissolutione, esse non possit." Kircher 1671a, pp. 399–400. Father Athanasius also invokes this idea in his explanation of the method of the *Ars magna sciendi*; Kircher 1669, p. 2.

24. Leinkauf 1993.

25. Kircher 1667b, p. 19.

26. Baldwin 1995.

27. "Quod vero proportiones imparium numerorum huic exacte quadrent a posteriori est; cum enim huiusmodi projectilium linae parabolae similissimae sint, ut parabolis veris, ita & projectilium lineis verisimillimis facile applicari possunt. Est enim Geometricis, & Arithmeticis rebus ita comparatum, ut physicis rebus quibuscunque facile applicentur, etiamsi nullum in physicis demonstratarum affectionum fundamentum sit." Kircher 1650a, vol. 2, p. 422.

28. The most important work summarizing Cusa's thought that is of interest in relation to this discussion is his *De Docta Ignorantia*. See Cusa 1932.

29. In fact, Kircher conceives the universe according to the terms formulated by Cardinal Nicholas of Cusa: the totality is *maximus contractus*, or indefinite finitude, in contrast with the *maximus absolutus*, God.

30. Camenietzki and Zeron 2000.

31. "Due nuove ci sono : la morte del Cardinale Pio, e la stampa, aspettatissima già sono anni del P. Atanasio Kircher. Questo è il gesuita matematico di Roma. L'opera stampata è un volume assai grosso sopra la calamita; volume arrichitto con una gran supelletile di bei rami. Sentirà astrolabii, horologii, anemoscopii, con una mano poi di vocabuli stravagantissimi. Fra l'altre cose vi sono moltissimi carraffe e carraffoni, epigrammi, distici, epitafii, inscrittioni, parte in latino, parte in greco, parte in arabico, parte in hebraico et altre lingue. Fra le cose belle vi è, in partitura, quella musica che dice esser antidoto del veleno della tarantola. Basta: il Sr Nardi e Maggiotti et io habbiamo riso un pezzo." Galilei 1968, vol. 18, p. 332.

32. Descartes 1974–89, vol. 5, pp. 548–549; Mersenne 1933–72, vol. 14, p. 636.

33. The text asks its readers to verify the following: "Whether there be found in the head of a certain snake, a stone, which laid upon a wound of any venomous creature, sticks fast to it, and draws away all the poysson: then, being put into milk, voids its poison, and turns the milk blue; and then applied again, draws many behind, till the wound be perfectly cured." Boyle 1692, p. 83.

34. Since the publication of Panofsky's study on Galileo's participation in discussions of painting and sculpture, several works have sought to understand the connections between Galileo's science and his aesthetics. Panofsky 1954; Damianaki 2000. This sort of reflection remains rather promising. But beyond the figurative arts and beyond Galileo and his surroundings, the relations between baroque literature and seventeenth-century natural philosophy await further work by other scholars.

35. See the essays by Michelle Molina and Paula Findlen in this volume for further discussion of Kircher's thought in New Spain. For a very interesting study of the use of astronomical themes in the sermons of the Portuguese master of letters António Vieira, see Carolino 1997. On the baroque in Brazil, see Coutinho 1994; and Hansen 1989.

36. In the first decades of the twentieth century, the discussions of the baroque took the opposition between Benedetto Croce and Eugenio D'Ors as their point of departure. Later, several scholars addressed the task of characterizing the most important traits of literature and arts in the seventeenth century. Within French scholarship, which appeared later than the work of the Italians and Spanish, the works of Victor L. Tapier, Marcel Raymond, and Jean Rousset are important for a more comprehensive exposition of the baroque. More recently, a new edition of the work of Claude-Gilbert Dubois has made available a rather clear exposition of the problem I am addressing; Dubois 1993. It is no exaggeration to say that the baroque remains a central problem for a number of scholars in France and elsewhere.

37. As one can easily imagine, the most important texts that discuss these figures of style in the baroque period were composed by writers who were furthest removed from this culture. See Tesauro 1654; Pellegrini 1650; and Gracián 1649. A recently published study reviews the debates on *pensiero peregrino*; Blanco 1992.

38. Graciàn 1984, p. 65.

39. "I have cited an illustrious example of a machinery that is powerful for action, impotent for production; the Jesuit order which, in three centuries of existence, has not produced one single man or one single book of genius." Michelet 1880, p. 41.

15

A Jesuit's Books in the New World

*Athanasius Kircher and His American Readers**

PAULA FINDLEN

1. Putting Kircher on the Shelf

Of all the libraries whose shelves buckled under the weight of Athanasius Kircher's hefty tomes, only two, to my knowledge, have been recorded for posterity. Around 1720, the Bolognese painter Giuseppe Crespi received a commission to decorate the cabinet doors of a music library.[1] Appropriately Crespi conceived of it as a trompe l'oeil, painting an image of a music library on the library itself (Figure 15.1). Sitting on the top shelf on the upper right is a fat, short volume, slightly recessed in relation to books that spill over its edge, but anchoring the entire row of books by being placed exactly in the middle. It is Kircher's *Musurgia universalis* (*Universal Music-making*) (1650), one of his most popular books in his lifetime and a standard work of music history and theory for the next century. Its presence in a painting of an early-eighteenth-century library reminds us just how canonical Kircher's encyclopedias were for many different disciplines in this period. Even as they ceased to be the latest summation of any particular branch of knowledge, they continued to represent the idea of the definitive text.

If Kircher's books were read enough to become part of a painting of a music library in Bologna, second city in the papal state, they were also symbolically important to the idea of erudition in other contexts that were considerably removed from his dynamic presence in seventeenth-century Rome. Kircher's reputation was not confined to the geographic boundaries of Europe. During his own lifetime his books could be found in libraries throughout the world. He had a global reputation that was virtually unsurpassed by any early modern author. "Here in Manila . . . I see many marvels which Your Reverence narrated in your books," wrote the Jesuit missionary Giovanni Montel in 1654. "I am the first to have brought one of them—the *Musurgia*—to the Indies. I do not doubt that it will be very useful for the Fathers in the missions where music is publicly taught." Montel, who died the following year in the Philippines, was an enthusiastic disciple who devoured Kircher's books before embarking on his mission, promising to write back to Rome about anything that he saw "in these lands that can confirm your doctrine."[2] He took Kircher's words and worldview with him—and the books as well.

Figure 15.1. Giuseppe Maria Crespi, *Music Library. Source:* Museo Bibliografico Musicale Rossini, Bologna. Courtesy of Scala/Art Resource.

Wherever Jesuit missionaries went, Kircher's books traveled. Kircher's *Musurgia* exemplifies the pattern of dispersion, though the specifics varied with each publication. Approximately 1,500 copies were printed in 1650. One was sent to every Jesuit college, a handful receiving an additional copy. Three hundred became gifts for the Jesuits who came to Rome to elect Goswin Nickel the new General of the Order in 1652. Another 352 were distributed throughout Europe, while 700 remained with the Amsterdam publisher Joannes Jansson, who, after all, was expecting a tidy profit from publishing Kircher. Where the French Jesuit Albert d'Orville acquired the 24 copies he took with him from Lisbon to China in October 1656 is uncertain, but he wrote of his satisfaction that Kircher's fame would "extend to the farthest edges of the earth." Kircher himself proudly advertised the fact that his books "were dispersed not so much in Europe but also in Africa, Asia, and America."[3] His accumulation of knowledge offered further proof of the post-Tridentine renewal of Catholic learning that reflected the unique role of the Society of Jesus as a vast and efficient machine for gathering, processing, and disseminating information.[4]

Kircher was such a lively and enduring presence in baroque Rome, visited by virtually everyone who came to the papal city, that it is easy for us to forget how many people encountered him primarily through his books and actually read these seemingly indigestible volumes. As early as the 1640s, the ships that departed from Lisbon and Seville carried Kircher's works to distant readers eager for his latest publication.[5] In the next few decades, his works were in great demand among readers outside Europe. In some instances, Kircher personally responded to requests for his publications, like Father Antonio Ceschi's 1648 letter from Agra (northern India) requesting a copy of his *Ars magnesia* (*Magnetic Art*) (1631), or as seen in Father Ignazio Arcamone's missive of 1671, expressing his gratitude that Kircher had sent copies of the *Ars magna lucis et umbrae* (*Great Art of Light and Shadow*) (1646) and *Obeliscus Pamphilius* (*Pamphilian Obelisk*) (1650) to Goa.[6] The majority of Kircher's New World readers, however, encountered Kircher's books as part of the Jesuit missionary network that routinely deposited them in colleges throughout the world and transported them from one place to another as Jesuits traveled. They did not get them directly from the famous author in Rome.

Distance seems to have magnified Kircher's reputation as one of the leading scholars of his day. "Oracle of sciences," pronounced one criollo reader after tasting the fruits of Kircher's erudition in Puebla. One Jesuit missionary joked that he was hoping to unearth "another Athanasius" in the Orient. "Perhaps one is not enough for Europe?"[7] The farther one traveled from Europe, the more printed books became scarce and precious commodities, even in places such as Mexico City, which had its own printing presses by 1539 but largely published devotional works.[8] Kircher's works were essential repositories of knowledge because they summed up so many other books that overseas readers could neither afford to take with them nor hope to acquire thousands of miles away from printing centers such as Amsterdam and Venice. They introduced readers to an infinity of subjects, providing definitive, up-to-date bibliographies on virtually every topic, intriguing descriptions of places and things, and beautifully engraved images of antiquities, curiosities, and instruments—a visual *wunderkammer* for the eyes to feast upon.

Equally important, the content of Kircher's books actively connected different parts of the world. Kircher routinely derived his information from missionary reports and overseas correspondents, making his books especially appealing to readers who might hope to participate in this new vision of knowledge. While he himself traveled very little, he understood the significance of travel to the pursuit of knowledge and responded to the growing curiosity about other cultures by providing his readers with tantalizing glimpses of the most interesting and less understood parts of the world. By the late seventeenth century, French and German Jesuits in China could read about Egypt and America in the pages of the *Oedipus Aegyptiacus* (*Egyptian Oedipus*) (1652–55); halfway around the world, Spanish criollos eagerly awaited the latest shipment of Kircher's China monumentis illustrata (*China Illustrated through its Monuments*) (1667) to learn more about Asia. The world did not grow smaller through Kircher's encyclopedias—quite the opposite, in fact—but he gave it a kind of philosophical intelligibility by providing a comparative framework through which to view cultures, languages, and artifacts and by insisting on the power of history and faith to unite disparate parts of the world.

Many of Kircher's most enthusiastic readers spent the majority or the entirety of their lives in the New World. His intellectual authority there seems to have persisted well after it declined within Europe, since American scholars continued to cite Kircher's works well into the early nineteenth century.[9] Readers who had the pleasure of paging through Kircher's books during his own lifetime were often compelled to write to Rome to tell him what his words meant to them. Juan Ramón de Coninck wrote from Peru in 1653 to tell Father Athanasius of the experience he had derived "from your books." He had read the *Prodomus Coptus (Coptic Forerunner)* (1636) and the first edition of the *Ars magna lucis et umbrae*—"which I possess"—and eagerly awaited the arrival of the *Oedipus*.[10] He wrote to Rome to offer his services as an observer of New World nature and culture, eager to become a footnote in one of Kircher's many projects. Coninck's pride in owning a copy of one Kircher's great encyclopedias of the natural world—surely one of the few examples in Peru at the time—mirrored Montel's satisfaction at being able to report to Kircher in 1654 that his copy of the *Musurgia* was circulating among the leading Jesuits in Manila. To possess one of Kircher's works "in the most remote corner of the world" was to own some tangible piece of the learned world.[11]

Getting a copy of Kircher outside of Europe was no easy matter. Since missionaries themselves had problems arriving successfully halfway around the world, the cost and difficulties of transporting books increased the value of those that survived the voyage. Even intimate disciples complained to Kircher about their problems acquiring his expensive tomes. Shipments arrived missing their precious cargo, like the copies of Kircher's *Historia Eustachio-Mariana (Marian-Eustachian History)* (1665) and *China monumentis illustrata* that mysteriously disappeared from their crate in Cadiz en route to New Spain (this is probably why one reader requested a copy of *El arte combinatoria* be sent in "a well closed chest").[12] In June 1670, the German Jesuit astronomer Valentin Stansel wrote from Salvador da Bahia to thank Father Athanasius for a copy of the most recent list of his publications. But he noted with some irony that this was all one could see of Kircher: "However, Brazil sees none of the books. Is Europe so greedy that it is unwilling to offer you to us?"[13] Staring at the titles of Kircher's publications, those in press and those yet to come, was part of the fantastic encounter with his mind. The publisher's list of the Kircherian corpus—a dynamic record of the fruits of his mind—was a challenge to the encyclopedic reader to possess it all, to read it all, to absorb every aspect of Kircher's wisdom as a prelude to one's own ascent to omniscience. It was a tantalizing advertisement that compelled potential readers to beg and borrow copies of the latest book from the next shipload of Jesuits disembarking in America.

The pages of Kircher's works offered a seemingly endless number of projects that his readers might realize—especially in the New World, where the possibilities for finding new information to add to the Kircherian corpus were particularly rich. Behind each of Kircher's works lay the Society of Jesus, which helped to finance their publication and ensured that each book had been vetted by the Jesuit censors.[14] But the Society also was an important community of potential readers, critics, and contributors to new and improved editions. Moreover, it expanded Kircher's readership in the New World, particularly in those parts of the Americas where Jesuits did not simply attempt to convert the indigenous population to Catholicism but participated in the creation and expansion of colonial society by playing a key role in the spiritual and intellectual life of the Spanish and Portuguese Americas. By the late seventeenth century, Kircher's books could be found in private libraries in the Americas. He was no longer read only by his fellow Jesuits but by European colonists and criollos whose own desire for erudition led them to engage with his works.[15]

For this reason, it is not surprising to discover that the other extant painting of Kircher's books depicts a library some six thousand miles west of Rome. In the first half of the eighteenth century, two painters put Kircher on the shelf in their depiction of one of the most discussed libraries in Mexico City. Their image of this library was copied by other artists during the next century. Quite curiously, it was one of the only libraries in New Spain owned by a woman. This particular reader played an especially memorable role in the reception of Kircher's thought not only due to the fame of her own writings but also because she was the only reader to transform his name into a verb. *Kirkerizar*, to kircherize, is a phrase that the Mexican nun, poet, philosopher, and theologian Sor Juana Inés de la Cruz (1651–95) bequeathed to posterity.[16] She was a sublime example of a reader who found a worldview in his books.

The story of Sor Juana Inés de la Cruz's fascination with the work of Kircher has become better known in the past two decades, thanks to Octavio Paz's marvelous biography of this Mexican nun, and to the work of various specialists in the poetry and prose of Sor Juana who in the 1930s first identified the importance of Kircher for her intellectual development.[17] But before discussing this subject, let us look at the two posthumous portraits of Sor Juana in her library. At least six years before Crespi decided to paint Kircher's *Musurgia*, the Mexican painter Juan de Miranda put the finishing touches on his portrait of Sor Juana; he completed it some time before his death in 1714 (Figure 15.2). In it, we see Sor Juana standing at a writing desk, looking out at us in the act of writing. To her right is her library, described by one biographer in the early eighteenth century as containing four thousand books, though others have estimated that it was no more than fifteen hundred, a large and impressive library at either end.[18] This imaginary library is a summation of the

Figure 15.2. Juan de Miranda, *Sor Juana Inés de la Cruz. Source:* Universidad Nacional Autónoma de México, Mexico City.

library that no longer existed by 1714, a selection of books representing different strands of Sor Juana's erudition. On the lowest shelf lie three volumes of her own writings. Behind them, shoved into a corner, is a book purporting to be the *Opera Kirkerio*.

Several decades later, Miguel Cabrera, described by his contemporaries as an American Kircher of the canvas, painted another important portrait of Sor Juana in her library.[19] He portrayed the Mexican nun in the act of reading rather than writing. Looking out at us, her hand is about to turn the page. This time, an even larger library forms the background of her portrait. Once again, Kircher is there. Just beyond the hefty tomes of medicine, represented especially by the works of Galen, lies a slim volume that is barely revealed by the raised red curtain. It is the only volume resting neither vertically nor horizontally on the shelf; in fact, it seems to float rather improbably in midair, as the spine never quite manages to touch the books below it—an appropriate way to depict the works of a natural philosopher who specialized in all sorts of optical illusions that made objects seem to levitate. Once again, it is the *Kirqueri Opera*.

The "works of Kircher" in Sor Juana's library were of course more than one book. In their entirety, a total of fifty-four printed volumes of some thirty books, they would have filled her imaginary library.[20] Both Miranda and Cabrera—

who knew something about the material appearance of these books and expected their viewers to get the joke—reduced some of the largest, most numerous, and weighty volumes ever to fill the shelves of any library down to a slim, inconsequential tome, just as Sor Juana condensed Kircher's ideas in her poems, transforming his prolix Latin sentences into short, elegant Castilian phrases. It is not certain how many of Kircher's books Sor Juana personally owned, but quite a few copies of his books were available in the libraries and bookshops of Mexico City, though there is no statistical study of book collecting to give us a better estimate of how many. Nonetheless we can see traces of Kircher in book inventories of this period, such as Juan de Sotto Noguera's declaration to the Holy Office in June 1699 that he was transporting "Noah's Ark" to New Spain.[21]

Sor Juana epitomized the kind of American readership of Kircher's works that developed in the second half of the seventeenth century. She repeatedly pulled his books down from the shelf in order to become learned. Mastering their content, evoking key ingredients, and ultimately critiquing the limits of Kircher's vision of the world were all fundamental aspects of her own claims to be a scholar of some note. Kircher's ideas became an essential resource in the evolution of her own epistemology of knowledge. Both Miranda and Cabrera understood this fact about Sor Juana when they painted her as a learned woman shaped by her encounter with the works of Kircher. There were many other books in her library, but Kircher's were among the most important.

2. Dreaming of Kircher

If Sor Juana were the only disciple of Kircher's in New Spain, we might consider her an anomaly—there were many other books to read. But she was hardly alone in her fascination with Father Athanasius. Instead we should see her as the culmination of a half-century's intellectual encounter with his encyclopedias. Between the 1650s and 1690s, there were a number of candidates for the title of the American Kircher—men and at least one woman who were so inspired by what they read that they tried to emulate it, building cabinets of curiosities filled with instruments and inventions lifted out of the pages of Kircher's books, pursuing and refining the ideas that he valued, and writing encyclopedic works of their own to rival those of Father Athanasius. In contrast to those owners of Kircher's book who saw them as lavishly illustrated coffee-table books, to be admired rather than read, the American Kircherians read Kircher with passion and erudition, agreeing with their Jesuit master that knowledge could not be confined to a single discipline but became tangible only when one sought out the connections among things.

Puebla, second city in the viceroyalty of New Spain, was home to two such individuals. The criollo cleric Alejandro Favián (b. 1624) was not a Jesuit but knew a number of the learned Jesuits who brought Kircher to America. One of them even had a personal connection with Kircher, since the French Jesuit François Guillot (1601–86) had briefly been Kircher's colleague and disciple at the Jesuit college in Avignon before departing for New Spain in 1635. He rebaptized himself Francisco Ximénez in the New World. Eight years later, the German Jesuit Walter Sonnenberg let him borrow a copy of Kircher's *Magnes, sive de arte magnetica* (*The Magnet, or the Magnetic Art*) (1641), which was already in its second edition by 1643, as Sonnenberg passed through Mexico on his way to the Philippines.[22]

During the following decade, Ximénez finally acquired a personal copy of one of Kircher's works, in all likelihood the *Musurgia*. In 1654, he moved to Puebla to become rector of the Colegio del Espíritu Santo. One year later, he reintroduced himself to Kircher as an old friend, speaking of his admiration for the German's books. It was early spring in Puebla, and the French Jesuit was nostalgic for youthful conversations of science in Avignon. He craved some reading material that reminded him of those days and added variety to his steady diet of Spanish books that emphasized, as he told Kircher, too much moral theology. "I . . . will procure all of the works of Your Reverence by every means that they may be sent to me." He offered to send Kircher "chocolate, multicolored feathered images, and some images in gold" in exchange for copies of his books.[23]

By July 1656, Ximénez seemed to have collected a good number of Kircher's books, save for the *Magnes*, but he had written to the Seville booksellers in hope of obtaining a copy. He continued to build his library over the next decade, though he often did not have time to read the books with any care, comparing the act of reading Kircher to the experience of being enclosed inside a small shell trying to see the vastness of the ocean.[24] Ximénez corresponded with Kircher until 1672, by which time he had become an ecclesiastical figure of note in New Spain, having moved to the Colegio Máximo de San Pedro y San Pablo in Mexico City in 1663, become confessor to the Spanish viceroy and vicereine (1665–73), and ultimately been elected the Provincial for New Spain (1674–77).[25] He continued to encourage Kircher to improve the quality of his information on the Americas through more regular contact with the missionary fathers.

Ximénez's decision to constitute a Kircherian library at the Jesuit college in Puebla created a nucleus of information about Kircher's projects that attracted other readers. In February 1661, he described the reaction of a "certain noble priest, avid for good books" who, after seeing "the index of Your Reverence's works, *Oedipum Egyptiacum*, *Itinera statica*, *Pestem, ac Misurgiam*" that Kircher had sent Ximénez, "burned with a vehement desire to buy all of Your Reverence's works at whatever price they are sold."[26] The eager Mexican reader was his younger friend Favián, who had already written to Rome several weeks earlier to express his utter admiration for Kircher's intellect.

Favián's encounter with Kircher was nothing short of prophetic. In Father Athanasius, he found the mentor he had always dreamed of. Favián had never seen anything like the four books that Ximénez showed him; he was fascinated and inspired. Initially Ximénez removed from his shelf the work that he thought would most intrigue his friend, an accomplished musician. As Favián later told Kircher, "the first [book] that he placed in my hands was the one of which I had dreamed, and it was the *Misurgia universal.*" Then Ximénez tantalized him by revealing "the catalogue of the rest that have seen the light in print and those that you were trying to print." Favián was awestruck that such erudition could exist. "Truly without exaggeration I say that nothing better has ever happened to me in my life."[27]

Dreaming of Kircher was one of the great intellectual fantasies of baroque Mexico. What did Favián find inside Father Athanasius's books that so excited him? In part, it was confirmation of his own ideas about the harmonic convergences of the world. But it was also Kircher's descriptions of musical instruments that helped Favián to understand the mechanism of a music box that made nine figurines dance to three different tunes. "At this time, one night I happened to dream that I had a wonderful book that described the composition of the said artificial instrument that had only vexed me, sketching and depicting it in its pages."[28] Shortly thereafter he found himself at the Colegio, where the book of his dreams materialized in Ximénez's library. Reading the catalogue of Kircher's books, he began to construct a list of the encyclopedias he needed to realize his own ambitions: *Mundus subterraneus* (*Subterranean World*), which did not appear until 1665, *Ars magna quam combinatoriam appellamus* (*The Great Art That We Call Combinatorial*), which eventually appeared as *Ars magna sciendi* (*The Great Art of Knowing*) in 1669, and especially the *Musurgia*. Favián also indicated an interest in two of Kircher's early publications that highlighted their shared interest in mathematical and astronomical instruments. He wanted to know how clocks ran and how magnets worked; he craved understanding of the properties of light, the mysteries of sound, and the secrets of language.[29] In Kircher, he had found the man he began to call his intellectual "father." Favián simply could not wait to become Kircher's "disciple."[30]

It seems curious that the one book absent from Favián's list had been the direct inspiration for the description of his dream. No reader of his letter of 2 February 1661 could miss the explicit reference to one of Kircher's most popular books, *Itinerarium exstaticum* (*Ecstatic Journey*), which originally appeared in 1656, followed by the *Iter ecstaticum ii* (*Second Ecstatic Journey*) (1657), which recounted Kircher's imaginary subterranean explorations. Cast in the form of a dream, this controversial work was especially popular with Kircher's American readers and spawned several imitations in Brazil and New Spain.[31] The year before Favián initiated his correspondence with Kircher, the Jesuit's disciple Kaspar Schott unified both in a revised edition that included a preface by Schott, which began by recounting a conversation he had purportedly had with Kircher that started with the Jesuit uttering the following words to his German disciple: "Father, last night I dreamed a remarkable dream."[32] Favián did not find the *Musurgia* by chance. In all probability, he was looking for it because he had read the *Iterinerarium exstaticum coelestis*, which was one of the four original books that Ximénez had showed him.

Favián corresponded regularly with Kircher until 1674, sending him money for books and instruments, samples of his own writings, gifts of chocolate, and other American curiosities that he thought might please his master. He became obsessed with the material replication of Kircher's world, describing in his letters "a new museum of magnificent architecture and genius that I have built in a most appropriate and delightful location, in imitation of Your Reverence." All it lacked were artifacts of science—clocks, telescopes, microscopes, magnetic machines, and other curious instruments that were the mainstay of Kircher's museum—because the New World, as Favián observed, was not sufficiently populated with artisans who knew how to make "such artificial things."[33] Reading Kircher's encyclopedias introduced him to a paper world of machines he considered essential to the realization of his own intellectual ambitions in Puebla. Favián filled his correspondence with specific questions about Kircher's machines. He was fascinated by the singing mechanical rooster on page 343 of the *Musurgia* (Figure 15.3). The images in the *Magnes* inspired him to think of building a magnetic machine. After reading the *Ars magna lucis et umbrae*, Favián wanted a catoptric theater, while the *Mundus subterraneus* inspired an interest in hydraulic devices. He begged Kircher for a good crystals and "those vitreous gradated lenses" and repeatedly reminded him to send a telescope—which finally arrived in 1667—so that he might show readers the power of Kircherian optics.[34]

Quite astutely, Favián understood the value of what he might offer Kircher. If Kircher helped him create a European cabinet of curiosities to rival the one at the Roman College, then Favián promised to "adorn yours with the most singular things that one can find here."[35] In exchange for transmitting American marvels to Europe, he anticipated the emergence of a scientific America that organized itself around collections of European books and machines such as the clock Kircher sent in 1662, which, disappointingly, was broken when it arrived, providing an opportunity for Favián to test his own mechanical skills when he fixed it.[36] Favián conceptualized this project through the reading practices he developed turning the large folio pages of Kircher's books, where his eye was drawn repeatedly to beautifully engraved images of machines. A Mexican reader such as Favián was acutely sensitive to the technical aspects of Kircher's books, which were increasingly works of art. His books, filled with copperplate engravings, *looked* different from the rougher printed volumes that rolled off the local presses. In an environment defined by the uniqueness

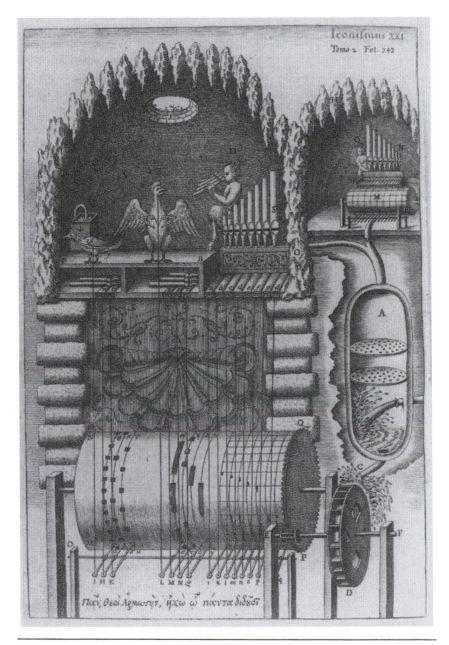

Figure 15.3. Kircher's singing mechanical rooster. *Source:* Athanasius Kircher, *Musurgia universalis* (Rome, 1650). Courtesy of Special Collections, Stanford University Libraries.

of American nature, Kircher offered his New World readers the fantasy of technology as well as the promise of omniscience.[37]

But it was Kircher the person who most filled his Mexican disciple with wonder. Favián treasured the letters he received from Rome, placing them in a bronze casket like precious relics. What he wanted most from Father Athanasius was his portrait (Figure 15.4). He first asked for a copy in 1663, promising that he would put it "in the main entry to my library as the greatest marvel that I have in the world." When he finally received a copy of the *Mundus subterraneus*, he greatly admired the portrait of Kircher that appeared at its beginning, describing it as "that perfect and beautiful print of your most beloved effigy." Did he hang it on his wall? This seems quite possible since, toward the end of 1665, he described the effects of meditating on Kircher's portrait in his library-museum:

> Only thinking about your ideas and admiring your portrait amuses and calms me. I am spending my life alone, withdrawing and amusing myself with reading and studying your books, which are my entire joy and pleasure, continuing to take advantage of them with my rough writings.[38]

Increasingly Kircher was Favián's world. He could think of no one else with whom he would rather discuss his ideas, transforming Kircher's portrait into a kind of Delphic oracle that spoke to him in private. While the intensity of their relationship initially flattered Kircher, it ultimately alarmed him. What was he to do with this American reader?

In November 1667, Favián wrote to Kircher regarding his plans for the portrait: "I decided to remove it from the book, since God told me what I can do with it." He gave the engraving to the *amanteca*, the native Christian artists at the church in Michoacán, and asked them to transform it into a brilliant feathered portrait of Kircher adorned with gold. Like the sheet of glyphic writing filled with images of Aztec idols that Favián enclosed in a box and sent to Kircher on the ships that left for Seville in May 1666, the portrait exemplified the best of what America could offer to a European. Favián hoped it would eventually find its place in the Roman College museum "in eternal memory of our friendship, as the greatest and most expensive thing that I can send you from these kingdoms."[39]

Let us stop for a moment to conjure up this American portrait of Kircher, which unfortunately never made it to Rome, if it was ever finished. Favián literally transformed Kircher into a brilliant, technicolor icon of knowledge to rival the feathered portraits of saints, popes, and rulers that were mass-produced in Mexico in this period.[40] Perhaps we should consider the impact of the words that accompanied the engraved portrait, written by Kircher's colleague James Alban Gibbes, professor of eloquence at the Roman College: "HERE HE IS: even the Antipodes know his face and name." What might these words have

Figure 15.4. Portrait of Athanasius Kircher, age sixty-two. *Source:* Athanasius Kircher, *Mundus subterraneus* (Amsterdam, 1665). Courtesy of Bancroft Library, University of California, Berkeley.

suggested to his American readers? At the most basic level, Kircher was a cultural icon worthy of appropriation. Just as he derived his status from the fact that his books traveled to the Antipodes, those places the ancients thought humans could not inhabit, his readers understood that the voyage was not complete unless they sent him home. Favián wanted to make the European Kircher anew. Having Kircher in New Spain was not enough. Giving Kircher back his American image was the culmination of their relationship, the best possible gift that Favián could imagine arriving in Rome from the marvel-laden New World.

The lost portrait was a fitting accompaniment to Favián's intellectual homage to his master: his "rough writings" inspired by Kircher. Around 1667, he completed his *Tautología extática universel* (*Universal Ecstatic Tautology*). A five-volume encyclopedia of some three thousand pages that continued the dialogue between Cosmiel and Theodidactus, the protagonists of the *Itinerarium exstaticum*, it was an alarmingly Kircherian product that purported to be a universal encyclopedia of absolutely everything. Favián wrote it in homage to Kircher, who that same year dedicated his *Magneticum naturae regnum* (*Magnetic Kingdom of Nature*) (1667) to "the illustrious and distinguished Alejandro Favián, native of the New World," praising him as the most enthusiastic reader that he had ever had.[41] Favián's fondest hope was that Kircher would help him find a European publisher, preferably Joannes Jansson, whom he approvingly described in 1661 as "the best artisan of printing I think we have today in the world."[42] Quite simply, he needed Kircher's help to understand the practicalities of publishing. How much would the printing of such a large book cost? How many copies should he print? Trying to understand the economics of printing, he boldly asked Kircher to tally up the cost of *all* of the books he had published with Jansson.

Favián badgered Kircher with questions about printing his first book while planning an equally Borgesian *Tratado de la luz* (*Treatise on Light*), which grew to an immodest 2,500 pages by 1672, far larger than the hefty second edition of the *Ars magna lucis et umbrae* (*Great Art of Light and Shadow*) that Jansson printed in 1671.[43] There was no denying the intensity of Favián's passion— some might even say insanity—for Kircher. He had re-created Kircher's museum in Puebla, read all of Father Athanasius's books, and effectively rewritten them, making them larger and even more preposterous than the works of his master. Now he expected Kircher to help him become a published author, while also asking him for other favors such as access to the Jesuit General Gian Paolo Oliva, whom Favián believed to be a Genoese relative, and assistance in his ascent through the ecclesiastical hierarchy of New Spain, where he aspired to become bishop of Michoacán. For him, Kircher represented access to Rome, the center of learning, faith, and power from which all good things might emanate.

The American Kircher, however, remained an unpublished author. Today all we have left of Favián's encyclopedias are their descriptions in his letters, and his museum has long since disappeared. There were limits to becoming Kircher in the New World. Favián did not become bishop of Michoacán or even of Puebla. He incited the wrath of church elders such as Ximénez who disliked his immodesty, disapproved of his ambitions, and ultimately felt that a criollo should not aspire to such things. "This is the barbarous genius of the Americans," observed Ximénez to Kircher in May 1672, reminding his German confrere that it was unwise to trust the American-born son of a Genoese merchant.[44] The last we hear of Favián is in 1681, a year after Kircher's death, when he was still trying to persuade General Oliva of the merits of his candidacy for a bishopric.

3. Kircherizing in America

Two years after Favián disappeared from public view, an ex-Jesuit in Mexico City inscribed his personal copy of the 1660 edition of Kircher's *Iter extaticum coelestis* with his name and the date of its purchase.[45] By 1684, Carlos Sigüenza y Góngora (1645–1700) was one of the most learned scholars in New Spain, a criollo polymath of great cultural authority at the viceregal court and a correspondent of scholars in other parts of the world. He was already a royal cosmographer (1680) and later served as a book censor for the Holy Office (1699). Professor of mathematics and astrology at the Royal University of Mexico since 1672, he was a passionate collector of books and manuscripts, including many pre-conquest codices and manuscripts in Nahuatl, and the author of numerous works of prose and poetry. His study was also filled with curiosities—natural objects such as a giant's tooth and a mamut's fossilized jawbone, Mexican antiquities, instruments, and maps.[46] In every respect, he was the sort of American scholar whom Kircher would have admired and sought out.

Sigüenza y Góngora conceived a youthful passion for Kircher. "Incredibly addicted to Father Kircher," was how one eighteenth-century biographer described him.[47] So we must ask ourselves exactly how and where he encountered him. Having entered the Society of Jesus in 1660, the twenty-two-year-old Sigüenza y Góngora was a student at the Colegio del Espíritu Santo until he was expelled for various infractions on 3 August 1667.[48] He had been in Puebla at the height of Favián's friendship with Kircher, and perhaps had seen the fruits of this elder polymath's kircherizing and Ximénez's contributions to the Jesuit college library. This first American library of Kircher inspired subsequent collections of his books—and projects from them.

In the viceregal capital of New Spain, Sigüenza y Góngora became a central participant in the lively intellectual and cultural life of the Athens of America.[49] He knew the Mercedarian fray Diego Rodríguez (1596–1668), who was the first person to hold the university chair in mathematics and astrology in Mexico City and was a reader of Kircher's mathematical and astronomical works.[50] Sigüenza y Góngara had an even closer assocation with the learned Luis Becerra Tanco (1603–72), a formidable linguist who briefly occupied the same professorship for less than three months before his death. At the time, Becerra Tanco was in the midst of applying certain theories described in Kircher's *Ars magna lucis et umbrae* to one of the most fundamental religious debates in the viceroyalty of New Spain: the veracity of the miraculous image of the Virgin of Guadalupe that had appeared to the Nahua convert Juan Diego in December 1531. The role of Kircher's works in this important episode reminds us that it was his combination of religious and scientific learning and his standing within the Society of Jesus that made Kircher a prominent intellectual authority in the Spanish and Portuguese Americas.

In 1666, the cathedral chapter of Mexico City decided to investigate the origins of the cult of the Virgin of Guadalupe, calling upon Becerra Tanco to give expert testimony as a historian and linguist who had taught Nahuatl for many years. Becerra Tanco believed in the veracity of the miracle and set to work expanding his testimony into a book, *Felicidad de México* (*Mexico's Happiness*), which appeared posthumously in 1675. He argued that "pictures" were comparable to "writings" in the American tradition, making the image a legitimate message even in the absence of contemporary written accounts of the appearance of the Virgin. He celebrated the fact that the Virgin had first appeared to Diego in the form of "celestial music" before becoming an image imprinted on his cloak, painted with the flowers he clutched to his chest as he attempted to convince the bishop of Mexico that a miracle had occurred. Finally, he used his expert mathematical abilities to affirm that the image had appeared on the cloak much like the images generated from a convex mirror.[51] Kircher's *Ars magna lucis et umbrae*, which included lengthy passages on the miraculous paintings of nature in addition to discussing the myriad properties of lenses and mirrors in the production of images as a means of understanding light, was the principal source for Becerra Tanco's explanation of the divine physics of the image of the Mexican Virgin.[52] But the contents of his *Oedipus Aegyptiacus* and *Musurgia* also provided essential ingredients for making the miracle of the Virgin of Guadalupe culturally intelligible in a world in which images and sounds had greater authority than written words.

Perhaps we should revisit Favián's *Tratado de la luz* for just a moment. Why was light worth some 2,500 pages of his Kircherian prose when his summation of all the arts and sciences had required only 500 additional pages to complete? The answer seems to lie in the controversy over the Virgin of Guadalupe in Mexico City. In the late 1660s, the divinity of light was one of the most important religious subjects in the viceroyalty of New Spain. Understanding its specific properties might help to explain how a brilliant image of the Virgin had appeared without human intervention on a piece of cloth. This was the world in which Sigüenza y Góngora became a scholar, and it left a deep and lasting imprint on him.

In July 1672, Sigüenza y Góngora succeeded Becerra Tanco as professor of mathematics and astrology, inheriting a university position that had already been held by three other readers of Kircher.[53] In light of the previous decade's controversy, he had begun to consider the idea of writing an epic poem in praise of the Virgin of Guadalupe, *Primavera indiana* (*Indian Spring*), which appeared in 1680. Sigüenza y Góngora filled it with literary allusions to Kircher, including a poetic rendition of Becerra Tanco's explanation of what happened when a ray of divine light hit the convex mirror that God held up to the world, dispersing its radiance so that flowers would paint an image of the Virgin. The generative strength of divine light seemed almost alchemical, since it produced miraculous transformations of substance. "Beautiful Mary . . . even the Phoenix is reborn at the sight of your light." Imagining the moment at which the Virgin descended from the heavens with a chorus of song on the hilltop before Juan Diego, Sigüenza y Góngora used one of Kircher's favorite words to describe the scene: "Ecstatic."[54] The harmonious union of God and Nature was a subject that Kircher had perfected in his many publications—and his approach to such issues was appreciated by American readers in search of scholarly authorities to justify their view that the New World produced powerful Christian miracles.

In the fall of 1680, as Kircher lay on his deathbed in Rome, Sigüenza y Góngora found himself consulting Kircher's *Oedipus Aegyptiacus* in order to prepare a triumphal arch in the plaza of Santo Domingo for the entry of a new viceroy and vicereine, who arrived on 30 November, three days after Kircher's death (though news of his passing surely did not reach the American Kircherians for at least several months). The resulting publication, *Teatro de virtudes políticas* (*Theater of Political Virtues*) (1680), presented Mexico City as the new Rome, since both were cities of great empires that had successfully made the transition from paganism to Christianity. Sigüenza y Góngora wanted to show the count and countess of Paredes that they were not arriving in a country without a past, but participating in the continuation of its glorious political history. That history, of course, was found in the ancient codices, filled with glyphic writings that scholars were then in the process of deciphering.

Sigüenza y Góngora could not resist a commentary on Kircher's account of America. On the one hand, Kircher's history appealed to Sigüenza y Góngora because it made the perceived similarities between Egyptian and Aztec rituals a proof of the universality of faith and culture. America was decisively part of Kircher's history of the world. But the criollo scholar was equally inclined to note the limits of Kircher's knowledge, highlighting the German Jesuit's "numerous improprieties" in his interpretation of Mesoamerican codices in the Vatican Library.[55] He esteemed Kircher as Europe's foremost living authority on symbolic wisdom, but did not think that a German Jesuit who misread the texts of *his own* culture could tell him that American "hieroglyphs" were simply a barbarous imitation of the Egyptian ones, lacking their subtlety and erudition.[56] Ultimately, Kircher did not know America, even if America knew him.

This more critical reading of Kircher signaled the emergence of a new kind of relationship between Father Athanasius and his American readers. While Sigüenza y Góngora boasted that he corresponded with Kircher, no evidence survives that suggests he actually did.[57] His relationship with Kircher seems to have existed solely through the printed page and in the steady addition of Kircher's books to his considerable library. By the end of his life, he owned all but four of the *Opera Kirkerio*. When he donated his library and instruments to the Colegio Máximo de San Pedro y San Paulo, he made a point of singling out his gift of "my set of the works of Father Athanasius Kircher." Sigüenza y Góngora knew the Jesuit library contained the four books he was missing. Perhaps they owned them because Ximénez's considerable library had been deposited there after his death in 1686, bringing to mind the enticing prospect that his gift was an attempt to unify their two collections. It gave him enormous satisfaction to report that, following his donation, "the said set will be complete."[58]

The opportunity to bring forth new knowledge from the latest Kircherian library in New Spain presented itself in the summer of 1681, when a German Jesuit who had desperately wanted to be an overseas missionary arrived in Mexico City. Eusebio Francisco Kino (1645–1711) counted himself a disciple once removed of Kircher, since he had been a student in Ingolstadt of the Jesuit mathematician Wolfgang Leinberer, "who was a most enthusiastic, even ingenious disciple in Rome of the famous mathematician Father Athanasius Kircher, admiration of our century in that Apostolic Curia and City of the Christian World."[59] Early in his training at the Jesuit college, Kino had discovered his talent for mathematics and his vocation to go to the Indies. He exercised the former only to pursue the latter, initially in hope of going to China, though the fact that he spent part of his time in Seville in 1679 making "various mathematical instruments of small size in order to meet the needs of clerics," in imitation of the ones he had seen in Ingolstadt, suggests that he considered carefully how scientific knowledge might be profitably employed in a missionary context.[60]

In November 1680, Kino was stuck in Seville, wondering if he would ever get to the New World. The month of Kircher's death greatly improved his mood because it produced a spectacular comet that was seen all over the world by astronomers. Kino observed it in Spain during November through January, and then continued to chart its course across the Atlantic in February, following his departure from Cadiz for Vera Cruz. Shortly after his arrival in Mexico City in June 1681, Kino composed his *Exposición astronómica de el cometa* (As-

tronomical Exposition of the Comet). And it was in this work that he cited "the most learned mathematician of our age Father Athanasius Kircher" as the source of his ideas that comets were either new terrestrial or celestial exhalations, depending on whether they were sublunar or supralunar, and not "stars created at the beginning of the world."[61] He also insisted that Kircher agreed with him that comets portended terrible events such as the earthquake that had just devastated Mexico City on 23 June 1681.

There were already several opinions on the 1680 comet in circulation in Mexico City. One of them was Sigüenza y Góngora's *Manifiesto filosófico contra los cometas despojados del imperio que tenían sobre los tímidos* (*Philosophical Manifesto against Comets, Stripped of Their Dominion over the Fearful*) (1681). It appeared in January 1681, preceding Kino's arrival, and engendered a lively pamphlet war among those who believed in the traditional view of comets as God's omens and those who championed a more modern interpretation of comets as natural phenomena.[62] Intentionally or unintentionally, Kino became Sigüenza y Góngora's adversary, at least on paper—he left for California as the copies of the *Exposición astronómica* began to circulate in Mexico City. It earned the approval of the aging Ximénez, who praised Kino for his "perfect knowledge of geometry, arithmetic, optics and the fundamental sciences of astrology" and inspired a poem by Sor Juana.[63]

By the end of 1681, Sigüenza y Góngora had produced a new and improved version of his book, entitling it *Libra astronómica y filosófica* (*Astronomical and Philosophical Balance*) in memory of Galileo's famous debate with the Jesuit Orazio Grassi earlier in the century.[64] While the work was approved for publication in 1682, it did not appear until 1690. In composing it, Sigüenza y Góngora explicitly challenged Kino's claim to have understood Kircher well. Kino may have studied with one of his German disciples, but the criollo scholar had the books in hand to consult as he prepared his counterassault. Turning the pages of the *Mundus subterraneus*, he found confirmation of his theory that terrestrial exhalations were an appropriate model for understanding celestial phenomena. In a tour de force reading of Kircher's encyclopedias, he combined data from the *Oedipus Aegyptiacus*, *Obeliscus Pamphilius* (*Pamphilian Obelisk*) (1650), *Scrutinium pestis* (*Investigation of Plague*) (1656), and *Arca Noë* (*Noah's Ark*) (1675) to create a complete chronology of natural disasters preceding the Flood. And of course he referred repeatedly to the *Itinerarium extaticum* as a principal source for his astronomy.[65] "I recognize the authority of the most erudite Athanasius," Sigüenza y Góngora told his readers.[66]

How could Kino, European disciple of Kircher, be wrong, and Sigüenza y Góngora, his American counterpart, be right? Lest his readers did not know, the criollo polymath provided the answer: Kino had misused Kircher and misread the *Itinerarium exstaticum*. The German Jesuit's Kircher was antiquated—an astronomical ancient who advocated an outmoded view of comets. But Sigüenza y Góngora had more faith in Kircher's ability to change with the times because he understood Kircher to be a scholar fascinated with new ideas, even if he did not always have reliable information. Sigüenza y Góngora found evidence of Kircher's modernity, drawing his readers' attention to a passage in the *Scrutinium pestis* where Kircher disavowed the opinion that comets indicated the course of the future. "Therefore if the Reverend Father would read the most diverse works of the said author," he commented in regard to Kino's interpretation of Kircher's theory of comets, he would discover that Kircher possessed a complex and fertile intellect.[67]

The conflicting accounts that Sigüenza y Góngora offered of Kircher's erudition in the year following his death serve to remind us of how fundamental the early 1680s were for the future of the Jesuit polymath's reputation. On the one hand, Kircher did not know enough about America; increasingly his encyclopedias looked quaint and incomplete. On the other hand, he continued to offer his readers thousands of pages of valuable and often contradictory information, since he indiscriminately summarized, synthesized, and imperfectly translated both ancient and modern authors, and a great deal in between. In this respect, Kircher could indeed assist his American readers in besting an astronomer from the Old World.

There was one consistent thread unifying Sigüenza y Góngora's use of the works of Athanasius Kircher. He had read them and re-read them. And he kept collecting them. Between drafting the *Libra* in 1681 and seeing it into print in 1690, he obtained the copy of Schott's edition of the *Iter exstaticum*, adding further weight to his claim to be a superior reader of Kircher because he now had the most up-to-date copy of the central book in the debate. Europeans, Sigüenza y Góngora affirmed, believed that "Americans don't know how to read."[68] The response to such unbridled arrogance was to read Kircher better than his European disciples.

4. Sor Juana's Kircher, or Egypt in Mexico

It is time to return to the presence of Kircher's books in the library of Sigüenza y Góngora's contemporary, Sor Juana Inés de la Cruz, a woman born in sight of a Mexican volcano, Popocatépetl, worthy of celebration in Kircher's *Mundus subterraneus*.[69] Sor Juana, too, arrived in Mexico City in the 1660s, when Kircher's reputation was at its apex. She developed an epistemology of knowledge that drew inspiration from Kircher's unique vision of the world. The library she created in her rooms at the Hieronymite convent of Santa Paula was decidedly Kircherian. Containing musical and scientific instruments and other curiosities such as the countess of Paredes's gift of a feathered Aztec headdress, it was another monastic *wunderkammer*. Sor Juana owned at least six or seven of Kircher's books, which she read, along with the other books in her considerable library, as inspiration for her ideas about nature, history, religion, music, optics, and astronomy. Whatever the exact size of her collection of Kircher's works, it played a disproportionately large role in her intellectual activities.[70] In fact, it is no exaggeration to say that a Mexican nun was one of the best readers Kircher ever had.

Sor Juana's reading of Kircher spanned the entirety of the period in question, occurring primarily in Mexico City between the mid-1660s and 1691. The chronology of her reading is not unimportant because it identifies her as a reader who first encountered a mature Kircher at the height of his fame. She grew up on Kircher in a region whose libraries were filled with his works, and whose leading intellectuals avidly consumed his ideas. She never corresponded with him, though she knew some of the Mexican scholars who did.[71] Twenty-nine years old at the time of his death in 1680, and already famous for her poetry and erudition, Sor Juana was well situated to appreciate fully the impact of Kircher on his reading public. But she did more than that, since she was one of the few to articulate how the act of reading Kircher transformed her life.

We cannot reconstruct a specific chronology of Sor Juana's reading of Kircher. Since all but two books from her library have disappeared, we cannot know in a material sense exactly *how* she read Kircher. The two surviving works suggest, however, that she was an interesting annotator of her books. In her grandfather's copy of Octaviano della Mirandola's *Illustrium poetarum flores* (Lyon, 1590), Sor Juana noted her possession of this book by writing "of Juana Inés de la Cruz, the worst" on a page. In a copy of Pietro Domenico Cerone's 1613 musicological treatise, she identified herself in the margins as "his disciple, Juana Inés de la Cruz."[72] This brief annotation suggests something important about Sor Juana that bears mentioning in relation to her fascination with Kircher. Sor Juana was a reader who chose and declared her masters. She did this, in part, as she explained on numerous occasions, because she had been educated "with no other teacher but my books."[73] Sor Juana frequently reminded her readers that she had not become learned by frequenting the seminaries, colleges, and universities where men studied, but in a virtual university of her own design created by the libraries and scholars she frequented. Writing about Kircher, borrowing key images from his works, and ultimately celebrating the significance of kircherizing in her life allowed Sor Juana to indicate how central his books had been to her intellectual formation. He created an encyclopedic approach to learning that she revised.

Sor Juana's first public expression of her admiration for Kircher appeared, not coincidentally, in her first major publication, *Neptuno alegórico* (*Allegorical Neptune*). She composed this work for the triumphal arch erected before the west door of the metropolitan cathedral in celebration of the arrival of the new viceroy and vicereine, the count and countess of PAREDES, in Mexico City in 1680. It was specifically this work and its celebration of "the magnifi-

Figure 15.5. Kircher's image of an Aztec temple. *Source:* Athanasius Kircher, *Oedipus Aegyptiacus* (Rome, 1652–55). Courtesy of Special Collections, Stanford University Libraries.

cent Mexican temple" as a New World pyramid (Figure 15.5) that provoked Sigüenza y Góngora's observation in his *Teatro de virtudes políticas*, written for another triumphal arch, that Kircher did not understand enough about the Americas to become its supreme authority.[74] To understand the dialogue about Kircher between these two great scholars, we need to envision Sor Juana's Kircher in relationship to other readings of Kircher in New Spain.

While Sigüenza y Góngora's *Teatro de virtudes políticas* pointedly presented the superior virtues of the Americas in relationship to Europe's past and present, Sor Juana's *Neptuno alegórico* used the arrival of the viceroy, allegorized as Neptune, as an opportunity to connect the Old World and the New by celebrating the presence of Egypt in Mexico. Offering up her own version of the kind of hieroglyphic wisdom that made Kircher famous, Sor Juana argued that Neptune was but another name for Horus, son of Isis. She celebrated Isis as the Great Mother (*Magna Mater*) of whom many ancients and Renaissance authors had written, siding with those authorities who argued she was the template of Minerva. Citing Plato, she made Isis into a poet, also reminding listeners that Isis was the "inventor of Egyptian writing." She classified Isis among the "learned women" as an uncommon deity in possession of all parts of knowledge who represented knowledge herself.[75] Isis became the mirror of her own erudition.

Sor Juana culled the specific ingredients for her description of Isis from many different sources. But the image that best encapsulated her vision of Isis could be found on page 189 of the first volume of Kircher's *Oedipus* (Figure 15.6), just as she also drew inspiration for her account of the Mexican temple from the engraving on page 422 of the same volume. Kircher's polyvalent Isis, literally a *polymorphus Daemon*, was the origin of all female divinity, a fact he illustrated by connecting her name to those of many other Greco-Roman goddesses. Most importantly, he identified her as Minerva, the goddess of wisdom. The image of female wisdom that Kircher created, and used as an allegory of the arrival of Queen Christina of Sweden in Rome in 1655, became the model for Sor Juana's own understanding of herself as the Minerva of New Spain.[76] Possibly she knew something of the Roman celebration of Christina as the new Isis upon her conversion to Catholicism, since Sor Juana explicitly mentioned the Swedish queen as a living example of female learning in her *Respuesta de la poetisa a la muy illustre Sor Filotea de la Cruz* (*Response of the Poetess to the Most Illustrious Sor Filotea de la Cruz*) of 1691.[77] Isis, a woman who knew everything, was a worthy progenitor of Sor Juana, the criolla who had successfully defended her learning in public in 1668 when no less than forty scholars questioned her on virtually every imaginable subject. Mastering Kircher became the supreme declaration of her own omniscience.

While Sor Juana read many different kinds of books to construct her image of knowledge, she exhibited a special affection for the illustrated encyclopedia. As Dario Puccini aptly observes, she transformed many of Kircher's best images into her poetic expressions as an exercise of her "iconic imagination."[78] Like many early modern scholars, Sor Juana appreciated Renaissance emblem books and cited them frequently as the source of her allegories and mythologies. Her mastery of their difficult combination of words and images demonstrated a kind of erudition that she, and her society, especially valued because it was knowledge whose truth appeared in multiple guises. Kircher's *Oedipus* seems to have held a special fascination for her. Not only was it a Catholic encyclopedia that proclaimed the Jesuit philosophy of universalism by identifying traces of Egypt, the font of Kircher's *prisca theologia*, in Asia and America, but it was also one of the greatest Catholic emblem books ever produced.[79] While scholars such as her contemporary Sigüenza y Góngora looked closely at Kircher's words, Sor Juana derived inspiration from his images. She was not alone in this approach to his books.[80] For a poetic philosopher with a highly visual imagination, his books were encyclopedias of images to conjure up for the pleasure of her listeners, many of whom shared her knowledge of his books. Her reading of

Figure 15.6. Kircher's Isis. *Source:* Athanasius Kircher, *Oedipus Aegyptiacus* (Rome, 1652–55). Courtesy of Special Collections, Stanford University Libraries.

Kircher was a virtuoso display of ecphrasis, the art of drawing images with words.

Like many American readers of Kircher, Sor Juana also treasured Kircher's *Itinerarium exstaticum* (1656), whose preface explicitly connected the discovery of the New World with the equivalent celestial novelties discovered with the assistance of the telescope, as Kircher argued that both expanded our understanding of the cosmos.[81] It is not unreasonable for us to imagine that the work held an additional resonance for her, since Kircher had dedicated this work of astronomy to Queen Christina of Sweden, the only instance when he acknowledged a female patron. One way for Sor Juana to become Kircher's Isis—outdoing Kircher in her kircherizing—was to embark on her own ecstatic journey. She wrote her most famous poem, *Primero sueño* (*First Dream*), also known simply as *El Sueño*, around 1685 and published it in 1692. Describing it as "the only piece I remember having written for my own pleasure," Sor Juana distinguished it from the hundreds of other poems she composed for patrons and admirers.[82] It has been described as her philosophical summa, an extended meditation on the limits and possibilities of knowledge.

While the fictional Kircher of the *Itinerarium exstaticum* discovered a cosmos that shattered the old Aristotelian-Ptolemaic cosmology in favor of the Tychonic compromise that incorporated elements of Copernican astronomy into geocentrism, Sor Juana's poetic alter ego, a female Soul who "cast her gaze across all creation," advocated no particular system of the world.[83] Her ambitions were far greater and more deeply philosophical. The infinity of Kircher's system that troubled Jesuit censors was also present in her dream as her "soaring intellect," freed of all corporeal constraints, measured "the vastness of the Sphere."[84] But Sor Juana's soul did not find any resolution to her questions through a cosmic voyage. If anything, kircherizing produced further uncertainties. The struggle for knowledge, as she reminded her readers, was a battle from which reason did not always emerge the simple victor. Hers was a soul cast adrift in an ocean of knowledge, a ship periodically run aground "upon the mental shore," in search of a method yet unwilling to believe that even the most structured approach to knowing could construct a satisfyingly complete system of knowledge when it had difficulty explaining the smallest, simplest parts of nature.[85] In the end, we must see Sor Juana's *Primero sueño* as a respectful, admiring, but ultimately devastating critique of Kircher's own intellectual assumptions.

The world that Sor Juana presented her readers was an edifice built by Kircher. Its tallest natural monuments were his volcanoes; its tallest human monuments were the Egyptian pyramids and "that blasphemous, arrogant Tower" he had written of in his *Turris Babel* (*Tower of Babel*) (1679).[86] It was a universe with a Kircherian geometry, illuminated by his optics, composed of two intersecting pyramids of light and shadow inscribed within the perfection of a circle that contained "the sublime pyramid of the mind"[87] (Figure 15.7). The *Primero sueño* allowed Sor Juana to combine her appreciation of Kircher's *Oedipus* with a

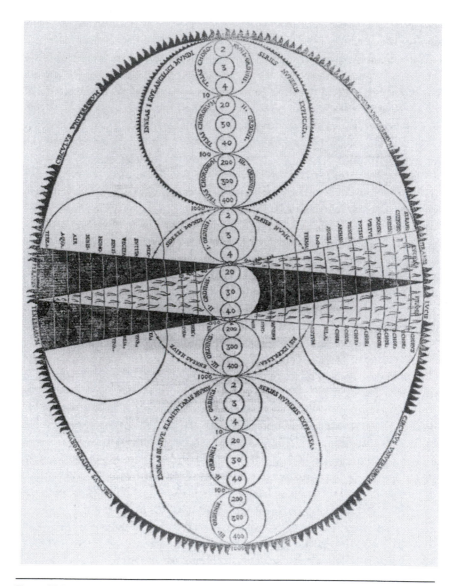

Figure 15.7. Kircher's intersecting pyramids of light and shadow. *Source:* Athanasius Kircher, *Musurgia universalis* (Rome, 1650). Courtesy of Special Collections, Stanford University Libraries.

sophisticated reading of his *Ars magna lucis et umbrae*, the same book that had fascinated earlier readers like Favián. The conclusion of her dream immersed her audience in some of the most memorable pages of this book, conjuring up one of Kircher's most famous machines—the magic lantern of the Collegio Romano (Figure 15.8). Gradually awaking from her dream, Sor Juana's Soul opened her

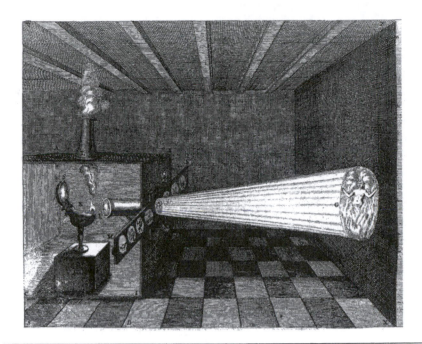

Figure 15.8. Kircher's magic lantern in the Collegio Romano. *Source:* Giorgio de Sepibus, *Romani Collegii Societatis Iesu Musaeum Celeberrimum* (Amsterdam, 1678). Courtesy of Special Collections, Stanford University Libraries.

eyes. The first thing she saw was the flight of "ghostly figures" (*las fantasmas*). Sor Juana explained that they resembled the images produced by an optical machine:

> In this same way, the magic lantern throws
> on a white wall
> the contours of delineated figures
> in thrall as much to shadow as to light,
> trembling reflections maintained by guarding
> a proper distance
> according to *docta perspectiva*
> and precise measurements
> derived from various experiments.[88]

Sor Juana's dream was not simply an ecstatic journey taken from the peak of Kircher's pyramid, but a voyage that allowed her to travel across his books. When asked if anyone had attempted to make the world of shadows visible in this earthly world, she responded, yes, in the museum of Father Athanasius in Rome. And then she opened one of his encyclopedias with her words.

Kircher confidently proclaimed in his many publications that he held the key to the "great art of knowing."[89] Sor Juana was not so sanguine that anyone could claim such authority when knowledge was so opaque, so subtle, so multifarious. But this did not stop her from trying to achieve the sort of omniscience that Kircher celebrated, even as she voiced the opinion that it was perhaps more productive to learn the arts and sciences one by one rather than to begin with the premise that all knowledge had but one key.[90] Yet when asked to defend her own learning in 1691, under mounting pressure to renounce her worldliness for a more spiritual life, she found justification for her methodology in yet another of Kircher's books.

On 1 March 1691, Sor Juana composed her *Respuesta a Sor Filotea de la Cruz*, responding to the pseudonym under which the bishop of Puebla, Manuel Fernández de Santa Cruz, had written a published letter to her, dated 25 November 1690. The debate about Sor Juana's learning became public with the appearance of her *Carta atenagórica* (*Letter Worthy of Athena*), published together with Fernández's letter in Puebla in 1690, which critiqued the theology of one of great preachers of the late seventeenth century, the Portuguese Jesuit António Vieira (1608–97). Vieira was a powerful figure within the Society of Jesus, a charismatic preacher and missionary who returned to Brazil in 1681 after a lengthy residence in Rome, where he had been Queen Christina's and Gian Paolo Oliva's confessor and surely encountered Father Athanasius in the corridors of the Collegio Romano.[91] It is in this document that Sor Juana declared herself a "daughter" of the Jesuits, implying that she argued dispassionately with Vieira because they shared a common parentage.[92]

Sor Juana's understanding of herself as a progeny of the Society of Jesus reappeared prominently in her *Respuesta*. "You have spent much time in the study of philosophy and poetry," commented Fernández. "Now it is only right that you improve your occupation and better your choice of books." He advised Sor Juana to follow the path of Boethius the medieval philosopher. "You have spend no small amount of time on these curious sciences. Move along now, like the great Boethius, to the more beneficial ones, joining the utility of moral philosophy to the subtleties of natural philosophy."[93] Egypt was learned, he reminded the nun, but it was also barbarously unchristian.

But the new Egypt that Sor Juana inhabited was a gloriously Catholic empire in which the Jesuits repeatedly found glimmerings of Christianity in pagan doctrines and philosophized about nature without impunity. More than any other religious order, they justified the necessity of studying the entire encyclopedia of knowledge as a prerequisite to knowing God in the structure of their curriculum.[94] Sor Juana argued that she studied all the arts and sciences, rather than concentrating solely on theology, because they were the stepping stones in the ascent to wisdom. Each kind of learning shed light on different aspects of divinity because they provided the tools for understanding diverse elements of the Bible that Sor Juana described as "the book that encompasses all books, the science that embraces all the sciences."[95] Since the Bible was the ultimate encyclopedia, it was necessary to become an encyclopedist in order to comprehend it.

Kircher provided the supreme model for this kind of Catholic understanding of the world, since he was the best-known Jesuit natural philosopher of the second half of the seventeenth century, demonstrating the compatibility of knowledge and faith in every word he wrote. Sor Juana reminded her critics of this fact by describing her own intellectual cursus as a realization of yet another key Kircherian image: "The world is bound by secret knots."[96] She confessed that the absence of a formal structure to her learning had led her to study "diverse things without having any particular inclination for any of them but for all in general." Even if she had not found the key to knowledge, she reveled in its quest. Chance—or was it the unseen hand of God?—brought books to her attention. She read what came her way, studying "diverse things at the same time."[97] What initially seemed to be a defect of her education became its virtue. Sor Juana explained that her encyclopedism allowed her to discern the

> hidden links that were placed in this universal chain by the wisdom of their Author in such a way that they conform and are joined together with admirable unity and harmony. This is the very chain the ancients believed did issue from the mouth of Jupiter, from which were suspended all things linked one with another, as is demonstrated by the Reverend Father Athanasio Quirquerio in his curious book, *De Magnete*. All things issue from God, who is at once the center and the circumference from which and in which all lines begin and end.[98]

Kircher had no book by this particular title, though he had written several works on magnetism, which he believed to be the natural proof of divine action in the world.[99] Mostly likely, Sor Juana was thinking of the *Magneticum naturae regnum* (*Magnetic Kingdom of Nature*) (1667), whose frontispiece evoked so well the idea she put into words regarding her epistemology of knowledge. Appropriately, this little book was dedicated to the criollo Favián, whose intensity for Kircher rivaled her own and who had proved to their common master that his best readers lived in the New World.

Eight months after writing her *Respuesta*, Sor Juana composed her *villancicos* in celebration of the feast of Saint Catherine of Alexandria in the church of Oaxaca on 25 November 1691. In this bittersweet account of a biblical Egypt in which a learned Christian woman convinced "all the sages of Egypt . . . that sex is not the essence of understanding," Sor Juana invoked the martyrdom of Saint Catherine as the template for her own struggle with the Catholic Church over the use of her learning.[100] Kircherizing had brought her knowledge and fame, but it was only through the renunciation of this learning that she could achieve a full reconciliation with her faith.

There has been much debate regarding the exact meaning of her profession of 5 March 1694, in which she wrote in blood of her intent to "abandon humane studies."[101] Until recently we have taken literally the words of her biographer Diego Calleja, who declared that she sold all her worldly goods, reserving for herself only a few devotional works from the splendor of her library. But we now know that approximately 180 books and some of her unpublished writings remained in her convent cell until her death in 1695.[102] Were Kircher's among those that remained or those she gave away? Unfortunately, we will probably never know.

All we can say is that artists who sought to capture Sor Juana's spirit kept his books in her library. Both during her lifetime and after her death, her secular writings circulated more widely in Spain, where they were published, than in New Spain, where only a single devotional work went into multiple editions. But as of 1700, when her *Fama y obras póstumas* (*Fame and Posthumous Works*) first appeared, readers in Spain could open a volume of Sor Juana's writings and find the following words in her fiftieth *Romance*, a poem written to the count of Granja in Peru during or shortly after 1692:

> Certainly, if the Combinatorial Art,
> with which I sometimes *kircherize*,
> does not deceive in its calculation
> and does not err in its numbers,
> One of the Anagrams
> that appears to be more meaningful
> in your lengthy summation
> that would occupy many books,
> says . . .
> But will I say it? I'm very much afraid
> that you would be angry with me,
> if I discover you from the Title
> just like it says on your baptismal certificate.[103]

Poetry, as Sor Juana observed in this witty response to an anagram buried in a poem, was but another form of kircherizing.

In the 1725 edition of her complete works, readers were allowed to connect this poem for the first time with one she had written prior to 1689 for the birthday of the viceroy, the marquis de la Laguna, count of Paredes.

> Your age, great Sire, so exceeds
> the capacity of zero
> that Kircher's combinatorial art
> cannot multiply its quantity.[104]

Thinking with Kircher was indeed a cultural exercise of no small significance in New Spain during the second half of the seventeenth century. But as Sor

Juana discovered, it came with a high price. Just as Favián could not become bishop of Michoacán and Sigüenza y Góngora, once expelled for his sins, could not return to the Society of Jesus, Sor Juana's kircherizing was a perilous if pleasurable occupation for a nun who was perceived to be too worldly. Kircher's disciple Kino praised her warmly when they met shortly after his arrival in Mexico City and probably facilitated her contact with his patron, the duchess of Aveiro.[105] But that was 1681, a year of hopes and ambitions for both of them. Within a decade, Kino was establishing missions and mapping Baja California and Pimería Alta, fulfilling his lifelong ambition to apostolize the Indies. Instead, Sor Juana found herself publicly defending the use of her intellect by invoking Kircher's magnetic and combinatorial arts in the service of her image of Egypt as a place in which wise men were humbled by a young woman of true faith and no small learning.

*****

There was a rumor in circulation in New Spain regarding how to get to Rome. The Nahua told the story of a magic chest that transported anyone who got inside it all over the world, "going by way of Rome."[106] Such tales remind us that the idea of global travel was not simply a European fantasy, but a shared vision of many peoples whose lives were transformed by the overseas empires of the early modern world. By the middle of the seventeenth century, that magic chest was filled with books to spur the imagination of New World readers on the journey to the Eternal City. Chief among them were the works of Father Athanasius.

In 1694, one year before Sor Juana's death, yet another curious book appeared in New Spain that evoked the specter of Kircher. Engraved by the artist Miguel Guerrero, the frontispiece of the Jesuit Francisco de Florencia's *Historia de la provincia de la Compaña de Jesús de Nueva España* (*History of the Province of the Society of Jesus in New Spain*) was an explicit homage to Kircher's *Ars magna lucis et umbrae* (Figure 15.9). At the center Saint Francisco de Borja, the Jesuit General who inaugurated missions in Florida, Peru, and Mexico, rests atop a globe that depicts the majority of the southern hemisphere above Mexico as *terra incognita* because it has not yet been christianized. Light emanates from this recently canonized Jesuit, bringing the word of God to the natives of New Spain via the saintly offices of Ignatius of Loyola and Francis Xavier. God is indeed the Father of Light and the Jesuits its bearers throughout the world.

No reader of this book could see it without thinking of Kircher's optics.[107] To explain the transmission of light was to explain divine action in the universe. In the context of the overseas missions, Kircher became a cultural authority without parallel because he offered a persuasive explanation of the scientific underpinnings of faith that engravers in Jansson's printing house in Amsterdam transformed into some of the most powerful images of knowledge in the mid–seventeenth century. Those images lay inside the books that mis-

Figure 15.9. Kircherian account of the transmission of Christianity in New Spain. *Source:* Francisco de Florencia, S.J., *Historia de la provincia de la Compaña de Jesús de Nueva España* (Mexico City, 1694). Courtesy of Bancroft Library, University of California, Berkeley.

sionaries packed in chests and took to America. Others opened them and preserved them in the libraries of the New World. The result was an exuberant half-century of kircherizing, a transatlantic encyclopedic encounter without parallel in the early modern world.

Notes

*   My thanks to Jorge Cañizares-Esguerra, Antonella Romano, Barbara Fuchs, Ben Schmitt, Susan Deans-Smith and audiences at New York University, University of Washington, Stanford University, and the Ecole des Hautes Études en Sciences Sociales for their comments on earlier versions of this essay.
1.   Pajes Merriman 1980, p. 319.
2.   Archivio della Pontificia Università Gregoriana, Rome (hereafter **APUG**), *Kircher*, MS. 567, fol. 155r (Manila, 15 July 1654).
3.   APUG, *Kircher*, MS. 561, fol. 79r (Kircher to Joannes Jansson, n.d.); MS. 568, fol. 73r (Albert d'Orville, Lisbon, 18 October 1656). The 1656 China mission also took one dozen copies of the *Oedipus Aegyptiacus* with them as well as four other unspecified works by Kircher. See Fletcher 1968, pp. 110, 112.
4.   See especially Harris, 1996, 1999, and forthcoming.
5.   The earliest example of Kircher's books reaching the New World seems to have occurred in 1643 when the German Jesuit Walter Sonnenberg stopped in Mexico en route to the Philippines; APUG, *Kircher*, MS. 567, fol. 267r (Teopzothan, 27 February 1643).
6.   APUG, *Kircher*, MS. 567, fol. 154 (Agra, India, 24 September 1648); MS. 565, fol. 96 (Salsette, Goa, 1 September 1671). The most comprehensive discussion of Kircher's relations with missionaries remains Wicki 1968.
7.   Osorio Romero 1993, p. 11; APUG, *Kircher*, MS. 568, fol. 73r (Albert d'Orville, Lisbon, 18 October 1656).
8.   Leonard 1959, pp. 79–80. See also Torre Revello 1940; and Osorio Romero 1986.
9.   Cañizares-Esguerra 2001, pp. 212–213, 248, 295–299; Bargellini 2001, p. 90. Juan Bautista Muñoz referred to Kircher's *China illustrata* as late as 1797 in his discussion of figured stones relating to the Virgin of Guadalupe; de la Torre Villar and Navarro de Anda 1982, p. 851.
10. APUG, *Kircher*, MS. 567, fol. 135r (Julì, Peru, 20 July 1653). In all likelihood the "arte Copticam" is the *Prodromus Coptus* (Rome, 1636), but it is possible that it was another of Kircher's works, the *Lingua Aegyptiaca restituta* (Rome, 1643).
11. Ibid. The most extensive study of Kircher in America to date is Kramer 1997, but see also the valuable studies of Beuchot 1994; and Bargellini 2001.
12. Osorio Romero 1993, pp. 162–163. *El arte combinatoria* was probably the *Ars magna sciendi* (Amsterdam, 1669).
13. APUG, *Kircher*, MS. 560, fol. 93r (Salvador da Bahia, 9 June 1670). Kircher's first list of his projected publications appeared in the *Ars magna lucis et umbrae* (Rome, 1646), p. 936. For more on Stansel, see Carlos Ziller Camenietzki's contribution to this volume.
14. See Harald Siebert's contribution to this volume and Stolzenberg, forthcoming.
15. Kircher's readership in British North America, where scholars such as John Winthrop and Cotton Mather also owned his books, will have to await another study, since this essay is primarily concerned with his readership in the Spanish and, to a lesser degree, Portuguese Americas.
16. This phrase appears in her poem: "Allá va, aunque no debiera" in Juana Inés de la Cruz 1951–57, vol. 1, p. 158 (Romance no. 50). Despite its significance both to her work and the reception of Kircher's thought, it has not received extensive analysis. See Trabulse 1982, p. 90; Bénassy-Berling 1982, pp. 146, 161; Beuchot 1999, p. 74; and Bargellini 2001, p. 89.
17. Paz 1988. The literature on Sor Juana has grown considerably over the past decade. This essay will cite only those parts that seem directly relevant to a philosophical investigation of Sor Juana's activities. In addition to the fundamental work of Paz, I have found the following studies especially useful: Bénassy-Berling 1982; Sabat de Rivers 1992; Los Empeños 1995; Beuchot 1995 and 1999; Trabulse 1996; Puccini 1996; Kirk 1998; Martínez-San Miguel 1999; and Merrim 1991 and 1999.

18. The most comprehensive study of Sor Juana's library remains Abreu Gomez 1934a.

19. Regarding Cabrera as an American Kircher, see Francisco Xavier Lazcano's remarks in Cabrera 1756, preface. The paintings are especially well discussed in Abreu Gomez 1934b; Scott 1995; and Trabulse 1996.

20. Fletcher 1968; Hein 1993; Nummedal and Findlen 2000, p. 186.

21. Torre Revello 1940, p. CXLVII. See also Osorio Romero 1986; and Leonard 1959. *Arca Noë* (Amsterdam, 1675) was one of Kircher's last publications.

22. On Sonnenberg, see Hausberger 1995, pp. 310–311.

23. Osorio Romero 1993, pp. 4–5.

24. Ibid., p. 134.

25. Bargellini 2001, p. 86.

26. Ibid, p. 18. Also discussed in Kramer 1997, p. 327; and Bargellini 2001, p. 86.

27. Ibid., pp. 8–9. For a discussion of Jansson's printed advertisements of Kircher's publications, see Stolzenberg 2001a, p. 9 and the introduction to this volume. A good example can be found in Sepibus 1678, p. 61: "Elenchus librorum a P. Athanasio Kirchero."

28. Osorio Romero 1993, p. 9.

29. Favián expressed a desire to see Kircher's *Primitiae gnomonicae catoptricae* (1635) and *Specula melitensis* (1638).

30. Osorio Romero 1993, p. 17.

31. Camenietzki, 1995a; and his essay in this volume.

32. Kircher 1660, p. ** 2r.

33. Osorio Romero 1993, p. 46.

34. Ibid., pp. 12, 30, 45, 60, 141.

35. Ibid, p. 46. On Kircher's museum, see Findlen 1994, 1995, 2001a and 2001b and Lo Sardo 2001.

36. Osorio Romero 1993, pp. 21–23.

37. Understanding how readers in different parts of the world responded to European printing is surely another dimension of the argument put forward about technology in a global context in Adas 1989.

38. Osorio Romero 1993, p. 65.

39. Ibid., pp. 21, 147; see Bargellini 2001, p. 87. In addition to transforming Kircher's image into a work of American art, Favián had had images of Saint Athanasius, Saint Peter, four church fathers, Ignatius Loyola, and Pope Alexander VII reworked in feathers.

40. Castelló Yturbide 1993.

41. Kircher 1667b, n.p.

42. Osorio Romero 1993, p. 25.

43. Ibid., pp. 142–143, 148–150, 162.

44. Ibid., p. 169

45. Sigüenza y Góngora's 1684 inscription in his copy of Kircher's *Iter* can be consulted in the Biblioteca Nacional de México; Mayer 1998, p. 87.

46. The literature on Sigüenza y Góngora has enjoyed a revival in the past decade. For the purposes of this study, I have relied especially on Perez Salazar 1928; Leonard 1929; Lafuente and Catalá 1992; Trabulse 1998; Lorente Medina 1996; and Mayer 1998 and 2000. The objects in his collection are discussed in Cañizares-Esguerra 2000, p. 819; and Mayer 1998, p. 99.

47. Eguira y Eguren 1944, p. 77.

48. Burrus 1953, p. 387. There seems to be some debate about the beginning of Sigüenza y Góngora's novitiate; cf. Trabulse 1988, p. 21.

49. Leonard 1959, p. 78. For a more general discussion of scientific culture in the Spanish Americas, see Cañizares-Esguerra 2000. On the general cultural and political climate, see Brading 1991.

50. Trabulse 1982, pp. 86–87n16; Beuchot 1995, p. 36.

51. De la Torre Villar and Navarro de Anda 1982, pp. 324, 327, 332. See Poole 1995 for the contested history of the Virgin of Guadalupe in the seventeenth and eighteenth centuries.

52. Kircher 1646, pp. 69–106, 190–191 (on miraculous paintings of nature), pp. 917–935 (on the mystical and metaphorical qualities of light). See Trabulse 1994, pp. 275–278.

53. The Dominican mathematician fray Ignacio Muñoz (1668–72), who succeeded Rodríguez (1630–68) and preceded Becerra Tanco (1672), was also a reader of Kircher; Victor Navarro Brotóns, "La *Libra astronómica y filosofica* de Sigüenza y Góngora," in Mayer 2000, p. 147.

54. Sigüenza y Góngora, *Primavera indiana*, in De la Torre Villar and Navarro de Anda 1982, pp. 341 (XIX), 349 (XLVII). There are many other passages that describe light in terms that Kircher would have understood well. See Elías Trabulse, "La obra científica de Carlos Sigüenza y Góngora," in Lafuente and Catalá 1992, p. 235.

55. Sigüenza y Góngora 1984, p. 181. For a close reading of this episode, see Kramer 1997, pp. 334–359. The subsequent history of the movement to create an indigenous history of the Americas is discussed in Cañizares-Esguerra 2001.

56. Kircher 1652–55, vol. 3, p. 33. See Kramer 1997, pp. 361–362; and Bargellini 2001, p. 89. For a comparative study of the emergence of criollo consciousness in scientific debates, see Cañizares-Esguerra 1999; and more generally, Brading 1991.

57. Leonard 1929, p. 49; Trabulse, "La obra científica de Don Carlos de Sigüenza y Góngora (1667–1700)," in Mayer 2000, p. 100. It is highly unlikely that Kircher would have neglected to save letters from Sigüenza y Góngora, making their absence from his surviving correspondence in the Gregorian University all the more telling.

58. See "Testamento de Don Carlos de Sigüenza y Góngora," in Pérez Salazar 1982, pp. 171–172. As translated in Paz 1988, p. 176.

59. Eusebio Kino, *Exposición astronómica de el cometa* (1681), in Montané Martí 1997, p. 154. The entire text is reproduced in a modern edition in this volume.

60. Kino 1998, p. 54. On Kino's activities in New Spain, see Hausberger 1995, pp. 204–218; and Bolton 1984 [1936].

61. Kino, *Exposición*, in Montané Martí 1997, p. 197. This argument made comets equivalent to the sunspots that Jesuit astronomers such as Christoph Scheiner, Giambattista Riccioli, and Kircher described as exhalations that only *appeared* to mar the perfect surface of the sun rather than actual features of the sun, as Galileo and his disciples thought.

62. Navarro Brotáns, "La *Libra astronómica y filosofica*," in Mayer 2000, pp. 145–185, is the best account of this fascinating debate. See also Bolton 1984 [1936], pp. 77–83; Paz 1988, pp. 261–263; Trabulse 1974, pp. 21–23, 29, 56, 82; and Trabulse 1982, pp. 86–87n16.

63. As quoted in Bolton 1984 [1936], p. 79. For Sor Juana's poem praising Kino, whom she described somewhat ambiguously as the "Icarus of rational discourse," see Juana Inés de la Cruz 1951–57, vol. 1, p. 309. Kino proudly mentioned that he had earned their approval for his other writings; Bolton 1984 [1936], p. 82; Kino 1998, p. 109n3.

64. Drake and O'Malley 1960. Sigüenza y Góngora's title was taken from Orazio Grassi's *Libra astronomica ac philosophica* (Perugia, 1626), though he essentially took Galileo's position in relationship to Kino's arguments.

65. Sigüenza y Góngora 1984, pp. 256, 267, and *passim*. All totaled, Sigüenza y Góngora referred to Kircher's works twenty-one times in the *Libra*. Trabulse 1974, p. 187n69.

66. Ibid., p. 279.

67. Ibid, p. 273.

68. Montané Martí 1997, p. 206.

69. Kircher 1665c.

70. The exact size of Sor Juana's library is unknown. Her earliest biographer, the Jesuit Diego Calleja, estimated its contents as 4,000 books, but more recent estimates have suggested that it may have been closer to 1,500–3,000 volumes; Paz 1988, pp. 248–260; Abreu Gomez 1934a. For female reading practices and book collecting in New Spain, see Muriel 1994; and Ibsen 1999, pp. 9–10.

71. For Sor Juana's association with the Society of Jesus, see Zertuche 1961.

72. Paz 1988, pp. 78, 238. See also Abreu Gomez 1934a, pp. 329–346, for a more complete discussion of her library and the fascimile of these pages (pp. 451, 453).

73. Juana Inés de la Cruz, 1951–57, vol. 4, p. 447. Also discussed in Kirk 1998, pp. 131–137, 149.

74. Kirk 1998, p. 30. In 1680, Sor Juana composed a poem in Sigüenza y Góngora's honor; Juana Inés de la Cruz 1951–57, vol. 1, p. 380.

75. Ibid., vol. 4, pp. 360, 362 (quotes), 362–366.

76. See Findlen 1995 and 2001a for further discussion of Kircher's role in Christina of Sweden's entry into Rome.

77. Juana Inés de la Cruz, 1951–57, vol. 4, p. 462.

78. Puccini 1996, p. 87.

79. For the role of the Jesuits in producing emblem books, see Manning and van Vaeck 1999. See Pastine 1978; and Stolzenberg, forthcoming, as well as his essay in this volume for further discussion of the *Oedipus*.

80. Trabulse 1995, pp. 68, 75.

81. Kircher 1656, p. 12, 1–2. See Trabulse 1982, pp. 75–91.

82. Juana Inés de la Cruz 1951–57, vol. 4, p. 471. I have used the translation in Juana Inés de la Cruz 1997, p. 65. This poem has been discussed in detail in numerous publications, including Carilla 1952; Gaos 1960; Sabat de Rivers 1976 and 1992; Bénassy-Berling 1982, esp. pp. 147–159; Paz 1988, pp. 357–386; Soriano Vallès 1996; and Merrim 1999, pp. 241–243.

83. In this respect, we should distinguish her reading from that of Sigüenza y Góngora's in his debate with Kino because the *technical* aspects of Kircher's cosmology did not interest Sor Juana.

84. Juana Inés de la Cruz 1997, pp. 101 (line 445), 93 (lines 301–302). On the problems with the *Iter*, see Camenietzki 1995a; and Ingrid Rowland's essay in this volume.

85. Juana Inés de la Cruz 1997, p. 107 (line 566). See Beuchot 1995 and 1999 for further discussion of the philosophical complexity of Sor Juana's image of knowledge.

86. Juana Inés de la Cruz 1997, p. 99 (line 414). The pyramids are discussed intermittently from the first lines of the poem (lines 1–4) until the reference to the Tower of Babel (lines 340–413), and the volcano on one occasion (line 319).

87. Ibid., p. 101 (line 424). See Dixon 1984.

88. Ibid., p. 125 (lines 873–881). I have modified the translation slightly.

89. See especially Kircher 1669.

90. Juana 1997 p. 109 (lines 575–599). Cf. Kircher 1665c, vol. 2, p. iii.

91. On Vieira's life and work, see Cohen 1998; and Carvalho Da Silva 2000. Sor Juana chose to emphasize Christ's divinity in response to Vieira's demonstration of Christ's love of humanity.

92. Juana Inés de la Cruz 1951–57, vol. 4, p. 413.

93. Ibid., vol. 4, pp. 695–696.

94. Romano 1999 discusses the growth of Jesuit science and offers an extensive bibliography on pedagogy within the colleges; see also Giard 1995.

95. Juana Inés de la Cruz 1951–57, vol. 4, p. 449. Also discussed in Merrim 1999, p. 202.

96. Kircher 1667b, frontispiece. Puccini 1996, p. 77n39, believes that Sor Juana owned this work and read it carefully.

97. Juana Inés de la Cruz 1951–57, vol. 4, p. 449.

98. Ibid., vol. 4, p. 450. I have used the translation in Juana Inés De la Cruz 1997, p. 23.

99. Baldwin 1987 and 2001a.

100. Juana Inés de la Cruz 1951–57, vol. 2, p. 171. See Paz 1988, pp. 434–435; Kirk 1998, pp. 144–146; and Martínez-San Miguel 1999, pp. 60–63. Other translators have rendered this passage as "gender is not the essence in matters of intelligence" (Paz 1988, p. 435), but I have preferred the more literal use of *el sexo* and *lo entendido*.

101. Paz 1988, pp. 461–462.

102. Trabulse 1996, p. 26; Paz 1988, pp. 467–468; Kirk 1998, pp. 147–149. For the different biographies of Sor Juana after her death, see Maza 1980.

103. Juana Inés de la Cruz 1951–57, vol. 1, p. 158: "Pues si la Combinatoria, / en que a veces *kirkerizo*, / en el cálculo no engaña / y no yerra en el guarismo, / uno de los Anagramas / que salen con más sentido, / de su volumosa suma / que ocupara muchos libros, / dice . . . ? Dirélo? Mas temo / que os enojaréis conmigo, / si del Título os descubro / la fe, come del Bautismo." For the dating, see ibid., p. 443. Thanks to Antonio Barrera for his help with the translation.

104. Ibid., p. 302 (Soneto 193).

105. Montané Martí 1997, p. 102.

106. As quoted in Gruzinski 1993, p. 228.

107. I am indebted to Trabulse 1995, pp. 72, 74, for bringing this fascinating image to my attention. There are also other examples of painters and engravers copying images from Kircher's books in Mexico, such as José de Alzíbar's marvelous painting of *El ministerio de San José*, through the first half of the eighteenth century, also discussed in Trabulse 1995.

16

True Lies

Athanasius Kircher's China Illustrata *and the Life Story of a Mexican Mystic*

J. MICHELLE MOLINA

This essay charts the circulation of knowledge compiled and diffused through Jesuit global networks, at a moment in history when evangelization kept company with science. The story is now familiar: Jesuit missionaries like Matteo Ricci relied as much on the latest European scientific discoveries to impress the Chinese as they did Christian doctrine. Further, not only did Jesuits bring science overseas, but they assembled new bodies of knowledge out of their missionary experiences, for in order to better convert "pagan" communities, Jesuits compiled information ranging from language grammars to geographic descriptions. In the story I tell the components remain the same: Jesuits, faith, and science. Yet they materialize in a surprising mix, as the latest geographic discoveries were put to use by a Jesuit priest in New Spain—not in a scientific treatise or another description of geographic discoveries—but to meet the new demands for "evidence" in the increasingly rigorous standards of Catholic Reformation hagiography.

Hagiography is not the usual place where scholars look for evidence about the uses of early modern scientific and geographic findings. And yet in a seventeenth-century hagiography of a Mexican mystic, a Jesuit priest named Alonso Ramos drew upon Athanasius Kircher's *China illustrata* (*China Illustrated*) (1667), a descriptive account of Asia. Ramos studied Kircher's work to construct the early life history of Catarina de San Juan (1608–88), a woman who was born in India, captured by half-caste Portuguese pirates, sold as a slave in Manila, and sent to New Spain on the Manila Galleon. Ramos was the primary confessor to Catarina de San Juan in the final fifteen years of her life. In the biography, he presented Catarina de San Juan as his "spiritual daughter" and a potential saint, but his work served two additional purposes. First he described the Society of Jesus as the vanguard of the drive for a universal Christian empire. Second, Ramos elevated New Spain, and particularly, Puebla de Los Angeles within that empire. Thus the telling of her life was informed not only by the universal Christian mission of the Jesuits, but also by creole identity formation in New Spain. This essay treats the social and cultural history of New

Spain, while simultaneously unveiling its links to the Asian world, especially significant because they were not mediated by the Spanish metropole. Further, I have approached the material with an eye to the contingent nature of individuals' choices and actions, as well as the hegemonic shape that narratives—both geographic and hagiographic—were required to take to be considered successful.

In the standard story about Europe's consumption of facts and fantasies about China, we seldom consider the role of New Spain. One has a mental image of Europeans—Kircher and others—sitting at their library windows, looking toward the East. New Spaniards, too, looked from their library windows, but toward the West and across the Pacific. From both vantage points, China and Japan dominated the horizon and overshadowed the view of India, explaining why Catarina de San Juan, a woman known to be from India, was still referred to as a *china*—a Chinese woman.[1]

We ought also to recall that New Spain held a strategic geographic location as an intermediary nodal point between Europe and Asia, and served as an important point of transport and communication.[2] As such, New Spaniards had a view of the newly global world that was not limited to information found in books like Kircher's *China illustrata*. Although often relying upon networks of Jesuit information, many citizens of New Spain imagined themselves as belonging to a world community of Catholics that included Christians in Asia.

The essay is divided into three parts: first, I discuss the information about India that Ramos would have found by reading Kircher's *China illustrata*; second, I show *how* Ramos drew upon Kircher's work and suggest reasons *why* he needed to do so in the first place; finally, I point to evidence suggesting that Asia had a hold on the imagination of people in New Spain that did not depend upon books like the *China illustrata*.

Searching for India in the Shadow of Egypt

Kircher's *China illustrata* traced the trajectories of individual Jesuits to advertise their latest geographic discoveries and to plot the growth of a global Christianity. Kircher completed the *China illustrata* in 1666; it was published in 1667. It was a more synthetic than creative work. From his library and museum in Rome, Kircher maintained contacts with many of the missionaries returning from or embarking upon their journeys to Jesuit mission stations. Drawing upon the materials written or collected by other Jesuits, the *China illustrata* was a compilation of facts and reports about the Asian world made by Jesuit missionaries that included contributions from Michael Boym, Johan Grueber, and Henry Roth, among many others, and assembled previously unpublished relations and singular writings on Asian regions, including geography, botany, zoology, languages, religion, and antiquities. Kircher was motivated to publicize the findings of his Jesuit brethren in Asia "only so that the notes made with so much labor and exertion shouldn't be left to the roaches and worms."[3] Indeed, many of the letters from Asia included entreaties to Kircher to oversee the publication of a tract or treatise. For example, the French Jesuit Aimé Chezaud wrote: "I have composed in Persian several tracts concerning disputes about the law. These are called *Reply to the Mirror Polisher*. I do not know anyone better qualified to publish this at Rome than you. I beg you to inform me if there is any hope of printing such books there."[4] Publishing from colonial outposts was not the optimal choice. First, although the Jesuits had printing presses in Japan and Goa, their primary purpose was printing Christian tracts in local languages. They were intended for limited use and a circumscribed audience.[5] Second, as Father Chezaud's letter makes clear, many individual missionaries hoped not simply to see their work in print, but also to reach a European audience. In this regard, Kircher's book was a resounding success: European scholars in the seventeenth and early eighteenth centuries considered the *China illustrata* to be a very important source of information about Asia, even after Kircher himself had fallen in stature.[6] The book provided numerous new and detailed visual images of China, in addition to rendering images of the Society's most heroic figures, from Ricci to Kircher himself![7] Kircher was keen to broadcast the gains made for the Catholic Church by his companions in the field, to share knowledge about the world, and also to promote vocations of future missionaries, for as he insisted throughout the *China illustrata*, the "shortage of workers in the field" caused the decline of Christianity in Asia in centuries past, a strong hint that the same fate should not come to pass in his own time.

The majority of the *China illustrata* was devoted to documenting the various interactions of European Christians in China. What could Alonso Ramos have learned about India from reading a book about China? The answer was, very little. In most chapters India was described as an intermediary node in the story of the spread of Christianity and idolatry to eastern Asia. The same could be said of the place India held in the aims of many Jesuit missionaries: it was a passage to China and Japan. A brief survey of the book's contents is illustrative. In the first section, Kircher defended the authenticity of the Sino-Syrian monument, a tablet discovered in the Shensi province in 1625 that documented the establishment of a seventh-century community of Nestorian Christians with imperial support.[8] There was little room for mention of India; rather, Kircher was preoccupied with conveying the correct interpretation of the Syriac inscription on the monument, reflecting his own keen interest in languages.

The latter half of the *China illustrata* was similarly devoid of information about India. Rather, it described the exotic plants, animals, political systems, peoples, and architecture of China. The closing chapter was devoted to Chinese literature. Here Kircher sought the origins of the beliefs and practices of "the kingdoms of Asia" but was clearly most interested in tracing the linguistic origins of Chinese characters back to their Egyptian "source." As such, Kircher did more than simply publish his colleagues' findings on China; his comments and organization of the material lead the reader directly to Egypt and reflect what Kircher saw as Egypt's role as the source of both knowledge and paganism. In fact, for Kircher, all things Asian sprang forth from an Egyptian cradle, and his driving interest was to harmonize Chinese language and culture with that of ancient Egypt.[9] For example, regarding Chinese temples he commented: "Who could fail to see this place, so full of fortune tellers, as just another face of Egypt?"[10] Although he wrote the book to fulfill obligations to his informants in the field, it was hardly surprising that his preoccupation with Egypt would surface in the *China illustrata*. Thus, it has been argued that the *China illustrata*, with its comparison of Egyptian hieroglyphics to Chinese characters, was the culmination of his work on Egypt that began in the 1630s and was published in *Oedipus Aegyptiacus* (*Egyptian Oedipus*) (1652–55) and *Lingua Aegyptiaca restituta* (*Egyptian Language Restored*) (1643).[11]

If China, in Kircher's telling, was a mere shadow of Egypt, then was there any room for India? The most promising section from which Ramos might have gleaned information about India was a section titled "For What Reasons, by Whom, and by Which Journeys at Various Times the Sacred Gospel of Christ Was Taken to the Farthest Regions of the Orient, India, Tartary, China, and the Other Regions of Asia." Kircher compared Jesuit discoveries with those of the well-known medieval traveler Marco Polo. This portion of the book is fascinating because it helps to illuminate what counted as "eyewitness" knowledge worthy of publication. Similar standards, we will see later, guided Ramos's use of the *China illustrata*. Kircher advertised the talents of Jesuits as explorers and geographers, showing how Jesuit findings clarified the cartographic contours of Asia that Marco Polo had left vague. Kircher drew upon the travel narrative of the Jesuit Benedict Goës, who had set out at the order of the viceroyalty of India and the Mughal emperor on an overland route to China. Goës was to confirm that Polo's "Cathay" and Ricci's "China" were one and the same place. The arduous journey was considered a success in this regard, even though Goës died before reaching Peking. What Kircher does not reveal was that Goës himself never wrote the intended record of their travels; instead, his servant, Isaac, an Armenian Christian, not only completed the journey but also composed the narrative, which was later translated by Nicolas Trigault, S.J. Although Trigault informed the reader that Isaac wrote the report, the language was edited to maintain the narrative as if it were a first-person account written by Goës. Kircher, however, made no mention of Isaac as the author of the work, truncating the story with Goës's death, implicitly suggesting that the "eyes" in eyewitness accounts were more authoritative if they were European.[12] Kircher's collection of "eyewitness" accounts in the *China illustrata* will serve the same purpose for Ramos, lending credibility to an account that was told to him by a low-status *casta* servant.

In Kircher's telling of Goës's travels to China, India served as a stopping ground and as a point of departure. India played the same role in his understanding of the trajectory that Christianity took on its way to China. Kircher addressed the evangelization of the early apostolic fathers, Saint Thomas in particular, and the existence of a remnant of the Syrian Church, called the Saint Thomas Christians.[13] "Finally," Kircher remarked,

> Divine Mercy had pity on the ruin of so many souls, and at the predetermined times sent apostolic men to replace the trampled vines with new ones, and to tend them. . . . This occurred when it pleased Him who holds the times and moments in His power, and the desired, but not really expected, event came to pass through the agency of the Jesuit order.[14]

Kircher explained that the teachings of Christ had been introduced in India by the descendants of the early apostolic fathers. While certainly not a descriptive account of the customs and geography of India, the history of the Saint Thomas Christians allowed Kircher to emphasize the key role the Society of Jesus played in reintroducing an "uncorrupted" Christianity to the region. Importantly, we shall see, this history formed a significant part of Ramos's understanding of Catarina de San Juan's introduction to Catholicism.

Kircher gave more information about the Mughal emperor Akbar's wealth, including the number and quality of elephants he owned, than any other aspect of Indian life, culture, and geography. He was an eloquent prince, who had strength of character:

> Gems of speech seemed to fall from his mouth both to aid the memory of what he had said and to show the extent of his majesty. The listeners silently paid great attention to his words, which were written down. Although he was so great, yet in his private conversations with the fathers he put aside all his majesty.[15]

Kircher also commented on Akbar's physical strength, his military training, and his penchant for dressing well. Adorned in jewels, his feet were washed in "an expensive liquid"; he sat on silk cushions that were embroidered in gold; and he wore a cloth woven from gold thread on his head. The descriptions of gold accoutrements were never-ending. The king's usual recreation was riding an elephant covered, of course, with a golden carpet and "a throne of inestimable cost." "Numberless such stories could be told," Kircher commented, "but let us return to the point."

The point, for Kircher, was that India was full of wonders. The snakestone was one such wonder: it was a stone said to suck venom from a snakebite.[16] Kircher also described a story about a boy who ate only snakes because his mother had been frightened by a snake during her pregnancy. Kircher's readers were next edified about the "flying cats" of Kashmir. These, he assured Europeans, were really just bats. Now crocodiles and tigers, on the other hand, could present a real problem, as one Jesuit priest discovered when both animals were poised to attack him as he explored the mouth of the Indus River. Due to the divine intervention of the Virgin Mary, the priest stepped aside just in time to see the crocodile devour the tiger. "Later," Kircher assured the reader, "there will be more information about animals."[17]

In sum, Kircher paid scant attention to India, which was eclipsed by China. This was not due to lack of information available to him, but rather reflected his own interests and those of the literate public in the events and information that came out of China and Japan. Certainly reports about East Asia outstripped the number of accounts of India; however, Kircher could have drawn upon the constant stream of new books that updated information about European trade and mission efforts in India. One example of a book written by one of Kircher's contemporaries was *Viaggi* by Pietro de Valle, who devoted an entire volume to India. De Valle discussed Hinduism and social and cultural practices, and he included maps and drawings of the places he visited. This very popular book was published in Italy in 1650 and reissued in several other European languages. Giuseppe Sebastiani wrote another account of India, published in 1665, the same year that *China illustrata* appeared in print. Sebastiani wrote quite a different story about India, focusing on the revolt of the Saint Thomas Christians and the Dutch conquest of parts of India. When Kircher did discuss India, he, unlike de Valle, expressed no interest in the "stupid superstitions" of Hindus. And unlike Sebastiani, an Italian Carmelite, Kircher turned a blind eye to the decline of Jesuit and Portuguese supremacy in India, but rather focused on a golden period when Jesuits held a favored place in the Mughal court.[18]

Kircher's disinterest in India was characteristic of many Jesuits who, until the mid-seventeenth-century suppression of Christianity in Japan, placed much hope upon both Japan and China as educated nations with the rationality and capacity for conversion. East Asians were considered "white"—or in the exact words of the Italian Jesuit Alessandro Valignano, a visitor to India and Japan, "as if they were white and well-formed."[19] By the time Kircher published *China illustrata*, such hopes had long since been lost as far as Japan was concerned. Japanese leaders had tolerated Christianity or, more accurately, the Jesuits, to assure the continuance of the Macao-Nagasaki silk trade, but eventually all of the European religious orders were expelled from Japan (1614), and efforts were made to root out remaining vestiges of Christianity. This resulted in the persecution of countless Japanese converts to Christianity, which in the period from 1614 to 1650 led to the martyrdom of an estimated 2,128 Japanese Christians and 71 European missionaries.[20] Now all eyes turned away from Japan, and ambitions were pinned instead on a massive conversion of Chinese to Christianity. The driving forces behind the *China illustrata* were Jesuit intellectual and missionary efforts in support of global Christianity. Kircher's collection of descriptions demonstrated how scientific knowledge was born of evangelical encounters. There is every reason to believe that published descriptions like the *China illustrata*—similar to the popular Jesuit letter books—would have been valuable in gaining financial and vocational support for an overseas Christian triumph focused on the Chinese mission.

It is difficult to ascertain the moment when the *China illustrata* arrived in New Spain. Kircher's work on magnetism arrived in Puebla in 1655 among the possessions of a Jesuit who was in transit to a mission in the Philippines. This unnamed Jesuit was housed at the Colegio del Espíritu Santo in Puebla. François Guillot "Ximénez" was the current director of the Jesuit college and was intrigued by the book, for he had once met Kircher as a young man in France. He showed the book to Alejandro Favián, who was a former student at the Jesuit college. Favián maintained a lively correspondence with Kircher over the next decade, and Kircher sent him not only books on mathematics and watchmaking, but also a wide array of mechanical instruments, with which Favián attempted to reproduce for Puebla a library akin to Kircher's famous Roman showpiece.[21] He made a gift of his duplicate copies to Diego Ossorio de Escobar, bishop of Puebla.[22] Interestingly, there is evidence connecting Catarina de San Juan to this same bishop. In the dedication to Catarina's biography, Ramos wrote that Escobar had called Catarina de San Juan to his bedside when he was dying "to aid him with her prayers and, with her tears, which might serve as letters of favor before the Supreme Judge."[23] Here we have the convergence of patronage: an admirer of Jesuit science was also a devotee of Catarina de San Juan. It is likely that the *China illustrata* arrived among the many books solicited by Favián. It was probably read with enthusiasm by his mentor, Ximénez, who himself had been interested in Asia and had requested but was denied a post in the Japan mission. Again the matter of circulation is difficult to discern. Kircher's works might have been held in the collections of the Colegio del Espíritu Santo. It is also possible that although held privately by men like Favián and Escobar, the books circulated nonetheless. Given the absence of large public research institutes, the tradition of making available one's private collection to scholars was common.[24] The library of the Jesuit Colegio de Mexico had a complete set of Kircher's works by 1700 when Sigüenza y Góngora "completed the set" by bequeathing his entire collection to the Jesuit fathers.[25] Even if only a few copies of Kircher's works arrived in Puebla, they may indeed have circulated widely among local scholars. We know, at least, that Alonso Ramos was able to consult a copy of Kircher's *China illustrata* when he wrote the life story of Catarina de San Juan in 1689 because he quotes from it, as we shall see, quite strategically.

Catarina de San Juan: A Map Imbued with Virtue

Thus far, I have discussed the *China illustrata* and provided a hypothesis as to how the work might have come into Ramos's possession. But the fact remains that what Ramos held in his hands was a description of a wealthy and magnanimous Mughal, a serpent's stone, some crocodiles on the banks of the river, and promises of more descriptions of animals—although most of these would have been found not in India, but in China. How does Ramos utilize what little about India he discovered in Kircher's book to talk about Catarina de San Juan's life?

Catarina de San Juan arrived in Puebla in 1624 as a slave. Following her master's death, she was freed and worked as a servant for a priest, who arranged for her marriage to his slave, a man named Diego who was also a slave from Asia. Catarina agreed to this marriage, which took place in 1626, on the condition that she remain a virgin. In the struggle to maintain her vow of chastity within the vows of marriage, she began to perform miracles to keep her husband out of her bedroom. This brought her to the attention of local priests, who determined that they had a holy woman in their midst.[26]

Ramos himself arrived in New Spain in 1658 and did not become Catarina's confessor until approximately 1673, so many of the details of the story were told to him by an elderly Catarina looking back on her life. It is unclear when she began to gain notoriety among the general population of Puebla. Upon her death in 1688, when Ramos took up his pen to convince the Church hierarchy that a local holy woman and his own spiritual daughter was worthy of sainthood, it was no doubt with great enthusiasm and perhaps with grand visions of his career. He invested considerable emotional and intellectual resources, as well as more than one thousand sheets of expensive paper, in writing the most voluminous life story of a religious woman ever to be published in the Americas.[27] The first volume was published in 1689, with two more volumes appearing in 1690 and 1693.

To begin, Ramos played with a notion of mapping the world, promising that the reader would not lack descriptions of the two worlds of Catarina, this luminous star from the Orient who came to the Occident. Her travels give him the opportunity to tell of ports in both globes, land and sea, and of course, to put Puebla de Los Angeles on the map. Indeed, in quoting the *China illustrata*, Ramos passed the most up-to-date knowledge about Asia to the reader. He stressed that the narration of the life and death of "this prodigious flower who tread the earth in the Orient until she arrived at the pinnacle of perfection in this Occident, has, resulting from her journeys, bestowed upon us a Map imbued with virtue, providing a sure path with which to guide our way." Here Ramos played with a dual notion of Catarina's life experiences as both providing a map of the physical world and charting a moral or spiritual route.

Fascinated though he was with making poetic observations about Catarina's journey, Ramos had a very local problem. His descriptions of this mysterious place served not merely to provide rare information about India, but facilitated the critical function of verifying Catarina's lineage. Catarina's status as a slave and servant would have been an issue in a society highly concerned with social standing. In fact, the eight celebrated mystics in colonial Puebla were almost entirely of the elite classes. Catarina de San Juan provided the only exception. The other seven had taken vows, an indication of social as well as of religious standing, as joining a convent required a dowry.[28]

"Perhaps even more intriguing," writes a scholar of early modern female piety, "is the broader question of why the Jesuits and Puebla itself would fervently promote a nonwhite, lay holy woman when she deviated so vividly from the model of female saint promoted by the Counter Reformation church?"[29] If we step back to encompass the global dimensions of her life story, we find at least one answer to the question: her story highlighted the history of evangelization of the Society of Jesus in Asia and its promotion of universal Christian empire. Notably, this aspect of her life was relatively unexplored by her other, non-Jesuit biographer, a priest named Graxedo, who in fact skips over the majority of her Asian background altogether.[30]

Nonetheless, it was likely her status as a *casta* servant that accounted for Ramos's eagerness to provide Catarina with royal ancestry. He informed us that although her mother came from a line of Arab emperors, her father was of the more illustrious and prominent Mughal kingdom. "Comparing all of the historical information which we have about Catarina," Ramos wrote, "including chronicle and philosophical evidence which I discuss, I intend to show that the subject of this history was the niece or joined very closely with the unvanquished Mughal emperor, Mahameth Zeladin Ecchabar, or Akbar, who died in the year 1605." Ramos added that he would give "a brief notice of the grandeur of his person and his Empire." Anyone who wanted to read in greater detail, he advised, should consult Kircher's *China illustrata* as well as Daniello Bartoli's biography of the martyr Rudolfo Aquaviva.[31]

Ramos claimed that he offered details about Akbar in honor of the loving affection Catarina de San Juan had received from the Mughal, but given the dearth of information about India in the *China illustrata*, he could have told of little other than the grandeur of Akbar. In sum, there were at least three reasons that Ramos called upon the legacy of Akbar. First, in Ramos's struggle to account for Catarina's social background in a status-conscious society, it helped if he could trace her to royalty. Second, this move to document her status was, in part, circumscribed by the kind of information available to him. Nonetheless, this worked in his favor because, third, it reinforced the image of the Jesuits, special friends of Akbar, as key players in the struggle for universal Christian empire.

The narrative structure of hagiography demands a story that includes the birth of the saint, his or her life of progress along a path of virtue, and an edifying death.[32] Ramos had the life and death, but required information about the birth of Catarina de San Juan and the signs of grace that accompanied her entry into the world. Reference to Kircher's work, while showcasing his familiarity with the most recent knowledge of Asia, was also quite useful in providing Ramos the necessary facts to narrate Catarina's signs of grace at birth and during her childhood. This seemingly outlandish narrative actually provided the typical components of a saint's life story.[33] For example, Mary appeared to her mother before and after her birth; she was miraculously saved from drowning in a nearby river; while lost in the forest, she remained unscathed even though she fell into a pit of vipers. (Was she healed by the marvelous snakestone?) Her mother had a vision that foretold Catarina's sanctity as well as the fact she would travel to many foreign lands.

But in naming Akbar or a close relative as her father, Ramos put himself into yet another bind. Now he had a problem greater than simply providing a complete life history for Catarina de San Juan. Her given name was Myrrah. This was a Muslim name. She was not a Hindu—described by Kircher as "modern barbarians"—but fell into the much more maligned category of "Moor." The *China illustrata* came to the rescue, as Kircher's map of the spread of Christianity provided Ramos with a graceful exit. Ramos claimed that Catarina's antecedents "had heard and knew of the Apostle St. Thomas whose preaching in the Orient reached the Mughal Empire, as is expressly affirmed by Padre Athanansio Kircherio."[34] These "glimmers of the true Faith" were evident in their lives. Her father, although not Christian, was sympathetic to Christianity. Not only did her mother have visions of Mary, but Ramos assured the reader, the entire family was forced to throw their riches into a deep lake and flee when their homeland was invaded by Turks. Ramos writes that the piety of Catarina's father infuriated the Devil, who feared the ruin of his infernal dominion in those lands. Thus the Devil provoked the Turks to take up arms against "this enemy of Idolatry" and invade his lands. Although Ramos drew many of his speculations about the Mughal empire and its relation to Catarina de San Juan from Kircher's *China illustrata*, he concocted many others, including this invasion. What could be a greater sign of their Christian status than an invasion by the infidel?[35] Ramos was also careful to note that Catarina was either in the crib or in her mother's arms. She was not cared for by the idolatrous servants, whose false gods her mother despised. In fact, Catarina only took the sweet milk of her mother and refused the breasts of other women.[36] Here Ramos marked not only the religious but the "biological" segregation of Catarina from the Muslim majority.

Despite the limited information available in the *China illustrata*, Kircher provided Ramos the necessary tools to navigate the societal demands of New Spain's literate public.[37] Ramos still had to deal with the issue of credibility. One of the introductory letters to the biography written by the Jesuit Antonio Núñez de Miranda suggested as much,[38] who titled his letter: "Some Difficulties That May Result Upon the First Reading of This History":

> The mere telling does not assure its truth, if it is lacking in prudent opinions. Is one gullible, does one take things lightly, to believe such praiseworthy things about a poor Chinese slave, only because she imagined it and recounted it? It is divine prudence and canonical opinion to believe that matters of the Soul do not have the possibility of witnesses. Nor is there an informant other than her con-

fessor, the sole arbitrator, supreme and truly divine conscience in the Sacrosanct law and venerated court of the Confession.[39]

Núñez de Miranda was interested in the theological correctness of the biography and rightly so, for as we shall see, the Inquisition ultimately suppressed the book because the descriptions of her visions were considered blasphemous. Yet something analogous was true of Catarina de San Juan's early life in India: just as "matters of the Soul" could not be witnessed, for most people in New Spain, matters pertaining to India were quite difficult to verify. While Núñez de Miranda deferred to God, Ramos tried to augment the story of God's grace in Catarina's life with a dose of Kircher. This points to a tension in the definition of "truth" in the seventeenth century. On one hand, ultimate authority rested with God, yet at the same time, scholars increasingly established legitimacy with documentary evidence and eyewitness accounts.[40] Further, as we have seen, the authority of the eyewitness was to be carefully weighed. Like Isaac, Goës's servant, Catarina de San Juan was a "poor Chinese slave" and lacked an authoritative voice. Kircher may have given Ramos precious little to go on, but he was a credible "informant" and his book spoke volumes in terms of authority.

Imagining Asia in New Spain

When he read the *China illustrata*, Ramos may have imagined that he, too, in writing the story of Catarina de San Juan, could participate in the heady world of great Jesuit explorers and intellectuals, who discussed discoveries of the natural phenomena and curious customs of a world apart. We might ask, was he not already a participant in the Jesuit project of attempting to realize a universal Christian empire? He was active in the distant Americas. He was a rector of a college in the city of Puebla, and although not evangelizing natives like his Jesuit brethren on the northern frontier, his role at the college was central to the Jesuit missionary system as a whole. Serving as a nodal point of communication and transport between Asia and Europe, New Spain had an integral geographic role in unifying the Jesuit empire.

Yet there was something more fantastic and captivating about the world described by Kircher. One sign of Ramos's emulation of Kircher's fascination with Egypt appeared in the biography. He described the saintly models for Catarina de San Juan and mentioned her namesake, Saint Catherine. This would not have been surprising had he been referring to Saint Catherine of Genoa, a woman who maintained her vow of chastity within her marriage, or to Saint Catherine of Siena, a mystic and an important model for female piety in New Spain. Saint Catherine of Siena's pictures adorned the walls of many churches. Her life story was popular among young women, along with the *vida* of Saint Teresa of Avila. However, Ramos surprised the reader by claiming that she was named not for Catherine of Siena, but Saint Catherine of Alexandria, an early Christian martyr and saint from Egypt.[41]

Both Catarina de San Juan and Catherine of Alexandria were royalty from the Orient. They were both converts to Christianity. They had similar visions. For example, Catarina de San Juan had a vision in which she saw Mary holding the Christ child. Mary offered her the opportunity to hold Jesus, but Catarina refused, protesting that she was unworthy. This corresponded to a moment when the young Catherine of Alexandria was captivated by a painting of Mary with the child Christ, but the baby turned away from her, indicating that as a non-Christian, she was unworthy. Most important, Ramos' mention of Catherine of Alexandria tapped into the existing interest in Egypt among the educated of both Europe and New Spain and reminds us of an early modern "orientalism" that was based not only on new geographic discoveries but also upon a common heritage of saints and martyrs, both ancient and contemporary.

As such, the popular imagination of Asia was not limited to the wealthy and the literate who had access to the rarefied world of ideas about Egyptian hieroglyphics available in Jesuit libraries. Rather, a distinct vision coexisted that focused on the stories of the Japanese Christians martyred in the late sixteenth and early seventeenth centuries. Stories of these deaths were depicted in church paintings and sermons. Competing religious orders sponsored campaigns to support the canonization of their priest-martyrs. In fact, in 1686, just a few years before Ramos wrote the biography of Catarina de San Juan, there was renewed activity surrounding the memory of the Japanese martyrs as the Augustinians sought to have their own martyr in Japan, a priest born in New Spain, declared a saint.[42] Further signs of local interest in the death of Japanese Christians could be found in the fact that a Jesuit mission rectory in Sonora was named "The Mission of the Japanese Martyrs."[43]

Further, in a powerful example of imagined community, laypersons in New Spain formed a Congregation whose members dedicated themselves to prayer for the martyred souls of a Jesuit Congregation in Japan. Although the Jesuits in Japan focused their conversion efforts on the Japanese leadership, the most enduring converts consisted of peasants, artisans, and merchants. These persons made up the majority of Japanese Christian martyrs. The brothers and sisters of the Congregation of Our Lady of Cumi in Mexico City claimed to be moved by the bravery and zeal shown by both men and women of the Japanese Congregation of Cumi, "who risked losing their businesses, haciendas, homes, and even their children" and "who suffered the most cruel torments in defense of their faith, eight of whom were burned alive" and many were killed in the persecution of "the twenty thousand."[44]

At first sight, this latter number appears to be a gross exaggeration. Scholars estimate the actual number of martyrs was approximately five thousand throughout the whole of the seventeenth century in Japan. Were the Congregation founders in New Spain misinformed about the number of Christians who died in Japan? Upon closer inspection, this document probably refers to the Shimabara rebellion of 1637–38, in which approximately twenty thousand crypto-Christians overthrew local authorities, fought off Japanese soldiers, and held their ground for several months before they were starved out, brutally crushed, and killed.[45] The Jesuit congregants in New Spain were correct about the twenty thousand deaths, but deceived about one aspect of the uprising. According to the Catholic norms pertaining to sainthood, those who resorted to the sword to combat religious persecution could not be counted among the martyrs. The congregants in New Spain, however, disregarded the theological details and stated what to them seemed quite apparent: these Christians had died defending their faith and were thus called martyrs. Unlike Ramos's depiction of India, this popular vision of Japan paid no attention to emperors or princesses, but rather, as the document maintains, expressed concern about the lives and deaths of common people, men and women with businesses and homes and children. This serves as a testament to the flow of information that traveled from Asia to New Spain, much of which bears the markings of the Society of Jesus, but shows how this information played out in the thoughts and prayers of particular Christians in New Spain.

Ramos, however, remained enthralled by royalty, as can be seen in his efforts to tie Catarina's travels to the history of Jesuit martyrdom in Japan. He described how one of Catarina's suitors in Manila was a descendant of a Japanese emperor, a Christian who had been converted by the Jesuits in Nagasaki. On a visit to the Philippines, this Christian prince became enraptured by her beauty and wanted to marry her. But her jealous master intervened and hid her away in another house. The Christian prince, despite his best efforts, was forced to leave Manila without seeing her again. Ramos commented that, ultimately, this benefited the people of New Spain: otherwise she would have been martyred among the Christians in Japan, and Puebla would not have been favored by her presence.

Kircher and Ramos were connected by a thread that was the *China illustrata*, but apart from that, they have little in common but their mutual membership in the Jesuit Order. In reference to their careers as Jesuits, the two could not have been more different. Kircher was a source of pride for the Jesuits in Rome and abroad. If Ramos achieved any notoriety during his life, it was the dismal status of having authored the only published life story of a holy person to be suppressed during the colonial period.[46] The volumes were not merely censored, but completely prohibited from being owned or read. In 1693, just as he was publishing the final volume of the biography, the Spanish Inquisition placed the first volume on the *Index of Prohibited Books*. Although the unorthodoxy of some of her spiritual visions is beyond the scope of this essay, the edict made clear that these are the object of their criticism:

Written by Padre Alonso Ramos, a professed member of the Society of Jesus, printed in Puebla in the printing plant of Diego Fernández de León, 1689; for containing revelations, visions, and apparitions that are useless, untrue, full of contradictions and comparisons that are improper, indecent and fearful, and that are almost blasphemies . . . abusive of the highest and ineffable ministry of the Incarnation of the Son of God, and of other parts of the holy scripture, and containing doctrines that are fearful, dangerous, and contrary to the sense of the doctors and practice of the Universal Church, without more basis than the vain credulity of the author.[47]

The Inquisition laid the blame square at the feet of the author, Ramos. In an interesting twist to this tale, however, it was only in 1696, several years after the publication of the edict, that the Inquisition in New Spain carried out the orders of its superior office in Spain. The book had garnered significant public support in Puebla and Mexico City prior to publication, and according to Myers, given the status of Catarina's patrons, the issue might have been "too hot to handle" in New Spain.[48] One patron, Núñez de Miranda, who wrote the introduction discussed earlier, was a *calificador* (inquisitorial censor) of the Holy Office of the Inquisition, and thus particularly well positioned to ignore orders from Spain. It might be mere coincidence, but he died in 1695; the decision to finally heed the Inquisitorial edict from Spain and formally suppress the biography in New Spain was taken in 1696.[49] Did the death of one of Catarina de San Juan's patrons ring the death knell on Ramos's hopes for the biography?

Ramos was bitterly disappointed and drank away the remainder of his life. The dissolute Jesuit was now an embarrassment to his brethren and locked in a cell to be kept out of public view. He might be returned to Spain, but for what purpose? His superiors thought it best to let him live out his final days in his cell in Puebla.

Telling Catarina de San Juan's story had multiple dimensions. Her travels made Catarina de San Juan a global phenomenon, a fact used well by Ramos in support of the Jesuit global mission. Yet she died a much loved holy woman of Puebla de Los Angeles in Mexico. Ramos waxed poetic about her ability to prepare chocolates and mole, the typical dish of Puebla. Her body was interred behind the altar of the Jesuit cathedral in Puebla. Her funeral drew thousands among the citizens of Puebla. An image circulated portraying her alongside the much beloved bishop of Puebla, Juan de Palafox y Mendoza (1600–1659), who was a candidate for sainthood—and who, it should be noted, had been embroiled in a bitter feud with the Jesuits in the late 1640s.[50]

Spanish Americans struggled to have the Americas included in the sacred history of the Catholic Church. The shape of this contest changed according to the type of claim asserted. Ramos may have portrayed Catarina de San Juan as a Jesuit symbol, but her appearance with Palafox signaled a sense of spiritual superiority that belonged to the city of Puebla alone.[51] In Pueblan politics, the Jesuits and Palafox were enemies, but when confronted with an edict from Spain, the pictures of Palafox and Catarina represented the united face of Puebla. New Spaniards insisted upon their right to be included in the universal history of the Catholic Church and to have local saints as their representatives.

Catarina de San Juan was not a typical holy woman, and Alonso Ramos labored to make her life conform to the standards of hagiography. A most peculiar feature of his biography was the presence of scientific and geographic discoveries in what typically would have been a simpler narrative of the miraculous events associated with a religious woman's life. As such, Catarina's story was not simply constructed out of local knowledge of a woman from Puebla. In Ramos's attempts to meet the demands of hagiography, the biography overflowed the boundaries of a traditional saint's life story. For the historian, it serves as a record of a collective imagining of the Asian world—"collective" because as the nature of the biography makes clear, Ramos incorporated in his understanding of Catarina's past the information produced by Jesuit missionaries in Asia. It should not be forgotten that Jesuits were active in India, Japan, and China, as well as the Philippines and Mexico, at the behest of the Portuguese and Spanish crowns with the goal of Christianizing and stabilizing overseas colonies. This essay has traced the ways in which knowledge in Europe was produced out of particular colonial relationships and, in the case of Ramos, consumed in yet another colonial setting. The Jesuit world mission made possible the collection of information in the *China illustrata*, but it also dictated the narrative structure of Catarina's story. The global nature of Catarina's journeys around the sea of Bengal, to Cochin India, to Manila, and then to Acapulco was equally the product of early modern commerce and serves as a record of trade in human capital in Asia. Yet Ramos neatly compressed her journey into the contours of a saga that announced the inevitability of a universal Christian empire and the singularity of Puebla as the "new Jerusalem" within that dominion. In the end, the biography tells us little about Asia but says a great deal about the way in which Asia was imagined from the vantage point of New Spain.

Notes

1. Ironically, the Chinese and Japanese men who attended San Gregorio, a Jesuit college for Indians in Mexico City, were referred to as the "indios" of Japan and China. Specifically, the document states that the student Congregations were divided into two parts, the "indios naturales" (natives to Mexico) and the others from Japan and China. Archivum Romanum Societatus Iesu (hereafter **ARSI**), Mex 15, Carta Annua 1615, fol. 11v.
2. Considered the more reliable mail route, and often the Portuguese would send two copies of mail back to Europe, one by the India route and one through New Spain. See Dingping 2000, p. 48.
3. Kircher 1987, Introduction, n.p.
4. Kircher 1987, p. 78.
5. Priolkar 1958; Boxer 1951.
6. Szczesniak 1952, p. 388. See the essay by Florence Hsia in this volume.
7. Szczesniak 1952, p. 410.
8. Mungello 1985, p. 167.

9.   For the centrality of Egypt in Kircher's career, see Stolzenberg 2001c.
10. Kircher 1987, p. 125.
11. Mungello 1985, pp. 137, 146, 151, 153.
12. Billings 1997, pp. 106–117.
13. See the chapter titled "The Propagation of the Gospel in All of the Regions of Eastern Asia by St. Thomas the Apostle and His Successors." Myths about the travels of Saint Thomas to the Americas began to increase in New Spain during the seventeenth century, but Kircher denied such a possibility point-blank. He established that the earliest Christians to travel East would not have been Saint Thomas himself, but rather his descendants, the Coptic monks: "It is evident that the Coptic-Ethiopian Church (which all the world calls only Syrian.) . . . Was the first to found colonies, first in India and later in China and other regions of Asia. . . . I find some controversy among the interpreters as to where Ophir was located. . . . others designate as Ophir that region of America which people commonly call Peru. However, I don't see why a ship would go from Palestine to the other side of the world, since the lands are not joined and the sphere of the world was unknown to men at that time. Also, they had no magnet or other aids which helped our sailors to discover the world. Yet these ancients are said to have been able to reach America safely and in very little time. Moreover, why would they seek gold, gems, and precious woods in such distant regions with so much peril when nearer regions such as the Chersonese and Ethiopia abound in gold? This doesn't make sense and I think the theory ought to be rejected." Kircher 1987, p. 53. Nonetheless, the myth of Saint Thomas's travels to the New World continued to circulate in the Americas, as it served the important purpose of including New Spain in the sacred history of the Church. See Lafaye 1976; and Rubial Garcia 1999, p. 63.
14. Kircher 1987, pp. 4, 83.
15. Kircher 1987, pp. 71–72.
16. See Baldwin 1995.
17. Kircher 1987, p. 73.
18. For de Valle, see Lach 1993, p. 380; for Sebastiani, see p. 383; for all of the publications on India in seventeenth-century Europe, see pp. 306–547. For sixteenth-century publications, see Lach 1965, pp. 148–468.
19. ARSI, Goa 7, "Valignano's Summario," capitulo 17. See also Schutte 1980, pp. 170–172, for Valignano's division of the Portuguese dominions into the white nations of Japan and China and the black nations of India and Africa.
20. Boxer 1951, especially chapter VII, "The Palme of Christian Fortitude," pp. 308–361, and appendix XIV, "Summary Martyrology, 1614–1650," p. 448.
21. Findlen 1995.
22. Osorio Romero 1993, p. 10–12.
23. Ramos 1689, dedication.
24. O'Neill 1986, p. 281.
25. Paz 1988, pp. 176–177. See also Paula Findlen's essay in this volume.
26. Morgan 1998; Myers 1999; Maza 1990; Castillo Graxeda 1987.
27. Myers 1999.
28. Destefano 1977, p. 28. Uncloistered women were considered a social threat, especially women like Catarina de San Juan, who lived alone, and not communally with other *beatas*. In Inquisition trials, lone *beatas* were twice as likely to be convicted than women who lived communally. See Jaffary 1999.
29. Myers 1999, p. 294.
30. The fact that Graxedo was not a Jesuit could explain why he would not refer to the very Jesuit-laden story of her earlier life.
31. Bartoli 1663b.
32. Rubial Garcia 1999, p. 42.
33. Sanchez Lora 1988.
34. Ramos 1689, p. 7.
35. Bailey 1997, p. 47.
36. Ramos 1689, p. 14.
37. For a very interesting discussion of how Ramos negotiates the racial politics of a hagiography about a woman of color, see Morgan 1998, pp. 194–242.

38. Most famous as a confessor to Sor Juana Inés de la Cruz, Núñez de Miranda was interested in issues pertaining to female piety, and he also knew Catarina de San Juan. He also wrote a book adapting the Jesuit *Spiritual Exercises* for women in convents.
39. Antonio Núñez de Miranda, S.J., "Carta y discuros preocupativo, de algunas dificultades, que pueden resaltar luego a la primera vista de esta historia," in Ramos 1689, n.p.
40. For issues of "truth" and credibility in sixteenth-century New World histories, see Pagden 1993, pp. 51–88.
41. Ramos 1689, pp. 25–26. In Brad Gregory's study of early modern martyrdom, he writes that Catholic martyrs drew upon and were encouraged by the stories of the early Christian martyrs. Gregory 1999, p. 281.
42. Rubial Garcia 1999, p. 140.
43. ARSI, Mex 18, "De la Mission de este Rectorado de los SS. Martiros del Japon en esta Provincia de Sonora desde el ano de 1716 hasta 6 de Sept de 1720," fol. 45.
44. ARSI, Mex 16, "Congregacion de Nuestra Senora de Cumi establecida en Japon y establecida en Mejico," fol. 192. No date. Probably seventeenth century.
45. Boxer 1951, pp. 375–383.
46. Myers 1999, p. 276.
47. As quoted in Destefano 1977, p. 68.
48. Myers 1999, p. 293.
49. Zambrano 1961–77.
50. See Brading 1991, pp. 228–252.
51. See Rubial Garcia 1999, pp. 63, 78–79.

17

Athanasius Kircher's
China Illustrata (1667)
An Apologia Pro Vita Sua

FLORENCE HSIA

As was true of so many early modern books, the long title of the *China, Illustrated with Monuments Both Sacred and Profane, and Various Spectacles of Nature and Art, and Proofs of Other Memorable Matters* (1667) promised much to the curious seventeenth-century reader. The title's broad brief allowed Kircher wide latitude in shaping his fellow Jesuits' reports from the remote provinces of an expanding Christendom into an erudite travel guide across continents, centuries, and cultures. Published in 1667 toward the end of a long and illustrious career, the volume reflected many of the intellectual obsessions that had patterned Athanasius Kircher's own remarkably polymathic oeuvre, from the twinned histories of Christianity and paganism to the mechanical arts, natural history, and historical linguistics. But in publishing a volume of Jesuit missionary reports on the exotic East, Kircher faced a variety of challenges. Some involved his own scholarly reputation, while others implicated members of the Society of Jesus in general.

Although English natural philosophers awaited the arrival of Kircher's *Subterranean World* (1665) from Amsterdam with bated breath, a quick perusal led Henry Oldenburg, secretary of the Royal Society, to fear that Kircher had again provided "rather Collections, as his custom is, of what is already extant and knowne, yn any considerable new Discoveryes."[1] Contemporary scholars have repeated Oldenburg's criticism, characterizing Kircher's oeuvre as consisting of "massive encyclopedias" compiled with "a total lack of discrimination" and with "no suggestion that some authorities might be more reliable than others; every fact or observation seems to be given equal weight."[2] Given Kircher's heavy reliance throughout the text on a wide range of Jesuit missionary "authorities" concerning the East, the *China* hardly seems to be the sort of book to counter such evaluations. By far the most frequently excerpted text in the *China* was the *New Chinese Atlas* (1655) by Martino Martini (1614–61), a work well-known to European readers.[3] The renowned Dutch mapmaker Joan Blaeu published Martini's text as part of his own massive surveys of the globe, the *Theater of the Countries of the World* (1655) and the *Great Atlas* (1662), which were translated into numerous vernacular editions before 1667.[4]

Kircher also drew on two widely translated works by Jesuit missionaries: the journals of Matteo Ricci (1552–1610), edited by Nicolas Trigault (1577–1628) as *Of the Christian Expedition among the Chinese, Undertaken by the Society of Jesus* (1615), and the *Empire of China* (1642) by Alvaro Semedo (1586–1658). Even the *Chinese Flora* (1656) of Michael Boym (1612–59)—a comparatively rare Viennese imprint—reappeared in a popular French collection of voyages compiled by Melchisédech Thévenot in 1664.[5] Indeed, Kircher borrowed freely from a century's worth of Jesuit "histories and letters" on the exotic East, ranging from a Jesuit letter book published at the Portuguese city of Évora in 1565, to the *History and Relation of Tonkin and Japan* by Giovanni Filippo de Marini (1608–82), most recently reprinted at Rome in 1665.[6] Yet Kircher meant his contribution to the growing library of Jesuit books to be unique, not encyclopedic. Counseling the curious reader to consult Trigault, Semedo, Martini, and other works for comprehensive accounts of China, Kircher bracketed issues already widely known or related by others, and deliberately focused his text on rare, recondite, and secret matters in the kingdoms of the East.[7]

The novelty of the material Kircher selected for inclusion in the *China* undoubtedly heightened the volume's appeal, but did little to bolster its veracity. Europe's literary heritage concerning the kingdoms of the East was a superb mélange of fantastic lore stemming from a wide variety of classical and medieval sources, from Pliny the Elder's first-century *Natural History* to the thirteenth- and fourteenth-century accounts of Marco Polo and John de Mandeville.[8] Traditional "marvels of the East" included astonishing phenomena of natural and artificial origin and putative miracles of Christian and pagan character.[9] Jesuit texts concerning missionary experience in Asia traversed much the same conceptual territory. The new and extraordinary phenomena that Kircher culled from Jesuit experiences in Agra, Lhasa, and Beijing fell as well into the category of implausible "travelers' tales" about the exotic East.[10]

Nor were the observational and experimental reports that Kircher recounted in his own studies of the natural world above suspicion. Early in his career, Kircher had deeply impressed the savant Nicolas-Claude Fabri de Peiresc as a man possessing such "beautiful secrets of nature" as clocks powered by the heliotropic tendencies of sunflowers, but after observing Kircher's clocks at work, Peiresc soon doubted the significance of the Jesuit's experimental claims.[11] In 1661, an Englishman making the Grand Tour of the Continent confided to Robert Boyle that Kircher "is reputed very credulous, apt to put in print any strange, if plausible, story, that is brought unto him."[12] The variety of protocols for crediting reports of "strange facts" made Kircher as vulnerable to challenge as any other early modern natural philosopher, but the bizarre phenomena retailed in Kircher's works proved to be notably less robust.[13] It was not long after Kircher's death that the erudite Jesuit was transformed into the "prototype of the foolish polymath," a charlatan unable to discern truth from fiction.[14]

Gullibility, however, was a relatively kind characterization in comparison with the charges of outright fraud that both wary Protestants and hostile co-religionists launched at Jesuit opponents throughout the early modern era. Protestant suspicion concerning a wide range of Catholic deceptions—from exorcisms and relics to the ritual incantations of the Roman Mass—found a particular target in Jesuit missionaries, who concealed their very identity as priests from English interrogators by resorting to techniques of mental reservation and verbal equivocation.[15] Jesuit suppleness drew fire from Catholic critics as well. In his *Provincial Letters* (1656–57), Blaise Pascal accused Jesuits in China of having "even allowed Christians to practice idolatry, by the ingenious idea of getting them to hide under their clothes an image of Christ, to which they are taught to apply mentally the worship paid publicly to the idol Chacim-Choan and their Keum-fucum [Confucius]."[16] Thanks to a virtual torrent of anti-Jesuit literature, the myth of Jesuit duplicity was firmly entrenched in the early modern European imagination.[17]

Deciphering the Sino-Syrian Monument: The History of Christianity

Kircher faced his critics squarely. He informed his readers from the outset that the immediate "purpose and occasion" of the *China*'s publication was the resolution of a long-standing scholarly controversy. Three decades earlier, Kircher had presented the "Sino-Syrian monument" to European scholars in his *Coptic or Egyptian Forerunner* (1636). The monument itself was an eighth-century stone stele, with Chinese and Syrian inscriptions testifying to the presence of Christianity in Tang-dynasty China. Not all of Kircher's readers accepted his initial description of the stele at face value; one critic even declared that the purported monument was nothing more than a "Jesuit fraud" devised to deceive the Chinese. Kircher refrained from naming the critic in question—"partly," as he explained, "out of Christian charity"—but it was a Protestant scholar, Georg Horn, who had lodged the accusation of Jesuit duplicity.[18]

In mounting a collective Jesuit defense against such criticisms, Kircher drew on one of his own self-images of scholarly brilliance—that of a "new Oedipus" gifted with the ability to decipher the hidden meanings of Egyptian hieroglyphs.[19] In his lengthy reexamination of the Sino-Syrian monument, Kircher married claims of Jesuit linguistic prowess to apologetic strategies characteristic of ecclesiastical history and antiquarianism. Neither church scholars advocating rival histories of doctrines, rituals, or institutions, nor antiquarians concerned with reconstructing the ancient past, relied on rhetorical power to argue their positions. Rather, they turned to documentary evidence, compiling a variety of materials—private letters, official records, inscriptions, and other monuments of the past—to make their case.[20] Kircher likewise deployed "a model of history . . . characterized by an encyclopedic willingness to accomodate the incongruous and the alien, one that allowed many voices to speak, and many alphabets to appear, on the same page."[21]

Citing accounts of the Sino-Syrian monument's rediscovery in 1625 from Semedo's and Martini's books on China, Kircher produced a barrage of eyewitness testimony and corroboratory evidence in order to properly interpret the stele's inscriptions: a letter from Michael Boym (1612–59) describing the events surrounding the monument's discovery; a transcription of its texts, made by Boym's Chinese companion; Boym's transliteration of each character's pronunciation; and Boym's word-for-word Latin translation.[22] These elaborate preliminaries preceded a more fluent paraphrase of the Chinese text and Kircher's own translation of the Syriac inscriptions.[23] Having painstakingly laid out the proper evidentiary framework for interpreting the stele's inscriptions, Kircher finally fulfilled the controversial claim he had made concerning the stele at the beginning of the book: that Christian doctrine preached in China a millennium ago was as orthodox as that still taught by the Roman Catholic Church.[24] Though Kircher had declared his confessional intentions at the outset, the elaborate scholarly apparatus he constructed around the stele dwarfed the relatively brief conclusions he ultimately drew from it concerning "articles of faith and other ceremonies and rites," from the doctrine of the Incarnation and the efficacy of prayers for souls in purgatory, to the real presence of Christ's body and blood in the sacrifice of the Mass.[25] Instead of defending the content of the Sino-Syrian monument's inscriptions on the basis of their intrinsic theological truth, Kircher drew out the stele's lessons for modern-day heretics as a matter of textual authenticity.

Yet the Sino-Syrian monument (Figure 17.1) was but one landmark in Kircher's longer perspective on the history of Christianity in Asia. Using the same interpretative strategies he had used to authenticate the Sino-Syrian monument, Kircher went on to explore "by what means, by whom, by which routes, and at what different times the holy gospel of Christ" had been transmitted to the farthest shores of the Asian continent.[26] Advancing a thesis of cultural diffusion on so grand a scale was admittedly an "abstruse matter" of considerable controversy. Its clarification depended on correctly reading sources in a staggering array of languages.[27] Kircher met the challenge handily, treating disagreement over the site of Thomas's martyrdom, for instance, as a problem of linguistic confusion to be resolved with the help of missionary expertise. Had the apostle died in some Indian city named Calamina, or in the city of Salamina on the island of Cyprus? Kircher explained that *Calamina* was a corruption of the word *Calurmina*, which in the language of Malabar meant "above the stone." According to Peter Paul Godigny, rector of the Jesuit college at Cochin in southern India, the term referred to the rock on which Thomas was in the habit of making

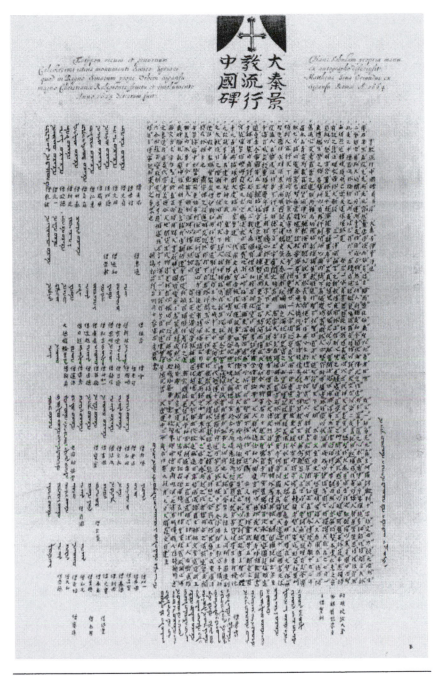

Figure 17.1. Transcription of the Sino-Syrian monument. *Source:* Athanasius Kircher, *China monumentis illustrata* (Amsterdam, 1667). Courtesy of Special Collections, Stanford University Libraries.

his daily prayers and on which he was martyred, not the name of the city in which he died.[28]

Interpreting Chinese Rites: The History of Superstition

But by the mid–seventeenth century, similar controversies over the meaning of exotic terms and the significance of ritual practices had ensnarled the Society of Jesus into shockingly public clashes with its competitors in the Asian missions. Dominican and Franciscan missionaries sharply criticized what they saw as Jesuit misuse of Chinese terms for proselytization, as well as Jesuit permissiveness in allowing Chinese converts to participate in a variety of traditional and seemingly superstitious ceremonies, including rites centered on the philosopher Confucius.[29] In 1645, the papal congregation charged with overseeing Catholic missions, Propaganda Fide, responded to a series of specific questions submitted by the Dominican friar, Juan Bautista de Morales, by prohibiting Chinese Christians from participation in most of the rituals as described by Morales.[30] Yet the text of the 1645 decree reflected the congregation's caution in evaluating such weighty cases of conscience on the basis of a single report on Chinese culture. In deciding whether Chinese Christians should be permitted to contribute toward certain communal activities—New Year's celebrations, sacrifices, idolatrous worship, and so on—Propaganda Fide declared that such payments could be made with pure intentions, "*supposing* that the situation is as it is described in the question."[31] The congregation reserved judgment altogether on whether the Chinese term "*king*" (*sheng*, holy), used by some missionaries with respect to the Holy Trinity, Christ, the Virgin Mary, and other Christian saints, could be applied to Confucius and emperors regarded as holy by the Chinese. The decree stated that "nothing can be declared concerning this word or its use, except with knowledge of the idiom, and of its true and and proper meaning," knowledge that Propaganda Fide clearly did not think it possessed.[32]

When Martino Martini returned to Europe as procurator for the Jesuit vice-province of China, he carried a brief to defend Jesuit evangelical efforts, presenting a memorial on the subject to Propaganda Fide in 1655. Martini explained that the rites performed by Chinese scholars in receiving their degrees were meant to honor Confucius as their teacher, not as a god. The papal congregation of the Holy Office decreed in 1656 that the rituals enumerated in Martini's petition seemed to be "merely civil and political" in nature, and hence were permissible.[33] But even though the decree was a putative victory for Jesuit missionary methods, it did not constitute anything like verification of Jesuit reports concerning Chinese culture. Roman theologians evidently granted Martini's characterization of Chinese customs a certain level of plausibility, but the language of their deliberations tells us that their decision endorsing particular missionary methods was premised on the assumed veracity of Martini's descriptions.[34] No conclusion could be drawn from the Holy Office's decree as to Jesuit veracity in describing Chinese culture. When the Holy Office was asked in

1669 whether their decision superceded the decision issued by Propaganda Fide in 1645, it replied that both decrees were still in effect, since each decree supposed a different set of facts concerning Chinese customs.[35]

Hence the credibility of Jesuit reports from the Asian missions was still an unsettled question by the time Kircher sat down to compose the *China*. In comparison with contemporary Jesuit defenses of missionary practice in tolerating certain Chinese ceremonies as free from superstition, Kircher's interpretation of Chinese rituals seems oddly idiosyncratic.[36] Although Kircher also relied heavily on Trigault's 1615 publication of Matteo Ricci's journals for descriptions of the "Literati" sect and its veneration of Confucius, he ignored the features of Chinese ceremonial life that Martini had defended as licit practices, selecting examples that supported his own claims for the Egyptian origins of Chinese idolatry. Kircher annotated excerpts from Trigault in such a way as to suggest similarities between animal sacrifices made to the "Lord of Heaven" (*Regem Coelorum*) worshipped by the Chinese literati, and those offered to the Egyptian god Osiris, as well as between the bimonthly rituals carried out by officials and scholars in Confucian temples, and the monthly rites celebrated in Egypt to the god Thoth, known to the Greeks as Hermes Trismegistus.[37] Indeed, Chinese idolatry was but one strand in a web of superstitious filiations that Kircher ultimately traced back to Egypt, part of the universal history of Christianity and paganism that Kircher had begun in his earlier works on Egypt, and that he would continue to elaborate in his *Noah's Ark* (1675) and *Tower of Babel* (1679).[38]

Kircher's emphasis on the illicit elements in Chinese ceremonial practices satisfied more than his own predilection for grand historical schemas.[39] At the end of the seventeenth century, a commentator on the Chinese rites controversy wrote succinctly that "The whole question boils down to a point of fact: to know what the Chinese think about their Confucius and their ancestors, and what they intend by the ceremonies with which they honour them."[40] The entire debate turned on whether missionary informants accurately grasped native beliefs and practices. Kircher answered that his fellow Jesuits could and did, because they possessed the requisite linguistic facilities. Kircher relentlessly praised the linguistic skills of the Jesuits on whom he depended for his discussion of Chinese, Japanese, Tartar and Indian idolatry, describing Bento de Goës (1562–1606) as "versed in the Persian speech," Giovanni Maria Campori (1574–1621) as "absolutely expert in the language of the Chaldeans," and Robert Nobili (1577–1656) as "most learned in the language and genealogy of the Brahmans."[41] Heinrich Roth (1620–68) similarly excelled in his knowledge of Sanskrit and the other languages of Mughal India, the Persian of the court, and the Hindi of the common people.[42] Kircher devoted one chapter to examples of Brahminical teachings on incarnation provided by Roth, whose knowledge of Sanskrit allowed him to draw out "the principal doctrines from their more arcane books," and another to Roth's brief introduction to the language itself, which concluded with an interlinear rendering of the *Pater Noster* and the *Ave Maria* in Latin and Sanskrit.[43]

Chinese was a particularly difficult language for Europeans to master, given the vast number of characters and the comparatively small number of phonetic sounds, yet members of the Society of Jesus willingly devoted themselves to its study.[44] Nicolas Trigault acquired his Chinese abilities thanks to a "tireless devotion"; Giacomo Rho (1592–1638) had made "so much progress in the Chinese language that whether you consider writing or speech, in China he was seen as a native"; and Michael Boym was "most expert in the Chinese tongue," as well as in "all matters concerning the mores and customs of the said Kingdom."[45] Kircher relied on such expertise and his own knowledge of Egyptian hieroglyphs to demonstrate the derivation of Chinese writing from Egyptian sources, one of the chief proofs Kircher adduced for the diffusion of idolatry from Egypt to China.[46] The extended study of Asian idolatry in Kircher's *China* demonstrated that Jesuits in the Asian missions were equipped with the linguistic skills needed to correctly identify superstition in its many manifestations through time and space, and to distinguish superstition from indigenous beliefs and practices that posed no threat to Christianity.

Unmaking the Marvelous East: Natural History

Collective Jesuit expertise in so many exotic languages made it possible for Kircher to clarify "confusion and doubt concerning the equivocation of words," a major source of controversy for the history of religion and superstition. Kircher promised, however, that he would also examine Eastern "prodigies of nature and art."[47] Surveying the Middle Kingdom with an eye that had long studied wonders of both the natural world and human ingenuity, Kircher acknowledged that reports of such matters previously retailed by Jesuit informants had been criticized as "manufactured, false, and unbelievable". In response to such slurs, Kircher took it upon himself to "distinguish the true from the false, the certain from the uncertain" in his fellow Jesuits' reports of Asian marvels.[48]

Only rarely in the *China* did Kircher challenge the intrinsic plausibility of some strange Asian phenomenon solely on the grounds that it was naturally impossible. Referring the reader to his extended discussion of alchemy in the *Subterranean World*, Kircher flatly rejected the "tricks" of Chinese alchemists who claimed to have discovered the secrets of gold-making and immortality.[49] Kircher also categorically denied the existence of winged tortoises, flying cats with feathered wings, birds born from leaves or flowers, and wool-bearing chickens as phenomena "contrary to the intention of Nature," explaining away reports of such oddities as mistakes of identification.[50] But on the whole, Kircher preferred to winnow the accounts that his Jesuit colleagues provided with a comparative sieve. In the section of the *China* devoted to "physical investigations concerning the rarer spectacles of nature," Kircher set out to show that these purportedly rare sights were in fact not rare at all, through a systematic comparison of marvelous Asian phenomena with their European analogues.[51] The squarish stones found on Mount Queyu were miracles of nature that could also be seen in the mountains of Calabria, a phenomenon Kircher himself noted in his *Subterranean World*. The astoundingly loud din of the storms that loomed over Mount Paoki resembled the thunderous sounds that the archbishop of Uppsala, Olaus Magnus (1490–1557), attributed to the Swedish mountains bordering the Gulf of Bothnia in his *History of the Northern Peoples* (1555).[52] A greenish lake in the coastal province of Fujian that reportedly turned iron into copper had its counterparts in Europe, "chiefly in those places where much copper is extracted from the mountains."[53] If Chinese roses that changed in color with sunrise and sunset were "prodigies of nature," violets in the garden of the Roman botanist Francisco Corvino exhibited similar transformations.[54] Jesuits in China reported having seen "wells of fire" in Shansi Province, emitting heat sufficient for cooking food. Recalling the observations he himself had made in Italy and Sicily several decades earlier, as well as his own studies of the subterranean world, Kircher reminded the reader that such "prodigies of nature" could be found in Europe, "and in fact the matter is seen to be not so much wondrous, as unfamiliar to us."[55]

In some cases Kircher's investigations led him to revise the accounts of "strange facts" he received from his fellow Jesuits. Chinese sailors claimed, for instance, that a plant from Guangdong Province could be used to predict the weather. The fewer the number of nodes on the plant, the fewer the storms that year, while the distance between the nodes and the root was said to indicate the month in which the storms would occur. Although Kircher denied this particular correspondence between macrocosmos and microcosmos, he allowed that other sympathetic relationships might exist, such that a plant might continually turn itself toward the wind; Kircher referred the reader to just such a phenomenon as described in his own *Magnet, or of the Magnetic Art*.[56] A certain stone discovered in Shensi Province was said to increase and diminish in size according to the waxing and waning of the moon. In experiments with its European counterpart, Kircher found that the stone reflected moonlight like a mirror, so much so that the moon's phases could be clearly distinguished, and suggested that it was this phenomenon that had given rise to the notion that the stone itself changed in size.[57]

For the most part, however, Kircher's discussions of Eastern marvels amplified the essential elements of his confreres' reports. Kircher complemented the Chinese stories that Martini related in his *New Chinese Atlas* (1655) about fossilized crabs with notices of parallel specimens on display in his museum at the Collegio Romano, a brief suggestion as to the cause, and references to more extended treatments of the same phenomenon in his other writings.[58] On occasion Kircher pointed to experimental evidence to support the plausibility of Asian phenomena, as when he commented that repeated experiments with the effects of ammonia salts and sulfur had led him to the cause of the Chinese rose's strange metamorphoses. More rarely, Kircher had the opportunity to examine actual Asian specimens, as when he wrote of his tests with snakestones, widely reputed in both India and China to be an antidote against poison, or when he promised the reader an investigation of the "wondrous qualities" ascribed to hippopotamus teeth, which Boym reported as possessing the power to stop the flow of blood.[59] Set within the context of a deflationary approach to the marvels of the East, such experimental trials, causal explanations, and collected objects served to accentuate the comparative framework Kircher laboriously constructed for evaluating the plausibility of Eastern wonders.

Jesuits in the Republic of Letters

Compiling a credible natural and religious history of the East depended on a process of mutual legitimation. Missionary informants drew on written sources as well as oral reports, on their own experiences as well as indigenous traditions, to compose their accounts of the marvelous East, which Kircher examined in turn with the help of a similarly broad range of European resources, including his own studies of natural phenomena. Even instances in which Kircher himself had no direct role in verifying phenomena were presented in terms of collective judgement, as when Kircher credited his fellow Jesuits with having finally resolved controversies over the fabrication of porcelain, thanks to their "sensory and ocular experience" of its manufacture.[60] Kircher similarly wove a complex tapestry of Christian and idolatrous belief in Asia by drawing judiciously on the disparate materials provided by his Jesuit counterparts in the missions, as well as his own massive works on early Christianity and paganism. In short, the *China* was a text uniquely shaped by the global breadth of the Society of Jesus's missionary enterprises, and by the scholarly depth of its educational institutions.[61]

Kircher took particular pains to emphasize the willingness of his fellow Jesuits to take part in a scholarly enterprise. Notably, he did not do so by pointing to the wide-ranging epistolary networks through which he solicited the cooperation of far-flung correspondents, including many of his Jesuit brethren.[62] Rather, Kircher explained that those who had "excited and joined in the writing of this work" were Jesuits with whom he had personally discussed the sacred and secular history of Asia when they passed through Rome on official business for the Society of Jesus.[63] Describing Martino Martini with evident pride as "once my private student in mathematics" at the Collegio Romano, Kircher remarked on the conversations he enjoyed with his former pupil when Martini returned to Rome in the mid-1650s as procurator for the Jesuit vice-province of China.[64] A "bond of friendship" likewise linked Kircher to Alvarez Semedo, who visited Rome as procurator for the Chinese vice-province a decade earlier.[65] Michael Boym went to Rome with an urgent mission to Pope Innocent X from Christian converts of the Ming court, then in flight from the new Manchu rulers of China, but found time to prepare his translation of the monument's text in Kircher's presence.[66] Kircher learned much in conversations with Giovanni Filippo de Marini during the latter's stay in Rome as procurator, and with Johann Grueber (1623–80) and Heinrich Roth when they returned to Rome after an exhaustive overland journey from India.[67] Peter Paul Godigny likewise shared his expertise with Kircher when he visited Rome as procurator for the Malabar Province, as did the procurator for the Philippines, Juan Lopez (1584–1659).[68] Kircher pointed out that he printed Boym's manuscript material with Boym's assent; that Grueber had "faithfully" complied with Kircher's request to make observations en route to China; and that Grueber and Roth had bequeathed their notes to him for publication. Roth readily granted Kircher's desire for the text of a rare document concerning Saint Thomas's route from Judea to India, and Kircher even cited Grueber's own words as having "gladly" sent Jesuit observations of longitude and latitude from India to Rome.[69]

When Kircher listed the medicinal benefits of tea for "learned men" and those whose affairs called for "prolonged wakefulness," he wrote that he had been persuaded of these virtues only after having sampled the drink at the "frequent invitation" of his fellow Jesuits[70] (Figure 17.2). The description calls up images of Kircher in a room at the Collegio Romano, sharing a cup of tea with a former student or friend as they pored together over some obscure text or natural oddity. Kircher's intimations of scholarly conviviality were meant to be suggestive. Despite the prescriptive force of the Society of Jesus's normative documents and its mechanisms for inculcating corporate goals, Jesuits in general and Kircher in particular were by no means unfamiliar with the difficulties of harnessing individual wills to a collective project.[71] Nonetheless, Kircher deliberately painted a harmonious picture of scholarly fellowship within the Society of Jesus, while also explicitly inviting the participation of the learned world at large. While discussing the possibility of plants moving in accord with other natural phenomena, for instance, Kircher wrote that "for fifteen years, to this day, we exhibit a prodigy of similar nature in our museum for visitors," suggesting that the curious reader of the *China* was welcome to take a more active role in examining exotica on display in the Collegio Romano museum, from hippopotamus teeth and birds' nests to fossilized crabs and samples of asbestos.[72] Kircher effectively extended the same invitation with respect to his histories of Eastern Christianity and superstition. Kircher's museum featured books by leading Chinese converts concerning the Sino-Syrian monument, together with an "autograph" copy—probably an ink rubbing—of its inscription; a rubbing of a stele placed at the entrance of the Jesuit church in Beijing, inscribed with an imperial edict praising both the astronomy and religion of the Jesuits; as well as illustrations of pagan deities. These curiosities were available "for examination by all" at the Collegio Romano museum, already a well-established locus for learned sociability.[73]

Figure 17.2. Chinese tea. *Source:* Athanasius Kircher, *China monumentis illustrata* (Amsterdam, 1667). Courtesy of Special Collections, Stanford University Libraries.

By emphasizing the amicability, generosity, and openness of Jesuit scholarship, Kircher laid the moral foundations for broader Jesuit participation within the Republic of Letters, that ideal community in which bonds of friendship and a shared commitment to the common good linked individuals in a collaborative search for knowledge.[74] Indeed, Kircher made explicit claims to Jesuit citizenship in the Republic of Letters. He described his former pupil Martino Martini as "not satisfied" with merely investigating the curiosities and customs of the Middle Kingdom; to the contrary, Martini decided to publish his findings in his *New Chinese Atlas* "for the benefit of the Republic of Letters."[75] Martini's noble sentiments were apparently shared by his fellow Jesuits in China, who feared their observations would fall victim to "moths and worms." In his preface, Kircher explained that he had published their materials at their behest for the public good, thus casting himself and his fellow Jesuits in thoroughly conventional roles as hardworking Republicans of Letters.[76]

Jesuits in China wore their success on their sleeves. Prior to the fall of the Ming dynasty in 1644, members of the Society of Jesus dressed in the long silken robes that Kircher described as appropriate for "Doctors of the great

West"[77] (Figure 17.3). In fact, this style of attire was proper to the Chinese learned elite, whose long study of the Chinese classics prepared them to take the examinations that qualified them for government service.[78] Jesuits had initially entered China with shaven heads and faces, and worn robes similar to those of Buddhist priests. But Matteo Ricci's growing sensitivity to the social distinctions marked by such outward appearances led to a deliberate shift in Jesuit missionary strategy during the 1590s. By growing their hair and beards, by wearing long silk robes with wide sleeves, and by exhibiting their mastery of both Chinese and European knowledge traditions, Jesuits presented themselves as learned men, worthy Western counterparts to the Chinese scholars and officials whose support they sought.[79] Imperial recognition of Jesuit learning also found sartorial expression. As Kircher explained, Adam Schall's robes bore the insignia denoting his rank as an official in the Qing bureaucracy.[80]

Both men appear in the frontispiece to the *China*, together with visual references to the technical skills and secular knowledge with which they laid the foundations of the Chinese Christian Church. Standing beneath their Jesuit forebearers, Ignatius of Loyola (1491–1556) and Francis Xavier (1506–52), Ricci and Kircher—the rightful inheritors of an apostolic succession—hold open a map of China to the view of the curious European reader as well the eager Jesuit missionary. In the *China*, Kircher chronicled evangelical journeys to the East made by a series of "apostolic men," from Saint Thomas to the apostle's modern successors, the Jesuits. Already "chosen by God as an Apostle for the salvation of the Indians" as well as the Japanese, Francis Xavier was the first Jesuit to turn his attention toward China. Though he died on a small island off the Chinese coast, his hopes were fulfilled by Kircher's own contemporaries in the Society of Jesus.[81]

In a chapter on "the manner in which Our Fathers are accustomed to proceed in the conversion of the Chinese," Kircher described the program of studies followed by Jesuits preparing to enter the China mission. According to Kircher, his fellow Jesuits began by first striving for a command of the language equivalent to that of the Chinese scholar-official, a task that required an "Apostolic perseverance" for success.[82] They then studied neither "metaphysical speculations," nor "scholastic subtleties," nor "lofty theories," but rather "sensible things" unknown to the Chinese that could induce admiration and raise the repute of Europeans in China.[83] Such items included the clocks, prisms, and mappamundi with which Matteo Ricci—once a student of Kircher's predecessor as professor of mathematics at the Collegio Romano, Christopher Clavius (1538–1612)—had "enticed the minds of many learned men, not only in the Province of Guangdong, but throughout the entire Empire," and so obtained a hearing for the Christian religion.[84] Similar potential lay in more specialized study of astronomy and mathematics, expertise for which Jesuits sought imperial patronage. Kircher told of how Schall's abilities had led the emperor to appoint the European priest to the highest position in

Figure 17.3. Jesuit missionaries in Chinese dress. *Source:* Athanasius Kircher, *China monumentis illustrata* (Amsterdam, 1667). Courtesy of Special Collections, Stanford University Libraries.

the imperial Astronomical Bureau, charged with annual preparation of the official Chinese calendar.[85] Next, missionaries-in-training turned their attention to moral philosophy, a topic of great interest to the Chinese; only then did they finally proceed to the delicate issue of how to instruct the Chinese in Christian doctrine and how to refute Chinese superstitions.

Having sketched an ideal training regimen for missionaries to China, Kircher pointed out that sustained proselytization depended on books as well, and proceeded to provide a "Catalogue of books by our Fathers, written for the growth of the Chinese church".[86] A testament to their mastery of the Chinese language, the list indicated the range of Western learning that Jesuit missionaries wished to present to a Chinese readership. Ricci's oeuvre included several books drawn from Clavius's texts in pure and mixed mathematics, as well as books on geography, natural philosophy, music, ethics, and a catechism attributed to the Jesuit cardinal Robert Bellarmine (1542–1621). Trigault prepared an ecclesiastical calendar, while Giacomo Rho produced works on catechetical and spiritual subjects, and more than a hundred texts on mixed mathematics in collaboration with Johann Adam Schall von Bell (1592–1666) on the calendar reform. Alfonso Vagnone (1568/9–1640) wrote several lives of the saints and other religious figures, devotional and catechetical writings, as well as books on political, moral, and natural philosophy. By 1636—after a half-century of evangelical work in China—Kircher's confreres had composed some 340 books in the Chinese language on religious, moral, natural, and mathematical subjects.[87] Illustrative rather than exhaustive, Kircher's bio-bibliography of the Jesuit mission in China provided pointillistic detail to a collective portrait of the Jesuit missionary as a man of broad learning, engaged in a scholarly apostolate.[88]

Defending a Life

The *China* was a remarkably popular work by an author who had experienced remarkable success in the early modern marketplace of the printed book. In the space of a decade, the *China* appeared in four separate folio editions and in more languages than any of Kircher's other works.[89] Kircher preferred to write in Latin—the language of the cosmopolitan *Respublica litterarum*—and even received praise for his Ciceronian style.[90] But Dutch competition and success in marketing exotic literature quickly procured a wider audience for Kircher's study of the mysterious East. When Kircher's designated printer, Joannes Jansson van Waesberghe, published the *China* in 1667, a rival Amsterdam bookseller rushed a reprint into production before the end of the year.[91] Jansson quickly brought out vernacular editions in Dutch (1668) and French (1670). In 1669 and again in 1673, substantial excerpts from the *China* crossed the Channel in John Ogilby's English translations of contemporary Dutch narratives concerning the Middle Kingdom.[92]

In its very popularity, the *China* well represents the early modern efflores-cence in Jesuit literary production that aimed at the tastes as well as the souls of learned lay audiences.[93] Yet Kircher's ability to compose a work like the *China* suggests his own alienation from the ideal of "apostolic mobility" that invoked the wanderings of Saint Paul as a model of ministry unique to the Je-suit vocation.[94] Like so many of his confreres, whose petitions to enter the mis-sions of the Society of Jesus are still preserved by the thousands, the youthful Kircher dreamed of the mission fields. Their requests testified to the continu-ing appeal of the Jesuit missionary ideal and a rhetoric of self-sacrifice, peril, and martyrdom sustained by the very literature on which Kircher drew in writing the *China*.[95] As a young man in the Society of Jesus, Kircher petitioned his superiors to be sent to China as a missionary, but was twice denied.[96] Kircher's journeys as a Jesuit effectively ended in 1634, when his superiors, pa-trons, and even divine providence directed Kircher to a life of scholarly fame as professor of mathematics at the Collegio Romano. There, Kircher enjoyed pre-cisely the "freedom from affairs" to write and publish for the Republic of Let-ters that was denied to his confreres in the mission fields, "occupied with attending to the salvation of souls."[97]

Kircher himself admitted a certain ambivalence about how to make proper use of his scholarly gifts. In his autobiography, he explained that during his early philosophical studies at the Jesuit college at Paderborn, he deliberately hid his abilities to avoid the sin of vanity, succeeding so well that his Jesuit in-structor thought him dull-minded. When Kircher took up his first teaching post as a professor of Greek, he felt obligated to reveal his talents for the good repute of the Society of Jesus, a decision that apparently gave rise to jealousy from others.[98] Kircher's difficulties mirrored those he attributed to his fellow Jesuits. Johann Schreck (Terrentius, 1576–30), for instance, was famed "through-out Germany as Philosopher, Physician and Mathematician, and most wel-come among princes" thanks to his learning. Schreck, like Galileo, was an early member of the Accademia dei Lincei, founded by the Roman prince Federico Cesi to reform natural philosophy.[99] "Weary of fame and honor, and sated with the world," Schreck decided to enter the Society of Jesus so that he could "de-vote his talent toward the conversion of the infidels," carrying out his later studies of natural history, medicine, and calendrical reform for the benefit of the "Christian Republic."[100] Thanks to "divine benevolence," Kircher realized that he, too, was meant to work "not only for the advancement of the Republic of Letters, but also to benefit souls and excite devotion in humankind." While searching for some classical ruins as part of his research for an antiquarian work on ancient Rome, Kircher found an abandoned church, built by Con-stantine the Great in memory of the place where the Roman general Eu-stachius had experienced a miraculous conversion to Christianity. Determined to revive the shrine, Kircher "set aside his other studies" and turned his atten-tion to composing a learned history of the site. Its publication in 1665 resulted in a shower of contributions from Kircher's patrons for the restoration of the church, which was thereafter served by an annual "Apostolic Mission" established by members of the Society of Jesus.[101]

Kircher's own literary labors at the very heart of the Catholic world thus bore a striking resemblance to the scholarly apostolate that Kircher attributed to his colleagues in the remote provinces of Christendom. Jesuits were men knowledgeable not only in Christian doctrine, but also in a wide range of secular disciplines. They used their learning to draw the attention of the learned elite, counting on natural human curiosity to excite patronage and hopefully devotion as well from emperors, princes, officials, and scholars.[102] Kircher's privileged and worldly position in the Republic of Letters was not without its ambiguities. He sought refuge from the strain of entertaining a constant stream of curious visitors by returning to the shrine he had rescued from obscurity. There in the Roman countryside, Kircher tried—not always successfully—to set aside his "usual employments and engage entirely in those of God."[103] Yet Kircher seems to have been largely at peace with his fusion of scholarship and spirituality. In his dedication for the *China*, Kircher wrote unapologetically to the General of the Society of Jesus, Gian Paolo Oliva (1600–1681), that the volume was "a new offspring of my genius."[104] The lessons that Kircher spelled out in the *China* for an aspiring missionary went well beyond practical recommendations to study the vernacular and written languages, forms of superstition, and other cultural features specific to a mission field. Kircher invested the scholarly apostolate with the same emotional fervor as the traditional ideal of apostolic journeying, declaring that Ricci had suffered "countless hardships, perils, and persecutions" in leaving behind a written oeuvre "for the good of the Chinese Church."[105] Apropos of his Jesuit bio-bibliography, Kircher even cited Paul's second letter to the Corinthians on an apostle's willingness to prove himself as a minister of God, patiently enduring all sorts of hardship "through glory and obscurity, infamy and renown" in order to bear witness to the suffering of Christ.[106] Together with his fellow Jesuits, Kircher persevered in the face of scorn, criticism, and even accusations of fraud for the benefit of both "the Christian Religion and the Republic of Letters."[107] Articulating and enacting a scholar's version of the *imitatio Christi*, Kircher defended both the religious order to which he belonged, as well as the life he lived within it.

Notes

1. Henry Oldenburg to Robert Boyle (25 August 1664), in Oldenburg 1966, vol. 2, p. 532.
2. Ashworth 1986, p. 155.
3. Kircher 1667a, "Prooemium ad lectorem," sig. **v.
4. Martini 1655; see Koeman 1970.
5. See Szczesniak 1955, pp. 491–494, 501–503.
6. Kircher 1667a, p. 120: "Non dicam hic de *Annalibus Sinensibus, Literisque ad diversos ex* China *tum ad superiores, tum ad amicos particulares de rebus Sinensibus conscriptis*, quorum non est numerus"; see also p. 140.

7. Ibid., p. 2, 237.
8. Recent analyses of this literature include Daston and Park 1998; and Campbell 1988.
9. For taxonomies of the medieval marvelous, see Le Goff 1988; and Larner 1999, pp. 80–81.
10. On the perceived credibility of travelers' tales in early modern Europe, see Shapin 1994, pp. 243–258; and generally, Adams 1962.
11. Hankins and Silverman 1995, pp. 14–30.
12. Robert Southwell to Robert Boyle (30 March 1661), in Boyle 2001, Vol. 1, p. 451.
13. On the emergence and verification of "strange facts" in seventeenth-century natural philosophy, see Daston and Park 1998, chapter 6; and Daston 1994, pp. 37–63.
14. Findlen 2000, p. 222.
15. See Iliffe 1999a and 1999b; and Zagorin, 1990, chapters 8–9.
16. Pascal 1967, p. 76.
17. For a convenient survey, see O'Malley 1999b.
18. Kircher 1667a, p. 1: "Quos inter quidam ex modernis Scriptoribus fuit, qui exiguo suo honore huius Monumenti veritatem omni conatu, insolenti sanè scommate elidere non est verecundatus, dum id modò Jesuiticâ fraude introductum, modò purum putum figmentum à Jesuitis, tum ad Sinenses decipiendos, tum ad thesauros eruendos confictum asserit: cuius nomini partim ex Christiana charitate parco." For a survey of early modern reactions to the Nestorian monument, see Mungello 1989, pp. 164–172.
19. On Kircher as the "new Oedipus," see Findlen 1994, p. 338; for his various linguistic studies, see Wilding 2001a; and Stolzenberg 2001c.
20. See Grafton 1999, chapter 6.
21. Ibid., p. 153.
22. Kircher 1667a, pp. 6–10; 13–21 ("Interpretatio I," the transliteration of the Chinese text); 22–28 ("Interpretatio II," Boym's literal translation).
23. Ibid., pp. 29–35 ("Interpretatio III," the Latin paraphrase); pp. 41–45 (Syriac inscriptions).
24. Ibid., p. 2.
25. Ibid., p. 33: "De Articulis fidei caeterisque cerimoniis & ritibus in Monumento contentis"; pp. 38–40.
26. Ibid., p. 46: "Qua ratione, & à quibus, quibusque itineribus, diversis temporibus Sacrosanctum Christi Evangelium in ultimas Orientis Regiones, Indiam, Tartariam, Chinam, caeterasque Asiae Regiones fuerit illatum." See also p. 2.
27. Ibid., p. 46.
28. Ibid., p. 53.
29. For some recent evaluations of the controversy over Chinese "terms" and "rites," see Mungello 1994; Rule 1986, chapters 2–3; and Minamiki 1985.
30. The text of the 1645 decree is available in Propaganda Fide 1907, vol. 1, no. 114, pp. 30–35.
31. Ibid., vol. 1, p. 32: "Censuerunt posse christianos chinenses pecunias contribuere dummodo per huiusmodi contributiones non intendant ad actus idololatricos, et superstitiosos concurrere, supposita causa quae narratur in dubio." Emphasis added.
32. Ibid., vol. 1, p. 34: "Censuerunt, non posse aliquid firmari circa vocem hanc (*King*), eiusve usum. nisi praehabita cognitione idiomatis, eiusque verae et propriae significationis: coeterum si eadem vox in Regno Chinarum habet latitudinem, posse ministros ea uti; si vero restringatur ad significandam veram et perfectam sanctitatem, nullatenus posse."
33. The text of the 1656 decree is available in Propaganda Fide, 1907, vol. 1, no. 126, pp. 36–39; the quotation is on p. 38. The decree, together with Martini's memorial to the congregation and related documents, is also reproduced in Martini 1998, vol. 1, pp. 367–444. Rule traces the gradual evolution of Jesuit views on Chinese "rites" and "terms," beginning with Trigault's editing of Ricci's manuscript memoirs as *De christiana expeditione apud Sinas* (1615); see Rule 1986, chapters 1–2.
34. See Martini 1998, vol. 1, pp. 374, 377, 383, 388, 389, 425, 427.
35. Rule 1986, p. 98.
36. The leading Jesuit chronicler of the Society's missions, Daniello Bartoli (1608–85), felt compelled to review the issues in some detail when he turned his attention to China in 1663; see Bartoli 1829, book 1, chapters 81–84, 142–147. Giovanni Filippo de Marini translated a major Jesuit response to mendicant criticisms; see Rule 1986, pp. 92–97.
37. Kircher 1667a, pp. 131–132; cf. Trigault, 1615, book 1, chapter 10. Kircher's discussion of Chinese ritual practices did not, however, actually conflict with the decisions made in Rome concerning the Chinese rites. Of the two ceremonies Kircher ascribed in the *China* to

the Chinese literati, the bimonthly ritual seems to correspond to a ritual already proscribed in 1645 by Propaganda Fide; the other, involving animal sacrifice to the "Lord of Heaven," is not described in either decree. Conversely, Kircher did not mention the Confucian rite permitted by the Holy Office in 1656 at Martini's instigation. Cf. Kircher 1667a, pp. 131–132, and the texts of the 1645 and 1656 decrees.

38. Kircher 1667a, pp. 2, 46, 129. See Stolzenberg 2001b; and Pastine 1978.

39. Cf. the analysis of Kircher's views offered in Mungello 1989, pp. 157–164, 172–173.

40. *Prejugez legitimes en faveur du decret de N.S. Père Alexandre VII et de la pratique des Jésuites au sujet des honneurs que les Chinois rendent à Confucius et à leurs ancestres* (1700), p. 2, as cited in Rule 1986, p. 70.

41. Kircher 1667a, p. 63: "*Benedicto Goësio* viro prudenti & cordato, nec non linguâ Persica"; p. 57, "*Pater Joannes Ma. Compori* . . . Sermonis Chaldaei oppidò peritus"; p. 152: "*P. Robertus Nobilis* Societatis IESU . . . nec non linguae & Brachmanicae genealogiae consultissimus."

42. Ibid., p. 80, 162, 156; sig. **2r: "*P. Henricum Roth* . . . trium linguarum, Persicae, Indostanicae, & Brachmanicae, instructissimus."

43. Ibid., p. 156: "P. Henricus Roth Augustanus Patriâ, Mogoricae Missionis in defessus operarius, qui uti Brachmanicae linguae est peritissimus, ita quoque ex ipsorum arcanioribus libris praecipua extraxit dogmata, ea intentione, ut nostris inter *Brachmanes* versantibus modum, quo tantas absurditates facilius confutare possent, traderet." See also pp. 162–163 (part 3, chapter 7, "De Literis Brachmanum" and plates), and p. 80. For Robert Nobili's dual expertise in Sanskrit and Brahmin theology, see p. 152.

44. For testimonies to Jesuit study of Chinese, see Kircher 1667a, pp. 97–98, 116, 235–236; on the difficulty of the language, see pp. 10–12, 235–236. Mungello surveys early modern European notions of the Chinese language; Mungello 1989.

45. Kircher 1667a, p. 118: "*Pater Nicolaus Trigautius Duacensis Belga*, uti melioris notae Linguae Sinicae, quam indefesso studio sibi compararat, peritissimus"; p. 119: "*P. Jacobus Rho Mediolanensis.* . . . tantos derepentè in Lingua Sinica progressus fecit, ut sive scripturam sive loquelam attendas, in *China* natus videretur"; p. 2: "*P.* verò *Michaële Boimo* Sinicae linguae peritissimo"; p. 225: "R.P. Michael Boym Polonus è Soc. IESU, tùm linguae Sinicae, tum rerum omnium ad dicti *Regni* mores & consuetudines pertinentium peritissimus."

46. See Ibid., pp. 225–236 (part 6, "De Sinensium literatura"); see also p. 134.

47. Ibid., p. 2: "Nostrum erit ea solummodo quae uti controversa sunt, ita quoque Lectores mirè circa nominum aequivocationem dubios perplexosque reddunt, explicare, nec non rariora, & ab aliis non tacta, reconditarum rerum in eo Regno, aliisque vicinis observatarum arcana, tum naturae, tum artis prodigia hoc opere, veluti opportuno loco, in curiosi Lectoris gratiam adducere."

48. Ibid., p. 164: "Cum in Patrum Nostrorum Operibus admiranda quaedam, quae tum in Indicis Regnis, tum in Sinarum Imperio occurrunt, Artis, & Naturae miracula, à nonnullis Criticastris veluti conficta, falsa, & nulla fide digna carpantur; ea hoc loco opportuno, ad eorum sincerae fidei integritatem contestandam, denuo ad incudem reducenda duxi; ut verum à falso, certum ab incerto sejunctum, rerum perperam intellectarum veritas, sublato fuco, innotescat"; see also prooemium, sig. **2v.

49. Ibid., p. 209; see Nummedal 2001, pp. 43–45.

50. Kircher 1667a, p. 204 ("testitudines alatae"); 84–85 ("Catti volantes"); 178 ("Folia arborum in aquis in hirundines animantur"); 198 ("Avicula ex flore nascens"); 197 ("Gallinae Lanigerae"); 196–197 ("monstruosum Naturae partum praeter intentionem Naturae produci"). For an Asian instance of "wondrous metamorphosis" that Kircher admitted as naturally possible, see pp. 199–201.

51. Ibid., p. 169: "Disquisitiones physicae de rarioribus naturae spectaculis, quae in *China* reperiuntur"; p. 164: "Omnibus que luculenter constet, nil in iis adeò insolitum atque spectari; quod tum in Europâ, tum caeteris Mundi partibus non reperiatur."

52. Ibid., p. 170; see Magnus 1555, book 2, chapter 4.

53. Ibid., p. 175: "Est in provincia *Fokien* Lacus, qui ferrum in cuprum vertit, totus viridi colore imbutus, cuius quidem rei ratio alia non est, nisi quod aqua tota vitrioli constet corpusculis; & color viridis eius manifestum indicium est, cuiusmodi in *Europae* quoque nulli non occurrunt, in iis potissimum locis, ubi copiosum è montibus cuprum extrahitur. Vide *Mundum Subterraneum Lib. 10 de Fodinis Cupri.*"

54. Ibid., p. 177: "Neque in *China* solum huiusmodi Naturae prodigia reperiri putes; habet hîc *Romae* nobilis Botanicus Franciscus Corvinus in suo horto, omni quae desiderari possunt,

plantarum genere instructissimo plantam, quam violam nocturnam vocat, qui diversos pro Solis ascensu aut descensu colores ad sensum mutat . . . de quibus vide fusiùs actum in *nostra Philosophia lib.* XII. *Mundi Subterranei* inserta."

55.   Ibid., p. 211: "atque adeo res non tam mira, quàm insolita nobis esse videtur"; pp. 209–211. See Nummedal 2001.

56.   Kircher 1667a, p. 177.

57.   Ibid., pp. 205–206.

58.   Ibid., p. 202.

59.   Ibid., pp. 176–177 (rose); 80–82, sig. Hh 3v (snakestones); 192–193 (hippopotamus teeth). On the broader context and *fortuna* of Kircher's claims concerning the snakestone, see Baldwin 1995.

60.   Kircher 1667a, p. 108: "Non desunt, qui fabulis quoque propudiosis annexis, nescio ex qua materia eam oriri velint, sed Patres nostri experientiâ sensatâ, ocularique docti, quaenam illa sit materia, quis eam elaborandi modus, & ratio, tandem detecta varietate nos ab omnibus falsitatis conceptae erroribus liberarunt."

61.   For an analysis of how such Jesuit networks patterned early modern Jesuit science, see Harris 1999.

62.   For appreciations of Kircher's correspondence, see Fletcher 1988c; and Wilding 2001b.

63.   Kircher 1667a, "Prooemium ad lectorem," sig. ** v: "P.P. qui sua ad hoc opus scribendum contulerunt & sollicitarunt." On the Jesuit office of procurator, see Dehergne 1973, pp. 314–315. Cf. Kircher 1667b, "Praefatio ad lectorem," sig. *8r–*9r.

64.   Kircher 1667a, p. 6: "*Pater Martinus Martinius* post Semedum Romam veniens, non solùm Monumenti rationem oretenus mihi retulit, sed & *in suo Atlante* ejusdem fusè meminit his verbis. . . ."; "Prooemium ad lectorem," sig. ** v: "olim privatus meus in Mathematicis discipulus." Kircher introduced Martini with the same phrase when he published his former pupil's observations of magnetic declination and lunar eclipses, made en route to China, in the third edition of his *Magnet, or of the Magnetic Art* (1654), p. 316. See Martini 1998, vol. 1, p. 511. For Martini's earlier contacts with Kircher, see Szczesniak 1960.

65.   Kircher 1667a, p. 6: "*P. Alvarus Semedus* Lusitanus, cuius verba tantò libentius hîc produco, quantò majori necessitudinis vinculo, dum hîc Romae Procuratorem ageret, mihi obstrictus fuit, nec non omnia mihi oretenus, quae circa hoc Monumentum observarat, recensuit."

66.   Ibid., "Prooemium ad lectorem," sig. ** v; p. 7.

67.   Ibid., "Prooemium ad lectorem," sig. ** v–** 2r; p. 81, 148, 150, 156, 193.

68.   Ibid., p. 53, 147.

69.   Ibid., p. 7 (Boym); "Prooemium ad lectorem," sig. **2r (Grueber), 66 (Grueber and Roth); p. 91: "[Roth] quod cum vehementer desiderarem, votis meis non illibenter annuit"; p. 222: "*Epistola P. Gruberi* ad Authorem. *Petit, ut sibi quaedam ibi petita transmittam, quodlibenter facio.*" See also pp. 86–87.

70.   Ibid., pp. 179–180: "Planta dicitur *Chà* . . . virtute sanè praestantissimâ pollet, quam nisi saepius Patrum nostrorum invitatione didicissem, vix ad id credendum induci potuissem, cum enim diureticae facultatis sit, omnes meatus nephriticos seu renum mirificè aperit, caput ab omni vaporum fuligine liberat, adeò ut Viris literatis, nec non magna negotiorum mole distentis ad vigilias continuandas nobilius aptiusque remedium à natura non concessum videatur."

71.   Grueber was deeply disappointed when he saw how his contributions had been edited for the *China*. He wrote to Kircher suggesting that corrections were needed and declaring his intent to publish his material himself. See Wessels 1924, pp. 164–170. For similar difficulties in Jesuit cooperative scholarship, see Gorman's contribution to this volume; Hsia 1999b; and more generally, Feingold 2005.

72.   Kircher 1667a, p. 177: "in hunc usque diem Musaeum nostrum visitantibus similis Naturae prodigium iam ab annis quindecim exhibemus." See pp. 193 (hippopotamus teeth); 198 (birds' nests); 202 (crabs); 207 (asbestos). For Kircher's magnetic explanations of plant motion, see Baldwin 2001a and 1987.

73.   See Grafton 1999, p. 152; and Kircher 1667a, pp. 1, 6–8 (Sino-Syrian monument); 105–106 (imperial edict); 136 (Chinese deities); 143 (Japanese deities); 105: "In ingenti lapide marmoreo prae foribus Ecclesiae nostrae erecto, suam in universo Imperio fidei Christianae propagandae voluntatem per edictum Regium ad aeternam rei memoriam partim Tar-

tarico, partim Sinico Characthere atque idiomate incidi voluit, quod in hunc usq; diem in *China* carta impressum, in Collegii Romani Musaeo omnibus spectandum exponitur." On Kircher's museum as a social space, see Findlen 1995.

74. On the intellectual sociability of the Republic of Letters, see Findlen 1994; Goldagar 1995; Bots and Waquet 1997; and Miller 2000.

75. Kircher 1667a, "Prooemium ad lectorem," sig. ** v: "Undè rerum inquisitione non contentus, inquisita propriis oculis examinanda examinata in Reip. Litterariae emoulumentum conscribenda censuit, quod & in *Atlante* suo egregiè praestitit."

76. Ibid., "Prooemium ad lectorem," sig. **2r. See note 97. See Noel Malcolm's essay in the volume for further discussion of this theme in Kircher's work.

77. Ibid., pp. 113–114: "vides habitum P. Matthaei Riccii magni Occidentis Doctoribus proprium & peculiarem, quo P.P.N.N. ut plurimum ante Tartarorum irruptionem uti solebant." Cf. p. 111.

78. For Kircher's description of the Chinese examination system, see ibid., pp. 115–116.

79. On the social significance of this change in dress, see especially Peterson 1994. For an extended study of Ricci's efforts to present himself as a man of learning, see Spence 1984.

80. Kircher 1667a, p. 113.

81. Ibid., p. 5: "Apostolo Sancto Thoma," "viros Apostolicos"; p. 97: "S. Franciscus Xaverius à Deo in *Indiarum* salutem electus Apostolus."

82. Ibid., p. 115: "De modo, quo in conversione Sinensium N.N.P.P. procedere solent"; p. 116: "spiritus Apostolici constantia"; see also pp. 97–98.

83. Ibid., p. 116: "non hîc Metaphysicarum speculationum, quas non capiunt; non Scholasticarum subtilitatum studium, aut sublimioris Theoriae ostentatio locum habet, sed sensibilium rerum ipsis incognitarum tum ad admirationem concitandam, tum ad *Europaei* nominis existimationem comparandam, instituta specimina ex Mathematica palaestra deprompta prodenda sunt."

84. Ibid., p. 98: "Sparsa itaque tantarum rerum fama, multorum quoque Literatorum, qui non solum in Regno *Cantoniensi*, sed in toto Imperio existentium animos allexit. . . ." See pp. 97–99; cf. Trigault 1615, book 2, chapter 6, and book 4, chapter 4.

85. Ibid., p. 104, and in general, pp. 108–115 (part 2, chapter 9, "De Correctione Calendarii Sinici, & quanta indè Bona emerserint").

86. Ibid., p. 117: "Catalagus [sic] Librorum à Patribus nostris in Chinensis Ecclesiae incrementum conscriptorum."

87. Ibid., pp. 117–121.

88. On the Jesuit apostolate to the Chinese literati and the imperial court, see Trigault 1615; Martini 1654; Bartoli 1829; and Schall's manuscript, "Historica relatio eorum quae contigerunt occasione concertationis Calendarii Sinici [1658]," published as Schall von Bell 1665, and reprinted in 1672. See Kircher 1667a, p. 112. For an introduction to this topic and to the Jesuit "apostolate through books," see Peterson 1973 and 1998; and Standaert 2001, pp. 474–502, 600–631.

89. See Nummedal and Findlen 2000, pp. 185–187, and Fletcher 1988d.

90. Fletcher 1988c, p. 140.

91. On Kircher's contract and later relations with Jansson, see Fletcher 1988b, pp. 8–10; and Fletcher 1968, pp. 116–117. For the commercial rivalry between Jansson and Jacob van Meurs, see Van Eeghen 1972; on the Dutch exotic book trade in general, see Schmidt 2002.

92. See Ogilby 1669.

93. For some preliminary studies of this phenomenon, see Harris 1996; and Van Damme 1999.

94. O'Malley 1984, p. 5. On the centrality of the missionary ideal to Jesuit spirituality, see Dompnier 1996, pp. 164–171; and Certeau 1974, pp. 61–65.

95. See Lamalle 1968; and Masson 1974.

96. See Fletcher 1988b, p. 2.

97. See Kircher's autobiography, 1684b, pp. 52–53; and Kircher, 1667a, "Prooemium ad lectorem," sig. **2r: "Quoniam verò Patribus continuò in salute animarum procuranda distentis, neque otium tempusque & media, ad rariorum quarundam rerum, quas in suis per vastissimas illas Mundi Regiones susceptis itineribus observârunt, notitias tum describendas, tum in lucem edendas suppetat, hoc unum à me contenderunt, ut illa, quae tanto labore & sudore compererant, scriptis commissa blattis & tineis non cederent, sed in unum volumen congesta, in Reipub. Litterariae bonum publicae luci traderem; quod hoc Opere me praestiturum pollicitus sum."

98. Kircher 1684b, pp. 17–18 ("non audebam ingenii talentum ostendere"; "divinarum in me donorum influxum minuerem"); 28 ("Venit itaque tempus, quô ingenii talenta huiusque abscondita ex obligatione manifestare cogerer, non tam mei intuitu, quàm bona Societatis aestimatione in publica professione praestanda.")

99. See Iannaccone 1998.

100. Kircher 1667a, p. 110: "Erat P. Joan. Terentius *Germanus*, patria *Constantiensis*, antequam Societatem ingrederetur, Philosophus, Medicus & Mathematicus totâ *Germaniâ* celeberrimus, nec non Principibus ob insignium Naturae arcanorum exactam notiatam medicandique felicitatem gratissimus, is tandem famae honorisque, quo eum cuncti prosequebantur, pertaesus Mundoque satur, Societatem ingressus, ut talentum suum in conversione infidelium salubriùs impenderet, Indicam expeditionem petiit, quam & haud magno labore obtinuit"; p. 111: "incredibili cum fructu & Christianae Reipublicae incremento." Cf. p. 119.

101. Kircher 1684b, p. 62: "Porrò Anno 1661 aliud accidit Divinae Bonitatis ostentum, quod me non solùm in reipublicae litterariae promotione laborare voluit, sed & animarum fructum, & ad devotionem in Hominibus excitandum eligere voluit, cum dicto anno Tyber virium instaurandarum causâ me conferrem, eodemque tempore materiam antiquitatum pro Latii Opere conficiendo colligerem, audieram in vicinis montibus insignia Empolitanae Vrbis à Livio saepius allegatae rudera latere"; p. 65: "Ego . . . depositis aliis omnibus Studiis, minimè otiosus coepi SS. huius loci Historiam, cui Titulus est: *Historia Eustachio-Mariana*, describere, impressamq."; p. 69: "hinc Missionem Apostolicam, sive communionem nostrorum Patrum ope institui, ad quem quotannis in Festo S. Michaelis Archangeli cum solemni indulgentiarum promulgatione ad multa millia hominum utriusque sexus ad participanda Sacramenta confluunt. . . ." See Kircher 1665b.

102. Kircher 1667a, 112: "Quod verò Regem ex se & natura sua curiosissimum, ad Patribus tantoperè favendum impulerat, erat ingens librorum ad Astronomiam Sinicam reformandam apparatus, quem plurimis libris comprehensum Regi obtulerant"; for related references to curiosity and wonder, see pp. 98–99, 104.

103. Findlen 1994, pp. 343–344.

104. Kircher 1667a, "Dedicatio," sig. *3r.

105. Ibid., p. 117: "Venerabilis *Pater Matthaeus Riccius Maceratensis* post S. Xaverium Chinensis Expeditionis fundator, post innumeros labores, pericula, persecutiones, sequentes post se Libros in bonum Sinicae Ecclesiae reliquit"; see also p. 119: "Vir fuit Apostolico Spiritu plenus, incredibili in adversis animi constantiâ" (of Giacomo Rho); "donec post 35 annos in Sinica expeditione transactos tot laborum, periculorum, persecutionum pro Christo toleratarum coronam gloriae, uti piè credimus, meruit, in *Chianceu* 9. Aprilis 1640" (of Alfonso Vagnone).

106. Ibid., p. 117: "Itaque in omnibus exhibeamus nosmetipsos, sicuti Dei Ministros in multa patientia, in tribulationibus . . . per gloriam & ignobilitatem, per infamiam & bonam famam . . . semper mortificationem Domini nostri IESU Christi in copore nostro circumferentes, ut vita IESU manifestetur in carne nostra mortali." [2 Corinthians 4]

107. Ibid., p. 237: "Christianae Religioni & Reip. Leterariae"; see also "Prooemium ad lectorem," sig. **2r ("Reip. Litterariae"); **2v ("Reipublicae Christianae").

Epilogue
Understanding Kircher in Context*

ANTONELLA ROMANO
TRANSLATED BY PAULA FINDLEN AND DERRICK ALLUMS

Athanasius Kircher's life, world, and work belong, without a doubt, to a universe to which we have lost the key. His is a spectacular and extraordinary world, in which one gets easily lost like his fictional protagonists of the *Itinerarium exstaticum* (1656), wandering throughout the celestial universe or lost in the depths of universal time. His world is conspicuously luxurious—consider, for example, the rich illustrations that signpost his many books. In Kircher's world, the boundaries between entertainment and science, between religion and other means of understanding the supernatural, and between legend and history are often blurred. This exuberance awakens not only our fascination but our scholarly interest as well. One needs only read or re-read the pages that the famous Italian ethnologist Ernesto De Martino devoted to the tarantella—the dance of healing and exorcism that Apulian people who have been bitten by a tarantula still perform today—to discover that Kircher's musical treatise, *Musurgia universalis* (1650), was, in the middle of the twentieth century, one of his major sources.[1] In the middle of the 17th century already, Alejandro Favián, a priest living in the province of Michoacán in central Mexico and who imagined himself the local Kircher, requested this very same work from its author.[2]

The question deserves to be asked: when we study Kircher, what exactly are we studying? Following a volume as rich and varied as this one conceived by Paula Findlen, the question is not entirely without legitimacy, especially since such work provokes numerous different reflections: on the disciplinary fields summoned by such a study, on the historiographical approaches it puts into play, and on the objectives of the various contributions.

The recent renewal of interest in Athanasius Kircher—a project that follows its own rhythm in relation to the general history of the Jesuits, an issue to which I will have occasion to return—is based on an implicit principle that seems strikingly evident in all publications on Kircher.[3] There is no question of totally embracing the man or his work, since the polymorphous character of the one and the other forbids any total or global comprehension. The world of which they are an incarnation—and this is another implicit postulate that has yet to be demonstrated—remains impossible for us to grasp. Thus Kircher, both the man and his work, becomes the subject of a series of partial interrogations whose overlapping in the context of a collective effort such as this eventually might be able to shed some light on this strange and singular complexity.

Perhaps my own incompetence with regard to such a project authorizes a certain freedom that itself guarantees a kind of nonchalance that is sometimes necessary in the face of such overwhelming productions—that of the man and of his commentators. I have no intention of proposing an alternative to this consensual *modus operandi* and still less of critiquing it. Kircher the individual—*la machine Kircher*—fascinates me less than other subjects that this kind of project raises, which is why I prefer to focus my remarks on those aspects of this volume that highlight the "Kircherian moment"—the world that encompassed him. In other words, following a method that the Jesuit father himself suggests, I will take a stroll in that distant galaxy of which Kircher is but one of the constellations and seek to understand the brightness of his star measured against that of thousands of others that fill the skies.[4]

1. Trompe l'œil: Effects of the Sources

If the trompe l'œil was supposed to constitute one of the principal figures of the baroque, then we can speak about a "baroque Kircher" provided we look for the trompe l'œil where it can be found: as a historian, I see it first and foremost in the sources. I am not suggesting we deny the importance of the historical figure Athanasius Kircher, but rather that we start from a basic observation: the quality and variety of surviving sources concerning him facilitate the study of him. One needs only investigate the contributions that make up this volume to realize the extent to which it is possible, in Kircher's case, to resolve all of the questions one could ever want to raise regarding such a historical figure. This is not simply the effect of Kircher the polymath, but of the Society of Jesus of which he was a member. In addition to the considerable printed work, which is exceptional neither for his Order nor for his time, we have the numerous other documentary resources provided by the Society. The traces he left behind in the administrative archives are abundant, including ample material for intellectual history in the form of the Jesuit censorship reports on Kircher's books, among others.[5] This state of affairs owes less to individuals than to an institution.

Let me invoke an example of the presence of Kircher in the "ordinary sources" of the Society—one that sheds light on the development of mathematics instruction in early-seventeenth-century France.[6] It regards the city of Aix-en-Provence, a dynamic center among the cities of southwestern France. The scholarly community in Aix enjoyed numerous exchanges with its counterparts in Avignon, Digne, and Lyon, and engaged in intense scientific activity led by such figures as Peiresc and Gassendi.[7] The Jesuit college at Aix, which the Society acquired in 1621, began teaching mathematics through the efforts of Prior Jean-Louis de Revillas—in other words, because of an impetus external to the Order.[8] According to the establishment's chronicle of 1633:

> After Easter of this year, the Father Rector, on the way to the provincial congregation which was taking place in Lyon, passed by way of Avignon where he met with Monsignor Jean-Louis de Revillas, prior of the Priory of Saint-Pierre in Tourves, who handed his priory over to the hands of Our Holy Father in favor of the College at Aix. The whole affair was sent to Rome and authorized by Monsignor the Provost of Pignans who conferred the benefice. The only remaining business was the expedition of the bulls, which was done the following year.[9]

On 10 October 1633, the priory of Tourves was annexed and united with the buildings of the Jesuit college of Aix. The income that it generated was intended to contribute to the support of the students and to the foundation of a new chair in mathematics.[10] The letter of Revillas that follows, addressed to General Muzio Vitelleschi and preserved in the Jesuit archives, constitutes not only direct testimony of the way a chair was endowed, but it especially explains the motivations of its founder—and inadvertently offers us an early glimpse of Kircher:

> Most Illustrious and Reverend Father,
>
> It has been two months since I sent to Rome the act of renunciation of my priory at Tourves in favor of the College at Aix in order to establish two very necessary classes—mathematics and casuistry. The first one will be greatly esteemed by all the nobles of this province, and the Senate will value it as well since the Reverend Father Athanasius Kirker, who is a very great mathematician and very knowledgeable in letters and languages, is in Avignon. I judged it expedient, both for the utility of the College as well as for public satisfaction, to have Father Athanasius start teaching mathematics in this College at the start of classes next year. It will provide a wonderful inauguration for the course because of the worth of this great Father. He is much beloved by many great minds of this region, particularly by the Most Reverend Signor Abbot and Senator Peiresc, who himself is one of the greatest and most curious minds in all of France and beyond and is very well-known and loved by His Holiness and our patron, the Most Eminent Cardinal Barberini. [Peiresc] has a universal and curious library, well-furnished with manuscripts and other things that, I believe, cannot be found either in the Vatican or other Italian libraries, or in France and other realms. This library will be most useful to Father Athanasius, allowing him to complete his wonderful compositions. He will not find such a convenience anywhere else. Beyond this fact, the said Signor Abbot will also serve him well with conversation since he is quite a universal man, well versed in the most curious things. Monsignor the Abbot strongly desires that the said Father remain at this College.[11]

Without a doubt, this letter sketches the outlines of a network that was decisive in structuring intellectual exchange between France and Italy during the 1630s. Two of the major figures within this exchange already played a crucial role that was well understood by the prior of Tourves when he wrote to Rome: Peiresc, on the French side, and Francesco Barberini, the twenty-sixth nephew of Urban VIII, on the Italian side.[12] Moreover, the letter provides us with one of the first portraits of Kircher, before his entry onto the Roman scene. It is a document in which the founder of the chair of mathematics in Aix, mindful of the scholarly networks that structured his world, demonstrated his particular interest in the presence of the German Jesuit who was in the region at that time and whose culture and encyclopedic curiosity were well-known even before his arrival there.[13] Revillas's letter speaks to the importance of reputation in the *ethos* of the Republic of Letters as well as its determining weight in the founder's motivations for selecting Kircher.

To conclude, this letter alludes to an economy of direct exchange centered on a place of sociability that was still largely inscribed in the domain of private life—the library.[14] The library supposes three actors: the powerful patron, in this case, a great prelate; the intermediary of a less elevated rank whose role was to valorize both the patron and the scholar; and the man of science. In this sense, it prefigures what will be called *la machine Kircher*, the Kircherian project of knowledge and publication whose implementation in Rome is documented by many of the contributions to the present volume.

The project outlined in the letter was not realized.[15] The first professors of mathematics at the College in Aix did not have Kircher's stature. In order for the project launched in 1633 to be realized, we must await the arrival of François de Saint-Rigaud in 1637 and the nomination of Pierre Le Roy, a more competent and experienced teacher, in the following year. Nonetheless it was the reputation of one of the mathematicians of the Society, Kircher, that led to its creation. This was the work of a man little known to historians, but who nevertheless represented that class of learned clerics, friends of the arts and sciences at the juncture between France and Italy in the early seventeenth century.[16]

Kircher was able to take advantage of these intersections, both on the French and Italian sides of the exchange. In France, he certainly benefited from his German status, since the Society had been forbidden to recruit and host foreigners there for thirty years.[17] Moreover, he arrived at a moment when the plan for training mathematicians was not yet fixed. The names of more local mathematicians such as Pierre Bourdin and Jacques de Billy were barely known, mainly in the French countryside, and Charles de la Faille had left Burgundy for Spain. Despite its well-known Jesuit colleges and the existence of a flourishing, if local, scholarly milieu, the south of France had only a handful of proper chairs of mathematics and very few real mathematics teachers. The interest of the prior in a trained scholar who already enjoyed a reputation as a mathematician and whose interests were diverse but also complementary to those of local scholars such as Peiresc is therefore understandable. In Italy,

Kircher was able to use the support he had garnered in France, but this aspect of his story is both better known and better documented.

2. Kircher, a Jesuit among Jesuits

The letter of Prior Jean-Louis de Revillas allows me to take up the metaphor of the trompe l'œil again: this source has been preserved not because it concerns Kircher, but rather because it was addressed to the Father General. The Jesuits offer us a textual patrimony that owes its existence less to the personalities attracted to the Society than to the very ways in which the Order functioned and was organized.[18] Kircher becomes visible, in part, because he belonged to this system.

The "centralized" character of the Society, which placed each Jesuit establishment within an administrative hierarchy that oversaw a relay of information from the provinces at the regional level to the assistancies at the level of the state, is well-known. Exchange of information was absolutely central to the Society from its foundation. The concern for both the control and the rationalization of the relations between establishments required the creation of a complex network of relations and communications consisting of different types of documents. While this is not the place for a detailed analysis of this network, it is worth noting, as we remarked above, that Kircher owed his fortune, at least in part, to its existence.[19] Thus the very means by which relations were organized, between hundreds of houses spread all over the world, played a specific role in the kinds of sources they produced.

However, beyond these aspects of the Society, maintaining the unity of the body of the Order was the real challenge. The risks—that this unity would rupture or that the homogeneity of the Order might disappear, taking with it any sense of belonging to the whole—were always there but undoubtedly exacerbated in the middle of the seventeenth century.[20] In his own fashion, by placing his writings in circulation within the Jesuit network, Kircher too worked toward the formation of this unity. A full century after the foundation of the Order, beyond the profound modifications put into place by the Ignatian project and in the footsteps of key Jesuits such as Christoph Clavius and Antonio Possevino, Kircher was able to activate certain institutional ways of thinking, without himself having invented them.[21] Following others, he was able to conceive of ways of optimizing the institution as well as realizing the universal dimension of the Jesuit project. This is, at least, one way of viewing his efforts to put his works into circulation.

Indeed, by looking too much at the ways in which Kircher was exceptional, we end up forgetting one of his essential characteristics, that is, his membership in the Jesuit Order and his full participation in Jesuit culture. Harald Siebert, Michael John Gorman, Paula Findlen, and Florence Hsia, in particular, remind us of these things in this volume. In other words, it seems to me that the very exuberance of Kircher's work and his activity—too often analyzed in terms of their singularity—allows us to comprehend Kircher as a Jesuit, for this exuberance constituted one of the thousand manifestations of the universalizing ambition of Ignatius's order. In this sense, Kircher can be viewed as little more than a paradigmatic incarnation of the Society, wherein the threads by which we aim to grasp him, to master him, cross. Could what we call his "encyclopedism" in a scholarly mode, or "baroque" in a more popular account be little more than an updated version of the apostolic ideal on which the project of the first Jesuits was based? We must attempt to understand this ideal in both its spatial and temporal dimensions because the universality that the first Jesuits constructed encompassed the world and all the activities that were possible within it.

From its inception, the Society and its members participated in a system of exchange. We need to investigate all the elements of this exchange from the double point of view of its participants and the places where it was in effect. For the history of the Society is no longer self-contained or understandable in terms stipulated within and by its own structure, nor did the members of the Society work in the shadows cast by the walls that cloistered their houses. Kircher and men like him were profoundly conscious of what it specifically meant to be a Jesuit and the possibilities it offered for them.

The specific configuration of the Society of Jesus is not simply a matter of historical interpretation alone. The crucial characteristics of the Society—that is, the very ones that it developed from the moment of its foundation and that owe much to its missionary vocation and to the role that this vocation played in the identity of the young Order—inform this specificity.[22] Before the Society became a teaching order, and later involved itself in intellectual and even scientific activities, it was founded as a missionary order. It is precisely the influence of this activity on the Society's identity that I would like to evoke here as a legacy for Kircher.[23] Like the Jesuits who preceded him and those who succeeded him, Kircher carried with him, and in him, the heritage aptly summarized by Jérôme Nadal's superb formula: *Totus mundus nostra habitatio fit* (Our home is all the world).[24] To be sure, arrogance is mixed with utopia in this saying, but it also indicates the scale on which the Society intended to operate from the start. Kircher is a worthy inheritor of both this arrogance and the utopia. He made the whole world of knowledge his home. There he established the utopia of his linguistic program, and there he enacted the arrogance of his pretension to explain the entire world, from the mysterious caverns of the earth to the no less enigmatic celestial spheres.

Both the variety of Kircher's projects—demonstrated in this volume in the essays by Daniel Stolzenberg, Anthony Grafton, Haun Saussy, and Nick Wilding, to cite only a few—and the diversity of his past and contemporary interlocutors—men of erudition such as Joseph Scaliger, Giordano Bruno, and Leibniz[25]—resonate profoundly with the ideal of mobility that undergirded the Jesuit apostolic missions.[26] His approach to knowledge was supported by another type of heritage as well, that is, the one Clavius constructed with tenacity and conviction as professor of mathematics in the Roman College: over a half-century of engagement in the structuring of the teaching mission of the young Order. Kircher participated in this tradition as well when he inherited Clavius's position in 1639.

The point here is not to engage in an exercise characteristic of an older historiography by determining too literal a genealogy or charting the invention of a tradition that begins with Clavius and ends with Kircher. Such an approach misses the ways in which both Kircher himself and a subsequent Jesuit historiography made this seem self-evident when it was, in fact, part of the mythmaking of the Order. It was nevertheless difficult for Kircher, and generally the Jesuit mathematicians and philosophers in the generations born after 1560, to escape comparison with the great astronomer and mathematician Clavius, just as it is inevitable for the contemporary researcher to notice the connections between them. This is precisely what Angela Mayer-Deutsch's essay in this volume invites us to do, when she refers to the presence of Clavius's portrait in the production of that of his successor. Understanding the relationship between the two Jesuits is all the more important, since Clavius was himself German—from Bamberg—and seems incontestably the founder of the Jesuit scientific tradition that began in the 1580s. Through his institutional and political actions and based on his epistemological conviction of the value of mathematics, Clavius, with the notable support of Antonio Possevino and later his first students, was able to put into place a course of study in mathematics independent of philosophy by promoting the establishment of "mathematics academies."[27] Without returning to many aspects of recent work on the history of the early Society, it seems important to recall the ways in which Kircher resembled his predecessor and fit the expectations of his Order regarding who should hold this position in Rome while also recalling his many other activities that were quite independent of these preconceptions and equally important to his success in Rome.

To establish the legitimacy of the "scientist" within the Jesuit Order, Clavius mobilized a series of resources both internal and external to the organization. Internally, he worked toward the construction of a most efficient network of information exchange that progressively expanded beyond the confines of the Society.[28] He also benefited from the growing need for a culture of science in civil society. Clavius used the patronage of important men to combat those within the Society who resisted his vision of the relations between fields of knowledge, that is, his proposition of a new hierarchy of knowledge that privileged mathematically based disciplines but also raised the question of theology's supremacy.[29] For example, having earned Pope Gregory XIII's gratitude during the reform of the Julian calendar, he used it to good advantage in the debate over the *Ratio Studiorum*.[30] Furthermore, his concern for Jesuit universalism, which might almost be understood as a geopolitical vision of the space of the construction of scientific knowledge, is evident in his unflagging interest in the mission, not only as a space for the reception of European science but also as a reservoir for knowledge and as an observatory of natural phenomena, especially astronomical ones. The Chinese horizon was already present in Clavius's thought, as it would later be in Kircher's.

In light of this brief sketch of Clavius's activities and interests, we can understand more concretely the ways in which the Jesuits inserted themselves into intellectual networks that largely exceeded the boundaries of the Society. Moreover, we can see them beginning to take their place in the European-wide scholarly community—that was also of worldwide scale as Europe ventured out onto the other continents—that gradually and slowly became the "Republic of Letters."[31] This observation goes beyond the figure of Kircher. On the one hand, it highlights the importance of the Society in the constitution of modern Western culture. On the other hand, it throws into relief the other cultural resources upon which he and some other members of his Order were able to draw. In particular, I am thinking of the institutional construction of publishing within the Jesuit Order in which the conditions for the emergence of the figure of the writer were also being constructed: an established internal zone for the circulation of authorized books as well as a potential external space for the production of various printed matter.[32] Jesuits such as Daniello Bartoli and Antonio Vieira, to cite only two of Kircher's contemporaries, were active in this domain.[33] In short, even Kircher's style of writing and publishing was not his alone.

3. The Roman Face of Kircher

We cannot complete this re-reading of Kircher without alluding to another one of his attachments: the city of Rome. In fact, to neglect it would be a serious misinterpretation of what shaped and informed his outlook on the world, since it completes the other aspects of Kircher's world that I have already invoked. While he was a descendant of Ignatius and of Clavius, Athanasius Kircher was also a son of Rome, that elusive *Urbs*, the thousand-year seat of Western culture prior to the arrival of Christianity, later the centuries-old capital of Christianity, and finally the young capital of a Catholic world on the defensive. Kircher's intellectual production is simultaneously the product, the result, and a new episode in these overlapping and intermingling histories that are so obvious in the city's topography.

The Rome of the 1630s in which Kircher arrived was undergoing profound intellectual and architectural changes.[34] It was a city that continued to attract European scholars because it harbored not only artistic but also scientific treasures. Finally, it was also a city in which the Society of Jesus occupied a visible place but no longer the unique one it had held for the previous fifty years. To be sure, the Society was the only institutional actor, in this city as in many others, that was capable of intervening in many different levels of intellectual life, from the education of the lay elite to the international training of the clergy, and from the production of missionaries to that of experts in all areas for the papacy. But particularly, in this most cosmopolitan and aristocratic of cities, the Society multiplied the means by which its presence was felt within the various social networks, working to consolidate its prestige and its own image of power.

Numerous accounts of Rome, from Montaigne's celebrated portrayal in his *Journal de voyage* to the different reports dispersed throughout historical memoirs and guides to the early modern city, bear witness to the importance of the Collegio Romano in the intellectual life of early modern Rome from the moment of its foundation.[35] In its own way, the Society sustained this vision, which certainly corresponded to the early stages of its efforts to secure its institutional identity, as evidenced in Ignatius's correspondence.[36] We can see the centrality of Rome in still more spectacular fashion by looking at the *Roma ignaziana* (1610)[37] (Figure 18.1). This map, which systematically oversized Jesuit buildings and spaces in Rome to make them more visible, accentuates the variety of ways in which the new Order inserted itself into the social and urban fabric of the city. Ignatian Rome was a city filled with new religious establishments that the map itemizes: the house in which Ignatius professed his faith and its church, the Roman College, the Saint Peter's *collegium penitentieriae,*[38] the novitiate, the orphanages, the houses of the Catechumins, of Saint Martha, for the reformed prostitutes, the German and English colleges,[39] and finally, the Maronite and Roman seminaries.[40] The care with which each of their buildings is identified demonstrates their importance, and generally the importance of the sites of culture and learning, in relation to the overall Jesuit plan of action in Rome. The appearance of each of these centers resulted in a concentration of competent men and of books, and each played a role in facilitating networks of intellectual exchange, both within the Order and beyond.[41] Just as buildings secured the Jesuit presence in Rome, the canonization of Ignatius and Francis Xavier in 1622 seemed to assure the legitimacy of the new Order.[42] Festivals in Paris, Bahia, and Goa in 1640, following the model of those that took place in Rome, celebrated its first centenary and its global influence. In this sense, the inauguration of the Roman College museum in 1651 constituted yet another element in the Order's politics of spectacular visibility.[43]

This strategy, however, was all the more necessary by the mid–seventeenth century, when the Jesuits were no longer the sole actors in the scientific drama of Rome and competed actively with other scholarly communities for patrons and students. The three decades between 1630 and 1660 in pontifical Rome were not only characterized by the "failure" of Prince Federico Cesi's Accademia dei Lincei (1603–30), which had opened up a rather uncertain space for lay forms of scientific sociability,[44] but also enlivened by the presence in Rome of a diverse array of noteworthy scholars with varied scientific interests: Michelangelo Ricci, Giovani Giustino Ciampini,[45] Gasparo Berti,[46] Raffaele Magiotti,[47] as well as numerous foreigners who passed through the city, such as the celebrated Marin Mersenne, and those who moved there more permanently, as was

Figure 18.1. Ignatian Rome, seventy years after the Society of Jesus was founded. *Source: Roma ignaziana* (Antwerp, 1610).

the case with Gabriel Naudé.[48] The French Minims of Trinità dei Monti participated as well in the artistic and cultural networks of those successors of Galileo known as the *novatores*.[49] The young Congregation of Propaganda Fide (f. 1622) asserted itself as the main actor in the elaboration and application of a new missionary politics of the Holy See in which the Society played, with others, merely a supporting role.[50] The sheer variety of institutional affiliations and the complexity of the ties that bound these scholars and their institutions together means we cannot simply categorize any of them as belonging to a single community, Jesuit or otherwise, nor should we think of them in terms of simple oppositions—Jesuits versus Minims, ecclesiastical versus lay scholars. What is certain, however, is that the Society of Jesus no longer enjoyed the virtual cultural monopoly that it had had in Rome since 1540.

A precise history of the intellectual milieus of Rome during the seventeenth century remains to be written. Current research tends to highlight the richness, complexity, and variety of intellectual interests, among which natural philosophy certainly had its place. It would now be premature to conclude that Galileo's condemnation had the effect of concentrating the "new science" in Medicean Florence alone. Such a conclusion undervalues the importance that Rome in particular enjoyed, precisely because it was the papal capital as well as the hub of all the aristocratic clients seeking favors in the Italian peninsula. In other words, Rome offered a kind of political, social, and cultural polycentrism that sustained the intellectual vitality of the Eternal City.[51] The sheer number of intellectual centers in Rome led to lively exchanges among them. This intellectual vitality took varying forms in different contexts: numerous academies that were the mainstay of aristocratic social life organized around salons; a rich sense of pedagogy, in which context the chairs in philosophy and mathematics provide a good vantage point from which to observe the place the Jesuits continued to occupy in Roman intellectual life; and scholarly debates, which involved the international Republic of Letters as well.[52] I would like to emphasize that the knowledge and learning that this city stimulated and cultivated were, like it, universal in scope. In this sense, the variety of the interests of a Kircher or a Ciampini or a Christina of Sweden reflected *all* of Rome's possibilities: those that had been bequeathed by its past as well as those that emerged from the peculiar organization of an early modern state that was, at that time, the only centralized and universal monarchy in the world.[53]

I will venture the hypothesis that Roman scientific life in this period, which has been undervalued and largely reduced to its artistic manifestations as well as the growth of collecting culture, owes its originality to the unprecedented convergence of social groups within this urban fabric.[54] This complex society produced a new cultural and intellectual patrimony that was without equivalent in the early modern world. It conditioned and provided the context for scholarly activity.[55] This unique intellectual production was direct result of the political functioning of the papal capital; it alone sanctioned the variety of

Kircher's intellectual activities. The point here is not to reduce Rome's cultural identity as a city of scholars obsessed with antiquarian pursuits, which it certainly was, but rather to understand the boom these disciplines experienced in this period by focusing on the other domains of knowledge that also concerned themselves with questions of time and temporality that promoted the emergence of new epistemological paradigms. In this sense, archaeology, geology, debates on fossils, the study of biblical exegesis, and astronomy can all be understood as participating in the same intellectual matrix in which the "scientific revolution" played a part. [56] Would such subjects have intersected so fruitfully in a city less ancient or less modern, or in a city that functioned on so many different levels as a capital? Therein lies the specificity of Rome; and in just this sense, Kircher was profoundly Roman.

An alternative formulation of this hypothesis would run as follows: like all of his contemporaries, Kircher concerned himself with the problem of how to gain experience of things, but he did not use the experimental method solely to elaborate and explain the natural world. This was the strict domain of experimentation for those scholars of his generation who applied themselves to the physico-mathematical sciences only. Kircher instead also experimented with time. For him, the relevant questions lay no longer in understanding and critiquing Aristotelian cosmology, as they had been in Clavius's day. Instead for Kircher, both as a cleric and as a participant in the Roman scholarly community, the burning issue was sacred chronology: how should he reconcile this traditional Christian cosmology with the new science of biblical exegesis, the further elaboration of ancient and pagan history, the recent acquisitions from other civilizations (particularly those from China), and the earliest data about the history of the earth? His work and his museum—that unique inquiry he conducted—charted a path both from the subterranean world to the superlunary spheres and from Rome to its peripheries, all within a rediscovered Christian chronology. Kircher studied both fossils and obelisks not because his interests were varied, but because he wished to plot an intellectual course between the two, one that would end by attributing the same meaning to the mark of time embedded in stone that fashioned both of them. In this sense, traveling through time and reasoning chronologically, Kircher metaphorically speaking fused the relations between these two objects. Without a doubt, the Kircherian research program, both arrogant and utopian, was a project on the scale of Rome eternal itself.

Kircher put this program into effect in his publishing and in his museum. In both locations, fossils and ancient inscriptions lay side by side, allowing us as much as his contemporaries to view them in a most spectacular fashion. One could re-read the museum that bears his name as a microcosm of the man, the figure par excellence of his polymathy, but it could also stand for the microcosm of Rome, this *Urbs* that welcomed him and all the other foreigners of the earth with all the forms of knowledge that abounded in it. Kircher's museum was perhaps the last attempt to reconcile the Jesuit concept of universalism with the universalism of the post-Tridentine Church. We must see Athanasius Kircher's grasp of all these threads as a fleeting moment in the larger history of Roman universalism. Shortly thereafter, the papacy vested a new sense of its universality in the Congregation of the Propaganda Fide. The treasures of the world now came to them rather than to the Jesuits. And soon a new publishing venture was under way to convey the results of all the knowledge collected in Rome—catechisms, bibles, dictionaries, and scholarly work in many languages emerged from the polyglot press of the Propaganda Fide by the end of the seventeenth century, overshadowing the work of a single Jesuit who had attempted to know and publish everything for the greater glory of God.

Notes

*   I would like to thank Paula Findlen for inviting me to write this text. By doing so, she permitted me to read closely all the contributions that make up this volume, which expanded my understanding of Kircher considerably. She also encouraged me to participate in the current rethinking about a rich and complex moment of the early modern period—the seventeenth century. Finally, I am grateful to her for forcing me to hypothesize about this moment and Rome's place within it, especially since the Eternal City seems to me the veritable heroine of this volume.

1.   De Martino 2002. My profound thanks to Alice Ingold, who read me these passages of Kircher.

2.   See Paula Findlen's contribution to this volume.

3.   Since each of the contributions of this volume make the point, even if they rely principally on English-language sources, there is no need to present the bibliography here. However, Michael John Gorman's and Nick Wilding's project of making Kircher's correspondence available online has greatly fueled recent interest in the man and his work.

4.   I have in mind Kircher 1656.

5.   Harald Siebert's contribution to this volume uses these sources to excellent advantage, distinguishing between the institution of censorship and the censors' interest in quality control. He offers a more nuanced view of censorship and the disciplining process it represents by demonstrating that guaranteeing orthodoxy, religious and ideological, was not its only goal.

6.   By "ordinary sources," I am referring to the vast collection of documents, which are of a mainly administrative nature, preserved at the Archivum Romanum Societatis Iesu (hereafter **ARSI**) in Rome. These constitute the daily bread of historians of the Society who study less famous members of the Order.

7.   On the precise nature of the relations between Kircher and Peiresc, see the excellent contribution by Peter Miller in this volume. Dainville 1978; and Homet 1982 have already commented on the scientific dynamism of this area of Provence. The most recent work on Gassendi confirms these elements. See the worthwhile contribution of Galluzzi 1993, pp. 86–119.

8.   Compère and Julia 1984, p. 30. On the question of the social and political demands placed on the Society, I refer the reader to Romano 2002a.

9.   Méchin 1890, p. 80.

10.   Ibid., p. 349.

11.   ARSI, LUGD. 11, fol. 133r. On the stimulating intellectual environment of Aix in these years, the correspondence of Peiresc is particularly enlightening. See Peiresc 1893, which includes the letters addressed to Jean-Jacques Bouchard, a close acquaintance of Francesco Barberini, and those exchanged with Gassendi. Several of them make reference to Athanasius Kircher.

12.   Francesco Barberini's (1597–1679) fortune was tied to the ascent of his uncle to the papal throne in 1623. He became a cardinal, was elected to the celebrated Accademia dei Lincei in 1623, and assumed many important responsibilities, among them prefect of the Vatican Library (1627–34). Barberini's first important post was the legation to France in 1625. While a mediocre diplomat, he was intensely active in the cultural domain, as seen most notably in his uncle's private library, whose size and value he increased considerably. He thus appears as one of the most important actors in this French-Italian network, in which aristocrats, both

of the Church and of society, mingled with artists, natural philosophers, and scholars. An active member of the pro-French party in Rome, he was, in the tradition of Roman patronage, both host and protector to numerous French scholars: for example, he commissioned works from Poussin. The Frenchman Bouchard his secretary for Latin letters, wrote from, Rome the eulogy of his friend Peiresc. It is unfortunate that no monograph has been devoted to Bouchard, who died prematurely in Rome in 1641 at the age of thirty-five. By way of bibliographic references, see Redondi 1983; Bellini 1997; and Ferrier 1988.

13. During his brief visit to Avignon, Kircher set up an observatory in the tower of the college. See Dainville 1978, p. 313.

14. Among the numerous works on this subject, see Chartier 1986 and 1987; and notably, Roche 1987.

15. Material problems that hinder the donation dominate much of the remainder of the letter before mention is again made of Athanasius Kircher and of the donor's express demand that the German Jesuit be sent from Avignon to Aix.

16. More research is needed on the organization of the networks of exchange between the two countries, since the examples above point to their centrality for scientific pursuits. On the second half of the century, see Waquet 1989a.

17. This national peculiarity was the result of the suppression of 1593 and of the Edict of Restoration of 1603.

18. I refer the reader to the *Constitutions*, whose eighth part is entitled, "That which helps to unite with their head and those who have been divided." It is entirely devoted to this theme. The opening chapter broaches the question: "What can assist the union of hearts?" See Luce Giard's fine analysis of the correspondence; Giard 1993, p. 140: "The system of sustained correspondence had a rhythm dictated by Ignatius himself.... Information about professors, the doctrines to be taught, curriculum materials, the amount of time to devote to them, the manuals to be used, the methods and results to be obtained—all this circulated throughout the entire network. Here practice was structured according to the principles, and the periphery was in dialogue with the center, demanding modifications, advice, and directives. Writers from the periphery recounted personal conflicts between individual actors, explained local difficulties, ... suggested new procedures, and related decisions that had to be made urgently and hence without consultation with Rome." See also her worthwhile introduction to the letters of Ignatius, Giard 1991, as well as Giard 1995.

19. On the precise aspects of the organization of these archives, see Romano 1999, pp. 16–27. For an analysis of the role these sources have played in the reinvigoration of Jesuit studies, see Fabre and Romano, 1999.

20. The question of maintaining Jesuit identity ought to be considered in both its spiritual and political dimensions. Not only do the analyses of Pierre-Antoine Fabre and Luce Giard suggest this way of looking at the problem, but the *Constitutions* framed this way as well. The changing political dynamic within the Catholic Church that followed the Thirty Years' War constitutes a decisive element in the evolution of the Society. A long-term study of the relations between the nationalities represented in the Society would no doubt test this hypothesis. For the first decades concerning the writing of the *Constitutions*, see Fabre 1991; and Giard 1996.

21. I will have occasion to return to Clavius below. Despite his importance, scholarship on Possevino is uneven and rather weak. The polymorphous character of his work—diplomacy, confessional meditation, intellectual production—has not yet been given the attention it deserves. Still, for a first approach, see Balsamo 1994; Biondi 1981; Piaia 1973; and Ceccarelli 1993.

22. For the work of the research group on the history of Iberian missions in the modern era, see Fabre-Vincent, forthcoming.

23. I have developed this point in Romano, forthcoming.

24. As cited by Ines Zupanov in "Politiques missionnaires," 1999, p. 296.

25. See the contributions of Anthony Grafton and Ingrid Rowland to this volume.

26. In fact, the question of settling down varied according to the type of apostleship mission. For example, in provinces outside of Europe, the key question was indigenous languages. In many Jesuit sources, we can see the contradictions inherent to the linguistic question in missionary work, because missionaries could not really convert without knowing the languages but learning them was a real investment of time and resources in a context in which, throughout the entire history of the Society, men were too few in number. On the politics of the Society and the question of the "management of the missionary personnel," see Demoustier 1995, pp. 3–33; and Castelnau-L'Estoile 2000, pp. 175–198. The recent use of the *Indipetae*, these

typically Jesuit sources, have led to new lines of research. See notably Cappocia 2000. The remarks of Ines Zupanov on the difficulties associated with applying this ideal, especially because of the language problem that was central in particular to the extra-European missionary enterprise, are particularly interesting. See "Politiques missionaires," 1999.

27. Ugo Baldini was the first to elucidate this history. For a detailed analysis, see his two collections of articles: Baldini 1992 and 2000. See also the first part of Romano 1999. On the theme of the Jesuits as contributors to the scientific activity of the early modern world, see also Feldhay 1987, 1995, and 1999.

28. Ugo Baldini and Pier Daniele Napolitani created a critical edition of this correspondence, which has had a limited circulation. See Clavius 1992. Certain aspects of it are discussed in the second part of Romano 1999. In the correspondence of Clavius, we can see the emergence of an economy of information exchange in which both the letter and printed works play an equally constitutive role. In this volume, Nick Wilding touches on these matters with regard to Clavius, as does Noel Malcolm with reference to Kircher.

29. Romano 1999, chapter 3.

30. See Baldini 1983; and Romano 2002a.

31. Romano 1997 and 2000.

32. This area of research has recently enjoyed a profound and original revival in the unpublished work of Van Damme 2000.

33. Of the abundant work available on Vieira, notably in Brazil, I refer the reader to Carvalho Da Silva 2000.

34. See Insolera 1980; Bonnefoy 1970; and Frommel 2000.

35. I take the example of Ciappi 1596, pp. 16, 43–33; or, much later, of Piazza 1679. For an exhaustive list of these potential sources, see Rinaldi 1914, pp. 13–15.

36. See in particular the letter analyzed by Villoslada 1954, pp. 14–15.

37. See Frutaz 1952, vol. 2. That is where I found the reproduction of the *Roma ignaziana*.

38. The College of the Penitentiaries of Saint Peter (*Collegium Poenitentieriae*) was one of the three penitentiary colleges of the city, along with that of San Giovanni Laterano, entrusted to the Franciscans, and that of Santa Maria Maggiore, managed by the Dominicans. The penitentiary colleges of these three basilicas were organized by Pius V. See Moroni 1845, vol. 52, pp. 73–75.

39. Later the Greek, Irish, and Scottish colleges were added to those that already existed in 1610. For a detailed note on all of these establishments, see Moroni 1845, vol. 14, pp. 142–242.

40. Planned by Pius IV as a response to the problem of the training of the clergy, the Roman seminary opened its doors in 1564 under the direction of the Jesuits. The seminarians took courses at the Roman College, while the rehearsals and exercises took place at the seminary.

41. On the importance of the libraries of the Jesuit establishments in Rome, I refer the reader to descriptions of the period as well as to the work of Romani 1996. At the end of the eighteenth century, in his celebrated *Storia della letteratura italiana* (1784, vol. 7, part 1, p. 213), Girolamo Tiraboschi was still able to write: "Quella che avevano i Gesuiti nel loro Collegio Romano divenne presto una della più rinomate, per le copiose raccolte, che vi si mirono, di libri si stampati chae manoscritti."

42. On the complexity of the canonization of Ignatius, see Fabre 2000.

43. See Findlen 1995.

44. Among the abundant bibliographic references to the Lincei, I refer the reader in particular to Gabrieli 1989 and 1996; Gardair 1981; Ricci 1994; and Donato 2000.

45. On Ricci and Ciampini, see Gardair 1984.

46. See *Dictionary of Scientific Bibliography*, vol. 2, pp. 83–84.

47. See *Dictionary of Scientific Bibliography*, vol. 9, pp. 13–14. On these two figures, see Torrini's definitive contribution: Torrini 1979.

48. On the French in Rome during this period, see Pintard 1943.

49. See the contributions of Marianne Leblanc, Laurent Vignault, and Antonella Romano in Bruley 2002, pp. 131–153.

50. Pizzorusso 2000.

51. On this point, I refer the reader to Caffiero et al., forthcoming.

52. See Donato 2000.

53. Delumeau 1959; Labrot 1987.

54. See Visceglia 2001.

55. For a first approach to these infrastructures, see Romano 2002b.

56. See Stephen Jay Gould's contribution to this volume.

Bibliography

Primary Sources

Acta Eruditorum. 1685. Leipzig.

Alexandri ab Alexandro, 1532. *Genialium dierum*. Paris.

Alsted, Johannes Heinrich, 1652 [1608]. *Clavis artis Lullianae*. Strasburg.

Al-Suyuti; 1903. *Kitab husn al-muhadarah fi akbar misr wa al-qahira*. 2 vols. Misr: Matba'at Bashari.

Apin, Sigmund Jacob, 1728. *Anleitung wie man die Bildnüsse berühmter und gelehrter änner mit Nutzen sammeln . . . sol*. Nuremberg.

Aquin, Philippe d', 1625. *Interpretation de l'arbre de la cabale enrichy de sa figure tirée des plus anciens autheurs hebrieux*. Paris.

———, 1993. *Interpretazione dell'albero della Kabalah*. Trans. Andrea Forte. Rome: Atanòr.

Arcangelo da Borgonovo, 1557. *Dechiaratione sopra il nome di Giesu, secondo gli Hebrei Cabalisti, Greci, Caldei, Persi, & Latini*. Ferrara.

Bacon, Francis, 1968. *The Works of Francis Bacon*. 1872. Eds. James Spedding, Robert Ellis, and Douglas Heath. New York: Garrett Press.

Baldinucci, Filippo, 1682. *Vita del Cavalier Gian Lorenzo Bernino scultore, architetto e pittore scritta da Francesco Baldinucci*. Florence: Vincenzo Vangelisti.

———, 1845–47. *Notizie dei Professori del disegno da Cimabue in qua*. 5 vols. Florence: Batelli.

Bartoli, Daniello, 1663. *Missione al Gran Mogol del Ridolfo Aquaviva della Compagnia di Giesu, sua vita e morte*. Rome.

———, 1829. *Dell'istoria della Compagnia di Gesù: La Cina, Terza Parte dell'Asia*. Florence. Reprint of *Dell'Historia della Compagnia de Giesu: La Cina, Terza Parte dell'Asia*. Rome, 1663.

Bartolocci, Giulio, 1675–93. *Bibliotheca Magna Rabbinica*. 4 vols. Rome.

Becher, Johann Joachim, 1661. *Character pro notitia linguarum universali, inventum steganographicum hactenus inauditum*. Frankfurt.

Beringer, J. B. A., 1963. *Lithographiae Wirceburgensis*. 1726. Eds. and trans. Melvin Jahn and Daniel Woolf. Berkeley: University of California Press.

Bernini, Vita di, ed., 1948. *Scritta da Filippo Baldinucci con uno studio a cura di Sergio Samek Ludovici*. Milan: Edizioni del Milione.

Besnier, Pierre, 1675. *A Philosophical Essay for the Reunion of the Languages, or, the Art of Knowing All by the Mastery of One*. Trans. Henry Rose. Oxford.

Biancani, Giuseppe, 1615. *Aristotelis loca Mathematica*. Bologna.

Blaeu, Joan. 1649–1655. *Theatrum orbis terrarum, sive Atlas novus*. 6. vol. Amsterdam.

Blaeu, Joan, 1662. *Atlas maior, sive Cosmographia Blauiana: qua solum, salum, coelum, accuratissime describuntur*. Amsterdam.

Blauenstein, Salomon de, 1667. *Interpellatio brevis ad philosophos veritatis tam amatores, quam scrutatores pro lapide philosophorum contra antichymisticum Mundum subterraneum P. Athanasii Kircheri Jesuitae*. Biennae.

Bodin, Jean, 1579. *Methodus ad facilem historiae cognitionem. Artis historiae penus*. Ed. Johann Wolf. 2 vols. Basel.

Bouchard, Jean-Jacques, ed., 1638. *Monumentum Romanorum Nicolao Claudio Fabricio Perescio Senatori Aquensi Doctrinae Virtutisque Causa Factum*. Rome.

———, 1976. *Oeuvres*. Ed. Emmanuel Kanceff. Torino: G. Giappichelli.

Bourguet, L., 1729. *Lettres philosophiques sur la formation des sels et des crystaux . . . a l'occasion de la pierre belemnite*. Amsterdam.

Boyle, Robert, 1692. *General Heads for the Natural History of a Country, Great or Small; Draws out for the use of Travellers and Navigators*. London.

———, 1772. *The Works of the Honourable Robert Boyle*. 2nd edition. Ed. Thomas Birch. 6 vols. London.

421

————, 2001. *The Correspondence of Robert Boyle*. Eds. Michael Hunter et al. Vol. 1. London: Pickering & Chatto.

Boym, Michael, 1656. *Flora sinensis, fructus floresque*. Vienna.

Bresson, Agnès, ed., 1992. *Peiresc. Lettres à Claude Saumaise*. Florence.

Bruno, Giordano, 1884. "De Immenso et Innumerabilibus." In *Jordani Bruni Nolani Opera Latine Conscripta*. Ed. Francesco Fiorentino. Vols. 1–2. Naples: Domenico Morano.

Burckhardt, Jacob, 1744–46. "Athanasii Kircheri, S.I. . . . epistolae." In *Historiae Bibliothecae Augustae quae Wolffenbutteli est*. Vol. 2: 123–152. Leipzig.

Cabrera, Miguel, 1756. *Maravilla Americana*. Mexico City.

Cardano, Girolamo, 1550. *De subtilitate*. Nuremberg.

Carion, Joannes, 1557. *Chronicorum libri tres*. Paris.

Castillo Graxeda, Jose del, 1987. *Compendio de la vida y virtudes de la venerable Catarina de San Juan*. 1692. Puebla: Gobierno del Estado de Puebla.

Ceruto, B., and A. Chiocco, 1622. *Musaeum Francisci. Calceolari Veronensis*. Verona.

Ciappi, Marcantonio, 1596. *Compendio delle heroiche et gloriose attioni et santa vita di Gregorio XIII*. Rome.

Clavius, Christophus, 1992. *Corrispondenza*. Eds. Ugo Baldini and Pier-Daniele Napolitani. Pisa: Università di Pisa, Dipartimento di matematica.

Combe, Thomas, 1614. *The Theater of Fine Devices, containing an hundred morall Emblemes*. London. Reprinted 1983. San Marino: The Huntington Library.

Contucci, Contuccio de, 1763–65. *Musei Kirkeriani aerea notis illustrata*. Rome.

Corraro, Angelo, 1664. *Rome Exactly Describd, as to the Present State of it, Under Pope Alexandre the Seventh*. Trans. J. B. Gent. London.

Cusa, Nicolas de, 1932. *De Docta Ignorantia*. Heidelberg.

Decembrio, Angelo, 1540. *Politiae literariae libri septem*. Vienna.

da Borgonovo, Archangelo, 1569. *Cabalistarum selectiora, obscurioraque dogmata, a Ionne Pico ex eorum commentationibus pridem excerpta*. Venice.

De Dalmases, C., 1943–65. *Fontes Narrativi de S. Ignatio de Loyola et de Societate Iesu* (Monumenta Historica Societatis Iesu). 4 vols. Rome: Institutum Historicum Societatis Iesu.

de Florencia, Francisco, 1964. *Historia de la Provincia de la Compaña de Jesús de Nueva España*. Mexico.

De la Torre Villar, Ernesto, and Ramiro Navarro de Anda, eds., 1982. *Testamonios historicos guadalupanos*. Mexico City: Fondo de Cultura Económica.

Descartes, René, 1969. *Oeuvres de René Descartes*. Eds. Charles Adam and Paul Tannery. 10 vols. Paris: Vrin.

————, 1974–89. *Oeuvres de Descartes*. Eds. Charles Adam and Paul Tannery. 11 vols. Paris: Vrin.

————, 1985. *The Philosophical Writings of Descartes*. Trans. John Cottingham, Robert Stoothoff, and Dugald Murdoch. Cambridge: Cambridge University Press.

Desmaizeaux, Pierre, 1729. "Préface." In Pierre Bayle, *Lettres*, 3 vols. Vol. 1: i–xliv. Ed. P. Desmaizeaux. Amsterdam. 3 vols. I-xliv.

Devos, J. P., and H. Seligman, eds., 1967. *L'Art de deschiffrer. Traité du déchiffrement du XVIIe siècle*. Louvain: Publications Universitaires de Louvain.

Dobrzenski, Jacobo, 1657. *Nova et amenior de admirando fontium genio philosophia*. Ferrara.

Drake, Stillman, and Charles D. O'Malley, eds. and trans., 1960. *The Controversy on the Comets of 1618: Galileo Galilei, Horatio Grassi, Mario Guiducci, Johann Kepler*. Philadelphia: University of Pennsylvania Press.

Ecchellensis, Abraham, 1651. *Historiae orientalis supplementum ex ipsorummet orientalium mss. Monumentis, Chronicon Orientale*. Paris.

Eguira y Eguren, Juan José, 1944. *Prólogos a la Biblioteca Mexicana*. Mexico City: Fondo de Cultura Económica.

Encelius, C., 1557. *De re metallica*. Frankfurt.

Eusebius, 1923. *Chronici Canones*. Trans. St. Jerome. Ed. John Knight Fotheringham. London.

Evelyn, John, 1955. *Diary*. Ed. E. S. de Beer. 6 vols. Oxford: Clarendon Press.

Fabretti, Raffaele, 1741. "Sopra alcuni correzioni del Lazio del P. Atanasio Kircher." In *Saggi di Dissertazioni Accademiche, pubblicamente lette nella nobile Accademia Etrusca, dell'antichissima città di Cortona*, vol. 3. Rome.

Firpo, Luigi, 1993. *Il Processo di Giordano Bruno*. Rome: Salerno Editrice.

Fontenelle, Bernard Le Bouyer de, 1686. *Entretiens sur la pluralité des mondes*. Paris.

Gabrieli, Giuseppe, 1996. *Il carteggio linceo*. Rome: Accademia Nazionale dei Lincei.

Galatino, Pietro, 1518. *Opus toti christianae Reipublicae maxime utile, de arcanis catholicae veritatis.* Ortonae Maris.

Galilei, Galileo, 1968. *Opere.* 20 vols. Florence: Giunti-Barbèra.

———, 1975. *Dialogo sui massimi sistemi.* 1632. Ed. Libero Sosio. Turin: Einaudi.

Galluzzi, Paolo, and Maurizio Torrini, eds., 1975. *Le Opere dei discepoli di Galileo Galilei. Carteggio, 1642–1648.* 2 vols. Florence: Giunti-Barbèra.

Gassendi, Pierre, 1657. *The Mirrour of True Nobility and Gentility [Viri Illustris Nicolai Claudii Fabrici de Peiresc . . . Vita].* Trans. B. Rand. London.

———, 1658. *Opera omnia.* Lyons.

———, 1992. *Peiresc, 1580–1637. Vie de l'illustre Nicolas-Claude Fabri de Peiresc Conseiller au Parlement d'Aix.* Trans. Roger Lassalle with Agnès Bresson. Paris: Belin.

Gastaldi, Hieronymi, 1684. *Tractatus de avertenda et profliganda peste politico-legalis.* Bologna.

Gellibrand, Henry, 1635. *A Discourse Mathematical On the Variation of the Magneticall Needle. Together with its admirable Diminution lately discovered.* London. *Giornale dei Letterati.* 1673. Vol. IX.

Gracián, Baltasar, 1648. *Agudeza y Arte de Ingenio.* Huesca.

———, 1984. *El Criticón.* Madrid.

Grandamy, Jacques, 1645. *Nova demonstratio immobilitatis terrae.* La Flèche.

Grimaldi, Francesco Maria, 1665. *Physico-mathesis de lumine, coloribus, et iride.* Bologna.

Harsdörffer, Georg Philipp, 1651. *Fortsetzung der mathematischen und philosophischen Erquickstunden.* Nuremberg.

Holstenius, Lucas, 1817. *Epistolae ad diversos.* Ed. Jean François Boissonade. Paris.

Hugo, Hermannus, 1617. *De prima scribendi origine et universa rei literariae antiquitate.* Antwerp.

Huygens, Christiaan, 1888–. *Oeuvres complètes.* 22 vols. The Hague: Martinus Nijhoff. *Journal des Sçavants* vol. 15. 1685.

Juana Inés de la Cruz, Sor, 1951–57. *Obras Completas de Sor Juana Inés de la Cruz.* Ed. Alberto G. Salceda. 4 vols. Mexico City: Fondo de Cultura Económica.

———, 1988. *A Sor Juana Anthology.* Trans. Alan S. Trueblood. Cambridge, MA: Harvard University Press.

———, 1997. *Poems, Protest, and a Dream.* Trans. Margaret Sayers Peden. Introduction by Ilan Stavans. Harmondsworth, UK: Penguin.

Kepler, Johannes, 1610. *Dissertatio cum nuncio sidereo nuper ad mortales misso Galilaeo Galilaeo.* Florence.

———, 1634. *Somnium, seu opus posthumum de astronomia lunari.* Frankfurt.

Kestler, Johann Stephan, 1680. *Physiologia Kircheriana experimentalis.* Amsterdam.

Kino, Eusebio Francisco, 1954. *Kino Reports to Headquarters: Correspondence of Eusebio F. Kino, S.J., from New Spain with Rome.* Ed. and trans. Ernst J. Burrus, S.J. Rome: Institutum Historicum Societatis Jesu.

———, 1998. *Epistolario, 1670–1710.* Ed. Domenico Calarco. Bologna: Editrice Missionaria Italiana.

Kircher, Athanasius, 1631. *Ars magnesia.* Würzburg.

———, 1635. *Primitiae gnomonicae catoptricae.* Avignon.

———, 1636. *Prodromus Coptus sive Aegyptiacus.* Rome.

———, 1638. *Specula melitensis.* Naples.

———, 1641. *De arte magnetica opus tripartitvm.* Rome.

———, 1641. *Magnes, sive de arte magnetica.* Rome.

———, 1643a. *Lingua Aegyptiaca restituta.* Rome.

———, 1643b. *Magnes, sive de arte magnetica opus tripartitum.* Cologne.

———, 1646. *Ars magna lucis et umbrae.* Rome.

———, 1650a. *Musurgia universalis.* 2 vols. Rome.

———, 1650b. *Obeliscus Pamphilius.* Rome.

———, 1652–55. *Oedipus Aegyptiacus.* 3 vols. Rome. The title pages of the work's three "tomes" are dated 1562, 1653, and 1654; but much of the front-matter included in the first tome, such as the imprimatur and dedication, is dated 1655, the year that the book in fact appeared.

———, 1653. "Rituale Ecclesiae Aegyptiace." In Leone Allaci, *Summikta.* 236–267. Cologne.

———, 1654. *Magnes, sive de arte magnetica.* 3rd edition. Rome.

———, 1656. *Itinerarium exstaticum.* Rome.

———, 1657. *Iter exstaticum II qui & Mundi subterranei Prodromus dicitur.* Rome.

————, 1658. *Scrutinium physico-medicum contagiosae luis, quae dicitur pestis.* Rome.

————, 1659. *Scrutinium physico-medicum contagiosae.* Leipzig.

————, 1660. *Iter extaticum coeleste.* Würzburg.

————, 1661. *Diatribe de prodigiosis crucibus, quae tam supra vestes hominum . . . comparuerunt.* Rome.

————, 1663. *Polygraphia nova et universalis ex combinatoria arte detecta.* Rome.

————, 1665a. *Arithmologia, sive de abditis numerorum mysterijs.* Rome.

————, 1665b. *Historia Eustachio-Mariana.* Rome.

————, 1665c. *Mundus subterraneus.* 2 vols. Amsterdam.

————, 1666. *Ad Alexandrum VIII Pont. Max. Obelisci Aegyptiaci: nuper inter Isaei Romani rudera effossi interpretatio hieroglyphia.* Rome.

————, 1667a. *China monumentis . . . illustrata.* Amsterdam.

————, 1667b. *Magneticum naturae regnum.* Amsterdam.

————, 1669. *Ars magna sciendi.* Amsterdam.

————, 1671a. *Iter exstaticum coeleste.* Würzburg.

————, 1671b. *Latium, id est, nova et parallela Latii tum veteris tum novi descriptio.* Amsterdam.

————, 1672. *Principis christiani archetypon politicum.* Amsterdam.

————, 1673. *Phonurgia Nova.* Kempton.

————, 1675. *Arca Noë.* Amsterdam.

————, 1676. *Sphinx mystagoga.* Amsterdam.

————, 1678. *Mundus subterraneus.* Amsterdam. 2nd edition.

————, 1679a. *Turris Babel.* Amsterdam.

————, 1679b. *Tariffa Kircheriana id est inventum aucthoris novum expeditâ, & mirâ arte combinatâ methodo, universalem gemetriae, & arithmeticae practicae summam continens.* 2 vols. Rome.

————, 1684a. *Fasciculus epistolarum.* Ed. Hieronymus Langenmantel. Augsburg.

————, 1684b. "Vita admodum reverendi P. Athanasii Kircheri, Societ. Iesu, viri toto orbe celebratissimi." In *Fasciculus epistolarum adm. R.P. Athanasii Kircheri Soc. Iesu.* Ed. Hieronymus Langemantel. Augsburg.

————, 1987. *China Illustrata.* Trans. Charles D. Van Tuyl. Muskogee, OK: Indiana University Press.

Knittel, Caspar, 1682. *Via Regia ad omnes scientias et artes. Hoc est: Ars Universalis Scientiarum omnium Artiumque Arcana facilius penetrandi.* Prague.

Knorr, G. W., and J. E. I. Walch, 1768–77. *Recueil des monumens des catastrophes que la globe terrestre a éssuiées, contenant des pétrifications dessinées, gravées et enumirées.* 5 vols. Nuremberg.

Kuhlmann, Quirinus, 1674. *Epistolae duae, prior, de arte magna sciendi sive combinatoria, posterior de admirabilibus quibusdam inventis . . . cum responsoria . . . Athanasii Kircheri.* Leyden.

————, 1960. *Himmlische Libes-Küße.* Ed. Arnfrid Astel. [*Lyrische Hefte* 2, supplement.] Heidelberg: Astel.

————, 1998. *XLI. Libes-Kuß.* Trans. and combinatorial implementation by Ambroise Barras. Available on the Internet at http://infolipo.unige.ch/atelier/kuhlmann/kuhlmann.html.

Langenmantel, Hieronymus Ambrosius, ed., 1684. *Fasciculus epistolarum Adm. R. P. Athanasii Kircheri.* Augsburg.

Leclerc, Jean, 1701. *Parrhasiana, ou pensées diverses sur des matières de critique, d'histoire, de morale et de politique.* Amsterdam. 2nd edition.

Lefebvre, Tanneguy, ed., 1669. *Prima Scaligerana nusquam antehac edita, quibus adjuncta et altera Scaligerana.* Saumur.

Leibniz, Gottfried Wilhelm, 1768. *G. G. Leibnitii opera omnia.* Ed. Ludwig Dutens. 4 vols. Geneva.

————, 1903. *Opuscules et fragments inédits de Leibniz.* Ed. Louis Couturat. Paris: Alcan.

————, 1969 [1959]. *Philosophical Papers and Letters.* 2nd edition. Ed. and trans. Leroy E. Loemker. Dordrecht: D. Reidel.

————, 1981. *New Essays on Human Understanding.* Trans. Peter Remnant and Jonathan Bennett. Cambridge, UK: Cambridge University Press.

————, 1987. *Philosophischer Briefwechsel, Erster Band.* 1663–85. Berlin: Akademie Verlag.

————, 1994. *Writings on China.* Eds. and trans. Daniel J. Cook and Henry Rosemont Jr. Chicago: Open Court.

Llull, Ramon, 1617. *Raymundi Lulli Opera.* Eds. Giordano Bruno et al. Strassburg.

Loyola, St. Ignatius, 1903–11. *Monumenta Ignatiana, series prima: Sancti Ignatii de Loyola epistolae et instructiones.* Madrid: Gabriel Lopez del Horno.

————, 1991. *Ecrits*. Ed. Maurice Giuliani, Paris: Desclée de Brouwer.

————, 1996. *Saint Ignatius of Loyola: Personal Writings*. Trans. Joseph A. Munitz and Philip Endean. London: Penguin.

Maché, Ulrich, and Volker Meid, eds., 1980. *Gedichte des Barock*. Stuttgart: Reclam.

Magnus, Olaus, 1555. *Historia de gentibus septentrionalibus*. Rome.

Martini, Martino, 1654. *Brevis relatio de numero, & qualitate Christianorum apud Sinas*. Rome. Reprinted in Martini 1998, vol. 2, pp. 41–84.

————, 1655. *Novus atlas sinensis*. Amsterdam.

————, 1658. *Sinicae historiae decas prima*. Munich.

————, 1998. *Opera omnia*. Ed. Franco Demarchi: *Lettere e documenti*. Ed. Giuliano Bertuccioli. 4 vols. Trent: Università degli STUDI di Trento.

Mather, Cotton, 1994. *The Christian Philosopher*. Ed. Winton U. Solberg. Urbana: University of Illinois Press.

Mencke, Johann Burkhard, 1937. *The Charlatanry of the Learned* (*De charlataneria eruditorum, 1715*). Trans. Francis E. Litz. Ed. H. L. Mencke. New York: Knopf.

Mersenne, Marin, 1932–88. *Correspondance du P. Marin Mersenne, Religieux Minime*. Eds. Cornélis de Waard et al. 16 vols. Paris: G. Beauchesne.

Mirto, Alfonso, 1999. *Lucas Holstenius e la corte Medicea: Carteggio (1629–1660)*. Florence.

Montaigne, Michele de, 1942. *Journal de voyage en Italie par la Suisse et L'Allemagne, en 1580 et 1581*. Nouvelle édition, établie sur le texte de l'édition originale posthume de 1774. Ed. Maurice Rat. Paris: Garnier frères.

Morin, Jean, 1682. *Antiquitates Ecclesiae Orientalis*. London.

Müller, Theobald, 1577. *Musaei Joviani imagines*. Basel.

Nadal, Jeronimo, 1962. *P. Hieronymi Nadal Commentarii de Instituto Societatis Iesu*, ed. Michael Nicolau, S.J. (*Epistolae et Monumenta P. Hieronymi Nadal*, Tomus V). Rome: Monumenta Historica Societatis Iesu.

Neicklius, Caspar, 1727. *Museographia*. Leipzig and Breslau.

Newton, Isaac, 1687. *Philosophiae naturalis principia mathematica*. London.

Nicolson, Marjorie Hope, ed., 1992. *The Conway Letters*. Revised edition with an introduction and new materials edited by Sarah Hutton. Oxford: Clarendon.

Nieuhof, Johan, 1673. *An Embassy from the East-India Company of the United Provinces, to the Grand Tatar Cham Emperour . . . with an appendix of several remarks taken out of Father Athanasius Kircher*. 2nd edition. Trans. John Ogilby. London.

Ogilby, John, 1669. *An Embassy from the East-India Company of the United Provinces, to the Grand Tartar Cham Empereur of China*. London.

Oldenburg, Henry, 1966. *The Correspondence of Henry Oldenburg*. Eds. A. Rupert Hall and Maris Boas Hall. Madison: University of Wisconsin Press. Vol. 2.

Osorio Romero, Ignacio, 1993. *La Luz Imaginaria: Epistolario de Atanasio Kircher con los Novohispanos*. Mexico: Universidad Nacional Autonoma de Mexico.

Pascal, Blaise, 1967. *The Provincial Letters*. Trans. A.J. Krailsheimer. Baltimore: Penguin Books.

Peiresc, Nicolas-Claude Fabri de, 1888–98. *Lettres de Peiresc*. Ed. Philippe Tamizey de Larroque. 7 vols. Paris: Imprimerie Nationale.

————, 1983. *Lettres à Naudé (1629–1637)*. Ed. Phillip Wolfe. Paris and Seattle: Papers on French Seventeenth Century Literature.

————, 1989. *Lettres à Cassiano dal Pozzo (1626–1637)*. Ed. Jean-François Lhote and Danielle Joyal. Clermont-Ferrand: Éditions Adosa.

————, 1992. *Lettres à Claude Saumaise et a son entourage (1620–1637)*. Ed. Agnès Bresson. Florence: Olschki.

————, 1995. *Correspondance de Peiresc & Aleandro*. Ed. Jean-François Lhote and Danielle Joyal. 2 vols. Clermont-Ferrand: Éditions Adosa.

Pellegrini, Matteo, 1650. *Fonti dell'Ingenio Ridotti ad Arte*. Bologna.

Petau, Denis, 1757. *De doctrina temporum*. 3 vols. Venice.

Petrucci, Giuseffo, 1677. *Prodromo apologetico alli studi Chircheriani*. Amsterdam.

Pezron, Paul, 1687. *L'antiquité des temps rétablie et défendue contre les juifs et les nouveaux chronologistes*. Paris.

Piazza, Carlo Bartolomeo, 1679. *Opere pie di Roma descritte secondo lo stato presente*. Rome.

Pimenta, António, 1665. *Sciographia da Nova Prostimasia Celeste & Portentoso Cometa do Anno de 1664*. Lisbon.

Poe, Edgar Allen, 1978. "A Descent into the Maelström." In *Collected Works of Edgar Allen Poe*. Vol. 2. *Tales and Sketches, 1831–1842*. Ed. Thomas Olive Mabbott with Eleanor D. Kewer and Maureen C. Mabbott. 574–597. Cambridge, MA: Belknap.

Polanco, Juan de, 1903. *Reglas que deven observar acerca del escribir los de la Compañia que están esparzidos fuera de Roma*. In Loyola 1903–11, part 1, vol. 1, pp. 542–549.

Possevino, Antonio, 1593. *Bibliotheca selecta de ratione studiorum*. 1607. Cologne.

Propaganda Fide, 1907. *Collectanea S. Congregationis de Propaganda Fide seu decreta, instructiones, rescripta pro apostolicis missionibus*. Vol. 1. Rome: Typographia Polyglotta.

Raleigh, Walter, 1736. *History of the World*. 2 vols. London.

Ramos, Alonso, 1689. *Primera Parte de los prodigios de la omnipotencia, y milagros de la gracia en la vida de la venerable sierva de Dios Catharina de S. Joan; natural del Gran Mogor, difunta en esta imperial ciudad de la Puebla de los Angeles en la nueva Espana*. Puebla.

Reuchlin, Johannes, 1494. *De Verbo Mirifico*. Basel.

———, 1993. *On the Art of Kabbalah. De Arte Cabalistica*. 1517. Trans. Martin Goodman and Sarah Goodman. Lincoln: University of Nebraska Press.

Rhenanus, Beatus, 1551. *Rerum Germanicarum libri tres*. 2nd edition. Basel.

Ribadeneira, Petro, S.J., Philippo Alegambe, S.J., and Nathanaele Sotvello, S.J., 1676. *Bibliotheca Scriptorum Societatis Iesu*. Rome.

Riccioli, Giambattista, 1651. *Almagestum Novum*. Bologna.

———, 1661. *Geographiae et Hydrographiae reformatae [. . .] libri duodecim*. Bologna.

Rupprich, R. H., 1956. *Dürer. Schriftlicher Nachlaß*. 2 vols. Berlin: Deutscher Verein für Kulturwissenschaft.

Saavedra Fajardo, Diego de, 1670. *Republica literaria*. Alcala.

Saggi, 1735–41. *Saggi di dissertazioni accademiche pubblicamente lette nella nobile Accademia Etrusca dell'antichissima città di Cortona*. 3 vols. Rome.

Salianus, Jacobus, 1641. *Annales ecclesiastici veteris testamenti*. 6 vols. Paris.

Samotheus, Joannes Lucidus, 1545–46. *Opusculum de emendationibus temporum*. Venice.

Sandrart, Joachim von, 1675. *Teutschen Academie Zweiter Theil*. Nuremberg.

Saumaise, Claude, 1648. *De annis climactericis et antiqua astrologia diatribe*. Leiden.

Scaliger, Joseph. *Animadversiones in chronologica Eusebii, Thesaurus temporum*.

———, 1606. *Isagogici chronologiae canones, Thesaurus temporum*. Leiden.

———, 1610. *Opuscula*. Paris.

———, 1629. *Opus de emendatione temporum*. 3rd edition. Geneva.

Schall von Bell, Adam, 1665. *Historica narratio de initio et progressu missionis Societatis Iesu apud Sinenses ac praesertim in regia Pequinensi, ex litteris R. P. Joannis Adami Schall*. Vienna.

Scheuchzer, J. J., 1723. *Herbarium diluvianum, Editio novissima*. Leiden.

Schott, Kaspar, 1657. *Mechanica-Hydraulico Pneumatica*. Würzburg.

———, 1657–59. *Magia universalis naturae et artis*. 4 vols. Würzburg.

———, 1660. *Pantometrum Kircherianum*. Würzburg.

———, 1661. *Cursus mathematicus sive Absoluta omnium Mathematicum Disciplinarum Encyclopaedia*. Würzburg.

———, 1664. *Technica curiosa, sive mirabilia artis*. Würzburg.

———, 1665. *Schola steganographica*. Würzburg.

Schott, Kasper, 1667. *Physica curiosa*. Würzburg.

———, 1668. *Organum Mathematicum*. Würzburg.

Sebastiani, Giuseppi, 1672. *Il viaggio all'Indie Orientali*. Rome: Filippomaria Mancini.

Selenus, Gustavus (pseudonym of Duke August II of Braunschweig-Lüneburg), 1624. *Cryptomenytices et cryptographiae libri ix*. Lüneburg.

Semedo, Alvaro, 1642. *Imperio de la China: I cultura evangelica en èl, por los religios de la Compania de Iesus*. Madrid.

Seng, Nikolaus, 1901. *Selbstbiographie des P. Athanasius Kircher aus der Gesellschaft Jesu*. Fulda: Druck und Verlag der Fuldaer Actiendruckerei.

Sepibus, Giorgio de, 1678. *Romani Collegii Musaeum Celeberrimum*. Amsterdam.

Sigüenza y Góngora, Carlos de, 1984. *Seis Obras*. Ed. William G. Bryant. Caracas: Biblioteca Ayacucho.

Sorbière, Samuel, 1660. *Lettres et discours de M. Sorbiere sur diverses matieres curieuses*. Paris.

Sossus, Gulielmus, 1632. *De numine historiae liber*. Paris.

Spon, Jacob, 1673. *Recherches des antiquités et curiosités de la ville de Lyon*. Lyon.

Stansel, Valentin, 1658. *Orbe affonsino ou horoscopio universal.* Évora.
———, 1683. *Legatus uranicus ex orbe novo in veterem.* Praha.
———, 1685a. *Uranophilus Caelestis Peregrinus.* Gand.
———, 1685b. *Zodiacus divini doloris.* Évora.
Tamizey de Larroque, Philippe, ed., 1972. *Les Correspondants de Peiresc.* 1879. 2 vols. Geneva: Slatkine.
Tesauro, Emanuele, 1654. *Il Canocchiale Aristotelico.* Torino.
Tiraboschi, Girolamo, 1772–1782. *Storia della letteratura italiana.* 11 vol. Modena: presso la Società tipografica.
Thévenot, Melchisédech, 1663–1672. *Relations de divers voyages curieux, qui n'ont point esté publiées.* 4 vols. Paris.
Trigault, Nicolas, 1615. *De christiana expeditione apud Sinas, suscepta ab Societate Iesu. Ex P. Matthaei Ricii eiusdem Societatis comentariis, Libri V.* Augsburg.
Trithemius, Johannes, 1518. *Polygraphiae libri sex.* Oppenheim.
———, 1567. *De septem secundeis, id est, intelligentiis, sive spiritibus orbes post Deum moventibus.* Cologne.
———, 1608. *Steganographia: hoc est: Ars per occultam scripturam animi sui voluntatem absentibus aperiendi certa.* Frankfurt.
Turgot, Anne-Robert, 1970. *Remarques critiques sur les Réflexions philosophiques de Maupertuis sur l'origine des langues et la signification des mots* (1750). In *Varia linguistica.* Ed. Charles Porset. 24–66. Bordeaux: Ducros.
Uffenbach, Konrad Zacharias von, 1754. *Merkwürdige Reisen durch Niedersachsen, Holland and Engelland.* Ulm.
Valence, P. Apollinaire de, 1891. *Correspondance de Peiresc avec plusieurs Missionaires et Religieux de l'ordre des Capucins, 1631–1637.* Paris.
della Valle, Pietro, 1650. *Viaggi di Pietro della Valle il pelligrino: con minuto ragguaglio di tutti le cose notabili apresso.* Rome: Vitale Mascardi.
Vigenère, Blaise de, 1586. *Traicté des chiffres.* Paris.
"Vigneul-Marville" (pseudonym of Noël Bonaventure d'Argonne), 1699–1701. *Mélanges d'histoire et de littérature.* 3 vols. Paris and Rouen.
Walton, Brian, 1657. "Prolegomena." In *Biblia sacra polyglotta.* London.
Weinsheun, Stanislaus Mink von (pseudonym of Johann Just Winckelmann), 1657. *Proteus: Das ist, eine unglaubliche Lustnützliche Lehrart, in kurzer Zeit ohne Müh Deutsch und Lateinische Vers zu machen, auch einen Französischen und Lateinischen Brief zuschreiben.* Oldenburg.
———, 1692. *Dreyfache Kunst-Schnur.* Frankfurt and Leipzig.
Wilkins, John, 1668. *An Essay Towards a Real Character and a Philosophical Language.* London.
Woodward, J., 1728. *Fossils of all Kinds Digested into a Method.* London: W. Innys.

Secondary Sources

Abreu Gomez, Emilo, 1934a. *Sor Juana Inés de la Cruz bibliografia y biblioteca.* Mexico City: Monografías Bibliográficas Mexicanas, no. 29.
———, 1934b. *Iconografia de Sor Juana Inés de la Cruz.* Mexico City: Publicaciones del Museo Nacional de Mexico.
Adams, Frank Dawson, 1954. *The Birth and Development of the Geological Sciences.* New York: Dover.
Adams, Percy G., 1962. *Travelers and Travel Liars, 1660–1800.* Berkeley: University of California Press.
Adas, Michael, 1989. *Machines as the Measure of Man: Science, Technology and Ideologies of Western Dominance.* Ithaca, NY: Cornell University Press.
Åkerman, Susanna, 1991. *Queen Christina and Her Circle: The Transformation of a Seventeenth-century Philosophical Libertine.* Leiden: Brill.
Albani, Paolo, and Berlinghiero Buonarroti, 1994. *Aga Magéra Difúra—Dizionario delle Lingue Immaginarie.* Bologna: Zanichelli.
Alden, Dauril, 1996. *The Making of an Enterprise: The Society of Jesus in Portugal, Its Empire, and Beyond: 1540–1750.* Stanford, CA: Stanford University Press.
Allen, Don Cameron, 1949. *The Legend of Noah: Renaissance Rationalism in Art, Science and Letters.* Urbana: University of Illinois Press.
———, 1960. "The Predecessors of Champollion." *Proceedings of the American Philosophical Society* 104: 527–547.

————, 1970. *Mysteriously Meant: The Rediscovery of Pagan Symbolism and Allegorical Interpretation in the Renaissance.* Baltimore: Johns Hopkins Press.

Allen, E. John B., 1972. *Post and Courier Service in the Diplomacy of Early Modern Europe.* The Hague: Martinus Nijhoff.

Allen, Michael J.B., 2000. *Marsilio Ficino: The Philebus Commentary. A Critical Edition and Translation.* Tempe: Arizona Center for Medieval and Renaissance Studies.

Altmann, Alexander. "Lurianic Kabbalah in a Platonic Key: Abraham Cohen Herrera's *Puerta del Cielo.*" In *Jewish Thought in the Seventeenth Century.* Eds. Isadore Twersky and Bernard Septimus. 1–37. Cambridge, MA: Harvard University Press.

Andrewes, William J. H., ed., 1996. *The Quest for Longitude: The Proceedings of the Longitude Symposium.* Cambridge, MA: The Collection of Historical Scientific Instruments, Harvard University.

Apples to Atoms. Portraits of Scientists from Newton to Rutherford. 1986. NPG London: London.

Arnold, Klaus, 1971. *Johannes Trithemius.* Würzburg: Schöningh.

Arrhenius, Svante, 1908. *Worlds in the Making: The Evolution of the Universe.* Trans. H. Borns. New York: Harper.

Ashworth, William B., 1986. "Catholicism and Early Modern Science." In *God and Nature: Historical Essays on the Encounter between Christianity and Science.* Eds. David C. Lindberg and Ronald L. Numbers. 136–166. Berkeley: University of California Press.

————, 1989. "Light of Reason, Light of Nature—Catholic and Protestant Metaphors of Scientific Knowledge." *Science in Context* 3: 89–109.

Athanasius Kircher, 2001. *Athanasius Kircher y la ciencia del siglo XVII.* Madrid: Universidad Complutense de Madrid.

Aufrère, Sydney, 1990. *La Momie et la tempête: Nicolas-Claude Fabri de Peiresc et la "Curiosité Egyptienne" en Provence au début du XVIIᵉ siècle.* Avignon: Editions A. Barthélemy.

Bach, José Alfredo, 1985. *Athanasius Kircher and His Method: A Study in the Relations of the Arts and Sciences in the Seventeenth Century.* Ph.D. dissertation. University of Oklahoma.

Bailey, Gauvin Alexander, 1997. "A Mughal Princess in Baroque New Spain." *Anales del Instituto de Investigaciones Esteticas* 71: 37–73.

Baldini, Ugo, 1983. "Christoph Clavius and the Scientific Scene in Rome." In *Gregorian Reform of the Calendar: Proceedings of the Vatican Conference to Commemorate Its 400th Anniversary, 1582–1982.* Eds. George V. Coyne, Michael A. Oskin, and Olof Pedersen. 137–169. Vatican City: Specola Vaticana.

————, 1984a. "Additamenta galilaeana. I. Galileo, la nuova astronomia e la critica all'aristotelismo nel dialogo epistolare tra Giuseppe Biancani e i revisori romani della Compagnia di Gesù." *Annali dell'Istituto e Museo di storia della scienza di Firenze* 9: 13–43.

————, 1984b. "Su alcune fonti archivistiche per la storia della scienza." In *Scienza e letteratura nella cultura italiana del Settecento.* Eds. Renzo Cremante and Walter Tega. 567–574. Bologna: Il Mulino.

————, 1985. "Una fonte poco utilizzata per la storia intellettuale: le 'censurae librorum' e 'opinionum' nell'antica Compagnia di Gesù." *Annali dell'istituto storico italo-germanico in Trento* 11: 19–67.

————, 1992. *Legem Impone Subactis. Studi su filosofia e scienza dei gesuiti in Italia.* Rome: Bulzoni.

————, 1996. "La formazione scientifica di Giovanni Battista Riccioli." In *Copernico e la questione copernicana in Italia.* Ed. Luigi Pepe. 123–182. Florence: Olschki.

————, 2000. *Saggi sulla cultura della Compagnia di Gesù (secoli XVI–XVIII).* Padua: CLEUP.

Baldwin, Martha, 1987. *Athanasius Kircher and the Magnetic Philosophy.* Ph.D. dissertation. Chicago: University of Chicago, Department of History.

————, 1993. "Alchemy in the Society of Jesus in the Seventeenth Century: Strange Bedfellows?" *Ambix* 40: 41–64.

————, 1995. "The Snakestone Experiments: An Early Modern Medical Debate." *Isis* 86: 394–418.

————, 2001a. "Kircher's Magnetic Investigations." In Stolzenberg 2001a, pp. 27–36.

————, 2001b. "Matters Medical." In Stolzenberg 2001a. pp. 85–92.

————, 2002. "Pious Ambition: Natural Philosophy and the Jesuit Quest for the Patronage of Printed Books in the Seventeenth Century." In *Jesuit Science.* Ed. Mordechai Feingold. 285–329. Cambridge, MA: MIT Press.

Balsamo, Luigi, 1994. "Venezia e l'attività editoriale di Antonio Possevino." In *I Gesuiti a Venezia. Momenti e problemi di storia veneziana della Compagnia di Gesù. Atti del convegno di studi, Venezia, 2–5 ottobre 1990.* Ed. M. Zanardi. 629–660. Padua: Gregoriana Libreria Editrice.

Bann, Stephen, 1994. *Under the Sign: John Bargrave as Collector, Traveller, and Witness*. Ann Arbor: University of Michigan Press.

Barb, A. A., 1953. "Diva Matrix: A Faked Gnostic Intalgio in the Possession of P. P. Rubens and the Iconology of a Symbol." *Journal of the Warburg and Courtauld Institutes* 16: 193–238.

Bargellini, Clara, 2001. "Athanasius Kircher e la Nuova Spagna." In Lo Sardo 2001, pp. 86–91.

Bartola, Alberto, 1989. "Alessandro VII e Athanasius Kircher S.J.: Ricerche ed appunti sulla loro corrispondeza erudita e sulla storia di alcuni codi Chigiani." *Miscellanea Bibliothecae Apostolicae Vaticanae, Studi e Testi* 333: 7–105.

Battista, Anna Maria, 1966. *Alle origini del pensiero politico libertino: Montaigne e Charron*. Milan: Giuffrè.

Baumstark, Reinhold, ed., 1997. *Rom in Bayern: Kunst und Spiritualität der ersten Jesuiten*. Munich: Hirmer.

Bedini, Silvio A. 1991. *The Pulse of Time: Galileo Galilei, the Determination of Longitude, and the Pendulum Clock*. Florence: Olschki.

Beinlich, Horst, et al., 2002. *Spurensuche: Wege zu Athanasius Kircher*. Dettelbach: J. H. Röll.

Bellini, Erolamo, 1997. *Umanisti e Lincei. Letteratura e scienza a Roma nell'età di Galileo*. Padua: Antenore.

Belloni, Luigi, 1985. "Athansius Kircher: Seine Mikroscopie, die Animalcula und die Pestwürmer." *Medizinhistorisches Journal* 20: 58–65.

Bénassy-Berling, Marie-Cécile, 1982. *Humanisme et religion chez Sor Juana Inés de la Cruz*. Paris: Éditions hispaniques: Publications de la Sorbonne.

Benjamin, Walter, 1977. *The Origin of German Tragic Drama*. Trans. John Osborne. London: Verso.

Bennett, Jim, 1987. *The Divided Circle: A History of Instruments for Astronomy, Navigation and Surveying*. Oxford: Phaidon-Christie's.

Beuchot, Mauricio, 1994. "Kircher y algunos filósofos mexicanos en el siglo XVII." *Intersticios* 1: 87–95.

———, 1995. "El universo filosófico de Sor Juana." In *Memoria del Coloquio Internacional Sor Juana Inés de la Cruz y el pensamiento novohispano*. 29–40. Toluca: Instituto Mexiquense de Cultura.

———, 1999. *Sor Juana, una filosofia barocca*. Toluca: Universidad Autónoma del Estado de México.

Biale, David, 1979. *Gershom Scholem: Kabbalah and Counter-History*. Cambridge, MA.

Billings, Timothy James, 1997. "Illustrating China: Emblematic Autopsy and the Catachresis of Cathay." Ph.D. dissertation. Cornell University.

Biondi, Albano, 1981. "La *Bibliotheca selecta* di Antonio Possevino, un progetto di egemonia culturale." In *La "Ratio studiorum": Modeli culturali e pratiche educative dei Gesuiti in Italia fra Cinque e Seicento*. Ed. Gian Paolo Brizzi. 43–75. Rome: Bulzoni.

Blair, Ann, 1997. *Theater of Nature: Jean Bodin and Renaissance Science*. Princeton, NJ: Princeton University Press.

Blanco, Mercedes, 1992. *Les Réthoriques de la pointe: Baltasar Gracian et le conceptisme en Europe*. Paris: Champion.

Blau, Joseph, 1944. *The Christian Intepretation of the Kabbalah*. New York: Columbia University Press.

Blunt, Anthony, 1979. *Borromini*. London: Allen Lane.

Boehm, Gottfried, 1985. *Bildnis und Individuum: Über den Ursprung der Porträtmalerei in der italienischen Renaissance*. Munich: Beck.

Boge, Herbert, 1973. *Griechische Tachygraphie und Tironische Noten*. Berlin: Akademie-Verlag.

Bolton, Herbert Eugene, 1984 [1936]. *Rim of Christendom: A Biography of Eusebio Francisco Kino, Pacific Coast Pioneer*. 2nd edition. Tucson: University of Arizona.

Bonnefoy, Yves, 1970. *Rome, 1630: L'horizon du premier baroque*. Paris: Gallimard.

Borges, Jorge Luis, 1981. "El idioma analítico de John Wilkins." In Borges, *Otras Inquisiciones*. 102–106. Madrid: Alianza Editorial.

———, 1998. *Collected Fictions*. Trans. Andrew Hurley. New York: Penguin.

Borsi, F., 1980. *Borromini architetto*. Milano: Electa.

Bots, Hans, 1977. *Republiek der Letteren: Ideaal en werkelijkheid*. Amsterdam: APA-Holland Universiteits Pers.

Bots, Hans, and Françoise Waquet, 1997. *La République des Lettres*. Paris: Editions Belin.

Boxer, C. R., 1951. *The Christian Century in Japan, 1549–1650*. Berkeley and Los Angeles: University of California Press, 1951.

Brading, David A., 1991. *The First America: The Spanish Monarchy, Creole Patriots, and the Liberal State, 1492–1867*. Cambridge, UK: Cambridge University Press.

Brann, Noel, 1999. *Trithemius and Magical Theology: A Chapter in the Controversy over Occult Studies in Early Modern Europe*. Albany: State University of New York Press.

Bresson, Agnès, 1988. "Peiresc et les études coptes: Prolegomènes au déchiffrement des hieroglyphes." *XVIIᵉ Siècle* 40: 41–50.

Broekmans, Herman, Ton Gruntjes, and Hans Bots, 1976. "Het beeld van de Republiek der Letteren in het tijdschrift van H. Basnage de Beauval." In *Henri Basnage de Beauval en de Histoire des ouvrages des savans, 1687–1709*. Ed. Hans Bots. 2 vols. Vol. 1, pp. 109–136. Amsterdam: APA-Holland Universiteits Pers.

Brown, John Lackey, 1939. *The Methodus ad facilem historiae cognitionem of Jean Bodin: A Critical Study*. Washington, DC: The Catholic University of America Press.

Bruley, Yves, ed., 2002. *La Trinité-des-Montes redécouverte*. Rome: De Lucca.

Bruni, Silvia, 2001. "Le Museo Kircheriano e il Museo Nazionale Romano" in Lo Sardo 2001, pp. 335–342.

Burrus, E. J., S.J., 1953. "Sigüenza y Góngora's Efforts for Readmission into the Jesuit Order." *Hispanic American Historical Review* 33: 387–391.

Busti, Laurina, 2001. "Lettera scritta da Atanasio Kircher a Giovan Battista Orsucci, Roma 14 Maggio 1666." In Lo Sardo 2001, pp. 350–351.

Butterfield, H., 1931. *The Whig Interpretation of History*. London: G. Bell.

Caffiero, Marina, Maria Pia Donato, and Antonella Romano, forthcoming. "De la catholicité post-tridentine à la République Romaine: Splendeurs et misères des intellectuels courtisans." In *Florence, Rome, Naples: Une histoire comparée des milieux intellectuels italiens à l'époque moderne*. Eds. Jean Boutier, Brigitte Marin, and Antonella Romano. Rome: Ecole française de Rome.

Calvino, Italo, 1981. *If on a Winter's night a Traveller*. Trans. William Weaver. San Diego: Harcourt Brace.

Camenietzki, Carlos Ziller, 1995a. "L'Extase interplanetaire d'Athanasius Kircher: Philosophie, cosmologie et discipline dans la Compagnie de Jésus au XVIIe siècle." *Nuncius* 10: 3–32.

———, 1995b. *L'harmonie du monde au XVIIe siècle: Essai sur la pensée scientifique d'Athanasius Kircher*. Ph.D. dissertation. Universite de Paris IV-Sorbonne.

Camenietzki, Carlos Ziller, and Carlos Alberto Zeron, 2000. "Quem Conta um Conto Aumenta um Ponto: O mito do Ipupiara, a natureza americana e as narrativas da colonização do Brasil." *Revista de Indias* 60: 111–134.

Campbell, Mary B., 1988. *The Witness and the Other World: Exotic European Travel Writing, 400–1600*. Ithaca, NY: Cornell University Press.

Cañizares-Esguerra, Jorge, 1999. "New World, New Stars: Patriotic Astrology and the Invention of Indian and Creole Bodies in Colonial Spanish America, 1600–1650." *American Historical Review* 104: 33–68.

———, 2000. "Spanish America: From Baroque to Modern Colonial Science." In *The Cambridge History of Science*. Vol. 4. *The Eighteenth Century*. Ed. Roy Porter. 814–837. Cambridge, UK: Cambridge University Press.

———, 2001. *How to Write the History of the New World: Historiographies, Epistemologies, and Identities in the Eighteenth-Century Atlantic World*. Stanford, CA: Stanford University Press.

Cappocia, Anna Rita, 2000. "Per una lettura delle *Indipetae* italiane del Settecento: 'Indifferenza' e desiderio di martirio." *Nouvelles de la République des Lettres* 20: 7–43.

Carilla, Emilio, 1952. "Sor Juana: Ciencia y poesia (sobre el 'Primero Sueño')." *Revista de filologia española* 36: 287–307.

Carolino, Luís Miguel, 1997. "A Ciência e os topoi retóricos em António Vieira: Um caso de difusão cultural em Portugal e no Brasil durante o século XVII." *Revista da Sociedade Brasileira de História da Ciência* 18: 55–71.

Carvalho Da Silva, Paolo José, 2000. *A tristeza na cultura luso-brasileira. Os Sermões do padre Antonio Vieira*. São Paulo: Educ-Fafesp.

Casanovas, Juan, and Philip Keenan, 1993. "The Observations of Comets by Valentine Stansel, a Seventeenth Century Missionary in Brasil." *Archivum Historicum Societatis Iesu* 62: 319–330.

Casciato, Maristella, Maria Grazia Ianniello, and Maria Vitale, eds., 1986. *Enciclopedismo in Roma barocca: Athanasius Kircher e il Museo del Collegio Romano tra Wunderkammer e museo scientifico*. Venice: Marsilio.

Cascioli, V., 1915–16. "Il Santuario della Mentorella e il P. A. Kircher." *La Civiltà Cattolica* 66: 692–703; and 67: 168–176.

Castelló Yturbide, Teresa, ed., 1993. *The Art of Featherwork in Mexico*. Mexico: Fomento Cultural Banamex.

Castelnau-L'Estoile, Charlotte de, 2000. *"Les ouvriers d'une vigne stérile" Les jésuites et la conversion des Indiens au Brésil (1580–1620)*. Paris and Lisbon: Fondation Gulbekian.

Castrucci, Emanuele, 1981. *Ordine convenzionale e pensiero decisionista, saggio sui presupposti intellettuali dello stato moderno nel seicento francese*. Milan: Giuffrè.

Ceccarelli, Maria Grazia, 1993. *Storia della bibliografia. Cataloghi a stampa. Bibliografie teologiche. Bibliografie filosofiche. Antonio Possevino*. Vol. 4. Ed. Alfredo Serrai. Rome: Bulzoni.

Ceñal, Ramón, 1953. "Juan Caramuel: Su epistolario con Athanasio Kircher, S.J." *Revista de Filosofia* 44: 101–148.

Certeau, Michel de, 1974. "La Réforme de l'Intérieur au Temps d'Aquaviva." In *Les Jésuites: Spiritualité et Activités*. 53–69. Paris and Rome: Beauchesne/Centrum Ignatianum.

Chaine, M., 1933. "Une Composition oubliée du Père Kircher." *Revue de l'Orient Chretien* 29: 196–208.

Charles-Daubert, Françoise, 1985. "Le 'Libertinage érudit' et le problème du conservatisme politique." In *L'État baroque: Regards sur la pensée politique de la France du premier XVIIᵉ siècle*. Ed. Henri Méchoulan. 179–202. Paris: Vrin.

Chartier, Roger, 1986. "Pratiques de la lecture." In *Histoire de la vie privée*. Eds. Philippe Ariès and Georges Duby. Vol. 3: 126–144. Paris: Le Seuil.

———, 1987. *Lectures et lecteurs dans la France d'Ancien Régime*. Paris: Editions Promodis.

Cipriani, Giovanni, 1993. *Gli obelischi egizi. Politica e cultura nella Roma barocca*. Florence: Olschki.

City of Rastatt, 1981. *Universale Bildung im Barock: Der Gelehrte Athanasius Kircher. Eine Ausstellung der Stadt Rastatt in Zusammenarbeit mit der Badischen Landesbibliothek*. Rastatt: Stadt Rastatt; Karlsruhe: Bad. Landesbibliothek. The Cleveland Museum of Art, 1951. *Portrait Miniatures: The Edward B. Greene Collection*. Cleveland: The Cleveland Museum of Art.

Clough, Cecil H., 1993. "Italian Renaissance Portraiture and Printed Portrait-Books." In *The Italian Book, 1465–1800*. Ed. Denis Reidy. 183–224. London: The British Library.

Cohen, Thomas M., 1998. *The Fire of Tongues: António Vieira and the Missionary Church in Brazil and Portugal*. Stanford, CA: Stanford University Press.

Collani, Claudia von, 1996. "Theology and Chronology in *Sinicae historiae Decas Prima*." In Demarchi and Scartezzini 1996, pp. 231–244.

———, 1998. "Johann Adam Schall von Bell: Weltbild und Weltchronologie in der Chinamission im 17. Jahrhundert." In *Western Learning and Christianity in China: The Contribution and Impact of Adam Schall von Bell, S.J. (1592–1666)*. Ed. Roman Malek, S.V.D. 2 vols. Vol. 1: 79–100. Sankt Augustin.

———, 2000. "Theologie und Chronologie in Martinis *Sinicae historiae decas prima*" In *Martino Martini S.J. (1614–1661) und die Chinamission im 17. Jahrhundert*. Eds. Roman Malek and Arnold Zingerle. Sankt Augustin.

Compère, Marie-Madeleine, and Julia, Dominique, 1984. *Les collèges français, XVIe XVIIIe siècle: La France du midi*. Vol. 1. Paris: Editions du CNRS.

Cook, Michael, 1983. "Pharaonic History in Medieval Europe." *Studia Islamica* 57.

Corradino, Saverio, 1990. "Athanasius Kircher: Damnatio memoriae e revisione in atto." *Archivum Historicum Societatis Iesu* 59: 3–26.

———, 1993. "L''Ars magna lucis et umbrae' di Athanasius Kircher." *Archivum Historicum Societatis Iesu* 62: 249–279.

———, 1996. "Athanasius Kircher matematico." *Studi secenteschi* 37: 159–180.

Costantini, Claudio, 1969. *Baliani e i Gesuiti*. Florence: Giunti-Barbèra.

Coutinho, Afrânio, 1994. *Do Barroco, ensaios*. Rio de Janeiro: Editora UFRJ.

Couturat, Louis, and Léopold Leau, 1903. *Histoire de la langue universelle*. Paris: Hachette.

Cram, David, and Jaap Maat, 1999. "Universal Language Schemes in the Seventeenth Century." In *Geschichte der Sprachwissenschaften / History of the Language Sciences / Histoire des Sciences du Langage*. Eds. Sylvain Auroux, Konrad Koerner, Hans-Josef Niederehe, and Kees Versteegh. 2 vols. Vol. 1: 1030–1043. Berlin and New York: De Gruyter.

Crombach, Prf. 1932–1935. "Jesuitengeneral Goswin Nickel von Coslar. Erbauliches aus seinem Leben." *Mitteilungen aus den deutschen Provinzen* 13: 283–288.

Dainville, François de, 1978. "Foyers de culture scientifique dans la France méditerranéenne du XVIe au XVIIIfe siècle." In *L'éducation des Jésuites, XVIe–XVIIIe siècles*. Ed. Marie-Madeleine Compère. 311–322. Paris: Minuit.

Damianaki, Chrysa, 2000. *Galileo e le arti figurative*. Rome: Vecchiarelli.

Dan, Joseph, 1987. *Gershom Scholem and the Mystical Dimension of Jewish History*. New York: New York University Press.

Dan, Joseph, ed., 1997. *The Christian Kabbalah: Jewish Mystical Books and their Christian Interpreters*. Cambridge: Harvard College Library.

Darwin, C., 1859. *The Origin of Species*. London: Murray.

Daston, Lorraine, 1994. "Baconian Facts, Academic Civility, and the Prehistory of Objectivity." In *Rethinking Objectivity*. Ed. Allan Megill. 37–63. Durham, NC: Duke University Press.

———, 2000. "Preternatural Philosophy." In *Biographies of Scientific Objects*. Ed. Lorraine Daston. 15–41. Chicago and London: University of Chicago Press.

Daston, Lorraine, and Katharine Park, 1998. *Wonders and the Order of Nature, 1150–1750*. New York: Zone Books.

Daut, R., 1975. *Imago: Untersuchungen zum Bildbegriff der Römer*. Heidelberg: Winter.

David, Madeleine V., 1965. *Le Débat sur les écritures et l'hieroglyphe aux XVIIᵉ et XVIIIᵉ siècles et l'application de la notion de déchiffrement aux écritures mortes*. Paris: S.E.V.P.E.N.

Dear, Peter. 1995. *Discipline and Experience: The Mathematical Way in the Scientific Revolution*. Chicago and London: University of Chicago Press.

Dehergne, Joseph, 1973. *Répertoire des Jésuites de Chine de 1552 à 1800*. Rome and Paris: Institutum Historicum S.I./Letouzey & Ané.

Delattre, Pierre, 1949–57. *Les établissements des jésuites en France depuis quatre siècles: Répertoire topo-bibliographique*. 5 vols. Enghien: Institut supérieur de théologie.

Deleuze, Gilles, 1993. *The Fold: Leibniz and the Baroque*. Trans. Tom Conley. Minneapolis University: University of Minnesota Press.

Della Vida, Giorgio Levi, 1939. *Ricerche sulla formazione del più antico fondo dei manoscritti orientali della Biblioteca Vaticana*. Vatican City: Biblioteca Apostolica Vaticana.

Delumeau, Jean, 1959. *Vie économique et sociale dans la Rome de la seconde moitié du XVIe siècle*. Paris: De Boccard.

Demarchi, Franco, and Scartezzini, Riccardo, eds., 1996. *Martino Martini: A Humanist and Scientist in Seventeenth Century China*. Trent: Università degli Studi di Trento.

De Martino, Ernesto, 2002. *La terra del rimorso. Il Sud tra religione e magia*. Milan: Net.

Demel, Walter, 1986. "Antike Quellen und die Theorien des 16. Jahrhunderts zur Frage der Abstammung der Chinesen: Überlegungen zu einem frühneuzeitlichen Diskussionsthema." *Saekulum* 37: 199–211.

Démoustier, Adrien, 1995. "La distinction des fonctions et l'exercice du pouvoir selon les règles de la Compagnie de Jésus." In *Les Jésuites à la Renaissance: Système éducatif et production du savoir*. Ed. Luce Giard. 3–33. Paris: PUF.

Démoustier, Adrien, and Dominique Julia, eds. 1997. *Ratio studiorum: [Version de 1599], édition bilingue latin-français*. Paris: Belin.

Depéret, Charles, 1909. *The Transformations of the Animal World*. London: Kegan Paul, Trench, Trübner.

Destefano, Michael Thomas, 1977. "Miracles and Monasticism in Mid-Colonial Puebla, 1600–1750: Charismatic Religion in a Conservative Society." Ph.D. dissertation. University of Florida.

Dibon, Paul, 1990. *Regards sur la Hollande du siècle d'or*. Naples: Vivarium.

Diepenbroick-Grüter, Hans Dietrich von, 1954–63. *Porträtsammlung*. Teckenburg: Selbstverlag.

Dingping, Shen, 2000. "La relacion entre la Iglesia mexicana y la evangelizacion en China en los siglos XVI y XVII: Un estudio comparativo sobre sus estrategias." *Estudios de Asia y Africa* 35: 47–76.

Dinis, Alfredo de Oliveira, 1989. *The Cosmology of Giovanni Battista Riccioli (1598–1671)*. Ph.D. dissertation, Cambridge, UK: Cambridge University.

Dixon, Paul, 1984. "Balance, Pyramids, Crowns, and the Geometry of Sor Juana Inés de la Cruz." *Hispania* 67: 560–566.

Dompnier, Bernard, 1996. "La Compagnie de Jésus et la Mission de l'Intérieur." In *Les Jésuites à l'Age Baroque (1540–1640)*. Eds. Luce Giard and Louis de Vaucelles. 155–179. Grenoble: Jérôme Millon.

Donato, Maria Pia, 2000. *Accademie romane. Una storia sociale (1671–1824)*. Rome: Edizioni Scientifiche Italiane.

Draper, J. W., 1874. *History of the Conflict between Religion and Science*. New York: Appleton.

Droixhe, Daniel, 1978. *La linguistique et l'appel de l'histoire (1600–1800)*. Geneva.

Dubois, Claude-Gilbert, 1993. *Le Baroque: Profondeurs de l'apparence*. 1973. Bordeaux: Presses Universitaires de Bordeaux.

Duhr, Bernhard, S.J, 1928. *Geschichte der Jesuiten in den Ländern deutschsprachiger Zunge im 18. Jahrhundert*. Munich and Regensburg: Verlagsanstalt vorm. G. J. Manz.

Eamon, William, 1995. *Science and the Secrets of Nature*. Princeton, NJ: Princeton University Press.

Eco, Umberto, 1989. *Foucault's Pendulum*. Trans. William Weaver. New York: Harcourt Brace Jovanich.

———, 1995. *The Search for a Perfect Language*. Oxford: Blackwell.

———, 2001. "Kircher tra steganografia e poligrafia." In Lo Sardo 2001, pp. 209–213.

Eisenstein, Elizabeth, 1979. *The Printing Press as an Agent of Change*. 2 vols. Cambridge, UK: Cambridge University Press.

Elm, Susanna et al, eds, 2000. *Orthodoxie, christianisme, historie*. Rome: Ecole Française de Rome.

Evans, R. J. W., 1979. *The Making of the Habsburg Monarchy, 1550–1700: An Interpretation*. Oxford: Clarendon Press.

Fabre, Pierre-Antoine, 1991. "Constitutions et règles: Introduction." In Ignace de Loyola, *Ecrits*. Ed. Maurice Giuliani. 385–391. Paris: Desclée de Brouwer.

———, 2000. "Ignace de Loyola en procès d'orthodoxie (1525–1622)." In *Orthodoxie, christianisme, historie*. Eds. Susanna Elm, Eric Rebillard, and Antonella Romano. 101–124. Rome: Ecole française de Rome.

Fabre, Pierre-Antoine, and Vincent Bernard, forthcoming. *Histoire culturelle et histoire sociale: les missions religieuses dans le monde ibériques: Actes du colloque international de Paris, 25–27 mai 2000*. Paris: éditions de l'EHESS.

Fabre, Pierre-Antoine, and Antonella Romano, 1999. "Introduction." *Revue de Synthèse* 120 [Special issue on *Les Jésuites dans le monde moderne: Nouvelles approches historiographiques*].

Faivre, A., and F. Tristan, eds., 1979. *Kabbalistes Chrétiens*. Paris: Albin Michel.

Feingold, Mordechai, ed., 2003. *Jesuit Science and the Republic of Letters*. Cambridge, MA: MIT Press.

Feldhay, Rivka, 1987. "Knowledge and Salvation in Jesuit Culture." *Science in Context* 1: 195–213.

———, 1995. *Galileo and the Church: Political Inquisition or Critical Dialogue*. Cambridge, UK: Cambridge University Press.

———, 1999. "The Cultural Field of Jesuit Science." In O'Malley et al. 1999, pp. 107–130.

Ferrier, Jacques, 1988. "Du côté de chez Peiresc avec J.-J. Bouchard." In *L'été Peiresc. Fioretti II. Nouveaux mélanges composés et offerts sous la direction de J. Ferrier*. 50–53. Avignon: Aubanel.

Findlen, Paula, 1994. *Possessing Nature: Museums, Collecting, and Scientific Culture in Early Modern Italy*. Berkeley: University of California Press.

———, 1995. "Scientific Spectacle in Baroque Rome: Athanasius Kircher and the Roman College Museum." *Roma moderna e contemporanea* 3: 625–665. Longer version reprinted in *Jesuit Science and the Republic of Letters*. Ed. Mordechai Feingold. 225–284. Cambridge, MA: MIT Press, 2002.

———, 2000. "The Janus Faces of Science in the Seventeenth Century: Athanasius Kircher and Isaac Newton." In *Rethinking the Scientific Revolution*. Ed. Margaret J. Osler. 221–246. Cambridge, UK: Cambridge University Press.

———, 2001a. "Un'incontro con Kircher a Roma." In Lo Sardo 2001, pp. 39–48.

———, 2001b. "Science, History, and Erudition: Athanasius Kircher's Museum at the Collegio Romano." In *The Great Art of Knowing: The Baroque Encyclopedia of Athanasius Kircher*. Ed. Daniel Stolzenberg. 17–26. Stanford, CA: Stanford University Libraries.

Fletcher, John, 1968. "Athanasius Kircher and the Distribution of His Books." *The Library*, ser. 5, 23: 108–117.

———, 1970. "Astronomy in the Life and Work of Athanasius Kircher." *Isis* 61: 52–67.

———, 1972. "Claude Fabri de Peiresc and the Other French Correspondents of Athanasius Kircher (1602–1680)." *Australian Journal of French Studies* 9: 250–273.

———, 1982. "Drei unbekannte Briefe Athanasius Kirchers an Fürstabt Joachim von Gravenegg." *Fuldaer Geschichtsblätter* 58: 92–104.

———, 1986. "Kircher and Duke August of Wolfenbüttel: Museal Thoughts." In Casciato et al., 1986, pp. 282–294.

———, ed., 1988a. *Athanasius Kircher und seine Beziehungen zum gelehrten Europa seiner Zeit*. Wiesbaden: Harrassowitz.

————, 1988b. "Athanasius Kircher: A Man under Pressure." In Fletcher 1988a, pp. 1–15.

————, 1988c. "Athanasius Kircher and His Correspondence." In Fletcher 1988a, pp. 139–178.

————, 1988d. "Kircher's Works." In Fletcher 1988a, pp. 179–189.

Foucault, Michel, 1966. *Les Mots et les choses*. Paris: Gallimard.

Freedberg, David, 2002. *The Eye of the Lynx: Galileo, His Friends, and the Beginnings of Modern Natural History*. Chicago: University of Chicago Press.

Friedlander, Paul, 1937. "Athanasius Kircher und Leibniz: Ein Beitrag zur Geschichte der Polyhistorie im XVII. Jahrhundert." *Rendiconti della Pontificia Accademia Romana di Archeologia* 13, f. 3–4: 229–247

Frommel, Christoph L., ed., 2000. *Francesco Borromini e l'universo barroco*. Milan: Electa.

Frutaz, Antonio Pietro, ed., 1952. *Le piante di Roma*. Vol. 2. Rome: Istituto di studi romani.

Fück, Johann, 1944. "Die arabischen Studien in Europa vom 12. bis in den Anfang des 19. Jahrhunderts." In *Beiträge zur Arabistik, Semitistik und Islamwissenschaft*. Eds. Richard Hartmann and Helmuth Scheel. 85–253. Leipzig.

Fumaroli, Marc, 1997. "La République des Lettres redécouverte." In *Il vocabolario della République des Lettres: terminologia filosofica e storia della filosofia*. Ed. M. Fattori. 41–56. Florence: Olschki.

Gabrieli, Giuseppe, 1989. *Contributi alla storia dell'Accademia dei Lincei*. Rome: Accademia Nazionale dei Lincei.

Galassi Paluzzi, Carlo, ed., 1930. *Mostra di Roma secentesca*. Rome: Istituto di Studi Romani.

Galluzzi, Paolo, 1977. "Galileo contro Copernico." *Annali dell' Istituto e Museo di Storia della Scienza di Firenze* 2: 87–148.

————, 1993. "Gassendi e l'affaire Galilée delle legi del moto." *Giornale critico della filosofia italiana* 74: 86–119.

Gambaro, Ivana, 1989. *Astronomia e Tecniche di Ricerca nelle lettere di G.B. Riccioli ad A. Kircher*. Genova: Quaderni del Centro di studio sulla storia della tecnica del Consiglio Nazionale delle Ricerche.

Gaos, José, 1960. "El sueño de un sueño." *Historia Mexicana* 10: 54–71.

García Villoslada, Ricardo, 1954. *Storia del Collegio Romano dal suo inizio (1551) alla soppressione della Compagnia di Gesù (1773)*. Rome: Universita Gregoriana.

Gardair, Jean-Michel, 1981. "I Lincei: I soggetti, i luoghi, le attività." *Quaderni storici* [Special issue on *Accademie scientifiche del' 600*. Eds. Paolo Galluzzi, Carlo Poni, and Maurizio Torrini]: 763–787.

————, 1984. *Le "Giornale de' Letterati" de Rome (1668–1681)*. Florence: Olschki.

Garin, Eugenio, 1973. *Umanesimo italiano*. Bari: G. Laterza.

Gatti, Hilary, 2000. *Giordano Bruno and Renaissance Science*. Ithaca, NY: Cornell University Press.

Geoffroy, E. "Al-Suyuti." In *The New Encyclopedia of Islam*. Cyril Glassé Atta Nira Press, 2001 Walnut Creek, CA.

Giard, Luce, 1991. "Lettres et instructions: Introduction." In Ignatius de Loyola, *Ecrits*. Ed. Maurice Giuliani. 619–627. Paris: Desclée de Brouwer.

————, 1993. "La constitution du système éducatif jésuite." In *Etudes sur le vocabulaire intellectuel du Moyen Age, VI, Vocabulaire des collèges universitaires (XIII–XVIe siècles): Actes du colloque de Leuven 9–11 avril 1992*. Ed. Olga Weijers. 131–148. Turnhout: Brepols.

————, ed., 1995. *Les Jésuites à la Renaissance: Système éducatif et production du savoir*. Paris: PUF.

————, 1996. "Relire les Constitutions." In *Les Jésuites à l'âge baroque (1540–1640)*. Eds. Luce Giard and Louis de Vaucelles. 37–60. Grenoble: Jérôme Millon.

Gibbon, Edward, 1966. *Memoirs of My Life*. Georges A. Bonnard, ed. London: Nelson.

Gillespie, Charles C., ed. 1970– *Dictionary of Scientific Bibliography*. New York: C. Scribner's Sons.

Gillespie, Gerald, 1978. "Primal Utterance: Observations on Kuhlmann's Correspondence with Kircher, in View of Leibniz' Theories." In *Wege der Worte: Festschrift für Wolfgang Fleischhauer*. Ed. Donald C. Riechel. 27–46. Cologne: Böhlau.

Godman, Peter, 2000. *The Saint as Censor: Robert Bellarmine between Inquisition and Index*. Leiden: Brill.

Godwin, Joscelyn, 1979. *Athanasius Kircher: A Renaissance Man and the Quest for Lost Wisdom*. London: Thames and Hudson.

————, 1988. "Athanasius Kircher and the Occult." In Fletcher 1988a, pp. 17–36.

Goldberg, Edward, 1988. *After Vasari: History, Art and Patronage in Late Medici Florence*. Princeton, NJ: Princeton University Press.

Goldgar, Anne, 1995. *Impolite Learning: Conduct and Community in the Republic of Letters, 1680–1750*. New Haven, CT: Yale University Press.

Gómez de Liaño, Ignacio, 1986. *Athanasius Kircher: Itinerario del éxtasis o las imagines de un saber universal*. 2 vols. Madrid: Ediciones Siruela.

Goodman, Dena, 1994. *The Republic of Letters: A Cultural History of the French Enlightenment*. Ithaca, NY: Cornell University Press.

Gorman, Michael John, 1996. "A Matter of Faith? Christoph Scheiner, Jesuit Censorship and the Trial of Galileo." *Perspectives on Science* 4: 283–320.

———, 1998. *The Scientific Counter-Revolution: Mathematics, Natural Philosophy and Experimentalism in Jesuit Culture, 1580–c.1670*. Ph.D. dissertation. European University Institute: Florence.

———, 1999. "From 'The Eyes of All' to 'Usefull Quarries in philosophy Sciences, and the Arts.'" In O'Malley et al., 1999a, pp. 170–189.

———, 2001. "Between the Demonic and the Miraculous: Athanasius Kircher and the Baroque Culture of Machines." In Stolzenberg 2001a, pp. 59–70.

———, 2002. "Mathematics and Modesty in the Society of Jesus: The Problems of Christoph Grienberger." In *Archimedes*. Ed. Mordechai Feingold.

Gorman, Michael John, and Nick Wilding, 2000. *La Technica Curiosa di Kaspar Schott*. Rome: Edizioni dell'Elefante.

———, 2001. "Athanasius Kircher e la cultura barocca delle macchine." In Lo Sardo 2001, pp. 217–237.

Gould, Stephen Jay, 1998. *Leonardo's Mountain of Clams and the Diet of Worms*. New York: Harmony.

———, 2002a. "Both Neonate and Elder: The First Fossil of 1557." *Paleobiology* 28: 1–8.

———, 2002b. "Drawing a Gloriously False Inference." *Paleobiology* 28: (2), pp. 179–183.

Grafton, Anthony, 1983–93. *Joseph Scaliger: A Study in the History of Classical Scholarship*. 2 vols. Oxford: Oxford University Press.

———, 1990. *Forgers and Critics*. Princeton, NJ: Princeton University Press.

———, 1991. *Defenders of the Text*. Cambridge, MA: Harvard University Press.

———, 1995. "Tradition and Technique in Historical Chronology." In *Ancient History and the Antiquarian: Essays in Memory of Arnaldo Momigliano*. Eds. Michael H. Crawford and C. R. Ligota. 15–31. London: Warburg Institute, University of London.

———, 1997a. "*Fragmenta historicorum Graecorum*: Fragments of Some Lost Enterprises." In *Collecting Fragments / Fragmente Sammeln*. Ed. Glenn Most. 124–143. Göttingen.

———, 1997b. *The Footnote: A Curious History*. Cambridge, MA: Harvard University Press. also 1999

Gravit, Francis W., 1938. "Peiresc et les études coptes en France au XVIIe siècle." *Bulletin de la société d'archéologie copte* 4: 1–21.

Gregory, Brad S., 1999. *Salvation at Stake: Christian Martyrdom in Early Modern Europe*. Cambridge, MA:, and London: Harvard University Press.

Grell, Chantal, 1995. *Le Dix-huitième siècle et l'antiquité en France, 1680–1789*. 2 vols. Oxford: Voltaire Foundation.

Griggs, Tamara, 2000. "Antiquaries and the Nile Mosaic: The Changing Face of Erudition." *Ricerche di storia dell'arte* 72: 37–48.

———, 2002. *The Changing Face of Erudition: Antiquaries in the Age of the Grand Tour*. Ph.D. dissertation. Princeton University.

Gruzinski, Serge 1993. *The Conquest of Mexico: The Incorporation of Indian Societies into the Western World, 16th–18th Centuries*. Trans. Eileen Corrigan. Cambridge, UK: Polity Press.

Haakman, Anton, 1995. *Il mondo sotteraneo di Athanasius Kircher*. Milan: Garzanti. [Italian translation of *De onderaardse wereld van Athanasius Kircher*. Amsterdam, 1991.]

Habermas, Jürgen, 1989. *The Structural Transformation of the Public Sphere*. Trans. Thomas Burger and Frederick Lawrence. Cambridge, UK: Polity Press.

Hankins, Thomas L., and Robert J. Silverman, 1995. *Instruments and the Imagination*. Princeton, NJ: Princeton University Press.

Hansen, João Adolfo, 1989. *A sátira e o engenho: Gregório de matos e a Bahia do século XVII*. São Paulo: Companhia das Letras, Secretaria de Estado da Cultura.

Harris, Steven J., 1989. "Transposing the Merton Thesis: Apostolic Spirituality and the Establishment of the Jesuit Scientific Tradition." *Science in Context* 3: 89–108.

————, 1996. "Confession-Building, Long-Distance Networks, and the Organization of Jesuit Science." *Early Science and Medicine* 1: 287–313.

————, 1998. "Long-Distance Corporations, Big Sciences, and the Geography of Knowledge." *Configurations* 6: 269–304.

————, 1999. "Mapping Jesuit Science: The Role of Travel in the Geography of Knowledge." In O'Malley et al. 1999a, pp. 212–240.

————, forthcoming. "Center, Periphery, and Networks of Exchange: The Circulation of Natural Knowledge in the Society of Jesus." In *From Rome to Eternity: The Catholic Imagination in Early Modern Italy*. Eds. Pamela M. Jones and Thomas Worcester. Cambridge, UK: Cambridge University Press.

Haskell, Francis, 1993. *History and Its Images: Art and the Interpretation of the Past*. New Haven, CT, and London: Yale University Press.

Hausberger, Bernd, 1995. *Jesuiten aus Mitteleuropa im kolonialen Mexico: Eine Bio-Bibliographie*. Vienna: Verlage für Geschichte und Politik.

Heigel, Theodor, 1881. "Zur Geschichte des Censurwesens in der Gesellschaft Jesu." *Archiv für Geschichte des Deutschen Buchhandels* 6: 162–167.

Heilbron, John L., 1989. "Science in the Church." *Science in Context* 3.1: 9–29.

————, 1999. *The Sun in the Church*. Cambridge, MA: Harvard University Press.

Hein, Olaf, 1993. *Die Drucker und Verleger der Werke des Polyhistors Athanasius Kircher S.J.* Cologne: Böhlau.

Heinrich, Georges, 1892. *Lateinisch-Deutsches Handwörterbuch*. Hannover: Hahn.

Hellyer, Marcus, 1996. "'Because the Authority of My Superiors Commands': Censorship, Physics and the German Jesuits." *Early Science and Medicine* 1: 319–354.

————, 1998. "The Last of the Aristotelians: The Transformation of Jesuit Physics in Germany, 1630–1773." Ph.D. dissertation. University of California at San Diego.

————, 1999. "Jesuit Physics in Eighteenth-Century Germany." In O'Malley et al. 1999a, pp. 538–554.

Hine, William, 1988. "Athanasius Kircher and Magnetism." In Fletcher 1988a, pp. 79–99.

Hofmann, Siegfried, 1994. "Das Orban'sche Museum in Ingolstadt." In *Macrocosmos in Microcosmo: Die Welt in der Stube. Zur Geschichte des Sammelns, 1450–1800*. Ed. Andreas Grote. 661–677. Opladen: Leske und Budrich.

Homet, Jean-Marie, 1982. *Astronomie et astronomes en Provence, 1680–1730*. Aix-en-Provence: Publisud.

Hsia, Florence, 1999a. "Jesuits, Jupiter's Satellites, and the Académie Royale des Sciences." In O'Malley et al. 1999a, pp. 241–257.

————, 1999b. "Some Observations on the *Observations*: The Decline of the French Jesuit Scientific Mission in China." *Revue de synthèse* 4: 305–333.

Iannaccone, Isaia, 1998. *Johann Schreck Terrentius: Le scienze rinascimentali e lo spirito dell'Accademia dei Lincei nella Cina dei Ming*. Naples: Istituto universitario orientale, Dipartimento di studi asiatici.

Ibsen, Kristine, 1999. *Women's Spiritual Autobiography in Colonial Spanish America*. Gainesville: University Press of Florida.

Idel, Moshe, 1988. *Kabbalah: New Perspectives*. New Haven, CT: Yale University Press.

Iliffe, Robert, 1999a. "Foreign Bodies: Travel, Empire and the Early Royal Society of London. Part II. The Land of Experimental Knowledge." *Canadian Journal of History / Annales Canadiennes d'Histoire* 34: 23–50.

————, 1999b. "Lying Wonders and Juggling Tricks: Religion, Nature, and Imposture in Early Modern England." In *Everything Connects*. Eds. James E. Force and David S. Katz. 185–209. Leiden: Brill.

Insolera, Italo, 1980. *Le città nella storia d'Italia: Roma*. Bari: Laterza.

Institutum, 1892–93. *Institutum Societatis Iesu*. Florence: Ex typographia a SS. Conceptione.

Iverson, Erik, 1968. *Obelisks in Exile*. Vol. 1. *The Obelisks of Rome*. Copenhagen: G. E. C. Gad.

————, 1993 [1961]. *The Myth of Egypt and Its Hieroglyphs in European Tradition*. Princeton, NJ: Princeton University Press.

Jaffary, Nora, 1999. "Virtue and Transgression: The Certification of Authentic Mysticism in the Mexican Inquisition." *The Catholic Southwest* 10: 9–28.

Jaffé, David, 1988. "Peiresc's Famous Men Picture Gallery." In *L'Eté Peiresc: Fioretti II: nouveaux mélanges*. 133–140. Aubanel [Avignon]: Académie du Var.

————, 1994. "Wissenschaftlicher Betrieb in einem Raritätenkabinett." In *Macrocosmos in Microcosmo: Die Welt in der Stube. Zur Geschichte des Sammelns, 1450–1800*. Ed. Andreas Grote. 301–322. Opladen: Leske und Budrich.

Jahn, M. E., and D. J. Woolf, 1963. *The Lying Stones of Johann Bartholomew Adam Beringer*. Berkeley: University of California Press.

Jensen, Lionel, 1997. *Manufacturing Confucianism: Chinese Traditions and Universal Civilization*. Durham, NC: Duke University Press.

Johns, Adrian, 1998. *The Nature of the Book: Print and Knowledge in the Making*. Chicago: Chicago University Press.

Kantola, Ilkka, 1994. *Probability and Moral Uncertainty in Late Medieval and Early Modern Times*. Helsinki: Luther-Agricola Society.

Kathke, Petra, 1997. *Porträt und Accessoire: Eine Bildnisform im 16. Jahrhundert*. Berlin: Reimer.

Keohane, Nannerl O., 1980. *Philosophy and the State in France: The Renaissance to the Enlightenment*. Princeton, NJ: Princeton University Press.

Kirk, Pamela, 1998. *Sor Juana Inés de la Cruz: Religion, Art, and Feminism*. New York: Continuum.

Klempt, Adalbert, 1960. *Die Säkularisierung der universalhistorischen Auffassung*. Göttingen.

Klinger, Linda Susan, 1991. *The Portrait Collection of Paolo Giovio*. Ph.D. dissertation. Princeton University.

Knowlson, James, 1975. *Universal Language Schemes in England and France, 1600–1800*. Toronto and Buffalo, NY: University of Toronto Press.

Koeman, Cornelis, 1970. *Joan Blaeu and His Grand Atlas*. Amsterdam: Theatrum Orbis Terrarum.

Koselleck, Reinhart, 1988. *Critique and Crisis: Enlightenment and the Pathogenesis of Modern Society*. Oxford: Berg.

Koyré, Alexandre, 1953. "An Experiment in Measurement." *Proceedings of the American Philosophical Society* 97: 222–237.

Kramer, Roswitha, 1997. " '. . . ex ultimo angulo orbis': Atanasio Kircher y el Nuevo Mundo." In *Pensamiento europeo y cultura colonial*. Eds. Karl Kohut and Sonia V. Rose. 320–377. Frankfurt: Vervuert.

Krempel, Ulla, 1968. "Die Orbansche Sammlung, eine Raritätenkammer des 18. Jahrhunderts." *Münchner Jahrbuch der bildenden Kunst* 19: 169–184.

Kühn-Hattenhauer, Dorothee, 1979. *Das graphische Oeuvre des Francesco Villamena (1538–1607)*. Ph.D. dissertation. Freie Universität: Berlin.

Kuntz, Marion Leathers, 1987. "Guillaume Postel and the Syriac Gosepls of Athanasius Kircher." *Renaissance Quarterly* 40: 465–484.

Labrot, Gérard, 1987. *L'image de Rome: Une arme pour la Contre-Réforme*. Seyssel: Champ Vallon.

Lach, Donald, 1965. *Asia in the Making of Europe*. Vol. 1. *The Century of Discovery*. Chicago: University of Chicago Press.

————, 1993. *Asia in the Making of Europe*. Vol. 3. *Century of Advance*. Chicago, University of Chicago Press.

Lafaye, Jacques, 1976. *Quetzalcoatl and Guadalupe: The Formation of Mexican National Consciousness, 1531–1813*. Trans. Benjamin Keen. Chicago: University of Chicago Press.

Lafuente, Antonio, and José Sala Catalá, eds., 1992. *Ciencia colonial en America*. Madrid: Alianza.

Lamalle, Edmond, 1968. "La Documentation d'Histoire Missionnaire dans le 'Fondo Gesuitico' aux Archives Romaines de la Compagnie de Jésus." *Euntes docete* 21: 131–176.

————, 1981. "L'archivio di un grande ordine religioso: L'Archivio Generale della Compagnia di Gesù." *Archivia Ecclesiae* 82: 92–120.

Larner, John, 1999. *Marco Polo and the Discovery of the World*. New Haven, CT: Yale University Press.

Lantschoot, Arnold van, 1948. *Un Précurseur d'Athanase Kircher: Thomas Obicini et la Scala Vat. Copte 71*. Louvain: Bureaux du Muséon.

Latanza, Antonio, 1995. *Il ripristino dell'organo idraulico del Quirinale*. Rome.

Latour, Bruno, 1996. *Aramis, or the Love of Technology*. Trans. Catherine Porter. Cambridge, MA: Harvard University Press.

Lattis, James, 1994. *Between Copernicus and Galileo: Christoph Clavius and the Collapse of Ptolomaic Cosmology*. Chicago: Chicago University Press.

Le Blanc, Charles, 1854. *Manuel de l'Amateur d' Estampes*. Paris: Jannet.

Le Goff, Jacques, 1988. "The Marvelous in the Medieval West." In *The Medieval Imagination*. Trans. Arthur Goldhammer. 27–44. Chicago: University of Chicago Press.

Leinkauf, Thomas, 1993. *Mundus combinatus: Studien zur Struktur der barocken Universalwissenschaft am Beispiel Athanasius Kirchers SJ (1602–1680)*. Berlin: Akademie Verlag.

Leonard, Irving A., 1929. *Don Carlos de Sigüenza y Góngora: A Mexican Savant of the Seventeenth Century*. Berkeley: University of California Press.

———, 1959. *Baroque Times in Old Mexico*. Ann Arbor: University of Michigan Press.

Lorente Medina, Antonio, 1996. *La prosa de Sigüenza y Góngora y la formación de la conciencia criolla mexicana*. Mexico City: Fondo de Cultura Económica.

Lo Sardo, Eugenio, 1993. *L'atlante della Cina di Michele Ruggieri, Poligrafico dello Stato*. Rome.

———, ed., 1999. *Iconismi e mirabilia da Athanasius Kircher*. Rome: Edizioni dell'Elefante.

———, ed., 2001. *Athanasius Kircher: Il Museo del Mondo*. Rome: Edizioni de Luca.

Los Empeños, 1995. *Los Empeños: Ensayos en Homenaje a Sor Juana Inés de la Cruz*. Mexico City: Universidad Autónoma de México.

Lucas, Thomas M., ed., 1993. *Saint, Site and Sacred Strategy: Ignatius, Rome and Jesuit Urbanism*. Vatican City: Biblioteca Apostolica Vaticana.

Lugli, Adalgisa, 1986. "Inquiry as Collection." *RES* 12: 109–124.

Luisetti, Federico, 2001. *Plus Ultra. Enciclopedismo barocco e modernità*. Turin: Trauben.

Lukács, Ladislaus, 1965–92. *Monumenta Paedagogica Societatis Iesu*. 7 vols. Rome: Institutum Historicum Societatis Iesu.

Magie des Wissens, 2003. *Magie des Wissens: Athanasius Kircher (1602–80) Jesuit und Universalgelehrter*. Fulda: Michael Imhof.

Malcolm, Noel, 2002. *Aspects of Hobbes*. Oxford: Oxford University Press.

Mancia, Anita, 1992. "Il Concetto di 'dottrina' fra gli *Esercizi Spirituali* (1539) e la *Ratio Studiorum* (1599)." *Archivum Historicum Societatis Jesu* 61: 3–70.

Manning, John, and Marc van Vaeck, 1999. *The Jesuits and the Emblem Tradition*. Turnhout : Brepols.

Marrone, Caterina, 1986. "Lingua Universale e Scrittura Segreta nell'Opera di Kircher." In Casciato et al. 1986, pp. 78–86.

———, 2002. *I geroglifici fantastici di Athanasius Kircher*. Viterbo: Stampa Alternativa & Graffitti.

Martínez-San Miguel, Yolanda, 1999. *Saberes americanos: Subalternidad y epistemología en los escritos de Sor Juana*. Pittsburgh: Nuevo Siglo/Internacional de Literature Iberoamericana.

Mascardi, Agostino, 1859. *Dell'Arte Istorica*. Ed. Adolfo Bartoli. Florence: F. Le Monnier.

Masson, Joseph, 1974. "La perspective missionnaire dans la spiritualité des Jésuites." In *Les Jésuites: Spiritualité et activités*. Paris: Beauchesne; Rome: Centrum Ignatianum. 135–154.

Mayer, Alicia, 1998. *Dos Americanos, dos pensamientos: Carlos de Sigüenza y Góngora y Cotton Mather*. Mexico City: Universidad Autónoma de México.

———, ed., 2000. *Carlos de Sigüenza y Góngora: Homenaje, 1700–2000*. 2 vols. Mexico City: Universidad Autónoma de México, 2000.

Maza, Francisco de la, ed., 1980. *Sor Juana Inés de la Cruz ante la historia*. Mexico City: Universidad Autónoma de México.

———, 1990. *Catarina de San Juan: Princesa de la India y visionaria de Puebla*. Mexico: Cien de Mexico.

Mazza, Claudia, 2001. "Le antichità imperiali e i culti orientali: L'Iseo Campense." In Lo Sardo 2001, pp. 133–141.

McCracken, George, 1948. "Athanasius Kircher's Universal Polygraphy," *Isis* 39: 215–227.

Méchin, Edouard, 1890. *L'enseignement en Provence avant la Révolution: Annales du Collège Royal Bourbon d'Aix depuis les premières démarches faites pour sa fondation jusqu'au 7 ventôse an III, époque de sa suppression*. Vol. 1. Marseille.

Mély, Fernand de., 1922. *La Virga Aurea du Fr. J.-B. Hepburn d'Écosse*. Paris: Éditions Ernest Leroux.

Mercati, Angelo, 1951. "Notizie sul gesuita Cristoforo Borri e su sue 'inventioni' da carte finora sconosciute di Pietro della Valle, il pellegrino." *Pontificia Academia Scientiarum, Acta* 15: 25–45.

Merrill, Brian L., ed., 1989. *Athanasius Kircher (1602–1680): Jesuit Scholar*. An Exhibition of his Works in the Harold B. Lee Library Collections at Brigham Young University. Provo, UT: Friends of the Brigham Young University Library.

Merrim, Stephanie, ed., 1991. *Feminist Perspectives on Sor Juana Inés de la Cruz*. Detroit: Wayne State University Press.

———, 1999. *Early Modern Women's Writing and Sor Juana Inés de la Cruz*. Nashville: Vanderbilt University Press.

Mertens, Dieter, 1997. "Oberrheinische Humanisten im Bild: Zum Gelehrtenbildnis um 1500." In *Bild und Geschichte. Studien zur politischen Ikonographie*. Eds. Konrad Krimm and Herwig John. 221–248. Sigmaringen: Jan Thorbecke.

Michelet, Jules, 1880 [1843]. *Des Jésuites*. Paris: Calmann Lévy.

Miller, Peter N., 1997a. "An Antiquary between Philology and History: Peiresc and the Samaritans." In *History and the Disciplines*. Ed. Donald R. Kelley. 163–184. Rochester, NY: Rochester University Press.

———, 1997b. "Les origines de la Bible Polyglotte de Paris: Philologia sacra, Contre-Reforme et raison d'état." *XVIIᵉ Siècle* 194: 57–66.

———, 2000. *Peiresc's Europe: Learning and Virtue in the Seventeenth Century*. New Haven, CT: Yale University Press.

———, 2001a. "The Antiquary's Art of Comparison: Peiresc and *Abraxas*." In *Philologie und Erkenntnis: Beiträge zu Begriff und Problem frühneuzeitlicher "Philologie"*. Ed. Ralph Häfner. 57–94. Tübingen: Max Niemeyer Verlag.

———, 2001b. "A Philologist, a Traveller and an Antiquary Rediscover the Samaritans in Seventeenth-Century Paris, Rome and Aix: Jean Morin, Pietro della Valle and N.-C. Fabri de Peiresc." In *Die Praktiken der Gelehrsamkeit in der Frühen Neuzeit*. Eds. Helmut Zedelmaier and Martin Mulsow. 123–146. Tübingen: Max Niemeyer Verlag.

———, 2001c. "Making the Paris Polyglot Bible: Humanism and Orientalism in the Early Seventeenth Century." In *Die europaische gelehrtenrepublik im Zeitalter des Konfessionalismus*. Ed. Herbert Jaumann. 59–85. Wiesbaden: Harrassowitz.

———, 2004. "The Mechanics of Christian-Jewish Intellectual Collaboration in Seventeenth-Century Provence: N.-C. Fabri de Peiresc and Salomon Azubi." In *Hebraica Veritas? Christian Hebraists, Jews, and the Study of Judaism in Early Modern Europe*. Eds. Allison Coudert and Jeffrey Shoulson. Philadelphia: University of Pennsylvania Press.

Minamiki, George, 1985. *The Chinese Rites Controversy from Its Beginning to Modern Times*. Chicago: Loyola University Press.

Miniati, Mara, 1989. "Les *Cistae Mathematicae* et l'organisation des connaissances au XVIIe siècle." In *Studies in the History of Scientific Instruments*. Eds. Christine Blondel, Françoise Parot, Anthony Turner, and Mari Williams. 43–51. London: Turner Books.

Mirto, Alfonso, 1989. "Le Lettere di Athanasius Kircher della Biblioteca Nazionale di Firenze." *Atti e Memorie dell'Accademia Toscana di Scienze e Lettere La Colombaria* LIV (Nuove Serie XL): 129–165.

———, 2000. "Lettere di Athanasius Kircher dell'Archivio di Stato di Firenze." *Atti e Memorie dell'Accademia Toscana di Scienze e Lettere La Colombaria* LXV (Nuove Serie LI): 217–240.

Momigliano, Arnaldo, 1966. "Ancient History and the Antiquarian." In *Studies in Historiography*. 1–39. London: Weidenfeld and Nicolson.

———, 1990. "The Rise of Antiquarian Research." In *The Classical Foundations of Modern Historiography*. 54–79. Berkeley: University of California Press.

Montané Martí, Julio César 1997. *Intriga en la corte: Eusebio Francisco Kino, Sor Juana Inés de la Cruz y Carlos de Sigüenza y Góngora*. Hermosillo: Universidad de Sonora.

Monumenta Ignatiana, 1934–38. *Monumenta Ignatiana: Ex autographis vel ex antiquioribus exemplis collecta*. Series tertia. Rome: Typis Pontificiae Universitatis Gregorianae.

Morgan, Ronald J., 1998. *Saints, Biographers and Creole Identity Formation in Colonial Spanish America*. Ph.D. dissertation. University of California at Santa Barbara.

Moroni, Gaetano, 1845. *Dizionario di erudizione storica-ecclesiastica da S. Pietro sino ai nostri giorni*. Vol. 52. Venezia. Vol. 14. Printed 1840–61.

Mortzfeld, Peter, ed., 1986–. *Die Porträtsammlung der Herzog August Bibliothek Wolfenbüttel*. Munich: Saur.

Mungello, David E., 1985. *Curious Land: Jesuit Accommodation and the Origins of Sinology*. Honolulu: University of Hawaii Press, 1989.

———, ed., 1994. *The Chinese Rites Controversy: Its History and Meaning*. Nettetal: Steyler Verlag.

Muriel, Josefina, 1994. "Lo que leían las mujeres de la Nueva España." In *La literatura novohispana*. Eds. José Pascual Buxó and Arnulfo Herrara. 159–173. Mexico City: Universidad Nacional Autónoma de México.

Myers, Kathleen, 1999. "Testimony for Canonization or Proof of Blasphemy? The New Spanish Inquisition and the Hagiographic Biography of Catarina de San Juan." In *Women in the Inquisition: Spain and the New World*. Ed. Mary E. Giles. 270–295. Baltimore: Johns Hopkins University Press. 1999.

Nicolson, Marjorie Hope, 1948. *Voyages to the Moon*. New York: Macmillan.

Nocenti, Luca, 2002. "Vedere mirabilia: Kircher, Redi, anatre settentrionali, rarità orientali e mosche nel miele." *Rivista di estetica*, n.s., 19: 36–60.

Nummedal, Tara, 2001. "Kircher's Subterranean World and the Dignity of the Geocosm." In Stolzenberg 2001a, pp. 37–47.

Nummedal, Tara, and Paula Findlen, 2000. "Words of Nature: Scientific Books in the Seventeenth Century." In John L. Thornton, *Thornton and Tully's Scientific Books, Libraries, and Collectors.* 4th edition. Ed. Andrew Hunter. 164–215. Aldershot: Ashgate.

O'Malley, John, 1984. *To Travel to Any Part of the World: Jerónimo Nadal and the Jesuit Vocation.* Studies in the Spirituality of Jesuits. Vol. 16, no. 2. St. Louis: American Assistancy Seminar on Jesuit Spirituality.

———, 1993. *The First Jesuits.* Cambridge, MA: Harvard University Press.

——— Gauvin Alexander, Bailey, Steven S. Harris, T. Frank Kennedy, eds., 1999a. *The Jesuits: Cultures, Sciences, and the Arts, 1540–1773.* Toronto: University of Toronto Press.

———, 1999b. "The Historiography of the Society of Jesus." In O'Malley et al., 1999a, pp. 3–37.

Omont, Henri, 1892. "Procédé d'imprimerie pour les langues orientales communiqué a Peiresc par le P. Gilles de Loches (1634)." *Revue des langues romanes,* ser. 4, 36: 488–495.

O'Neill, Robert K., 1986. "The Role of Private Libraries in the Dissemination of Knowledge about Asia in Sixteenth Century Europe." In *Asia and the West: Encounters and Exchanges from the Age of Explorations: Essays in Honor of Donald F. Lach.* Ed. Edwin J. Van Kley. 277–308. Notre Dame: Cross Cultural Publications.

Osorio Romero, Ignacio, 1986. *Historia de las bibliotecas novohispanas.* Mexico City: Sep. Dirección General de Bibliotecas.

Pachtler, G. M., 1887–94. *Ratio studiorum et institutiones scholasticae Societatis Iesu.* 4 vols. Berlin: A. Hofmann.

Pagden, Anthony, 1993. *European Encounters with the New World.* New Haven, CT, and London: Yale University Press.

Pajes Merriman, Mira, 1980. *Giuseppe Maria Crespi.* Milan: Rizzoli.

Paleotti, Gabriele, 1961. "Discorso intorno alle imagini sacre e profane (Bologna 1582)," in Paola Barocchi (Ed.): *Trattati d'arte del Cinquecento fra manierismo e controriforma.* Bari: G. Laterza. Vol. 2, 117–509.

Panofsky, Erwin, 1954. *Galileo as Critic of the Arts.* The Hague: Nijhoff.

Pascual-Buxó, José, 1989. "Sor Juana egipciana (Aspectos neoplatónicos de El sueño)." *Mester* 18: 1–17.

Pastine, Dino, 1978. *La nascita dell'idolatria: L'Oriente religioso di Athanasius Kircher.* Florence: La Nuova Italia.

Pastor, Ludwig Von, 1961. *Storia dei papi.* Vol. 14 (1644–1700). Rome: Desclée.

Pavoni, Rosanna, 1985. "Paolo Giovio et son musée de portraits: A propos d'une exposition." *Gazette des beaux-arts,* 6e série, 105: 109–116.

Paz, Octavio, 1988. *Sor Juana, or, The Traps of Faith.* Trans. Margaret Sayers Peden. Cambridge, MA: Belknap Press.

Peirce, Charles Sanders, 1887. "Logical Machines." *American Journal of Psychology* 1: 165–170.

Perez Salazar, Francisco, 1928. *Biografia de D. Carlos de Sigüenza y Góngora seguida de varios documentos ineditos.* Mexico City: Antigua Imprenta de Murguia.

Petech, L., 1971. "Borri, Cristoforo." In *Dizionario biografico degli italiani.* Vol. 13: 3–4. Rome: Istituto della Enciclopedia italiana.

Peterson, Willard J., 1973. "Western Natural Philosophy Published in Late Ming China." *Proceedings of the American Philosophical Society* 117: 295–322.

———, 1994. "What to Wear? Observation and Participation by Jesuit Missionaries in Late Ming Society." In *Implicit Understandings: Observing, Reporting, and Reflecting on the Encounters between Europeans and Other Peoples in the Early Modern Era.* Ed. Stuart B. Schwartz. 403–421. Cambridge, UK: Cambridge University Press.

———, 1998. "Learning from Heaven: The Introduction of Christianity and Other Western Ideas into Late Ming China." In *Cambridge History of China.* Vol. 8:789–839. Eds. Denis Twitchett and Frederick W. Mote. Cambridge, UK: Cambridge University Press.

Piaia, Gregorio, 1973. "Aristotelismo, 'heresia' e giuridizionalismo nella polemica del P. Antonio Possevino contro lo studio di Padova." *Quaderni per la storia dell'Università di Padova* 6: 125–145.

Pinot, Virgile, 1932. *La Chine et la formation de l'esprit philosophique en France (1640–1740).* Paris: P. Geuthner.

Pintard, René, 1943. *Le Libertinage érudit dans la première moitié du XVIIᵉ siècle.* Paris: Boivin.

Pizzorusso, Giovanni, 2000. "Agli antipodi di Babele. Propaganda Fide tra immagine cosmopolita e orizzonti romani (XVII–XIX secolo)." In *La città del papa. Vita civile e religiosa dal*

Giubileo di Bonifacio VIII al Giubileo di Papa Wojtila. Eds. Luigi Fiorani and Adriano Prosperi. *Storia d'Italia. Annali 16.* Torino: Einaudi.

Polgár, Lászlo, 1980–90. *Bibliographie sur l'histoire de la Compagnie de Jésus, 1901–1980.* 3 vols. Rome: Institutum Historicum Societatis Iesu.

Politiques missionnaires, 1999. "Politiques missionnaires sous le pontificat de Paul IV. Un document interne de la Compagnie de Jésus en 1558." *MEFRIM* 111: 277–344.

Pommier, Eduard, 1998. *Théories du portrait de la Renaissance aux Lumières.* Paris: Gallimard.

Poole, Stafford, 1995. *Our Lady of Guadalupe: The Origins and Sources of a Mexican National Symbol, 1531–1797.* Tuscon: University of Arizona Press.

Portoghesi, Paolo, 1992. "Il palazzo della Sapienza." In *L'Archivio di Stato di Roma.* Ed. Lucio Lume. 189–243. Florence: Nardini editore.

Preimesberger, Rudolf, Hannah Baader, Nicola Suthor, 1999. *Porträt: Geschichte der klassischen Bildgattungen in Quellentexten und Kommentaren.* Vol. 2. Berlin: Reimer.

Prinz, Wolfram, 1979. "La série gioviana o la collezione dei ritratti degli uomini illustri." In *Gli Uffizi Catalogo generale.* Ed. Galleria degli Uffizi. 603–664. Florence: Centro Di.

Priolkar, Anant Kakba, 1958. *The Printing Press in India: Its Beginnings and Early Development.* Bombay: Marathi Samshodhana Mandala.

Procacci, Giuliano, 1965. *Studi sulla fortuna del Machiavelli.* Rome: Istituto storico italiano per l'età moderna e contemporanea.

Puccini, Dario, 1996. *Una donna in solitudine. Sor Juana Inés de la Cruz. Un'eccezione nella cultura e nella letteratura barocca.* Bologna: Edizioni Cosmopoli.

Pumfrey, Steven, 1989. "'O tempora, O magnes!' A Sociological Analysis of the Discovery of Secular Magnetic Variation in 1634." *British Journal for the History of Science* 22: 181–214.

Purcell, Rosamond Wolff, and Stephen Jay Gould, 1992. *Finders, Keepers.* New York: W. W. Norton.

Ramsay, Rachel, 2001. "China and the Ideal of Order in John Webb's *An Historical Essay.*" *Journal of the History of Ideas* 62: 483–503.

Raskolnikoff, Mouza, 1992. *Histoire romaine et critique historique dans l'Europe des Lumières.* Rome: Ecole française de Rome.

Redondi, Pietro, 1983. *Galileo eretico.* Torino: Einaudi

Reichmann, Matthias, 1914. "Ordenszensur und persönliche Verantwortlichkeit in der Gesellschaft Jesu." *Stimmen aus Maria-Laach* 87: 151–160.

Reilly, P. Conor, S.J., 1958. "A Catalogue of Jesuitica in the 'Philosophical Transactions of the Royal Society of London.'" *Archivum Historicum Societatis Iesu* 27: 339–362.

———, 1974. *Athanasius Kircher, S. J., Master of a Hundred Arts.* Rome-Wiesbaden: Edizioni del Mondo.

Ricci, Saverio, 1994. *Una filosofica milizia: Tre studi sull'Accademia dei Lincei.* Udine: Campanotto editore.

Rietbergen, Pieter J. A. N., 1989. "A Maronite Mediator between Seventeenth-Century Cultures: Ibrahim al-Hakilani, or Abraham Ecchellense (1606–1664) between Christendom and Islam." *Lias* 16.

Rinaldi, Ernesto, 1914. *La fondazione del Collegio Romano. Memorie storiche.* Arezzo: Cooperativa tipografica.

Rivière, Ernest-M., 1910. "Le scandale du P. Francois Duneau." *Documents d'histoire* 1: 469–473.

Rivosecchi, Valerio, 1982. *Esotismo in Roma Barocca. Studi sul Padre Kircher.* Rome: Bulzoni.

Robinet, André, 1988. *G. W. Leibniz Iter Italicum (Mars 1689–Mars 1690): La dynamique de la République des Lettres.* Florence: Olschki.

Roche, Daniel, 1987. "Du livre au lire: Les pratiques citadines de l'imprimé." In *Lectures et lecteurs dans la France d'Ancien Régime.* Ed. Roger Chartier. 165–222. Paris: Le Seuil.

Roethlisberger, Marcel Georges, 1993. *Abraham Bloemaert and His Sons.* 2 vols. Doornspijk: Davaco Publishers.

Romani, Valentino, 1996. *Biblioteche romane del Sei e Settecento.* Manziana: Vecchiarelli.

Romano, Antonella, 1997. "Les collèges jésuites, lieux de sociabilité scientifique (1540–1640)." *Bulletin de la Société d'histoire moderne et contemporaine* 44: 6–20.

———, 1999. *La contre-réforme mathématique: Constitution et diffusion d'une culture mathématique jésuite à la Renaissance (1560–1640).* Rome: Ecole française de Rome.

———, 2000. "Entre collèges et académies: Esquisse de la place des jésuites dans les réseaux européens de la production scientifique (XVIIe–XVIIIe siècles)." In *Académies et sociétés savantes en Europe, 1650–1800: Actes du colloque international de Rouen (14–17 novembre 1995).* 387–407. Paris: Champion.

————, 2000. "Pratiques d'enseignment et orthodoxie intellectuelle en milieu jésuite (seconde moitié du XVIe siècle.) In Elm, et al, ed. 2000, 241–260.

————, 2002a. "Modernité de la *Ratio Studiorum* (Plan raisonné des études): Genèse d'un texte normatif et engagement dans une pratique enseignante." In *Tradition jésuite et pratique pédagogique: Histoire et actualité.* Eds. Étienne Ganty, Michel Hermans, and Pierre Sauvage. 44–87. Namur-Bruxelles: Presses Universitaires de Namur / Éditions Lessius.

————, 2002b. "Il mondo della scienza." In *Storia di Roma.* Vol. 5. Ed. Giorgio Cuccio. Roma: Laterza.

————, forthcoming. "Les jésuites entre apostolat missionnaire et activité scientifique (XVIe–XVIIIe siècles)." In *The Jesuits as Intermediaries in Early Modern World.* Ed. Diogo Curtado.

Rosenthal, Franz, 1968. *A History of Muslim Historiography.* 2nd edition. Leiden: E. J. Brill.

Rossi, Paolo, 1960. *Clavis Universalis: arti mnemoniche e logica combinatoria da Lullo a Leibniz.* Milan: Ricciardi.

————, 1984. *The Dark Abyss of Time.* Trans. Lydia Cochrane. Chicago and London.

————, 2000. *Logic and the Art of Memory: The Quest for a Universal Language.* Chicago: University of Chicago Press.

Rostenberg, Leona, 1989. *The Library of Robert Hooke: The Scientific Book Trade of Restoration England.* Santa Monica, CA: Modoc Press.

Rowland, Ingrid, 1998. *The Culture of the High Renaissance: Ancients and Moderns in Sixteenth-Century Rome.* Cambridge, UK: Cambridge University Press.

————, 2000. *The Ecstatic Journey: Athanasius Kircher in Baroque Rome.* Chicago: University of Chicago Press.

Rozsa, Gyoergy, 1973. *Magyar történetábrázolás a 17. Században.* Budapest: Akadémiai Kiadó.

Rubial Garcia, Antonio, 1999. *La santidad controvertida.* Mexico: Universidad Nacional Autonoma de Mexico.

Rudwick, Martin J. S., 1972. *The Meaning of Fossils.* London: Macdonald.

Rule, Paul A., 1986. *K'ung-tzu or Confucius? The Jesuit Interpretation of Confucianism.* Sydney: Allen & Unwin.

Rupprich, Hans (Ed.), 1956. *Dürer, schriftlicher Nachlaß*, Vol. 1, 259, Nr. 36.

Sabat de Rivers, Georgina, 1976. *El "Sueño" de sor Juana Inés de la Cruz: tradiciones literarias y originalidad.* London: Tamesis.

————, 1992. *Estudios de Literatura Hispanoamericana: Sor Juana Inés de la Cruz y otros poetas barrocos de la colonia.* Barcelona: PPU.

Salem, Marlis, 2001. "Al-Suyuti and His Works: Their Place in Islamic Scholarship from Mamluk Times to the Present." *Mamluk Studies Review* 5: 73–89.

Sanchez Lora, Jose Luis, 1988. *Mujeres, conventos y formas de la religiosidad barroca.* Madrid: Fundacion Universitaria Espanola.

Sarasohn, Lisa T., 1993. "Nicolas-Claude Fabri de Peiresc and the Patronage of the New Science in the Seventeenth Century." *Isis* 84: 70–90.

Sartain, E. M., 1975. *Jalal al-din al-Suyuti, I: Biography and Background.* Cambridge, UK: Cambridge University Press.

Scavizzi, Giuseppe, 1992. *The Controversy on Images from Calvin to Baronius.* New York: Peter Lang.

Schäfer, Peter, and Gary Smith, eds., 1995. *Gershom Scholem: Zwischen den Disziplinen.* Frankfurt: Suhrkamp.

Scharlau, Ulf, 1969. *Athanasius Kircher (1601–1680) als Musikschriftsteller: Ein Beitrag zur Musikanschauung des Barock.* Kassel: Bärenreiter-Antiquariat.

Schatzberg, Walter, Ronald Waite, and Jonathan Johnson, 1987. *The Relations of Literature and Science: An Annotated Bibliography of Scholarship, 1880–1980.* New York: The Modern Language Association of America.

Scher, Stephen K., 1994. *The Currency of Fame: Portrait Medals of the Renaissance.* New York: Harry N. Abrams.

Schmidt, Benjamin, 2002. "Inventing Exoticism: The Project of Dutch Geography and the Marketing of the World, circa 1700." In *Merchants and Marvels: Commerce, Science, and Art in Early Modern Europe.* Eds. Pamela H. Smith and Paula Findlen. 347–369. New York: Routledge.

Schnapper, Antoine, 1988. *Le Géant, La Licorne, La Tulipe. Collections et Collectionneurs Francaises au XVIIe siècle.* Paris: Flammarion.

Scholem, Gershom, 1978. *Kabbalah.* New York: Meridian.

————, 1997. "The Beginnings of the Christian Kabbalah." In Dan 1997, pp. 17–51.

Schutte, Josef Franz, 1980. *Valignano's Mission Principles for Japan. Vol. I. From His Appointment as Visitor until His First Departure from Japan. Part I. The Problem (1573–1580)*. Trans. John J. Coyne, S.J. St. Louis: The Institute of Jesuit Sources.

Scott, Nina, 1995. "Imágenes de Sor Juana." In *Memoria del Coloquio Internacional Sor Juana Inés de la Cruz y el pensamiento novohispano*. 425–431. Toluca: Instituto Mexiquense de Cultura.

Secret, François, 1974. "Notes sur quelques kabbalistes chrétiens." *Bibliothèque d'humanisme et Renaissance* 36: 67–82.

————, 1977. "Un Épisode oublié de la vie de Peiresc: Le sabre magique de Gustave Adolphe." *XVIIᵉ Siècle* 117: 49–52.

————, 1985. *Les Kabbalistes Chrétiens*. Milan: Archè.

————, 1992. *Hermétisme et Kabbale*. Naples: Bibliopolis.

Seelig, G., 1995. "Bloemaert, Cornelis (II)." In *Saur Allgemeines Künstlerlexikon: Die Bildenden Künstler aller Zeiten und Völker*. Ed. Günter Meißner. 549–550. Munich and Leipzig: Saur.

Shapin, Steven, 1994. *A Social History of Truth: Civility and Science in Seventeenth-Century England*. Chicago and London: University of Chicago Press.

Shapin, Steven, and Simon Schaffer, 1985. *Leviathan and the Air-Pump: Hobbes, Boyle and the Experimental Life*. Princeton, NJ: Princeton University Press.

Siebert, Harald, 2002. "Vom römischen Itinerarium zum Würzburger Iter-Kircher, Schott und die Chronologie der Eregnisse." In Beinlich et al, eds, pp. 163–188.

Sigila, 2001. Vol. 8.

Singer, Hans Wolfgang, 1931. *Allgemeiner Bildniskatalog*. Leipzig: Hiersemann.

Smith, Richard, 2002. "The Jesuits and Evidential Research in Late Imperial China: Some Reflections." *Ex/Change* 3: 7–12.

Sommervogel, Carlos, S.J., 1890. *Bibliothèque de la Compagnie de Jésus*. 10 vols. Paris.

Soriano Vallès, Alejandro, 1996. *La invertida escala de Jacob: Filosofía y teología en El Sueño de Sor Juana Inés de la Cruz*. Toluca: Instituto Mexiquense de Cultura.

Spence, Jonathan D., 1984. *The Memory Palace of Matteo Ricci*. New York: Viking.

Standaert, Nicolas, ed., 2001. *Handbook of Christianity in China*. Vol. 1. Leiden: Brill.

Stillman, Robert E., 1995. *The New Philosophy and Universal Languages in Seventeenth-Century England*. Lewisburg, PA: Bucknell University Press.

Stolzenberg, Daniel, ed., 2001a. *The Great Art of Knowing: The Baroque Encyclopedia of Athanasius Kircher*. Stanford: Stanford University Libraries.

————, 2001b. "Kircher among the Ruins: Esoteric Knowledge and Universal History." In Stolzenberg 2001a, pp. 127–139.

————, 2001c. "Kircher's Egypt." In Stolzenberg 2001a, pp. 115–125.

————, 2003. "*Lectio Idealis:* Theory and Practice in Athanasius Kircher's Translations of the Hieroglyphs." In *Philosophers and Hieroglyphs*. Eds. L. Morra, C. Bazzanella, and P. Gallo. Turin: Rosenberg & Sellier.

————, 2004. "Oedipus Censored: *Censurae* of Athanasius Kircher's Works in the Archivum Romanum Societatis Iesu." *Archivum Historicum Societatis Iesu*.

————, forthcoming. "Utility, Edification, and Superstition: Jesuit Censorship and Athanasius Kircher's *Oedipus Aegyptiacus*." In *The Jesuits II: Cultures, Sciences, and the Arts, 1540–1773*. Eds. John O'Malley, Steven Harris, Gauvin Bailey, and T. Frank Kennedy. University of Toronto Press.

Strasser, Gerhard F., 1979. "Geheimschrift." In *Sammler, Fürst, Gelehrter: Herzog August zu Braunschweig und Lüneburg, 1579–1666*. (Kataloge der Herzog-August-Bibliothek, 27.) Eds. Paul Raabe and Eckhard Schinkel. 181–191. Wolfenbüttel: Herzog August Bibliothek.

————, 1988a. "La contribution d'Athanase Kircher a la tradition humaniste hiéroglyphique." *XVIIᵉ Siècle* 40: 79–92.

————, 1988b. *Lingua Universalis: Kryptologie und Theorie des Universalsprachen im 16. Und 17. Jahrhundert*. Wiesbaden: Harrassowitz.

————, 1996. "Science and Pseudoscience: Athanasius Kircher's *Mundus Subterraneus* and His *Scrutinum . . . Pestis*." In *Knowledge, Science and Literature in Early Modern Germany*. Eds. Gerhild Scholz Williams and Stephan K. Schnindler, Chapel Hill: University of North Carolina Press, 1996. 219–240.

Strathman, Ernst, 1951. *Sir Walter Raleigh: A Study in Elizabethan Skepticism*. New York: Columbia University Press.

Stumpo, Enrico, 1985. *Il capitale finanziario a Roma fra fine Cinquecento e Seicento. Contributo alla storia della fiscalità pontificia in età moderna (1570–1660).* Milan: A. Giuffrè.

Sturm, Edwin, 1982. "Die Ölgemälde des Fuldaer Priesterseminars, Fuldaer Geschichtsblätter 58, 1982, 1, 1–26."

———, 1984. *Die Bau- und Kunstdenkmäler der Stadt Fulda.* Fulda: Parzeller.

Szczesniak, Boleslaw, 1952. "Athanasius Kircher's China Illustrata." *Osiris* 10: 385–411.

———, 1955. "The Writings of Michael Boym." *Monumenta serica* 14: 481–538.

———, 1960. "A Note on the Studies of Longitudes Made by M. Martini, A. Kircher, and J.N. Delisle from the Observations of Travellers to the Far East." *Imago mundi* 15: 89–93.

———, 1981/2. "Die Ölgemälde des Fuldaer Priesterseminars." *Fuldaer Geschichtsblätter* 58: 1–25.

Taranto, Domenico, 1994. *Pirronismo ed assolutismo nella Francia del '600: studi sul pensiero politico dello scetticismo da Montaigne a Bayle (1580–1697).* Milan: Franco Angeli.

Thorndike, Lynn, 1923–58. *A History of Magic and Experimental Science.* 8 vols. New York: Columbia University Press.

Torre Revello, José, 1940. *El libro, la imprenta y el periodismo en América durante la dominación española.* Buenos Aires: Casa Jacobo Peuser.

Torrey, H. B., 1938. "Athanasius Kircher and the Progress of Medicine." *Osiris* 5: 246–275.

Torrini, Maurizio, 1979. "Due galileiani a Roma: Raffaello Magiotti e Antonio Nardi." In *La scuola galileiana: Prospettive di ricerca.* Eds. Gino Arrighi, Paolo Galluzzi, and Maurizio Torrini. 53–88. Florence: La nuova Italia.

Trabulse, Elías, 1974. *Ciencia y religión en el siglo XVII.* Mexico City: El Colegio de México.

———, 1980. "Sor Juana Inés de la Cruz y Athanasius Kircher." *Vuelta* 38: 47–48.

———, 1982. *El Círculo roto: Estudios históricos sobre la ciencia en México.* Mexico: Fondo de Cultura Económica.

———, 1988. *Los manuscritos perdidos de Sigüenza y Góngora.* Mexico City: El Colegio de México.

———, 1994. *Los orígenes de la ciencia moderna en México (1630–1680).* Mexico City: Fondo de Cultura Económica.

———, 1995. *Arte y ciencia en la historia de México.* Mexico City: Fomento Cultural Banamex, A. C.

———, 1996. *La memoria transfigurada: Tres imágenes histórica de Sor Juana.* Mexico City: Universidad del Claustro de Sor Juana.

Trabulse, Elias, with Alberto Sarmiento and María Pardo, 1984. *Historia de la ciencia en México: Estudios y Textos. Siglo XVII.* Vol. 2. Mexico City: Fondo de Cultura Económica.

Treu, Erwin, 1959. *Die Bildnisse des Erasmus von Rotterdam.* Basel: Gute Schriften.

Ultee, Maarten, 1987. "The Republic of Letters: Learned Correspondence, 1680–1720." *The Seventeenth Century* 2: 95–112.

Van Damme, Stéphane, 1999. "Ecriture, institution et société: Le travail littéraire dans la Compagnie de Jésus en France (1620–1720)." *Revue de synthèse* 4: 261–283.

———, 2000. *Savoirs, culture écrite et sociabilité urbaine: L'action des enseignants jésuites du collège de la Trinité de Lyon (1630–1730).* Ph.D. dissertation. Université de Paris I.

Van de Vyver, Omer, 1977. "Lettres de J.-Ch. della Faille S.I., cosmographe du roi à Madrid, à M. -F. Van Langren, cosmographe du roi à Bruxelles, 1634–1645." *Archivum Historicum Societatis Iesu* 46: 73–183.

Van Eeghen, Isabella H, 1972. "Arnoldus Montanus's Book on Japan." *Quaerendo* 2: 250–272.

Van Helden, Albert, 1996. "Longitude and the Satellites of Jupiter." In *The Quest for Longitude: The Proceedings of the Longitude Symposium.* Ed. William J. H Andrewes. 81–100. Cambridge, MA: The Collection of Historical Scientific Instruments.

Van Kley, Edwin, 1971. "Europe's 'Discovery' of China and the Writing of World History." *American Historical Review* 76: 358–385.

Van Lantschoot, Arnold, 1948. *Un Précurseur d'Athanase Kircher: Thomas Obicini et la scala Vat. copte 71.* Louvain: Bureaux du Muséon.

Vasoli, Cesare, 1978. *L'Enciclopedismo del Seicento.* Naples: Bibliopolis.

Victor, Joseph M., 1978. *Charles de Bovelles: An Intellectual Biography.* Geneva: Droz.

Villari, Rosario, 1987. *Elogio della dissimulazione. La lotta politica nel Seicento.* Rome: Laterza.

Villoslada, Riccardo, 1954. *Storia del Collegio Romano dal suo inizio (1551) alla sorpressione della Compagnia di Gesù (1773).* Rome: Università Gregoriana.

Visceglia, Maria Antonietta, ed., 2001. *La nobiltà romana in età moderna. Profili istituzionali e pratiche sociali.* Rome: Carocci.

Walker, D. P., 1972. *The Ancient Theology: Studies in Christian Platonism from the Fifteenth to the Eighteenth Century.* London: Duckworth.

Waquet, Françoise, 1985. "Charles Patin (1633–1693) et la République des Lettres." *Lias* 12: 115–136.

——, 1989a. *Le modèle français et l'Italie savante: Conscience de soi et perception de l'autre dans la République des Lettres.* Rome: Ecole française de Rome.

——, 1989b. "Qu'est-ce que la République des Lettres? Essai de sémantique historique." *Bibliothèque de l'École des Chartes* 147: 473–502.

——, 1993. "Les Éditions de correspondances savantes et les idéaux de la République des Lettres." *XVIIᵉ Siècle* 45: 99–118.

Wessels, Cornelius, 1924. *Early Jesuit Travellers in Central Asia, 1603–1721.* The Hague: Martinus Nijhoff.

White, A. D., 1896. *A History of the Warfare of Science with Theology in Christendom.* 2 vols. New York: Appleton.

Wicki, Josef, S.J., 1968. "Die *Miscellanea Epistolarum* des P. Athanasius Kircher, S. J. in Missionarischer Sicht." *Euntes Docete* 21: 221–254.

Wilding, Nick, 1998. "The Catalogue and the Collection—Romani Collegii Societis Jesu Musaeum Celeberrimum, & Musaeum Regalis Societatis. Or a catalogue & Discription of the Natural and Artificial Rarities Belonging to The Royal Society and Preserved at Gresham Colledge. (1681)." Unpublished paper.

——, 2000. *Writing the Book of Nature: Natural Philosophy and Communication in Early Modern Europe.* Ph.D. dissertation. Fiesole: European University Institute.

——, 2001a. "'If You Have a Secret, Either Keep It, or Reveal It': Cryptography and Universal Language." In Stolzenberg 2001a, pp. 93–103.

——, 2001b. "Kircher's Correspondence." In Stolzenberg 2001a, pp. 141–146.

Williamson, George L. 1964. *Bryan's Dictionary of Painters and Engravers.* Port Washington, NY: Kennikat Press.

Wilson, Catherine, 1995. *The Invisible World: Early Modern Philosophy and the Invention of the Microscope.* Princeton, NJ: Princeton University Press.

Wirszubski, Chaim. "Francesco Giorgi's Commentary on Pico's Kabbalistic Theses." *Journal of the Warburg and Courtauld Institutes* 37 (1974): 145–56.

Wirszubski, Chaim, 1989. *Pico Della Mirandola's Encounter with Jewish Mysticism.* Cambridge, MA: Harvard University Press.

Witek, John W., S.J., 1983. "Chinese Chronology: A Source of Sino-European Widening Horizons in the Eighteenth Century." In *Actes du IIIe Colloque international de Sinologie: Appréciation par Europe de la tradition chinoise à partir du XVIIe siècle.* Paris: Belles Lettres.

Wittkower, Rudolph, 1958. *Art and Architecture in Italy, 1600 to 1750.* Harmondsworth, UK, and Baltimore: Penguin.

Woolf, D. R., 1990. *The Idea of History in Early Stuart England: Erudition, Ideology, and "The Light of Truth" from the Accession of James I to the Civil War.* Toronto: Toronto University Press.

Wurzbach, Alfred von, 1906: *Niederländisches Künstler-Lexikon.* 2 vols. Vienna and Leipzig: Von Halm und Goldmann.

Yates, Frances, 1964. *Giordano Bruno and the Hermetic Tradition.* London: Routledge.

——, 1971. *The Art of Memory.* London: Penguin.

Zagorin, Perez, 1990. *Ways of Lying: Dissimulation, Persecution, and Conformity in Early Modern Europe.* Cambridge, MA: Harvard University Press.

Zambrano, Francisco, 1961–77. *Diccionario bio-bibliografico de la Compania de Jesus en Mexico.* 16 vols. Mexico City: Editorial Jus.

Zertuche, Francisco, 1961. *Sor Juana y la Compañía de Jesús.* Mexico City: Universidad de Nuevo León, Departamento de Extensión Universitaria.

Zika, Charles, 1976. "Reuchlin's *De Verbo Mirifico* and the Magic Debate of the Late Fifteenth Century." *Journal of the Warburg and Courtauld Institutes* 39: 104–138.

Zittel, K. A. von, 1899. *Geschichte der Geologie und Palaontologie bis Ende des 19 Jahrhunderts.* Munich: Oldenbourg.

Notes on Contributors

Martha Baldwin teaches history of science at Stonehill College and is the author of many articles on Athanasius Kircher's magnetic philosophy and medicine, including "The Snakestone Experiments: An Early Modern Medical Debate," *Isis* 86 (1995): 394–418.

Paula Findlen is Ubaldo Pierotti Professor of Italian History and Director of the Science, Technology and Society Program at Stanford University. She is the author of *Possessing Nature: Museums, Collecting and Scientific Culture in Early Modern Italy* (Berkeley, 1994); (with Pamela H. Smith, ed.), *Merchants and Marvels* (New York, 2001); and *The Italian Renaissance: The Essential Readings* (2002).

Michael John Gorman completed his PhD at the European University Institute and is a Lecturer in the Science, Technology and Society Program at Stanford University. He is the co-editor of the Athanasius Kircher Correspondence Project and the author of various essays on Jesuit science and mathematics.

Stephen Jay Gould was Agassiz Professor of Zoology and Adjunct Professor of the History of Science at Harvard University and the author of numerous books and essays dealing with the history and culture of science in addition to his well-known works as a paleontologist.

Anthony Grafton is the Dodge Professor of History at Princeton University where he teaches European intellectual history. His books include *Joseph Scaliger* (Oxford, 1983–93); *Leon Battista Alberti* (New York, 2000); and *Bring Out Your Dead* (Cambridge, Mass., 2001).

Florence Hsia teaches in the Department of the History of Science at the University of Wisconsin, Madison. She is completing a book entitled *Enlightened Mission* which explores the fate of the French Jesuit overseas scientific missions in China in the seventeenth and eighteenth centuries.

Eugenio Lo Sardo is the Ispettore Generale of the Archivio di Stato in Rome. He curated the 2001 exhibit at Palazzo Venezia that reconstructed the Roman College museum. He is the editor of *Il Museo del Mondo* (Rome, 2001); and *Iconismi e mirabilia da Athanasius Kircher* (Rome, 1999).

Noel Malcolm is a general editor of the Clarendon Edition of the *Works of Thomas Hobbes* (Oxford, 1994). He has edited Hobbes's complete correspondence for that series, and is now preparing an edition of *Leviathan*. A former Fellow of Gonville & Caius College, Cambridge, he has been a Visiting Lecturer at Harvard and Carlyle Lecturer at Oxford. He was elected to the British Academy in 2001.

Peter N. Miller is Professor of Cultural History at the Bard Graduate Center in New York. He is the author of, most recently, *Peiresc's Europe: Learning and Virtue in the Seventeenth Century* (Yale University Press, 2000). This essay, and others on Peiresc's Samaritan, Hebrew, Gnostic, Ethiopic and African studies, reflect work towards *Peiresc's Orient: The Antiquarian Imagination* (Yale University Press, forthcoming).

Angela Mayer-Deutsch studied Psychology and History of Art and is currently writing her Ph.D. dissertation in the History of Art at the University of Frankfurt am Main on the uses of objects in seventeenth-century collections, with a focus on the "Musaeum Kircherianum."

J. Michelle Molina is a graduate student in the Department of History at the University of Chicago. She is completing a dissertation entitled "Visions of God, Visions of Empire: Jesuit Spirituality and Colonial Governmentality."

Ingrid Rowland is the Mellon Professor at the American Academy in Rome and has taught art history at the University of Chicago. She is the author of *Ecstatic Journey: Athanasius Kircher in Baroque Rome* (Chicago, 2000); and *The Culture of the High Renaissance* (Cambridge, U. K., 1999).

Antonella Romano is Chargée de recherche at the Centre Alexandre Koyré, CNRS, Paris. She is the author of the *La contre-réforme mathématique: Constitution et diffusion d'une culture mathématique jésuite à la Renaissance (1540–1640)* (Rome, 1999) and the editor, with Pierre-Antoine Fabre, of *Les Jésuites dans le monde moderne : nouvelles approches, Revue de synthèse*, n° 120/2-3, Paris, 1999; and, with S. Elm and É. Rebillard, of *Orthodoxie, christianisme, histoire* (Rome, 2000). Most recently she has edited *Sciences et mission, le cas jésuite (XVIe-XVIIIe siècles)* in the *Archives Internationales d'Histoire des Sciences* 148 (2002).

Haun Saussy is Professor of Asian Languages and Comparative Literature at Stanford University. He is the author of *The Problem of a Chinese Aesthetic* (1993) and *Great Walls of Discourse* (2001).

Harald Siebert studied Physics, Philosophy and Classics in Augsburg, Philosophy and History of Science in Munich, Paris, and Berlin (Maître in Philosophy, Paris IV). He is current finishing a dissertation on Athanasius Kircher's natural philosophy at the Technische Universität Berlin.

Daniel Stolzenberg, a postdoctoral fellow at the Max Planck Institute for the History of Science recently completed a dissertation on Kircher called "Egyptian Oedipus: Antiquarianism, Oriental Studies, & Occult Philosophy in the Work of Athanasius Kircher." He is the editor of *The Great Art of Knowing: The Baroque Encyclopedia of Athanasius Kircher* and has an M.A. in the History and Philosophy of Science from Indiana University, Bloomington.

Nick Wilding is the co-editor of the Athanasius Kircher Correspondence Project. He is currently a British Academy Postdoctoral Fellow at the Department of History and Philosophy of Science at Cambridge University, working on a study of pseudonymous and anonymous scientific authorship in early modern Europe.

Carlos Ziller Camenietzki is a researcher at the Museu de Astronomia e Ciências Afins, Rio de Janeiro, Brazil. He received his doctorate from the University of Paris IV in 1995, with a dissertation on Kircher, and works on the history of early modern science and culture, in particular, the Jesuits and Portuguese culture in the seventeenth century. His recent essays include "Dissimulações honestas e cultura científica na Idade Barroca," *Sigila* 8 (2001): 81–91; "Jesuits and Alchemy in the Early Seventeenth Century: Father Johannes Roberti and the Weapon-Salve Controversy," *Ambix* 48 (2001): 83–101, 2001; "La poudre de madame: la trajectoire de la guérison magnétique des blessures en France," *XVIIe Siècle* 211 (2001): 285–305; "Quem conta um conto aumenta um ponto: o mito do Ipupiara, a natureza americana e as narrativas da colonização do Brasil," *Revista de Indias* 60 (2000): 111–134.

Index

Made in the USA
Lexington, KY
30 September 2017